Eros at the Banquet

Oklahoma Series in Classical Culture

Eros at the Banquet

Reviewing Greek with Plato's *Symposium*

Louise Pratt

University of Oklahoma Press : Norman

Library of Congress Cataloging-in-Publication Data

Pratt, Louise H., 1960–
    Eros at the banquet : reviewing Greek with Plato's Symposium / Louise Pratt.
        p. cm. — (Oklahoma series in classical culture ; v. 40)
    English and Greek, Classical.
    Includes bibliographical references and index.
    ISBN 978-0-8061-4142-8 (pbk. : alk. paper)
    1. Greek language—Textbooks for foreign speakers—English. 2. Greek language—Problems, exercises, etc.
    3. Greek language—Grammar. I. Plato. Symposium. II. Title.
    PA258.P76 2011
    488.2'421—dc22
                                                                                    2010032806

Eros at the Banquet: Reviewing Greek with Plato's Symposium is Volume 40 in the Oklahoma Series in Classical Culture.

The paper in this book meets the guidelines for permanence and durability of the Committee on Production Guidelines for Book Longevity of the Council on Library Resources, Inc. ∞

1 2 3 4 5 6 7 8 9 10

Philology is that venerable art which demands of its votaries one thing above all: to go aside, to take time, to become still, to become slow—it is a goldsmith's art and connoisseurship of the *word* which has nothing but delicate, cautious work to do and achieves nothing if it does not achieve it *lento*. But for precisely this reason it is more necessary than ever today, by precisely this means does it entice and enchant us the most, in the midst of an age of "work," that is to say, of hurry, of indecent and perspiring haste, which wants to "get everything done" at once, including every old or new book: —this art does not easily get anything done, it teaches to read *well*, that is to say, to read slowly, deeply, looking cautiously before and aft, with reservations, with doors left open, with delicate eyes and fingers.

—F. Nietzsche, *Daybreak: Thoughts on the Prejudices of Morality*
(trans. R. J. Hollingdale)

Contents

Appendixes

Figures

Suggestions for Using This Book

This textbook is intended to create a bridge between first-year Greek and the reading of demanding Greek texts. In my view, this transitional stage is particularly difficult for students. They want to read something engaging and important as a reward for the considerable effort they have expended to acquire a reading knowledge of Greek. Unfortunately, they do not have enough knowledge of basic Greek vocabulary to read fluently, and, particularly if a summer has interrupted their study of Greek, their knowledge of basic forms and syntax is often shaky—or at least not firm enough to read authors in dialects other than the Attic they were taught in first year. This text is intended to address these issues.

The imagined course that this textbook is intended to serve (second-year Greek) falls into two parts. In the first part, students review first-year grammar and strengthen their vocabularies by reading edited selections from the *Symposium* (readings 1–5) and by doing review exercises. I have chosen selections that are representative of the early part of the *Symposium*, but have condensed them by omitting sentences and passages that are likely to frustrate students at this early stage. I have also rewritten selected sentences to make them more accessible and more typical of standard Attic practice, though I have tried to keep such changes minimal. In the second part of the course, the class reads selections from the Oxford Classical Text of the *Symposium* (Burnet 1901) with the assistance of notes and glossary. My choices for this second part are the complete myth of Aristophanes (reading 6), the entrance and speech of Alcibiades (reading 10), and the dialogue's ending (reading 11), supplemented by selections from Diotima's speech (reading 9) or Agathon's speech (reading 7) if time permits. At the advice of several readers, I have included the last two thirds of the *Symposium* in its entirety so that teachers may select from their favorite parts. It is very unlikely that all the readings in the book can be completed in a nonintensive one-semester course unless the review exercises are omitted.

Suggested Reviews

All of the early readings and some of the later ones include a list of suggested review topics. These are only suggestions. The lists may be modified to suit the needs of particular classes. To do all these topics with perfect thoroughness would be very challenging and would probably slow the pace of the class unduly. I strive to improve, but not to perfect, students' recollection of these matters—to a point at which they can read more fluently and confidently. Because much is gained by reading, it is important not to become bogged down in reviewing but to get to the reading as soon as possible. In general, I ask students to spend a limited amount of time prior to each reading refreshing their memories of forms and syntax. For this, I use my *Essentials of Greek Grammar: A Reference for Intermediate Readers of Attic Greek* (Norman: University of Oklahoma Press, 2010), to which the notes and exercises are keyed; some of the most difficult examples found in the *Symposium* are translated there. I ask students to do selected exercises after the readings to reinforce grammatical principles and vocabulary.

Vocabulary

A section of vocabulary to be learned or reviewed precedes each reading. Although these words are available in the glossary, ideally some effort should be made to learn them before embarking on the reading. These words are not provided in the notes and are either used repeatedly in the *Symposium* or are such basic words in Greek that it is worth making an extra effort to learn them by rote. Homemade flashcards work very well for most students. Frequent vocabulary quizzes can provide additional incentive, if needed, and I recommend them. Plato did not compose the *Symposium* to give modern students vocabulary practice, so some additional effort beyond the reading is probably needed if students want to expand their vocabularies. The exercises that accompany readings 1–6 are also meant to provide additional practice with vocabulary.

Some of the vocabulary should already be known to the student; which and how many words will depend on what first-year textbook students have used (as well as other factors, such as how well they have retained what they were asked to learn). Teachers may wish to adapt the lists, depending on student background and ability.

Words not listed prior to the reading or glossed in the notes are words that students should already know, because they are required by most first-year Greek textbooks in common use for speakers of English. Students should make a concentrated effort to learn any words they have to look up: these are the most basic elements of Greek vocabulary and will be a constant source of frustration if not mastered.

If a prefix does not appreciably alter the familiar meaning of a word or alters it in a predictable way, I do not normally gloss the word (e.g., I assume that a student can look at εἰσέρχομαι and deduce that it means "enter, go in," even if s/he has never seen that word before). A few words should be recognizable from close English derivatives (e.g., I assume a student can look at φιλοσοφία and recognize "philosophy," especially in the context of a sentence). Before looking up a word in the glossary, students should always attempt to derive its meaning from context, from English derivatives, from breaking its down into components, or from trying to visualize what it would look like in a dictionary.

An asterisk (*) on words in the notes and exercises indicates a common Greek word that is not used frequently enough in the textbook to demand learning it; however, motivated students who are otherwise managing reviews and vocabulary well may want to learn these words in order to prepare themselves better for future reading in Greek. I also expect my own students to be able to recognize vocabulary that they have not been asked to learn in the context of passages that they have prepared.

Principal Parts

I have included principal parts when I think it useful. Some of these are necessary because they are so irregular that the student will not be able to recognize the verb without knowledge of its parts, but I have also included many examples of regular sets of principal parts to help students solidify their familiarity with the most common patterns. I do not typically include the principal parts on verbs with prefixes; these can usually be found in the glossary under the form without the prefix. I also have not provided complete sets of principal parts of verbs that occur only once or twice in the *Symposium* or of verbs that have regular but incomplete (because unattested in some tenses) sets of principal parts; the latter should be recognizable to students who know the patterns.

Notes

I provide notes on vocabulary and grammar on pages facing the readings to reduce the amount of time looking things up in the back of the book. Students should, however, take care not to become overly dependent on these notes. By consistently reviewing readings with a piece of paper covering the notes, students can be sure that they are developing the ability to read and translate independently. Rereading with the notes covered cannot be done too often; it is a reliable way to improve knowledge of all aspects of Greek. Students who thrive on challenge may want to cover the notes at all times and use them only when they are stuck. References to my *Essentials of Greek Grammar: A Reference for Intermediate Readers of Attic Greek* (Norman: University of Oklahoma Press, 2010), abbreviated *Essentials*, are provided for students who need additional help with basic forms and grammar and to Smyth 1956 for students who want to learn more about the less common grammatical features, but students who are reading well need not consult such references.

Exercises

The exercises are designed to give practice with both the vocabulary lists and the grammar subjects suggested for review with each chapter. They were originally inspired by M. G. Balme and J. H. W. Morwood's *Cupid and Psyche* (Oxford: Oxford University Press, 1976). Teachers should, of course, feel free to skip them or to do them in a different order when time or student preparation makes that advisable. Generally, I assign none or a very few to accompany a full reading, more on days when a vocabulary quiz and/or review is the main purpose of the class. They can also be sight-read together when class translation suggests a concept that needs immediate review. Challenge passages may be done together or assigned to especially good students or classes. It is not necessary—or even desirable—to do all of the exercises.

Glossary

I included in the glossary all words that are used in the textbook, except those in the exercises that are glossed *ad loc*. Although I have tried to be inclusive, I do not include all forms of every word. If students do not find a word, they should consider whether it might be found in a different place if its temporal augment were removed.

Stephanus Numbers

In referring to Plato's dialogues, it is conventional to use the page numbers of a sixteenth-century edition of Plato printed by Stephanus.[1] These are used in all standard texts of Plato, in most translations, and in all secondary references to Plato. Each section of a dialogue is labeled with a number followed by a letter, as Stephanus broke each page into five approximately equal sections, each labeled with a letter (a–e). I use the Stephanus numbers consistently beginning in reading 6, where I preserve the complete Oxford Classical Text. In readings 1–5, I give prior to each reading the Stephanus numbers of the part of the dialogue on which that reading is based, but I have not used them in the text itself lest confusion arise. Although many of the sentences are identical to those of the standard text, others are not. Teachers or students should use the Stephanus numbers given at the beginning of readings 1–5 to locate the full text on which those readings are based.

---

1. Stephanus is the Latin name of Henri Estienne (died 1598) and his father, Robert (1503–59), who ran a printing house in Paris.

Acknowledgments

I owe thanks to many people for their help with this project. First, I owe the greatest thanks to all my students who have helped me to think about teaching Greek. For their initial suggestions about what features they would like to see in a second-year Greek text, I thank in particular Sarah Hitch, Julie Jun, and Eric Weilnau; this book originated in their thoughts about what they needed and wanted in second-year Greek. Great thanks are also due the first group of students I taught using the text: Adam Davie, Wes Easom, J. T. Fetter, Richard Hu, and Greg Williams, for their patience with the weaknesses of the first draft and their enthusiasm, which made it seem worth continuing. Debbie Fetter, who put the entire first draft into braille for her son, was an amazing resource and inspiration to me; she called attention to numerous inconsistencies with tact and unbelievable patience.

Mike Lippman, who taught the text on its second round, was also a great resource; the text has profited in various ways from his suggestions and knowledge of the dialogue. His class, in particular Sharon Hsu, Cami Koepke, and Valerie Prochaska, also provided valuable feedback. I am grateful to the readers for the University of Oklahoma Press, particularly Reader #1, who offered comments on virtually every page of the original manuscript, and to my editors, David Aiken, John Drayton, and Alice Stanton, for their help at various stages of the manuscript's development. I thank my excellent research assistants, David Litwa and Benjamin Cook, for providing careful reading and detailed suggestions; my colleagues Peter Bing, Sandra Blakely, George Conklin, Kevin Corrigan, Richard Patterson, and Garth Tissol for reading and commenting on parts of the manuscript; Jasper Gaunt and Stacey Gannon-Wright of the Michael C. Carlos Museum and my colleague Katrina Dickson for their help with images from the Carlos collection.

The Perseus Digital Library Project (ed. Gregory R. Crane; copyright the Trustees of Tufts University; http://www.perseus.tufts.edu) was very useful at several stages of the project. In particular, I used the Vocabulary Tool in 2003 to construct a preliminary glossary and to get counts of words used in the *Symposium*, but I have relied on it throughout the project to locate examples and find other kinds of information.

A grant from the Emory Center for Teaching and Curriculum brought needed financial support at an early stage of this project; I doubt I would have pursued it without this crucial support. I also thank the Emory College of Arts and Sciences and the Laney School of Graduate Studies of Emory University for the financial support they gave to the publication of this project.

Finally, I thank my family, who spent many hours waiting for me to join them as I labored to complete my work on this textbook, for their love, patience and support.

Bibliography

Allen, Reginald E. 1991. *The Dialogues of Plato*, vol. 2: *The Symposium*. New Haven: Yale University Press.

Bing, Peter, and Rip Cohen. 1991. *The Games of Venus: An Anthology of Greek and Roman Erotic Verse from Sappho to Ovid*. New York: Routledge.

Breitenberger, Barbara. 2007. *Aphrodite and Eros: The Development of Erotic Mythology in Early Greek Poetry and Cult*. New York: Routledge.

Bremmer, Jan. 1990. "Adolescents, Symposion, and Pederasty." Pp. 135–48 in *Sympotica: A Symposium on the Symposion*. Edited by Oswyn Murray. Oxford: Oxford University Press.

Burkert, Walter. 1985. *Greek Religion*. Translated by John Raffan. Cambridge: Harvard University Press.

Burnet, J. 1901. *Plato: Symposium*. Oxford Classical Texts. Oxford: Oxford University Press.

Burnyeat, M. F. 1977. "Socratic Midwifery, Platonic Inspiration." *Bulletin of the Institute for Classical Studies* 24:7–17.

Bury, R. G., ed. 1973. *The Symposium of Plato*. 2nd ed. Cambridge: Heffer (reprint of 1932 edition).

Calame, Claude. 1999. *The Poetics of Eros in Ancient Greece*. Princeton: Princeton University Press.

Carnes, Jeffrey. 1998. "This Myth Which Is Not One: Construction of Discourse in Plato's Symposium." Pp. 104–21 in *Rethinking Sexuality: Foucault and Classical Antiquity*. Edited by D. Larmour, P. Miller, and C. Platter. Princeton: Princeton University Press.

Carpenter, Thomas H., and Christopher A. Faraone. 1993. *Masks of Dionysus*. Ithaca: Cornell University Press.

Carson, Anne. 1986. *Eros the Bittersweet: An Essay*. Princeton: Princeton University Press.

Clay, Diskin. 1975. "The Tragic and Comic Poet of the Symposium." *Arion* 2:238–61.

Connelly, Joan Breton. 2007. *Portrait of a Priestess: Women and Ritual in Ancient Greece*. Princeton: Princeton University Press.

Corrigan, Kevin, and Elena Glazov-Corrigan. 2004. *Plato's Dialectic at Play: Argument, Structure, and Myth in the Symposium*. University Park: Pennsylvania State University Press.

Craik, Elizabeth. 2001. "Plato and Medical Texts: Symposium 185c–193d." *Classical Quarterly* n.s. 51/1:109–14.

Davidson, James. 1997. *Courtesans and Fishcakes: The Consuming Passions of Classical Athens*. New York: St. Martin's.

———. 2007. *The Greeks and Greek Love: A Radical Reappraisal of Homosexuality in Ancient Greece*. London: Weidenfeld & Nicholson.

Denniston, J. D. 1950. *The Greek Particles*. 2nd ed. Revised by K. J. Dover. Indianapolis: Hackett.

Dover, Kenneth J. 1966. "Aristophanes' speech in Plato's Symposium." *Journal of Hellenic Studies* 86:41–50.

———. 1978. *Greek Homosexuality*. Cambridge: Harvard University Press.

———. 1980. *Plato: Symposium*. Cambridge: Cambridge University Press.

Edelstein, Ludwig. 1945. "Eryximachus in Plato's *Symposium*." *Transactions of the American Philological Association* 76:85–103.

Fehr, Burkhard. "Entertainers at the Symposion: The Akletoi in the Archaic Period." Pp. 185–95 in *Sympotica: A Symposium on the Symposion*. Edited by Oswyn Murray. Oxford: Oxford University Press.

Foucault, Michel. 1985. *The Use of Pleasure: The History of Sexuality*, vol. 2. Translated by Robert Hurley. New York: Vintage.

Gagarin, Michael. 1977. "Socrates' Hybris and Alcibiades' Failure." *Phoenix* 31:22–37.

Gantz, Timothy. 1993. *Early Greek Myth: A Guide to the Literary and Artistic Sources.* Baltimore: Johns Hopkins University Press.

Gould, Thomas. 1963. *Platonic Love.* London: Routledge & Paul.

Halperin, David. 1985. "Platonic Eros and What Men Call Love." *Ancient Philosophy* 5:161–204.

———. 1990. "Why Is Diotima a Woman? Platonic Eros and the Figuration of Gender." Pp. 257–308 in *Before Sexuality: The Construction of Erotic Experience in the Ancient Greek World.* Edited by David M. Halperin, John J. Winkler, and Froma I. Zeitlin. Princeton: Princeton University Press.

———. 2002. *How to Do the History of Homosexuality.* Chicago: University of Chicago Press.

Hubbard, Thomas K., ed. 2000. *Greek Love Reconsidered.* New York: Wallace Hamilton.

———, ed. 2003a. *Homosexuality in Greece and Rome: A Sourcebook of Basic Documents.* Berkeley: University of California Press.

———. 2003b. Review of Halperin 2002. *Bryn Mawr Classical Review* 9:22.

Hunter, Richard. 2004. *Plato's Symposium.* Oxford Approaches to Classical Literature. Oxford: Oxford University Press.

Jameson, Michael. 1993. "The Asexuality of Dionysus." Pp. 44–64 in *Masks of Dionysus.* Edited by Thomas H. Carpenter and Christopher A. Faraone. Ithaca: Cornell University Press.

Kannicht, R., and B. Snell. *Tragicorum Graecorum fragmenta*, vol. 2. Göttingen: Vandenhoeck & Ruprecht, 1981.

Kidd, Ian. 1995. "Some Philosophical Demons." *Bulletin of the Institute of Classical Studies* 40:217–24.

Konstan, David, and E. Young-Bruehl. 1982. "Eryximachus' Speech in the *Symposium.*" *Apeiron* 16:40–46.

Konstan, David. 2002. "Enacting Eros." Pp. 354–73 in *The Sleep of Reason: Erotic Experience and Sexual Ethics in Ancient Greece and Rome.* Edited by Martha Nussbaum and Juha Sihvola. Chicago: University of Chicago Press (available online at http://www.stoa.org/diotima/essays/).

Lear, Andrew, and Eva Cantarella. 2008. *Images of Ancient Greek Pederasty: Boys Were Their Gods.* New York: Routledge.

Lissarague, François. 1987. *The Aesthetics of the Greek Banquet: Images of Wine and Ritual.* Translated by Andrew Szegedy-Maszak. Princeton: Princeton University Press.

———. 1990a. "Around the Krater: An Aspect of Banquet Imagery." Pp. 196–209 in *Sympotica: A Symposium on the Symposion.* Edited by Oswyn Murray. Oxford: Oxford University Press.

———. 1990b. "Why Satyrs Are Good to Represent." Pp. 228–36 in *Nothing to Do with Dionysos? Athenian Drama in Its Social Context.* Edited by John J. Winkler and Froma I. Zeitlin. Princeton: Princeton University Press

Mattingly, H. B. 1958. "The Date of Plato's *Symposium.*" *Phronesis* 3:31–39.

McClure, Laura. 2003. *Courtesans at Table: Gender and Greek Literary Culture in Athenaeus.* New York: Routledge.

Murray, Oswyn, ed. 1990. *Sympotica: A Symposium on the Symposion.* Oxford: Oxford University Press.

Nails, Debra. 2002. *The People of Plato: A Prosopography of Plato and Other Socratics.* Indianapolis: Hackett.

———. 2006. "Tragedy Off-Stage." Pp. 179–207 in *Plato's Symposium: Issues in Interpretation and Reception.* Edited by J. H. Lesher, Debra Nails, Frisbee C. C. Sheffield. Hellenic Studies 22. Washington DC: Center for Hellenic Studies, Harvard University Press.

Nehamas, Alexander, and Paul Woodruff. 1989. *Symposium/Plato: Translated, with Introduction and Notes.* Indianapolis: Hackett.

Nussbaum, Martha. 1986. "The Speech of Alcibiades: A Reading of the Symposium." Pp. 165–99 in Nussbaum's *The Fragility of Goodness: Luck and Ethics in Greek Tragedy and Philosophy.* Cambridge: Cambridge University Press.

Patterson, Richard. 1982. "The Platonic Art of Comedy and Tragedy." *Philosophy and Literature* 6:76–93.

———. 1991. "The Ascent in Plato's Symposium." *Proceedings of the Boston Area Colloquium in Ancient Philosophy* 7:193–214.

Riginos, Alice Swift. 1976. *Platonica: The Anecdotes concerning the Life and Writings of Plato.* Leiden: Brill.

Rose, Gilbert P., ed. 1985. *Plato's Symposium.* 2nd ed. Bryn Mawr: Bryn Mawr Classical Commentaries.

Rosen, Stanley. 1987. *Plato's Symposium*. 2nd ed. New Haven: Yale University Press.

Rowe, C. J., ed. 1998. *Plato: Symposium*. Warminster: Aris & Phillips.

Ruprecht, Louis A., Jr. 1999. *Symposia: Plato, the Erotic, and Moral Value*. Albany: State University of New York Press.

Rutherford, R. B. 1995. "The Symposium." Pp. 179–205 in Rutherford's *The Art of Plato*. London: Duckworth.

Seaford, Richard. 2006. *Dionysos*. New York: Routledge.

Sider, David. 1980. "Plato's Symposium as Dionysian Festival." *Quaderni urbinati di cultura classica* 33:41–56.

Slater, William J., ed. 1991. *Dining in a Classical Context*. Ann Arbor: University of Michigan Press.

Smyth, Herbert Weir. 1956. *Greek Grammar*. Revised by Gordon M. Messing. Cambridge: Harvard University Press.

Snell, Bruno, ed., with R. Kannicht. 1986. *Tragicorum Graecorum fragmenta*, vol. 1. Göttingen: Vandenhoeck & Ruprecht.

Sparkes, Brian A., and Lucy Talcott. 1951. *Pots and Pans of Classical Athens*. Princeton: American School of Classical Studies at Athens.

West, M. L., ed. 1966. *Hesiod: Theogony*. Oxford: Clarendon.

EROS AT THE BANQUET

Introduction

Overview of the Dialogue

The *Symposium* is one of Plato's dialogues, a series of works he wrote in the first half of the fourth century B.C.E. following the death of Socrates in 399 B.C.E. Socrates appears in most of the dialogues, usually as the central character; their typical action is dialogue between the philosopher and various individuals, many of whom are important historical figures in their own right. The dialogues are, however, generally assumed to be fictional. Although they may refer to real people and events, they should be taken not as historical accounts, but as imaginative recreations, including plenty of deliberate invention and careful reshaping to fit Plato's larger purposes. Appendix 1 contains biographical sketches of all the major characters in the *Symposium*, but readers should use these details with caution, remembering that Plato is not necessarily interested in historical accuracy.

Plato's original purpose in the dialogues appears to have been to help his readers appreciate, or at least confront, the complex figure of Socrates: his strange teaching technique of relentless questioning; his idiosyncratic personality, lifestyle, and ethical beliefs; and his alienation from mainstream Athenian culture—all of which resulted in his state-mandated suicide following his conviction for impiety and corrupting the young. This purpose is clearest in Plato's early dialogues, which look at events surrounding the trial of Socrates (*Apology, Crito*) or depict question-and-answer sessions that expose the reader to Socrates' methods and values (*Ion, Euthyphro, Lysis*). Plato sometimes appears to be directly addressing the specific charges made against Socrates at his trial (he did not acknowledge the gods of the city, he introduced new divinities, he corrupted the youth) or to be correcting popular beliefs about Socrates found in contemporary sources (that Socrates took pay for his teaching, that he was a teacher of rhetoric). Other representations of Socrates by those who knew him survive—Aristophanes' comedy the *Clouds* (first performed in 423 B.C.E.) and Xenophon's Socratic dialogues (ca. 394–354 B.C.E.), including another *Symposium*—but Plato's versions are generally considered the most successful. Plato's Socrates is more interesting and complex than either Aristophanes' intellectual buffoon or Xenophon's tedious moralizer. Plato thus makes clearer how Socrates simultaneously attracted so many followers and so much ire. Plato also seeks in the dialogues to explore philosophical questions of various kinds. Some of these were apparently of interest to Socrates himself, though the later dialogues are generally thought to reflect Plato's own philosophical concerns rather than those of the historical Socrates.

The *Symposium*, probably written about 384–379 B.C.E.,[1] is from the middle of Plato's career, approximately the same period that saw the production of his other great masterpiece, the *Republic*. It recounts the story of a drinking party (Greek *symposium*) that took place in 416 B.C.E.[2] in Athens at the home of a fifth-century writer of tragedies, Agathon. It certainly contributes much to Plato's two characteristic goals. We learn about Socrates both through what we witness in the dialogue and from what is said about him by his friends and close associates, particularly by the outspoken Alcibiades, who, because he is drunk, tells more than an inhibited speaker might. The dialogue emphasizes some of the most idiosyncratic features of Socrates' character: his sudden immersions into strange trancelike states, his flirtatious behavior with young men, his resistance to strong human impulses, such as fear and desire. The *Symposium* also explores the philosophical concept of ἔρως (*eros*, erotic love), apparently a real concern to the historical Socrates throughout his life. This dialogue is also considered philosophically important for what most interpreters see as a highly developed statement on the nature of the forms, a philosophical concept central to Plato's philosophy as interpreters understand it (see reading 9 with introduction).

Major as these achievements are, the *Symposium* goes beyond them to engage readers with little interest in philosophy as normally conceived, through its many comedic touches, its drinking party setting, and its erotic subject matter. It is generally considered Plato's literary masterpiece. Containing some of the most memorable passages ever written on the subject of erotic love, it has been highly influential on later literature and thought.[3] The mix of narrative styles, including casual banter, witty mythmaking, personal narrative, Socratic cross-examination, and polished rhetorical speeches, keeps the *Symposium* constantly fresh and engaging, as does the broad range of sources it draws on: traditional myths, contemporary scientific and medical theories, laws, and social practices. Moreover, the various parts seem carefully arranged to stimulate thought, without permitting readers to draw a simple or obvious conclusion. Unlike many Socratic dialogues in which Socrates dominates the discussion, the *Symposium* includes a full cast of engaging characters who compete with Socrates for our attention. It is in this way perhaps the most "dialogic" of Plato's dialogues, as the characters emerge as fully realized participants in the discussion rather than as subordinates to Socrates.

In addition, Plato considers many of the most essential aspects of Athenian life in the fifth century, making it a treasure trove of information for students of the ancient Greek world. Set at a critical moment in Athenian history, it includes one of its most colorful and controversial political figures, Alcibiades (see introduction: "Historical Context of the Dialogue"). It engages the two most significant literary genres of fifth-century Athens: drama and rhetoric (see introduction:

---

1. For the dating, see the brief account and references in Dover 1980: 10n1. See Corrigan and Glazov-Corrigan 2004 for arguments that Plato conceived and composed the *Symposium* and *Republic* simultaneously.

2. Our source for the date is Athenaeus, *Deipnosophists* 5.217a. Athenaeus is, however, here discussing Plato's unreliability as a chronologist, something that should perhaps trouble commentators more than it has.

3. Xenophon's *Symposium* is probably the earliest example of its pervasive influence; *Hedwig and the Angry Inch*, a rock musical now available in film, is a relatively recent response to Aristophanes' speech in the dialogue that students may find interesting. Allen 1991: vii–viii contains a very brief summary of its philosophical importance; Hunter 2004: 113–35 includes an excellent overview of its afterlife.

"Literary Themes and Context"). The *Symposium* also offers a glimpse of two major social institutions of fifth-century Athens: the symposium, the all-male Greek drinking party (see introduction: "The Symposium as a Social Institution"), and pederasty, an erotic relationship between an older male and younger teenaged male, an institution regularly associated with the aristocratic world of the Athenian symposium (see introduction: "Pederasty at Athens"). Although far from straightforward in its approach to these two social institutions, the *Symposium* is a major source for our understanding of them and for our understanding of Greek social and sexual beliefs and practices.

Platonic Love

The *Symposium* is also largely responsible for the widespread conception of Platonic love, now popularly considered a nonsexual form of love, a surprising thing given that the dialogue sets out to discuss specifically a kind of love that is commonly associated with sexual desire (ἔρως) rather than the more general conception of love represented by the Greek word φιλία, which covers a much wider range of human relations, including love between parents and children and among friends (see introduction: "The Greek Vocabulary of Love"). The teachings of a woman named Diotima (reading 9) and the behavior of Socrates, as reported by Alcibiades in the final speech (reading 10), supported by the views of other speakers that erotic love should not be selfishly directed toward sexual gratification but should contribute to the virtue and education of the beloved, contribute to the paradoxical notion that Plato's ideal of erotic love is often best expressed in relationships that do not involve sexual acts.

Further Reading on Platonic Love

- primary—on ἔρως: Plato, *Phaedrus*; on φιλία: Plato, *Lysis*
- secondary—Gould 1963; Halperin 1985

Religion in the *Symposium*: Δαίμονες, Eros, and Dionysus

The dialogue also offers original perspectives on Greek divinities. Socrates reports the teachings of a woman, Diotima, apparently a priestess, who offers the intriguing idea of a δαίμων as a figure midway between the gods and humans (reading 9B), a simplified way of looking at the Greek idea of the δαίμων that proved very influential. In earlier texts, there is no simple consistent division between god and δαίμων; the term tends to be used in connection with a particular kind of divine activities rather than with a distinct class of divine beings, so that Homer, for example, refers to the Olympian gods in certain contexts as δαίμονες (Burkert 1985: 179–81). The *Symposium*'s conception of the δαίμων (Latin *daemon*) ultimately evolved into the European notion of the demon, a much more negative figure than the Greek δαίμων, which can bring good fortune as well as bad to human beings.

In addition, the *Symposium* has a great deal to say about two Greek gods: Eros, the boy-god of love, and Dionysus, god of wine and theater. When compared to his mother, the goddess of love, Aphrodite, Eros is a relatively minor figure in Greek literature before the *Symposium*. Absent from Homer epic and other early mythical narratives, he appears briefly in Hesiod's *Theogony* as a parentless cosmic force essential to the divine reproduction that created the ordered universe; he is most beautiful of the immortals and a looser of limbs (λυσιμελής) who overpowers the sense and thoughtful counsel of the gods (*Theogony* 120–22). Lyric poetry and art of the archaic and classical periods build on this characterization of the god in the image of love itself, making Eros a handsome, cunning, and seductive youth rather than the chubby baby (the Latin Cupid) of later times.

Although this youthful Eros may be playful, he may also be dangerous, an inducer of madness and pain. In one poetic fragment, Anacreon, a sixth-century lyric poet, describes Eros tossing a ball to the lover and inviting him out to play with a girl (PMG 358). In another, he compares Eros to a blacksmith who batters the lover with an axe and douses him in an ice-cold bath (PMG 413). Eros is a boxer (PMG 396), a hunter (Ibycus PMG 287), a mountain wind that smashes oaks (Sappho 47 L-P), the nursling of the Frenzies (Μανίαι), the destroyer of Troy and many heroes (Theognis 1231–34).[4] In Euripides' tragedy *Hippolytus*, the chorus sings a remarkable ode concerning Eros, calling him a "tyrant over men" who "breathes disaster" (525–64). Anacreon captures the paradox of Eros in this brief fragment: "The dice that Eros plays with / are raving madness and battle din" (PMG 398; translation by Bing and Cohen 1991: 91). Although they build on these traditional representations, the characters of the *Symposium* present more benign views of this boy-god.

Dionysus, too, though not as overtly the subject of the dialogue as Eros, is frequently evoked as the god of theater, as the god of wine and therefore the natural overseer of drinking parties, and as the patron god of the satyrs. The *Symposium* thus takes a place beside Euripides' *Bacchae* and Aristophanes' *Frogs* (both 405 B.C.E.) as one of the great results of reflection on the nature of that enigmatic god. With a dramatic date close to the dates of these two dramatic productions, the *Symposium* appears to join in the late-fifth-century discussion of Dionysus.

Further Reading on Religion in the Symposium

- primary—on Dionysus: Euripides, *Bacchae* and *Cyclops*; Aristophanes, *Frogs*; *Homeric Hymn to Dionysus*; on Eros: Sappho 130 L-P; Ibycus PMG 286, 287; Anacreon PMG 357, 358, 398, 413; Theognis 1231–34, 1275–78 (all of which can be found in English translation in Bing and Cohen 1991); Hesiod, *Theogony* 120–22. Euripides has many fragments on the subject of Eros in addition to his hymn to the powerful and destructive Eros (*Hippolytus* 525–62), some of which are included as challenge passages in the exercises. *Lexicon iconographicum mythologiae classicae* (1981–97) has articles on both Dionysus and Eros; although the articles are not in English, students will profit from the abundant artistic representations.

---

4. Ibycus, Sappho, and Theognis are all major lyric poets whose writings are worth exploring further for early Greek ideas about love.

Fig. 1. Eros as a young man, with Aphrodite, looking more like her husband than her son. Detail from bronze hydria (water vessel), fourth century B.C.E. Inv. 2001.12.1. Courtesy of the Michael C. Carlos Museum of Emory University, Atlanta, Georgia. Photo by Bruce M. White, 2005.

- secondary—general information: Burkert 1985; on δαίμονες: Kidd 1995; on Dionysus: Seaford 2006, Carpenter and Faraone 1993; on Eros: Carson 1986, Breitenberger 2007

Drama of the *Symposium*: A Brief Summary of Its Action

The *Symposium* is arguably the most dramatic of Plato's dialogues.[5] In antiquity Plato was said to be writing tragedies before he met Socrates and was converted to philosophy. Although modern scholars are skeptical of this claim, the *Symposium* certainly not only shows considerable interest in drama but demonstrates Plato's skills at plotting and characterization.[6]

The occasion for the *Symposium* is a banquet in celebration of Agathon's first victory two days earlier in the tragic contests at the Lenaea, a festival celebrating the god Dionysus, one of the two venues for tragic performance at Athens.[7] All dramatic performances in Athens in this period were part of competitions, and this competitive context is also evident in the *Symposium*, whose speakers openly compete to give the best performance. Indeed, Agathon says early in the dialogue that the god Dionysus himself will judge the contest in wisdom between Socrates and Agathon.

We learn (reading 2) that most of the men present at Agathon's party had drunk a great deal of wine at a victory celebration the night before. When some of them confess that they are still hungover, they decide that they will forego serious drinking for the night and drink only for pleasure (on drinking practices at symposia, see "The Symposium as a Social Institution"). They decide to pass the time by making speeches in praise of Eros, who, they agree, has been neglected by the poets, traditionally responsible for the praise of gods. There follows a series of five speeches on the subject of Eros the god and ἔρως the concept (Greek writing conventions of the period do not distinguish capital and lowercase letters). These speeches offer a noteworthy array of different views, both popular and idiosyncratic, on both Eros and ἔρως, from the point of view of Athenian men of the fifth century. Interesting in their own right, they are also useful as sources for Athenian beliefs about love and sexual practices. The speeches are carefully arranged in a sequence that appears to be taking steps toward defining a new philosophical notion of love. A highly inventive and amusing myth tracing the origins of human love, recounted by Aristophanes, the famous writer of comedies, is one of the most successful achievements of the dialogue (reading 6). The series of speeches climaxes in a highly rhetorical and artful speech in praise of Eros by the host and honoree, Agathon (reading 7).

---

5. Some suggest the *Protagoras* as a possible contender; the *Protagoras* is set some fifteen to twenty years earlier, when Alcibiades is first getting his beard (309a) and Agathon is still a youth (μειράκιον; 315d–e), but includes many of the same characters as the *Symposium* so appears to be thematically linked (Rutherford 1995: 181–82).

6. See Riginos 1976: 43–51 for the anecdotes linking Plato with various kinds of poetry, particularly tragedy, and for her arguments against them.

7. The other is the City Dionysia, a still larger festival of Dionysus and a more competitive context for tragedies. At the City Dionysia there were three days of tragedy, each day devoted to a performance of three tragedies and one satyr-play by a single tragedian. At the Lenaea only two tragic poets competed with two tragedies and no satyr-play. Comedies were more important than tragedies at the Lenaea, the reverse at the City Dionysia. Sider 1980 suggests that Plato invokes elements of the City Dionysia to enhance the importance of the occasion.

Immediately following the applause that greets Agathon's speech, Socrates steps forward to question Agathon in his characteristic way (reading 8). As elsewhere in Plato's dialogues, Socrates explicitly rejects speechmaking as a method for arriving at the truth. Instead, by leading Agathon through a series of questions, Socrates shows that Agathon does not know what he is talking about and that many of his assumptions about Eros and ἔρως are false. Socrates then proceeds to offer the views of a woman named Diotima (reading 9), who, he claims, taught him all about love when he was younger. He confesses that he himself once thought as Agathon does but that Diotima taught him otherwise. Diotima appears to be a Platonic invention; she is particularly interesting as the only woman represented in the all-male context of the *Symposium*. Many scholars consider her to be the mouthpiece of Plato himself; her views are the most overtly philosophical views presented.

Shortly after Socrates' account of Diotima's speech to him, there is a terrible noise, and Socrates' young associate Alcibiades crashes the party, clearly extremely drunk. After much lively banter and jesting, Alcibiades embarks on a speech in praise of, not Eros, but Socrates (reading 10). In addition to reporting several interesting episodes in Socrates' life, the speech develops a memorable comparison of Socrates to a satyr, a mythological half-man/half-horse follower of the god Dionysus, known for frequently comical expressions of drunkenness and sexual desire.

Following Alcibiades' speech, we get a brief glimpse of Socrates, Aristophanes, and Agathon drinking and discussing whether the same person can write both tragedies and comedies (reading 11). The rest of the group has fallen asleep after drinking considerable amounts of wine, and our source admits that he soon joined them. The dialogue ends with Socrates resuming his normal life at daybreak, unaffected by having been awake all night drinking.

This summary addresses the main features of the narrative, but the *Symposium* is further complicated by an unusually elaborate introductory section that presents two separate narrators, Apollodorus, who was not himself present at the party but is telling the story to an unnamed companion (ἑταῖρος) and to us, and Aristodemus, who was present at the party as a follower of Socrates himself and who originally reported the tale to Apollodorus (reading 1). This introductory frame certainly suggests Plato's interest in the nature of narrative and its problematic relationship to truth. It also establishes a second dramatic date, the time of narration, some ten to fifteen years after the party itself, as a frame of reference.

Historical Context of the Dialogue

Although written in the first half of the fourth century, the dialogue is set in the final two decades of the fifth. The introductory frame (reading 1) occurs somewhere near the end of the fifth century. The conversation makes it clear that Socrates is still alive, so it must be prior to his death in 399 B.C.E., but our narrator suggests that the events that he is about to describe took place long before, so it is hard to imagine that this discussion took place much earlier than 405 B.C.E. This puts it toward the end of the Peloponnesian War, the great conflict between the two major Greek city-states, Athens and Sparta, and their allies. The war ended in 404 B.C.E. with the Athenians' defeat at the hands of the Spartans and their subsequent loss of political dominance in Greece. This defeat also contributed to a cultural decline in Athens. Without the revenues flowing in from its tribute-paying allies, Athens did not have the finances to support the public building projects that, under the leadership of fifth-century statesmen such as Pericles, led to the Parthenon and other architectural masterpieces. Moreover, in 406/405 B.C.E., both Sophocles and Euripides died, leaving Athens bereft of its most prominent tragic playwrights. Aristophanes continued to write comedies, but apart from the brilliant *Frogs*, written in response to the death of Euripides, none of the later Aristophanic comedies have quite the brilliance or political punch of those from the war years. Thus, Athens was significantly diminished. Although Menander and Plato, in particular, reinvigorated Athenian culture to some degree with their literary innovations in the fourth century, the final years of the fifth century must have been dispiriting for Athenians, particularly as they looked back on the previous century of achievement. Thucydides, a contemporary chronicler of the Peloponnesian War, clearly interprets the downfall of Athens as tragic. Thus, the introductory section provides a tragic frame for the bright comedy of the drinking party, set in the period before Sparta's defeat of Athens.

Although the date of the introductory frame is imprecise, most of the action of the *Symposium* can be set very precisely in 415 B.C.E. This is a crucial moment of Athenian history: Athens seemed to be asserting military and cultural dominance over the other Greek city-states, but the Athenians' disastrous expedition to Sicily in 415 would signal the end of their aggressive campaign.[8] Moreover, Alcibiades, who plays a major part in this dialogue, played a major role in the fiasco in Sicily. Initially, he was one of the great supporters of the Sicilian Expedition and was one of three generals chosen to lead it. Shortly after the expedition set out, however, he was recalled to Athens to stand trial on a charge that he had "profaned the Eleusinian Mysteries," apparently by participating in some kind of staged initiation into this secret cult in honor of the goddess Demeter in front of onlookers who had not been initiated, possibly at a symposium very like the one described here.

The charge against Alcibiades may have received additional weight owing to another event: the so-called mutilation of the herms. The herms were stone statues, representations of the god Hermes, consisting of a head and a set of genitals on a stone plinth (fig. 2). Herms stood in doorways and at the entrances to public spaces, offering luck to passersby. The night before the Athenian fleet was due to sail to Sicily, these were mutilated, perhaps by drunken revelers following a symposium, perhaps by political rivals of Alcibiades seeking to undermine the expedition. This was seen as a bad omen for the expedition, tempting retribution from the gods. Informants who came forward during the inquiry into the mutilation accused Alcibiades both of the sacrilege (which would seem to work strangely against his own aims) and of involvement in the mocking of the mysteries, apparently associating both acts of impiety with a plot to overthrow the democracy (Thucydides 6.27–29). Two other guests at Agathon's party, Phaedrus and Eryximachus, were accused by different informants of participating in the sacrilege (Andocides, *On the*

---

8. Dover 1980: 9n1 points out that it is somewhat over a year until the Sicilian Expedition, but that time frame might seem short to someone writing so many years later. Moreover, this is presumably a liberty we can permit a writer of what is a kind of fiction.

Fig. 2. Ithyphallic herm from Siphnos. Archaic, ca. 510 B.C.E. Inv. 3728. National Archaeological Museum, Athens, Greece. Photo credit: Bridgeman-Giraudon/Art Resource, New York.

Mysteries 15, 35).[9] These events consequently lurk in the shadowy political and social background of Agathon's party.

The recall of Alcibiades was particularly unfortunate as one of the other two generals in charge of the Sicilian Expedition, Nicias, had argued in the Athenian assembly against undertaking it, accusing Alcibiades of supporting it out of a selfish desire for profit and fame (Thucydides 6.12). Alcibiades' recall therefore left the Athenian army with weak and uninspired leadership. Moreover, Alcibiades did not accept his recall with grace; he ran away to Sparta and gave the Spartans and their commander Gylippus advice that helped them to corner and massacre a large part of the Athenian army in Sicily. Athens never seems to have recovered its confidence following this devastating defeat, though the war dragged on for some ten years.

By setting the party in the period immediately before the Sicilian Expedition and by giving such prominence to Alcibiades, Plato seems to be commenting on the broader historical circumstances that led Athens from the pinnacle of its power and influence to the low point of the turn of the century. Many scholars think that Alcibiades' role in the Peloponnesian War and in contemporary politics was instrumental to the charge in Socrates' trial that he was guilty of corrupting young men. Plato seems to be considering the relationship between the two very carefully in the *Symposium*.

Further Reading on Historical Context

- primary—most standard histories of Athens contain good accounts of these events, but a wealth of excellent primary sources are available, of which Thucydides' *Peloponnesian War*, especially book 6, and Plutarch's *Life of Alcibiades* probably make the most interesting reading. Additional primary sources worth consulting are Andocides, *On the Mysteries*; Xenophon, *Hellenica* 1; and Plato, *Alcibiades* 1.

Literary Themes and Context

Throughout the *Symposium*, Plato plays with different literary genres and styles. For example, a doctor, Eryximachus, gives a polished speech that uses vocabulary and forms of expression characteristic of the most developed scientific and medical writers of the day; in its interest in elements and opposites, such as the cold and the hot, the wet and the dry, it has close affinities with the surviving writing of the presocratic philosophers and the Hippocratic corpus. But, above all, the dialogue emphasizes the two most prominent literary genres of the period: rhetoric and drama. All of the six speechmakers in the *Symposium*, except for the comic poet Aristophanes, are also depicted in Plato's *Protagoras* listening intently to prominent sophists. These sophists were professional teachers of wisdom on many topics, but were known particularly for their expertise in public speaking, a skill for which they were well paid in Athens, where public

---

9. See Murray 1990: 149–61 for a discussion of the political significance of these two events and their connection to *symposia*. But Nails 2002: 223–24, 143 points out that, though there is solid evidence connecting Phaedrus to the profanation of the Mysteries, connecting either character to the mutilation of the herms is less certain.

speaking had so many important uses, both in politics and in the courtroom. Thus, all of the speakers but Aristophanes are closely associated elsewhere in Plato with rhetorical training. Agathon's showy style, the climax of the first part of the dialogue, is explicitly associated with that of Gorgias, arguably the most prominent fifth-century rhetorician and the subject of another major Platonic dialogue on the subject of rhetoric. The style of Agathon's speech is strikingly distinct, but each speaker has a characteristic style particular to himself, and Plato has clearly given considerable thought to the techniques and effects of rhetoric.

The setting for the party, a celebration of Agathon's first victory in the tragic contests, makes the importance of the dramatic theme clear. In addition, two major Athenian dramatists of the period play central roles in the dialogue: Agathon, a tragedian, competitive with his better known contemporaries Euripides and Sophocles; and Aristophanes, the best known writer of comedies from antiquity. Their two juxtaposed speeches are the climax of the first set of speeches in the dialogue; moreover, only these two remain awake at the end, arguing with Socrates over tragedy and comedy. In addition, Socrates explicitly identifies the third major Athenian form of drama, satyr-play, with the final speech of the dialogue, in which Alcibiades develops his comparison between Socrates and a satyr. Satyr-play, named after the chorus of satyrs that appeared in each play of this type, had some of the same seriocomic elements as Alcibiades' speech, as we can see in the only complete surviving example, Euripides' *Cyclops*. Moreover, satyr-play was normally performed immediately following a tragic poet's three tragedies, thus bringing a cheerier mood to the end of a day of dramatic performances. Alcibiades' drunken, Dionysus-inspired, satyr-filled speech plays the same role in the dialogue.

The inclusion of Aristophanes is also striking, as, unlike the other characters in the *Symposium*, Plato does not portray him as a friend of Socrates elsewhere. Moreover, in his *Clouds*, a play first performed in 423 B.C.E., Aristophanes pillories Socrates as a fuzzy-headed intellectual and a dangerous and immoral sophist. In Plato's *Apology*, a fictional version of the defense speech that Socrates gave at his trial, Socrates implies that the *Clouds* was a major factor in Socrates' bad reputation in Athens and therefore contributed to his death (18b, 19b–c). In his *Thesmophoriazusae*, produced in 411 B.C.E., Aristophanes also mocks the host of the party, Agathon, for an effeminate personal and poetic style. But there are no obvious signs of tension between these characters in the *Symposium*, nor does Plato characterize Aristophanes in an obviously disrespectful way. Indeed, Aristophanes gives one of the most engaging speeches of the dialogue. Although he is the butt of jokes and raillery, anecdotal evidence suggests that this kind of mockery was intended and accepted in a friendly spirit and was a natural part of the social institution of the symposium (see reading 1 introduction).

Further Reading on Literary Themes

- on rhetoric—speeches of Lysias and Gorgias's brief *Encomium on Helen* are useful samples of contemporary rhetoric for readers of the *Symposium*. Plato's *Phaedrus* discusses Lysias as a rhetorician. See also Plato, *Gorgias*.
- on comedy—Aristophanes' *Clouds*, *Frogs*, and *Thesmophoriazusae* are good examples of Aristophanic comedies and offer comic takes on Socrates, Agathon, and Alcibiades. Reading

Aristophanes' *Thesmophoriazusae* is probably the best way to get an impression of how Agathon's tragedies might have compared to other surviving Greek tragedies, as none by Agathon himself exist (see appendix 1).

- on satyr-play—Euripides' *Cyclops* is the only surviving example.

The Symposium as a Social Institution

The symposium (literally "drinking-together") is an important Greek social institution defined primarily by the practice of drinking while reclining on couches (κλῖναι). The practice appears to have begun in Greece as early as the eighth century B.C.E. and to have remained important among Greek males of the social elite at least through the late Roman period.

The guests at Agathon's symposium are all male, and the symposium is traditionally a male domain. An Athenian man would not take his wife—or any other respectable female relative—to a symposium. Non-Athenian women or women of lower social classes were sometimes present. Flute-girls (αὐλητρίδες), women who played an αὐλός, a double-reed wind instrument similar to an oboe but usually translated "flute," appear in vase paintings and other representations of symposia, as do female dancers, but they are paid entertainers, not guests (figs. 4 and 5). We also hear of *hetaerae* (ἑταῖραι), female companions, at the symposium; these again are not legitimate Athenian wives, but are courtesans or mistresses, like Pericles' mistress, Aspasia, Neaera in the speech *Against Neaera*, and many of the female love interests of New Comedy. Typically, they are foreign-born women, often quite well educated, but they are treated as distinct from the daughters and wives of Athenian citizens, whose contact with men was carefully regulated to ensure their chastity before marriage and, later, their marital fidelity and the legitimacy of their children. *Hetaerae* are commonly depicted in vase paintings of the symposium and are addressed in the erotic lyric poetry that was performed at symposia. Literary sources show *hetaerae* engaged in the sexual jokes and banter—often showing considerable sophistication and a wide knowledge of literature—that were part of the symposium.

The men reclined on couches, arranged in a rectangle around the perimeter of specially designed rooms (the *andron*, the men's room), in uneven numbers, usually seven or eleven, sometimes as many as fifteen or as few as three. Two men normally shared a couch, though at the end of the *Symposium* Alcibiades joins Socrates and Agathon on the couch they are sharing, suggesting that they were roomy enough for three. There seems to have been a conventional hierarchy in the seating: the person on the right (probably) of the doorway was in the first position, moving in a counterclockwise direction around the room (see appendix 3). Often a symposiarch, the leader of the symposium, was chosen by lot or acclaim to direct the drinking and other activities of the group. In the *Symposium*, Eryximachus is acting as an exceptionally sober symposiarch until the drunken Alcibiades enters and appoints himself symposiarch.

The symposium normally began with a libation and a prayer to a god or gods. A dinner might precede the libation as it does in the *Symposium*, or food might be present as an accompaniment to the drinking.

Fig. 3.   Men reclining among characteristic accoutrements of the symposium; silhouettes of characteristic vessels on inner band. Detail from red-figure kylix (drinking cup), ca. 480 B.C.E. Inv. 1998.8. Courtesy of the Michael C. Carlos Museum of Emory University, Atlanta, Georgia. Photo by Bruce M. White, 2005.

It is clear, however, that wine drinking was the defining element of most symposia. The wine was mixed with either cold or warm water in a mixing bowl (*krater*) before being ladled into a wine pourer (*oinochoe*) and then poured, by a slave, into individual drinking cups (*kylixes*). The drinker propped himself up on his left elbow and held his cup with his right.

Greek literature contains numerous warnings against drinking too much. A number of poems recommend specific ratios of water to wine (ranging from half-wine/half-water to even more moderate proportions of wine to water).[10] We also have discussions of the disastrous results of excessive drinking, such as the poem below, by the comic poet Eubulus, defining how many *kraters* of wine it is safe for men to partake of—and the results of surpassing his recommended measures.

10. Davidson 1997: 46 suggests that five parts water to two parts wine was the most widely accepted proportion, about as potent as beer, given the greater potency of Greek wine.

Fig. 4.   Reclining man and woman playing the aulos. Interior of red-figure cup by the Colmar Painter, archaic period, ca. 490 B.C.E. From Vulci. Location: Louvre, Paris, France. Photo credit: Réunion des Musées Nationaux/ Art Resource, New York.

Fig. 5.   A scantily dressed flute-girl plays for men reclining and drinking in characteristic postures. The guests are drinking from rhytons. Detail from red-figure Attic terracotta bell crater, fourth century B.C.E. Inv. IV 910. Kunsthistorisches Museum, Vienna, Austria. Photo credit: Erich Lessing/Art Resource, New York.

This poem is quoted by Athenaeus as follows (the god Dionysus is speaking):

> Three bowls only do I mix for men of good sense.
> One is for health: the first one they quaff.
> The second is for love and pleasure, the third for sleep.
> Having drunk this down, those called wise
> go home. The fourth bowl no longer is our own,
> but hubris's. The fifth is shouting's,
> the sixth revel's, the seventh black eyes',
> the eighth is the lawsuit's, the ninth belongs to violent rage,
> the tenth to madness that leads to hurling![11]

11. It is not clear how the verb ἐκβάλλει is to be interpreted here. There are passages that suggest it can mean vomit, a translation hard to resist in the context. But others interpret it to mean "throw furniture," a result of excessive drinking well represented in Greek texts, or to mean that some unspecified member of the party throws the drunkard out.

So too much poured into one small cup
very easily knocks out the legs from under those who have drunk.[12]

It is clear from the poem itself that all men did not drink in the moderate way recommended by Dionysus. In addition, vase paintings show young men throwing up or otherwise carousing after a symposium (fig. 6).

The Greek name for such a carousing in the streets is a *komos*. (The poem above sees the *komos*, the revel, as the result of the sixth *krater*.) Alcibiades is clearly participating in a *komos* when he enters near the end of the dialogue. The *komos*-song, the drinking song following a symposium, is the etymological origin of the word *comedy*, and thus the themes of drinking and drama are entangled in Greek culture just as they are in the dialogue itself. In the *Symposium*, the guests decide early in the evening to drink only for pleasure. Dionysus of the poem associates the second *krater* with pleasure and, perhaps not coincidentally, *eros*. In fact, the results of the first six *kraters* in the poem are all mentioned in the dialogue: from health (at the beginning embodied by the doctor Eryximachus) to Alcibiades' shouting and the entrance of disorderly revelers at the end.

Besides drinking, eating, and ogling and/or listening to flute-girls, the guests at symposia enjoyed conversation, poetry, and musical performances of various kinds, including performances by the guests. Erotic and playful themes were clearly prominent. We also hear of drinking games, such as *kottabos*, in which drinkers, using the lees of their wine, attempted to hit a target (fig. 7).

Further Reading on the Background of the Symposium

• Davidson 1997: 43–49 is a valuable starting place for more background on the symposiastic context of the work. Sparkes and Talcott 1951 provides nice examples of the important pottery and cups used at the symposium as well as some amusing vase paintings illustrating their uses. Murray 1990 and Slater 1991 contain scholarly essays on various aspects of the symposium, including valuable essays on the archeological context. On women at the symposium, see Davidson 1997: 73–136, especially 91–97. McClure 2003 offers a detailed examination of the evidence of Athenaeus's *Deipnosophists* on *hetaerae* at the symposium.

Pederasty at Athens

The *Symposium* is written in a social context that recognizes erotic relationships between males as commonplace, though scholars find it difficult to agree on the precise nature of the relationship to which the term *pederasty* is applied. Several features are, however, characteristic of the relationship in Athens during the fifth century, the time in which the dialogue is set. There is normally an older male called the ἐραστής (lover) and a younger male, the ἐρώμενος (beloved) or the παιδικά (darling), implying a lopsided level of desire. The older male is assumed to

---

12. The Greek version is the challenge passage in review exercise 6.

Fig. 6. Boy assisting a vomiting drinker. Attic red-figure kylix (drinking cup) attributed to the Dokimasia Painter. From Capua, ca. 490 B.C.E. Inv. F2309. Photo: Johannes Laurentius. Location: Antikensammlung, Staatliche Museen zu Berlin, Berlin, Germany. Photo credit: Bildarchiv Preussischer Kulturbesitz/Art Resource, New York.

experience sexual desire or at least intensely strong admiration for a more beautiful and enticing younger one. The elder is presumed to be less physically attractive but to offer other kinds of benefits, at least when the relationship is between social equals, as the *Symposium* generally assumes. In vase painting, ἐρασταί are typically shown offering gifts of various kinds—fighting cocks, hares, lyres, and other small presents;[13] elsewhere, lovers implicitly or explicitly offer their beloveds fame or other kinds of social or political advancement. In the context of the symposium, the role of the ἐραστής seems to have been conceived of as educational and initiatory,

13. See Lear and Cantarella 2008: 39 for courting gifts depicted in vase painting.

Fig. 7. Man playing kottabos. Detail from red-figure kylix (drinking cup), ca. 480 B.C.E. Inv. 1998.8. Courtesy of the Michael C. Carlos Museum of Emory University, Atlanta, Georgia. Photo by Bruce M. White, 2005.

at least in the loose sense of introducing young men to the world of manhood and male behavior appropriate to their social class; some of the speakers in the *Symposium* use these traditional elements to support a fuller notion of the ἐραστής as a teacher of true virtue.

Pederasty as a social institution is closely associated with the aristocratic domain of the symposium, but many Greek texts, particularly Aristophanic comedies, treat sexual attraction to boys aged approximately thirteen to twenty years as a natural form of desire in adult males of all classes. Indeed, boys of this age, particularly athletes, are highly eroticized through the art of the period, much as teenage girls (and, increasingly, boys) are in contemporary popular culture. Infrequently mentioned, however, is a desire for boys that excludes an erotic attraction to women. Many texts assume that men are attracted to both women and boys. Greek mythology presents the god Zeus engaged in liaisons with multiple women, but also so interested in the beautiful Trojan youth Ganymede that he abducts him to be his cupbearer on Olympos. Bisexual attractions are accepted as the norm, and Zeus is exceptional only in how many relationships he cultivated successfully. Greek texts acknowledge that this was not necessarily beneficial to his relationship with his wife, Hera, but otherwise offer little critical comment on his choices. Like Zeus, men involved in pederastic relationships are not assumed to be uninterested in women; married men or men with female lovers might also admire or even pursue younger males. Ancient debates about which is the "better" object of love exist, however, and the *Symposium* is one of several texts that recognize that some men are more attracted to one gender than the other.

It is a little more difficult to pin down securely the ages at which males were involved in pederastic relationships. Texts suggest that boys just getting a first beard are particularly attractive; in fact, the sentiment is common that once a male experienced full beard growth, he was no longer desirable. The general assumption is that this means that males primarily between approximately thirteen and eighteen years of age were παιδικά;[14] Davidson 2007 argues that puberty took place considerably later in antiquity than in modern times, perhaps as late as age twenty-two or so, which would make the range a bit later than previous scholars thought. In addition, the *Symposium* treats Agathon as a young ἐρώμενος, though he must be close to thirty, if we can trust the evidence of the *Protagoras*, set some fifteen to twenty years earlier, in which he appears explicitly as the παιδικά of Pausanias.[15] Of course, in his *Thesmophoriazusae* of 411 B.C.E., Aristophanes implies that Agathon is effeminate and lacks a beard. If Agathon didn't experience the beard growth that normally marked maturity in Greek culture, his "shelf life" would have been extended. Or Plato may not be paying close attention to chronology, something that Athenaeus complains about in the passage on which we base our dating of the party.

Agathon and Pausanias appear to be atypical of pederastic couples in their long-term monogamy. Other texts imply that once a boy got full beard growth, his lover would turn his attention to younger boys, while the former ἐρώμενος would in turn become himself an ἐραστής, pursuing younger boys and/or women. The pederastic relationship is thus normally seen as transitory rather than permanent. Pausanias (reading 4) argues explicitly against this apparent norm, inspired no doubt partly by his own experience.

Debatable too is what kinds of behaviors were seen as socially acceptable ways for men to express their sexual desire for boys or young men. Texts tend to be discreet on this subject, and vase paintings, though occasionally very explicit, are not always easy to interpret.[16] There is a

---

14. Support for these ages can be found in Strato, *Palatine Anthology* 12.4, but this is a very late text, and there are some solid reasons to think that in fifth-century Athens, *eromenoi* were generally older.

15. Because the *Protagoras* reports that Alcibiades is just getting his beard, scholars date it some fifteen to twenty years earlier than the *Symposium*. Phaedrus, who likewise appears very young in the *Symposium*, is also present in the *Protagoras*.

16. Dover 1978 argues convincingly, primarily from the evidence of vase paintings, that intercrural (between the thighs) sex was a socially acceptable expression of pederasty. (Davidson 2007 argues that the fifth-century vases that depict intercrural sex are critical of this practice, though he seems to accept that earlier ones are not.) There is no evidence that it was ever

strong tendency, however, particularly in the philosophical tradition, to value resistance to sexual desire, and many texts that acknowledge male desire of boys as natural also clearly see resistance to the physical gratification of such desire as a form of manly strength. In addition, upper-class fathers tried to protect their sons who had not yet reached maturity from older sexually predatory males by making a slave, a *pedagogus*, attend them when going to and from school. Laws in Athens intended to prevent older males from mixing with boys under eighteen in the gymnasium and in other places that might allow sexual contact, and it seems clear that considerable social disapproval fell on men even for talking privately with underage boys of protected social classes. At symposia, boys under eighteen would not have reclined with other men on couches, but would have been seated or standing and chaperoned, typically by their fathers. Consequently, we should not imagine a world in which men were allowed to gratify their desire for teenage boys in any context and in anyway they wished. Although it is reasonably clear that there was little stigma attached to sexual acts involving boy slaves, the social and legal restrictions on the physical expression of erotic love within the context of pederasty were significant. Despite these restrictions, the symposium clearly was a context in which men felt comfortable openly expressing erotic feelings for younger men and even boys (*paides*), as vase paintings and lyric poetry clearly attest. The *Symposium* is no anomaly in this respect but is characteristic of Athenian culture and indeed of Greek culture more generally; homoerotic relationships were not only widely acknowledged but often highly valued as relationships central to the social and political order.

Further Reading on Pederasty

• Hubbard 2003a is an invaluable sourcebook of ancient sources pertaining to homosexual relations in antiquity. Dover's magisterial 1978 study remains the standard secondary work on Greek homoeroticism. Davidson 2007 offers an impassioned critique of many of Dover's most influential claims and will lead to some reevaluation as well as more detailed discussion of many aspects of Greek homosexuality. The work of Halperin and Hubbard, especially Halperin 2002 and Hubbard 2000 and 2003b, is also useful for those who want to acquaint themselves with some of the remaining controversies and issues. Bremmer 1990 gives a concise chronological survey of pederasty within the symposiastic context; the introduction in Bing and Cohen 1991 offers a brief overview of ancient erotic conceptions and customs. Foucault 1985 is important in defining issues that recur frequently in the discussion.

---

acceptable for men to perform oral sex on individuals of any age, class, or gender. The evidence for anal sex is ambiguous. Certainly, it is often presented as degrading and effeminizing to be the passive partner in such couplings, which would seem to make it unacceptable in the pederastic context of the symposium. Halperin implies (in 1990: esp. 266–67; and 1985) that it was acceptable to be the penetrating partner in anal copulation, but the evidence for this seems far from clear, particularly in the fifth century. Depictions of sodomy in fifth-century vase painting associate it with satyrs, figures of excess who draw derisive laughter; in comedy, sodomy is a form of insult or punishment, not an expression of erotic love. But a passage from Aristotle (fourth century) seems to take anal sex for granted, and erotic epigrams of later periods show considerable interest in the attractions of boys' anuses. And we do need to remember that the same act could have a different connotation in a different context even in the same time period. See also Lear and Cantarella 2008: 106–38 for a detailed discussion of the evidence from vase painting.

The Greek Vocabulary of Love: Ἔρως and Φιλία

Greek uses several distinct words for love. Ἔρως, the primary concept of love under scrutiny in the *Symposium*, and the corresponding verb ἐράω refer primarily to erotic love, though they can also be used to describe strong desires of a nonsexual kind. Homer speaks of an ἔρως for food and drink, for example. In his description of the preparations for the Sicilian Expedition, Thucydides describes an ἔρως for war taking hold of the citizens of Athens to suggest the irrationality in the enthusiasm with which they took up that highly dangerous and ultimately self-destructive mission: "An eros for the expedition overcame everyone alike" (ἔρως ἐνέπεσε τοῖς πᾶσιν ὁμοίως ἐκπλεῦσαι; 6.24.3). Diotima's speech in the *Symposium* explicitly extends the meaning of ἔρως beyond the merely sexual realm, but at the same time acknowledging that the word is normally used of erotic relationships. Although ἔρως is not exclusively sexual then, something clearly compulsive and overpowering about it makes it akin to sexual passion. It implies a strong desire or need, not merely affection or warmth.

The word φιλία, which also is regularly translated "love," and the corresponding verb φιλέω refer to a more general form of love that exists between family members and friends, though it can also apply to erotic relationships. Generally, φιλία is conceived of as a more symmetrical and mutual relationship with less connotation of strong passion than is ἔρως. Φίλοι (family members and friends) are presumed to both love and be loved; we do not see the strong distinction evident in the words ἐραστής and ἐρώμενος (see previous section). There are clearly contexts in which both φιλία and ἔρως apply to the same relationship, but these words should be kept distinct in discussions of the dialogue. A third word for love, ἀγαπή (only the verb ἀγαπάω occurs in Plato), has often been of particular interest to Christian interpreters. It is associated with an unselfish and giving form of love distinct from the passionate form represented by ἔρως. Ἀγαπάω is used in only a limited way in the *Symposium* and is hard to distinguish from φιλέω; it does not yet have the distinct connotations it would be given later by Christian thinkers.

Further Reading on Ἔρως

- Davidson 2007: 11–37 has an extended meditation on ἔρως and related words. Konstan 2002 offers interesting reflections on *eros* and reciprocity. Calame 1999 offers a book-length treatment that, though challenging, is much broader.

Bibliography

- text: Plato's *Symposium* is cited from Burnet 1901.
- commentaries on the *Symposium*: Rowe 1998 is particularly useful for students, because it contains a complete translation with the complete Greek text, as well as more detailed explanatory notes helpful to interpretation. Of the book-length studies, Hunter 2004 is specifically directed to first-time readers of the *Symposium*; Allen 1991 gives an excellent,

concise overview accessible to beginners as well as a translation; Nehamas and Woodruff's 1989 translation is particularly accessible and engaging. For those who want full interpretations, both Corrigan and Glazov-Corrigan 2004 and Rosen 1987 offer thorough and thought-provoking discussions of the whole.

Part 1
Readings and Notes

Reading 1. The Frame

The dialogue has an elaborate introductory section. It begins abruptly with a character, Apollodorus, a close associate of Socrates, speaking in response to an unnamed interlocutor's[17] unreported question about an event in the past, a dinner party at the house of the tragic poet Agathon. The unnamed interlocutor is later labeled simply ἑταῖρος (companion, friend); he is apparently a wealthy businessman (χρησματιστικός) (reading 1B.18–19). Apollodorus reports that he has recently told this story to Glaucon, presumably the brother of Plato, known to us from other dialogues, and in fact he begins with the story of that previous telling. The whole structure conveys great interest in the process of narrating itself, a characteristic feature of this dialogue, much of which is told in indirect statement and by narrators reporting what other narrators have said. In addition to establishing a specific time frame for the events described and their distance from the time of narration (see introduction: "Historical Context of the Dialogue"), Plato seems to be concerned in this opening section with establishing the sources for the account he gives in the dialogue, presumably as a way of suggesting something about its truth value.[18]

The choice of Apollodorus as narrator may be intended to remind the reader of Socrates' trial and death, since this same Apollodorus was present at both and, at least according to Plato's *Phaedo*, was particularly and memorably affected by Socrates' death, crying throughout the extended discussion before breaking down entirely and making everyone else cry too, except, of course, for Socrates (*Phaedo* 117d). This behavior is presented earlier in the *Phaedo* (59a–b) as characteristic of Apollodorus's "softness" (mentioned also in *Symposium* 173d). Xenophon in his version of Socrates' defense speech also associates him with tenderheartedness and the tears surrounding Socrates' death and also suggests that he is a bit naïve or simple (εὐήθης; *Apology* 27–28). The hint at Socrates' death combined with the general time frame of this introductory conversation (see introduction: "Historical Context of the Dialogue") gives a serious, even a tragic, frame to the generally light and comic events of the main narrative.[19]

---

17. This is not Glaucon, as Dover 1980: 8 suggests. Glaucon, who is presumably the same Glaucon who appears in Plato's *Republic* and is therefore Plato's brother, is rather one of the people to whom Apollodorus has previously addressed the story, as we learn below.

18. On this feature of the dialogue, see Corrigan and Glazov-Corrigan 2004: especially 7–20; and Hunter 2004: 22–29, which discusses Plato's interest in narrative form.

19. See Nails 2006 for more on the tragic consequences of the *Symposium*.

Fig. 8. Let us embark! Dionysus in his ship. Interior of kylix (drinking cup), ca. 540 B.C.E. by Exekias. Inv. 2440. Staatliche Antikensammlung, Munich, Germany, Photo credit: Bildarchiv Preussischer Kulturbesitz/Art Resource, New York.

Fig. 9.   Eyecup in resting position. This cup is decorated with ships, appropriate to a common conception of the drinking party as a sea voyage. The travelers must be careful to avoid a shipwreck. Inv. 2000.1.3. Courtesy of the Michael C. Carlos Museum of Emory University, Atlanta, Georgia. Photo by Bruce M. White, 2005.

The tragic and the comic, the serious and the laughable, are juxtaposed throughout the dialogue. So the second sentence of the dialogue mentions teasing (παίζων), an important element of symposia in general and the *Symposium* in particular, evident in the mocking banter exchanged by the guests at the party. Such teasing is accepted as part of the fun and camaraderie of the party. We hear a revealing anecdote about a man who asked Socrates whether he was upset about the "hubris" to which Aristophanes subjected him in the *Clouds* (see introduction: "Literary Themes and Context"). Apparently Socrates responded, "Not I. I am mocked in the theater as though at a giant symposium" (pseudo-Plutarch, *Moralia* 10cd). The symposiastic context makes the mockery playful rather than painful. The anecdote also suggests that the Athenians could see a natural analogy between drama and the symposium despite the much more public nature of drama and the obvious differences of scale (Hunter 2004: 13–14). The connection of both occasions to the god Dionysus and to various forms of playful disorder and performance encourage this. The so-called eyecups, which allow the drinker to take on a new identity as he drinks his wine, just as the actor does when he puts on his mask and costume, are a nice physical representation of the connection (figs. 9 and 10).

Fig. 10. Eyecup in drinking position creates a mask for the drinker with the cup's stem resembling a snout and handles representing ears. Inv. 2000.1.3. Courtesy of the Michael C. Carlos Museum of Emory University, Atlanta, Georgia. Photo by Bruce M. White, 2005.

Reading 1A

Apollodorus responds to an unreported question he has just been asked, by telling the story of his recent conversation with Glaucon and some other businessmen on the subject of the same dinner party.

Suggested Reviews

- indirect statement with the infinitive (*Essentials* §184)
- syntax (*Essentials* §§166–75) and declension (*Essentials* §§25–40) of participle
- forms of irregular verbs, especially εἰμί and φημί (*Essentials* §§65–66)
- second declension nouns θεός -οῦ ὁ/ἡ and δεῖπνον -ου τό (*Essentials* §43) and third declension neuter noun ἔτος -ους τό (*Essentials* §45.3d); learn to distinguish these noun types from one another using their glossary entries
- principal parts and meanings of ἀκούω, γίγνομαι, μένω, and πυνθάνομαι

  ἀκούω ἀκούσομαι ἤκουσα ἀκήκοα — ἠκούσθην = hear, listen
  γίγνομαι γενήσομαι ἐγενόμην γέγονα γεγένημαι = arise, happen, become, be
  μένω μενῶ ἔμεινα μεμένηκα = remain, wait, stay
  πυνθάνομαι πεύσομαι ἐπυθόμην — πέπυσμαι = learn by hearsay or by inquiry; ask (about), inquire (about); hear (about)

Vocabulary

ἄρτι *adv.*: recently, just now
δεῖπνον -ου τό: dinner, dinner party, feast
διηγέομαι διηγήσομαι διηγησάμην — διήγημαι: narrate, relate, tell, describe
ἔοικα: seem, resemble (perf. forms with pres. meaning); *often used impers.*: it seems, it appears
  (e.g., ὡς ἔοικε: as it seems; ὡς ἔοικε ἔμοιγε: as it seems to me at any rate)
ἐρωτικός -ή -όν: erotic, amatory, having to do with love or desire
ἔτος -ους τό: year
ἔχω + *inf.*: be able to ——

ἦ δ᾽ ὅς: he said (occasionally ἦ δ᾽ ἥ: she said; it does occur in reading 9, one of the few places in the *Symposium* where a woman speaks. Ἦ is not from εἰμί but from another -μι verb, ἠμί, which is used almost exclusively in this phrase and in another common phrase, ἦν δ᾽ ἐγώ: I said).

-θεν *as suffix*: from —— (e.g., πόθεν: from where?; οἴκοθεν: from home; πόρρωθεν: from afar, from a distance; Ἀθήνηθε(ν): from Athens)

μήν *particle*: indeed, truly; *especially common as* καὶ μήν: and indeed, moreover, what is more, and in fact (Denniston 1950: 108–11)

ὄπισθε(ν) *prep. + gen., or adv.*: behind, in back of *gen.*

οὔπω/οὐδέπω *adv.*: not yet (*πω: yet)

παίζω παίσομαι ἔπαισα πέπαικα πέπαισμαι: tease, joke, play (cf. παῖς ὁ/ἡ); παίζω . . . πρός *acc.*: make fun of *acc.*

παντάπασι(ν) *adv.*: all in all, in every way, completely, entirely (cf. πάντα-πᾶσι)

παραγίγνομαι παραγενήσομαι παρεγενόμην —— παρεγενήθην: be present, be by or near, come to, arrive at *dat.*

πόρρω *adv.*: far, far off, afar

πρό *prep. + gen.*: before, in front of, for, on behalf of (*note especially* πρὸ τοῦ: before this, previously; προ- is also found as a prefix: before, forward, in advance)

πρῴην *adv.*: lately, just now, day before yesterday

σαφής -ές: clear, plain, distinct, sure, unerring

συνουσία -ας ἡ: being together with, get-together, association, gathering

Reading 1A (based on *Symposium* 172a1–173a3)

ΑΠΟΛΛΟΔΩΡΟΣ Δοκῶ μοι οὐκ ἀμελέτητος εἶναι περὶ ὧν πυνθάνεσθε.   1

καὶ γὰρ ἐτύγχανον πρῴην εἰς ἄστυ οἴκοθεν ἰὼν Φαληρόθεν· τῶν οὖν   2

γνωρίμων τις ὄπισθεν ἰδών με πόρρωθεν ἐκάλεσε, καὶ παίζων· "Ὦ   3

Φαληρεύς," ἔφη, "οὗτος Ἀπολλόδωρος, οὐ μενεῖς;" Ἐγὼ οὖν ἔμεινα.   4

   Καὶ ὅς, "Ἀπολλόδωρε," ἔφη, "καὶ μὴν καὶ ἄρτι σε ἐζήτουν,   5

βουλόμενος πυθέσθαι τὴν Ἀγάθωνος συνουσίαν καὶ Σωκράτους καὶ   6

---

1 ˮ   δοκῶ μοι . . . εἶναι = I seem to myself to be; i.e., I think that . . . I am
      ἀμελέτητος -ον = unprepared, unpracticed
      περὶ ὧν = περὶ ἐκείνων ἅ: an example of suppressed antecedent and attraction of the relative
         pronoun (*Essentials* §§131–33)

2   καὶ γάρ = for in fact (καί often best translated "even" or "in fact" when it is not connecting two
         syntactically parallel things)
      ἰών: supplementary part. of εἶμι with ἐτύγχανον (*Essentials* §170)
      Φαληρόθεν = from Phalerum, one of the Athenian demes (political districts) outside the city on
         the coast (on the suffix -θεν, see vocabulary)

3   γνώριμος -ου ὁ = acquaintance; τῶν γνωρίμων is a partitive genitive with indefinite pronoun
         τις (*Essentials* §93); as often, the definite article has possessive force
      ἰδών: aor. circumstantial part. of ὁράω (*Essentials* §171)

4   Φαληρεύς -εως ὁ = man from Phalerum. Why this is teasing (παίζων) is unclear. Perhaps it is
         "the mock-official tone of the address." Other suggestions are that the speaker mocks
         Apollodorus for baldness (φαλαρός = bald) or that the phallus is suggested, which would fit
         the dramatic themes that pervade the *Symposium* (phallic processions were a standard part of
         dramatic festivals) and its often comic mood. Bury 1973: 1–2 discusses several possibilities.
      οὗτος = hey you! (here colloquially); common in Attic drama, where it is often accompanied by a
         name in the nominative (rather than the voc.), as here
      οὐ μενεῖς; οὐ + future in a question is a polite way of making a request

5   ὅς = he (nom.), subje. of ἔφη; the relative pronoun here and in similar contexts substitutes for a
         demonstrative pronoun; compare the common expression: ἦ δ' ὅς = he said
      καὶ μήν: this combination of particles normally indicates a transition; regularly used in drama to
         introduce a new scene, marking an entrance with a note of surprise or recognition (Smyth
         1956: §2921 and Denniston 1950: 355, who suggests "Why!")
      καὶ ἄρτι: as often when not being used as a connective, καί emphasizes the word that follows it:
         "even, just"

6   Ἀγάθων -ωνος ὁ = Agathon, host of the party (see appendix 1)

Ἀλκιβιάδου καὶ τῶν ἄλλων τῶν τότε ἐν τῷ δείπνῳ παραγενομένων· 7

βούλομαι δὲ μάλιστα πυθέσθαι περὶ τῶν ἐρωτικῶν λόγων τίνες ἦσαν. 8

ἄλλος γάρ τίς μοι διηγεῖτο ἀκηκοὼς Φοίνικος τοῦ Φιλίππου, ἔφη δὲ 9

καὶ σὲ εἰδέναι. ἀλλὰ οὐδὲν εἶχε σαφὲς λέγειν. σὺ οὖν μοι διήγησαι. 10

ἑταῖρος γὰρ Σωκράτους ὤν, δικαιότατος εἶ τοὺς λόγους αὐτοῦ 11

ἀπαγγέλλειν. πρότερον δέ μοι," ἦ δ᾽ ὅς, "εἰπέ, ἆρα σὺ αὐτὸς 12

παρεγένου τῇ συνουσίᾳ ταύτῃ ἢ οὔ; 13

---

7   Ἀλκιβιάδης -ου ὁ = Alcibiades, the most prominent Athenian political figure of his generation, a controversial figure (see appendix 1 and introduction)

    τῶν . . . παραγενομένων: the definite article τῶν goes with participle παραγενομένων, attributive with τῶν ἄλλων (*Essentials* §168)

8   πυθέσθαι περὶ τῶν ἐρωτικῶν λόγων τίνες ἦσαν = πυθέσθαι τίνες ἦσαν οἱ ἐρωτικοὶ λόγοι. τῶν ἐρωτικῶν λόγων = speeches about Eros. Instead of saying "to learn what the speeches about Eros were," Plato says "to learn the speeches about Eros, what they were" (prolepsis or anticipation; *Essentials* §208)

9   ἄλλος . . . τις = someone else; note this common use of τις with ἄλλος

    ἀκηκοώς: perf. act. part. nom. masc. sing. of ἀκούω

    Φοίνιξ Φοίνικος ὁ = Phoinix (otherwise unknown); ἀκούω usually takes the genitive of the person from whom something is heard: hear from *gen.*

    τοῦ Φιλίππου = [son] of Philip; it is common to see a man's name in the genitive accompanying a proper noun to refer to the father or husband

10   καὶ σέ = you too. Καί here is not connective but adverbial; καί means "and" only when it connects two things that are syntactically the same (i.e., subjects, verbs, direct objects, predicates, etc.).

    σὲ εἰδέναι: indir. statement (acc. + inf.) (*Essentials* §184)

    ἔχω + *inf.* = I am able to ——. Be sure to learn this special meaning of ἔχω with the infinitive.

    διήγησαι: aor. mid. impera. 2nd pers. sing. Remember that an imperative has only aspect, not tense. The aorist imperative suggests simple action, not past tense.

11   δικαιότατος + *inf.* = the most appropriate one to ——, the right one to ——. This common use of the infinitive with adjectives and adverbs denotes fitness or capacity (epexegetical or explanatory inf.) (*Essentials* §181).

    εἶ: from εἰμί (*Essentials* §65)

12   ἀπαγγέλλω = announce publicly, make public

    ἦ δ᾽ ὅς: see vocabulary

    αὐτός: as always in the nominative, αὐτός here intensifies the subje. σύ = you yourself (*Essentials* §200)

Κἀγὼ εἶπον ὅτι "Παντάπασιν ὁ διηγούμενός σοι ἔοικεν οὐδὲν   14

διηγεῖσθαι σαφές, εἰ νεωστὶ ἡγῇ τὴν συνουσίαν γεγονέναι ταύτην ἣν   15

ἐρωτᾷς, ὥστε καὶ ἐμὲ παραγενέσθαι. οὐκ οἶσθ', ὦ Γλαύκων, ὅτι   16

πολλῶν ἐτῶν Ἀγάθων ἐνθάδε οὐκ ἐπιδεδήμηκεν; οὐδέπω δὲ   17

τρία ἔτη ἐστίν ἀφ' οὗ ἐγὼ Σωκράτει συνδιατρίβων ἠρξάμην καὶ   18

ἐπιμελὲς πεποίημαι ἑκάστης ἡμέρας εἰδέναι ὅ τι ἂν λέγῃ ἢ πράττῃ.   19

---

14   κἀγώ = καὶ ἐγώ, a common instance of crasis (*Essentials* §207)

      ὅτι: frequently used in the *Symposium* to introduce a direct statement; it is virtually a punctuation
      mark: do not translate in these contexts

      ὁ διηγούμενος: the definite article preceding the participle makes clear that this is a substantive
      participle (*Essentials* §169); on the tense, see note on διηγεῖσθαι in line 15

15   διηγεῖσθαι: in the absence of an imperfect infinitive, Greek regularly uses a present infinitive in
      indirect statement to reflect an original imperfect indicative; the continuing aspect is more
      important than the past tense; context calls for translation as a past tense

      *νεωστί *adv.* = recently

      ἡγῇ from ἡγέομαι = think, consider. What must the subject be? Hint: review the middle endings
      of epsilon-contract verbs (*Essentials* §58).

      γεγονέναι: perf. inf. of γίγνομαι in indir. statement

16   ὥστε καὶ ἐμὲ παραγενέσθαι: natural result clause with acc. subje. (ἐμέ), inf. verb (*Essentials*
      §185). As Apollodorus was *not* actually present, and there is no actual fact to record, he uses
      the infinitive characteristic of the natural result clause rather than the indicative of the actual
      result clause. Latinists may wish to note the difference between Latin and Greek here (Latin
      result clauses use the subju.).

      οἶσθ' = οἶσθα from οἶδα (*Essentials* §65)

      Γλαύκων -ωνος ὁ = Glaucon, presumably the brother of Plato, who appears in the *Republic*

17   πολλῶν ἐτῶν = for many years; gen. of time within which. Although we might expect an accusa-
      tive to express duration, the genitive can be used to denote the time since an action has happened
      (Smyth 1956: §1447).

      ἐπιδημέω = be at home, come home [from foreign travel]

18   ἀφ' οὗ = ἀπὸ τοῦ χρόνου οὗ = from the time when, i.e., since

      συνδιατρίβω + *dat.* = spend time with. συνδιατρίβων is a supplementary participle with
      ἠρξάμην (*Essentials* §170)

19   ἐπιμελὲς ποιέομαι + *inf.* = make it a practice to ——

      ἑκάστης ἡμέρας: gen. of time within which (*Essentials* §95)

      ὅ τι ἂν λέγῃ ἢ πράττῃ: subju. + ἄν in an indef. rel. clause (*Essentials* §152; also §160)

πρὸ τοῦ δὲ ἐποίουν οὐδέν, ἀλλὰ ἀθλιώτατος ἀνθρώπων ἦ, ὥσπερ   20
σὺ νυνί, οἰόμενος δεῖν πάντα μᾶλλον πράττειν ἢ φιλοσοφεῖν."   21

---

20   πρὸ τοῦ = before this. This common expression (which should be learned) preserves the original
demonstrative function of the definite article (ὁ ἡ τό), a use still found in Homer.
*ἄθλιος -α -ον = wretched, miserable
ἦ: from εἰμί (*Essentials* §65)

21   νυνί = right now. The so-called deictic iota is added to various words in Greek and serves as a kind
of pointer. It is common with οὗτος (οὑτοσί = this one here; οὑτωσί = in this very way, etc.).
δεῖν: inf. of the impersonal verb δεῖ in indir. statement (*Essentials* §183)
φιλοσοφέω = love knowledge and pursue it, philosophize, be a philosopher

Reading 1B

Apollodorus gives a precise date and setting for the dinner party and describes his source, Aristodemus, a lover of Socrates and an eyewitness to the dinner party. We also hear a little more about Apollodorus himself and his unnamed companion (ἑταῖρος).

Suggested Reviews

- forms of relative pronouns (*Essentials* §§4–5) and syntax of relative clauses (*Essentials* §§129–35)
- syntax of genitive absolute (*Essentials* §176)
- irregular verbs, especially εἰμί, οἶδα, φημί (*Essentials* §§65–66)
- third declension names Ἀγάθων -ωνος ὁ (regular third declension) and Σωκράτης -ους ὁ

nominative	ὁ Ἀγάθων	ὁ Σωκράτης
genitive	τοῦ Ἀγάθωνος	τοῦ Σωκράτους
dative	τῷ Ἀγάθωνι	τῷ Σωκράτει
accusative	τὸν Ἀγάθωνα	τὸν Σωκράτη

- third declension adjectives κακοδαίμων -ον and σαφής -ές (*Essentials* §14, §17)

Vocabulary

ἄθλιος -α -ον: wretched, miserable, subject to toils and struggles (cf. English "athlete" and ἆθλος -ου ὁ: contest, conflict, competition and *ἆθλον -ου τό: prize)

ἄλλως *adv.*: otherwise, in another way or manner (learn common idiom ἄλλως τε καί: especially, particularly)

ἄρα: so, then, therefore (particle implying inference; distinguish from the question word ἆρα)

δέομαι δεήσομαι — — δεδέημαι ἐδεήθην: want, need, ask for (usually with gen. obj.) (pass. deponent: uses pass. forms with act. meaning; *Essentials* §138)

διανοέομαι διανοήσομαι — — διανενόημαι διενοήθην: think, have in mind, intend (cf. νοῦς/νόος) (pass. deponent; *Essentials* §138)

ἐλεέω, *aor.* ἠλέησα: pity, show mercy to (cf. *ἔλεος -ου ὁ: pity, mercy, compassion) ἔνιοι -αι -α *pl. adj.*: some

ἔχω + *adv.*: be (a certain way); e.g., πῶς ἔχεις: How are you? καλῶς ἔχω: I am well.

ἥδομαι ἡσθήσομαι — — — ἥσθην: enjoy (cf. English "hedonist" and ἡδύς -εῖα -ύ and ἡδέως) (pass. deponent; *Essentials* §138)

ἦν δ᾽ ἐγώ: I said

ἠρόμην *aor.*: I asked (stem ἐρ-); *also fut.*: ἐρήσομαι, but not in other tenses, where the verb ἐρωτάω is used instead

καθά (καθ᾽ ἅ, κατὰ ἅ) *adv.*: as (*recognize also* καθάπερ: just as)

κακοδαίμων -ον: unfortunate, unlucky, unhappy (cf. εὐδαίμων -ον)

μαίνομαι μανήσομαι/μανοῦμαι ἐμηνάμην μέμηνα μεμάνημαι ἐμάνην: be mad, be insane, rage, rave, be madly drunk (cf. *μανία -ας ἡ: mania, insanity, craziness)

μέντοι *part.*: (1) certainly, at any rate; (2) still, however, nevertheless

οἴομαι/οἶμαι οἰήσομαι — — — ᾠήθην: think (pass. deponent; *Essentials* §138)

ὁμολογέω ὁμολογήσω ὡμολόγησα ὡμολόγηκα ὡμολόγημαι ὡμολογήθην: agree (with), say the same (as), speak as one (with); *dat. pers. agreed with and/or acc. thing agreed to* (cf. prefix ὁμο-: same + λόγος)

πάλαι *adv.*: long ago (cf. English "paleontology" and "Paleozoic" and παλαιός -ά -όν)

πάντως *adv.*: entirely, altogether, completely

πειράω πειράσω ἐπείρασα πεπείρακα πεπείραμαι ἐπειράθην: attempt, endeavor, try, test; more common in the middle with same meaning as active (cf. English "empirical" and *πεῖρα -ας ἡ: trial, attempt, experiment, experience and *ἔμπειρος -ον: experienced)

-περ/περ: indeed, the very (enclitic particle adding force to the word it follows, common with a relative pronoun; e.g., ὅσπερ: the very one who; ὅπερ: the very thing which/that; ὥσπερ: just as)

πλήν *prep. + gen.*, or *adv.*: except, besides

πλούσιος -α -ον: wealthy, rich (cf. *πλοῦτος -ου ὁ: wealth)

πορεύομαι πορεύσομαι ἐπορευσάμην — πεπόρευμαι: go, travel, journey

ὑστεραία -ας ἡ: day after, following day (cf. ὕστερος -α -ον) (abbreviated from ἡ ὑστεραία ἡμέρα)

χωρίς *adv.*: separately, apart; *prep. + gen.*: apart from, without, far from

ὠφελέω ὠφελήσω ὠφέλησα ὠφέληκα ὠφέλημαι ὠφελήθην: help, benefit

Reading 1B (based on *Symposium* 173a3–174a1)

Καὶ ὅς, "Μὴ παῖζε," ἔφη "ἀλλ᾽ εἰπέ μοι πότε ἐγένετο ἡ συνουσία αὕτη."   1

Κἀγὼ εἶπον ὅτι "Παίδων ὄντων ἡμῶν ἔτι, ὅτε τῇ πρώτῃ τραγῳδίᾳ   2

ἐνίκησεν Ἀγάθων, τῇ ὑστεραίᾳ ἢ ᾗ τὰ ἐπινίκια ἔθυεν αὐτός τε καὶ οἱ   3

χορευταί."   4

"Πάνυ," ἔφη, "ἄρα πάλαι, ὡς ἔοικεν. ἀλλὰ τίς σοι διηγεῖτο; ἢ αὐτὸς   5

Σωκράτης;"   6

"Οὐ μὰ τὸν Δία," ἦν δ᾽ ἐγώ, "ἀλλ᾽ ὅσπερ Φοίνικι διηγεῖτο. Ἀριστόδημος ἦν   7

τις, Κυδαθηναιεύς, σμικρός, ἀνυπόδητος ἀεί· παρεγεγόνει δ᾽ ἐν τῇ συνουσίᾳ,   8

Σωκράτους ἐραστὴς ὢν ἐν τοῖς μάλιστα τῶν τότε, ὡς ἐμοὶ δοκεῖ. ἀλλὰ καὶ   9

---

1   ὅς = he (the rel. pron. frequently serves as a simple demonst.)

    αὕτη: the breathing mark and accent make clear that this is a form of οὗτος αὕτη τοῦτο, not of αὐτός

2   παίδων ὄντων ἡμῶν ἔτι: this genitive absolute (*Essentials* §176) answers the question asked by Glaucon in the previous sentence. There is no main clause in this sentence; the main clause is implied by the question. Successive clauses become increasingly specific about the time frame.

3   τῇ ὑστεραίᾳ ἢ ᾗ = τῇ ὑστεραίᾳ ἢ [τῇ ἡμέρᾳ] ᾗ = *literally* on the day later than the day on which (dat. of time when) (*Essentials* §112)

    τὰ ἐπινίκια = sacrifices in thanks for victory (internal acc.) (functions like cognate acc.; *Essentials* §77)

    αὐτός: as always in the nominative, αὐτός here intensifies the understood subject (he) = he himself (*Essentials* §200)

4   χορευτής -οῦ ὁ = member of a chorus; the singular verb (ἔθυεν) suggests that they are added as an afterthought

7   Φοίνιξ -ικος ὁ: see note on reading 1A.9

8   Κυδαθηναιεύς -έως ὁ: = man from Kydathenaion, one of the city demes (districts) of Athens

    σμικρός = μικρός

    ἀνυπόδητος -ον + shoeless, unshod; *literally* without [ἀν-] binding [δη-/δε-] below [ὑπό]; shoelessness is a recurring motif in the dialogue, so this word is worth noting, though it is not otherwise a particularly common word in Greek

    παρεγεγόνει: what is this relatively rare form (*Essentials* §55)?

9   ἐραστής -οῦ ὁ = lover (specifically, the older male in a homosexual pair), passionate follower

    ἐν τοῖς μάλιστα = ἐν τοῖς μάλιστα ἐρασταῖς = among those who were particularly lovers

    τῶν τότε: partitive gen. (*Essentials* §93), def. art. + adv. (*Essentials* §189)

Σωκράτη γε ἔνια ἤδη ἠρόμην ὧν ἐκείνου ἤκουσα, καί μοι ὡμολόγει καθάπερ   10
ἐκεῖνος διηγεῖτο."   11

"Τί οὖν," ἔφη, "οὐ διηγῇ μοι; πάντως δὲ ἡ ὁδὸς ἡ εἰς ἄστυ ἐπιτηδεία   12
τοῖς πορευομένοις καὶ λέγειν καὶ ἀκούειν."   13

Οὕτω δὴ ἰόντες ἅμα τοὺς λόγους περὶ αὐτῶν ἐποιούμεθα, ὥστε οὐκ   14
ἀμελετήτως ἔχω, ὅπερ ἀρχόμενος εἶπον. εἰ οὖν δεῖ καὶ ὑμῖν διηγήσασθαι,   15
ταῦτα χρὴ ποιεῖν. καὶ γὰρ ἔγωγε, ὅταν μέν τινας περὶ φιλοσοφίας   16
λόγους ἢ αὐτὸς ποιῶμαι ἢ ἄλλων ἀκούω, χωρὶς τοῦ οἴεσθαι ὠφελεῖσθαι   17

---

10   Σωκράτη ... ἔνια ἠρόμην = I asked Socrates some things ... (the verb takes a double acc.)

   ὧν: gen. pl. neut. rel. pron.; partitive gen. with ἔνια = some of those things which/that. What is
   this use of the relative pronoun (*Essentials* §133)?

   ἐκείνου: what is this use of the genitive (*Essentials* §100 or note on reading 1A.9)?

12–13   ἐπιτηδεία: predicate adj.; + dat. + inf. = good for *dat.* to use for ——ing, suitable for *dat.'s* ——ing.
   What is this use of the infinitive (*Essentials* §181)?

15   ἀμελέτητος -ον = without practice, unpracticed

   ἔχω: review common meaning of ἔχω + *adv.* (see vocabulary)

   ὅπερ: neut. sing. acc. rel. pron. with intensifying suffix = the very thing which/that. Here the
   phrase οὐκ ἀμελετήτως ἔχω is the antecedent of the relative clause (*Essentials* §131).

   καὶ ὑμῖν; how should καί be translated here (note on reading 1A.10)?

16   ταῦτα χρὴ ποιεῖν: compare English "if I must, I must"

16–17   ὅταν μέν ... ποιῶμαι ἢ ... ἀκούω: subju. + ἄν in an indef. rel. clause (*Essentials* §152, §160)

   τινας περὶ φιλοσοφίας λόγους: τινας agrees with λόγους. The phrase περὶ φιλοσοφίας is
   nested in between because it functions like an attributive adjective (compare to examples in
   Essentials §189)

17   ἢ ... ἢ = either ... or

   αὐτός: how should αὐτός be translated here (*Essentials* §200)?

   χωρὶς τοῦ οἴεσθαι = apart from thinking; articular infinitive in genitive depending on the
   preposition χωρίς (*Essentials* §182)

   ὠφελεῖσθαι: inf. in indir. statement with οἴεσθαι. What must the subject of the indirect statement be (*Essentials* §184)?

χαίρω· ὅταν δὲ ἄλλους τινάς, ἄλλως τε καὶ τοὺς ὑμῶν τῶν πλουσίων   18

καὶ χρησματιστικῶν, αὐτός τε ἄχθομαι ὑμᾶς τε τοὺς ἑταίρους ἐλεῶ, ὅτι   19

οἴεσθε τὶ ποιεῖν οὐδὲν ποιοῦντες. καὶ ἴσως αὖ ὑμεῖς οἱ πλούσιοι ἐμὲ ἡγεῖσθε   20

κακοδαίμονα εἶναι, καὶ οἴομαι ὑμᾶς ἀληθῆ οἴεσθαι· ἐγὼ μέντοι ὑμᾶς οὐκ   21

οἴομαι, ἀλλ᾽ εὖ οἶδα.   22

ἙΤΑΙΡΟΣ· Ἀεὶ ὅμοιος εἶ, ὦ Ἀπολλόδωρε· ἀεὶ γὰρ σαυτόν τε κακηγορεῖς   23

καὶ τοὺς ἄλλους, καὶ δοκεῖς μοι ἀτεχνῶς πάντας ἀθλίους ἡγεῖσθαι πλὴν   24

Σωκράτους, ἀπὸ σαυτοῦ ἀρξάμενος. καὶ ὁπόθεν ποτὲ ταύτην τὴν ἐπωνυμίαν   25

---

18   ὅταν δέ balances ὅταν μέν in lines 16–17. The parallelism allows the reader to infer ἄλλους ... τινας [λόγους ... ἀκούω], contrasting with τινας περὶ φιλοσοφίας λόγους from the previous sentence: "But whenever I hear ... some other [kind of] speeches. ..."

ἄλλως τε καί = especially, particularly. The literal meaning of this common expression is "both otherwise and . . ."; this word order creates emphasis rather than afterthought in Greek.

τοὺς ὑμῶν τῶν πλουσίων καὶ χρησματιστικῶν: τούς refers back to λόγους; τῶν πλουσίων καὶ χρησματιστικῶν (moneymaking) in line 19 is in apposition to ὑμῶν (*Essentials* §120). So translate: "the speeches of you wealthy [and] moneymaking types."

19   χρηματιστικός -ή -όν: involving χρήματα = moneymaking, having to do with business

τε ... τε = both ... and. τε should normally be translated before the word it follows (like the Latin suffix *-que*), thus creating the following structure: both [αὐτός ἄχθομαι] and [ὑμᾶς τοὺς ἑταίρους ἐλεῶ].

*ἄχθομαι = be vexed, weighed down, be burdened, aggrieved

τοὺς ἑταίρους is in apposition to ὑμᾶς (*Essentials* §120)

20   τί is the enclitic τι, accented here for emphasis (rare) = something! i.e., really something, something big. It is the object of ποιεῖν here. What must the subject of this infinitive in indirect statement be (*Essentials* §184)?

οἱ πλούσιοι is in apposition to ὑμεῖς (*Essentials* §120)

21–22   ἐγώ ... ὑμᾶς οὐκ οἴομαι [supply κακοδαίμονας εἶναι]: the bracketed elements can be supplied from parallel with the previous sentence

23   κακηγορέω = abuse, speak badly of

24   *ἀτεχνῶς *adv.* = simply, absolutely

25   ὁπόθεν ποτέ = from wherever! (ποτέ adds a wondering or surprised tone to an interrogative, like the English suffix *-ever*)

ἐπωνυμία -ας ἡ = nickname

ἔλαβες τὸ μαλακὸς καλεῖσθαι, οὐκ οἶδα ἔγωγε. ἐν γὰρ τοῖς λόγοις ἀεὶ   26
τοιοῦτος εἶ, σαυτῷ τε καὶ τοῖς ἄλλοις ἀγριαίνεις πλὴν Σωκράτους.   27
ΑΠΟΛΛΟΔΩΡΟΣ· Ὦ φίλτατε, καὶ δῆλόν γε δὴ ὅτι οὕτω διανοούμενος καὶ   28
περὶ ἐμαυτοῦ καὶ περὶ ὑμῶν μαίνομαι καὶ παραπαίω;   29
ΕΤΑΙΡΟΣ· Οὐκ ἄξιον περὶ τούτων, Ἀπολλόδωρε, νῦν ἐρίζειν· ἀλλ᾽ ὅπερ   30
ἄρτι ἐδεόμεθά σου, μὴ ἄλλως ποιήσῃς, ἀλλὰ διήγησαι τίνες ἦσαν οἱ λόγοι.   31
ΑΠΟΛΛΟΔΩΡΟΣ· Ἐξ τοίνυν ἀρχῆς ὑμῖν ὡς ἐκεῖνος διηγεῖτο καὶ ἐγὼ πειράσομαι   32
διηγήσασθαι.   33

---

26   τὸ μαλακὸς καλεῖσθαι: artic. inf. in apposition to ἐπωνυμίαν (*Essentials* §182)

μαλακός -ή -όν = soft; nominative because it is a predicate of the subject (*Essentials* §123). On Apollodorus's softness, see reading 1 introduction. Some texts read μανικός = crazy (cf. English "manic"), but that does not seem to fit the immediate context as well (unless the comment is intended to be heavily ironical). See line 29 for Apollodorus's "mania."

27   ἀγριαίνω + *dat.* = get angry at, be aggravated by

28   ὦ φίλτατε: these extravagantly affectionate forms of address are highly characteristic of Platonic dialogue and typically have a slightly ironical or gently mocking tone

καὶ ... γε δή: Rose 1985: 5 (note on §173e1) suggests that the combination of particles here lends both an indignant and ironical tone to the question: "and is it really so clear . . . ?"

29   παραπαίω = be out of one's wits. Apollodorus's "mania" should probably be connected to the philosophical mania mentioned by Alcibiades in the final speech of the dialogue (reading 10E, especially line 47).

30   ἐρίζω = argue, quarrel, contest (cf. Eris, goddess of strife and discord)

31   μὴ ... ποιήσῃς: prohibitive subju. (*Essentials* §149)

32   τοίνυν = then, okay then.

καὶ ἐγώ: καὶ is not connective here, but adverbial

Reading 2. The Drinking Party

The narrator is the character Aristodemus, who has been described in reading 1B.8 as σμικρός, ἀνυπόδητος ἀεί.[20] This theme of shoelessness is repeated several times in the dialogue. Socrates is regularly portrayed as shoeless, an aspect of his lack of fashion consciousness that is mocked in the *Clouds*; in this reading he departs from custom in an effort to appear καλός before the καλός Agathon. An interest in the καλός boy is a standard feature of the literature and art of the symposium. In general, Greek texts tend to present beauty (κάλλος) more than any other quality of a human being as engendering ἔρως. Although this is normally assumed to be physical beauty, the word καλός actually has a much broader application in Greek that allows for other kinds of thinking to emerge in the dialogue. There is also play in this section on the name of Agathon and the Greek adjective ἀγαθός.

Aristodemus has not actually been invited to the party at Agathon's so he goes along "uninvited" (ἄκλητός). Traditionally, such uninvited guests have a very low social status; without property or marketable skills, they are parasites who attend the parties of the wealthy hoping to get a meal (Fehr 1990). Although in fact Socrates does invite Aristodemus and he is welcomed as a friend at Agathon's, there is clearly some humor in portraying the small, shoeless, and altogether unassuming Aristodemus as ἄκλητός. Moreover, as an uninvited guest, Aristodemus invites comparison with Alcibiades, who also makes an uninvited appearance later in the dialogue (Allen 1991: 6). Modest in appearance and personality, Aristodemus is the precise opposite of the outgoing, vibrant, and self-absorbed Alcibiades. But both men are lovers of Socrates. Apollodorus describes Aristodemus in reading 1B.9 as Σωκράτους ἐραστὴς ὢν ἐν τοῖς μάλιστα τῶν τότε; Alcibiades openly professes his love for Socrates in his speech at the end of the dialogue. We also witness in this reading Socrates' strange habit of suddenly becoming so absorbed in thought as to stop whatever he is doing and stand motionless for extended periods of time.

In the original, this section is narrated by Apollodorus in the third person, most of it in indirect discourse. I have reworded it in the first person to make it more straightforward and easily comprehensible. This obviously is a significant change in the way Plato presented this part of the narrative. But there are many quotations in Apollodorus's report of Aristodemus's narrative, and many of these I have preserved unedited, so that much of this section is unchanged from the original.

---

20. In Xenophon, *Memorabilia* 1.4.2, he is called τὸν μικρόν.

Fig. 11. Underside of red-figure cup, ca. 480 B.C.E., showing men drinking and playing kottabos among characteristic accoutrements of the symposium, silhouettes of characteristic vessels. Inv. 1998.8. Courtesy of the Michael C. Carlos Museum of Emory University, Atlanta, Georgia. Photo by Bruce M. White, 2005.

Reading 2A

Aristodemus reports how he meets Socrates, who invites him to Agathon's house for dinner.

Suggested Reviews

- forms and common uses of the subjunctive (*Essentials* §§147–49, §§152–54)
- forms of irregular verb εἶμι (*Essentials* §§65–66)
- principal parts and meanings of ἄγω, λέγω, τυγχάνω

> ἄγω ἄξω ἤγαγον ἦχα ἦγμαι ἤχθην = lead or carry, convey, bring; live (a particular way),
> e.g., ἄγω εἰρήνην = live in peace; ἄγε (impera.) = come!
> λέγω ἐρῶ/λέξω εἶπον/ἔλεξα εἴρηκα εἴρημαι ἐρρήθην/ἐλέχθην = say, speak, talk, tell
> τυγχάνω τεύξομαι ἔτυχον τετύχηκα/τέτευχα + *gen. obj.* = happen upon, meet with by
> chance, gain, obtain; + *supplemental part.* = happen to be ——ing, happen to ——; + *dat.*
> *pers.* = happen to, befall

Vocabulary

αὐτίκα *adv.*: straightaway, at once, immediately, directly

αὐτόθι *adv.*: there, on the very spot (the suffix -θι generally signals place where; cf. *ἀλλόθι:
elsewhere); *recognize also* αὐτοῦ: at the very place, there, here, on the spot (can, of course,
also be the gen. of αὐτός)

γέλοιος -α -ον: causing laughter, laughable, ridiculous, funny (cf. γελάω)

δειπνέω δειπνήσω ἐδείπνησα δεδείπνηκα δεδείπνημαι ἐδειπνήθην: dine; *recognize also*
συνδειπνέω: dine with

δεῦρο *adv.*: here

διαλέγομαι διαλέξομαι/διαλεχθήσομαι— —διείλεγμαι διελέχθην: discuss, converse (pass.
deponent) (cf. English "dialogue")

ἐάω ἐάσω εἴασα εἴακα εἴαμαι εἰάθην: let, allow, permit; leave be, let go

ἔθος -ους τό: habit, custom

εἰς + *gen. name*: to gen.'s, to gen.'s house; *also* ἐν + *gen. name*: at gen.'s, at gen.'s house

ἐντυγχάνω -τεύξομαι -ἔτυχον -τετύχηκα/-τέτευχα: light upon, meet, encounter *dat.*

κατακλίνω -κλινῶ -ἔκλινα -κέκλικα—— -εκλίνην: lay down; *mid.-pass.*: lie down, recline

κεῖμαι κείσομαι: lie, lie dead, be placed, be made, be established; *recognize also* κατακεῖμαι: lie down, recline

Forms of κεῖμαι (with slight irregularities):

	pres. indic.	imperf. indic.	pres. subju.	pres. opt.	pres. impera.
1st pers. sing.	κεῖμαι	ἐκείμην	κέωμαι	κεοίμην	—
2nd pers. sing.	κεῖσαι	ἔκεισο	κέῃ	κέοιο	κεῖσο
3rd pers. sing.	κεῖται	ἔκειτο	κέηται	κέοιτο	κείσθω
1st pers. pl.	κείμεθα	ἐκείμεθα	κεώμεθα	κεοίμεθα	—
2nd pers. pl.	κεῖσθε	ἔκεισθε	κέησθε	κέοισθε	κεῖσθε
3rd pers. pl.	κεῖνται	ἔκειντο	κέωνται	κέοιντο	κείσθων
pres. inf.	κεῖσθαι				
pres. part.	κείμενος -η -ον				

κινέω κινήσω ἐκίνησα κεκίνηκα κεκίνημαι ἐκινήθην: set in motion, move [someone or something else (*act.*) *or* oneself (*mid.*)], urge on (cf. English "kinetic")

-κις *as suffix*:——times (ὀλιγάκις: few times, seldom; πολλάκις: many times, often; δεκάκις: ten times; ὁσάκις: as many times; etc.)

μηδαμῶς/οὐδαμῶς *adv.*: emphatic form of μή/οὐ: in no way, not at all

οἷός τ᾽ [εἰμί] + *inf.*: be able to——

ὅποι *rel. adv.*: [to] where, whither; to wherever (indir. version of ποῖ)

οὗ *rel. adv.*: where (can also be the gen. sing. rel. pron.)

οὐδαμοῦ *adv.*: nowhere (-ου often signals place "where"; cf. ποῦ; οὗ, πανταχοῦ: everywhere; πολλαχοῦ: in many places; αὐτοῦ: on the very spot, here, there)

προσέχω τὸν νοῦν + *dat.*: pay attention to; *literally* hold one's mind to

πρόσθε(ν) prep. + *gen.*, or *adv.* (as though from πρό + θεν): before, forward, in front; *recognize also* ἔμπροσθεν = πρόσθεν

σκέπτομαι/σκοπέω σκέψομαι ἐσκεψάμην——ἔσκεμμαι: look around carefully, contemplate, survey (cf. English "skeptic" and "telescope")

σύν prep. + *dat.*: along with, in company with, together with

συν-/συμ- (less commonly συγ-/συλ-) *as a prefix*: together with, fellow——(e.g., συνουσία -ας ἡ: being together, gathering, party; συμπόσιον -ου τό: symposium, drinking together, drinking party; συμπότης -ου ὁ: fellow-drinker; σύνεργος -ου ὁ: colleague, fellow-worker; σύνειμι: be together; σύμφημι: speak together, i.e., agree; συνδειπνέω: dine with; σύμμαχος -ου ὁ: ally)

τοι *enclitic particle*: well then, accordingly, so, then, therefore (*recognize also* stronger version combined with enclitic νυν: τοίνυν)

χθές *adv.*: yesterday

χωρέω χωρήσομαι/χωρήσω ἐχώρησα κεχώρηκα κεχώρημαι ἐχωρήθην: go, give way, advance; *recognize also* ἀναχωρέω: go up, go back, retreat

Reading 2A (based on *Symposium* 174a3–175b5)

Σωκράτης ἐνέτυχέ μοι λελουμένος τε καὶ τὰς βλαύτας　　　　1
ὑποδεδεμένος, ἃ ἐκεῖνος ὀλιγάκις ἐποίει· καὶ ἠρόμην αὐτὸν ὅποι　2
ἴοι οὕτω καλὸς γεγενημένος.　　　　3

Καὶ οὗτος εἶπεν ὅτι "Ἐπὶ δεῖπνον εἰς Ἀγάθωνος. χθὲς γὰρ　4
αὐτὸν διέφυγον τοῖς ἐπινικίοις, φοβηθεὶς τὸν ὄχλον. ὡμολόγησα δ'　5
εἰς τήμερον παραγενήσεσθαι. ταῦτα δὴ ἐκαλλωπισάμην, ἵνα καλὸς　6
παρὰ καλὸν ἴω. ἀλλὰ σύ," ἦ δ' ὅς, "ἐθέλεις ἰέναι ἄκλητος ἐπὶ δεῖπνον;"　7

Κἀγὼ δὲ πρῶτον ἠπόρουν, ἐρωτῶν ἐμαυτόν, "Τί εἴπω; ἴω　8
ἄκλητος ἢ οὔ;" τέλος δ' εἶπον ὅτι "Ὅπως ἂν σὺ κελεύῃς οὕτως πράξω."　9

"Ἕπου τοίνυν," ἔφη, "καὶ ἴωμεν ἀγαθοὶ ἐπὶ δεῖπνον εἰς Ἀγάθωνος."　10

1　*λούω = wash
　βλαύτη -ης ἡ = sandal or slipper
2　ὑποδέομαι = bind below; *mid.* = strap on [oneself] (*δέω = bind)
3　ἴοι: from εἶμι; optative in indir. question after verb in secondary sequence; translate like corresponding tense of indicative after past tense main verb (*Essentials* §158)
5　διαφεύγω: strengthened version of φεύγω = avoid
　τοῖς ἐπινικίοις = at the sacrifices of victory; this use of the dative without a preposition expresses place where (more common in poetry)
　φοβηθείς: from φοβέομαι (pass. deponent) (*Essentials* §138)
　*ὄχλος -ου ὁ = crowd, mob
6　εἰς τήμερον = τήμερον
　ταῦτα δή = for *these* reasons, i.e., that's why (adverbial acc., with emphasis given by δή; see Smyth 1956: §1610)
　καλλωπίζω = make beautiful, adorn; *mid.* = make oneself καλός
7　παρὰ καλόν: he means to the side of Agathon, who was famously καλός
　ἴω: subju. in a purpose clause (*Essentials* §153) Though the optative normally replaces the subjunctive when the main verb is in a secondary (past) tense (*Essentials* §1596), the subjunctive may accompany past tense verbs, especially when, as here, the purpose has not yet been fulfilled but lies still in the future. (See Smyth 1956 §2197 for additional examples and contexts.)
　ἄκλητος -ον = uninvited (cf. κληθείς from καλέω)
8　*ἀπορέω = be at a loss
　εἴπω and ἴω: deliberative subju. (*Essentials* §148). In the original, Aristodemus accepts Socrates' suggestion with alacrity, showing his devotion.
9　ἂν ... κελεύῃς: subju. in an indef. rel. clause (*Essentials* §151)
10　ἴωμεν: hortatory subju. (*Essentials* §157)

Τοιαῦτα δὲ διαλεχθέντες ἦμεν. ὁ οὖν Σωκράτης ἑαυτῷ πως   11

προσέχων τὸν νοῦν κατὰ τὴν ὁδὸν ἐπορεύετο ὑπολειπόμενος, καὶ   12

περιμένοντος ἐμοῦ ἐκέλευσε προιέναι εἰς τὸ πρόσθεν. ἀφικόμενος δ᾽   13

ἐπὶ τῇ οἰκίᾳ τῇ Ἀγάθωνος, τι αὐτόθι γελοῖον ἔπαθον. ἐμοὶ γὰρ εὐθὺς   14

παῖς τις ἀπαντήσας ἤγαγεν οὗ κατέκειντο οἱ ἄλλοι μέλλοντες δειπνεῖν·   15

εὐθὺς δ᾽ οὖν ὡς εἶδεν με Ἀγάθων, "Ὦ," ἔφη "Ἀριστόδημε,   16

εἰς καλὸν ἥκεις ὅπως συνδειπνήσῃς· εἰ δ᾽ ἄλλου τινὸς ἕνεκα ἦλθες,   17

εἰς αὖθις ἀναβαλοῦ, ὡς καὶ χθὲς ζητῶν σε ἵνα καλέσαιμι, οὐχ οἷός τ᾽ ἦ   18

εὑρεῖν. ἀλλὰ Σωκράτη ἡμῖν πῶς οὐκ ἄγεις;"   19

Καὶ ἐγὼ μεταστρεφόμενος οὐδαμοῦ ὁρῶ Σωκράτη ἑπόμενον·   20

εἶπον οὖν ὅτι καὶ αὐτὸς μετὰ Σωκράτους ἥκοιμι, κληθεὶς ὑπ᾽ ἐκείνου   21

δεῦρ᾽ ἐπὶ δεῖπνον.   22

"Καλῶς γ᾽," ἔφη Ἀγάθων, "πεποίηκας σύ· ἀλλὰ ποῦ ἔστιν οὗτος;"   23

"Ὄπισθεν ἐμοῦ ἄρτι εἰσῄει· ἀλλὰ θαυμάζω καὶ αὐτὸς ποῦ ἂν εἴη."   24

---

11   διαλεχθέντες from διαλέγομαι: like φοβέομαι, this verb uses aorist passive forms with active
        meaning (see note on φοβηθείς in line 5)
        ἦμεν from εἶμι: review *Essentials* §§65–66 if necessary

12   προσέχω τὸν νοῦν: this common Greek phrase normally means "pay attention," but in the context
             with ἑαυτῷ obviously means something more like "become lost in one's own thoughts"
        ὑπολείπω = leave behind
        περιμένω = wait around. (The *case* of the participle offers a clue to syntax here. See *Essentials* §176.)

13   πρόειμι εἰς τὸ πρόσθεν = go on ahead

15   *ἀπαντάω = meet with *dat.*
        οὗ: see vocabulary

16   ὡς (here) = when

17   εἰς καλόν = at a good time
        συνδειπνήσῃς: subju. in a purpose clause (*Essentials* §153)

18   εἰς αὖθις ἀναβαλοῦ = put it off until another time (ἀναβαλοῦ: aor. mid. impera.)
        ὡς (here) = as, since
        καλέσαιμι: optative in a purpose clause in secondary sequence (*Essentials* §159b)

19   πῶς . . . ; = how come . . . ? how is it that . . . ? (as often in Greek)

20   μεταστρέφομαι = turn (oneself) around
        ὁρῶ: the present tense is often used in narrating past events to give vividness (historical pres.);
             normally translated as past

21   ἥκοιμι: optative in indir. statement after verb in secondary sequence; translate like corresponding
             tense of indicative after past tense verb (*Essentials* §158)

24   εἰσῄει: from εἰσ-εἶμι (*Essentials* §65)
        ἂν εἴη = could/might be; potential optative (*Essentials* §156; also §161)

"Οὐ σκέψῃ," ἔφη, "παῖ, καὶ εἰσάξεις Σωκράτη; σὺ δ᾽, Ἀριστόδημε,   25
παρ᾽ Ἐρυξίμαχον κατακλίνου."   26

Ἄλλος δέ τις τῶν παιδῶν ἦλθεν ἀγγέλλων ὅτι "Σωκράτης οὗτος   27
ἀναχωρήσας ἐν τῷ τῶν γειτόνων προθύρῳ ἕστηκεν, κἀμοῦ καλοῦντος   28
οὐκ ἐθέλει εἰσιέναι."   29

"Ἄτοπόν γ᾽," ἔφη Ἀγάθων, "λέγεις· οὔκουν καλεῖς αὐτὸν καὶ   30
μὴ ἀφήσεις;"   31

Κἀγὼ εἶπον "Μηδαμῶς, ἀλλ᾽ ἐᾶτε αὐτόν. ἔθος γάρ τι τοῦτ᾽ ἔχει·   32
ἐνίοτε ἀποστὰς ὅποι ἂν τύχῃ ἕστηκεν. ἥξει δ᾽ αὐτίκα, ὡς ἐγὼ οἶμαι.   33
μὴ οὖν κινεῖτε, ἀλλ᾽ ἐᾶτε."   34

"Ἀλλ᾽ οὕτω χρὴ ποιεῖν, εἰ σοὶ δοκεῖ," ἔφη, "ἀλλ᾽ ἡμᾶς, ὦ παῖδες,   35
τοὺς ἄλλους ἑστιᾶτε."   36

---

25   Οὐ σκέψῃ ... εἰσάξεις: on οὐ + future in a question, see note on reading 1A.4
26   Ἐρυξίμαχος -ου ὁ = Eryximachus, a doctor (see appendix 1)
28   *γείτων -ονος ὁ = neighbor
      πρόθυρον -ου τό = porch, vestibule
      ἕστηκεν (perf. of ἵστημι) = has taken a stand; i.e., is standing
      κἀμοῦ = καὶ ἐμοῦ (crasis; *Essentials* §207)
30   *ἄτοπος -ον = strange, odd
      οὔκουν introducing a question = then won't . . . ? (see note on line 25)
31   μή: οὐ μή + *fut. indic.* = a strong prohibition (Smyth 1956: §1919); despite the question form, this
         is a command (see note on line 25)
      ἀφήσεις (fut. of ἀφίημι) = let go, release; leave alone
32   ἔθος τι: in apposition to τοῦτ᾽; as often with apposition, supply "as"
33   *ἐνίοτε = sometimes (cf. ἔνιοι, ὅτε)
      ἀποστάς from ἀφίστημι: aor. part. (intrans.)
      ἂν τύχῃ: explain the syntax (hint: see note on line 9)
35   Ἀλλά: following a command, indicates consent (Denniston 1950: 16–20)
36   ἑστιάω = entertain hospitably, serve a feast to

Reading 2B

Socrates at last arrives at the party. Agathon, who is reclining alone on the farthest couch, invites Socrates to join him, in order that Agathon may profit from whatever piece of wisdom Socrates has just obtained in his trance. Socrates rejects the notion that wisdom can be transferred by personal contact in the manner of a siphon sucking liquid from a fuller to an emptier vessel. In so doing, he implicitly rejects a traditional assumption of the Greek symposium that young men become better by associating with older and hence presumably wiser—or at least more socialized—men of their social class. Agathon introduces the theme of Socrates' hubris, which runs throughout the *Symposium*, and suggests that Dionysus will serve as a judge in a contest between Agathon and Socrates over who is the wisest. The competitive context and the role of Dionysus as judge are important to the overall interpretation of the dialogue.

Suggested Reviews

- uses of the optative (*Essentials* §§155–59)
- forms and uses of ἵστημι (set, place); στήσω (shall set); ἔστησα (set, caused to stand); ἔστην (root aor.) (stood); ἕστηκα (perf. with pres. meaning) (stand); ἑστώς (perf. part.); ἕσταμαι, ἐστάθην (was set); in general, *causal* (make to stand, set, place, appoint, establish); *intrans.* (stand, take a stand, stop, be set, be placed) (*Essentials* §§60–64)
- first declension nouns σπονδή -ῆς ἡ, σοφία -ας ἡ, and ὑβριστής -οῦ ὁ (*Essentials* §42)
- third declension nouns μάρτυς μάρτυρος ὁ and ὕδωρ ὕδατος τό (*Essentials* §44)

Vocabulary

- Make a particular effort to learn the principal parts of ᾄδω/ἀείδω and πίνω.

ᾄδω/ἀείδω* ᾄσομαι/ἀείσομαι* ᾖσα/ἤεισα* —— -ῇσμαι ᾔσθην: sing (* = non-Attic forms)
ἀμφότεροι -αι -α *pl. adj.*: both, each (of two)
ἅπτομαι ἅψομαι ἡψάμην —— -ῆμμαι: touch, grasp, attain, overtake *gen.*, take hold of *gen.*
δικαστής -οῦ ὁ: judge, juror, dikast
δυνατός -ή -όν: strong, mighty, able, possible; + *inf.*: able to——, capable of —— ing; *recognize also* ἀδύνατος (cf. δύναμαι): incapable, impossible, unable to

50

εἶεν *particle*: very well then, so far so good (context should distinguish this from the 3rd pers. pl. opt. of εἰμί, εἶεν)

ἔσχατος -η -ον: last (cf. English "eschatology")

καθίζομαι/καθέζομαι καθιζήσομαι ἐκαθισάμην: sit down, be seated, take a resting position; *recognize also* perf. κάθημαι: have taken a seat; i.e., be sitting

κενός -ή -όν: empty, void; + *gen.*: void of, empty of (cf. English "cenotaph")

μάρτυς μάρτυρος ὁ: witness (cf. English "martyr")

ὁπότερος -α -ον: which (of two) (indir. version; cf. πότερος -α -ον)

πάρειμι (παρεῖναι): be present, common as a substantive participle: οἱ πάροντες: those being present, those in attendance; τῷ πάροντι: at the present (time)

πίνω πίομαι ἔπιον πέπωκα πέπομαι ἐπόθην: drink (cf. English "potable" and "symposium")

πλέων πλέον (or πλείων πλεῖον): more (irreg. compar. of πολύς)

πλήρης -ες: full; + *gen.*: full of

πληρόω πληρώσω ἐπλήρωσα πεπλήρωκα πεπλήρωμαι ἐπληρώθην: make full; + *gen.*: fill (with) *gen.*

ῥᾴων -ον and ῥᾷστος -η -ον: easy (irreg. compar. and superl. of ῥᾴδιος -α -ον)

ῥέω ῥυήσομαι/ῥεύσομαι* ἔρρευσα* ἐρρύηκα——ἐρρύην: flow, run, stream, gush (cf. English "diarrhea") (Attic uses aor. pass. forms for act.; * = non-Attic forms)

σπονδή -ῆς ἡ: libation

σφόδρα *adv.*: very, very much, exceedingly

τῷ ὄντι: truly, really, in truth

ὑβριστής -οῦ ὁ: one who commits hubris, violent, overbearing person, insolent fellow, criminal (cf. ὕβρις)

ὕδωρ ὕδατος τό: water

φαῦλος -η -ον: slight, paltry, insignificant; *of people*: worthless, common, vulgar

Reading 2B (based on *Symposium* 175c5–176c5)

Μετὰ ταῦτα ἡμεῖς μὲν ἐδειπνοῦμεν, ὁ δὲ Σωκράτης οὐκ εἰσῄει.   1

ὁ οὖν Ἀγάθων πολλάκις ἐκέλευε μεταπέμψασθαι τὸν Σωκράτη, ἐγὼ δὲ   2

οὐκ εἴασα. τέλος μὲν αὐτὸς ἀφίκετο, ἡμεῖς δὲ μάλιστα ἐμεσοῦμεν   3

δειπνοῦντες. ὁ οὖν Ἀγάθων—ἐτύγχανε γὰρ ἔσχατος κατακείμενος   4

μόνος——"Δεῦρ'," ἔφη, "Σώκρατες, παρ' ἐμὲ κατάκεισο, ἵνα καὶ τοῦ σοφοῦ   5

ἁπτόμενός σου ἀπολαύσω, ὅ σοι προσέστη ἐν τοῖς προθύροις.   6

δῆλον γὰρ ὅτι ηὗρες αὐτὸ καὶ ἔχεις· οὐ γὰρ ἂν προαπέστης."   7

Καὶ ὁ Σωκράτης καθιζόμενος εἶπεν ὅτι "Εὖ ἂν ἔχοι, ὦ Ἀγάθων,   8

---

2   ἐκέλευε: understand as the object τὸν παῖδα or τοὺς παῖδας; these words are frequently omitted
    *μεταπέμπω = send after, send for

3   μάλιστα + *numerals and other kinds of measurement* = about, approximately; *so:* "when we were
    about in the middle . . ."
    μεσόω + *supplemental part.* = be in the middle of ——ing

4   ἔσχατος = last, i.e., the furthest to the right, in the rectangular room, the seat normally taken by
    the host (see appendix 3)

5   τοῦ σοφοῦ neut. (as ὅ, to which it is the antecedent, makes clear) = the wise thing which/that—
    the object of ἀπολαύω, but Plato may be exploiting the ambiguity of the form so that it may
    at first appear to be in apposition to σοῦ

6   σοῦ: obj. of ἅπτομαι (verbs that mean "touch" or "take hold of" frequently take gen. objects; cf.
    λαμβάνομαι)
    *ἀπολαύω = enjoy, benefit from *gen.*
    προσίστημι *intrans.* = come to
    τὰ προθύρα = porch, vestibule; used in both singular and plural apparently without distinction.
    What is the etymology of this word?

7   προαπέστης (from προ-αφ-ίστημι) = stop first, leave off; aor. indic. + ἄν = past contrary-to-
    fact (with protasis implied: εἰ μὴ εὗρες αὐτό or similar); ἄν + indic. (*Essentials* §162)

8–9   ἂν ἔχοι . . . εἰ . . . εἴη: opt. in future-less-vivid ("should . . . would") condition (*Essentials* §161;
    also §157)

εἰ τοιοῦτον εἴη ἡ σοφία ὥστ᾽ ἐκ τοῦ πληρεστέρου εἰς τὸ κενώτερον   9

ῥεῖν ἡμῶν, ἐὰν ἁπτώμεθα ἀλλήλων, ὥσπερ τὸ ἐν ταῖς κύλιξιν ὕδωρ   10

τὸ διὰ τοῦ ἐρίου ῥέον ἐκ τῆς πληρεστέρας εἰς τὴν κενωτέραν. εἰ γὰρ   11

οὕτως ἔχει καὶ ἡ σοφία, πολλοῦ τιμῶμαι τὴν παρὰ σοὶ κατάκλισιν. οἶμαι   12

γὰρ με παρὰ σοῦ πολλῆς καὶ καλῆς σοφίας πληρωθήσεσθαι. ἡ μὲν γὰρ   13

ἐμὴ σοφία φαύλη τις ἂν εἴη, ἢ καὶ ἀμφισβητήσιμος ὥσπερ ὄναρ οὖσα,   14

ἡ δὲ σὴ λαμπρά τε καὶ πολλὴν ἐπίδοσιν ἔχουσα, ἥ γε παρὰ σοῦ νέου   15

ὄντος οὕτω σφόδρα ἐξέλαμψεν καὶ ἐκφανὴς ἐγένετο πρῴην ἐν μάρτυσι   16

9–10   ὥστ᾽ ... ῥεῖν: natural result clause. The infinitive implies not an actual result but a possible or natural one; neut. τοιοῦτον (the sort of thing) anticipates the result clause: "the sort of thing that could flow . . ." or "the kind of thing that [naturally] flows . . ." (*Essentials* §185)

10   κύλιξ -ικος ἡ = kylix, drinking cup

11   ἐρίον -ου τό = piece of wool
   ῥέον: neut. part. with ὕδωρ. It is unclear whether Socrates is describing an actual siphoning device used by the ancients or is merely hypothesizing. There is no obvious practical purpose in moving liquid from one drinking cup to another via a piece of wool.

12   πολλοῦ (gen. of value) = greatly
   κατάκλισις -εως ἡ = reclining

13   με: an accusative subject of indirect discourse is unusual in Greek when the subject of an indirect statement is the same as the subject of the main verb, but the accusative pronoun is sometimes used for emphasis, as here (Smyth 1956: §1974)

14   φαύλη τις = a worthless thing, something worthless (pred.)
   ἂν εἴη: ἂν makes clear that this is a potential optative (*Essentials* §156; also §161)
   ἀμφισβητήσιμος -ον = dubious, doubtful, debatable
   ὄναρ τό = dream. Socrates seems to play here with the notion, found in Homer (especially *Odyssey* 19.562–67), that dreams may be either true or false.

15   ἡ δὲ σή: σοφία can be understood from the context, gender, and parallelism with ἡ μὲν ... ἐμὴ [σοφία]
   *λαμπρός -ά -όν = glorious, shining
   ἐπίδοσις -εως ἡ = potential for growth

16   ἐκλάμπω = shine forth
   ἐκφανής -ές = manifest, apparent

τῶν Ἑλλήνων πλέον ἢ τρισμυρίοις." 17

"Ὑβριστὴς εἶ," ἔφη, "ὦ Σώκρατες," ὁ Ἀγάθων. "καὶ ταῦτα μὲν 18

καὶ ὀλίγον ὕστερον διαδικασόμεθα ἐγώ τε καὶ σὺ περὶ τῆς σοφίας, 19

δικαστῇ χρώμενοι τῷ Διονύσῳ· νῦν δὲ πρὸς τὸ δεῖπνον πρῶτα τρέπου." 20

Μετὰ ταῦτα, κατακλινέντος τοῦ Σωκράτους καὶ δειπνήσαντος, 21

σπονδάς τε ἐποιησάμεθα καὶ τἆλλα τὰ νομιζόμενα, καὶ ᾄσαντες τὸν θεὸν 22

ἐτρεπόμεθα πρὸς τὸν πότον. 23

Ὁ οὖν Παυσανίας, "Εἶεν, ἄνδρες," ἔφη, "τίνα τρόπον ῥᾷστα 24

πιόμεθα; ἐγὼ μὲν οὖν λέγω ὑμῖν ὅτι τῷ ὄντι πάνυ χαλεπῶς ἔχω ὑπὸ 25

τοῦ χθὲς πότου καὶ δέομαι ἀναψυχῆς τινος, οἶμαι δὲ ὑμῶν τοὺς πολλούς· 26

---

17   τρισμυρίοι -αι -α = 30,000 (Dover 1980: 84: "Thirty thousand is the traditional number of male citizens of Athens even in the fourth century"). Here Socrates is clearly referring to Agathon's victory at the tragic festival two days before. As Sider 1980: 45 points out, however, mention of τῶν Ἑλλήνων rather than τῶν Ἀθηναίων strongly suggests the City Dionysia, the larger and more significant festival for tragedy in the fifth century, than the Lenaea festival, where Agathon actually won, which was attended almost exclusively by Athenians. Sider suggests that Plato deliberately exaggerates the importance of the occasion.

18   Ὑβριστής: this strong word is no doubt partly teasing in the characteristic manner of symposiastic banter, but Socrates' hubris is a theme in the dialogue (Gagarin 1977)
       ταῦτα = on these matters (acc. of respect) (*Essentials* §82)

19   διαδικάζομαι = contest, compete

20   δικαστῇ = [as a] judge—the predicate of τῷ Διονύσῳ after χράομαι (which takes a dat.), as the absence of the definite article makes clear (*Essentials* §188; Smyth 1956: §1509)
       Διόνυσος -ου ὁ = Dionysus, god of wine and theater, and thus especially appropriate for the context
       πρῶτα = πρῶτον

22   τὰ νομιζόμενα = the customary things

24   Παυσανίας -ου ὁ = Pausanias, lover of Agathon and another major figure of the dialogue (see appendix 1)
       τίνα τρόπον = in what way? *adverbial acc.* = τίνι τρόπῳ (line 27)

26   ἀναψυχή -ῆς ἡ = a breather, a break
       οἶμαι δὲ ὑμῶν τοὺς πολλούς [χαλεπῶς ἔχειν . . . καὶ ἀναψυχῆς τινος δεῖσθαι]: the bracketed phrase can be supplied through the parallelism implied by the δέ that answers the μέν of line 25. Watch for the way in which μέν . . . δέ frequently allows the reader to fill in missing elements through parallels.

παρῆστε γὰρ χθές. σκοπεῖσθε οὖν τίνι τρόπῳ ἂν ὡς ῥᾷστα πίνοιμεν." 　27

Ὁ οὖν Ἀριστοφάνης, "Τοῦτο μέντοι," ἔφη, "εὖ λέγεις, ὦ Παυσανία. 　28

καὶ γὰρ αὐτός εἰμι τῶν χθὲς βεβαπτισμένων." 　29

Ὁ δ' Ἐρυξίμαχος "'Ἕρμαιον ἂν εἴη ἡμῖν," ἔφη, "ὡς ἔοικεν, ἐμοί τε καὶ 　30

Ἀριστοδήμῳ καὶ Φαίδρῳ καὶ τοῖσδε, εἰ ὑμεῖς οἱ δυνατώτατοι πίνειν νῦν 　31

ἀπειρήκατε· ἡμεῖς μὲν γὰρ ἀεὶ ἀδύνατοι. Σωκράτη δ' ἐξαιρῶ λόγου· 　32

ἱκανὸς γὰρ καὶ ἀμφότερα, ὥστ' ἐξαρκέσει αὐτῷ ὁπότερ' ἂν ποιῶμεν." 　33

27　παρῆστε: from παρ-εἰμί. What is the form (*Essentials* §65)?

　　ἂν … πίνοιμεν: what kind of optative is this (*Essentials* §156)?

28　Ἀριστοφάνης -ους ὁ = Aristophanes, the most outstanding fifth-century comic dramatist and a
　　major character of the dialogue (see appendix 1)

　　μέντοι = certainly (here), though a more common meaning of the particle is "however, and yet"

29　βαπτίζω = dip in liquid, immerse completely (cf. English "baptize"); here metaphorical for
　　drunkenness; τῶν χθὲς βεβαπτισμένων is a partitive genitive (*Essentials* §93)

30　ἕρμαιον -ου τό = godsend, windfall, piece of luck (Hermes is the god of lucky finds)

31　Φαῖδρος -ου ὁ Phaedrus, another major character of the dialogue (see appendix 1)

32　ἀπειρήκατε: perf. from ἀπεῖπον = renounced

　　ἐξαιρέω = exempt, exclude

　　λόγου: here probably more like "reckoning, account" rather than "speech"

33　ἀμφότερα: acc. of respect (*Essentials* §82)

　　*ἐξαρκεῖ: used impersonally = it is enough for *dat.*, it satisfies

　　ἂν ποιῶμεν: what form is ποιῶμεν and, therefore which use of ἂν is this (*Essentials* §160 or
　　§152)?

Reading 2C

Eryximachus, the doctor, continues to speak, advocating sobriety. At Eryximachus's suggestion, they dismiss the flute-girl and, responding to an observation by Phaedrus, agree to offer speeches in praise (encomia) of Eros, the boy-god of love.

Suggested Reviews

- uses of ἄν and conditional sentences (*Essentials* §§160–65)
- principal parts and meanings of αἱρέω, ἔρχομαι, and ὁράω

    αἱρέω αἱρήσω εἷλον ᾕρηκα ᾕρημαι ᾑρέθην = take, capture, grasp; *in erotic contexts =* seduce, conquer; *mid.* = choose, elect
    ἔρχομαι εἶμι/ἐλεύσομαι ἦλθον ἐλήλυθα = come or go
    ὁράω ὄψομαι εἶδον ἑώρακα ὦμμαι ὤφθην = see

- forms of contract verbs (*Essentials* §§57–59)

Vocabulary

ἀμελέω ἀμελήσω ἠμέλησα ἠμέληκα ἠμέλημαι ἠμελήθην: neglect, have no care for; + *gen. obj.*: be neglectful of (cf. *ἀμελεία -ας ἡ: carelessness, neglect; *ἐπιμελέομαι: take care of, be attentive to)

ἀντιλέγω: speak against, oppose, disagree, contradict

βουλεύω βουλεύσω ἐβούλευσα βεβούλευκα βεβούλευμαι ἐβουλεύθην: take counsel, deliberate, plan; *recognize also* συμβουλεύω + *dat.*: take counsel with another, advise, recommend (distinguish from βούλομαι)

δεξιός -ά -όν: right; *frequently in fem.*: right hand (because ἡ χείρ is understood); recognize recurrent phrase in *Symposium*: ἐπὶ δεξιά: to the right, in the right-hand direction (i.e., moving around the circle of guests from left to right, probably indicating counterclockwise, though some scholars interpret as clockwise; appendix 3)

ἐγκωμιάζω ἐγκωμιάσομαι/ἐγκωμιάσω ἐνεκωμίασα ἐγκεκωμίακα ἐγκεκωμίασμαι
ἐνεκωμιάσθην: praise, give an encomium, laud; *recognize also* ἐγκώμιον -ου τό: encomium, speech of praise

ἑκών -οῦσα -όν: willing(ly)

ἐνάντιος -α -ον: opposite, opposing, hostile

ἔνδον *adv.*: within, in the house, at home

ἔρως -ωτος ὁ: love, desire

Ἔρως -ωτος ὁ: Eros, boy-god of love and desire, traditionally son of Aphrodite, goddess of love

ἡδονή -ῆς ἡ: pleasure (cf. English "hedonist" and ἥδομαι and ἡδύς)

μεθύω: be drunk, be intoxicated; *recognize also* μέθη -ης ἡ: drunkenness, intoxication; strong
drink and μεθύσκομαι: become drunk

μέμνημαι: remember (perf. forms with pres. meaning); strictly speaking this is the perfect of
μιμνήσκω: have recalled; *usually + gen.* (like most verbs of remembering and forgetting),
but sometimes with accusative.

Here are other common perfect verbs with present meaning:

οἶδα: know (have seen)

τέθνηκα (from θνήσκω): be dead (have died)

ἕστηκα (from ἵστημι): stand (have stood)

βέβηκα (from βαίνω): be in (a place) (have come to it)

ἔγνωκα (from γιγνώσκω): know (have learned)

πέφυκα (from φύω): be [by nature]

οἶνος -ου ὁ: wine

που/πού *enclitic indef. adv.*: anywhere, somewhere; *but more frequently simply introduces a
speculative note*: I suppose, I guess

πρόθυμος -ον: eager, willing, ready (with forward spirit)

πω *enclitic particle*: yet, up to this time (cf. οὔπω)

πώποτε *adv.*: ever yet, ever (cf. πω/οὔπω/οὔποτε)

σύμφημι: speak together with; i.e., agree, assent, approve

ὑμνέω ὑμνήσω ὕμνησα ὕμνηκα ὕμνημαι ὑμνήθην: sing, hymn (cf. English "hymn")

Reading 2C (based on *Symposium* 176c5–178a4)

"Ἐπειδὴ οὖν μοι δοκεῖ οὐδεὶς τῶν παρόντων προθύμως ἔχειν πρὸς   1
τὸ πολὺν πίνειν οἶνον, ἴσως ἂν ἐγὼ λέγοιμι ἀληθῶς περὶ τοῦ μεθύσκεσθαι.   2
ἐμοὶ γὰρ δὴ τοῦτό γε κατάδηλον γέγονεν ἐκ τῆς ἰατρικῆς, ὅτι χαλεπὸν   3
τοῖς ἀνθρώποις ἡ μέθη ἐστίν. καὶ οὔτε αὐτὸς ἑκὼν ἐθελήσαιμι ἂν πιεῖν   4
πόρρω οὔτε ἄλλῳ συμβουλεύσαιμι, ἄλλως τε καὶ κραιπαλῶντι ἔτι ἐκ τῆς   5
προτεραίας."   6
Πάντες οὖν ὡμολογήσαμεν μὴ πίεσθαι ὑπὲρ μέτρον, ἀλλ' οὕτω   7
πίνοντες πρὸς ἡδονὴν μόνην. ὁ δ' Ἐρυξίμαχος ἐκέλευσεν ἡμᾶς τὴν ἄρτι   8
εἰσελθοῦσαν αὐλητρίδα χαίρειν ἐᾶν, αὐλοῦσαν ἑαυτῇ ἢ ταῖς γυναιξὶ   9
ταῖς ἔνδον, ἵνα ἀλλήλοις συνεῖμεν διαλεγόμενοι.   10
Πάντων δ' ὁμολογησάντων ὁ Ἐρυξίμαχος εἶπε ὅτι, "Ἡ μέν μοι ἀρχὴ   11
τοῦ λόγου ἐστὶ κατὰ τὴν Εὐριπίδου Μελανίππην· 'οὐ γὰρ ἐμὸς ὁ μῦθος,'   12

---

1   Eryximachus is still the speaker.

2   τὸ ... πίνειν and τοῦ μεθύσκεσθαι: articular infinitives (*Essentials* §182)

3   κατάδηλος -ον: strengthened form of δῆλος; as a prefix, κατά sometimes only strengthens the word
      ἡ ἰατρική = ἡ ἰατρική τέχνη = the medical art (Eryximachus is a doctor)

4   μέθη -ης ἡ = strong drink, drunkenness (cf. English "meth-")

5   πόρρω *adv.* = far, far off, i.e., beyond what is moderate, too much
      κραιπαλάω = be hungover

6   *προτεραία -ας ἡ = the previous day, the day before (cf. ὑστεραία -ας ἡ)

7   *μέτρον -ου τό = measure, moderation

9   αὐλητρίς -ίδος ἡ = girl who plays the aulos (a wind instrument similar to an oboe), flute-girl
      (see introduction)
      χαίρειν ἐάω = allow to say farewell; i.e., send away, dismiss
      αὐλέω = play the aulos; αὐλοῦσαν is a present participle, but here seems to carry the idea of
      purpose more commonly associated with a future participle

10   συνεῖμεν: see Rowe 1998: 135 for possible sexual innuendo here. What is the form of this word
      (*Essentials* §65)?

11   μοι: dat. of the possessor (*Essentials* §107)

12   κατὰ τὴν Εὐριπίδου Μελανίππην = according to Euripides' Melanippe, in the words of
      Euripides' Melanippe. Eryximachus quotes from the beginning of a well-known speech given by
      Euripides' character, Melanippe. Euripides wrote two plays on Melanippe, neither of which
      survives, except in fragments.
      *μῦθος -ου ὁ = tale, story (myth)

ἀλλὰ Φαίδρου τοῦδε, ὃν μέλλω λέγειν. Φαῖδρος γὰρ πολλάκις πρός με   13
λέγει, 'Οὐ δεινόν,' φησίν, 'ὦ Ἐρυξίμαχε, ἄλλοις μέν τισι θεῶν ὕμνους καὶ   14
παιῶνας εἶναι ὑπὸ τῶν ποιητῶν πεποιημένους, τῷ δὲ Ἔρωτι, τηλικούτῳ   15
καὶ τοσούτῳ θεῷ, μηδὲ ἕνα πώποτε τοσούτων γεγονότων ποιητῶν   16
πεποιηκέναι μηδὲν ἐγκώμιον; ἔγωγε ἤδη τινὶ ἐνέτυχον βιβλίῳ ἀνδρὸς   17
σοφοῦ, ἐν ᾧ ἐνῆσαν ἅλες ἔπαινον θαυμάσιον ἔχοντες πρὸς ὠφελίαν.   18
Ἔρωτα δ' οὐδείς πω ἀνθρώπων τετόλμηκεν ἀξίως ὑμνῆσαι· οὕτως   19
δ' ἠμέληται τοσοῦτος θεός.' ταῦτα δή μοι δοκεῖ εὖ λέγειν Φαῖδρος.   20
δοκεῖ οὖν μοι χρῆναι ἕκαστον ἡμῶν λόγον εἰπεῖν ἔπαινον Ἔρωτος   21
ἐπὶ δεξιὰ ὡς ἂν δύνηται κάλλιστον, ἄρχειν δὲ Φαῖδρον πρῶτον,   22
ἐπειδὴ καὶ πρῶτος κατάκειται καὶ ἔστιν ἅμα πατὴρ τοῦ λόγου."   23
Ὁ δὲ Σωκράτης "Οὐδείς σοι, ὦ Ἐρυξίμαχε," ἔφη, "ἐναντία ψηφιεῖται.   24

---

13   ὃν μέλλω λέγειν: the antecedent of the relative clause here is not Φαίδρου but the more distant
       μῦθος, as the context makes clear

14   οὐ δεινὸν [ἐστι]: as usual when the verb is missing, supply a form of "to be." Technically the
       infinitives that follow are the subject of the sentence, but it may be easier to treat the accusatives
       and infinitives that follow like accusatives and infinitives in indirect statement: "Is it not
       terrible that . . ."
       *ὕμνος -ου ὁ = hymn, song of praise (cf. ὑμνέω)

15   παιών -ῶνος ὁ = paean, song of praise
       τηλικοῦτος -αύτη -οῦτο = of such an age, of so great an age

16   μηδὲ ἕνα: emphatic version of μηδένα = not even one; both οὐδέ and μηδέ frequently mean
       "not even" as well as "and not, nor." μή rather than οὐ is regularly used after adjectives and
       other words that take an infinitive not in indirect discourse (see Smyth 1956: §2713)

18   ἐνῆσαν: from ἐν + εἰμί. What is the form (*Essentials* §65)?
       ἅλες from ἅλς ἁλός ὁ = salt (pl. used where English uses a sing. collective noun; translate as a
       sing.). A speech or treatise in praise of a mundane object like salt allowed the sophists to show
       off their rhetorical skill.
       *ἔπαινος -ου ὁ = praise (cf. ἐπαινέω)
       *θαυμάσιος -α -ον = wondrous, amazing (cf. θαυμάζω)
       πρὸς ὠφελίαν = for its usefulness, for its benefit (cf. ὠφελέω)

19   *τολμάω = dare, undertake

21   χρῆναι: inf. of χρή
       ἔπαινον: in apposition to λόγον = a speech of praise

22   ὡς ἂν δύνηται κάλλιστον = as beautifully as he can

23   πατὴρ τοῦ λόγου: because he got Eryximachus started thinking about this

24   *ψηφίζομαι ψηφιοῦμαι ἐψηφισάμην—ἐψήφισμαι = vote

οὔτε γὰρ ἄν που ἐγὼ ἀποφήσαιμι, ὃς οὐδέν φημι ἄλλο ἐπίστασθαι   25

ἢ τὰ ἐρωτικά, οὔτε που Ἀγάθων καὶ Παυσανίας, οὐδὲ μὴν Ἀριστοφάνης,   26

ᾧ περὶ Διόνυσον καὶ Ἀφροδίτην πᾶσα ἡ διατριβή, οὐδὲ ἄλλος οὐδεὶς   27

τουτωνὶ ὧν ἐγὼ ὁρῶ. ἀλλὰ τύχῃ ἀγαθῇ καταρχέτω Φαῖδρος καὶ   28

ἐγκωμιαζέτω τὸν Ἔρωτα."   29

Ταῦτα δὴ καὶ οἱ ἄλλοι πάντες ἄρα συνέφασάν τε καὶ ἐκέλευον   30

ἅπερ ὁ Σωκράτης. πάντων μὲν οὖν ἃ ἕκαστος εἶπεν οὔτε πάνυ μέμνημαι   31

οὔτ᾽ ἐρῶ πάντα· ἃ δὲ μάλιστ᾽ ἔδοξέ μοι ἀξιομνημόνευτα, ταῦτα ὑμῖν ἐρῶ.   32

---

26   Ἀγάθων καὶ Παυσανίας: who apparently had a reputation as particularly devoted lovers

27   ᾧ: dat. of possessor (*Essentials* §107)

      Ἀφροδίτη -ης ἡ = Aphrodite, goddess of love

      *διατριβή -ῆς ἡ = way of life, pastime

28   ὧν: explain the case of this relative pronoun (*Essentials* §132)

      τύχῃ ἀγαθῇ = with good fortune. With the third person imperative here, this is essentially an expression of goodwill toward Phaedrus as he begins; dative of accompanying circumstance (Smyth 1956: §1527).

      κατάρχω = ἄρχω (strengthened)

      καταρχέτω and ἐγκωμιαζέτω: both 3rd pers. imperatives

31   ἅπερ ὁ Σωκράτης [ἐκέλευσε]: the missing word can be understood from context

      πάντων: obj. of μέμνημαι (verbs of remembering and forgetting regularly use gen. objects)

32   ἀξιομνημόνευτος -ον = worthy of mention

Reading 3. The Speech of Phaedrus

Although Eryximachus calls him the father of the discussion (reading 2C.23), Phaedrus is also the youngest speaker at the *Symposium*. This creates a connection between Phaedrus and the god he is praising. As Phaedrus notes, Hesiod and other early mythological writers place Eros among the earliest gods, as sexual love needs to be present to generate other gods; in this sense Eros is the "father" of the other gods. But, as Agathon will tell us later, Phaedrus's description of Eros as the eldest (πρεσβύτατος) is contradicted by Eros's youthful image in vase paintings and poetic texts. Like Phaedrus, Eros is a young progenitor.

Phaedrus is probably the ἐρώμενος (beloved) of Eryximachus, as their frequent discussions of Eros and their close relationship suggest (see appendix 1). This would make Phaedrus's speech offer the perspective of the younger partner in the relationship, a relatively rare phenomenon in Greek literature. Rosen 1987: 50–54 argues that this gives Phaedrus too narrow a perspective on Eros, but for those acquainted with the traditional erotic poetry of the symposium, which shows considerable self-absorption on the part of the ἐραστής (lover) and very little interest in the feelings of the ἐρώμενος (beloved), this may have been a refreshing change.

Phaedrus appears in Plato's *Protagoras*, alongside Eryximachus, listening to the sophist Hippias; he is, like most of the other speakers in the dialogue, part of an elite group interested in and influenced by these prominent intellectuals. Phaedrus also appears in Plato's *Phaedrus*, another dialogue on the subject of *eros*, where he is depicted as an ardent admirer of the rhetorician Lysias, one of the most successful and wealthiest resident aliens (*metics*) of the period (ca. 412–388 B.C.E.). Many of the speeches written by Lysias survive; their style is clear and relatively simple, and it is possible that Phaedrus's style in this dialogue is meant to imitate Lysias's.[21] This provides a striking contrast to the final speech in the series, Agathon's, which explicitly imitates the showier and more playful style of the more radical sophist and rhetorician Gorgias. Given that Agathon is another *eromenos* known for his youth and beauty and that Agathon explicitly hearkens back to Phaedrus's speech by criticizing his argument about Eros's age, it seems likely that Plato wants us to see these two speeches as forming a frame for the group of speeches leading up to Socrates' (see appendix 4).

Phaedrus's speech uses many of the conventions of Athenian rhetoric. As was common rhetorical practice, he relies heavily on mythical accounts to support his case, citing the most traditional poetic sources for Greek mythology, Homer and Hesiod (though also Parmenides and Acusilaus), and

---

21. This effect may be slightly exaggerated here, as, in my endeavor to make this speech accessible, I have simplified the syntax of several sentences.

Fig. 12.   Achilles binding Patroclus's wounds. Red-figure kylix (drinking cup) by Sosias, from Vulci, ca. 500 B.C.E. Inv. F2278. Antikensammlung, Staatliche Museen zu Berlin, Berlin, Germany. Photo credit: Bildarchiv Preussischer Kulturbesitz/Art Resource, New York.

referring to a traditional Greek tragedian, Aeschylus (though to criticize him). He focuses on two elements standard in Greek encomia: the subject's lineage and his contributions to the city (Dover 1980: 90). His emphasis on the way *eros* creates virtue in the form of shame (αἰσχύνη) and competitive love of honor (φιλοτιμία) in both lover and beloved seems to be related to a common assumption about the social purposes of the symposium and the relationships formed there: that by associating with older men of the same social station (καλοὶ κἀγαθοί) the young man would learn the virtues appropriate to his class. Phaedrus's heavy emphasis on shame and on a love of honor that makes people strive to appear good in the eyes of others is highly characteristic of Greek society and has led to its being classified as a "shame" culture. The final point of his speech, that love encourages the ultimate sacrifice, the willingness to die for another, allies Phaedrus with traditional forms of heroism in Greek society.

The name Phaedrus (Greek Φαῖδρος) means "shining, bright," and although Phaedrus is a historical character, Plato may still be interested in the name's significance, as he clearly is in Agathon's. Scholars have pointed out that virtually all of Phaedrus's arguments are systematically undermined in the remainder of the dialogue (Corrigan and Glazov-Corrigan 2004: 54–56); the promise of his youth and glorious appearance thus would appear to be entirely superficial (unlike the fundamental "goodness" of Agathon?).

Further Reading on the Speech of Phaedrus

- Plato's *Phaedrus* complements the *Symposium* well, for those looking for additional readings on Platonic love or on Plato's version of traditional Greek pederasty. For detailed discussion of Phaedrus's speech, see Allen 1991: 12–14; Corrigan and Glazov-Corrigan 2004: 51–56; and Rosen 1987: 39–59.

Suggested Reviews

- common uses of the accusative (*Essentials* §§76–88)
- common uses of the genitive (*Essentials* §§89–105)
- declension of τάξις -εως ἡ (*Essentials* §46.3e)
- principal parts of βάλλω, ἔχω, and θνῄσκω

  βάλλω βαλῶ ἔβαλον βέβληκα βέβλημαι ἐβλήθην = throw, hurl, shoot at, take a shot at, hit, strike

  ἔχω (*imperf.* εἶχον) ἕξω/σχήσω ἔσχον ἔσχηκα -ἔσχημαι ἐσχέθην = (1) have, hold; (2) + *inf.* = be able; (3) + *adv.* = be [such], be in [such a] state; e.g., πῶς ἔχεις; = How are you? εὖ ἔχω = I am well; χαλεπῶς ἔχω = I am in a bad state; (4) οὐκ ἔχω + ὅπως, πῶς, ποῦ, etc. = I don't know how/where/etc. . . .

  θνῄσκω -θανοῦμαι -ἔθανον τέθνηκα = die, be dying

- forms of ἵημι ἥσω -ἧκα/(-ἐ) -εἷκα -εἷμαι -εἵθην (set going, put in motion) (*Essentials* §§60–63)

Reading 3A

Phaedrus begins his speech by claiming that Eros is among the eldest of the gods and responsible for the greatest goods to humankind.

Vocabulary

- Make an effort to learn the forms of ζάω.

αἰσχύνη -ης ἡ: shame, disgrace (cf. αἰσχύνομαι, αἰσχρός, αἰσχίων, αἴσχιστος)

αἰσχύνομαι αἰσχυνοῦμαι ᾐσχυνάμην— —ᾐσχύνθην: feel shame before *acc.*, be ashamed

ἀνανδρία -ας ἡ: cowardice, lack of manliness (cf. ἀνήρ ἀνδρός ὁ; *ἀνδρεῖος -α -ον: brave, courageous; *ἀνδρεία -ας ἡ: bravery, courage)

γένεσις -εως ἡ: origin, source, birth, race, descent (cf. English "Genesis" and aorist stem of γίγνομαι γεν-)

δήπου *particle*: indeed perhaps, I would indeed suppose, it indeed may be (δή + που)

διαφερόντως *adv.*: in a different way, differently from, at odds with, extremely, extraordinarily

ἔπος -ους τό: word; restricted in the *Symposium* to the phrase ὡς ἔπος εἰπεῖν: so to speak, virtually, practically, almost—a phrase that students should recognize—but common in other authors in a broader range of uses (cf. English "epic" and εἰπεῖν)

ἐραστής -οῦ ὁ: lover (standard term for the older male in male couples), passionate follower

ἐράω (*imperf.* ἤρων): be in love with, have a passion for; + *gen. obj.*: love desirously; distinguish from ἐρέω, the future of λέγω, to which it is often similar and occasionally identical

ἐργάζομαι ἐργάσομαι ἠργασάμην—εἴργασμαι ἠργάσθην: work, do, accomplish, produce, perform; *recognize also stronger* version ἐξεργάζομαι: fully accomplish, bring to completion, work thoroughly, work out (cf. ἔργον -ου τό)

ἐρώμενος -ου ὁ: beloved (subst. pass. part. from ἐράω, standard term for the younger male in male couples)

ἔστιν + *acc.* + *inf.*: it is possible for *acc.* to——

ζάω ζήσω (*pres.* ζῶ ζῇς; *imperf.* ἔζων ἔζης; *part.* ζῶν ζῶσα ζῶν; *inf.* ζῆν): live

ἥκιστος -η -ον: least; *neut. pl.* ἥκιστα *used adverbially*: least of all, not at all (cf. μάλιστα)

θαυμαστός -ή -όν/θαυμάσιος -α -ον: to be wondered at, wondrous, wonderful (cf. θαυμάζω)

θνήσκω θανοῦμαι ἔθανον τέθνηκα (= ἀποθνήσκω): die; *perf.* to have died, i.e., be dead; *note also* irreg. perf. inf. τεθνάναι

64

ἰδιώτης -ου ὁ: private person, nonprofessional, layman, person lacking specialized σοφία of various kinds (cf. English "idiot")

μή + *part.*: if not——ing; μή normally gives a conditional force to the participle that is not found when οὐ accompanies the participle

μηχανή -ῆς ἡ: device, scheme, instrument, machine, contrivance (cf. English "mechanism")

παιδικά -ῶν τά *pl. used for sing.*: darling, the beloved in a pederastic relationship, favorite, young beloved

πλοῦτος -ου ὁ: wealth (cf. πλούσιος -α -ον)

πρεσβύτερος -α -ον: older, elder, superior, more esteemed/important; πρεσβύτατος -η -ον: oldest, eldest, best, most esteemed/important

τάξις -εως ἡ: arrangement, order, battle order, line of battle

τεκμήριον -ου τό: sure sign or token, evidence, proof

τίμιος -α -ον: prized, valued, honored, honorable (cf. τιμάω, τιμή ἡ, ἀτιμάζω)

χρηστός -ή -όν: worthy, good, valuable, useful, upright, helpful; *recognize also* χρήσιμος -η -ον: useful, good

Reading 3A (based on *Symposium* 178a6–179a5)

Μέγας θεός ἐστιν ὁ Ἔρως καὶ θαυμαστὸς ἐν ἀνθρώποις τε καὶ   1

θεοῖς, πολλαχῇ μὲν καὶ ἄλλῃ, οὐχ ἥκιστα δὲ κατὰ τὴν γένεσιν. τὸ γὰρ   2

ἐν τοῖς πρεσβύτατον εἶναι τὸν θεὸν τίμιον, τεκμήριον δὲ τούτου· γονεῖς   3

γὰρ Ἔρωτος οὔτ᾽ εἰσὶν οὔτε λέγονται ὑπ᾽ οὐδενὸς οὔτε ἰδιώτου οὔτε   4

ποιητοῦ, ἀλλ᾽ Ἡσίοδος πρῶτον μὲν Χάος φησὶ γενέσθαι—   5

αὐτὰρ ἔπειτα   6

Γαῖ᾽ εὐρύστερνος, πάντων ἕδος ἀσφαλὲς αἰεί,   7

ἠδ᾽ Ἔρος.   8

---

2   πολλαχῇ καὶ ἄλλῃ = in many other ways. Feminine dative adjectives are frequently used as virtual adverbs. As often, καί is used to connect another adjective to a form of πολύς and may be omitted in translating for more idiomatic English. Also common: the generalization precedes and the most important instance is placed last for emphasis, the reverse of normal English practice.

     ἥκιστα = adverbial

2–3   τὸ . . . εἶναι: articular infinitive serving as a subject; the accusative τὸν θεόν is the subject of the infinitive. Adding "the fact that . . ." to the translation of the articular infinitive may help to get it into English (*Essentials* §182). τίμιον is a predicate; the main verb ἐστί can be inferred from the sentence's structure.

     ἐν τοῖς πρεσβύτατον = ἐν τοῖς πρεσβυτάτοις (idiomatic)

3   τεκμήριον δὲ τούτου: supply ἔστι = there is *or* τόδε ἐστί = this is

     γονεύς -εως ὁ = father, ancestor, parent (declines like βασιλεύς; *Essentials* §46.3g)

4   ἰδιώτου . . . ποιητοῦ: in apposition to οὐδενός.

     Ἡσίοδος -ου ὁ = Hesiod, traditional Greek poet; author of *Theogony*, the traditional account of the genealogies of the Greek gods

5   Χάος -ους τό = Chaos, both a god and a part of the original structure of the universe, according to Hesiod. Chaos appears as a gaping hole or Chasm in the *Theogony* (West 1966: 192–93n116). Although Χάος precedes the verb φησί, it is the subject of the indirect statement introduced by Ἡσίοδος . . . φησί.

6–8   Quotation of *Theogony* 116–17, 119. The dialect is virtually identical to that of Homeric epic.

6   *αὐτάρ: epic for ἀτάρ (common in Homer)

7   Γαῖ᾽ = *Γαῖα = Gaia, Earth (= γῆ)

     εὐρύστερνος -ον = broad-breasted

     ἕδος -ους τό = seat

     *ἀσφαλής -ές = unshakeable, firm, steadfast

     *αἰεί = ἀεί

8   *ἠδ᾽ = ἠδέ = and (common in poetry)

     Ἔρος = Ἔρως

Ἡσιόδῳ δὲ καὶ Ἀκουσίλεως σύμφησιν μετὰ τὸ Χάος δύο τούτω γενέσθαι,   9

Γῆν τε καὶ Ἔρωτα.   10

   Πρεσβύτατος δὲ ὢν μεγίστων ἀγαθῶν ἡμῖν αἴτιός ἐστιν. οὐ γὰρ   11

ἔγωγ᾽ ἔχω εἰπεῖν ὅτι μεῖζόν ἐστιν ἀγαθὸν νεανίᾳ ἢ ἐραστὴς χρηστός—   12

καὶ ἐραστῇ παιδικά. ἀνθρώποις γὰρ τοῖς μέλλουσι καλῶς πάντα τὸν βίον   13

ζήσειν οὕτω χρήσιμον οὔτε τιμαὶ οὔτε πλοῦτος οὔτ᾽ ἄλλο οὐδὲν ὡς ἔρως.   14

ἐμποιεῖ γὰρ τὴν ἐπὶ μὲν τοῖς αἰσχροῖς αἰσχύνην, ἐπὶ δὲ τοῖς καλοῖς   15

φιλοτιμίαν. οὐ δ᾽ ἔστιν ἄνευ τούτων οὔτε πόλιν οὔτε ἰδιώτην μεγάλα   16

---

9 Ἡσιόδῳ δὲ καί: the dative ending makes clear that καί does not connect Hesiod to the nominative Ἀκουσίλεως but must be adverbial. The dative is explained by σύμφησί = agrees with *dat*.

Ἀκουσίλεως -ω ὁ = Acusilaus of Argos, of whom little is known. According to Josephus, he lived before the Persian Wars and compiled Γενεαλογίαι, offering translations and corrections of Hesiod.[22]

τούτω: masc. dual acc. of οὗτος, subje. (with acc. δύο) of the indirect statement here. Dual endings, used as an alternative to plural endings for things that are found in pairs, are used intermittently in the *Symposium* (*Essentials* §§67–69).

11 μεγίστων ἀγαθῶν: gen. with the adj. αἴτιος (*Essentials* §102)

αἴτιος: presumably because he helped engender them

12 ὅτι = ὅ τι (is conventionally printed as one word in Plato, despite the confusion that can result)

νεανίᾳ: dat. with ἀγαθόν = good for *dat*. (*Essentials* §116)

13 μέλλουσι (dat. pl. part. with τοῖς, not 3rd pers. pl. indic.) depends on χρήσιμον = useful for *dat*. (*Essentials* §116); χρήσιμον is a pred. adj. (*Essentials* §123)

14 οὕτω . . . ὡς *correl.* = as . . . as

15 ἐμποιέω = create in, implant

ἐπὶ . . . τοῖς αἰσχροῖς: what must the position of this phrase between the definite article τήν and the noun αἰσχύνην mean? How should that affect the translation (*Essentials* §187)?

τοῖς αἰσχροῖς and τοῖς καλοῖς: neut.

16 *φιλοτιμία -ας ἡ = love of honor, competitive spirit, desire to excel

ἔστιν + *acc.* + *inf.* = it is possible for *acc.* to —— (see vocabulary)

τούτων: i.e., τῆς αἰσχύνης καὶ τῆς φιλοτιμίας

καὶ καλὰ ἔργα ἐξεργάζεσθαι. φημὶ τοίνυν ἄνδρα ὅστις ἐρᾷ, εἴ τι αἰσχρὸν   17

ποιῶν κατάδηλος γίγνοιτο ἢ πάσχων ὑπό του δι' ἀνανδρίαν μὴ ἀμυνόμενος,   18

οὔτ' ἂν ὑπὸ πατρὸς ὀφθέντα οὕτως ἀλγῆσαι οὔτε ὑπὸ ἑταίρων οὔτε   19

ὑπ' ἄλλου οὐδένος ὡς ὑπὸ παιδικῶν· ὁ δ' ἐρώμενος διαφερόντως τοὺς   20

ἐραστὰς αἰσχύνεται, ὅταν ὀφθῇ ἐν αἰσχρῷ τινι ὤν. εἰ οὖν πόλις τις   21

γένοιτο ἢ στρατόπεδον ἐραστῶν τε καὶ παιδικῶν, αὕτη ἂν εἴη πολλῷ   22

---

17   φημί: enclitics retain their accent at the beginning of a sentence or clause (Smyth 1956: §187a)

    ἄνδρα: subje. of the indir. statement

17–18   εἰ . . . ἀνανδρίαν: the syntax of the if-clause is unaffected by the indirect statement, but the main clause of this same sentence uses the accusative + infinitive construction; this is normal for indirect statements.

18   κατάδηλος γίγνομαι + *supplemental part.* = be clearly ——ing, be caught ——ing

    *ὑπό + *gen.* accompanying πάσχω = at the hands of —— (ὑπό + gen. is regularly used to express agency with πάσχω, which implies passivity even though not pass. in form)

    *του = τινός

    μή: what does μή before a participle imply (*Essentials* §173)?

    *ἀμύνομαι = defend oneself

19   ὀφθέντα: participle with conditional force; accusative because it agrees with the subject of the indirect statement, ἄνδρα (see note on line 17)

    ἀλγέω = feel pain (here clearly refers to a feeling of shame so acute as to be painful); ἀλγῆσαι: aorist infinitive in indirect statements; ἄν and the optative in the protasis make clear that this represents an original aorist optative in a future-less-vivid condition (*Essentials* §157)

19–20   οὕτως . . . ὡς *correl.* = so much . . . as

21   *στρατόπεδον -ου τό = army camp. In the early fourth century, there was actually such an army at Thebes, the so-called Sacred Band.

22   πολλῷ = by far (dat. of degree of difference) (*Essentials* §111)

ἀρίστη πασῶν. οἱ γὰρ τοιοῦτοι ἀπέχοιντο ἂν πάντων τῶν αἰσχρῶν   23

καὶ φιλοτιμοῖντο πρὸς ἀλλήλους, καὶ μαχόμενοί γε μετ' ἀλλήλων νικῷεν   24

ἂν ὀλίγοι ὄντες ὡς ἔπος εἰπεῖν πάντας ἀνθρώπους. ἐρῶν γὰρ ἀνὴρ   25

ὑπὸ παιδικῶν ὀφθῆναι ἢ λιπὼν τάξιν ἢ ὅπλα ἀποβαλὼν ἧττον ἂν δήπου   26

δέξαιτο ἢ ὑπὸ πάντων τῶν ἄλλων, καὶ πρὸ τούτου τεθνάναι ἂν πολλάκις   27

ἕλοιτο.   28

---

23 *ἀπέχομαι + *gen.* = hold (oneself) back from

24 φιλοτιμέομαι πρός + *acc.* = compete with *acc.* in seeking honor

25 ὡς ἔπος εἰπεῖν: the phrase qualifies πάντας (as is typical of this phrase) and so means something more like "virtually" or "almost" than one might think from a more literal translation of the phrase

26 ὀφθῆναι: complementary inf. with δέξαιτο (δέχομαι + *inf.* = be glad to ——, choose to ——, but here paired with ἧττον = choose less, be less glad)

27 πολλάκις: take with τεθνάναι (paradoxical)

28 ἕλοιτο: from αἱρέω (*mid.* = choose)

Reading 3B

Phaedrus draws on several mythological examples that would have been familiar to his audience. The first is that of Alcestis, wife of Admetus. According to the story as presented in Euripides' *Alcestis*, the earliest full account we have, the god Apollo, because of Admetus's past generous hospitality to him (some later versions suggest he was Apollo's ἐρώμενος), gave Admetus the right to postpone his imminent death if he could find someone to die in his place. His parents refused, but his young wife, Alcestis, agreed, prompting much praise of her virtue as well as lamenting of her loss. Heracles descended into the Underworld and brought Alcestis back from the dead providing a reward for her virtue. The inclusion of Alcestis as exemplary of traditional heroic virtue acknowledges that women are capable of love and virtue, something only rarely acknowledged by the other speakers.

Phaedrus compares Alcestis's self-sacrifice favorably with that of Orpheus, the famous singer, who made a descent into the Underworld but did not actually sacrifice his own life. According to the standard version of the myth, Orpheus descended into the Underworld alive to retrieve his dead wife Eurydice. There he was able to win over even the implacable ruler of the dead with his song and was allowed to bring his wife back on the condition that he did not turn around to look at her until he reached the world of the living above. But he was unable to restrain himself, and his wife was snatched back to the Underworld. It is not clear that Plato knew all of those elements; certainly, Phaedrus tells a somewhat different version of the story, according to which the gods of the Underworld tricked Orpheus with a phantom (φάσμα) of his wife. Orpheus was said to have lost his life, torn to death by maenads, female followers of Dionysus, an event to which Phaedrus clearly alludes as a contrast to Alcestis's death.

Finally, Phaedrus speaks of Achilles, the greatest Greek warrior of the Trojan War, whose mother, Thetis, predicted that if he killed the greatest Trojan warrior, Hector, he would soon die. The alternative was that Achilles would live a long life without fame. But when Hector killed Patroclus, Achilles' closest friend, Achilles went into a rage and killed Hector, thus hastening his own death. In the *Iliad*, Homer does not say that Achilles and Patroclus were lovers, though he presents them as deeply attached to one another. But in the fifth century, their relationship was clearly interpreted by many as erotic. Aeschylus's tragedy on the subject, of which we have only fragments, clearly made Achilles the ἐραστής (lover) and Patroclus the ἐρώμενος (beloved).

Fig. 13. The god Apollo holding a kithara. Athenian red-figure pelike, 460–450 B.C.E.
Inv. 1843,1103.28. British Museum, London, England. © Trustees of the British Museum.

Vocabulary

ἄγαμαι, *aor.* ἠγάσθην: wonder at, be astonished at, admire. Like δύναμαι, ἄγαμαι conjugates like the middle of ἵστημι (*Essentials* §60).

ἀγαπάω ἀγαπήσω ἠγάπησα ἠγάπηκα ἠγάπημαι ἠγαπήθην: love (typically, of a more disinterested, less passionate sort than ἐράω), be fond of

ἀλλότριος -α -ον: alien to, foreign to, unfriendly to (opposite of φίλος)

ἅτε + *part.*: because of ——ing, on account of ——ing

βοηθέω βοηθήσομαι ἐβοήθησα βεβοήθηκα βεβοήθημαι ἐβοηθήθην: come to aid, assist, help *dat.*

εὐδαιμονία -ας ἡ: prosperity, good fortune, happiness (cf. εὐδαίμων -ον)

θεῖος -α -ον: divine, holy, sacred (cf. θεός ὁ/ἡ, θεά ἡ)

ἵημι -ἥσω -ἧκα/ (-ἕ) -εἷκα -εἷμαι -εἵθην: send, send away, let go, let go forth, throw, hurl, release; *mid.*: feel an impulse toward a thing, yearn for; *most often used in compounds, especially ἀνίημι*: send up; ἀφίημι: send away, send forth, let go, permit, neglect; παρίημι: pass over, neglect (*Essentials* §§60–63)

κύριος -α -ον: important, critical, authoritative, masterly

μάκαρ (*gen.* μάκαρος): blessed, happy

μαρτυρία -ας ἡ: witnessing, testimony, evidence (cf. μάρτυς)

μηχανάομαι μηχανήσομαι ἐμηχανσάμην—μεμηχάνημαι: devise, bring about, contrive; *recognize also* διαμηχανάομαι

ὅθεν *rel. adv.*: from whom, from which, from where; *often used as demonst. rather than rel.*: from this, hence

πάλιν *adv.*: back, again (cf. English "palindrome" and "palinode")

παρέχω: provide, furnish (see ἔχω for principal parts)

σπουδή -ῆς ἡ: haste, eagerness, zeal, effort, seriousness

τελευτάω τελευτήσω ἐτελεύτησα τετελεύτηκα τετελεύτημαι ἐτελευτήθην: complete, finish, accomplish, end, die (cf. τέλος)

τιμωρέω τιμωρήσω ἐτιμώρησα τετιμώρηκα τετιμώρημαι ἐτιμωρήθην: avenge, help; *mid.*: exact vengeance on, avenge oneself upon, punish

τοιγάρ: so then, accordingly, therefore, wherefore; *recognize also stronger version* τοιγάρτοι

τολμάω τολμήσω ἐτόλμησα τετόλμηκα τετόλμημαι ἐτολμήθην: dare, undertake, venture

φάσκω: say, affirm, assert (pres. and imperf. only)

φιλία -ας ἡ: friendship, affection, friendly or familial love

ψυχή -ῆς ἡ: soul, breath, life (cf. English "psyche" and "psychology")

Reading 3B (based on *Symposium* 179b4–180b8)

Καὶ μὴν ὑπεραποθνῄσκειν γε μόνοι ἐθέλουσιν οἱ ἐρῶντες, οὐ μόνον   1

ἄνδρες, ἀλλὰ καὶ αἱ γυναῖκες. τούτου δὲ καὶ ἡ Πελίου θυγάτηρ Ἄλκηστις   2

ἱκανὴν μαρτυρίαν παρέχεται, ἐθελήσασα μόνη ὑπὲρ τοῦ αὑτῆς ἀνδρὸς   3

ἀποθανεῖν, ὄντων αὐτῷ πατρός τε καὶ μητρός, οὓς ἐκείνη τοσοῦτον   4

ὑπερεβάλετο τῇ φιλίᾳ διὰ τὸν ἔρωτα, ὥστε ἀποδεῖξαι αὐτοὺς ἀλλοτρίους   5

ὄντας τῷ ὑεῖ καὶ ὀνόματι μόνον προσήκοντας. τοῦτο δ᾽ ἐργασαμένη τὸ   6

ἔργον οὕτω καλὸν ἔδοξεν ἐργάσασθαι οὐ μόνον ἀνθρώποις ἀλλὰ καὶ θεοῖς,   7

ὥστε αὐτῇ ἔδοσαν τοῦτο γέρας οἱ θεοί, τὸ ἐξ Ἅιδου ἀνεῖναι πάλιν τὴν   8

ψυχήν, ἀγασθέντες τῷ ἔργῳ· οὕτω καὶ θεοὶ τὴν περὶ τὸν ἔρωτα σπουδήν   9

τε καὶ ἀρετὴν μάλιστα τιμῶσιν. Ὀρφέα δὲ τὸν Οἰάγρου ἀτελῆ ἀπέπεμψαν   10

ἐξ Ἅιδου, φάσμα δείξαντες τῆς γυναικὸς ἐφ᾽ ἣν ἧκεν, αὐτὴν δὲ οὐ δόντες,   11

1	καὶ μήν = moreover; it typically introduces a new line of argument
	ὑπεραποθνῄσκω = ὑπέρ + ἀποθνῄσκω = die for someone else, die on behalf of another
2	Πελίης -ου ὁ = Pelias, son of the god Poseidon and a mortal woman Tyro
	Ἄλκηστις -ιδος ἡ = Alcestis (see introduction)
4	αὐτῷ: dat. of possessor (*Essentials* §107), refers to Alcestis's husband, Admetus
	τοσοῦτον: adverbial
5	ὑπερβάλλομαι = surpass
	τῇ φιλίᾳ: = in her [affectionate] love (dat. of respect) (*Essentials* §110)
6	ὑεῖ = υἱῷ
	ὀνόματι = in name (dat. of respect) (*Essentials* §110)
	*προσήκω = be related to
8	*γέρας -αος τό = prize of honor; γέρας is a predicate of τοῦτο: "this as a prize of honor"—as shown by the absence of the definite article (τοῦτο τὸ γέρας = this prize of honor) (*Essentials* §188)
	Ἅιδης -ου ὁ = Hades, god of the Underworld
	ἀνεῖναι from ἀνίημι: artic. inf. serving as a noun in apposition to γέρας
9	ἀγασθέντες from ἄγαμαι (deponent: pass. form with act. meaning)
	τῷ ἔργῳ = because of the deed (dat. of cause). This is particularly common with verbs of emotion, expressing the occasion or the motive for the emotion (Smyth 1956: §§1517–20).
10	Ὀρφεύς -έως ὁ = Orpheus (see introduction)
	Οἴαγρος -ου ὁ = Oiagrus, father of Orpheus
	ἀτελής -ές = without τέλος, without end or goal, unaccomplished, unfulfilled
11	φάσμα -ατος τό = apparition, phantom

ὅτι μαλθακίζεσθαι ἐδόκει, ἅτε ὢν κιθαρῳδός, καὶ οὐ τολμᾶν τοῦ ἔρωτος   12

ἕνεκα ἀποθνῄσκειν ὥσπερ Ἄλκηστις, ἀλλὰ διαμηχανᾶσθαι ζῶν εἰσιέναι   13

εἰς Ἅιδου. τοιγάρτοι διὰ ταῦτα δίκην αὐτῷ ἐπέθεσαν, καὶ ἐποίησαν τὸν   14

θάνατον αὐτοῦ ὑπὸ γυναικῶν γενέσθαι.   15

διαφερόντως δ’ οἱ θεοὶ Ἀχιλλέα τὸν τῆς Θέτιδος υἱὸν ἐτίμησαν καὶ   16

εἰς μακάρων νήσους ἀπέπεμψαν, ὅτι πεπυσμένος παρὰ τῆς μητρὸς ὡς   17

ἀποθανοῖτο ἀποκτείνας Ἕκτορα, μὴ ποιήσας δὲ τοῦτο οἴκαδε ἐλθὼν   18

γηραιὸς τελευτήσοι, ἐτόλμησεν ἑλέσθαι βοηθήσας τῷ ἐραστῇ Πατρόκλῳ   19

καὶ τιμωρήσας οὐ μόνον ὑπεραποθανεῖν ἀλλὰ καὶ ἐπαποθανεῖν   20

τετελευτηκότι· ὅθεν δὴ καὶ ὑπεραγασθέντες οἱ θεοὶ διαφερόντως αὐτὸν   21

ἐτίμησαν, ὅτι τὸν ἐραστὴν οὕτω περὶ πολλοῦ ἐποιεῖτο. Αἰσχύλος δὲ   22

---

12 μαλθακίζομαι = be softened, be soft (*μαλακός -ή -όν = soft, weak, cowardly)
    κιθαρῳδός -οῦ ὁ = kithara player; a kithara is a stringed instrument resembling a harp (fig. 13)

14 δίκην . . . ἐπιτίθημι = impose punishment on *dat.*

15 ὑπὸ γυναικῶν = at the hands of women (cf. ὑπό + gen. with πάσχω in reading 3A.18)

16 Ἀχιλλεύς -έως ὁ = Achilles (see introduction)
    Θέτις -ιδος ἡ = Thetis, Achilles' mother, a sea goddess

17 μακάρων νήσους = Isles of the Blessed, where a pleasant afterlife is reserved for a very small
    number of privileged mortals (in contrast to the unpleasant Underworld), often compared to
    the Elysian plain (mentioned in the *Odyssey* 4.561–69); see Gantz 1993: 1.132–35

18–19 ἀποθανοῖτο and τελευτήσοι: take note of the tense of optative. Why optative here (*Essentials*
    §158)?

18 Ἕκτωρ -ορος ὁ = Hector, the greatest Trojan warrior
    μή: what does μή before a participle imply (*Essentials* §173)?

19 γηραιός -ά -όν = aged, in old age (*γῆρας -ως τό = old age)
    τελευτήσοι see note on lines 18–19

20 ὑπεραποθανεῖν and ἐπαποθεῖν: both infinitives are dependent on ἑλέσθαι. ἐπαποθνῄσκω =
    die in addition to, die with or after *dat. obj.*; for meaning of ὑπεραποθνῄσκω, see note on line
    1. Since Achilles dies after Patroclus, he doesn't actually save his lover's life, as Alcestis does for
    Admetus. Phaedrus implies that this is even more of a self-sacrifice.

21 τετελευτηκότι: what is this form (*Essentials* §33)?
    ὑπεράγαμαι = ὑπερ + ἄγαμαι = admire excessively (note this additional meaning of ὑπέρ as a
    prefix; cf. English "hyper-")

22 *περὶ πολλοῦ ποιέομαι = value much, consider important
    Αἰσχύλος -ου ὁ = Aeschylus, the tragic playwright. The play (*Myrmidons*) survives only in brief
    fragments.

φλυαρεῖ φάσκων Ἀχιλλέα Πατρόκλου ἐρᾶν, ὃς ἦν καλλίων οὐ μόνον   23

Πατρόκλου ἀλλὰ καὶ τῶν ἡρώων ἁπάντων, καὶ ἔτι ἀγένειος, ἔπειτα   24

νεώτερος πολύ, ὥς φησιν Ὅμηρος. ἀλλὰ γὰρ τῷ ὄντι μάλιστα μὲν ταύτην   25

τὴν ἀρετὴν οἱ θεοὶ τιμῶσιν τὴν περὶ τὸν ἔρωτα, μᾶλλον μέντοι θαυμάζουσιν   26

καὶ ἄγανται καὶ εὖ ποιοῦσιν ὅταν ὁ ἐρώμενος τὸν ἐραστὴν ἀγαπᾷ ἢ ὅταν   27

ὁ ἐραστὴς τὰ παιδικά. θειότερον γὰρ ἐραστὴς παιδικῶν· ἔνθεος γάρ ἐστι.   28

διὰ ταῦτα καὶ τὸν Ἀχιλλέα τῆς Ἀλκήστιδος μᾶλλον ἐτίμησαν, εἰς μακάρων   29

νήσους ἀποπέμψαντες.   30

Οὕτω δὴ ἔγωγέ φημι Ἔρωτα θεῶν καὶ πρεσβύτατον καὶ τιμιώτατον   31

καὶ κυριώτατον εἶναι εἰς ἀρετῆς καὶ εὐδαιμονίας κτῆσιν ἀνθρώποις καὶ ζῶσι   32

καὶ τελευτήσασιν.   33

---

23   *φλυαρέω = talk nonsense

24   *ἥρως ἥρωος ὁ = warrior, hero
      ἀγένειος -ον = beardless

25   Ὅμηρος -ου ὁ = Homer, poet of the *Iliad* and *Odyssey*
      ἀλλὰ γάρ = but anyway, to return to my point. He resumes his argument following the digression about Aeschylus.

27   εὖ ποιοῦσιν: with an adverb, ποιέω normally means "treat." The understood objects must be members of the pairs described in the ὅταν-clause. Phaedrus argues that the gods honor the ἐρώμενος who sacrifices himself for his lover more than the lover who makes a similar sacrifice, because the ἐρώμενος, who is not conceived of as being in love, is not filled with Eros and therefore has less divine inspiration to assist and motivate his actions.

28   ἔνθεος -ον = full of the god, inspired, possessed (because he is full of Eros)

32   *κύριος . . . εἰς (of things) = critical to, important for
      κτῆσις -εως ἡ = possessing, possession (κτῆσιν not ἀρετῆς is the obj. of εἰς, which takes an accusative obj.)
      ζῶσι: dat. pl. part. from ζάω

Reading 4. Pausanias's Purified Pederasty

We know little of Pausanias of Cerameis beyond his long-lasting relationship with Agathon, unusual in a culture where most homoerotic relationships were short-term ones. Pausanias is clearly the older male (*erastes*) in this pair, so his speech here offers an immediate contrast with the perspective given in the previous speech by the young *eromenos*, Phaedrus. In Plato's *Protagoras* (315de), set some fifteen to twenty years earlier, Pausanias appears alongside a young Agathon as a follower of the sophist Prodicus. Prodicus was particularly known for drawing precise distinctions between words that were similar, and Pausanias too shows an interest in making fine distinctions. Prodicus was also a moralist of a traditional kind, a lover of virtue, hard work, and postponed gratification, as seen in his famous allegorical fable "The Choice of Heracles" (mentioned at *Symposium* 177b),[23] and a strongly moralistic tone is also evident in Pausanias's speech. Pausanias's particular interests in laws and in cultural practices and his lawyerly tone further define the speech and provide a contrast with the speech of the doctor Eryximachus that follows.

Pausanias's arguments that there are good and bad forms of Eros are worth careful consideration. In certain ways, the distinctions he draws between the bad Eros that is short-term, promiscuous, and sexual and a good Eros that is monogamous, lifelong, and transcends the purely sexual may seem very familiar to contemporary students. More startling perhaps may be his argument that, when pederasty is practiced correctly, it alone is an admirable form of Eros. His rejection of heterosexual relationships has to do with his perception that women are not the intellectual or social equals of men, as indeed would have been difficult to achieve in Athenian society. This made erotic relationships between men and women in general more narrowly sexual and consequently less virtuous by Pausanias's standards than is his ideal. But, as many readers have noted, Pausanias's interest in the gratification of the *erastes*, which commentators have understood to mean sexual gratification, shows him to be self-interested; for all his emphasis on virtue there is something crassly commercial about his suggestion that the beloved can offer sexual gratification in exchange for an education. In Xenophon's *Symposium*, Socrates criticizes Pausanias for overstating the case for pederasty. Moreover, Socrates' behavior as reported later in the dialogue by Alcibiades confirms that, for all his flirtatiousness with young men and his interest in their education in virtue, Socrates explicitly rejected the kind of exchange that Pausanias here

---

23. The text is paraphrased in Xenophon's *Memorabilia* 2.1.21–34. It told an allegorical fable of how the feminine figures of Virtue (Ἀρετή) and Vice (Κακία) approached Heracles and asked him to choose between them, laying out the advantages of each way of life. The way of Vice appears easier, more seductive, and pleasurable in the short-term, but the life of Virtue holds greater long-term rewards. The fable was apparently popular and was frequently retold.

Fig. 14. The bad Eros? An *erastes* courts a boy, apparently with money, although scholars dispute the significance of these sacks. Red-figure lekythos. Inv. 2001.28.1. Courtesy of the Michael C. Carlos Museum of Emory University, Atlanta, Georgia. Photo by Bruce M. White, 2007. For discussion of such sacks in pederastic vase paintings, see Lear and Cantarella 2008: especially 78–86 and work cited there.

presents as a justification for pederasty. We should also remember that Pausanias's conception of pederasty is modeled on his own long-term, apparently monogamous, relationship with a man now in his late twenties or early thirties, not exactly "pederasty" as generally conceived.

Despite his atypical conception, Pausanias's speech remains an important source for our knowledge of the practices and ideology of classical pederasty, as he comments more directly than most Athenian sources on social practices both in Athens and elsewhere in Greece. Unfortunately, the most uncontroversial thing that Pausanias says is perhaps that attitudes toward pederasty in Athens are ποικίλος (complex) and hard to understand. These attitudes have certainly been hotly debated in scholarship over the last several decades.[24]

Pausanias ingeniously adapts Greek mythology and religious practice to his own end in creating the idea of two Erotes, a good and a bad. He uses Homer's and Hesiod's two quite different genealogies for Aphrodite to argue that there are in fact two Aphrodites: one described by Homer in *Iliad* 5 born from Zeus and Dione, hence the product of a heterosexual union, and one born from the foam of the sea and the castrated genitals of the god Ouranos, as described by Hesiod in the *Theogony*, hence motherless. The latter he calls Ourania ("Heavenly") using a standard cult name of Aphrodite, which he links to her birth from Ouranos. Moreover, he twists another cult title of Aphrodite, Pandemos (of the Entire People), by giving it the implication "Promiscuous" and applying it to the Homeric Aphrodite. He then argues that there must be an Eros that corresponds to each of the two Aphrodites, thus ingeniously imposing a coherence and logic on incoherent features of Greek mythology. The speech is typical of sophistic practices criticized by Plato and parodied by Aristophanes in the *Clouds*.

Suggested Reviews

- common uses of the dative (*Essentials* §§106–18)
- natural result clauses (*Essentials* §185)
- declension of εἷς μία ἕν (*Essentials* §71)
- forms of τίθημι θήσω ἔθηκα/(θε-) τέθηκα τέθειμαι ἐτέθην (set, put, place, arrange) (*Essentials* §§60–63)
- principal parts of λαμβάνω and μανθάνω

  λαμβάνω λήψομαι ἔλαβον εἴληφα εἴλημμαι ἐλήφθην = take, capture, grasp, understand; + δικήν παρά + *gen.* = punish *gen.*
  μανθάνω μαθήσομαι ἔμαθον μεμάθηκα = learn

---

24. Although it is criticized for overstating the case on certain points, K. J. Dover's *Greek Homosexuality* (1978) is still the standard work in the field. For some of the controversies, the writings of James Davidson, David Halperin, and Thomas Hubbard are thought-provoking (see bibliography).

Reading 4A

Pausanias distinguishes between two Erotes, a heavenly (*ouranios*) Eros and a promiscuous (*pandemos*) Eros, sons of two different Aphrodites.

Vocabulary

ἄδηλος -ον: unclear, uncertain

ἀδικία -ας ἡ: injustice, wrongdoing (cf. ἀδικέω)

ἀναγκάζω ἀναγκάσω ἠνάγκασα ἠνάγκακα ἠνάγκασμαι ἠναγκάσθην: force, compel

ἀναγκαῖος -α -ον: necessary (cf. ἀνάγκη ἡ and ἀναγκάζω); *especially common in impersonal use*: ἀναγκαῖον + *acc.* + *inf.*: it is necessary for *acc.* to ——

ἁπλοῦς -οῦν: simple (cf. ἁπλῶς: simply); *two-termination adj., endings contract from* -έος -έον (see Smyth 1956: §290 for full declension)

ἄρρην -εν: male (in some dialects: ἄρσην -εν)

βλέπω βλέψομαι ἔβλεψα βέβλεφα βέβλεμμαι ἐβλέφθην: look (at), see; *also common in compounds, especially* ἀποβλέπω: look off at, gaze fixedly at, look away from everything else at (not "look away" as we might expect)

διαπράττομαι διαπράξομαι διεπραξάμην — διαπέπραγμαι: bring about, accomplish, do (thoroughly)

εἷς μία ἕν: one; *should be distinguished from the prepositions* εἰς *and* ἐν, *which it resembles; if necessary, review the full declension, which is the same as* οὐδείς οὐδεμία οὐδέν

ἐντεῦθεν *adv.*: hence, from this point, from here

ἐξαπατάω ἐξαπατήσω ἐξηπάτησα ἐξηπάτηκα ἐξηπάτημαι ἐξηπατήθην: deceive (less common without the prefix: ἀπατάω)

θεά -ᾶς ἡ: goddess

θῆλυς -εια -υ: female

καταγελάω + *gen.*: laugh at, jeer or mock at, ridicule (see γελάω for principal parts)

κόσμιος -α -ον: well-ordered, regular, moderate (cf. *κόσμος ὁ: order, ornament)

μετέχω + *gen.*: partake of, share in, take part in (see ἔχω for principal parts)

οἴχομαι οἰχήσομαι: be gone, be off; *usually accompanied by a participle meaning or implying* "go away": οἴχομαι φεύγων: I am off and fleeing; ᾤχετο ἀπιών: [he] was off and gone; οἰχήσονται ἀποτρέχοντες: they will run away and be gone, etc.

ὄνειδος -ους τό: reproach, blame, disgrace

ὁρμάω ὁρμήσω ὥρμησα ὥρμηκα ὥρμημαι ὡρμήθην *trans.*: set in motion, stir up, rouse; *intrans. mid.-pass.*: hurry, rush, set off, begin

οὐράνιος -α -ον: having to do with Ouranos, heavenly

πάνδημος -ον: of or belonging to all the people, common, ordinary, vulgar

τέλος -ους τό: final outcome, end, result; *without def. art. as adv.*: finally

χαρίζομαι χαριοῦμαι ἐχαρισάμην—κεχάρισμαι + *dat.*: gratify, give pleasure to, do a favor for (cf. χάρις)

Reading 4A (based on *Symposium* 180c1–182a6)

Φαῖδρος μὲν τοιοῦτόν τινα λόγον εἶπε, μετὰ δὲ Φαῖδρον ἄλλοι   1
τινες ἦσαν ὧν οὐ πάνυ διαμνημονεύω· οὓς παρεὶς τὸν Παυσανίου λόγον   2
διηγήσομαι.   3

"Οὐ καλῶς μοι δοκεῖ, ὦ Φαῖδρε," ἦ δ' ὅς, "προβεβλῆσθαι ἡμῖν ὁ λόγος,   4
τὸ παρηγγέλθαι ἁπλῶς οὕτως ἐγκωμιάζειν Ἔρωτα. εἰ μὲν γὰρ εἷς ἦν ὁ   5
Ἔρως, καλῶς ἂν εἶχε, νῦν δὲ οὐκ ἔστιν εἷς· πάντες γὰρ ἴσμεν ὅτι οὐκ   6
ἔστιν ἄνευ Ἔρωτος Ἀφροδίτη. μιᾶς μὲν οὖν οὔσης εἷς ἂν ἦν Ἔρως· ἐπεὶ   7
δὲ δὴ δύο ἐστόν, ἀνάγκη καὶ δύο Ἔρωτε εἶναι. πῶς δ' οὐ δύο τὼ θεά;   8

---

2   (δια)μνημονεύω = μνημονεύω (= μέμνημαι): in general, μνη- signifies remembrance, reminding, or remembering. Mnemosyne is the goddess Memory. The prefix δια- suggests "thoroughly," as often.

οὕς = τούτους: a relative pronoun may begin a sentence in place of a demonstrative

παρείς: from παρίημι = pass over, skip over

4   προβάλλω = put forward, propose

ἡμῖν: dat. of agent with a perf. pass. (*Essentials* §114)

5   *παραγγέλλω = urge; τὸ παρηγγέλθαι ... Ἔρωτα: artic. inf. (*Essentials* §182) in apposition (*Essentials* §120) to ὁ λόγος. What is the tense of the infinitive παρηγγέλθαι?

ἁπλῶς: with ἐγκωμιάζειν

οὕτως: modifies ἁπλῶς; οὕτως + *adj. or adv. usually* = so

6–7   οὐκ ἔστιν ἄνευ Ἔρωτος Ἀφροδίτη: presumably Pausanias means that Eros is Aphrodite's constant companion (as well as her son). Or perhaps the names here reflect the concepts associated with each: i.e., there is no Sex (Aphrodite) without Desire (Eros).

7   μιᾶς ... οὔσης: gen. abs. serving as a protasis (if-clause) of this conditional sentence. What kind of condition must it be (*Essentials* §162)?

8   ἐστόν: 3rd pers. dual pres. indic. of εἰμί (*Essentials* §69)

ἀνάγκη = ἀνάγκη ἐστί

Ἔρωτε: acc. dual of Ἔρως (*Essentials* §67)

τὼ θεά: nom. dual of ἡ θεά. Rose 1985: 18 suggests that the two Erotes "are probably a take-off on Hesiod's two forms of Ἔρις 'Strife' (*Works and Days* 11–26)." The two Aphrodites arise from the inconsistent genealogies of Aphrodite offered by the two great traditional poets, Homer and Hesiod (see introduction).

ἢ μέν γέ που πρεσβυτέρα καὶ ἀμήτωρ Οὐρανοῦ θυγάτηρ, ἣν δὴ καὶ   9

Οὐρανίαν ἐπονομάζομεν· ἡ δὲ νεωτέρα Διὸς καὶ Διώνης, ἣν δὴ Πάνδημον   10

καλοῦμεν. ἀναγκαῖον δὴ καὶ Ἔρωτα τὸν μὲν τῇ ἑτέρᾳ συνεργὸν Πάνδημον   11

ὀρθῶς καλεῖσθαι, τὸν δὲ Οὐράνιον.   12

    Ὁ μὲν οὖν τῆς Πανδήμου Ἀφροδίτης ὡς ἀληθῶς πάνδημός ἐστι   13

καὶ ἐξεργάζεται ὅ τι ἂν τύχῃ· καὶ οὗτός ἐστιν ὃν οἱ φαῦλοι τῶν ἀνθρώπων   14

ἐρῶσιν. ἐρῶσι δὲ οἱ τοιοῦτοι πρῶτον μὲν οὐχ ἧττον γυναικῶν ἢ παίδων,   15

ἔπειτα δ᾿ ἐρῶσι τῶν σωμάτων μᾶλλον ἢ τῶν ψυχῶν, ἔπειτα τῶν   16

ἀνοητοτάτων ὡς ἂν δύνωνται, πρὸς τὸ διαπράξασθαι μόνον βλέποντες,   17

ἀμελοῦντες δὲ τοῦ καλῶς ἢ μή· ὅθεν δὴ συμβαίνει αὐτοῖς πράττειν ὅ τι   18

ἂν τύχωσι, ὁμοίως μὲν ἀγαθόν, ὁμοίως δὲ τοὐναντίον. οὗτος γὰρ ὁ Ἔρως   19

ἐστιν ἀπὸ τῆς θεοῦ νεωτέρας τε οὔσης πολὺ ἢ τῆς ἑτέρας καὶ μετεχούσης   20

ἐν τῇ γενέσει καὶ θήλεος καὶ ἄρρενος.   21

    Ὁ δὲ τῆς Οὐρανίας πρῶτον μὲν οὐ μετεχούσης θήλεος ἀλλ᾿ ἄρρενος   22

---

9   ἀμήτωρ: without a μήτηρ (nom. sing. adj.), motherless. Pausanias is referring to the account of Aphrodite's birth in Hesiod's *Theogony*, according to which she rises out of the sea-foam, engendered by the severed genitals of the castrated Ouranos (*Theogony* 178–95).

9–10   ἣν δὴ καὶ Οὐρανίαν: καί is not conjunctive but emphatic here. The two accusatives are related to one another by the verb (*Essentials* §78). On the two names for Aphrodite, see introduction.

10   ἐπονομάζω = name after or for *acc.*

    Διὸς καὶ Διώνης: the *Iliad* (5.370–72, 374) makes Aphrodite the daughter of the goddess Dione and Zeus

11   τῇ ἑτέρᾳ: the feminine gender shows that Aphrodite is meant

    τὸν . . . συνεργόν: in apposition to Ἔρωτα (συνεργός -οῦ ὁ = associate, partner)

12   τὸν δὲ Οὐράνιον = τὸν δὲ [τῇ ἑτέρᾳ συνεργόν] Οὐράνιον [ὀρθῶς καλεῖσθαι] from the parallel implied by τὸν μέν in the previous line

13   ὡς ἀληθῶς = in very truth, truly

15   ὅν: cognate acc. with ἐρῶσιν = the love which/that the worthless love (*Essentials* §77) (ἐράω takes a gen. of the person loved). For good English idiom in this context, translate ἐρῶσιν = experience *or* undergo.

17   ἀνόητος -ον = mindless, foolish

    διαπράττομαι in this context apparently refers to sexual activity or satisfaction

18   τοῦ καλῶς [διαπράξασθαι]: artic. inf. (*Essentials* §182)

    *συμβαίνει = befalls, falls randomly to *dat. + inf.*

μόνον—καὶ ἔστιν οὗτος ὁ τῶν παίδων ἔρως—ἔπειτα πρεσβυτέρας, ὕβρεως   23

ἀμοίρου· ὅθεν δὴ ἐπὶ τὸ ἄρρεν τρέπονται οἱ ἐκ τούτου τοῦ ἔρωτος ἔπιπνοι,   24

τὸ φύσει ἐρρωμενέστερον καὶ νοῦν μᾶλλον ἔχον ἀγαπῶντες. καί τις ἂν   25

γνοίη καὶ ἐν αὐτῇ τῇ παιδεραστίᾳ τοὺς εἰλικρινῶς ὑπὸ τούτου τοῦ   26

ἔρωτος ὡρμημένους· οὐ γὰρ ἐρῶσι παίδων, ἀλλ' ἐπειδὰν ἤδη ἄρχωνται   27

νοῦν ἔχειν, τοῦτο δὲ πλησιάζει τῷ γενειάσκειν.   28

Παρεσκευασμένοι γάρ εἰσιν, ὡς οἶμαι, οἱ ἐντεῦθεν ἀρχόμενοι ἐρᾶν   29

ὡς τὸν βίον ἅπαντα συνεσόμενοι καὶ κοινῇ συμβιωσόμενοι, ἀλλ' οὐκ   30

ἐξαπατήσαντες, ἐν ἀφροσύνῃ παῖδα λαβόντες ὡς νέον, καταγελάσαντες   31

οἰχήσεσθαι ἐπ' ἄλλον ἀποτρέχοντες. οὗτοι δὲ οἱ πάνδημοι ἐρασταί εἰσιν   32

---

23   ἔπειτα: δέ balancing πρῶτον μέν of the previous line can be understood from context, as in
       earlier lines (e.g., lines 15–16)

24   ἄμοιρος -ον = without any part of *gen*. The young were thought to be more hotheaded and
       therefore more inclined to hubris.
       ἐπίπνους -ουν (contracted from -οος -οον) = breathed upon, inspired

25   ἐρρωμένος -η -ον = in good health, strong, vigorous

26   γνοίη: aor. opt. of γιγνώσκω = recognize (as often in aor.)
       παιδεραστία -ας ἡ = pederasty, love of παῖδες
       εἰλικρινῶς = purely

27   ἀλλ' (here) = except

28   τοῦτο = τὸ νοῦν ἔχειν
       πλησιάζω = be near *dat*.
       γενειάσκω = grow a beard

29   ἐντεῦθεν: i.e., from the time when they are first getting a beard
       παρεσκευασμένοι . . . εἰσιν = are prepared (a compound form of the perf. indic. here best
       translated as a pres.); introducing inf. ἐρᾶν and οἰχήσεσθαι (line 32)

30   *κοινῇ = in common, in union (dat. fem. sing. used adverbially, as often)
       συμβιόω = live with
       ἀλλ' οὐκ: i.e., rather than (introducing the behavior the good kind of lover is not prepared to
       indulge in, but that is apparently the practice of οἱ πάνδημοι ἐρασταί)

31   ἀφροσύνη -ης ἡ = folly, thoughtlessness
       ὡς νέον = because of (being) young

32   οἰχήσεσθαι: depending on παρεσκευασμένοι . . . εἰσιν

οἱ καὶ τὸ ὄνειδος πεποιηκότες, ὥστε τινὰς τολμᾶν λέγειν ὡς αἰσχρὸν   33

χαρίζεσθαι ἐρασταῖς· λέγουσι δὲ εἰς τούτους ἀποβλέποντες, ὁρῶντες αὐτῶν   34

τὴν ἀκαιρίαν καὶ ἀδικίαν, ἐπεὶ οὐ δήπου κοσμίως γε καὶ νομίμως ὁτιοῦν   35

πρᾶγμα πραττόμενον ψόγον ἂν δικαίως φέροι.   36

---

35   ἀκαιρίαν -ας ἡ = poor timing, unseasonableness (cf. *καιρός -οῦ ὁ)
       *νομίμως = in accordance with νόμος, in a lawful way
       *ὁτιοῦν: neut. sing. adj. with πρᾶγμα = any . . . at all
36   *ψόγος -ου ὁ = reproach, blame, censure

Reading 4B

Pausanias goes on to describe contrasting sexual mores in Greek backwaters (Elis and Boeotia) and in places ruled by tyrants.

Vocabulary

- Make an effort to learn the principal parts of ὄμνυμι.

ἄλλοθι *adv.*: elsewhere (cf. αὐτόθι)

ἄνθος -ους τό: blossom, flower, bloom (an anthology is a collection of word "blossoms")

βέβαιος -ον (also -ος -α -ον): secure, firm, steadfast, sure

γενναῖος -α -ον: wellborn, noble

δουλεύω δουλεύσω ἐδούλευσα δεδούλευκα δεδούλευμαι ἐδουλεύθην: be a slave, perform the duties of a slave (cf. δοῦλος -ου ὁ)

δύναμις -εως ἡ: power, might, strength, capacity (cf. δύναμαι, δυνατός, ἀδύνατος)

ἐνθυμέομαι ἐνθυμήσομαι — — ἐντεθύμημαι ἐνεθυμήθην: have in mind, consider well, be concerned at (cf. *θυμός -οῦ ὁ: heart, spirit, emotion)

ἐπαινέω (or αἰνέω) ἐπαινέσω/ἐπαινέσομαι ἐπήνεσα ἐπήνεκα ἐπήνημαι ἐπηνέθην: praise, approve, applaud, commend; + *double acc.*: praise *acc. pers.* for *neut. acc. thing*

ἐπιχειρέω + *dat.*: put one's hand to or on, attack; + *inf.*: attempt, try

ἰσχυρός -ά -όν: strong (cf. *ἰσχύς -υος ὁ: strength)

καρπόομαι: reap, gather fruit (cf. *καρπός -οῦ ὁ: fruit, harvest)

λήγω λήξω ἔληξα: stop, cease, abate; + *gen.*: cease from *gen.*; + *supplemental part.*: stop ——ing, cease ——ing

μόνιμος -α -ον: staying in one place, stable, steadfast

νοέω νοήσω ἐνόησα νενόηκα νενόημαι ἐνοήθην: think, intend, perceive, understand; *recognize also* κατανοέω *and* ἐννοέω (cf. διανοέομαι *and* νοῦς)

ὄμνυμι ὀμοῦμαι ὤμοσα ὀμώμοκα ὀμώμο(σ)μαι ὠμό(σ)θην: swear

ὀνειδίζω ὀνειδιῶ ὠνείδισα ὠνείδικα—ὠνειδίσθην: reproach; reproach for *gen.* (cf. ὄνειδος)

ὅρκος -ου ὁ: oath

ὁστισοῦν ἡτισοῦν ὁτιοῦν: anybody/anything whatsoever, anybody/anything at all (declines like ὅστις + οὖν)

Fig. 15. The Tyrannicides Harmodius and Aristogeiton. Roman copy of Greek original. Museo Archeologico Nazionale, Naples, Italy. Photo credit: Alinari/Art Resource, New York. The original statues once stood in the Athenian agora, a symbol of the end of tyranny at Athens. They were stolen by the Persian army under Xerxes, but were replaced. Harmodius and Aristogeiton were lovers, popularly credited with putting an end to tyranny by killing Hipparchus, the brother of Hippias, the reigning member of the Peisitratid clan. Thucydides disputes the popular account (6.53–59), arguing that the entire affair originated in the wounding of a lover. Thucydides uses the story as an example of popular suspicion in his account of the recall of Alcibiades during the Sicilian Expedition (see introduction, "Historical Context of the Diologue").

οὗ *rel. adv.*: where (as well as gen. sing. masc. or neut. rel. pron.)

παιδαγωγός -οῦ ὁ: pedagogus, a person, usually a slave, in charge of accompanying children to and from school and elsewhere (cf. παίδ- and ἄγω)

παν- *as a prefix*: completely, all-, very (e.g., πάγκαλος: entirely καλός; πάμπολλοι: very many)

πολλαχοῦ *adv.*: in many places (cf. *παντάχου *adv.*: everywhere)

πονηρός -ά -όν: bad, wretched, wicked, toilsome

πρᾶξις -εως ἡ: deed, transaction, business

συμφέρω/συμφέρομαι: agree with, be agreeable to; hence, be beneficial to; *often used impers.* + *dat.* + *inf.*: it is beneficial, advantageous to *dat.* to ——

τύραννος -ου ὁ: tyrant, ruler who comes to power by unconstitutional means, ruler unrestrained by law; *recognize also* τυραννίς -ίδος ἡ: tyranny

φανερός -ά -όν: visible, manifest, evident (cf. φαίνω)

φιλέω + *inf.*: be inclined to, tend to, be accustomed to

ὧδε *adv.*: in this way, as follows, so, thus (ὧδε is to οὕτως as ὅδε is to οὗτος)

Reading 4B (based on *Symposium* 182a7–185c3)

Ὁ περὶ τὸν ἔρωτα νόμος ἐν μὲν ταῖς ἄλλαις πόλεσι νοῆσαι   1

ῥᾴδιος, ἁπλῶς γὰρ ὥρισται· ὁ δ᾽ ἐνθάδε καὶ ἐν Λακεδαίμονι ποικίλος.   2

ἐν Ἤλιδι μὲν γὰρ καὶ ἐν Βοιωτοῖς, καὶ οὗ μὴ σοφοὶ λέγειν, ἁπλῶς   3

νενομοθέτηται καλὸν τὸ χαρίζεσθαι ἐρασταῖς, καὶ οὐκ ἄν τις εἴποι οὔτε   4

νέος οὔτε παλαιὸς ὡς αἰσχρόν, ἵνα οἶμαι μὴ πράγματ᾽ ἔχωσιν λόγῳ   5

πειρώμενοι πείθειν τοὺς νέους, ἅτε ὄντες ἀδύνατοι λέγειν·   6

τῆς δὲ Ἰωνίας καὶ ἄλλοθι πολλαχοῦ αἰσχρὸν νενόμισται, ὅσοι ὑπὸ   7

βαρβάροις οἰκοῦσιν. τοῖς γὰρ βαρβάροις διὰ τὰς τυραννίδας αἰσχρὸν   8

---

2   ὁρίζω = define; *literally* = mark with a boundary

       ἐνθάδε: i.e., in Athens

       *ποικίλος -η -ον = complex, complexly wrought, ornate

3   Ἤλις -ιδος ἡ = Elis, a Greek city-state in the northwestern Peloponnesus. The Eleans are probably most important as the overseers of the ancient Olympics. Here they are lumped with the Boeotians as lacking eloquence.

       Βοιωτοί -ῶν οἱ = Boeotians, inhabitants of Boeotia, a large district in central Greece, bordering on Attica. An agricultural people, mocked by the Athenians as slow and backward—bovine perhaps, as the name suggests? Boeotia is also the native region of two important poets, Hesiod and Pindar.

       οὗ μή: use of μή rather than οὐ gives a conditional force to the indefinite relative clause (one with an indef. antecedent) = wherever [they are] not (Smyth 1956: §§2505–6). Remember οὗ = where.

       λέγειν: what use of the infinitive do you have here (*Essentials* §181)?

4   νενομοθέτηται (from νομοθετέω) = it has been made a law that . . .

5   οἶμαι = ὡς οἶμαι (as often)

       πράγματ᾽ ἔχω = have trouble

7   τῆς Ἰωνίας = in Ionia (gen. of place within which, relatively rare in prose) (Smyth 1956: §1448); from Ἰωνία -ας ἡ = Ionia, the large region of easternmost Greece, on the coast of Asia Minor (now Turkey). Because of their contact with Persia, Lydia, and other eastern non-Greek peoples, the Ionians are often considered soft and effete, but more civilized and articulate than the more militaristic Spartans or the more agricultural Boeotians.

       ἄλλοθι πολλαχοῦ = in many other places (the phrase anticipates the rel. clause introduced after the verb by ὅσοι)

       αἰσχρόν: pred. adj.; the subject must be the neuter articular infinitive of the previous paragraph: τὸ χαρίζεσθαι ἐρασταῖς

7–8   ὑπό + *dat.*: under [the control of] *dat.* At the time of composition (but not at the time of the dramatic date), Ionia was under Persian rule, one of several anachronisms in the dialogue.

τοῦτό γε καὶ ἥ γε φιλοσοφία καὶ ἡ φιλογυμναστία· οὐ γὰρ οἶμαι ὅτι   9

συμφέρει τοῖς ἄρχουσι φρονήματα μεγάλα ἐγγίγνεσθαι τῶν ἀρχομένων,   10

οὐδὲ φιλίας ἰσχυρὰς καὶ κοινωνίας, ὃ δὴ μάλιστα φιλεῖ τά τε ἄλλα πάντα   11

καὶ ὁ ἔρως ἐμποιεῖν. ἔργῳ δὲ τοῦτο ἔμαθον καὶ οἱ ἐνθάδε τύραννοι·   12

ὁ γὰρ Ἀριστογείτονος ἔρως καὶ ἡ Ἁρμοδίου φιλία βέβαιος γενομένη   13

κατέλυσεν αὐτῶν τὴν ἀρχήν.   14

Οὕτως οὗ μὲν αἰσχρὸν ἐτέθη χαρίζεσθαι ἐρασταῖς, κακίᾳ τῶν   15

θεμένων κεῖται, τῶν μὲν ἀρχόντων πλεονεξίᾳ, τῶν δ' ἀρχομένων ἀνανδρίᾳ·   16

---

9   τοῦτό γε: i.e., τὸ χαρίζεσθαι ἐρασταῖς

     φιλογυμναστία -ας ἡ = love of gymnastic exercise

10   συμφέρει used impers. + dat. = it is beneficial, advantageous to dat.

     φρονήματα μεγάλα ἐγγίγνεσθαι + gen. = that great (i.e., bold, ambitious) thoughts arise
     in gen.

11   κοινωνία -ας ἡ = fellowship, camaraderie

     ὅ: the singular treats the antecedents—φρονήματα μεγάλα, φιλίας, and κοινωνίας—as a
     single unit

     φιλεῖ + inf. = be inclined to, tend to. The singular verb with plural subject here is probably caused
     by the proximity to the neuter plural ἄλλα πάντα.

     τὰ ἄλλα πάντα: apparently refers back to ἡ φιλοσοφία καὶ ἡ φιλογυμναστία

12   ἔργῳ = by experience

13   Ἀριστογείτων -ονος ὁ = Aristogeiton, one of the Athenian tyrannicides, erastes of Harmodius

     Ἁρμόδιος -ου ὁ = Harmodius, one of the Athenian tyrannicides, eromenos of Aristogeiton.
     Harmodius and Aristogeiton were two male lovers, who were popularly credited with putting
     an end to tyranny at Athens. A famous statue of the Tyrannicides stood in the Athenian agora
     (fig. 15).

     ἡ Ἁρμοδίου φιλία: in using φιλία rather than ἔρως of the love experienced by the eromenos,
     Pausanias accepts the unreciprocal concept of love characteristic of Greek thinking about
     homoerotic relationships. The erastes experiences eros (erotic love), the eromenos experiences
     a generally unerotic form of love, friendship or affection (see introduction: "The Greek Vocab-
     ulary of Love").

14   καταλύω: dissolve, make an end of, destroy

15   ἐτέθη from τίθημι: review forms if necessary; κεῖμαι and passive forms of τίθημι are used
     virtually interchangeably to mean "be established"

     χαρίζεσθαι: inf. serving as the subje. of the rel. clause (Essentials §182); takes dat. obj.

15–16 κακίᾳ, πλεονεξίᾳ, and ἀνανδρίᾳ: dat. of cause = due to dat., because of dat. (Smyth 1956:
     §1517

     θεμένων from τίθημι: review forms if necessary (Essentials §62)

16   *πλεονεξία -ας ἡ = greed, lust for more (power, money, etc.)

οὗ δὲ καλὸν ἁπλῶς ἐνομίσθη, διὰ τὴν τῶν θεμένων τῆς ψυχῆς ἀργίαν.   17

Things that seem to favor the lover (*erastes*)

Ἐνθάδε δὲ πολὺ τούτων κάλλιον μὲν νενομοθέτηται, οὐ δὲ ῥᾴδιον   18

κατανοῆσαι. ἐνθυμήθητε γὰρ ὅτι λέγεται κάλλιον τὸ φανερῶς ἐρᾶν   19

τοῦ λάθρα, καὶ μάλιστα τῶν γενναιοτάτων καὶ ἀρίστων, κἂν αἰσχίους ὦσι.   20

ἡ αὖ παρακέλευσις τῷ ἐρῶντι παρὰ πάντων θαυμαστή, οὐχ ὥς τι αἰσχρὸν   21

ποιοῦντι. καὶ δὴ καὶ πρὸς τὸ ἐπιχειρεῖν ἑλεῖν ὁ νόμος δέδωκεν τῷ ἐραστῇ   22

ἐξουσίαν θαυμαστὰ ἔργα ἐργαζομένῳ ἐπαινεῖσθαι, ἃ εἴ τις τολμῴη ποιεῖν   23

διώκων ὁτιοῦν πλὴν τοῦτο, καρποῖτ᾽ ἂν τὰ μέγιστα ὀνείδη. εἰ γὰρ ἢ   24

χρήματα βουλόμενος παρά του λαβεῖν ἢ τινα ἄλλην δύναμιν ἐθέλοι ποιεῖν   25

οἷάπερ οἱ ἐρασταὶ πρὸς τὰ παιδικά, ἱκετείας τε καὶ ἀντιβολήσεις ποιούμενοι,   26

---

17   ἀργία -ας ἡ = laziness (ἀ-εργος)

18   τούτων: gen. of comparison; refers to the places, people, or laws just discussed, or to all three
        νενομοθέτηται = the law has been made

19   κατανοέω = understand
        ἐνθυμήθητε: aor. impera. of ἐνθυμέομαι = consider (pass. deponent)

20   τοῦ λάθρα = τοῦ λάθρα ἐρᾶν. What use of the genitive is this (*Essentials* §94)?
        *λάθρα = secretly, covertly
        τῶν γενναιοτάτων καὶ ἀρίστων: objects of ἐρᾶν in previous line
        αἰσχίους: here refers to physical appearance = rather ugly. What form is this (*Essentials* §24)?

21   παρακέλευσις -εως ἡ = encouragement, exhortation, cheering on
        ὥς = like, as though

22   ἑλεῖν: in an erotic context, αἱρέω normally means something like "seduce, win over, take in
            conquest"

23   *ἐξουσία -ας ἡ = means, resources, opportunity
        ἐπαινεῖσθαι: explanatory inf. with *ἐξουσία = the opportunity to be praised . . .

25   του = τινος (as often)

26   οἱ ἐρασταὶ πρὸς τὰ παιδικά: the missing verb can be inferred from context
        ἱκετεία -ας ἡ = supplication (cf. *ὁ ἱκέτης and *ἱκετεύω)
        ἀντιβόλησις -εως ἡ = entreaty, prayer

καὶ ὅρκους ὀμνύντες, καὶ κοιμήσεις ἐπὶ θύραις, καὶ ἐθέλοντες δουλείας   27

δουλεύειν οἵας οὐδ' ἂν δοῦλος οὐδείς, ἐμποδίζοιτο ἂν μὴ πράττειν οὕτω   28

τὴν πρᾶξιν καὶ ὑπὸ φίλων καὶ ὑπὸ ἐχθρῶν, τῶν μὲν ὀνειδιζόντων κολακείας   29

καὶ ἀνελευθερίας, τῶν δὲ νουθετούντων καὶ αἰσχυνομένων ὑπὲρ αὐτοῦ.   30

τῷ δ' ἐρῶντι πάντα ταῦτα ποιοῦντι χάρις ἔπεστι, καὶ δέδοται ὑπὸ τοῦ   31

νόμου ἄνευ ὀνείδους πράττειν, ὡς πάγκαλόν τι πρᾶγμα διαπραττομένῳ.   32

ταύτῃ μὲν οὖν οἰηθείη ἄν τις πάγκαλον νομίζεσθαι ἐν τῇδε τῇ πόλει καὶ   33

τὸ ἐρᾶν καὶ τὸ φίλους γίγνεσθαι τοῖς ἐρασταῖς.   34

Things that seem to discourage the lover (erastes)

Ἐπειδὰν δὲ παιδαγωγοὺς ἐπιστήσαντες οἱ πατέρες τοῖς ἐρωμένοις   35

μὴ ἐῶσι διαλέγεσθαι τοῖς ἐρασταῖς, καὶ τῷ παιδαγωγῷ ταῦτα   36

προστεταγμένα ᾖ, ἡλικιῶται δὲ καὶ ἑταῖροι ὀνειδίζωσιν ἐάν τι ὁρῶσιν   37

---

27   κοίμησις -εως ἡ = sleeping

27–28   δουλείας: cognate acc. with δουλεύω = perform slavish tasks (cf. δοῦλος)

28   οὐδέ = not even (as often)

          ἄν implies here a missing optative δουλεύοι (or similar)

          ἐμποδίζω μή + inf. = hinder from, prevent from

29–30   τῶν μέν . . . τῶν δέ: for def. art. + μέν . . . δέ see *Essentials* §190. Τῶν μέν refers to ἐχθρῶν, τῶν
          δέ refers to φιλῶν, creating a chiastic structure (forms a χ):

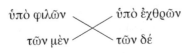

29   *κολακεία -ας ἡ = flattery

30   *νουθετέω = chastise

31   ἔπειμι = is upon, belongs to

33   *ταύτῃ = in this way (dat. fem. sing. used adverbially, as often)

          οἰηθείη from οἶμαι (pass. deponent)

35   ἐπιστήσαντες from *ἐφίστημι: trans. = put acc. in charge of dat.

37   προστεταγμένα ᾖ: perf. pass. subju. of *προστάττω = order, command

          ἡλικιώτης -ου ὁ = person of the same age as one, peer, age-mate (cf. *ἡλικία -ας ἡ)

τοιοῦτον γιγνόμενον, καὶ τοὺς ὀνειδίζοντας αὖ οἱ πρεσβύτεροι μὴ   38

διακωλύωσιν, εἰς δὲ ταῦτά τις αὖ βλέψας ἡγήσαιτ᾽ ἂν πάλιν αἴσχιστον   39

τὸ τοιοῦτον ἐνθάδε νομίζεσθαι.   40

Summing up: two kinds of lover

Τὸ δὲ οἶμαι ὧδ᾽ ἔχει· οὐχ ἁπλοῦν ἐστιν, ὅπερ ἐξ ἀρχῆς ἐλέχθη οὔτε   41

καλὸν εἶναι αὐτὸ καθ᾽ αὑτὸ οὔτε αἰσχρόν, ἀλλὰ καλῶς μὲν πραττόμενον   42

καλόν, αἰσχρῶς δὲ αἰσχρόν. αἰσχρῶς μὲν οὖν ἐστι πονηρῷ τε καὶ πονηρῶς   43

χαρίζεσθαι, καλῶς δὲ χρηστῷ τε καὶ καλῶς. πονηρὸς δ᾽ ἐστὶν ἐκεῖνος ὁ   44

ἐραστὴς ὁ πάνδημος, ὁ τοῦ σώματος μᾶλλον ἢ τῆς ψυχῆς ἐρῶν· καὶ γὰρ   45

οὐδὲ μόνιμός ἐστιν, ἅτε οὐδὲ μονίμου ἐρῶν πράγματος. ἅμα γὰρ τῷ τοῦ   46

σώματος ἄνθει λήγοντι, οὗπερ ἤρα, "οἴχεται ἀποπτάμενος," πολλοὺς   47

λόγους καὶ ὑποσχέσεις καταισχύνας· ὁ δὲ τοῦ ἤθους χρηστοῦ ὄντος   48

ἐραστὴς διὰ βίου μένει, ἅτε μονίμῳ συντακείς.   49

---

41   τὸ δέ = but the [actual] situation . . . [as opposed to what someone might think]. Pausanias now
    imposes an interpretation on the complex and contradictory details of Athenian attitudes.

42   καθ᾽ αὑτό = in and of itself, per se; in Attic, αὑτό (with rough breathing) is a contraction of
    ἑαυτό

43–44   αἰσχρῶς μὲν . . . καλῶς δέ: the previous sentence makes clear that πραττόμενον should be
    understood with each adverb

47   ἤρα: imperf. of ἐράω; review alpha-contract verbs if necessary (*Essentials* §77)
    οἴχεται ἀποπτάμενος = is off flying away . . . , a reference to the deceptive dream in *Iliad* 2.71

48   ὑπόσχεσις -εως ἡ = promise
    καταισχύνας: aor. act. part. masc. nom. sing. of καταισχύνω = shame, disgrace
    τοῦ ἤθους: gen. of description (*Essentials* §90), from ἦθος -ους τό = character

49   συντακείς: aor. pass. part. from συντήκω = melt together with, meld with, fuse with

Reading 5. Scientific and Medical Conceptions of Love: The Speech of the Doctor Eryximachus

The comic poet Aristophanes is next to Pausanias, but he is unable to speak due to a disabling attack of hiccups, so the doctor Eryximachus speaks in his place. The comic interlude allows Plato to poke fun at Aristophanes, perhaps suggesting that he has eaten or drunk too much, and it gives Eryximachus a chance to show off his medical knowledge, though perhaps not in the most dignified forum. In addition, because the attack of hiccups actually results in a change in the order of the speakers in a work in which considerable attention seems to have been given to that order, it may have a larger significance. Are we invited to consider two possible arrangements, one of the speeches and another of the speakers (see appendixes 3–4)? Is the injection of disorder perhaps a Dionysiac one, an acknowledgement of the presence of the god Dionysus and the importance of finding a place for disorder? Scholars have not agreed on the significance of this episode, nor even that it is anything more than playful, but it is certainly a moment that engages interest.

We have already met the doctor Eryximachus as the probable ἐραστής of Phaedrus and as the spokesman for sobriety. His father Acumenus was also a doctor, which may explain his son's rather surprising name; Eryximachus appears to mean something like "Belch-battler" or "Barf-battler,"[25] though the meaning of the "Eryxi-" prefix may in fact stretch to cover other kinds of discharges such as hiccups, offering clear motivation for the hiccups incident (though not necessarily for the rearrangement of speakers).

Eryximachus's speech offers the scientific and medical perspective on ἔρως. Elsewhere in his dialogues, Plato treats doctors as knowledgeable figures who know the best way to bring health to the body, as opposed to cooks, who know how to please the body without necessarily making it healthier. Consequently, despite the mocking banter of Aristophanes and the comedy of the hiccups incident that frames Eryximachus's speech, it is hard to dismiss his speech as worthless.[26] It must, like all the speeches, make a meaningful and useful contribution to the whole, and it is in fact the centerpiece of the opening group of speeches (see appendix 4). Perhaps one of the most important aspects of Eryximachus's speech is that it clearly presents love as a force with much broader significance and application than the previous two speeches, with their exclusive

---

25. It is possible that it was intended to have a more military sound to it, since the verb ἐρεύγομαι to which the noun ἔρευξις is related also refers to the roaring sound of battle. But, if so, Plato must be playing with the possible medical interpretations.
26. See arguments in Edelstein 1945 and Konstan and Young-Bruehl 1982.

Fig. 16.   Relief showing Asclepius, the hero-doctor, healing a patient accompanied by the goddess Hygeia. Archaeological Museum, Piraeus, Greece. Photo credit: Foto Marburg/Art Resource, New York.

focus on human forms of love, had suggested. In Eryximachus's speech, love is an overarching cosmic principle, not a narrow human concern, and this is an important contribution in a dialogue that seeks a full definition of ἔρως.

The language of the speech is similar to that of the medical writings attributed to the fifth-century doctor and medical writer Hippocrates.[27] It also resembles in language and content the fragments of the presocratic philosophers who wrote about the natural world. Interest in order (κόσμος), balance, and harmony (ἁρμονία) in the interactions of opposites (e.g., cold and hot, wet and dry) are highly characteristic of these texts. A striking oversight for a doctor talking about ἔρως is Eryximachus's failure to consider the opposition of male and female, an opposition that occurs in some early scientific writing; this oversight may be caused, as Rosen 1987: 101–7 suggests, by Eryximachus's personal commitment to pederasty and will be corrected in the next speech by Aristophanes. Eryximachus's speech shows awareness of a common presocratic technique of choosing one basic αἴτιον (cause) or ἀρχή (fundamental originating principle) to explain all things, but ingeniously here it is ἔρως. Also highly typical of Greek scientific and medical writing is the way the principle of analogy is used. Thus, Eryximachus uses analogies between human sexual behavior and the behavior of elements in the body to make points. For example, he takes Pausanias's argument that it is good to gratify good lovers and bad to gratify

27. Craik 2001 is a very useful starting place for students who want to examine the connection between medical texts and the *Symposium*.

bad lovers and applies it to the human body: in the same way, it is good to gratify the good (i.e., healthy) components of the body and bad to gratify the bad (i.e., sick) elements. In general, the good Eros promotes harmony and balance among the opposites that leads to good health; the bad encourages excesses that lead to disharmony and bad health. In reading 5B, Eryximachus applies principles that operate in the body to analyses of music and weather, again by analogy. Although this is an extremely important form of ancient reasoning, both scholars and students often find Eryximachus's arguments forbiddingly esoteric, and indeed, scholarly interpretation of Eryximachus's meaning does diverge in important details, suggesting that the precise meaning is hard to grasp. It is possible to shorten the readings or to skip the second reading without creating difficulties, though it will mean more words to look up in the glossary in subsequent readings.

Suggested Reviews

- uses of ὡς (*Essentials* §§192–99)
- verbal adjectives in -τέος/-τός (*Essentials* §§125–28)
- principal parts of λείπω, πίπτω, and φέρω

  λείπω λείψω ἔλιπον λέλοιπα λέλειμμαι ἐλείφθην = leave, abandon, leave out, omit
  πίπτω πεσοῦμαι ἔπεσον πέπτωκα = fall
  φέρω οἴσω ἤνεγκον/ἤνεγκα ἐνήνοχα ἐνήνεγμαι ἠνέχθην = bear, bring, lead, carry, wear; φέρε = come!

Reading 5A

Plato clearly enjoys playing with the names of his characters, and this reading begins with a play on Pausanias's name—Παυσανίου δὲ παυσαμένου ("when Pausanias paused" is my favorite English rendering)—and an unusual editorial comment that calls attention to the similarity of both sound and shape in the two words.

From this section on, I no longer alter the indirect statement that serves as the main form of narration outside reported speeches in the *Symposium*. Many accusatives serve as subjects, and infinitives serve as main verbs in the transitional sections between speeches. This passage begins with an extended sentence in indirect statement that is introduced by the phrase ἔφη ὁ Ἀριστόδημος, but the reader will frequently see just the accusative and infinitive and will need to supply the missing phrase ἔφη ὁ Ἀριστόδημος to make sense of the grammar.

Vocabulary

ἀκόλαστος -ον: undisciplined, intemperate; *recognize also* ἀκολασία -ας ἡ: intemperance, licentiousness (cf. *κολάζω: discipline, punish)

ἀνθρώπινος -η -ον: human (cf. ἄνθρωπος ὁ)

ἀνόμοιος -ον: dissimilar (to); different (from), unlike (ἀν-ὅμοιος)

ἅπαξ *adv.*: once (cf. ἁπλοῦς)

γλυκύς -εῖα -ύ: sweet (cf. English "glucose")

δημιουργός -οῦ ὁ: skilled workman, craftsman, maker, creator (δῆμος + ἔργον)

διπλοῦς -οῦν: double, twofold; *two-termination adj., endings contract from* -έος -έον (see Smyth 1956: §290 for full declension)

δίς *adv.*: twice

ἐπιθυμέω ἐπιθυμήσω ἐπεθύμησα ἐπιτεθύμηκα: desire *gen.*

ἐπιστήμη -ης ἡ: knowledge, understanding; *pl.*: sciences (cf. English "epistemology" and ἐπίσταμαι)

ἐχθίων -ιον and ἔχθιστος -η -ον: irreg. compar. and superl. of ἐχθρός -ά -όν

ζῷον -ου τό: living creature, animal (cf. English "zoology" and "zoo" and ζάω)

θερμός -ή -όν: hot, warm (cf. English "thermal" and "thermometer")

ἰατρός -οῦ ὁ: doctor, healer; *recognize also* ἰατρικός -ή -όν: medical, having to do with doctors or healing; *especially* ἡ ἰατρική = ἡ ἰατρικὴ τέχνη: the art of medicine, medicine

κτάομαι κτήσομαι ἐκτησάμην — κέκτημαι ἐκτήθην: acquire, procure for oneself, get, gain; *perf. with pres. meaning:* possess (cf. *τὸ κτῆμα: possession)

λύγξ λυγγός ἡ: hiccup(s), bout of hiccups

μέρος -ους τό: part, share, turn

νοσέω: be sick, be ill, ail (cf. νόσος -ου ἡ); *recognize also* νοσώδης -ες: sick, diseased, unhealthy

ξηρός -ά -όν: dry (cf. English "xeroscaping" and "xeroderma")

ὁμόνοια -ας ἡ: sameness of thought or mind, concord, unity

πικρός -ά -όν: bitter

πρόγονος -ου ὁ: forefather, ancestor, predecessor

ῥίς ῥινός ἡ: nose (cf. English "rhinoceros" and "rhinoplasty")

τείνω τενῶ -έτεινα -τέτακα τέταμαι -ετάθην: stretch, extend

ὑγιής -ές: healthy, sound; *recognize also* ὑγιεινός -ή -όν: good for the health, wholesome, healthy (cf. English "hygiene")

ὑγρός -ά -όν: wet, moist, fluid

φύω φύσω ἔφυσα: bring forth, produce, put forth; *mid.-pass. root aor.* ἔφυν: grow, be born, be made, arise, be [by nature]; *perf.* πέφυκα: be [by nature], be inclined [by nature]

ψυχρός -ά -όν: cold

Reading 5A (based on *Symposium* 185c4–186e3)

Παυσανίου δὲ παυσαμένου (διδάσκουσι γάρ με ἴσα λέγειν οὑτωσὶ   1
οἱ σοφοί) ἔφη ὁ Ἀριστόδημος δεῖν μὲν Ἀριστοφάνη λέγειν, τυχεῖν δὲ   2
αὐτῷ τινα λύγγα ἐπιπεπτωκυῖαν ἢ ὑπὸ πλησμονῆς ἢ ὑπό τινος ἄλλου καὶ   3
οὐχ οἷόν τε εἶναι λέγειν, ἀλλ᾽ εἰπεῖν αὐτόν—ἐν τῇ κάτω γὰρ αὐτοῦ τὸν   4
ἰατρὸν Ἐρυξίμαχον κατακεῖσθαι—"Ὦ Ἐρυξίμαχε, δίκαιος εἶ ἢ παῦσαί με   5
τῆς λυγγὸς ἢ λέγειν ὑπὲρ ἐμοῦ, ἕως ἂν ἐγὼ παύσωμαι."   6

Τὸν δ᾽ Ἐρυξίμαχον εἰπεῖν· "Ἀλλὰ ποιήσω ἀμφότερα ταῦτα· ἐγὼ μὲν γὰρ   7
ἐρῶ ἐν τῷ σῷ μέρει, σὺ δ᾽ ἐπειδὰν παύσῃ, ἐν τῷ ἐμῷ. ἐν ᾧ δ᾽ ἂν ἐγὼ λέγω, 8
ἐὰν μέν σὺ ἀπνευστὶ ἔχῃς πολὺν χρόνον, παύεσθαι ἐθελήσει λύγξ·   9
εἰ δὲ μή, ὕδατι ἀνακογχυλίασον. εἰ δὲ πάνυ ἰσχυρά ἐστιν,   10

1–2   διδάσκουσι... οἱ σοφοί: this is a rare editorial comment, presumably from Apollodorus, on the
      phrase Παυσανίου ... παυσαμένου, a perhaps extreme example of the balanced clauses
      taught by the rhetoricians (οἱ σοφοί).

      ἴσα: the words Παυσανίου and παυσαμένου are equal in length (four syllables) and metrical
      quantity (long-short-short-long), as well as similar in sound

3   ἐπιπεπτωκυῖαν: supplementary part. with τυχεῖν from ἐπιπίπτω = fall upon, befall (takes
      dat. obj.)

      πλησμονή -ῆς ἡ = fullness, satiety (presumably referring to Aristophanes' having eaten a lot) (cf.
      πληρής and πληρόω)

4   λέγειν ... εἰπεῖν: this is an interesting example of how aspect (pres. versus aor.) can give slightly
      different meanings to what otherwise might seem to be the same word. Aristophanes wasn't
      able to make his speech (λέγειν), but he said (εἰπεῖν)....

      ἐν τῇ κάτω αὐτοῦ: feminine definite article in this context allows the reader to infer κλίνη =
      couch (that is, on the couch next to him, on his right)

5   δίκαιος + *inf.* = the right one to —— (*Essentials* §181)

6   παύσωμαι: identify and explain the mood (*Essentials* §152); identify and explain the voice
      (*Essentials* §137)

8   μέρος -ους τό (here) = turn

      παύσῃ: identify and explain the mood and voice (see note on line 6)

      ἐν ᾧ = while; *literally* = in which (time)

9   ἀπνευστὶ ἔχω = hold one's breath (ἀπνευστί *adv.* = breathlessly)

      χρόνον: identify and explain the case (*Essentials* §80)

10   ἀνακογχυλίασον: aor. act. impera. (2nd pers. sing.) of ἀνακογχυλιάζω = gargle. Review
      imperatives if necessary.

ἀναλαβών τι τοιοῦτον οἵῳ κινήσαις ἂν τὴν ῥῖνα, πτάρε· καὶ ἐὰν τοῦτο   11

ποιήσῃς ἅπαξ ἢ δίς, καὶ εἰ πάνυ ἰσχυρά ἐστι, παύσεται."   12

"Οὐκ ἂν φθάνοις λέγων," φάναι τὸν Ἀριστοφάνη· "ἐγὼ δὲ ταῦτα   13

ποιήσω."   14

Extending love's domain

Εἰπεῖν δὴ τὸν Ἐρυξίμαχον, "Δοκεῖ τοίνυν μοι ἀναγκαῖον εἶναι,   15

ἐπειδὴ Παυσανίας ὁρμήσας ἐπὶ τὸν λόγον καλῶς οὐχ ἱκανῶς ἀπετέλεσε,   16

πειρᾶσθαι τέλος ἐπιθεῖναι τῷ λόγῳ. τὸ μὲν γὰρ διπλοῦν εἶναι τὸν Ἔρωτα   17

δοκεῖ μοι καλῶς εἰπεῖν· ὅτι δὲ οὐ μόνον ἐστὶν ἐπὶ ταῖς ψυχαῖς τῶν   18

ἀνθρώπων πρὸς τοὺς καλοὺς ἀλλὰ καὶ πρὸς ἄλλα πολλὰ καὶ ἐν τοῖς   19

ἄλλοις, τοῖς τε σώμασι τῶν πάντων ζῴων καὶ τοῖς ἐν τῇ γῇ φυομένοις   20

καὶ ὡς ἔπος εἰπεῖν ἐν πᾶσι τοῖς οὖσι, καθεωρακέναι μοι δοκῶ ἐκ τῆς   21

ἰατρικῆς, τῆς ἡμετέρας τέχνης, ὡς μέγας καὶ θαυμαστὸς καὶ ἐπὶ πᾶν ὁ θεὸς   22

τείνει καὶ κατ᾽ ἀνθρώπινα καὶ κατὰ θεῖα πράγματα.   23

---

11   τι τοιοῦτον οἵῳ = some such thing with which

     κινήσαις ἂν τὴν ῥῖνα: move one's nose presumably means to tickle it

     πταίρω = sneeze. πταρ- is the aorist stem; what is the precise form? (Hint: see note on
     ἀνακογχυλίασον in line 10.)

13   Οὐκ ἂν φθάνοις λέγων: idiomatic; Rose 1985: 24: "you could not speak too soon"; i.e., "the
     sooner you begin speaking the better."

16   ἀποτελέω = bring quite to an end, complete

17   ἐπιθεῖναι from ἐπιτίθημι = put acc. on dat.

18–21   ὅτι ... οὖσι: this whole clause is the object of καθεωρακέναι in line 21, and it looks more complicated
     than it is. It is simply a list of places where love is found. The list is structured first by οὐ μόνον ...
     ἀλλὰ καὶ ... καί (not only ... but also ... and ...), followed by a list of three things in apposition
     to τοῖς ἄλλοις, defined by the particles τε ... καὶ ... καί (... and ... and ...). Τε cannot be
     translated here, but helps to structure the list. Eryximachus is trying to shake off the narrow
     view of Pausanias by suggesting that *eros* has many objects and is found in many things other
     than humankind.

19   πρὸς τοὺς καλούς = for handsome males, toward handsome males; i.e., [love felt] for handsome
     young men, [love] directed at handsome young men

21   καθεωρακέναι from καθοράω = observe

22–23   ὡς ... πράγματα: this clause is also the object of καθεωρακέναι. For good English, it may be
     necessary to insert a conjunction (e.g., "and") before it.

23   κατά (here) = throughout

Love and medicine: creating harmony out of opposites in the body

Ἄρξομαι δὲ ἀπὸ τῆς ἰατρικῆς λέγων, ἵνα καὶ πρεσβεύωμεν τὴν   24
τέχνην. ἡ γὰρ φύσις τῶν σωμάτων τὸν διπλοῦν Ἔρωτα τοῦτον ἔχει·   25
τὸ γὰρ ὑγιὲς τοῦ σώματος καὶ τὸ νοσοῦν ὁμολογουμένως ἕτερόν τε καὶ   26
ἀνόμοιόν ἐστι, τὸ δὲ ἀνόμοιον ἀνομοίων ἐπιθυμεῖ καὶ ἐρᾷ. ἄλλος μὲν οὖν   27
ὁ ἐπὶ τῷ ὑγιεινῷ ἔρως, ἄλλος δὲ ὁ ἐπὶ τῷ νοσώδει. ἔστιν δή, ὥσπερ ἄρτι   28
Παυσανίας ἔλεγεν τοῖς μὲν ἀγαθοῖς καλὸν χαρίζεσθαι τῶν ἀνθρώπων,   29
τοῖς δ' ἀκολάστοις αἰσχρόν, οὕτω καὶ ἐν αὐτοῖς τοῖς σώμασιν τοῖς μὲν   30
ἀγαθοῖς ἑκάστου τοῦ σώματος καὶ ὑγιεινοῖς καλὸν χαρίζεσθαι καὶ δεῖ, καὶ   31
τοῦτό ἐστιν ᾧ ὄνομα τὸ ἰατρικόν, τοῖς δὲ κακοῖς καὶ νοσώδεσιν αἰσχρόν τε   32
καὶ δεῖ ἀχαριστεῖν, εἰ μέλλει τις τεχνικὸς εἶναι. ἔστι γὰρ ἰατρική, ὡς ἐν   33
κεφαλαίῳ εἰπεῖν, ἐπιστήμη τῶν τοῦ σώματος ἐρωτικῶν πρὸς πλησμονὴν   34

---

24   *πρεσβεύω = place as oldest, first, hold first in rank, honor (cf. πρεσβύτερος)

26   τὸ ὑγιές = τὸ ὑγιὲς μέρος
      τὸ νοσοῦν = τὸ νοσοῦν μέρος
      ὁμολογουμένως = by general agreement

30   *ἀκόλαστος -ον = undisciplined, intemperate, uneducated

30–31 τοῖς μὲν ἀγαθοῖς *neut.* = the good parts, the good elements or components; dat. with χαρίζεσθαι in
       line 31

31   ἑκάστου τοῦ σώματος: partitive gen. (which helps to explain why τοῖς μὲν ἀγαθοῖς = the good
      parts)

32   τοῦτο: i.e., the good and necessary kind of gratification
      ᾧ: dat. of possessor (*Essentials* §107)
      τοῖς δὲ κακοῖς καὶ νοσώδεσιν: see note on lines 30–31

33   ἀχαριστέω = not gratify, not indulge
      τεχνικός -ή -όν = skillful, skilled, knowledgable
      ἰατρική: the subje. of ἔστι, despite the absence of the definite article

33–34 ὡς ἐν κεφαλαίῳ εἰπεῖν = to summarize, to speak in summary. What follows is Eryximachus's
       concise definition of the medical art, one that would no doubt astound modern doctors, but it
       should be remembered that much of ancient medicine concerned what and how much to put
       into one's body (through, for example, diet and drugs) and what to remove from it (by, for
       example, purging or bleeding). The notion that it has to do with fullness and emptiness makes
       more sense in that context. It is quite consistent with Greek medical writing (e.g., Hippocratic
       corpus, *de flatibus*).

34   πλησμονή -ῆς ἡ = fullness, filling (cf. πλήρης and πληρόω)

καὶ κένωσιν, καὶ ὁ διαγιγνώσκων ἐν σώμασιν τὸν καλόν τε καὶ αἰσχρὸν   35

ἔρωτα, οὗτός ἐστιν ὁ ἰατρικώτατος, καὶ ὁ μεταβάλλειν ποιῶν, ὥστε ἀντὶ   36

τοῦ ἑτέρου ἔρωτος τὸν ἕτερον κτᾶσθαι, καὶ οἷς μὴ ἔνεστιν ἔρως ὁ   37

ἐπιστάμενος ἐμποιῆσαι ἔρωτα καὶ ἐνόντα ἐξελεῖν, ἀγαθὸς ἂν εἴη δημιουργός.   38

δεῖ γὰρ δὴ τὸν ἰατρὸν τὰ ἔχθιστα ὄντα ἐν τῷ σώματι φίλα οἷόν τ᾽ εἶναι   39

ποιεῖν καὶ ἐρᾶν ἀλλήλων. ἔστι δὲ ἔχθιστα τὰ ἐναντιώτατα, ψυχρὸν θερμῷ,   40

πικρὸν γλυκεῖ, ξηρὸν ὑγρῷ, πάντα τὰ τοιαῦτα· τούτοις ἐπιστηθεὶς ἔρωτα   41

ἐμποιῆσαι καὶ ὁμόνοιαν ὁ ἡμέτερος πρόγονος Ἀσκληπιός, ὥς φασιν οἵδε   42

οἱ ποιηταὶ καὶ ἐγὼ πείθομαι, συνέστησεν τὴν ἡμετέραν τέχνην.   43

---

35   κένωσις -εως ἡ = emptiness, emptying, purging (cf. κενός)

     διαγιγνώσκω = distinguish between two, decide (cf. English "diagnosis")

36   ὁ ... ποιῶν: subst. part. serving as subje. of ἂν εἴη δημιουργός in line 38

     *μεταβάλλειν ποιέω = make to change, effect changes, cause to change

37   κτᾶσθαι: infinitive in a natural result clause, with "bodies" as the implied subject

     οἷς μή: understand as the antecedent of the relative clause τοῖς σώμασι, with the inf. ἐμποιῆσαι in

       the next line = create *acc.* in *dat.*, implant *acc.* in *dat.*

41   ἐπιστηθείς from ἐπίσταμαι: pass. form with act. meaning

42   Ἀσκληπιός -οῦ ὁ = Asclepius, legendary physician, who was so good at curing people that he

       was said to have brought Hippolytus back from the dead. He was punished by the gods for

       violating the essential boundary between mortal and immortal. During classical times, he was

       still worshiped in cult and had a major sanctuary at Epidaurus. The tragedian Sophocles brought

       the cult of Asclepius to Athens.

     οἵδε: apparently referring to Aristophanes and Agathon, the two poets present

43   συνίστημι = establish (together), found

Reading 5B

Eryximachus applies his notion of medicine as the art of creating harmony out of opposites to some other fields: (1) music, which creates harmony out of opposites (e.g., low and high notes, fast and slow rhythms), and (2) farming, which uses the opposites found in weather and other conditions (e.g., wet and dry seasons, high and low temperatures) to create a climate conducive to growing plants. It is a good example of the kind of analogical reasoning characteristic of ancient science and medicine.

The passage begins with an analysis of a quotation from Heraclitus, a presocratic philosopher. Heraclitus's fragments, the most famous of which is "you can't step in the same river twice," have provoked a lot of thought, but even in antiquity he was considered hard to understand, so students should not be alarmed if they don't know precisely what is meant by the two quotations from Heraclitus, which I translate, "[the one] while being different agrees with itself" and "just like the harmony of the bow and the lyre." Eryximachus himself professes some uncertainty about their meaning. Ultimately, they have to do with Heraclitus's fundamental notion that everything depends on and comes out of opposites and tension, and that change and flux are the single constant.

Eryximachus's discussion of music depends on a fundamental Platonic principle: that music actually shapes the soul, and that it can be harmful as well as good, even when it brings pleasure. Plato's favorite analogy for this kind of harmful pleasure is the pleasure that comes from eating delicious things that are not good for one's health; Plato regularly contrasts cooking with medicine as an art that brings pleasure but not health.

Vocabulary

ἀνθρώπειος -α -ον: human (= ἀνθρώπινος -η -ον)
ἁρμονία -ας ἡ: harmony
βαρύς -εῖα -ύ: heavy, weighty, deep (cf. English "baritone")
βραδύς -εῖα -ύ: slow
διαφέρω/διαφέρομαι: differ, disagree (cf. διαφερόντως and its opposite: συμφέρω)
δικαιοσύνη -ης ἡ: justice, righteousness (cf. δική ἡ, δίκαιος, ἄδικος, etc.)
ἑκάτερος -α -ον: each (of two) (cf. ἕκαστος)
ἐνιαυτός -οῦ ὁ: year, any long period of time, cycle, period
ἐπιθυμία -ας ἡ: desire (cf. ἐπιθυμέω)

εὐλαβέομαι εὐλαβήσομαι — — — ηὐλαβήθην: take care, beware of

θηρίον -ου τό: wild animal, beast, game (cf. *θήρ -ός ὁ: wild beast, beast of prey)

κυβερνάω: steer, guide, govern (cf. *κυβερνήτης -ου ὁ: steersman, captain)

μεστός -ή -όν: full

μοῦσα -ης ἡ/Μοῦσα -ης ἡ: Muse, goddess of music, poetry, and dance; *recognize also* μουσικός -ή -όν: having to do with the Muses, musical; *especially* ἡ μουσική = ἡ μουσικὴ τέχνη: art of the Muses, music, poetry, and dance

ὁμιλέω: be in company with *dat.*, be with *dat.*; *recognize also* ὁμιλία -ας ἡ: being together, communion, companionship

ὁμολογία -ας ἡ: agreement (cf. ὁμολογέω)

ὀξύς -εῖα -ύ: sharp, keen, high-pitched (cf. English "oxytone," "oxymoron," and "oxygen")

πρόγονος -ου ὁ: forefather, ancestor, predecessor

σωφροσύνη -ης ἡ: temperance, prudence, self-control, moderation, chastity

σώφρων -ον: temperate, prudent, self-controlled, moderate, chaste, sober

ταχύς -εῖα -ύ: quick, swift; *recognize also* τάχα *adv.*: quickly, soon

ὑγίεια -ας ἡ: health (cf. English "hygiene" and ὑγιεινός and ὑγιής -ές)

φυτόν -οῦ τό: plant, tree (cf. φύω and φύσις ἡ)

ὥρα -ας ἡ: hour, season, time, youth (cf. English "hour")

ὡσαύτως *adv.*: in the same way as, in like manner, just as

Reading 5B (based on *Symposium* 186e4–188e4)

Ἥ τε οὖν ἰατρική, ὥσπερ λέγω, πᾶσα διὰ τοῦ θεοῦ τούτου   1

κυβερνᾶται, ὡσαύτως δὲ καὶ γυμναστικὴ καὶ γεωργία καὶ μουσική,   2

ὥσπερ ἴσως καὶ Ἡράκλειτος βούλεται λέγειν, καίπερ οὐ καλῶς λέγων.   3

τὸ ἓν γάρ φησι "διαφερόμενον αὐτὸ αὑτῷ συμφέρεσθαι," "ὥσπερ ἁρμονίαν   4

τόξου τε καὶ λύρας." ἔστι δὲ πολλὴ ἀλογία φάναι ἁρμονίαν διαφέρεσθαι   5

ἢ ἐκ διαφερομένων ἔτι εἶναι. ἀλλὰ ἴσως τόδε ἐβούλετο λέγειν, ὅτι ἐκ   6

διαφερομένων πρότερον τοῦ ὀξέος καὶ βαρέος, ἔπειτα ὕστερον   7

ὁμολογησάντων ἁρμονία γέγονεν ὑπὸ τῆς μουσικῆς τέχνης. τὴν γὰρ   8

ὁμολογίαν τοῖς διαφερομένοις—ὀξεῖ καὶ βαρεῖ, ταχεῖ καὶ βραδεῖ—   9

ἡ μουσικὴ ἐντίθησιν ἐνταῦθα, ὥσπερ ἐκεῖ ἡ ἰατρική, ἔρωτα καὶ ὁμόνοιαν   10

ἀλλήλων ἐμποιήσασα· καὶ ἔστιν αὖ μουσικὴ περὶ ἁρμονίαν καὶ ῥυθμὸν   11

ἐρωτικῶν ἐπιστήμη.   12

Ἐν δὲ τῇ μουσικῇ, ὥσπερ ἐν τῇ ἰατρικῇ, τοῖς μὲν κοσμίοις τῶν   13

ἀνθρώπων δεῖ χαρίζεσθαι καὶ φυλάττειν τὸν τούτων ἔρωτα, καὶ οὗτος   14

ἐστιν ὁ καλός, ὁ οὐράνιος, ὁ τῆς Οὐρανίας μούσης Ἔρως· ὁ δὲ Πολυμνίας   15

---

2   γυμναστική [supply τέχνή] = gymnastics, the science of exercise; γεωργία [supply τέχνή] = the
       science of farming (cf. *γεωργός -οῦ ὁ = farmer [from γῆ + ἔργον]; cf. English "George" and
       "*Georgics*")

3   Ἡράκλειτος -ου ὁ = Heraclitus of Ephesus, a presocratic philosopher, known for his obscurity
       and love of paradox
       βούλεται λέγειν: the English idioms that correspond to this are "is trying to say" or "means"

4–5   translations of these quotations are given in the introduction to this reading

5   *τόξον -ου τό = (archery) bow
       λύρα -ας ἡ = lyre
       ἔστι δὲ πολλὴ ἀλογία + *inf.* = it is very illogical to ——; there is great illogic in ——ing

6   ἔτι: Eryximachus adds this because he is going to say that harmony can be created out of what is
       originally in disagreement.

11–12 ἔστιν . . . ἐπιστήμη: compare the definition of medicine in reading 5A.33–35

11   ῥυθμός -οῦ ὁ = rhythm, meter

15   Οὐρανία = Heavenly; Πολυμνία = Of many songs. These are traditional names of two of the
       nine Muses. Eryximachus playfully exploits the correspondence between Οὐρανία and the
       adjective οὐρανία and the promiscuous connotations of the πολυ- prefix on Πολυμνία to
       create a correspondence with Pausanias's two Aphrodites and their corresponding Erotes.
       ὁ Πολυμνίας: identify the form of each word carefully before translating this phrase. Hint: compare
       the preceding phrase: ὁ τῆς Οὐρανίας μούσης Ἔρως.

ὁ πάνδημος μεγίστῃ εὐλαβείᾳ προσοιστέος, ὅπως ἂν τὴν μὲν ἡδονὴν   16
αὐτοῦ καρπώσηται, ἀκολασίαν δὲ μηδεμίαν ἐμποιήσῃ, ὥσπερ ἐν τῇ   17
ἡμετέρᾳ τέχνῃ μέγα ἔργον ταῖς περὶ τὴν ὀψοποιικὴν τέχνην ἐπιθυμίαις   18
καλῶς χρῆσθαι, ὥστ' ἄνευ νόσου τὴν ἡδονὴν καρπώσασθαι.   19
καὶ ἐν μουσικῇ δὴ καὶ ἐν ἰατρικῇ καὶ ἐν τοῖς ἄλλοις πᾶσι καὶ τοῖς   20
ἀνθρωπείοις καὶ τοῖς θείοις, καθ' ὅσον παρείκει, φυλακτέον ἑκάτερον τὸν   21
ἔρωτα· ἔνεστον γάρ.   22

Love and the seasons of the year

Ἐπεὶ καὶ αἱ ὧραι τοῦ ἐνιαυτοῦ μεσταί εἰσιν ἀμφοτέρων τούτων,   23
καὶ ἐπειδὰν μὲν πρὸς ἄλληλα τοῦ κοσμίου ἔρωτος τύχῃ ἃ νυνδὴ ἐγὼ   24
ἔλεγον, τά τε θερμὰ καὶ τὰ ψυχρὰ καὶ ξηρὰ καὶ ὑγρά, καὶ ἁρμονίαν καὶ   25
κρᾶσιν λάβῃ σώφρονα, ἥκει φέροντα εὐετηρίαν τε καὶ ὑγίειαν ἀνθρώποις   26
καὶ τοῖς ἄλλοις ζῴοις τε καὶ φυτοῖς, καὶ οὐδὲν ἠδίκησεν. ὅταν δὲ ὁ   27

---

16   *εὐλάβεια -ας ἡ = caution, discretion, care (cf. εὐλαβέομαι)

προσοιστέος -α -ον = must be approached, must be performed (verbal adj. in -τεος from προσφέρω = bring to, apply to, expose to, perform for; on verbal adjectives see *Essentials* §§125–27)

ὅπως ἂν = ὅπως: ἂν frequently accompanies ὅπως in introducing a purpose clause in Plato, Aristophanes, and formal documents (Smyth 1956: §2201a)

17   καρπώσηται ... ἐμποιήσῃ: both verbs seem to require an impersonal subject "one"

ἀκολασία -ας ἡ = licentiousness, intemperance

18   ὀψοποιικός -ή -όν = food-making, culinary

21   παρείκει = it is practicable

φυλακτέον = one must look out for (verbal adj. in -τεος from φυλάττω) (*Essentials* §127)

22   ἔνεστον: 3rd pers. dual indic. of ἔνειμι (*Essentials* §136)

24   πρὸς ἄλληλα: depends on ἔρωτος

τυγχάνω with gen. obj. = come upon *gen.* by chance, meet, find

24–27   τύχῃ/λάβῃ/ἥκει/ἠδίκησεν: all have neuter plural τὰ θερμά ... ὑγρά as their subjects. Neuter plural subjects use singular verbs. Identify the form and usage of τύχῃ and λάβῃ (*Essentials* §152, §160).

25   τά τε θερμά: τε simply introduces a string of connected words, the first unit of which is τὰ θερμά. Do not translate.

26   κρᾶσις -εως ἡ = mixing (cf. English "crasis," the grammatical term)

εὐετηρία -ας ἡ = a good year (for crops)

27   ἠδίκησεν is an instance of a gnomic aorist, an aorist used to express a general truth. It may be translated as a present indicative (*Essentials* §145). Smyth explains: "The aorist simply states a past occurrence and leaves the reader to draw the inference from a concrete case that what has happened once is typical of what often occurs" (1956: §1931).

μετὰ τῆς ὕβρεως Ἔρως ἐγκρατέστερος περὶ τὰς τοῦ ἐνιαυτοῦ ὥρας   28

γένηται, διέφθειρέν τε πολλὰ καὶ ἠδίκησεν. οἵ τε γὰρ λοιμοὶ φιλοῦσι   29

γίγνεσθαι ἐκ τῶν τοιούτων καὶ ἄλλα ἀνόμοια πολλὰ νοσήματα καὶ τοῖς   30

θηρίοις καὶ τοῖς φυτοῖς.   31

  Οὕτω πολλὴν καὶ μεγάλην, μᾶλλον δὲ πᾶσαν δύναμιν ἔχει   32

συλλήβδην μὲν ὁ πᾶς Ἔρως, ὁ δὲ περὶ τἀγαθὰ μετὰ σωφροσύνης καὶ   33

δικαιοσύνης ἀποτελούμενος καὶ παρ' ἡμῖν καὶ παρὰ θεοῖς, οὗτος τὴν   34

μεγίστην δύναμιν ἔχει καὶ πᾶσαν ἡμῖν εὐδαιμονίαν παρασκευάζει καὶ ἡμᾶς   35

ποιεῖ ἀλλήλοις δυναμένους ὁμιλεῖν καὶ φίλους εἶναι καὶ τοῖς κρείττοσιν   36

ἡμῶν θεοῖς. ἴσως μὲν οὖν ἐγὼ τὸν Ἔρωτα ἐπαινῶν πολλὰ παραλείπω,   37

οὐ μέντοι ἑκών γε. ἢ εἴ πως ἄλλως ἐν νῷ ἔχεις ἐγκωμιάζειν τὸν θεόν,   38

ἐγκώμαζε, ἐπειδὴ καὶ τῆς λυγγὸς πέπαυσαι.   39

---

28   ἐγκρατής -ές = strong, powerful; *in negative sense* = domineering

29   διέφθειρεν and ἠδίκησεν: both gnomic aorists (see note on line 27)

      οἵ τε . . . λοιμοί: τε serves to connect οἱ λοιμοί to the phrase καὶ ἄλλα ἀνόμοια πολλὰ
         νοσήματα in the next line

      *λοιμός -οῦ ὁ = plague, pestilence

30   νόσημα -ατος τό = νόσος -ου ἡ

32   *μᾶλλον δέ = or rather (as often)

33   συλλήβδην *adv.* = taken together

      συλλήβδην μὲν ὁ πᾶς Ἔρως: the whole Eros taken together is contrasted with the good Eros
         that is part of it (ὁ δέ)

34   ἀποτελέομαι = be fulfilled, be brought to fulfillment

Reading 6. Aristophanes' Comic Myth

From this point on, the text is complete and unadapted. It follows Burnet 1901 and uses the Stephanus numbers for reference. Teachers in a standard semester or quarter course may find it necessary to cut many of the readings for reasons of time. Most readers will want to read omitted sections in English translation.

Aristophanes, the famous Athenian writer of comedies (see appendix 1), now speaks out of turn. There may be some play here on the Greek word ἀτοπία (the state of being out of place), which is used several times in the *Symposium* to describe the strangeness of Socrates. And certainly Aristophanes has his own "strangeness" in the dialogue, due to his differences from the other speakers, all of whom are involved in pederastic relationships of some kind, all of whom appear in other dialogues as associates of Socrates, and all of whom appear in Plato's *Protagoras* as avid listeners to prominent sophists. In the *Clouds*, Aristophanes is clearly critical of the sophists, whom he does not bother to differentiate from Socrates; he is never associated with pederasty or with Socrates elsewhere, except as critics of both, and while he mocks and exaggerates most forms of human appetite, Aristophanes tends in his comedies to treat pederasty as characteristic of the aristocratic elite and to present himself as a champion of democracy. Aristophanes' speaking out of turn may be a play on other forms of his ἀτοπία in this group.

His hiccups have been cured, as we learn in the teasing banter that begins reading 6A, by the remedial application of a sneeze (as the poet puts it); his language mocks Eryximachus's theories, as the doctor protests. In response, Aristophanes draws a distinction between what is simply funny or laughable (*geloion*), a quality appropriate to a writer of comedies, and that which incites mocking or derisive laughter (*katagelaston*), something he seeks to avoid. This fundamental distinction may lie behind Plato's cleaned-up version of Aristophanic humor. Aristophanes' speech, though fanciful and inventive like Aristophanes' best plots, lacks the bathroom humor, sexual explicitness, and obvious political edge that are hallmarks of Aristophanic humor. At the end of the speech, Aristophanes gently teases Pausanias and Agathon and takes a dig at politicians, but the humor is subtle compared to most of that in Aristophanes' surviving plays.[28]

As he begins his speech (reading 6A), Aristophanes continues the medical theme with the suggestion that Eros is a healer—of a condition imposed in punishment long ago by the gods on the original humans, spherical beings with twice as many of all body parts as we now have. Aristophanes goes on to tell an etiological myth (readings 6B–D), one that accounts for our

---

28. For a more detailed examination of the relationship between Aristophanes' surviving plays and his speech, see Hunter 2004: 60–71.

Fig. 17. Fat grinning comic actor, wearing boots. Terracotta figurine, ca. 300 B.C.E. Inv. 1859,1226.830. British Museum, London, England. © Trustees of the British Museum.

current physical form and erotic psychology; many have found it the most compelling account of the state of being in love in the *Symposium*, expressing effectively the consuming experience of sexual desire. It represents a striking departure from much earlier Greek literature on the subject of erotic love, in offering a view of *eros* as mutual and reciprocal rather than following the hierarchical model that assumes a pursuing lover and a fleeing or passive beloved predominant in Greek literature. Moreover, Aristophanes' myth implies a view of sexual orientation as either fundamentally heterosexual or homosexual instead of reflecting the better-attested Greek assumption that men at least are bisexual and that preference for one gender over the other, when it occurs, is a choice made consciously and freely. The story also acknowledges lesbianism as a familiar category, something far from explicit elsewhere in Greek texts.

The attractiveness of Aristophanes' speech is undeniable. Its style is simple and effective; its content particularly original, amusing, and memorable. Scholars generally consider it the most successful of the first five speeches in the *Symposium*; some suggest that this most obvious fiction contains the dialogue's most profound truths.[29] This apparently flattering characterization of Aristophanes (despite his undignified hiccups) is perhaps surprising given that in the *Apology* Socrates suggests that Aristophanes' misrepresentation of him in the *Clouds* contributed to the bad reputation that led to his conviction and hence his death. But, though Plato presents Aristophanes remarkably well, we should not assume that the *Symposium* endorses his views, though many astute interpreters, including Freud and Jung, have thought so. However compelling, Aristophanes' account of Eros is narrowly focused on people, obviously so following the cosmic view of Eryximachus, and his view of love has been criticized as narcissistic, shallow, and ultimately unfulfillable, a longing for a kind of union we can never attain. For these reasons, the speech has also been taken as a dramatic representation of the deceptive power of art that Socrates points to in the *Republic*. But whether we regard the speech as profoundly true or dangerously deceptive, it stands in the dialogue as an important view that demands serious consideration as an alternative to the highly abstract view put forward through Socrates as the dialogue develops.

The transition (reading 6E) between Aristophanes' speech and the oration of the tragic poet and host, Agathon, reintroduces theatrical and competitive themes of the dialogue, setting up a dramatic competition between comic poet and tragic. It makes a point reiterated in Plato's dialogues: that a speaker should feel more fear and shame before a small, wise audience than a large undiscriminating one, such as that found in a theater. Although interesting as a sample of audience response, this final section of the reading can be omitted if scheduling demands.

29. See Corrigan and Glazov-Corrigan 2004 for a brief survey of interpretations.

Reading 6A

Banter occurs between Aristophanes and Eryximachus. The opening of Aristophanes' speech gives the characterization of Eros as a healer and a description of the original humans with three genders: male, female, and androgyne (half-male/half-female). The narrator and therefore the subject of ἔφη is Aristodemus, as elsewhere.

Suggested Reviews

- accusative absolute (*Essentials* §177)
- numerals (*Essentials* §§70–71)
- forms of δίδωμι δώσω ἔδωκα/(δο-) δέδωκα δέδομαι ἐδόθην (give, grant) (*Essentials* §§60–63)
- principal parts of φέρω

  φέρω οἴσω ἤνεγκα/ἤνεγκον ἐνήνοχα ἐνήνεγμαι ἠνέχθην: bear, bring, carry, lead, wear; imperative: come!

Vocabulary

ἀλλοῖος -α -ον: of another sort or kind, different (cf. ἄλλος)
αὐχήν -ένος ὁ: neck, throat
ἀφανίζω ἀφανιῶ ἠφάνισα ἠφάνικα ἠφάνισμαι ἠφανίσθην: make disappear, make unseen; *mid.*: disappear (cf. φαίνομαι)
εἶδος -ους τό: form, shape, figure
εἰκάζω εἰκάσω ἤκασα—— ἤκασμαι ἠκάσθην: liken, compare, infer from comparison, conjecture
θέλω = ἐθέλω
θυσία -ας ἡ: sacrifice, offering (cf. θύω)
ἰάομαι ἰάσομαι ἰασάμην—ἴαμαι ἰάθην: heal (cf. ἰατρός and ἰατρική)
ἱερός -ά -όν: holy, sacred, divine; *note especially* τὸ ἱερόν: temple, holy place; *in the plural can also and often does mean* sacred rites, sacrifices (cf. English "hieroglyphics")
ἴσος -η -ον: equal (to) *dat.*, the same (as) *dat.*, like *dat.*, even (cf. English "isosceles" and "isotope")
κατασκευάζω κατασκευάσω κατεσκεύασα κατεσκεύακα κατεσκεύασμαι κατεσκευάσθην: prepare, get ready, equip, build (cf. παρασκευάζω)

κεφαλή -ῆς ἡ: head

κύκλος -ου ὁ: circle, anything round (cf. English "cycle"); *note especially common dative use:* κύκλῳ: in a circle

λοιπός -ή -όν: left, left behind, remaining; οἱ λοιποί: the rest, those remaining (cf. λείπω)

ὅλος -η -ον: whole, entire

οὖς ὠτός τό: ear (cf. English "otology" or "otolaryngology")

πῃ: in some way, somehow; *recognize also the indirect version:* ὅπῃ: in whatever way, however; *in general, fem. sing. dat. adj.:* in ——way; e.g., ἄλλῃ: in another way; πάντῃ: in every way; ταύτῃ: in this way; οὐδάμῃ/μηδάμῃ: in no way; κοινῃ: in common

πρόσωπον -ου τό: face

σκέλος -ους τό: leg (cf. English "isosceles")

ψόφος -ου ὁ: noise, sound

Reading 6A (*Symposium* 189a1–190a7)

Ἐκδεξάμενον οὖν ἔφη εἰπεῖν τὸν Ἀριστοφάνη ὅτι "Καὶ   1   189a

μάλ' ἐπαύσατο, οὐ μέντοι πρίν γε τὸν πταρμὸν προσενεχθῆναι   2

αὐτῇ, ὥστε με θαυμάζειν εἰ τὸ κόσμιον τοῦ σώματος ἐπιθυμεῖ   3

τοιούτων ψόφων καὶ γαργαλισμῶν, οἷον καὶ ὁ πταρμός   4

ἐστιν· πάνυ γὰρ εὐθὺς ἐπαύσατο, ἐπειδὴ αὐτῷ τὸν πταρμὸν   5

προσήνεγκα."   6

Καὶ τὸν Ἐρυξίμαχον, " Ὠγαθέ," φάναι, " Ἀριστόφανες, ὅρα   7

τί ποιεῖς. γελωτοποιεῖς μέλλων λέγειν, καὶ φύλακά με τοῦ   8

λόγου ἀναγκάζεις γίγνεσθαι τοῦ σεαυτοῦ, ἐάν τι γελοῖον   9   189b

εἴπῃς, ἐξόν σοι ἐν εἰρήνῃ λέγειν."   10

Καὶ τὸν Ἀριστοφάνη γελάσαντα εἰπεῖν "Εὖ λέγεις, ὦ   11

Ἐρυξίμαχε, καί μοι ἔστω ἄρρητα τὰ εἰρημένα. ἀλλὰ μή με   12

---

1   ἐκδέχομαι = receive one's turn

2   καί with μάλα: strong affirmative = in fact (as often)

    ἐπαύσατο: the understood subject here is ἡ λύγξ = hiccups

    πταρμός -οῦ ὁ = sneeze

    προσενεχθῆναι from προσφέρω = bring to, apply to (here, as a remedy); what use of the infinitive is this (*Essentials* §185)?

3   τὸ κόσμιον = the orderly aspect (mocking Eryximachus's characterization)

4   γαργαλισμός -οῦ ὁ = tickling

    οἷον = such as. For the singular relative adjective with plural antecedent, see *Essentials* §135.

5   αὐτῷ: presumably refers to σῶμα (since hiccups [ἡ λύγξ] is fem.)

    πταρμός -οῦ ὁ = sneeze

6   προσήνεγκα: see note on προσενεχθῆναι in line 2

7   ὠγαθέ = ὦ ἀγαθέ (crasis) (*Essentials* §207)

8   γελωτοποιέω = incite laughter, make [people] laugh

10   ἐξόν: neut. acc. sing. part. of ἔξεστι introducing an acc. abs. (*Essentials* §177)

    ἐν εἰρήνῃ: that is, so as not to require Eryximachus to interfere

12   μοι: ethical dat. = for my sake (i.e., please) or a dat. of agent with ἄρρητα = by me. The ethical dative is common with an imperative, the dative of agent is standard with verbal adjectives (*Essentials* §§113–14).

    ἄρρητος -ον = unsaid

φύλαττε, ὡς ἐγὼ φοβοῦμαι περὶ τῶν μελλόντων ῥηθήσεσθαι,   13

οὔ τι μὴ γελοῖα εἴπω—τοῦτο μὲν γὰρ ἂν κέρδος εἴη καὶ τῆς   14

ἡμετέρας μούσης ἐπιχώριον—ἀλλὰ μὴ καταγέλαστα."   15

"Βαλών γε," φάναι, "ὦ Ἀριστόφανες, οἴει ἐκφεύξεσθαι·   16

ἀλλὰ πρόσεχε τὸν νοῦν καὶ οὕτως λέγε ὡς δώσων λόγον.   17

ἴσως μέντοι, ἂν δόξῃ μοι, ἀφήσω σε."   18   189c

"Καὶ μήν, ὦ Ἐρυξίμαχε," εἰπεῖν τὸν Ἀριστοφάνη, "ἄλλῃ   19

γέ πῃ ἐν νῷ ἔχω λέγειν ἢ ᾗ σύ τε καὶ Παυσανίας εἰπέτην.   20

ἐμοὶ γὰρ δοκοῦσιν ἄνθρωποι παντάπασι τὴν τοῦ ἔρωτος   21

δύναμιν οὐκ ᾐσθῆσθαι, ἐπεὶ αἰσθανόμενοί γε μέγιστ' ἂν   22

13–15   φοβοῦμαι οὔ . . . μή . . . ἀλλὰ μή . . . = I fear not . . . that [. . .] but that. . . . In fear clauses, μή
should be translated "that" or "lest" (*Essentials* §154).

14   οὔ τι = not at all, not in any way; as often following οὐ, τι is adverbial

*κέρδος -ους τό = profit (here = profitable thing, positive thing)

15   μοῦσα -ης ἡ = muse (i.e., the comic art of Aristophanes)

ἐπιχώριος -α -ον = appropriate to the location, fitting for the location; Rowe 1998: 49 cleverly
translates "in the province of my Muse"

καταγελαστός -όν = deserving mocking or derisive laughter (as opposed to γελοῖα = merely
funny, inspiring laughter)

ἀλλὰ μὴ καταγελαστά [supply εἴπω]: see note on lines 13–15 for the overall structure of this
sentence

16   βαλών . . . ἐκφεύξεσθαι = having taken a shot [at me], you think you will get away; Rose 1985:
29 nicely comments "as of a verbal hit-and-run"

ἐκφεύξεσθαι: fut. inf. in indir. statement after 2nd pers. mid. οἴει

17   δίδωμι λόγον = give an account, present one's case. The doctor seems to be using the language of
the law court or politician in this section.

ὡς δώσων: what is suggested by ὡς + future participle (*Essentials* §172)?

ἂν here is a contraction of ἐάν (common), as the subjunctive δόξῃ demands

ἀφήσω from ἀφίημι (here) = acquit

19–20   ἄλλῃ πῃ . . . ἢ ᾗ = in some way other than the way in which; other than as

20   εἰπέτην: aor. dual of λέγω (3rd pers. rather than the expected 2nd pers.)

21   ἄνθρωποι = οἱ ἄνθρωποι (crasis)

22   ᾐσθῆσθαι from αἰσθάνομαι: what must the tense be? Hint: the infinitive does not have a
temporal augment.

22–24   ἐπεὶ . . . μεγίστας: this dependent clause contains a condition in indirect statement (after ἐμοὶ
δοκοῦσι). The participle αἰσθανόμενοι serves as the protasis (if-clause). The apodosis (main
clause) is formed by ἂν + κατασκευάσαι in line 23, an aorist infinitive, consequently a past
contrary-to-fact condition. ἄνθρωποι or "they" carries over from the main verb as the subject.

αὐτοῦ ἱερὰ κατασκευάσαι καὶ βωμούς, καὶ θυσίας ἂν ποιεῖν   23

μεγίστας, οὐχ ὥσπερ νῦν τούτων οὐδὲν γίγνεται περὶ αὐτόν,   24

δέον πάντων μάλιστα γίγνεσθαι. ἔστι γὰρ θεῶν φιλανθρωπότατος,   25

ἐπίκουρός τε ὢν τῶν ἀνθρώπων καὶ ἰατρὸς   26   189d

τούτων ὧν ἰαθέντων μεγίστη εὐδαιμονία ἂν τῷ ἀνθρωπείῳ   27

γένει εἴη. ἐγὼ οὖν πειράσομαι ὑμῖν εἰσηγήσασθαι τὴν   28

δύναμιν αὐτοῦ, ὑμεῖς δὲ τῶν ἄλλων διδάσκαλοι ἔσεσθε.   29

Humans originally had three genders

Δεῖ δὲ πρῶτον ὑμᾶς μαθεῖν τὴν ἀνθρωπίνην φύσιν καὶ τὰ   30

παθήματα αὐτῆς. ἡ γὰρ πάλαι ἡμῶν φύσις οὐχ αὐτὴ ἦν   31

ἥπερ νῦν, ἀλλ' ἀλλοία. πρῶτον μὲν γὰρ τρία ἦν τὰ γένη   32

τὰ τῶν ἀνθρώπων, οὐχ ὥσπερ νῦν δύο, ἄρρεν καὶ θῆλυ,   33

---

23   αὐτοῦ ἱερά: the verb κατασκευάσαι that follows and pairing with βωμούς suggests this phrase
       means "his temples." (We would be more likely to say in this context "temples for him.")
       *βωμός -οῦ ὁ = altar
       ποιεῖν: inf. in indir. statement representing an original imperf. indic. With ἄν = present contrary-
       to-fact condition.
25   δέον: what kind of construction does this introduce? Hint: see note on line 10. This example has
       a concessive force: "although."
       πάντων: partitive gen. with the adv. μάλιστα
       φιλανθρωπότατος -ον: guess the meaning of this word by breaking it into parts
26   ἐπίκουρος -ου ὁ = helper, ally
27   τούτων here neut. = those things (refers to the entire human condition described by the myth
       that follows)
       ὧν ἰαθέντων = which, if healed; relative pronoun + aorist passive participle in a genitive absolute
       with conditional force, as the presence of ἄν (which should be taken with εἴη) in the main
       clause suggests
28   εἰσηγέομαι = introduce, explain
31   πάθημα -ατος τό = πάθος τό
       αὐτή = ἡ αὐτή (crasis): what does the def. art. + αὐτός -ή -ό mean (*Essentials* §203)? The breathing
       mark makes it clear that it is not αὐτός alone (only the refl., contracted from ἑαυτόν, which
       does not occur in the nom. case, has a rough breathing); the accent makes clear that it is not the
       feminine of οὗτος (αὕτη).

ἀλλὰ καὶ τρίτον προσῆν κοινὸν ὂν ἀμφοτέρων τούτων, οὗ   34   189e

νῦν ὄνομα λοιπόν, αὐτὸ δὲ ἠφάνισται· ἀνδρόγυνον γὰρ ἒν   35

τότε μὲν ἦν καὶ εἶδος καὶ ὄνομα ἐξ ἀμφοτέρων κοινὸν τοῦ   36

τε ἄρρενος καὶ θήλεος, νῦν δὲ οὐκ ἔστιν ἀλλ᾽ ἢ ἐν ὀνείδει   37

ὄνομα κείμενον.   38

The original human: what it looked like and how it traveled

Ἔπειτα ὅλον ἦν ἑκάστου τοῦ ἀνθρώπου τὸ   39

εἶδος στρογγύλον, νῶτον καὶ πλευρὰς κύκλῳ ἔχον, χεῖρας   40

δὲ τέτταρας εἶχε, καὶ σκέλη τὰ ἴσα ταῖς χερσίν, καὶ πρόσωπα   41

δύ᾽ ἐπ᾽ αὐχένι κυκλοτερεῖ, ὅμοια πάντῃ· κεφαλὴν δ᾽ ἐπ᾽   42   190a

ἀμφοτέροις τοῖς προσώποις ἐναντίοις κειμένοις μίαν, καὶ   43

ὦτα τέτταρα, καὶ αἰδοῖα δύο, καὶ τἆλλα πάντα ὡς ἀπὸ   44

τούτων ἄν τις εἰκάσειεν. ἐπορεύετο δὲ καὶ ὀρθὸν ὥσπερ   45

---

34   *τρίτος -η -ον = third
       πρόσειμι = be in addition, also be
       κοινὸν ὂν + *gen.* = sharing in
35   ἀνδρόγυνος -ον = having to do with both men and women, androgynous, hermaphroditic
36   εἶδος καὶ ὄνομα: either accusatives of respect or nominative neuter subjects; the neuter plural
           uses singular verbs
37   ἀλλ᾽ ἤ = except, other than
       ἐν ὀνείδει = in reproach, i.e., as an insult
40   στρογγύλος -η -ον = round, spherical
       *νῶτον -ου τό = back
       πλευρὰ -ᾶς ἡ = rib
42   κυκλοτερής -ές = circular, round
       πάντῃ = in every way, in every direction
       ἐπ᾽ = upon, atop
44   *αἰδοῖα -ων τά = genitals, set of genitals; *literally* = the shameful things, the shameful parts

νῦν, ὁποτέρωσε βουληθείη· καὶ ὁπότε ταχὺ ὁρμήσειεν θεῖν,   46

ὥσπερ οἱ κυβιστῶντες καὶ εἰς ὀρθὸν τὰ σκέλη περιφερόμενοι   47

κυβιστῶσι κύκλῳ, ὀκτὼ τότε οὖσι τοῖς μέλεσιν   48

ἀπερειδόμενοι ταχὺ ἐφέροντο κύκλῳ.   49

---

46   ὁποτέρωσε = to whichever of two sides, in which of two directions
       βουληθείη and ὁρμήσειεν: identify the forms and explain the usage here (*Essentials* §159a).
       *θέω = run
47   κυβιστάω = tumble, turn somersaults or cartwheels
       εἰς ὀρθόν = to the front, forward
48   *μέλος -ους τό = limb
49   ἀπερείδομαι = support oneself

Reading 6B

Zeus limits the power of the overweening original humans by cutting them in half. The original spherical humans come from the heavenly spheres of sun, earth, and moon. Twice as powerful as contemporary humans, the spherical humans become overconfident and attack the gods.

Suggested Review

- articular infinitive (τό + inf.) (*Essentials* §182)

Vocabulary

- Make an effort to learn the principal parts of πλέκω and τέμνω.

ἀπορέω ἀπορήσω ἠπόρησα ἠπόρηκα ἠπόρημαι ἠπορήθην: be without means or resources, be at a loss, be in grave distress, not know what to do (cf. *πόρος -ου ὁ: resource)

ἀριθμός -οῦ ὁ: number (cf. English "arithmetic")

ἀσθενής -ές: weak, without strength (cf. *σθένος -ους τό: strength)

γαστήρ γαστέρος/γαστρός ἡ: stomach (cf. English "gastro-")

δέρμα δέρματος τό: skin (cf. English "epidermis" and "dermatologist")

δίχα *adv.*: in two, asunder (cf. δίς)

ἐννοέω: have in mind, think, consider, intend (see νοέω for principal parts)

ἥμισυς -εια -υ: half (cf. English "hemisphere")

θεάομαι θεάσομαι ἐθεασάμην—τεθέαμαι: gaze at, look at, watch (cf. English "theater")

λιμός -οῦ ὁ: hunger, starvation, famine

μέσος -η -ον: middle (of); mid—— (e.g., ἐν μέσῃ τῇ γαστέρι: in midstomach, the middle of the stomach); *recognize also neut. subst.* τὸ μέσον: the middle

ὀμφαλός -οῦ ὁ: navel

πλέκω πλέξω ἔπλεξα πέπλεχα πέπλεγμαι ἐπλέχθην/ἐπλάκην: twine, weave, braid

σελήνη -ης ἡ: moon

στόμα -ατος τό: mouth

τέμνω τεμῶ ἔτεμον τέτμηκα τέτμημαι ἐτμήθην: cut; *recognize also* διατέμνω: cut in half, cut by dividing

Fig. 18.   Comic mask (Zeus). From a Gnathian column krater, ca. 470 B.C.E., inscribed ΔΙΟΣ ΣΩΤΗΡΟΣ.
Inv. 1856,1226.113. British Museum, London, England. © Trustees of the British Museum.

Reading 6B (*Symposium* 190a8–191b5)

ἦν δὲ διὰ ταῦτα τρία	1
τὰ γένη καὶ τοιαῦτα, ὅτι τὸ μὲν ἄρρεν ἦν τοῦ ἡλίου τὴν	2 190b
ἀρχὴν ἔκγονον, τὸ δὲ θῆλυ τῆς γῆς, τὸ δὲ ἀμφοτέρων μετέχον	3
τῆς σελήνης, ὅτι καὶ ἡ σελήνη ἀμφοτέρων μετέχει· περιφερῆ	4
δὲ δὴ ἦν καὶ αὐτὰ καὶ ἡ πορεία αὐτῶν διὰ τὸ τοῖς γονεῦσιν	5
ὅμοια εἶναι. ἦν οὖν τὴν ἰσχὺν δεινὰ καὶ τὴν ῥώμην, καὶ	6
τὰ φρονήματα μεγάλα εἶχον, ἐπεχείρησαν δὲ τοῖς θεοῖς,	7
καὶ ὃ λέγει Ὅμηρος περὶ Ἐφιάλτου τε καὶ Ὤτου, περὶ	8
ἐκείνων λέγεται, τὸ εἰς τὸν οὐρανὸν ἀνάβασιν ἐπιχειρεῖν	9

1–2   διὰ ταῦτα . . . ὅτι = because of this; for these reasons, namely

    ἦν . . . τρία τὰ γένη καὶ τοιαῦτα: the position of the definite article suggests something about the role of the adjectives τρία and τοιαῦτα (*Essentials* §123). What two syntactically identical things does καί connect?

2–3   τὴν ἀρχήν *adverbial acc.* = in the beginning, originally

3   ἔκγονος -ον = born of, sprung of *gen.*

4   περιφερής -ές = round (evidently means both "spherical" and "rotating")

5   καὶ . . . καί: what does this mean? What two things are joined here?

    αὐτά refers to τὰ γένη: what use of αὐτός is this (*Essentials* §200)?

    πορεία -ας ἡ = journey, mode of travel, way of moving (cf. πορεύομαι)

    γονεύς -έως ὁ = parent

6   εἶναι: what use of the infinitive is this (*Essentials* §182)? Several more examples of this same construction occur in the reading.

    τὴν ἰσχὺν . . . καὶ τὴν ῥώμην: accusatives of respect with δεινά (*Essentials* §82)

    *ἰσχύς -ύος ἡ = strength (cf. ἰσχυρός)

    *ῥώμη -ης ἡ = might

7   φρόνημα -ατος τό = spirit; *here with negative sense* = arrogance, insolence

    εἶχον: the shift to plural verbs without change of subject is probably caused by the move from describing τὰ γένη as abstract entities to narrating a story in which they perform actions like people. (See Smyth 1958: §959)

8–9   ὃ λέγει . . . Ὤτου: the relative clause serves as the subject of the verb λέγεται in the next line

    Ἐφιάλτης -ου and Ὦτος -ου ὁ = Ephialtes and Otos, two giants. At *Odyssey* 11.305–20, Homer tells of the pair's attempt to reach the gods by piling mountains on top of one another.

    περὶ ἐκείνων λέγεται: the absence of καί with ἐκείνων seems to imply that Homer's story about Otos and Ephialtes was actually about the original humans. Dover 1980: 115 comments: Plato "is interpreting the Homeric passage as a covert or confused allusion" to the story of the humans' attack on the gods.

9   ἀνάβασις -εως ἡ = ascent

ποιεῖν, ὡς ἐπιθησομένων τοῖς θεοῖς. ὁ οὖν Ζεὺς καὶ οἱ   10   190c

ἄλλοι θεοὶ ἐβουλεύοντο ὅτι χρὴ αὐτοὺς ποιῆσαι, καὶ ἠπόρουν·   11

οὔτε γὰρ ὅπως ἀποκτείναιεν εἶχον καὶ ὥσπερ τοὺς   12

γίγαντας κεραυνώσαντες τὸ γένος ἀφανίσαιεν—αἱ τιμαὶ   13

γὰρ αὐτοῖς καὶ ἱερὰ τὰ παρὰ τῶν ἀνθρώπων ἠφανίζετο—   14

οὔτε ὅπως ἐῷεν ἀσελγαίνειν. μόγις δὴ ὁ Ζεὺς ἐννοήσας   15

λέγει ὅτι "Δοκῶ μοι," ἔφη, "ἔχειν μηχανήν, ὡς ἂν εἶέν   16

τε ἄνθρωποι καὶ παύσαιντο τῆς ἀκολασίας ἀσθενέστεροι   17

γενόμενοι. νῦν μὲν γὰρ αὐτούς," ἔφη, "διατεμῶ δίχα ἕκαστον,   18   190d

---

10   ἐπιθησομένων from *ἐπιτίθημι = attack. What does ὡς + future participle imply?

11   *ὅτι = ὅ τι, traditionally written in Platonic texts as one word. Here introducing an indirect
        question after ἐβουλεύοντο.

        αὐτοὺς ποιεῖν = to do with them, to treat them

12–15   οὔτε ὅπως ... εἶχον ... οὔτε ὅπως ... = they did not know how ... nor how; ἔχω (with indir.
        question) = know

        ὅπως + opt.: not purpose clauses here, but, as the context suggests, deliberative indirect questions
        in secondary sequence = how they could kill [them] ... or how they could allow [them]. ...
        The original questions would be put in the subjunctive: πῶς ἀποκτείνωμεν; = How are we to
        kill them? or How can we kill them?

13   γίγας γίγαντος ὁ = giant

        κεραυνόω = strike with a lightning bolt (cf. *κεραυνός -οῦ ὁ = lightning bolt)

        ἀφανίσαιεν: the optative shows that this is part of the indirect question introduced by ὅπως at
        line 12

14   ἱερά: context suggests "rites" rather than "temples"

        ἠφανίζετο: context seems to demand "would disappear" as a translation. The imperfect indicative
        without ἄν is a little surprising, but there are parallels in Attic prose (Bury 1973: 59; Dover 1980:
        116). Rose 1985: 31 suggests: "The impf. may imply a danger, 'were likely to disappear.'"

15   ἐῷεν opt. of ἐάω: review alpha-contracts if necessary (*Essentials* §57). For usage, see note on
        lines 12–15.

        ἀσελγαίνω = behave licentiously

        *μόγις adv. = with toil and pain, scarcely, barely. Rose 1985: 31 suggests "at last" as an adverb
        more suitable to the king of the gods.

16   λέγει: historical present. The combination of λέγει and ἔφη to describe the same speech may give
        a somewhat conversational tone to the narrative.

        ὡς = how

        εἶέν ἄν = might exist (potential opt.); εἰμί is used existentially here

18   διατέμνω = διά + τέμνω

καὶ ἅμα μὲν ἀσθενέστεροι ἔσονται, ἅμα δὲ χρησιμώτεροι   19
ἡμῖν διὰ τὸ πλείους τὸν ἀριθμὸν γεγονέναι· καὶ βαδιοῦνται   20
ὀρθοὶ ἐπὶ δυοῖν σκελοῖν. ἐὰν δ' ἔτι δοκῶσιν ἀσελγαίνειν   21
καὶ μὴ θέλωσιν ἡσυχίαν ἄγειν, πάλιν αὖ," ἔφη, "τεμῶ δίχα,   22
ὥστ' ἐφ' ἑνὸς πορεύσονται σκέλους ἀσκωλιάζοντες."   23

    Ταῦτα εἰπὼν ἔτεμνε τοὺς ἀνθρώπους δίχα, ὥσπερ οἱ τὰ ὄα   24
τέμνοντες καὶ μέλλοντες ταριχεύειν, ἢ ὥσπερ οἱ τὰ ᾠὰ ταῖς   25   190e
θριξίν· ὅντινα δὲ τέμοι, τὸν Ἀπόλλω ἐκέλευεν τό τε   26
πρόσωπον μεταστρέφειν καὶ τὸ τοῦ αὐχένος ἥμισυ πρὸς   27
τὴν τομήν, ἵνα θεώμενος τὴν αὑτοῦ τμῆσιν κοσμιώτερος   28
εἴη ὁ ἄνθρωπος, καὶ τἆλλα ἰᾶσθαι ἐκέλευεν. ὁ δὲ τό τε   29

---

20   πλείους: pred. acc. with linking verb γεγονέναι
      τὸν ἀριθμόν: acc. of respect
      *βαδίζω βαδιοῦμαι = go, make one's way
21   σκελοῖν: dual of σκέλος
      ἀσελγαίνω = behave licentiously
22   θέλω = ἐθέλω: used throughout this speech and in many other Greek authors, including regularly
          in tragedy. Despite the speaker, it is not normally used in comedy except when parodying tragedy
          (LSJ under ἐθέλω).
      *ἡσυχία -ας ἡ = stillness, rest, peace; ἡσυχίαν ἄγω = live in peace, be peaceful
23   σχέλους: goes with ἑνός
      ἀσκωλιάζω = hop, dance as at the Ἀσκώλια, part of a Dionysiac festival in rural Attica
24   ὄα -ων τά = sorb-apples (small, speckled brown fruit, also known as a service berry)
25   ταριχεύω = preserve
      ᾠά -ῶν τά = eggs. The similarity of the word ᾠά to ὄα suggests that Aristophanes is free-
          associating. The homely examples are appropriate to comedy.
26   θρίξ τριχός ἡ = hair. Plutarch gives "dividing an egg with a hair" as a proverbial expression for
          the ease with which lovers can be divided over something trivial (*Moralia* 770b). The physical
          picture of Zeus dividing the spherical humans with ease also appears to have thematic
          relevance.
      Ἀπόλλων -ωνος ὁ = Apollo, traditionally the god of healing, but Aristophanes' myth implies
          that Eros is even more effective as a healer. This sets up claims made for Eros by Agathon in
          the next speech.
27   μεταστρέφω = turn around
28   τομή -ῆς ἡ = cut
      τμῆσις -εως ἡ = cut

πρόσωπον μετέστρεφε, καὶ συνέλκων πανταχόθεν τὸ δέρμα   30

ἐπὶ τὴν γαστέρα νῦν καλουμένην, ὥσπερ τὰ σύσπαστα   31

βαλλάντια, ἓν στόμα ποιῶν ἀπέδει κατὰ μέσην τὴν γαστέρα,   32

ὃ δὴ τὸν ὀμφαλὸν καλοῦσι. καὶ τὰς μὲν ἄλλας ῥυτίδας   33

τὰς πολλὰς ἐξελέαινε καὶ τὰ στήθη διήρθρου, ἔχων τι   34   191a

τοιοῦτον ὄργανον οἷον οἱ σκυτοτόμοι περὶ τὸν καλάποδα   35

λεαίνοντες τὰς τῶν σκυτῶν ῥυτίδας· ὀλίγας δὲ κατέλιπε,   36

τὰς περὶ αὐτὴν τὴν γαστέρα καὶ τὸν ὀμφαλόν, μνημεῖον   37

εἶναι τοῦ παλαιοῦ πάθους.   38

     Ἐπειδὴ οὖν ἡ φύσις δίχα   39

ἐτμήθη, ποθοῦν ἕκαστον τὸ ἥμισυ τὸ αὑτοῦ συνῄει, καὶ   40

περιβάλλοντες τὰς χεῖρας καὶ συμπλεκόμενοι ἀλλήλοις,   41

ἐπιθυμοῦντες συμφῦναι, ἀπέθνῃσκον ὑπὸ λιμοῦ καὶ τῆς   42

ἄλλης ἀργίας διὰ τὸ μηδὲν ἐθέλειν χωρὶς ἀλλήλων ποιεῖν.   43   191b

---

30 συνέλκω = draw together (*ἕλκω = draw, drag; cf. ἀφέλκω)

31 σύσπαστος -α -ον = sewn-together

32 βαλλάντιον -ου τό = little bag, purse, pouch

   ἀποδέω = bind fast (*δέω = bind)

33 ῥυτίς ῥυτίδος ἡ = wrinkle

34 ἐκλεαίνω = smooth out

   *στῆθος -ους τό = chest

   διαρθρόω = complete in detail

35 *ὄργανον -ου τό = tool, instrument

   σκυτοτόμος -ου ὁ = leather-cutter, shoemaker

   καλάπους καλάποδος ὁ = shoemaker's last, a form shaped like a foot to assist in making shoes

36 λεαίνω = smooth

   σκῦτος -ους τό = leather, piece of leather

   ῥυτίς ῥυτίδος ἡ = wrinkle

37 μνημεῖον -ου τό = monument, memorial, reminder

40 *ποθέω = long for, yearn after (ποθοῦν is a neut. part.)

   συνῄει from σύν + εἶμι (Essentials §65)

42 συμφύω = σύν + φύω

43 τῆς ἄλλης = the rest of; here = other forms of

   ἀργία -ας ἡ = inertia, inactivity, lack of ἔργα

καὶ ὁπότε τι ἀποθάνοι τῶν ἡμίσεων, τὸ δὲ λειφθείη, τὸ   44

λειφθὲν ἄλλο ἐζήτει καὶ συνεπλέκετο, εἴτε γυναικὸς τῆς   45

ὅλης ἐντύχοι ἡμίσει—ὃ δὴ νῦν γυναῖκα καλοῦμεν—εἴτε   46

ἀνδρός· καὶ οὕτως ἀπώλλυντο.   47

---

44   τι ... τό δέ = any one ... the other; similar to ὁ μὲν ... ὁ δέ, but τι emphasizes the indefiniteness
       of the example

       ἀποθάνοι ... λειφθείη: explain the mood and its use here (*Essentials* §159a)

46   ἡμίσει: dat. with ἐντύχοι

       τῆς ὅλης: added to γυναικός as an afterthought to remind the reader that half of a woman back
       then was half of a completely female sphere: "Half of a woman—that is, of the whole [i.e.,
       original] woman."

47   ἀπώλλυντο = they were dying (i.e., they kept on dying). The imperfect emphasizes the ongoing
       nature of the deaths.

Reading 6C

Aristophanes continues the story of the severing of the original humans, explaining how Zeus introduced sexual intercourse (by moving human genitals to the front) out of pity and as a form of consolation and temporary union for humans deprived of their other halves. Eros is thus the healer of our division and helps us to become whole again, to make us again one from two. It also appears to break humankind into three groups based on the original undivided forms from which we are descended: homosexual males (halves of the original men), lesbians (halves of the original women), and heterosexuals (halves of the original androgynes).

This passage has been used by some scholars to argue against the prevalent view that the ancient Greeks did not share our notions of sexual orientation; however, it is difficult to find parallels in Greek texts for the view of human sexuality implied here. Ancient Greek texts typically present bisexuality as the norm in adult males. Although there are arguments about which type of love (for boys or for women) is better, this is nowhere else presented as an unalterable biological or psychological fact but as a matter of taste that may be subjected to rational choice. Moreover, it is hard to find Greek texts in which two halves of a homosexual couple long for one another equally. Aristophanes' views are strikingly modern. Aristophanes is of course a comic poet, and some scholars have naturally raised questions about how seriously we are to take the views presented here.[30] Nonetheless, the story must be intelligible to the audience, and this suggests that perhaps there are a range of ancient views rather than a single one shared by all.

Vocabulary

- Make an effort to learn the principal parts of πλήττω and τίκτω.
- Students should be able to recognize compounds of familiar words such as φιλογύναικες, φίλανδροι, and ἀνδρόγυνον.

ἀνδρεία -ας ἡ: courage, manly spirit, bravery (cf. ἀνανδρία)
ἀνδρεῖος -α -ον: brave, courageous, manly, masculine
ἀρχαῖος -α -ον: original, ancient, old (cf. English "archaic" and ἀρχή)
ἀσπάζομαι ἀσπάσομαι ἠσπασάμην: welcome, greet; embrace, kiss; cling to
γεννάω γεννήσω ἐγέννησα γεγέννηκα γεγέννημαι ἐγεννήθην: beget, engender

---

30. Carnes 1998 is worth reading on the interpretation of the passage and its implications for ancient Greek view of sexuality.

γοῦν: at any rate, so at least

δράω δράσω ἔδρασα δέδρακα δέδραμαι ἐδράσθην: do (cf. δρᾶμα: drama, which Aristotle defines first and foremost as an action)

ἐκτός *adv.*: outside (cf. ἐκ)

ἐξαρκεῖ *used impers.* + *dat.*: it is enough for *dat.*; it satisfies *dat.*

θάρρος -ους τό/θάρσος -ους τό: courage, boldness

μαντεύομαι μαντεύσομαι ἐμαντευσάμην—μεμάντευμαι: communicate in the manner of an oracle, speak oracularly, prophesy (cf. English "mantic" and *μάντις -εως ὁ: prophet)

μειράκιον -ου τό: male of approximately 14–21, teenaged boy, young man

πλήττω/πλήγνυμι πλήξω ἔπληξα πέπληγα πέπληγμαι ἐπλήγην/-ἐπλάγην: strike; frequent in compound ἐκπλήττω/ἐκπλήγνυμι: strike out of one's senses, amaze, astound

πορίζω ποριῶ ἐπόρισα πεπόρικα πεπόρισμαι ἐπορίσθην: bring, convey; bring about, contrive; furnish, provide; *mid.*: procure, acquire, get resources (cf. ἀπορέω and *πόρος -ου ὁ: resource)

σφεῖς σφῶν σφίσι σφᾶς (neut. nom./acc.: σφέα) *3rd pers. pron.*: they

τίκτω τέξομαι ἔτεκον τέτοκα: give birth, bring into the world, bear

τμῆμα τμήματος τό: cut (cf. ἐτμήθην from τέμνω)

τόσος -η -ον: so great, so much; *pl.*: so many (cf. ὅσος and τοσοῦτος)

ψεύδομαι ψεύσομαι ἐψευσάμην—ἔψευσμαι: speak falsely, lie (cf. ψευδής -ές and English "pseudo-")

Reading 6C (*Symposium* 191b6–192d2)

Ἐλεήσας δὲ ὁ Ζεὺς ἄλλην	1
μηχανὴν πορίζεται, καὶ μετατίθησιν αὐτῶν τὰ αἰδοῖα εἰς	2
τὸ πρόσθεν—τέως γὰρ καὶ ταῦτα ἐκτὸς εἶχον, καὶ ἐγέννων	3
καὶ ἔτικτον οὐκ εἰς ἀλλήλους ἀλλ᾽ εἰς γῆν, ὥσπερ οἱ τέττιγες	4 191c
—μετέθηκέ τε οὖν οὕτω αὐτῶν εἰς τὸ πρόσθεν καὶ	5
διὰ τούτων τὴν γένεσιν ἐν ἀλλήλοις ἐποίησεν, διὰ τοῦ	6
ἄρρενος ἐν τῷ θήλει, τῶνδε ἕνεκα, ἵνα ἐν τῇ συμπλοκῇ	7
ἅμα μὲν εἰ ἀνὴρ γυναικὶ ἐντύχοι, γεννῷεν καὶ γίγνοιτο	8
τὸ γένος, ἅμα δ᾽ εἰ καὶ ἄρρην ἄρρενι, πλησμονὴ γοῦν γίγνοιτο	9
τῆς συνουσίας καὶ διαπαύοιντο καὶ ἐπὶ τὰ ἔργα τρέποιντο	10

---

1   ἐλεήσας ingressive aorist = taking pity. With a verb denoting a mental state or emotion or similar, the aorist often signals the initiation of that emotion or mental state; e.g., ἐδάκρυε imperf. = he was weeping, but ἐδάκρυσε aorist = he burst into tears.

2   *μετατίθημι = place elsewhere, move
αἰδοῖα -ων τά = genitals

3   *τέως = up to that time

4   *τέττιξ -ιγος ὁ = cicada. Cicadas are winged insects, similar in appearance to grasshoppers (though unrelated), known in antiquity for their loud, resonant, high-pitched song omnipresent in hot weather and for their desiccated, bloodless appearance, which makes them appear to subsist on air. Although cicadas generally lay eggs in trees, newborn nymph cicadas burrow into the ground and emerge only when they are close to adulthood, which gives rise to the misunderstanding here. Plato associates them elsewhere with song (see esp. *Phaedrus* 259b–d).

5   μετατίθημι = place elsewhere, move
αὐτῶν εἰς τὸ πρόσθεν: the echo of line 2 allows the reader to understand the missing words τὰ αἰδοῖα

7   τῶνδε ἕνεκα: anticipates everything that follows
συμπλοκή -ῆς ἡ = weaving together, embrace
ἵνα: what kind of clause does this introduce (*Essentials* §159b)?

8–9   ἅμα μὲν . . . ἅμα δέ . . . = at one and the same time both . . . and; both . . . and at the same time . . .

8–11   ἐντύχοι . . . γεννῷεν . . . γίγνοιτο: explain the optatives in this line and continuing to ἐπιμελοῖντο in line 11. Hint: see note on line 7 (*Essentials* §159b).

8   γεννῷεν: the subject must be "they" (the man and the woman)
γίγνοιτο: τὸ γένος (line 9) is the subject. The optative has present aspect, which suggests ongoing generation rather than an individual occurrence (i.e., "might continue to be born or arise").

9   πλησμονή -ῆς ἡ = satisfaction, fullness

10   διαπαύομαι = have some rest, get a break, get a respite

καὶ τοῦ ἄλλου βίου ἐπιμελοῖντο. ἔστι δὴ οὖν ἐκ τόσου   11

ὁ ἔρως ἔμφυτος ἀλλήλων τοῖς ἀνθρώποις καὶ τῆς ἀρχαίας   12   191d

φύσεως συναγωγεὺς καὶ ἐπιχειρῶν ποιῆσαι ἓν ἐκ δυοῖν καὶ   13

ἰάσασθαι τὴν φύσιν τὴν ἀνθρωπίνην.   14

Each of us seeks our other half, someone of the opposite sex if descended from an androgyne, someone of the same sex if descended from an all-male or all-female sphere.

                                          Ἕκαστος οὖν ἡμῶν   15

ἐστιν ἀνθρώπου σύμβολον, ἅτε τετμημένος ὥσπερ αἱ ψῆτται,   16

ἐξ ἑνὸς δύο· ζητεῖ δὴ ἀεὶ τὸ αὑτοῦ ἕκαστος σύμβολον.   17

ὅσοι μὲν οὖν τῶν ἀνδρῶν τοῦ κοινοῦ τμῆμά εἰσιν, ὃ δὴ   18

τότε ἀνδρόγυνον ἐκαλεῖτο, φιλογύναικές τέ εἰσι καὶ οἱ   19

πολλοὶ τῶν μοιχῶν ἐκ τούτου τοῦ γένους γεγόνασιν, καὶ   20

ὅσαι αὖ γυναῖκες φίλανδροί τε καὶ μοιχεύτριαι ἐκ τούτου   21   191e

τοῦ γένους γίγνονται. ὅσαι δὲ τῶν γυναικῶν γυναικὸς   22

τμῆμά εἰσιν, οὐ πάνυ αὗται τοῖς ἀνδράσι τὸν νοῦν προσέχουσιν,   23

---

11   ἐκ τόσου: the so-great thing meant here is the great division that occurred in our past

12   ἔμφυτος -ον = innate, inborn; pred. adj.

    ἀλλήλων: despite its position, the word is dependent on ὁ ἔρως

13   συναγωγεύς -έως ὁ = one who brings together, unifier, unifying force

    ἐπιχειρῶν: pred., parallel to ἔμφυτος and συναγωγεύς. Treat like a substantive participle (*Essentials* §169).

16   σύμβολον -ου τό: hard to translate into English; a symbolon is one piece of an object (typically a bone or a die) that two ξένοι, or any two contracting parties, broke, each person keeping one piece in order to have proof of the identity of the one presenting the other (cf. συμβάλλω and English "symbol"). Could be translated "symbolon" or "other half." "Significant other" loosely captures some of the word's significance here.

    ψῆττα -ης ἡ = flatfish. *Lysistrata* 115 also associates flatfish with cutting in two in a context that suggests it may have a sexual connotation, but the precise relevance eludes us. Perhaps it is just a familiar image.

17   σύμβολον completes τὸ αὑτοῦ

18   τῶν ἀνδρῶν: partitive with ὅσοι

    τοῦ κοινοῦ: depends on τμῆμα. The relative clause that follow offers clarification of what is meant by τοῦ κοινοῦ.

20   μοιχός -οῦ ὁ = adulterer, man who has sex with another man's woman

21   μοιχεύτρια -ας ἡ: a word apparently manufactured by Plato; by analogy with μοιχός, presumably referring to a woman who has sex with men outside of marriage

22–23 ὅσαι . . . εἰσιν: compare to the structure of ὅσοι . . . εἰσιν in line 18 ἀλλὰ μᾶλλον πρὸς τὰς γυναῖκας τετραμμέναι   24

εἰσί, καὶ αἱ ἑταιρίστριαι ἐκ τούτου τοῦ γένους γίγνονται.   25

ὅσοι δὲ ἄρρενος τμῆμά εἰσι, τὰ ἄρρενα διώκουσι, καὶ τέως   26

μὲν ἂν παῖδες ὦσιν, ἅτε τεμάχια ὄντα τοῦ ἄρρενος, φιλοῦσι   27

τοὺς ἄνδρας καὶ χαίρουσι συγκατακείμενοι καὶ συμπεπλεγμένοι   28

τοῖς ἀνδράσι, καὶ εἰσιν οὗτοι βέλτιστοι τῶν παίδων   29   192a

καὶ μειρακίων, ἅτε ἀνδρειότατοι ὄντες φύσει.   30

  Φασὶ δὲ δή τινες αὐτοὺς ἀναισχύντους εἶναι, ψευδόμενοι·   31

οὐ γὰρ ὑπ' ἀναισχυντίας τοῦτο δρῶσιν ἀλλ' ὑπὸ θάρρους καὶ ἀνδρείας   32

καὶ ἀρρενωπίας, τὸ ὅμοιον αὑτοῖς ἀσπαζόμενοι. μέγα δὲ   33

τεκμήριον· καὶ γὰρ τελεωθέντες μόνοι ἀποβαίνουσιν εἰς   34

τὰ πολιτικὰ ἄνδρες οἱ τοιοῦτοι. ἐπειδὰν δὲ ἀνδρωθῶσι,   35

παιδεραστοῦσι καὶ πρὸς γάμους καὶ παιδοποιίας οὐ προσέχουσι   36   192b

τὸν νοῦν φύσει, ἀλλ' ὑπὸ τοῦ νόμου ἀναγκάζονται·   37

ἀλλ' ἐξαρκεῖ αὐτοῖς μετ' ἀλλήλων καταζῆν ἀγάμοις. πάντως   38

μὲν οὖν ὁ τοιοῦτος παιδεραστής τε καὶ φιλεραστὴς γίγνεται,   39

ἀεὶ τὸ συγγενὲς ἀσπαζόμενος. ὅταν μὲν οὖν καὶ αὐτῷ   40

---

24   τετραμμένοι εἰσί from τρέπω = have turned themselves; i.e., are inclined

25   ἑταιρίστρια -ας ἡ: "lesbian" seems to be the implication of the word here, but there is scholarly
        debate over the meaning, which seems to have some of the implications of *hetaera* or courtesan

26   τέως = ἕως

27   τεμάχιον -ου τό = slice

28   συγκατακεῖμαι = συν + κατα + κεῖμαι
        συμπεπλεγμένοι: from συμπλέκομαι (takes dat. obj.)

31   ἀναίσχυντος -ον = shameless

32   ἀναισχυντία -ας ἡ = lack of shame, shamelessness

33   ἀρρενωπία -ας ἡ = masculinity (cf. ἄρρην)

34   τελεωθέντες = upon being completed (i.e., upon coming of age), from τελεόω = make perfect,
        complete

35   ἀνδρόω = rear to manhood, make a man; *pass.* = become a man, be made a man

36   παιδεραστέω = παίδων ἐράω
        παιδοποιία -ας ἡ = making children, having children

38   καταζάω = live one's life out
        ἄγαμος -ον = unmarried, unwed

40   *συγγενής -ές = akin, related, from the same stock

ἐκείνῳ ἐντύχῃ τῷ αὐτοῦ ἡμίσει καὶ ὁ παιδεραστὴς καὶ　　41

ἄλλος πᾶς, τότε καὶ θαυμαστὰ ἐκπλήττονται φιλίᾳ τε καὶ　　42

οἰκειότητι καὶ ἔρωτι, οὐκ ἐθέλοντες ὡς ἔπος εἰπεῖν χωρίζεσθαι　　43　　192c

ἀλλήλων οὐδὲ σμικρὸν χρόνον. καὶ οἱ διατελοῦντες　　44

μετ' ἀλλήλων διὰ βίου οὗτοί εἰσιν, οἳ οὐδ' ἂν ἔχοιεν εἰπεῖν　　45

ὅτι βούλονται σφίσι παρ' ἀλλήλων γίγνεσθαι. οὐδενὶ　　46

γὰρ ἂν δόξειεν τοῦτ' εἶναι ἡ τῶν ἀφροδισίων συνουσία, ὡς　　47

ἄρα τούτου ἕνεκα ἕτερος ἑτέρῳ χαίρει συνὼν οὕτως ἐπὶ　　48

μεγάλης σπουδῆς· ἀλλ' ἄλλο τι βουλομένη ἑκατέρου ἡ ψυχὴ　　49

δήλη ἐστίν, ὃ οὐ δύναται εἰπεῖν, ἀλλὰ μαντεύεται ὃ βούλεται,　　50　　192d

καὶ αἰνίττεται.　　51

42　θαυμαστά: adverbial acc. (cf. πολύ, μέγα, and πολλά)

43　οἰκειότης -τητος ἡ = family relationship, close relationship, kinship
　　χωρίζομαι + *gen.* = be apart from, be separate from (cf. χωρίς)

44　*διατελέω = bring to an end, carry through, continue

45　ἔχω: what does ἔχω + infinitive mean? Hint: it's not "have to —."

46　σφίσι: dat. of possession. σφεῖς is a third person plural personal pronoun, but it is used rarely in
　　Attic prose, where the demonstratives οὗτος and ἐκεῖνος and the oblique cases (all but nom.)
　　of αὐτός are far more commonly used. σφεῖς is used in poetry and in non-Attic prose.

47　τοῦτ': refers back to what precedes, i.e., the thing that everyone is longing for from one another
　　ἀφροδισία -ων τά = sex

47–48　ὡς ἄρα = as if

48　τούτου: refers back to ἡ τῶν ἀφροδισίων συνουσία; highly emphatic and somewhat
　　disparaging!

48–49　ἐπὶ μεγάλης σπουδῆς = with great eagerness

51　αἰνίττομαι = speak in a riddling or enigmatic way

Reading 6D

Aristophanes finishes his speech.

Vocabulary

ἀδικία -ας ἡ: injustice, wrongdoing, crime (cf. ἀδικέω)

αἴτιον -ου τό = αἰτία -ας ἡ

ἐγγύς *adv.*: nearby, near; *prep.* + *gen.*: near *gen.*

εὐσέβεια -ας ἡ: piety, reverence toward the gods

εὐσεβέω: be pious, act piously and reverently

ἡγεμών -όνος ὁ: leader (cf. ἡγέομαι and English "hegemony")

κωμῳδέω: represent in a comedy, make into a comedy, satirize, lampoon; *recognize also* κωμῳδία -ας ἡ: comedy

μακάριος -α -ον: blessed (cf. μάκαρ); *particularly frequent in vocative as a form of gently mocking address:* μακάριε, *when it is commonly translated "my friend."* (Rowe 1998: 107, 115 translates "my fine friend," which may capture better the mocking tone and preserve some of the original sense of the word.)

οἰκεῖος -α -ον: related, domestic, one's own

ὄργανον -ου τό: instrument, tool (cf. English "organ")

παρακελεύομαι: order, exhort, urge (cf. κελεύω)

ὑμνέω ὑμνήσω ὕμνησα ὕμνηκα ὕμνημαι ὑμνήθην: sing (of), hymn, laud; *recognize also* ὕμνος -ου ὁ: song, hymn

Fig. 19. The grave stele of an Athenian athlete named Glaukotas (Blue-ears), shows a young man in relief as though "cut through the nose," ca. 470–460 B.C.E. Inv. 2003.4.1. Courtesy of the Michael C. Carlos Museum of Emory University, Atlanta. Photo by Bruce M. White, 2004.

Reading 6D (*Symposium* 192d3–193e1)

Καὶ εἰ αὐτοῖς ἐν τῷ αὐτῷ κατακειμένοις   1

ἐπιστὰς ὁ Ἥφαιστος, ἔχων τὰ ὄργανα, ἔροιτο· "Τί   2

ἔσθ' ὃ βούλεσθε, ὦ ἄνθρωποι, ὑμῖν παρ' ἀλλήλων γενέσθαι;"   3

καὶ εἰ ἀποροῦντας αὐτοὺς πάλιν ἔροιτο· "Ἆρά γε   4

τοῦδε ἐπιθυμεῖτε, ἐν τῷ αὐτῷ γενέσθαι ὅτι μάλιστα ἀλλήλοις,   5

ὥστε καὶ νύκτα καὶ ἡμέραν μὴ ἀπολείπεσθαι ἀλλήλων;   6

εἰ γὰρ τούτου ἐπιθυμεῖτε, θέλω ὑμᾶς συντῆξαι καὶ   7

συμφυσῆσαι εἰς τὸ αὐτό, ὥστε δύ' ὄντας ἕνα γεγονέναι   8   192e

καὶ ἕως τ' ἂν ζῆτε, ὡς ἕνα ὄντα, κοινῇ ἀμφοτέρους ζῆν,   9

καὶ ἐπειδὰν ἀποθάνητε, ἐκεῖ αὖ ἐν Ἅιδου ἀντὶ δυοῖν ἕνα   10

εἶναι κοινῇ τεθνεῶτε· ἀλλ' ὁρᾶτε εἰ τούτου ἐρᾶτε καὶ   11

ἐξαρκεῖ ὑμῖν ἂν τούτου τύχητε·" ταῦτ' ἀκούσας ἴσμεν ὅτι   12

οὐδ' ἂν εἷς ἐξαρνηθείη οὐδ' ἄλλο τι ἂν φανείη βουλόμενος,   13

ἀλλ' ἀτεχνῶς οἴοιτ' ἂν ἀκηκοέναι τοῦτο ὃ πάλαι ἄρα ἐπεθύμει,   14

συνελθὼν καὶ συντακεὶς τῷ ἐρωμένῳ ἐκ δυοῖν εἷς   15

---

1   ἐν τῷ αὐτῷ: supply τόπῳ

2   ἐπιστάς from *ἐφίσταμαι = stand next to *dat.*
     Ἥφαιστος -ου ὁ = Hephaistos (Latin Hephaestus), god of fire and metalworking

5   ἐν τῷ αὐτῷ: see note on line 1
     ὅτι μάλιστα: ὅτι + superl. = ὡς + superl. (*Essentials* §198)

6   ἀπολείπεσθαι: inf. in a natural result clause (*Essentials* §185)

7   συντήκω = melt together, fuse together, weld together

8   συμφυσάω = blow together, conflate

8–11 γεγονέναι ... ζῆν ... εἶναι: why infinitives here (*Essentials* §185)?

11   τεθνεῶτε: dual part. acc. of θνῄσκω. The perfect means "having died," i.e., "dead."

12   ἄν ... τύχητε: what form is τύχητε, and what does this indicate about ἄν (*Essentials* §160)? See
     also note on ἄν at reading 6A.17.

13   ἐξαρνέομαι = deny (pass. deponent)
     φανείη βουλόμενος: φαίνομαι + *part.* = show oneself to ——, be openly ——ing (as opposed to
        φαίνομαι + *inf.* = appear to —— (but not really)

14   *ἀτεχνῶς *adv.* = simply

15   συντακείς: from συντήκω = melt together, fuse together, weld together. Infer the form from
     the ending.

γενέσθαι. τοῦτο γὰρ ἐστι τὸ αἴτιον, ὅτι ἡ ἀρχαία φύσις   16

ἡμῶν ἦν αὕτη καὶ ἦμεν ὅλοι· τοῦ ὅλου οὖν τῇ ἐπιθυμίᾳ   17

καὶ διώξει ἔρως ὄνομα. καὶ πρὸ τοῦ, ὥσπερ λέγω, ἓν   18   193a

ἦμεν, νυνὶ δὲ διὰ τὴν ἀδικίαν διῳκίσθημεν ὑπὸ τοῦ θεοῦ,   19

καθάπερ Ἀρκάδες ὑπὸ Λακεδαιμονίων· φόβος οὖν ἔστιν,   20

ἐὰν μὴ κόσμιοι ὦμεν πρὸς τοὺς θεούς, ὅπως μὴ καὶ αὖθις   21

διασχισθησόμεθα, καὶ περίιμεν ἔχοντες ὥσπερ οἱ ἐν ταῖς   22

στήλαις καταγραφὴν ἐκτετυπωμένοι, διαπεπρισμένοι κατὰ   23

τὰς ῥῖνας, γεγονότες ὥσπερ λίσπαι. ἀλλὰ τούτων ἕνεκα   24

πάντ' ἄνδρα χρὴ ἅπαντα παρακελεύεσθαι εὐσεβεῖν περὶ   25

θεούς, ἵνα τὰ μὲν ἐκφύγωμεν, τῶν δὲ τύχωμεν, ὡς ὁ Ἔρως   26   193b

---

16   τοῦτο is the predicate here; the ὅτι-clause explains what is meant by τοῦτο

18   διώξει: not a form of the verb διώκω but of the noun διώξις -εως ἡ = pursuit. It is a dative of
      reference = for the pursuit. The verb can be inferred (*Essentials* §73).

19   διοικίζω = make to live apart, disperse

20   Ἀρκάδες οἱ = Arcadians. In 385 B.C.E. the Spartans destroyed the city wall of Mantinea, a major
      Arcadian city-state and forced its population into four separate settlements. Most scholars take
      this line as an anachronistic reference to this event, perhaps introduced in anticipation of the
      appearance of the priestess, Diotima of Mantinea, later in the dialogue. Mattingly 1958 argues
      that the reference may actually be to a less well-known event in 416, one at which Aristophanes
      himself may have been present. Rowe 1998: 159 suggests a double resonance: one that is anach-
      ronistic and familiar, one less familiar but appropriate to the historical context.

21   ὅπως μή = μή (fear clause). ὅπως μή + fut. indic. is sometimes used instead of μή + subju. to
      express a fear for the future (Smyth 1956: §2231).

22   διασχίζω = cleave asunder, split apart
      ἔχοντες ὥσπερ: review meaning of ἔχω + adv., if necessary

23   *στήλη -ης ἡ = stele, post, block, slab
      καταγραφήν (adverbial) (from καταγραφή -ῆς ἡ) = in profile
      ἐκτυπόω = carve out in relief
      διαπρίω = saw through
      Plato here draws on an image familiar to this Greek audience, a human profile in relief on a
      funerary stele (fig. 19).

24   λίσπη -ης ἡ = die cut in half by two friends, each of whom kept one as a tally

26   τὰ μὲν ... τῶν δέ: what does it mean when the particles μὲν ... δέ are each preceded by a
      definite article (*Essentials* §190)?
      ὡς: translate as ὡς + indic. (*Essentials* §192)

ἡμῖν ἡγεμὼν καὶ στρατηγός. ᾧ μηδεὶς ἐναντία πραττέτω—   27

πράττει δ' ἐναντία ὅστις θεοῖς ἀπεχθάνεται—φίλοι γὰρ   28

γενόμενοι καὶ διαλλαγέντες τῷ θεῷ ἐξευρήσομέν τε καὶ   29

ἐντευξόμεθα τοῖς παιδικοῖς τοῖς ἡμετέροις αὐτῶν, ὃ τῶν νῦν   30

ὀλίγοι ποιοῦσι. Καὶ μή μοι ὑπολάβῃ Ἐρυξίμαχος, κωμῳδῶν   31

τὸν λόγον, ὡς Παυσανίαν καὶ Ἀγάθωνα λέγω—ἴσως μὲν   32

γὰρ καὶ οὗτοι τούτων τυγχάνουσιν ὄντες καὶ εἰσιν ἀμφότεροι   33   193c

τὴν φύσιν ἄρρενες—λέγω δὲ οὖν ἔγωγε καθ' ἁπάντων καὶ   34

ἀνδρῶν καὶ γυναικῶν, ὅτι οὕτως ἂν ἡμῶν τὸ γένος εὔδαιμον   35

γένοιτο, εἰ ἐκτελέσαιμεν τὸν ἔρωτα καὶ τῶν παιδικῶν τῶν   36

αὑτοῦ ἕκαστος τύχοι εἰς τὴν ἀρχαίαν ἀπελθὼν φύσιν. εἰ   37

δὲ τοῦτο ἄριστον, ἀναγκαῖον καὶ τῶν νῦν παρόντων τὸ   38

---

27   ᾧ = τούτῳ (referring to Eros in the previous sentence). The relative pronoun is frequently used as the first word of a sentence in place of a demonstrative pronoun.

28   *ἀπεχθάνομαι = is or becomes hateful to *dat.*

29   διαλλάττομαι = become reconciled to (pass. deponent)

30   ἡμετέροις αὐτῶν = our own. The genitive αὐτῶν reflects the idea of possession present in the possessive adjective ἡμετέροις, so that though they do not agree in case, they are taken together, a common way of expressing the reflexive for the personal pronoun.

   τῶν νῦν: partitive gen. with ὀλίγοι. The definite article can be followed by an adverb or a prepositional phrase to make a substantive (*Essentials* §189).

31   μὴ ... ὑπολάβῃ: what use of the subjunctive is this (*Essentials* §149)?

   μοι: ethical dat. (*Essentials* §113)

   *ὑπολαμβάνω = undercut, diminish

32   ὡς: introducing an implied indirect statement; supply λέγων before

   λέγω = I mean (as often)

33   τούτων = among these; partitive, refers to the ὀλίγοι who have attained their beloveds

34   τὴν φύσιν: acc. of respect (*Essentials* §82)

   ἄρρενες: descended from the all-male sphere; it may also be slightly humorous, given the characterization of Agathon in the *Thesmophoriazusae* as very effeminate

34   δὲ οὖν = even so (Rose 1985: 35 suggests "however true that may be")

   καθ' = κατά = concerning

36   ἐκτελέω = bring to an end, fulfill, accomplish, achieve (strengthened version of *τελέω)

37   ἀπέρχομαι = go back, revert

38   τῶν νῦν παρόντων = of the things now available (partitive gen. with superl.)

τούτου ἐγγυτάτω ἄριστον εἶναι· τοῦτο δ' ἐστὶ παιδικῶν τυχεῖν   39

κατὰ νοῦν αὐτῷ πεφυκότων· οὗ δὴ τὸν αἴτιον θεὸν ὑμνοῦντες   40

δικαίως ἂν ὑμνοῖμεν Ἔρωτα, ὃς ἔν τε τῷ παρόντι ἡμᾶς   41   193d

πλεῖστα ὀνίνησιν εἰς τὸ οἰκεῖον ἄγων, καὶ εἰς τὸ ἔπειτα   42

ἐλπίδας μεγίστας παρέχεται, ἡμῶν παρεχομένων πρὸς θεοὺς   43

εὐσέβειαν, καταστήσας ἡμᾶς εἰς τὴν ἀρχαίαν φύσιν καὶ   44

ἰασάμενος μακαρίους καὶ εὐδαίμονας ποιῆσαι."   45

  "Οὗτος," ἔφη, "ὦ Ἐρυξίμαχε, ὁ ἐμὸς λόγος ἐστὶ περὶ   46

Ἔρωτος, ἀλλοῖος ἢ ὁ σός. ὥσπερ οὖν ἐδεήθην σου, μὴ   47

κωμῳδήσῃς αὐτόν, ἵνα καὶ τῶν λοιπῶν ἀκούσωμεν τί ἕκαστος   48

ἐρεῖ, μᾶλλον δὲ τί ἑκάτερος· Ἀγάθων γὰρ καὶ Σωκράτης   49   193e

λοιποί."   50

---

39   ἐγγυτάτω: superl. adv. of ἐγγύς = nearest to *gen.*

40   κατὰ νοῦν αὐτῷ = with a mind attuned to him; i.e., most mentally attuned to him, most
        congenial with him

      οὗ = τούτου *neut.*: refers to the best thing described in the previous sentence and depends on the
        adjective αἴτιον

42   *ὀνίνημι ὀνήσω ὤνησα = profit, benefit, help, gratify
      εἰς τὸ ἔπειτα = for the future

45   ποιῆσαι: infinitive in indirect statement after ἐλπίδας μεγίστας παρέχεται, similar to a verb
        of promising

47–48   μὴ κωμῳδήσῃς: what use of the subjunctive is this (see note on line 31)?

49   ἑκάτερος: different from ἕκαστος only in that it always refers to two

Reading 6E

The transition between the speeches of the comic poet Aristophanes and of the tragic poet Agathon.

Vocabulary

ἀγνοέω ἀγνοήσω ἠγνόησα ἠγνόηκα ἠγνόημαι ἠγνοήθην: be ignorant of, not know
ἄφρων -ον: mindless, senseless; *recognize also the opposite* ἔμφρων -ον: sensible, thoughtful, prudent
ἐντυγχάνω: light upon, encounter, meet with *dat.*
θαρρέω: be bold, confident
θέατρον -ου τό: theater
θορυβέω: stir up, disturb, throw into confusion; make a noise or uproar, cheer
κωλύω κωλύσω ἐκώλυσα κεκώλυκα κεκώλυμαι ἐκωλύθην: prevent, hinder
παντοδαπός -ή -όν: of all kinds, of all varieties

Reading 6E (*Symposium* 193e2–194e2)

"Ἀλλὰ πείσομαί σοι," ἔφη φάναι τὸν Ἐρυξίμαχον· "καὶ	1
γάρ μοι ὁ λόγος ἡδέως ἐρρήθη. καὶ εἰ μὴ συνήδη Σωκράτει	2
τε καὶ Ἀγάθωνι δεινοῖς οὖσι περὶ τὰ ἐρωτικά, πάνυ	3
ἂν ἐφοβούμην μὴ ἀπορήσωσι λόγων διὰ τὸ πολλὰ καὶ	4
παντοδαπὰ εἰρῆσθαι· νῦν δὲ ὅμως θαρρῶ."	5
Τὸν οὖν Σωκράτη εἰπεῖν, "Καλῶς γὰρ αὐτὸς ἠγώνισαι,	6 194a
ὦ Ἐρυξίμαχε· εἰ δὲ γένοιο οὗ νῦν ἐγώ εἰμι, μᾶλλον δὲ	7
ἴσως οὗ ἔσομαι ἐπειδὰν καὶ Ἀγάθων εἴπῃ εὖ, καὶ μάλ᾽ ἂν	8
φοβοῖο καὶ ἐν παντὶ εἴης ὥσπερ ἐγὼ νῦν."	9
"Φαρμάττειν βούλει με, ὦ Σώκρατες," εἰπεῖν τὸν Ἀγάθωνα,	10

1–2   καὶ γάρ: offers an explanation of πείσομαι

       μοι: take with ἡδέως = in a manner pleasing to me. Plato's dialogues frequently criticize the way that words seduce and persuade the listener through pleasure alone.

2   συνήδη: from σύνοιδα. What is the form (*Essentials* §65)? Identify the type of condition completed by ἂν ἐφοβούμην in line 4 (*Essentials* §162).

       σύνοιδα + *dat.* + *part. in indir. statement* = share with *dat.* in the knowledge that. . . . The datives Σωκράτει and Ἀγάθωνι serve both as the persons sharing in the knowledge and as the subjects of the indirect statement with the participle οὖσι.

4   ἀπορήσωσι: identify the form and usage (*Essentials* §154). The type of condition (see note on line 2) explains why we are in primary sequence.

       ἀπορέω + *gen.* = be at a loss for *gen.*

5   εἰρῆσθαι: what use of the infinitive is this? Hint: it goes with τό in the previous line (*Essentials* §182).

6   ἀγωνίζομαι = take part in a contest, contend

7   οὗ = where (here and in the next line, as often)

7–8   μᾶλλον δὲ ἴσως: the equivalent of "or rather perhaps I should say" or similar. δέ makes it clear that this is not the apodosis, but a revised version of the previous clause.

8   καί with Ἀγάθων: not connective here

9   ἐν παντί = in extremity, in complete panic (idiomatic)

10   φαρμάττω = enchant, cast a spell on

"ἵνα θορυβηθῶ διὰ τὸ οἴεσθαι τὸ θέατρον προσδοκίαν μεγάλην   11
ἔχειν ὡς εὖ ἐροῦντος ἐμοῦ."   12

   "'Επιλήσμων μεντἂν εἴην, ὦ Ἀγάθων," εἰπεῖν τὸν   13
Σωκράτη, "εἰ ἰδὼν τὴν σὴν ἀνδρείαν καὶ μεγαλοφροσύνην   14   194b
ἀναβαίνοντος ἐπὶ τὸν ὀκρίβαντα μετὰ τῶν ὑποκριτῶν, καὶ   15
βλέψαντος ἐναντία τοσούτῳ θεάτρῳ, μέλλοντος ἐπιδείξεσθαι   16
σαυτοῦ λόγους, καὶ οὐδ' ὁπωστιοῦν ἐκπλαγέντος, νῦν   17
οἰηθείην σε θορυβήσεσθαι ἕνεκα ἡμῶν ὀλίγων ἀνθρώπων."   18

   "Τί δέ, ὦ Σώκρατες;" τὸν Ἀγάθωνα φάναι, "οὐ δήπου με   19
οὕτω θεάτρου μεστὸν ἡγῇ ὥστε καὶ ἀγνοεῖν ὅτι νοῦν ἔχοντι   20
ὀλίγοι ἔμφρονες πολλῶν ἀφρόνων φοβερώτεροι;"   21

---

11   τὸ θέατρον: Agathon suggests that his audience at the symposium is a theater audience
       προσδοκία -ας ἡ = expectation, anticipation
       ὡς εὖ ἐροῦντος ἐμοῦ: the genitives depend on προσδοκίαν; ὡς here, as is usual with the
           participle, distances the speaker (Agathon) from the thought and makes clear that the theater
           audience rather than Agathon himself holds high expectations for his performance. It may
           therefore introduce a note of modesty: "as if I were going to speak well" (Smyth 1956: §2086).
12   ἔχειν: inf. in indir. statement following οἴεσθαι (artic. inf.)
13   ἐπιλήσμων -ον = forgetful (cf. ἐπιλανθάνομαι)
       μεντἂν = μεντοι ἄν (crasis)
14   μεγαλοφροσύνη -ης ἡ = confidence
       ἀναβαίνοντος: the genitive participle modifies an understood σοῦ implied by the possessive
           adjective σήν, as do the other genitive participles in lines 16–17
15   ὀκρίβας -αντος ὁ = raised platform
       ὑποκριτής -οῦ ὁ = actor. Socrates appears to be referring to the proagon, an event that occurred
           the day before the tragic competitions when the playwright mounted a platform with his actors
           and gave a preview of coming attractions. In the year that Euripides died, Sophocles and his
           actors mounted the platform at the proagon in mourning, an effective tribute to his great rival.
           This practice is elsewhere attested only for the Greater Dionysia, not for the Lenaea (Sider 1980).
17   ὁπωστιοῦν = in anyway whatsoever
       ἐκπλαγέντος: aor. pass. part. of ἐκπλήττω
19   οὐ δήπου = surely not . . . ? Common as a way of introducing a question expecting a negative
           answer.
20   οὕτω θεάτρου μεστόν = so full of theater; i.e., so obsessed or focused on it
       νοῦν ἔχοντι = to a person who has sense (subst. part., but indef.; hence the absence of the def.
           art. expected with a subst. part.)
21   φοβερός -ά -όν = frightening

"Οὐ μεντἂν καλῶς ποιοίην," φάναι, "ὦ Ἀγάθων, περὶ σοῦ   22   194c

τι ἐγὼ ἄγροικον δοξάζων· ἀλλ' εὖ οἶδα ὅτι εἴ τισιν ἐντύχοις   23

οὓς ἡγοῖο σοφούς, μᾶλλον ἂν αὐτῶν φροντίζοις ἢ τῶν   24

πολλῶν. ἀλλὰ μὴ οὐχ οὗτοι ἡμεῖς ὦμεν—ἡμεῖς μὲν γὰρ   25

καὶ ἐκεῖ παρῆμεν καὶ ἦμεν τῶν πολλῶν—εἰ δὲ ἄλλοις   26

ἐντύχοις σοφοῖς, τάχ' ἂν αἰσχύνοιο αὐτούς, εἴ τι ἴσως   27

οἴοιο αἰσχρὸν ὂν ποιεῖν· ἢ πῶς λέγεις;"   28

"Ἀληθῆ λέγεις," φάναι.   29

"Τοὺς δὲ πολλοὺς οὐκ ἂν αἰσχύνοιο εἴ τι οἴοιο αἰσχρὸν   30

ποιεῖν;"   31

Καὶ τὸν Φαῖδρον ἔφη ὑπολαβόντα εἰπεῖν, "Ὦ φίλε   32   194d

Ἀγάθων, ἐὰν ἀποκρίνῃ Σωκράτει, οὐδὲν ἔτι διοίσει αὐτῷ   33

ὁπῃοῦν τῶν ἐνθάδε ὁτιοῦν γίγνεσθαι, ἐὰν μόνον ἔχῃ ὅτῳ   34

διαλέγηται, ἄλλως τε καὶ καλῷ. ἐγὼ δὲ ἡδέως μὲν ἀκούω   35

Σωκράτους διαλεγομένου, ἀναγκαῖον δέ μοι ἐπιμεληθῆναι   36

τοῦ ἐγκωμίου τῷ Ἔρωτι καὶ ἀποδέξασθαι παρ' ἑνὸς ἑκάστου   37

ὑμῶν τὸν λογον· ἀποδοὺς οὖν ἑκάτερος τῷ θεῷ οὕτως ἤδη   38

διαλεγέσθω."   39

---

23   ἄγροικος -ον = of the country, rustic; *hence* = crude, unsophisticated

     δοξάζω = think, imagine

24   φροντίζω + *gen.* = think of, be concerned about

25   μὴ οὐχ ... ὦμεν: subju. of cautious negation = I suspect we are not (*Essentials* §150)

26   ἐκεῖ παρῆμεν: he means at the theater yesterday when Agathon won

     τῶν πολλῶν: partitive gen.

32   ὑπολαμβάνω = take up (the argument)

33   *ἀποκρίνομαι = answer

     διοίσει: fut. of διαφέρει + *dat.* (impers.) = it makes a difference to *dat.*

34   ὁπῃοῦν = howsoever, in anyway whatsoever. The suffix -ουν strengthens indefinite words. See

     ὁτιοῦν below and ὁπωστιοῦν at line 17.

     τῶν ἐνθάδε ὁτιοῦν = any at all of the current matters

     ὅτῳ = ᾧτινι = someone with whom

37   ἀποδέχομαι = receive from, get from

"Ἀλλὰ καλῶς λέγεις, ὦ Φαῖδρε," φάναι τὸν Ἀγάθωνα,   40   194e

"καὶ οὐδέν με κωλύει λέγειν· Σωκράτει γὰρ καὶ αὖθις ἔσται   41

πολλάκις διαλέγεσθαι."   42

---

41   ἔσται: what is the form of this verb (*Essentials* §66)? What does this verb mean with an infinitive?

Reading 7. A Tragic Oration

Agathon is, of course, the host and honoree of the party, and his is the last of the speeches in praise of love. We can consequently expect his speech (readings 7A–C) to be the high point of this part of the dialogue. And it is certainly a rhetorical tour de force, as the response to it (readings 7C–D) suggests. Agathon is the first to raise the question of what an encomium should be and to focus his praise on the god himself rather than on what the god does for us. His characterization of Eros as young, handsome, soft, and supple both fits the characterization of Eros in lyric poetry and vase painting and mirrors the characteristics of Agathon himself. All of these speeches reflect their authors in certain ways, but the characterization of Eros as like Agathon is particularly important in that it will soon be directly contradicted by ideas advanced by Diotima, suggesting that Eros is in fact more like the tough, shoeless, homely Socrates than like the soft and handsome Agathon.

Agathon attributes (reading 7B) to Eros all four of the cardinal virtues—justice (δικαιοσύνη), temperance or moderation (σωφροσύνη), courage (ἀνδρεία), and wisdom (σοφία)—in a masterpiece of clever sophistical reasoning that shows the unexpected and paradoxical to be in fact true (e.g., love, which is not generally considered to foster intelligent and rational choices, is actually wise; love, resistance to which is normally seen as a kind of temperance, is actually temperate). Agathon provides a sustained discussion of love's virtue, twisting the evidence in striking ways to persuade his audience that the traditionally naughty god has it in abundance. The final part of his speech, the peroration (reading 7C.1–22), is highly polished and stylized and provides a wonderful example of a distinctive prose style for students beginning to think about Greek style. As Socrates comments (reading 7C.40–44), it is an outstanding example of the rhetorical style perfected by Gorgias of Leontini, one of the foremost sophists and rhetoricians of the time, with its balanced and carefully constructed antitheses, its short clauses, its love of paradox (e.g., Eros is more courageous than Ares, god of war) and of oxymoron (e.g., Eros is simultaneously fond of giving—φιλόδωρος—and stingy—ἄδωρος).

Since Agathon, a tragedian, directly follows Aristophanes, the foremost comic poet of Greece, we might expect his contribution to contend with that memorable comic myth on the tragic front, but Agathon's speech with its consistently cheerful and optimistic tone and its playful paradoxes is far from our modern conception of tragic. In a perhaps deliberate paradox, the comic poet's speech seems more tragic with its history of human suffering (πάθημα) and its picture of longing and constant need. But our modern perception perhaps fails to take account of the breadth of what was considered tragedy in antiquity and in particular of the developments introduced by

Fig. 20. Tragic mask with leaves and fruit. Detail of a Roman mosaic from the House of the Faun, Pompeii. Photo: Fotografica Foglia. Museo Archeologico Nazionale, Naples, Italy. Photo credit: Scala/Art Resource, New York.

some of its later practitioners, such as Euripides, a close associate of Agathon's, who wrote many tragedies that are not "tragic" by modern conceptions (e.g., *Helen, Iphigeneia among the Taurians*). Tragedy has in Agathon's time perhaps become as much a matter of style as of content. One defining feature of Greek tragedy identified by Aristotle is that it depicts worthwhile (σπουδαίους) rather than worthless (φαύλους) characters, or, as he puts it in a slightly different formulation, comedy imitates people who are worse (χείρους) than our contemporaries, tragedy people who are better (βελτίους) (*Poetics* 1448a). Agathon's Eros, who is entirely admirable and virtuous, certainly fits Aristotle's criterion for a tragic character. Moreover, it is clear that Gorgias was interested in tragedy and influenced it. Euripides' tragedies, *Helen* in particular, produced in 412 B.C.E., not too far distant in time from the *Symposium*'s setting, show clear traces of Gorgianic influence in their style and content, so that Agathon, in adhering close to Gorgias, is probably more representative of contemporary tragedy than we may immediately recognize.

When Socrates pointedly says in his response (reading 7D.1–28) that his oration will not be artful like Agathon's but rather truthful unlike all of those that preceded, this diminishes Agathon's achievement, and modern readers have overall been less impressed by Agathon's speech than was his audience at the symposium, who were brought up in a culture more appreciative of oratory as performance.

Reading 7A

Agathon begins his oration by explaining that it is necessary to describe the individual being praised: Eros is young, soft, fluid, and blooming, apparently much like Agathon himself. Our primary narrator, Apollodorus, who is apparently a lover of Socrates to judge from his own description, has the quality of softness, adding further support to this association between love and softness. Also important is the explicit discussion of what a proper encomium should be: Agathon's criticism of earlier speeches for being too focused on the benefits of love to humans rather than on the god himself is perceptive. The correction of Phaedrus's claim that Eros is the oldest of the gods helps give an overall structure to this part of the dialogue. The two youngest members of the group, both *eromenoi*, both associated with different rhetoricians, Lysias and Gorgias respectively, speak first and last, creating a ring composition and a clear beginning and ending to this section.

Suggested Review

- principal parts of εὑρίσκω and φεύγω

  εὑρίσκω εὑρήσω ηὗρον/εὗρον ηὕρηκα/εὕρηκα ηὕρημαι ηὑρέθην = find, discover
  φεύγω φεύξομαι ἔφυγον πέφευγα = flee, take flight, run away

Vocabulary

ἁπαλός -ή -όν: soft to the touch, tender, gentle, delicate; *recognize also the noun* ἁπαλότης -ητος ἡ: softness, tenderness
γῆρας -ως τό: old age (cf. γέρων ὁ and English "gerontology"); the declension of this noun, a variant on the third declension sigma stem, is probably too unusual to be worth memorizing (*Essentials* §45)
διέρχομαι: go through, narrate, relate, describe, tell thoroughly
ἐπιδείκνυμι: exhibit, show, demonstrate
ἦθος -ους τό: habit, custom; *pl.*: character, temperament
θάττων θᾶττον: swifter, quicker (irreg. compar. of ταχύς)

θέμις θέμιτος ἡ: right, law (frequently with ἐστι implied or expressed + inf.: it is right, it is
   lawful to ——)
μαλακός/μαλθακός -ή -όν: soft, gentle, mild
μισέω: hate (cf. English "misanthrope" and "misogynist")
παρέχω: provide
σκληρός -ά -όν: hard, harsh, rough, tough (opposite of ἀπαλός and μαλακός/μαλθακός)
τοιόσδε τοιάδε τοιόνδε: such as this (following), such as this (here); of the kind described
   next; pl.: such as these (cf. οἷος, τοιοῦτος; τοιόσδε is to τοιοῦτος as ὅδε is to οὗτος)
φυγή -ῆς ἡ: flight (cf. φεύγω)

Reading 7A (*Symposium* 194e4–196b3)

Ἐγὼ δὲ δὴ βούλομαι πρῶτον μὲν εἰπεῖν ὡς χρή με εἰπεῖν,   1

ἔπειτα εἰπεῖν. δοκοῦσι γάρ μοι πάντες οἱ πρόσθεν εἰρηκότες   2

οὐ τὸν θεὸν ἐγκωμιάζειν ἀλλὰ τοὺς ἀνθρώπους εὐδαιμονίζειν   3

τῶν ἀγαθῶν ὧν ὁ θεὸς αὐτοῖς αἴτιος· ὁποῖος δέ τις αὐτὸς ὢν   4

ταῦτα ἐδωρήσατο, οὐδεὶς εἴρηκεν. εἷς δὲ τρόπος ὀρθὸς παντὸς   5   195a

ἐπαίνου περὶ παντός, λόγῳ διελθεῖν οἷος οἵων αἴτιος ὢν   6

τυγχάνει περὶ οὗ ἂν ὁ λόγος ᾖ. οὕτω δὴ τὸν Ἔρωτα καὶ   7

ἡμᾶς δίκαιον ἐπαινέσαι πρῶτον αὐτὸν οἷός ἐστιν, ἔπειτα   8

τὰς δόσεις. φημὶ οὖν ἐγὼ πάντων θεῶν εὐδαιμόνων ὄντων   9

Ἔρωτα, εἰ θέμις καὶ ἀνεμέσητον εἰπεῖν, εὐδαιμονέστατον   10

εἶναι αὐτῶν, κάλλιστον ὄντα καὶ ἄριστον. ἔστι δὲ κάλλιστος   11

ὢν τοιόσδε. πρῶτον μὲν νεώτατος θεῶν, ὦ Φαῖδρε. μέγα   12

δὲ τεκμήριον τῷ λόγῳ αὐτὸς παρέχεται, φεύγων φυγῇ τὸ   13   195b

---

1   ὡς = how (context suggests)

1–2   Note the threefold repetition of εἰπεῖν. The addition of ἔπειτα further enhances the sound-play.

3   εὐδαιμονίζω = call *acc.* fortunate for *gen. cause*; congratulate *acc.* for *gen.* Note the sound-play of
      ἐγκωμιάζειν and εὐδαιμονίζειν (same metrical shape, same ending, similar sounds), which
      underscores the antithesis in τὸν θεόν … τοὺς ἀνθρώπους.

5   *δωρέομαι = give, present as a gift (cf. δῶρον -ου τό)

6   *ἔπαινος -ου ὁ = praise, speech of praise
      διελθεῖν (from διέρχομαι) defines εἷς … τρόπος ὀρθός
      οἷος οἵων: probably easiest to translate if καί is inserted between these two words: "what sort
      [he] is" and "for what sort of things he happens to be responsible"

7   ἡμᾶς = for us (acc. in an impers. construction) (*Essentials* §85). The preceding καί does not
      connect ἡμᾶς and τὸν Ἔρωτα but should be translated "also, too" ("we too").
      δίκαιον: the neuter adjective creates an impersonal construction (supply ἐστί)

9   δόσις -εως ἡ = gift

10   ἀνεμέσητος -ον = not prone to incur nemesis (divine punishment); i.e., not offensive to the gods

12   Phaedrus said in the first speech that Eros was the oldest (reading 3A.3, 11).

13   φεύγων φυγῇ = fleeing in flight, a poetic phrase. Greek erotic poetry typically presents love and
      old age as incompatible (e.g., Mimnermus, frag. 1). Hence Eros hates and avoids old age.

γῆρας, ταχὺ ὂν δῆλον ὅτι· θᾶττον γοῦν τοῦ δέοντος ἡμῖν   14

προσέρχεται. ὃ δὴ πέφυκεν Ἔρως μισεῖν καὶ οὐδ' ἐντὸς   15

πολλοῦ πλησιάζειν. μετὰ δὲ νέων ἀεὶ σύνεστί τε καὶ ἔστιν·   16

ὁ γὰρ παλαιὸς λόγος εὖ ἔχει, ὡς ὅμοιον ὁμοίῳ ἀεὶ πελάζει.   17

ἐγὼ δὲ Φαίδρῳ πολλὰ ἄλλα ὁμολογῶν τοῦτο οὐχ ὁμολογῶ,   18

ὡς Ἔρως Κρόνου καὶ Ἰαπετοῦ ἀρχαιότερός ἐστιν, ἀλλά   19

φημι νεώτατον αὐτὸν εἶναι θεῶν καὶ ἀεὶ νέον, τὰ δὲ παλαιὰ   20   195c

πράγματα περὶ θεούς, ἃ Ἡσίοδος καὶ Παρμενίδης λέγουσιν,   21

Ἀνάγκῃ καὶ οὐκ Ἔρωτι γεγονέναι, εἰ ἐκεῖνοι ἀληθῆ ἔλεγον·   22

---

14   δῆλον ὅτι: used often as the equivalent of "obviously." The notion that old age is swift is of course far from obvious, given that the elderly are better known for their slow pace. Agathon is being paradoxical in a way that Gorgias would have appreciated. Agathon goes on to explain the paradox by noting the speed at which old age comes upon us.

      τοῦ δέοντος = than it ought (subst. neut. part. from δεῖ; gen. of comparison)

15   *πέφυκα: perf. of φύω with pres. meaning = be [by nature]; + inf. = be inclined [by nature] to —, is [naturally] inclined to —

15–16   ἐντὸς πολλοῦ = very close

16   πλησιάζω = be or come near, draw near

      τε καὶ ἔστιν: context allows the reader to supply the pred. adj. νέος

17   πελάζω = draw near *dat.* The line paraphrases *Odyssey* 17.218: ὡς αἰεὶ τὸν ὁμοῖον ἄγει θεὸς ὡς τὸν ὁμοῖον.

19   Κρόνος -ου ὁ and Ἰαπετός -οῦ ὁ = Kronos (father of Zeus) and Iapetos (father of Prometheus), both Titans and thus members of the generation of gods who ruled prior to the current Olympians

21   πράγματα = troubles (here). For what he means by this, see notes to line 23.

      Ἡσίοδος -ου ὁ = Hesiod, author of the *Theogony*, used earlier by Phaedrus (reading 3) as an authority for the antiquity of Eros

      Παρμενίδης -ους ὁ = Parmenides, a presocratic philosopher, also cited earlier by Phaedrus to support his case (though omitted from reading 3). A quotation from Parmenides is used by Phaedrus: πρώτιστον μὲν Ἔρωτα θεῶν μητίσατο πάντων. Parmenides was particularly known in antiquity for his logical arguments establishing that there is no change or birth or death, but he also included an account of "human opinions" (δόξας . . . βροτείας) from which this quotation is presumably drawn.

22   Ἀνάγκῃ and Ἔρωτι: dat. of means (personified) or dat. of agent with the perf. γεγονέναι. Ἀνάγκη, the personified goddess "Necessity," is found in a few early philosophical texts including that of Parmenides.

οὐ γὰρ ἂν ἐκτομαὶ οὐδὲ δεσμοὶ ἀλλήλων ἐγίγνοντο καὶ ἄλλα   23

πολλὰ καὶ βίαια, εἰ Ἔρως ἐν αὐτοῖς ἦν, ἀλλὰ φιλία καὶ   24

εἰρήνη, ὥσπερ νῦν, ἐξ οὗ Ἔρως τῶν θεῶν βασιλεύει.   25

νέος μὲν οὖν ἐστι, πρὸς δὲ τῷ νέῳ ἁπαλός· ποιητοῦ δ᾽ ἔστιν   26

ἐνδεὴς οἷος ἦν Ὅμηρος πρὸς τὸ ἐπιδεῖξαι θεοῦ ἁπαλότητα.   27   195d

Ὅμηρος γὰρ Ἄτην θεόν τέ φησιν εἶναι καὶ ἁπαλήν—τοὺς   28

γοῦν πόδας αὐτῆς ἁπαλοὺς εἶναι—λέγων   29

   τῆς μένθ᾽ ἁπαλοὶ πόδες· οὐ γὰρ ἐπ᾽ οὔδεος   30

   πίλναται, ἀλλ᾽ ἄρα ἥ γε κατ᾽ ἀνδρῶν κράατα βαίνει.   31

καλῷ οὖν δοκεῖ μοι τεκμηρίῳ τὴν ἁπαλότητα ἀποφαίνειν,   32

ὅτι οὐκ ἐπὶ σκληροῦ βαίνει, ἀλλ᾽ ἐπὶ μαλθακοῦ. τῷ αὐτῷ   33

δὴ καὶ ἡμεῖς χρησόμεθα τεκμηρίῳ περὶ Ἔρωτα ὅτι ἁπαλός.   34   195e

---

23   ἐκτομή -ῆς ἡ = castration (probably refers to the story of Kronos's castration of Ouranos, told in
    Hesiod's *Theogony*)

    δεσμός -οῦ ὁ = binding (probably refers to the story of Prometheus's binding by Zeus in punish-
    ment for the Titan's theft of fire from the gods, told in *Prometheus Bound*, or to similar stories)

24   βίαιος -α -ον = forceful, violent

25   ἐξ οὗ = from which (time), from when, since

26   πρὸς δὲ τῷ νέῳ: in addition to his youth

27   *ἐνδεής -ές = in need of *gen.*

28   Ἄτη -ης ἡ = Ate, goddess of ruin. Agathon refers to and quotes from *Iliad* 19.91–94, where
    Agamemnon describes the swift and stealthy way this goddess overtakes men's senses.

30–31   A quotation from Homer, *Iliad* 19.92–93, though the text here is slightly different from the standard
    Homeric text.

30   τῆς = αὐτῆς or ταύτης (Homer uses the def. art. as a demonst. pron.)

    μένθ᾽ = μέντοι

    οὖδας -εος τό = ground, earth

31   πίλναμαι = draw near, approach

    ἥ = she (see note on τῆς in line 30)

    κατ᾽ (here) = upon *acc.*

    κράατα -ων τά = heads (Homeric form)

32   καλῷ: with τεκμηρίῳ

33   ἐπὶ μαλθακοῦ: susceptibility to Ate is presumably the "softness" of the heads, or does the hair on
    our heads make them soft? As Agathon comments in lines 35–36, heads are not particularly soft!

οὐ γὰρ ἐπὶ γῆς βαίνει οὐδ' ἐπὶ κρανίων, ἅ ἐστιν οὐ πάνυ   35

μαλακά, ἀλλ' ἐν τοῖς μαλακωτάτοις τῶν ὄντων καὶ βαίνει   36

καὶ οἰκεῖ. ἐν γὰρ ἤθεσι καὶ ψυχαῖς θεῶν καὶ ἀνθρώπων τὴν   37

οἴκησιν ἵδρυται, καὶ οὐκ αὖ ἑξῆς ἐν πάσαις ταῖς ψυχαῖς, ἀλλ'   38

ᾗτινι ἂν σκληρὸν ἦθος ἐχούσῃ ἐντύχῃ, ἀπέρχεται, ᾗ δ' ἂν   39

μαλακόν, οἰκίζεται. ἁπτόμενον οὖν ἀεὶ καὶ ποσὶν καὶ πάντῃ   40

ἐν μαλακωτάτοις τῶν μαλακωτάτων, ἁπαλώτατον ἀνάγκη   41

εἶναι. νεώτατος μὲν δή ἐστι καὶ ἁπαλώτατος, πρὸς δὲ   42   196a

τούτοις ὑγρὸς τὸ εἶδος. οὐ γὰρ ἂν οἷός τ' ἦν πάντῃ   43

περιπτύσσεσθαι οὐδὲ διὰ πάσης ψυχῆς καὶ εἰσιὼν τὸ πρῶτον   44

λανθάνειν καὶ ἐξιών, εἰ σκληρὸς ἦν. συμμέτρου δὲ καὶ   45

ὑγρᾶς ἰδέας μέγα τεκμήριον ἡ εὐσχημοσύνη, ὃ δὴ διαφερόντως   46

ἐκ πάντων ὁμολογουμένως Ἔρως ἔχει· ἀσχημοσύνη   47

---

35   κρανία τά = κράατα -ων τά (line 31) (cf. English "cranium")

35–36 Agathon outdoes the great poet, as Eros outdoes Ate by going upon something softer.

37   οἴκησις -εως ἡ = dwelling, house, residence
      ἵδρυμαι (perf. of ἱδρύω) = has established, has built, resides
      ἑξῆς *adv.* = in order, one after another (i.e., systematically without discrimination)

39   ᾗτινι: antecedent is implied ψυχῆς (obj. of ἀπέρχεται)
      σκληρόν: people who are "hardhearted" don't fall in love, Agathon implies

39–40 ᾗ δ' ἂν μαλακόν: supply ἦθος ἐχούσῃ ἐντύχῃ from earlier in line 39

40   οἰκίζομαι = make one's home
      καὶ ποσὶν καὶ πάντῃ = both with his feet (like Ate in Homer's description) *and* in every other
      way (Agathon's Eros outdoes Homer's Ate!)

43–45 Agathon describes the way love seems to creep into the very soul and later to leave it without the
      individual experiencing love being able to see it coming or going.

43   ὑγρός -ά -όν: seems to mean something more like "fluid, supple, flowing" than wet

44   περιπτύσσω = enfold, enwrap; presumably describing the all-encompassing feeling of being
      in love

45   σύμμετρος -ον = accommodating, harmonious, symmetrical

46   ἰδέα -ας ἡ = form, appearance
      εὐσχημοσύνη -ης ἡ = elegance, graceful manner

46–47 διαφερόντως = surpassingly; ἐκ πάντων ὁμολογουμένως = by general agreement. But the
      adverbs are also opposites to one another, creating a deliberate paradox, characteristically
      Gorgianic. Eros is at once different from and in agreement with all.

47   ἀσχημοσύνη -ης ἡ = inelegance, lack of grace

γὰρ καὶ Ἔρωτι πρὸς ἀλλήλους ἀεὶ πόλεμος. χρόας δὲ   48

κάλλος ἡ κατ᾽ ἄνθη δίαιτα τοῦ θεοῦ σημαίνει· ἀνανθεῖ γὰρ   49

καὶ ἀπηνθηκότι καὶ σώματι καὶ ψυχῇ καὶ ἄλλῳ ὁτῳοῦν οὐκ   50   196b

ἐνίζει Ἔρως, οὗ δ᾽ ἂν εὐανθής τε καὶ εὐώδης τόπος ᾖ,   51

ἐνταῦθα δὲ καὶ ἵζει καὶ μένει.   52

47–48   ἀσχημοσύνῃ, Ἔρωτι: What use of the dative is this? (*Essentials* §107)

48   χρόας: from χρώς ὁ = skin, complexion (acc. of respect with κάλλος)

49   *κάλλος -ους τό = beauty

δίαιτα -ας ἡ = mode of life, existence

σημαίνω = signify, indicate

ἀνανθής -ές = without bloom

50   ἀπανθέω = cease to bloom, wither, fade

51   ἐνίζω = sit on/in/among *dat.*

εὐώδης -ες = sweet-smelling, fragrant

52   ἐνταῦθα δέ = here (as opposed to where there are no blooms). Like καί and οὐδέ, δέ can be used adverbially to provide emphasis rather than as a connective. Here it also underscores the contrast with the places Eros avoids.

ἵζω = sit

Reading 7B

Agathon explains how Eros has the four cardinal virtues: justice (δικαιοσύνη), temperance (σωφροσύνη), courage (ἀνδρεία), and wisdom (σοφία). In addition to being a masterpiece of clever reasoning, Agathon shows his commitment to his art through his frequent citations from poetry and his artful arrangements of words. For example, lines 3–4 contain a nice example of chiasmus in an a-b-b-a arrangement:[31]

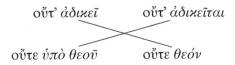

Suggested Reviews

- verbal adjectives in -τεος (*Essentials* §§125–27; also review exercise 5.b)
- declension of irregular comparative (*Essentials* §24, especially contracted forms in parentheses)

Vocabulary

βασιλεία -ας ἡ: kingdom, dominion, rule (cf. βασιλεύς ὁ)

βία -ας ἡ: force, strength (cf. βιάζομαι)

κάλλος -ους τό: beauty

κατασκευάζω κατασκευάσω κατεσκεύασα κατεσκεύακα κατεσκεύασμαι κατεσκευάσθην: prepare, equip or furnish fully, establish

κεφάλαιον -ου τό: gist, most important part; *note especially* the common expression ἐν κεφαλαίῳ: in sum

κρατέω κρατήσω ἐκράτησα κεκράτηκα κεκράτημαι ἐκρατήθην: rule *gen.*; control, have power over, be strong (cf. English "democracy" and "aristocracy")

ποίησις -εως ἡ: creation, making; poetry, the art of poetry (cf. ποιέω)

---

31. Chiasmus is so-called because when the words are written on separate lines, related items form the letter chi (χ).

Reading 7B (*Symposium* 196b4–197b9)

Περὶ μὲν οὖν κάλλους τοῦ θεοῦ καὶ ταῦτα ἱκανὰ καὶ ἔτι	1
πολλὰ λείπεται, περὶ δὲ ἀρετῆς Ἔρωτος μετὰ ταῦτα λεκτέον,	2
τὸ μὲν μέγιστον ὅτι Ἔρως οὔτ᾽ ἀδικεῖ οὔτ᾽ ἀδικεῖται οὔτε	3
ὑπὸ θεοῦ οὔτε θεόν, οὔτε ὑπ᾽ ἀνθρώπου οὔτε ἄνθρωπον. οὔτε	4
γὰρ αὐτὸς βίᾳ πάσχει, εἴ τι πάσχει—βίᾳ γὰρ Ἔρωτος οὐχ	5
ἅπτεται· οὔτε ποιῶν ποιεῖ—πᾶς γὰρ ἑκὼν Ἔρωτι πᾶν	6 196c
ὑπηρετεῖ, ἃ δ᾽ ἂν ἑκὼν ἑκόντι ὁμολογήσῃ, φασὶν "οἱ πόλεως	7
βασιλῆς νόμοι" δίκαια εἶναι. πρὸς δὲ τῇ δικαιοσύνῃ σωφροσύνης	8
πλείστης μετέχει. εἶναι γὰρ ὁμολογεῖται σωφροσύνη	9
τὸ κρατεῖν ἡδόνων καὶ ἐπιθυμιῶν, Ἔρωτος δὲ μηδεμίαν	10
ἡδονὴν κρείττω εἶναι· εἰ δὲ ἥττους, κρατοῖντ᾽ ἂν ὑπὸ Ἔρωτος,	11
ὁ δὲ κρατοῖ, κρατῶν δὲ ἡδονῶν καὶ ἐπιθυμιῶν ὁ Ἔρως διαφερόντως	12

---

1   ταῦτα ἱκανά: sense demands that ἱκανά is a predicate here, as is also suggested by the absence of the definite article. Supply the verb "are."

2   λεκτέον: verbal adj. of λέγω (*Essentials* §127)

3–4   οὔτ᾽ ἀδικεῖ ... θεόν: on the chiastic structure, see introduction

5   Ἔρωτος: obj. of ἅπτεται in line 6. Verbs implying physical touching often take genitive objects (cf. λαμβάνομαι = take hold of *gen.*).

6   οὔτε ποιῶν [τι] ποιεῖ [βίᾳ]: the missing words can be supplied from the parallel with the previous line: βίᾳ πάσχει, εἴ τι πάσχει

7   *ὑπηρετέω = serve *dat.*

     ἃ ... ὁμολογήσῃ: the relative clause is the subject of the indirect statement introduced by φασίν

7–8   οἱ πόλεως βασιλῆς νόμοι: a phrase from the orator, Alcidamas, a follower of Gorgias (Aristotle, *Rhetoric* 3.3.3 1406a3, where he gives the phrase as an example of Alcidamas's "frigid" [ψυχρά] style, due to the excessive use of ornamental epithets)

8   βασιλῆς: an alternative nom. pl. form

     νόμοι: in apposition to βασιλῆς

     πρός + *dat.* = in addition to

11   κρείττω and ἥττους: identify the form of each (*Essentials* §24)

12   ὁ δέ: i.e., Eros (ὁ δέ signals a change of subje. from the previous verb)

     κρατοῖ = κρατοίη: supply ἄν

ἂν σωφρονοῖ. καὶ μὴν εἴς γε ἀνδρείαν Ἔρωτι   13

"οὐδ' Ἄρης ἀνθίσταται." οὐ γὰρ ἔχει Ἔρωτα Ἄρης,   14   196d

ἀλλ' Ἔρως Ἄρη—Ἀφροδίτης, ὡς λόγος—κρείττων δὲ ὁ ἔχων   15

τοῦ ἐχομένου· τοῦ δ' ἀνδρειοτάτου τῶν ἄλλων κρατῶν πάντων   16

ἂν ἀνδρειότατος εἴη. Περὶ μὲν οὖν δικαιοσύνης καὶ σωφροσύνης 17

καὶ ἀνδρείας τοῦ θεοῦ εἴρηται, περὶ δὲ σοφίας λείπεται·   18

ὅσον οὖν δυνατόν, πειρατέον μὴ ἐλλείπειν. καὶ πρῶτον μέν,   19

ἵν' αὖ καὶ ἐγὼ τὴν ἡμετέραν τέχνην τιμήσω ὥσπερ Ἐρυξίμαχος   20

τὴν αὐτοῦ, ποιητὴς ὁ θεὸς σοφὸς οὕτως ὥστε καὶ ἄλλον   21   196e

ποιῆσαι· πᾶς γοῦν ποιητὴς γίγνεται, "κἂν ἄμουσος ᾖ τὸ πρίν," 22

---

13   σωφρονοῖ = σωφρονοίη
      *εἰς = in regard to

14   Ἄρης -εως ὁ = Ares, god of war
      ἀνθίσταμαι = stand up to, stand up against *dat.*
      The quotation is from Sophocles, *Thyestes*, frag. 235N, but Sophocles' version has πρὸς τὴν
      ἀνάγκην rather than Ἔρωτι. The idea that erotic love is irresistible and even a form of
      ἀνάγκη is certainly found in tragedy (as well as in Gorgias's *Encomium of Helen*).

14–15 ἔχω has an extended sense here of "have in one's power." It is characteristic of Greek thinking
      about love that it takes hold of a person.

15   Ἀφροδίτης: the genitive is dependent on Ἔρως and may play on Eros as the child of Aphrodite
      but more meaningfully in the context is an objective genitive (*Essentials* §92), an erotic passion
      for Aphrodite. The allusion is to the story of Ares and Aphrodite told by the poet Demodocus
      in the *Odyssey*, according to which Ares was involved in an adulterous love affair with the
      goddess Aphrodite (*Odyssey* 8.266–366).

16   τοῦ δ' ἀνδρειοτάτου: obj. of κρατῶν (nom. part.—not a genitive despite apparent similarity to
      the words surrounding it)

19   πειρατέον: verbal adj. of πειράομαι (*Essentials* §127)
      ἐλλείπω (ἐν + λείπω) = leave out; fall short

21   ἄλλον: what is the gender of this word? Hint: the dictionary entry is ἄλλος -η -ο. Supply as a
      pred. acc. ποίητην (implied by overall context).

22   κἂν = καὶ ἐάν (crasis)
      ἄμουσος -ον = without the Muses, Muse-less; i.e., uninspired, unpoetic
      τὸ πρίν = πρίν (adv. not conj.)
      The quotation is from Euripides, *Stheneboea*, frag. 663 Nauck, which begins ποιητὴν δ' ἄρα /
      Ἔρως διδάσκει. . . .

οὗ ἂν Ἔρως ἅψηται. ᾧ δὴ πρέπει ἡμᾶς   23

μαρτυρίῳ χρῆσθαι, ὅτι ποιητὴς ὁ Ἔρως ἀγαθὸς ἐν κεφαλαίῳ   24

πᾶσαν ποίησιν τὴν κατὰ μουσικήν· ἃ γάρ τις ἢ μὴ ἔχει ἢ   25

μὴ οἶδεν, οὔτ᾽ ἂν ἑτέρῳ δοίη οὔτ᾽ ἂν ἄλλον διδάξειεν.   26

καὶ μὲν δὴ τήν γε τῶν ζῴων ποίησιν πάντων τίς ἐναντιώσεται   27   197a

μὴ οὐχὶ Ἔρωτος εἶναι σοφίαν, ᾗ γίγνεταί τε καὶ φύεται   28

πάντα τὰ ζῷα; ἀλλὰ τὴν τῶν τεχνῶν δημιουργίαν οὐκ   29

ἴσμεν, ὅτι οὗ μὲν ἂν ὁ θεὸς οὗτος διδάσκαλος γένηται,   30

ἐλλόγιμος καὶ φανὸς ἀπέβη, οὗ δ᾽ ἂν Ἔρως μὴ ἐφάψηται,   31

σκοτεινός; τοξικήν γε μὴν καὶ ἰατρικὴν καὶ μαντικὴν   32

Ἀπόλλων ἀνηῦρεν ἐπιθυμίας καὶ ἔρωτος ἡγεμονεύσαντος,   33

---

23   ᾧ = τούτῳ

      πρέπει + *acc.* + *inf.* = it is fitting for *acc.* to ——

24   μαρτυρίῳ: pred. with ᾧ, from μαρτύριον -ου τό = testimony, proof "as proof"

25   πᾶσαν ποίησιν τὴν κατὰ μουσικήν = every kind of creation in the realm of the Muses' art;
      ποίησιν is accusative of respect with ἀγαθός. Agathon here seems to anticipate a point
      Diotima makes later—that the word ποίησις should mean not only poetic creation but all
      forms of creativity.

27-28 ἐναντιόομαι μὴ οὐχί = disagree that . . . , deny that. . . . As often following verbs and expressions
      with negative meaning, μὴ οὐχί is redundant here and should not be translated (Smyth 1956:
      §§2739-43).

29   τὴν τῶν τεχνῶν δημιουργίαν = the craftsmanship that belongs to the arts (acc. of respect)

29-32 οὐκ ἴσμεν . . . σκοτεινός; = don't we know . . . ? (rhetorical question)

31   ἐλλόγιμος -ον = worthy of note, famous, deserving of notice

      φανός -ή -όν = visible, bright, glorious

      ἐφάψηται from ἐφάπτομαι (ἐπί + ἅπτομαι)

      ἀπέβη = goes forth (gnomic aor.; *Essentials* §145)

32   σκοτεινός -ή -όν = dark, obscure, unknown

      τοξική -ῆς ἡ = the art of archery

      μαντική -ῆς ἡ = the art of prophecy (cf. μαντεύομαι)

      Ἀπόλλων ὁ = Apollo, god of archery, healing, and prophecy

33   ἐπιθυμίας . . . ἡγεμονεύσαντος: gen. abs.

      ἡγεμονεύω = act as ἡγεμών

      The erotic motivation of the invention of archery, medicine, and prophecy is not obvious in surviving
      mythology. Perhaps Agathon is referring to Apollo's engendering of Asclepius (the semidivine
      doctor hero), Iamos ("a seer preeminent among men"; Pindar, *Olympian* 6.34-70), and other
      human discoverers of these arts. Apollo is erotically connected with the female prophet Cassandra
      and to Daphne, who becomes the laurel, associated with prophecy. But perhaps the reasoning here
      is the same as for subsequent examples (see note on lines 37-42).

ὥστε καὶ οὗτος Ἔρωτος ἂν εἴη μαθητής, καὶ Μοῦσαι   34   197b

μουσικῆς καὶ Ἥφαιστος χαλκείας καὶ Ἀθηνᾶ ἱστουργίας   35

καὶ Ζεὺς "κυβερνᾶν θεῶν τε καὶ ἀνθρώπων." ὅθεν δὴ   36

καὶ κατεσκευάσθη τῶν θεῶν τὰ πράγματα Ἔρωτος ἐγγενομένου,   37

δῆλον ὅτι κάλλους—αἴσχει γὰρ οὐκ ἔπι ἔρως—πρὸ   38

τοῦ δέ, ὥσπερ ἐν ἀρχῇ εἶπον, πολλὰ καὶ δεινὰ θεοῖς ἐγίγνετο,   39

ὡς λέγεται, διὰ τὴν τῆς Ἀνάγκης βασιλείαν· ἐπειδὴ δ' ὁ   40

θεὸς οὗτος ἔφυ, ἐκ τοῦ ἐρᾶν τῶν καλῶν πάντ' ἀγαθὰ γέγονεν   41

καὶ θεοῖς καὶ ἀνθρώποις.   42

34–35   μαθητής is construed with two different kinds of genitive: with a genitive of person (μαθητής
        Ἔρωτος = Eros's student) and with a genitive of thing (μαθητής μουσικῆς = student of the
        musical art); translate as "a student of Eros in the art of music"
        Μοῦσαι μουσικῆς = Μοῦσαι μουσικῆς [ἂν εἶεν μαθηταὶ] Ἔρωτος

35   χαλκεία -ας ἡ = the art of bronze-working
        Ἀθηνᾶ: contracted nominative form of Athene, goddess of wisdom, weaving, and various other
        arts; the standard form in fourth-century prose, though other forms are more common in
        Homer and tragedy. For the contracted forms of first declension nouns, see Smyth 1956: §227.
        ἱστουργία -ας ἡ = the art of weaving

36   κυβερνᾶν: treat as parallel to other arts (i.e., τοῦ κυβερνᾶν = the art of steering)
        We don't know the source for the phrase in quotation marks here, but the change of construction
        from genitive to infinitive and the unusual genitive with κυβερνᾶν suggests that Agathon is
        quoting from a poet, as he is apt to do (Bury 1973: 80; Rowe 1998: 165).

37–42   Before Eros, there was no love, therefore there was no love of beauty, but, when Eros was born,
        love of beauty (the only kind of love there can be) was born, and therefore the gods began to
        pursue what is good and beautiful because they had desire for it.

37   τὰ πράγματα: contrasted to πολλὰ καὶ δεινὰ in line 39, so suggests something positive, stable,
        orderly, and good: "offices," "achievements," "business," possibly even "government"

38   κάλλους: obj. gen. with Ἔρωτος
        αἴσχει: obj. of ἔπι (as accent shows, an instance of anastrophe; Essentials §206); from αἶσχος
        -ους τό = ugliness

Reading 7C

As Agathon wraps up his speech, he pulls out all the rhetorical stops, and the speech becomes increasingly elaborate and Gorgianic in style. Although Agathon uses many uncommon words, the grammar of his peroration (final part of a speech) is fairly straightforward. Characteristic features are short parallel phrases with words of similar length and the same ending sound (homoeoteleuton) juxtaposed in balanced patterns, for example:

οὗτος δὲ ἡμᾶς ἀλλοτρι<u>ότητος</u> μὲν κεν<u>οῖ</u>, οἰκει<u>ότητος</u> δὲ πλη<u>ροῖ</u>

Antithesis, whereby words with opposite meanings balance one another, is also characteristic. So in the line above, the genitive noun ἀλλοτριότητος (estrangement, foreignness) is opposed to οἰκειότητος (kinship, intimacy), and the verb κενοῖ (empties) to πληροῖ (fills). Play with sound patterns is also evident in extended lists such as ἐν πόνῳ, ἐν φόβῳ, ἐν πόθῳ, ἐν λόγῳ and κυβερνήτης, ἐπιβάτης, παραστάτης. Almost the entire peroration uses metrical units known from Greek lyric poetry, giving a poetic sound to the whole (Dover 1980: 124).

Following Agathon's speech, Socrates reminds Eryximachus that all along he has been afraid of Agathon's powerful speaking style, which he compares to that of the sophist and rhetorician Gorgias. He plays on Gorgias's name, likening it to the mythological Gorgon's head, which turns a man to stone—in this case to speechlessness. Socrates' language in his response has Gorgianic touches that seem to render his claim ironic, but the implication that Agathon's style subdues the audience and renders them immobile rather than stimulating thought has a serious point.

Vocabulary

ἄνεμος -ου ὁ: wind, breeze

θορυβέω: make an uproar; *recognize also* θόρυβος -ου ὁ: din; ἀναθορυβέω: shout in applause, cheer; *note also* καταθορυβέω: shout down, boo

ἵμερος -ου ὁ: desire

κόσμος -ου ὁ: (1) order; (2) ornament, decoration; (3) universe (cf. κόσμιος and English "cosmology" and "cosmetics")

κυβερνήτης -ου ὁ: captain, steersman, guide, governor (cf. κυβερνάω)

μαντικός -ή -όν: of or for a soothsayer or his art, prophetic, oracular; ἡ μαντική = ἡ μαντική τέχνη (cf. μαντεύομαι and *μάντις ὁ: prophet and English "mantic") μέτριος -α -ον: moderate (cf. *μέτρον τό: measure, portion)

νεάνισκος -ου ὁ: young man (cf. νεανίας ὁ)

παντοδαπός -ή -όν: of every kind, of all sorts, manifold, varied

πόθος -ου ὁ: desire, yearning (cf. *ποθέω: desire, yearn for)

πόνος -ου ὁ: toil, pain, suffering, grief

ῥῆμα -ατος τό: that which is said or spoken, word, saying (cf. ἐρρήθην)

σωτήρ σωτῆρος ὁ: savior (cf. σῴζω and *σωτηρία ἡ: safety, deliverance)

τελευτή -ῆς ἡ: end (cf. τελευτάω)

ὕπνος -ου ὁ: sleep (cf. English "hypnotism")

ᾠδή -ῆς ἡ: song (cf. ᾄδω and English "ode")

Reading 7C (*Symposium* 197c1–198c5)

Οὕτως ἐμοὶ δοκεῖ, ὦ Φαῖδρε, Ἔρως πρῶτος αὐτὸς ὢν	1	197c
κάλλιστος καὶ ἄριστος μετὰ τοῦτο τοῖς ἄλλοις ἄλλων τοιούτων	2	
αἴτιος εἶναι. ἐπέρχεται δέ μοί τι καὶ ἔμμετρον εἰπεῖν, ὅτι	3	
οὗτός ἐστιν ὁ ποιῶν	4	
εἰρήνην μὲν ἐν ἀνθρώποις, πελάγει δὲ γαλήνην	5	
νηνεμίαν, ἀνέμων κοίτην ὕπνον τ’ ἐνὶ κήδει.	6	
οὗτος δὲ ἡμᾶς ἀλλοτριότητος μὲν κενοῖ, οἰκειότητος δὲ πληροῖ,	7	197d

---

1–2   πρῶτος ... μετὰ τοῦτο: the structure reminds us of how Agathon initially defined the task of the encomiast: first to describe the one being praised, then to talk about the things for which he is responsible.

3   ἐπέρχεται μοι ... εἰπεῖν: the infinitive is the subject of the verb here: *literally* = it comes over me to say *or better English* = I am inspired to say ...

ἔμμετρος -ον = in meter, in verse

4   οὗτος = Ἔρως

5–6   Although these lines appear complex, they are grammatically simple: a list of accusatives that serve as the direct object of the subst. part. ὁ ποιῶν in line 4. Agathon's comment leads scholars to believe that these lines are to be taken as his spontaneous composition, though they are Homeric in language and style and meter (dactylic hexameter rather than the iambic trimeter or lyric meters typical of tragedy). Bury 1973: 81 points out that the alliteration of the passage is typical of Gorgias, whose influence is overt here. The concentration of liquid (ρ, λ) and nasal (μ, ν, γ) sounds creates a soothing effect that supports the passage's sense.

5   πέλαγος -ους τό = sea

γαλήνη -ης ἡ = stillness of the sea, calm

6   νηνεμία -ας ἡ = state without ἄνεμοι, windlessness; in apposition to γαλήνην in the previous line = a calm [that is] windlessness. Translate as "a calm windlessness" or "a windless calm." Echoes *Odyssey* 5.391–92; 12.168–69.

κοίτη -ης ἡ = bed

ἐνί = ἐν (here) = amid

τ’ = τε: this word needs to be translated before the word it follows (so connects κοίτην and ὕπνον)

κῆδος -ους τό = care, concern

7   ἀλλοτριότης -ητος ὁ = alienation, estrangement, foreignness

κενόω = empty or drain *acc. of gen.*

οἰκειότης -τητος ὁ = kinship, family relationship, closeness, intimacy

τὰς τοιάσδε συνόδους μετ᾽ ἀλλήλων πάσας τιθεὶς συνιέναι,   8

ἐν ἑορταῖς, ἐν χοροῖς, ἐν θυσίαισι γιγνόμενος ἡγεμών·   9

πρᾳότητα μὲν πορίζων, ἀγριότητα δ᾽ ἐξορίζων·   10

φιλόδωρος εὐμενείας, ἄδωρος δυσμενείας· ἵλεως ἀγαθός· θεατὸς σοφοῖς,   11

ἀγαστὸς θεοῖς· ζηλωτὸς ἀμοίροις, κτητὸς εὐμοίροις· τρυφῆς,   12

ἁβρότητος, χλιδῆς, χαρίτων, ἱμέρου, πόθου πατήρ· ἐπιμελὴς   13

ἀγαθῶν, ἀμελὴς κακῶν· ἐν πόνῳ, ἐν φόβῳ, ἐν πόθῳ, ἐν   14

λόγῳ κυβερνήτης, ἐπιβάτης, παραστάτης τε καὶ σωτὴρ   15   197e

---

8   τοιάσδε: referring to the symposium itself

σύνοδος -ου ἡ = meeting, event that brings together

τίθημι + *acc.* + *inf.* = make *acc.* ——, cause *acc.* to ——

9   *ἑορτή -ῆς ἡ = feast, festival

*χορός -οῦ ὁ = round dance, choral dance or song, chorus

θυσίαισι = θυσίαις (Ionic dialect, common in Homer, Hesiod, and other poetry, is probably due to Homeric influence)

10   πρᾳότης -ητος ἡ = mildness, gentleness (cf. *πρᾷος -α -ον = gentle)

ἀγριότης -ητος ἡ = wildness, savagery (cf. *ἄγριος -α -ον = wild)

ἐξορίζω = banish

11   φιλόδωρος -ον = fond of giving *gen.*, bountiful in *gen.*, generous in *gen.*

εὐμένεια -ας ἡ = goodwill, favor, grace

ἄδωρος and δυσμένεια: meanings can be inferred from previous words (their opposites!)

ἵλεως -ων (endings contracted from -οος and -οου; see Smyth 1956: §289 for declension) = propitious, gracious

θεατός -ή -όν = watched, gazed upon (verbal adj. of θεάομαι) (*Essentials* §128). How should the dative with a verbal adjective be translated (*Essentials* §114)?

12   ἀγαστός -ή -όν = admired (verbal adj. of ἄγαμαι)

ζηλωτός -ή -όν = envied (verbal adj. of *ζηλόω = emulate, envy, strive to be)

*ἄμοιρος -ον = without any part of [him], without share [μοῖρα] in [him]

κτητός -ή -όν = held fast, clung to (verbal adj. of κτάομαι)

εὔμοιρος -ον: cf. ἄμοιρος -ον

τρυφή -ῆς ἡ = luxury, softness, delicacy, daintiness

13   ἁβρότης -ητος ἡ = delicacy, luxury

χλιδή -ῆς ἡ = delicacy, daintiness, luxury, effeminacy

*ἐπιμελής -ές = caring, concerned with *gen.* (cf. ἐπιμελέομαι)

14   *ἀμελής -ές = not caring for *gen.* (cf. ἀμελέω)

15   ἐπιβάτης -ου ὁ = one who mounts or embarks, the soldier on board a fighting ship, the warrior in a chariot

παραστάτης -ου ὁ = one who stands by, defender

ἄριστος, συμπάντων τε θεῶν καὶ ἀνθρώπων κόσμος, ἡγεμὼν   16

κάλλιστος καὶ ἄριστος, ᾧ χρὴ ἕπεσθαι πάντα ἄνδρα ἐφυμνοῦντα   17

καλῶς, ᾠδῆς μετέχοντα ἣν ᾄδει θέλγων πάντων θεῶν   18

τε καὶ ἀνθρώπων νόημα.   19

   "Οὗτος," ἔφη, "ὁ παρ' ἐμοῦ λόγος, ὦ Φαῖδρε, τῷ θεῷ   20

ἀνακείσθω, τὰ μὲν παιδιᾶς, τὰ δὲ σπουδῆς μετρίας, καθ'   21

ὅσον ἐγὼ δύναμαι, μετέχων."   22

   Εἰπόντος δὲ τοῦ Ἀγάθωνος πάντας ἔφη ὁ Ἀριστόδημος   23   198a

ἀναθορυβῆσαι τοὺς παρόντας, ὡς πρεπόντως τοῦ νεανίσκου   24

εἰρηκότος καὶ αὑτῷ καὶ τῷ θεῷ. τὸν οὖν Σωκράτη εἰπεῖν   25

βλέψαντα εἰς τὸν Ἐρυξίμαχον, "Ἆρα σοι δοκῶ," φάναι, "ὦ   26

παῖ Ἀκουμενοῦ, ἀδεὲς πάλαι δέος δεδιέναι, ἀλλ' οὐ μαντικῶς   27

ἃ νυνδὴ ἔλεγον εἰπεῖν, ὅτι Ἀγάθων θαυμαστῶς ἐροῖ, ἐγὼ δ'   28

ἀπορήσοιμι;"   29

---

16   κόσμος -ου ὁ: *here probably* = ornament—but perhaps carrying connotations of some of the
      word's other meanings

17   ἐφυμνέω = ἐπί + ὑμνέω

18   ᾄδει: context allows the reader to infer that the subject here must be Eros
      θέλγω = enchant, charm

19   νόημα -ατος τό = perception, thought

21   ἀνάκειμαι = be dedicated; *literally* = lay up
      τὰ μὲν . . . τὰ δέ = in part . . . in part (accusatives of respect)
      *παιδιά -ᾶς ἡ = childish play, sport, game; obj. of μετέχων (which takes a gen.)

21–22   καθ' ὅσον ἐγὼ δύναμαι: parenthetical

22   μετέχων: modifies ὁ λόγος not ἐγώ

24   ἀναθορυβέω = cheer, make a commotion in a positive way; ἀνά + *θορυβέω = make a
      commotion, create a disturbance
      *πρεπόντως = in fit manner, befittingly

27   Ἀκουμενός -οῦ ὁ = Akoumenos (Latin Acumenus), father of Eryximachus
      ἀδεής -ές = groundless (here); *literally* = fearless, without fear
      δέος -ους τό = fear, alarm, affright. Rose 1985: 41 points out that "ἀδεὲς δέος is an oxymoron, a
      deliberate, apparent contradiction for rhetorical effect. The entire phrase thus parodies
      Agathon's rhetoric."
      δεδιέναι: perf. inf. of δείδω = fear
      ἀλλ' οὐ = or . . . not. The adversative force of ἀλλά is probably best translated "or" in this rhetorical
      question: Ἆρα σοι δοκῶ . . . ἀλλ' οὐ; = Do I seem to you . . . or do I not seem . . . ? (Denniston
      1950: 1–2 under ἀλλά I.(ii)).

"Τὸ μὲν ἕτερον," φάναι τὸν Ἐρυξίμαχον, "μαντικῶς μοι   30

δοκεῖς εἰρηκέναι, ὅτι Ἀγάθων εὖ ἐρεῖ· τὸ δὲ σὲ ἀπορήσειν,   31

οὐκ οἶμαι."   32

"Καὶ πῶς, ὦ μακάριε," εἰπεῖν τὸν Σωκράτη, "οὐ μέλλω   33   198b

ἀπορεῖν καὶ ἐγὼ καὶ ἄλλος ὁστισοῦν, μέλλων λέξειν μετὰ   34

καλὸν οὕτω καὶ παντοδαπὸν λόγον ῥηθέντα; καὶ τὰ μὲν ἄλλα   35

οὐχ ὁμοίως μὲν θαυμαστά· τὸ δὲ ἐπὶ τελευτῆς τοῦ κάλλους   36

τῶν ὀνομάτων καὶ ῥημάτων τίς οὐκ ἂν ἐξεπλάγη ἀκούων;   37

ἐπεὶ ἔγωγε ἐνθυμούμενος ὅτι αὐτὸς οὐχ οἷός τ' ἔσομαι οὐδ'   38

ἐγγὺς τούτων οὐδὲν καλὸν εἰπεῖν, ὑπ' αἰσχύνης ὀλίγου   39

ἀποδρὰς ᾠχόμην, εἴ πη εἶχον. καὶ γάρ με Γοργίου ὁ λόγος   40   198c

ἀνεμίμνῃσκεν, ὥστε ἀτεχνῶς τὸ τοῦ Ὁμήρου ἐπεπόνθη·   41

30–31 τὸ μὲν ἕτερον . . . τὸ δέ = the one thing . . . the other

35–36 τὰ μὲν ἄλλα . . . μέν . . . τὸ δὲ ἐπὶ τελευτῆς = the rest [of the speech] . . . the part at the end. As often in Greek, the thing emphasized comes second and the rest comes first; English prefers to reverse the order. The second μέν (line 36) is unusual and puts additional emphasis on οὐχ ὁμοίως.

36 τοῦ κάλλους: gen. of cause (*Essentials* §98) with ἐξεπλάγη (from ἐκπλήττω). Review the principal parts of πλήττω (students should be able to infer the form from a general knowledge of verb form).

37 τῶν ὀνομάτων καὶ ῥημάτων = words and phrases

39 ὀλίγου *adv.* = almost, nearly (an abbreviation of the common expression ὀλίγου δεῖν = need a little)

40 ἀποδρὰς: aor. part. of *ἀποδιδράσκω = run away [in the manner of a slave]

εἶχον = I could (as though followed by an inf. οἴχεσθαι or ἀποδρᾶναι)

Γοργίης -ου ὁ: Gorgias, the famous rhetorician (see reading 7 introduction)

41 ἀτεχνῶς *adv.* = simply

τὸ τοῦ Ὁμήρου: *literally* = Homer's thing; i.e., the thing described by Homer, a common way of citing a passage. Here Socrates refers to Homer's lines at *Odyssey* 11.633–35 describing Odysseus's fear that Persephone will send up a monster with a Gorgon's head. Socrates is playing with Gorgias's name here.

ἐπεπόνθη: from πάσχω, a pluperfect that emphasizes the state in which Socrates found himself, one of frozen fear. Translate: "I found I had experienced. . . ."

ἐφοβούμην μή μοι τελευτῶν ὁ Ἀγάθων Γοργίου κεφαλὴν   42

δεινοῦ λέγειν ἐν τῷ λόγῳ ἐπὶ τὸν ἐμὸν λόγον πέμψας αὐτόν   43

με λίθον τῇ ἀφωνίᾳ ποιήσειεν."   44

---

42   μοι: ethical dat., not far in meaning from οἴμοι = oh my! (*Essentials* §113)

Γοργίου: can be understood both as the genitive of Gorgias the rhetorician's name and as an adjective = belonging to the Gorgon, i.e., Medusa's, the sight of whose head was supposed to turn people to stone. Translate: "Gorgian" to preserve the ambiguity.

43   λέγειν: take with δεινοῦ = clever at speaking; an explanatory infinitive (*Essentials* §181), but clearly playing on meaning of δεινός = awesome, terrifying

ἐν τῷ λόγῳ ἐπὶ τὸν ἐμὸν λόγον = in his speech against my speech. Modifies πέμψας. The phrase suggests the competition between Agathon and Socrates.

αὐτόν: intensifies με (*Essentials* §202)

44   ἀφωνία -ας ἡ = speechlessness (cf. φωνή -ῆς ἡ and *φωνέω = speak, make a sound)

ποιήσειεν: identify and explain the mood (*Essentials* §159c)

Reading 7D

Socrates acknowledges that he should never have agreed to participate in making encomia.

Vocabulary

ἄττα: Attic for τινά

γέλως -ωτος ὁ: laughter (cf. γελάω and γελοῖος)

ἡνίκα *conj.*: at which time, when

ὑπισχνέομαι ὑποσχήσομαι ὑπεσχόμην — ὑπέσχημαι: promise

φρονέω φρονήσω ἐφρόνησα πεφρόνηκα πεφρόνημαι ἐφρονήθην: think, have understanding, be wise or prudent; intend; + *neut. adj.*: think (a certain way), be disposed (a certain
way); e.g., φίλα φρονέω: be friendly (to); μέγα φρονέω: think big, be proud or arrogant

163

Reading 7D (*Symposium* 198c5–199c2)

Καὶ ἐνενόησα τότε ἄρα	1	
καταγέλαστος ὤν, ἡνίκα ὑμῖν ὡμολόγουν ἐν τῷ μέρει μεθ'	2	
ὑμῶν ἐγκωμιάσεσθαι τὸν Ἔρωτα καὶ ἔφην εἶναι δεινὸς τὰ	3	198d
ἐρωτικά, οὐδὲν εἰδὼς ἄρα τοῦ πράγματος, ὡς ἔδει ἐγκωμιάζειν	4	
ὁτιοῦν. ἐγὼ μὲν γὰρ ὑπ' ἀβελτερίας ᾤμην δεῖν τἀληθῆ	5	
λέγειν περὶ ἑκάστου τοῦ ἐγκωμιαζομένου, καὶ τοῦτο μὲν	6	
ὑπάρχειν, ἐξ αὐτῶν δὲ τούτων τὰ κάλλιστα ἐκλεγομένους	7	
ὡς εὐπρεπέστατα τιθέναι· καὶ πάνυ δὴ μέγα ἐφρόνουν ὡς εὖ	8	
ἐρῶν, ὡς εἰδὼς τὴν ἀλήθειαν τοῦ ἐπαινεῖν ὁτιοῦν. τὸ δὲ ἄρα,	9	
ὡς ἔοικεν, οὐ τοῦτο ἦν τὸ καλῶς ἐπαινεῖν ὁτιοῦν, ἀλλὰ τὸ ὡς	10	
μέγιστα ἀνατιθέναι τῷ πράγματι καὶ ὡς κάλλιστα, ἐάν τε ᾖ	11	198e
οὕτως ἔχοντα ἐάν τε μή· εἰ δὲ ψευδῆ, οὐδὲν ἄρ' ἦν πρᾶγμα.	12	

---

1   τότε: modifies ὤν (line 2), anticipating ἡνίκα

ἄρα = in fact. This particle is used repeatedly in this passage in this sense, as Socrates articulates what he came to realize.

2   καταγέλαστος -ον = ridiculous (verbal adj. of καταγελάω)

ὤν: what use of the participle is this (*Essentials* §178)?

4   ἄρα: see note on line 1

5   ἀβελτερία -ας ἡ = silliness, stupidity

7   *ὑπάρχω = begin, be fundamental

αὐτῶν τούτων: points back to τἀληθῆ in line 5

ἐκλεγομένους: from ἐκλέγομαι = pick or single out, select for oneself; the masculine plural accusative must be understood with δεῖν (line 5). Supply ἡμᾶς or understand an anonymous "people" (acc. masc. pl.).

8   εὐπρεπής -ές = attractive

8–9   ὡς εὖ ἐρῶν: ὡς + *fut. part. (here)* = on the grounds that [I would speak well] *or* because of expecting that [I would speak well]

9   τὸ δὲ ἄρα = but in fact (see note on line 1)

10   τὸ καλῶς ἐπαινεῖν: the subject

11   *ἀνατίθημι = lay upon, attribute, dedicate

12   πρᾶγμα -ατος τό = matter, issue, big deal

προυρρήθη γάρ, ὡς ἔοικεν, ὅπως ἕκαστος ἡμῶν τὸν Ἔρωτα   13

ἐγκωμιάζειν δόξει, οὐχ ὅπως ἐγκωμιάσεται. διὰ ταῦτα δὴ   14

οἶμαι πάντα λόγον κινοῦντες ἀνατίθετε τῷ Ἔρωτι, καί   15

φατε αὐτὸν τοιοῦτόν τε εἶναι καὶ τοσούτων αἴτιον, ὅπως ἂν   16

φαίνηται ὡς κάλλιστος καὶ ἄριστος, δῆλον ὅτι τοῖς μὴ γιγνώσκουσιν—   17   199a

οὐ γὰρ δήπου τοῖς γε εἰδόσιν—καὶ καλῶς γ᾽ ἔχει   18

καὶ σεμνῶς ὁ ἔπαινος. ἀλλὰ γὰρ ἐγὼ οὐκ ᾔδη ἄρα τὸν   19

τρόπον τοῦ ἐπαίνου, οὐ δ᾽ εἰδὼς ὑμῖν ὡμολόγησα καὶ αὐτὸς   20

ἐν τῷ μέρει ἐπαινέσεσθαι. ἡ γλῶσσα οὖν ὑπέσχετο, ἡ δὲ   21

φρὴν οὔ· χαιρέτω δή. οὐ γὰρ ἔτι ἐγκωμιάζω τοῦτον τὸν   22

τρόπον—οὐ γὰρ ἂν δυναίμην—οὐ μέντοι ἀλλὰ τά γε ἀληθῆ,   23

---

13   προυρρήθη ... ὅπως = it was preordained that ..., it was ordered in advance that ...

13–14   ὅπως ... ἐγκωμιάζειν δόξει and οὐχ ὅπως ἐγκωμιάσεται: the contrast is between the mere
         appearance of giving praise and the reality of it

15   πάντα: neut. acc. pl. (not with λόγον)

       κινοῦντες = set in motion, get *acc.* started (λόγον)

       ἀνατίθημι = lay upon, attribute, dedicate

16–17   ὅπως ἂν φαίνηται: Plato frequently uses ὅπως with ἂν + subju. in purpose clauses, though ἂν
         is typically not a feature of a purpose clause.

17   δῆλον ὅτι = clearly (frequent in Attic prose)

       γιγνώσκουσιν: dat. pl. part. with τοῖς (depending on φαίνηται)

19   σεμνός -ή -όν = august, dignified, majestic, pompous

21–22   ἡ γλῶσσα ... φρὴν οὔ: Socrates adapts a famous line from Euripides' *Hippolytus*, a line parodied
         by Aristophanes, apparently because it scandalized the Athenians with its sophistry and
         amorality: ἡ γλῶσσ᾽ ὀμώμοχ᾽, ἡ δὲ φρὴν ἀνώματος = My tongue has sworn, but my mind
         [is] unsworn (*Hippolytus* 612)

       *γλῶσσα -ης ἡ = tongue

       ὑπέσχετο: aor. of ὑπισχνέομαι

22   *φρὴν φρενός ἡ = mind, understanding

       χαιρέτω δή = good-bye to that! let it be gone! Given the invoking of Hippolytus (see note on lines
         21–22), it is tempting to see this as an allusion to another line in Euripides' *Hippolytus* in which
         Hippolytus roughly dismisses Aphrodite (= Cypris) as unworthy of his attention: τὴν σὴν δὲ
         Κύπριν πόλλ᾽ ἐγὼ χαίρειν λέγω = I say a big good-bye to your Cypris (*Hippolytus* 113)

       οὐ ... ἔτι ἐγκωμιάζω = I won't go on praising

22–23   τοῦτον τὸν τρόπον: adverbial acc. (*Essentials* §81); cf. τίνα τρόπον;

23   οὐ μέντοι ἀλλά = but nevertheless

εἰ βούλεσθε, ἐθέλω εἰπεῖν κατ᾽ ἐμαυτόν, οὐ πρὸς τοὺς   24   199b
ὑμετέρους λόγους, ἵνα μὴ γέλωτα ὄφλω. ὅρα οὖν, ὦ Φαῖδρε,   25
εἴ τι καὶ τοιούτου λόγου δέῃ, περὶ Ἔρωτος τἀληθῆ λεγόμενα   26
ἀκούειν, ὀνόμασι[32] δὲ καὶ θέσει ῥημάτων τοιαύτῃ ὁποία δἂν   27
τις τύχῃ ἐπελθοῦσα."   28

Τὸν οὖν Φαῖδρον ἔφη καὶ τοὺς ἄλλους κελεύειν λέγειν,   29
ὅπῃ αὐτὸς οἴοιτο δεῖν εἰπεῖν, ταύτῃ.   30

"Ἔτι τοίνυν," φάναι, "Φαῖδρε, πάρες μοι Ἀγάθωνα σμίκρ᾽   31
ἄττα ἐρέσθαι, ἵνα ἀνομολογησάμενος παρ᾽ αὐτοῦ οὕτως ἤδη   32
λέγω."   33

"Ἀλλὰ παρίημι," φάναι τὸν Φαῖδρον, "ἀλλ᾽ ἐρώτα." μετὰ   34   199c
ταῦτα δὴ τὸν Σωκράτη ἔφη ἐνθένδε ποθὲν ἄρξασθαι.   35

---

24   κατ᾽ ἐμαυτόν = in accordance with myself (i.e., in my own way)
      οὐ πρός = not in answer to (i.e., not in competition with)
25   ὄφλω: aor. subju. of ὀφλισκάνω = bring on oneself
26   τι adverbial = in any way, at all
      τοιούτου λόγου: δέομαι takes a gen. obj.
26–27 περὶ ... ἀκούειν: essentially in apposition to τοιούτου λόγου; the infinitive is complementary
      with the verb δέῃ, defining more precisely τοιούτου λόγου
27   θέσις -εως ἡ = setting, placing, arranging
      ὁποία: feminine nominative singular as the acute accent suggests (the neut. pl. would be ὁποῖα)
      so the antecedent is θέσει; correl. with τοιαύτῃ = some [= τις] such sort [of arrangement]
      however . . .
      δἂν = δὴ ἄν (crasis)
28   ἐπέρχομαι = come about, occur. The whole phrase is intended to suggest a lack of artfulness to
      Socrates' arrangement of words.
31   Φαῖδρε: Phaedrus is acting as the ἄρχων of the discussion, as was established at its outset.
      *πάρες: from παρίημι = permit (impera.)
      ἐρέσθαι: what verb is this? Hint: not a form of the future ἐρέω or ἐράω (use glossary if necessary).
32   ἀνομολογέομαι παρά = obtain an agreement from gen.
34   *παρίημι = permit
      ἐρώτα: the accent makes clear that, despite the resemblance, this word is not from the noun
      ἔρως but the imperative of the verb ἐρωτάω
35   *ἐνθένδε *ποθέν = from some such place as this (ποθέν is indef.; ἐνθένδε points to what follows)
      ἄρξασθαι: why an infinitive here (Essentials §184)?

---

32. I use Dover's text here rather than Burnet 1901.

Reading 8. Plain-Speaking: Socrates Responds

Socrates' way of communicating is distinct from that practiced by all the other speakers at the symposium. It thus underscores the difference between Socrates' values and those of other participants in this highly rhetorical culture. Socrates' conversational style and the simplicity of his vocabulary contrast particularly strikingly with the artful rhetoric of the previous speech. His habit of asking questions rather than making pronouncements is also characteristic. This does not always mean that Socrates is easier to understand than other speakers; in fact, students frequently struggle with the *concepts* when Socrates speaks, even when the grammar seems straightforward. This is no doubt because Socrates deliberately tries to subvert ordinary expectations and to make his audience reexamine their fundamental assumptions.

Suggested Review

- principal parts of κτάομαι, μιμνῄσκω, and πάσχω

  κτάομαι κτήσομαι ἐκτησάμην — κέκτημαι ἐκτήθην = procure for oneself, get, gain, acquire; *perf. forms with pres. meaning* = possess

  μιμνῄσκω μνήσομαι ἔμνησα — μέμνημαι ἐμνήσθην = remind, put in mind; *mid.-pass. deponent* = remember

  πάσχω πείσομαι ἔπαθον πέπονθα = suffer, experience

Fig. 21.   Hellenistic portrait bust of Socrates. Photo: Hervé Lewandowski. Inv. MA 59. Location: Louvre, Paris, France. Photo credit: Réunion des Musées Nationaux/Art Resource, New York.

Reading 8A

Socrates tries in his questioning of Agathon to establish four main points: (1) Eros is love of something, not of nothing. That is, love exists only in relation to another thing, not in isolation (like a parent or a sibling). (2) Eros must desire the thing of which it is love, because it wouldn't make sense to say it doesn't desire what it loves. (3) Eros must be lacking the thing it is love of, because it does not make sense to talk of desire for what we already have. (4) If we do say that we desire what we already have, what we mean is that we desire that what we have now will also be ours in the future.

Vocabulary

ἄλλο τι: something else, anything other, but frequently used to exclude all other possibilities (is it anything other than . . . ?) and thus in a question the virtual equivalent of "not" with the strong connotation that it would have to be this way: e.g., ἄλλο τι ὁμολογοῖ ἄν; Is it anything other than that he would agree? i.e., Would he not agree? Would he not have to agree? ἄλλο τι ἔστιν ὁ Ἔρως τινῶν; Is it anything other than that Eros is of something? i.e., Is Eros not of something? Mustn't Eros be of something?

ἀποκρίνομαι ἀποκρινοῦμαι ἀπεκρινάμην — ἀποκέκριμαι: answer

διέρχομαι: go through, narrate

εἰκός -ότος τό: what seems likely, the probable, the appropriate (cf. ἔοικα)

εἰς τὸν ἔπειτα χρόνον: in the future

ἐν τῷ [νῦν] παρόντι: in the present

ἐνδεής -ές: in need of *gen.*, lacking *gen.* (cf. δέομαι)

οὐκοῦν: then, therefore (particularly used to introduce questions expecting a "yes" answer)

πλουτέω: be wealthy (cf. πλοῦτος ὁ and πλούσιος)

τοσόσδε τοσήδε τοσόνδε: as great as this, as much as this; *pl.*: as many as these (cf. ὅσος, τόσος, τοσοῦτος, τοιόσδε)

ὑγιαίνω ὑγιανῶ ὑγίανα: be sound, be healthy (cf. English "hygiene" and ὑγιεινὰ ἡ, ὑγιής, ὑγιεῖνος)

Reading 8A (*Symposium* 199c3–200d7)

"Καὶ μήν, ὦ φίλε Ἀγάθων, καλῶς μοι ἔδοξας καθηγήσασθαι   1
τοῦ λόγου, λέγων ὅτι πρῶτον μὲν δέοι αὐτὸν ἐπιδεῖξαι   2
ὁποῖός τίς ἐστιν ὁ Ἔρως, ὕστερον δὲ τὰ ἔργα αὐτοῦ. ταύτην   3
τὴν ἀρχὴν πάνυ ἄγαμαι. ἴθι οὖν μοι περὶ Ἔρωτος, ἐπειδὴ   4
καὶ τἆλλα καλῶς καὶ μεγαλοπρεπῶς διῆλθες οἷός ἐστι, καὶ   5
τόδε εἰπέ· πότερόν ἐστι τοιοῦτος οἷος εἶναί τινος ὁ Ἔρως   6   199d
ἔρως, ἢ οὐδενός; ἐρωτῶ δ' οὐκ εἰ μητρός τινος ἢ πατρός   7
ἐστιν—γελοῖον γὰρ ἂν εἴη τὸ ἐρώτημα εἰ Ἔρως ἐστὶν ἔρως   8
μητρὸς ἢ πατρός—ἀλλ' ὥσπερ ἂν εἰ αὐτὸ τοῦτο πατέρα   9
ἠρώτων, ʽἎρα ὁ πατήρ ἐστι πατήρ τινος ἢ οὔ;' εἶπες ἂν   10
δήπου μοι, εἰ ἐβούλου καλῶς ἀποκρίνασθαι, ὅτι ἔστιν ὑέος   11
γε ἢ θυγατρὸς ὁ πατὴρ πατήρ· ἢ οὔ;"   12
"Πάνυ γε," φάναι τὸν Ἀγάθωνα.   13

---

1   καθηγέομαι + *gen.* = lead off, begin. Verbs of beginning tend to take genitive objects.
2   δέοι: what is the mood of this verb and why is it used here (*Essentials* §158)?
      αὐτόν: intensifies ὁ Ἔρως (prolepsis) (*Essentials* §208)
4   ἴθι: like ἄγε and φερέ, ἴθι is frequently used to introduce a second imperative = come!
5   τἆλλα = τὰ ἄλλα (crasis); acc. of respect (*Essentials* §82)
      μεγαλοπρεπής -ές = befitting a great man, magnificent
6   *πότερον: do not translate in direct questions. πότερον serves to introduce a question that
      poses two alternatives, here τινος or οὐδενός. (In an indir. question, πότερον = whether; see
      line 24.)
      τοιοῦτος οἷος εἶναι = the sort of thing such as to be. That is, is Eros the kind of thing that is
      defined by being love of something else, or does it exist independently (love of nothing)?
7–19 Socrates goes on to use family relations for comparison: a father is father of a son or daughter, he
      cannot be a father of nothing. Similarly, a brother is brother of a sister or a brother, not of
      nothing. The thought process here is complicated by the parenthetical joke in lines 7–9 that
      Eros is not love of a mother or father, presumably amusing because of *eros*'s sexual nature,
      though there has been scholarly debate (see discussion in Bury 1973: 89–90; with Dover 1980:
      134, for example, interpreting the genitives as genitives of source).
8   ἐρώτημα -ατος τό = question
9   πατέρα: about a father (second acc. with ἐρωτάω)
11   ὑέος: alternative gen. of υἱός -οῦ ὁ
13   *πάνυ γε = very much so (a common affirmative answer, used repeatedly in this reading)

“Οὐκοῦν καὶ ἡ μήτηρ ὡσαύτως;” Ὁμολογεῖσθαι καὶ τοῦτο.   14

“Ἔτι τοίνυν,” εἰπεῖν τὸν Σωκράτη, “ἀπόκριναι ὀλίγῳ πλείω,   15   199e
ἵνα μᾶλλον καταμάθῃς ὃ βούλομαι. εἰ γὰρ ἐροίμην, ‘Τί   16
δέ; ἀδελφός, αὐτὸ τοῦθ’ ὅπερ ἔστιν, ἔστι τινὸς ἀδελφὸς ἢ   17
οὔ;’ ” Φάναι εἶναι.   18

“Οὐκοῦν ἀδελφοῦ ἢ ἀδελφῆς;” Ὁμολογεῖν.   19

“Πειρῶ δή,” φάναι, “καὶ τὸν ἔρωτα εἰπεῖν. ὁ Ἔρως ἔρως   20
ἐστὶν οὐδενὸς ἢ τινός;”   21

“Πάνυ μὲν οὖν ἔστιν.”   22

“Τοῦτο μὲν τοίνυν,” εἰπεῖν τὸν Σωκράτη, “φύλαξον παρὰ   23   200a
σαυτῷ μεμνημένος ὅτου· τοσόνδε δὲ εἰπέ, πότερον ὁ Ἔρως   24
ἐκείνου οὗ ἔστιν ἔρως, ἐπιθυμεῖ αὐτοῦ ἢ οὔ;”   25

“Πάνυ γε,” φάναι.   26

“Πότερον ἔχων αὐτὸ οὗ ἐπιθυμεῖ τε καὶ ἐρᾷ, εἶτα ἐπιθυμεῖ   27
τε καὶ ἐρᾷ, ἢ οὐκ ἔχων;”   28

“Οὐκ ἔχων, ὡς τὸ εἰκός γε,” φάναι.   29

“Σκόπει δή,” εἰπεῖν τὸν Σωκράτη, “ἀντὶ τοῦ εἰκότος εἰ   30

---

15   ὀλίγῳ: dat. of degree of difference (*Essentials* §111)

16   βούλομαι: with λέγειν understood = I am getting at

16–17   τί δέ; = And what [about this]? Short questions consisting of τί + particle(s) are common in
          Greek. τί δέ; is used again later by Socrates (reading 8B.28) and by Diotima in her questioning
          of the young Socrates (reading 9E.22) and seems characteristic of their questioning style with
          its aggressive pursuit of truth and multiple follow-up questions.

17   ἀδελφός, αὐτὸ τοῦθ’ ὅπερ ἔστιν: a literal translation of the relative clause, which appears to be
          an accusative of respect, a bit unusual with a noun, does not convey a very clear meaning (“a
          brother, with respect to this very thing which/that it really is”). Rose 1985: 44 suggests using
          qua to translate the relative clause: “brother *qua* brother.” Rowe 1998: 71 translates: “Just insofar
          as he is a brother. . . .”

20   πειρῶ: impera. of πειράομαι

23–24   φύλαξον παρὰ σαυτῷ: i.e., keep in mind

24   μεμνημένος ὅτου = μεμνημένος ὅτου ἔρως ἐστίν
          τοσόνδε = as much as the following; i.e., this only (namely)

30   εἰ = whether (in an indir. question following σκόπει)

ἀνάγκη οὕτως, τὸ ἐπιθυμοῦν ἐπιθυμεῖν οὗ ἐνδεές ἐστιν, ἢ μὴ   31

ἐπιθυμεῖν, ἐὰν μὴ ἐνδεὲς ᾖ; ἐμοὶ μὲν γὰρ θαυμαστῶς δοκεῖ,   32   200b

ὦ Ἀγάθων, ὡς ἀνάγκη εἶναι· σοὶ δὲ πῶς;"   33

"Κἀμοί," φάναι, "δοκεῖ."   34

"Καλῶς λέγεις. ἆρ᾽ οὖν βούλοιτ᾽ ἄν τις μέγας ὢν μέγας   35

εἶναι, ἢ ἰσχυρὸς ὢν ἰσχυρός;"   36

"Ἀδύνατον ἐκ τῶν ὡμολογημένων."   37

"Οὐ γάρ που ἐνδεὴς ἂν εἴη τούτων ὅ γε ὤν."   38

"Ἀληθῆ λέγεις."   39

"Εἰ γὰρ καὶ ἰσχυρὸς ὢν βούλοιτο ἰσχυρὸς εἶναι," φάναι τὸν   40

Σωκράτη, "καὶ ταχὺς ὢν ταχύς, καὶ ὑγιὴς ὢν ὑγιής—ἴσως   41

γὰρ ἄν τις ταῦτα οἰηθείη καὶ πάντα τὰ τοιαῦτα τοὺς ὄντας   42

τε τοιούτους καὶ ἔχοντας ταῦτα τούτων ἅπερ ἔχουσι καὶ   43   200c

ἐπιθυμεῖν, ἵν᾽ οὖν μὴ ἐξαπατηθῶμεν, τούτου ἕνεκα λέγω—   44

τούτοις γάρ, ὦ Ἀγάθων, εἰ ἐννοεῖς, ἔχειν μὲν ἕκαστα   45

τούτων ἐν τῷ παρόντι ἀνάγκη ἃ ἔχουσιν, ἐάντε βούλωνται   46

ἐάντε μή, καὶ τούτου γε δήπου τίς ἂν ἐπιθυμήσειεν; ἀλλ᾽   47

ὅταν τις λέγῃ ὅτι ʻἐγὼ ὑγιαίνων βούλομαι καὶ ὑγιαίνειν,   48

καὶ πλουτῶν βούλομαι καὶ πλουτεῖν, καὶ ἐπιθυμῶ αὐτῶν   49

τούτων ἃ ἔχω,ʼ εἴποιμεν ἂν αὐτῷ ὅτι ʻσύ, ὦ ἄνθρωπε,   50

32–33   θαυμαστῶς . . . ὡς English word order: ὡς θαυμαστῶς [τοῦτο] δοκεῖ μοι εἶναι ἀνάγκη

38   ὅ γε ὤν: γε gives a causal force to the subst. part. = since at any rate he is [those things]

42   ταῦτα . . . τοιαῦτα = regarding these things and all such things (accusatives of respect)
         ἄν τις οἰηθείη: introducing an indir. statement with an acc. subje. (τοὺς ὄντας τε τοιούτους
             καὶ ἔχοντας ταῦτα) and inf. (ἐπιθυμεῖν)

43   τούτων ἅπερ ἔχουσι: obj. of ἐπιθυμεῖν

43–44   καὶ ἐπιθυμεῖν: καί not connective here = also

44   τούτου ἕνεκα: refers to the purpose clause preceding
         λέγω: supply an object, e.g., "these things"

45   τούτοις: the people previously described as τοὺς ὄντας τε τοιούτους καὶ ἔχοντας ταῦτα; dat.
             with ἀνάγκη [ἐστί] in the next line and infinitive ἔχειν

46   τούτων: partitive with ἕκαστα in the previous line; the antecedent of ἃ ἔχουσιν

πλοῦτον κεκτημένος καὶ ὑγίειαν καὶ ἰσχὺν βούλει καὶ εἰς   51   200d

τὸν ἔπειτα χρόνον ταῦτα κεκτῆσθαι, ἐπεὶ ἐν τῷ γε νῦν   52

παρόντι, εἴτε βούλει εἴτε μή, ἔχεις· σκόπει οὖν, ὅταν   53

τοῦτο λέγῃς, ὅτι 'ἐπιθυμῶ τῶν παρόντων,' εἰ ἄλλο τι λέγεις   54

ἢ τόδε, ὅτι 'βούλομαι τὰ νῦν παρόντα καὶ εἰς τὸν ἔπειτα   55

χρόνον παρεῖναι.' ἄλλο τι ὁμολογοῖ ἄν;"   56

    Συμφάναι ἔφη τὸν Ἀγάθωνα.   57

51	*ἰσχύς -ύος ἡ = strength
51–52	εἰς τὸν ἔπειτα χρόνον: see vocabulary
52–53	ἐν τῷ [νῦν] παρόντι: see vocabulary
54	εἰ: see note on line 30
56	ἄλλο τι: see vocabulary

Reading 8B

Socrates and Agathon build on the essential points of the previous reading: (1) love must be for something and cannot exist without an object, and (2) love is for something that is lacking and the lover doesn't have, so when it appears that someone desires something he already has, that must be considered a desire to possess that thing in the future. From here, Socrates takes up one of the points Agathon made in his speech, that love must be for beauty and not for ugliness, building on a fundamental assumption widespread in Greek culture that love is engendered by beauty. This brings them to the conclusion that love must actually lack beauty, undermining an essential point of Agathon's speech. In addition, Socrates argues that because good things (τὰ ἀγαθά) are beautiful, love must also lack them. The whole conversation is typically Socratic, leading to the doubting of everything the speaker once held secure.

Vocabulary

ἀναμιμνῄσκω: remind *acc.* of *gen.*; *mid.-pass.*: remember
δῆτα: certainly, be sure, of course (οὐ δῆτα: certainly not; τί δῆτα; what then?)
ἔνδεια -ας ἡ: want, need, lack (cf. δέομαι)
ἐπιεικής -ές: reasonable, fitting, meet, suitable (cf. εἰκός)
κινδυνεύω κινδυνεύσω ἐκινδύνευσα κεκινδύνευκα κεκινδύνευμαι ἐκινδυνεύθην: risk, venture; + *inf.*: be in danger of ——ing, risk or hazard ——ing, *often with idiomatic sense*: come close to ——ing, probably be ——ing, chance to —— (cf. ὁ κίνδυνος)

Reading 8B (*Symposium* 200d8–201c9)

Εἰπεῖν δὴ τὸν Σωκράτη, "Οὐκοῦν τοῦτό γ᾽ ἐστὶν ἐκείνου	1	
ἐρᾶν, ὃ οὔπω ἕτοιμον αὐτῷ ἐστιν οὐδὲ ἔχει, τὸ εἰς τὸν	2	
ἔπειτα χρόνον ταῦτα εἶναι αὐτῷ σῳζόμενα καὶ παρόντα;"	3	
"Πάνυ γε," φάναι.	4	200e
"Καὶ οὗτος ἄρα καὶ ἄλλος πᾶς ὁ ἐπιθυμῶν τοῦ μὴ ἑτοίμου	5	
ἐπιθυμεῖ καὶ τοῦ μὴ παρόντος, καὶ ὃ μὴ ἔχει καὶ ὃ μὴ ἔστιν	6	
αὐτὸς καὶ οὗ ἐνδεής ἐστι, τοιαῦτ᾽ ἄττα ἐστὶν ὧν ἡ ἐπιθυμία	7	
τε καὶ ὁ ἔρως ἐστίν;"	8	
"Πάνυ γ᾽," εἰπεῖν.	9	
"Ἴθι δή," φάναι τὸν Σωκράτη, "ἀνομολογησώμεθα τὰ εἰρημένα.	10	
ἄλλο τι ἔστιν ὁ Ἔρως πρῶτον μὲν τινῶν, ἔπειτα	11	
τούτων ὧν ἂν ἔνδεια παρῇ αὐτῷ;"	12	
"Ναί," φάναι.	13	201a
"Ἐπὶ δὴ τούτοις ἀναμνήσθητι τίνων ἔφησθα ἐν τῷ λόγῳ	14	
εἶναι τὸν Ἔρωτα· εἰ δὲ βούλει, ἐγώ σε ἀναμνήσω. οἶμαι	15	

---

1 τοῦτό: both looks back to what has preceded and is further defined by the articular infinitive
   τὸ . . . εἶναι in lines 2–3
   ἐκείνου: antecedent of ὃ . . . ἔχει, which defines it

2 ὃ: serves as both subje. of ἐστιν and direct obj. of ἔχει

3 ταῦτα: subje. of the articular infinitive τὸ . . . εἶναι; refers to the things a person has and wants
   (like strength, health, wealth)

5 οὗτος: the person described previously, namely, ὃς τοιοῦτος ὢν βούλεται τοιοῦτος εἶναι
   τοῦ μὴ ἑτοίμου: not the object of the participle ἐπιθυμῶν but of the main verb ἐπιθυμεῖ in the
   next line

10 ἀνομολογέομαι = agree upon, renew, or strengthen agreement of. Here Socrates undertakes a
   review of points already made to ensure Agathon's agreement.

11 ἄλλο τι: see vocabulary in reading 8A

14 ἐπὶ τούτοις = given these things
   ἀναμνήσθητι: aor. pass. impera. of ἀναμιμνήσκω
   τίνων: introducing an indir. question; gen. with τὸν ἔρωτα = for what

γάρ σε οὑτωσί πως εἰπεῖν, ὅτι τοῖς θεοῖς κατεσκευάσθη τὰ   16

πράγματα δι' ἔρωτα καλῶν· αἰσχρῶν γὰρ οὐκ εἴη ἔρως.   17

οὐχ οὑτωσί πως ἔλεγες;"   18

   "Εἶπον γάρ," φάναι τὸν Ἀγάθωνα.   19

   "Καὶ ἐπιεικῶς γε λέγεις, ὦ ἑταῖρε," φάναι τὸν Σωκράτη·   20

"καὶ εἰ τοῦτο οὕτως ἔχει, ἄλλο τι ὁ Ἔρως κάλλους ἂν εἴη   21

ἔρως, αἴσχους δὲ οὔ;" Ὡμολόγει.   22

   "Οὐκοῦν ὡμολόγηται, οὗ ἐνδεής ἐστι καὶ μὴ ἔχει, τούτου   23   201b

ἐρᾶν;"   24

   "Ναί," εἰπεῖν.   25

   "Ἐνδεὴς ἄρ' ἐστὶ καὶ οὐκ ἔχει ὁ Ἔρως κάλλος."   26

   "Ἀνάγκη," φάναι.   27

   "Τί δέ; τὸ ἐνδεὲς κάλλους καὶ μηδαμῇ κεκτημένον κάλλος   28

ἆρα λέγεις σὺ καλὸν εἶναι;"   29

   "Οὐ δῆτα."   30

   "Ἔτι οὖν ὁμολογεῖς Ἔρωτα καλὸν εἶναι, εἰ ταῦτα οὕτως ἔχει;"   31

   Καὶ τὸν Ἀγάθωνα εἰπεῖν, "Κινδυνεύω, ὦ Σώκρατες, οὐδὲν   32

εἰδέναι ὧν τότε εἶπον."   33

   "Καὶ μὴν καλῶς γε εἶπες," φάναι, "ὦ Ἀγάθων. ἀλλὰ   34   201c

σμικρὸν ἔτι εἰπέ· τἀγαθὰ οὐ καὶ καλὰ δοκεῖ σοι εἶναι;"   35

16–17 τοῖς θεοῖς . . . ἔρως: a close paraphrase of Agathon's words at reading 7B.37–38

17   εἴη: optative because an indirect statement in secondary sequence is implied by his paraphrase of
       Agathon (*Essentials* §158)

19   γάρ: common in brief answers, γάρ usually marks assent (Smyth 1956: §2806)

21   ἄλλο τι: see vocabulary in reading 8A

22   αἶσχος -ους τό = ugliness

31   ὁμολογεῖς = say the same [as you did before] ≠ agree [with me]

35   καί: not connecting τἀγαθά and καλά, as the absence of the definite article with καλά shows,
       but adverbial. What else does the absence of the definite article suggest about the grammatical
       function of καλά here (*Essentials* §123)?

"Ἔμοιγε."   36

"Εἰ ἄρα ὁ Ἔρως τῶν καλῶν ἐνδεής ἐστι, τὰ δὲ ἀγαθὰ   37

καλά, κἂν τῶν ἀγαθῶν ἐνδεὴς εἴη."   38

"Ἐγώ," φάναι, "ὦ Σώκρατες, σοὶ οὐκ ἂν δυναίμην ἀντιλέγειν,   39

ἀλλ᾽ οὕτως ἐχέτω ὡς σὺ λέγεις."   40

"Οὐ μὲν οὖν τῇ ἀληθείᾳ," φάναι, "ὦ φιλούμενε Ἀγάθων,   41

δύνασαι ἀντιλέγειν, ἐπεὶ Σωκράτει γε οὐδὲν χαλεπόν."   42

---

41   μὲν οὖν: in this context, the two particles work together to create a correction = no, but . . .
       (Smyth 1956: §2901b)

       φιλούμενε: voc. part., used attributively; the vocative does not use a definite article

42   Σωκράτει γε οὐδὲν χαλεπόν [ἐστιν ἀντιλέγειν]: characteristic Socratic modesty, perhaps
       ironical

Reading 9. A Woman Speaks: Diotima's Erotic Wisdom

Socrates introduces his fellow symposiasts to his own instructor in τὰ ἐρωτικά, a woman named Diotima from Mantinea. Most of this section is Socrates' report of Diotima's teaching about love when he was a young man. The introduction of Diotima further distances us from the narration: we are now getting Apollodorus's version of Aristodemus's report of Socrates' report of Diotima's speech in the still more distant past.

Since we have no other reference to Diotima in Greek literature, most scholars have assumed that Diotima is Plato's invention, and indeed there are hints in the text that she is a transparent fiction. For example, she refers directly to the myth just told by Aristophanes (reading 6), a myth as far as we know manufactured for this occasion. Diotima's name means "Zeus-Honoring" or "Zeus-Honored," and though Socrates never explicitly refers to her as a priestess, her reported actions in staving off the plague (reading 9A), the religious subject matter (especially reading 9C), and her talk of initiating Socrates into the mysteries (reading 9I) tend to suggest that she is a priestess of some kind, a high status role for women in ancient Greece. Notably, Mantinea, a region in central Greece, sounds very similar to μάντις (prophet), and the language of prophecy and divination is used heavily in this section of the dialogue and surrounding portions.[33] At the same time, Socrates appears in other dialogues being educated by *hetaerae* (Aspasia in *Menexenus* 235e–236b; Theodote in *Memorabilia* 3.11) (see introduction on *hetaerae*), and her knowledge of τὰ ἐρωτικά certainly suggests that as an intriguing alternative profession in the absence of her named one. Nussbaum 1986 points out that Alcibiades, who will figure prominently in the final part of the dialogue, was said to have had as a mistress a *hetaera* named Timandra; Diotima's name seems to be a clever reversal on that of the "man-honoring" or "man-honored" *hetaera*. Whether priestess or *hetaera*, Diotima appears to be taken quite seriously; her views are the most overtly philosophical views presented in the dialogue and the closest to Plato's own, as inferred by scholars studying Plato. Many scholars see her as the author's mouthpiece, though some prominent scholars disagree. Diotima is the only "female" voice in the dialogue, and Plato is careful to reflect that in her speech, which emphasizes sexual generation and makes heavy use of the language and imagery of pregnancy and childbirth.[34]

Parts of Diotima's speech are quite challenging, and though they may be worth doing at a measured pace with a motivated class with serious philosophical interests, they can overwhelm

---

33. See Ruprecht 1999: 44–50 for a stimulating discussion of the significance of Mantinea.

34. Halperin 1990 offers an interesting discussion of why Plato puts the most philosophical part of the dialogue in a woman's voice, the only "female" voice we hear in the work.

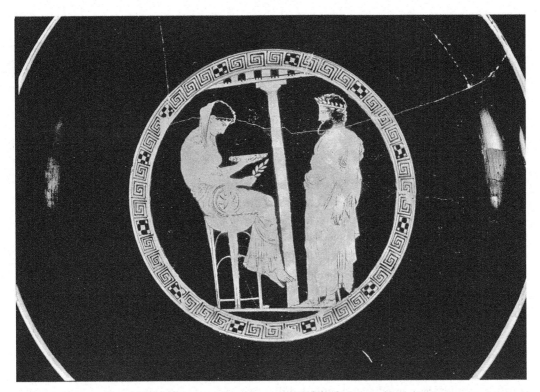

Fig. 22.   Priestess Themis delivering an oracle to Aegeus at Delphi, but suggesting a contemporary representation of the Pythia at Delphi performing her mantic duties. Kylix (drinking cup), from Vulci, ca. 440 B.C.E. Photo: Johannes Laurentius. Inv. F 2538. Antikensammlung, Staatliche Museen zu Berlin, Berlin, Germany. Photo credit: Bildarchiv Preussischer Kulturbesitz/Art Resource, New York. See Connelly 2007: 77 for discussion of the cup. This book is also a good resource for students wanting background on priestess figures like Diotima.

second-year students if the pace is too hasty or the philosophical background of the class or instructor is minimal (Allen 1991 is a helpful guide). Readings 9A–C—which offer an introduction to Diotima, a description of Eros's "demonic" character (see reading 9B introduction), and an allegorical myth of his birth to Poros and Penia—provide a nice sample for a class that does not have the time or inclination to probe the speech in depth. Readings 9I–J are particularly important philosophically: reading 9I contains a description of the initiation, and reading 9J a developed account of the so-called Platonic forms (εἴδη). These can also be read separately, assuming that previous parts of the speech are read in English translation.

Reading 9A

The precise time frame of Diotima's encounter with Socrates appears to be ten years before the outbreak of the plague in Athens in 430 B.C.E., when the historical Socrates would have been 29–30 years old, about the same age as Agathon appears to be in the dialogue, if Plato is historically accurate here. Diotima treats Socrates as very young, just as the dialogue treats Agathon as very young. Diotima's questioning shows Socrates to have been much like Agathon in his assumptions about love; Socrates acknowledges that he once shared Agathon's views that Eros was a great and beautiful god. His conversation with Diotima reveals Eros instead to be an in-between or intermediate figure: though not himself beautiful, he is not ugly either; though not wise, not ignorant either.

Vocabulary

ἀμαθής -ές: ignorant, uneducated, stupid, dull
ἀμαθία -ας ἡ: ignorance, stupidity, want of learning
μεταξύ *adv.,* or *prep. + gen.*: between
σχέδον *adv.*: nearly, almost
φρόνησις -εως ἡ: intention, thought, sense; good sense, thoughtfulness, wisdom, understanding;
　　also sometimes with negative sense: pride, presumption, arrogance

Reading 9A (*Symposium* 201d1–202b9)

Καὶ σὲ μέν γε ἤδη ἐάσω· τὸν δὲ λόγον τὸν περὶ τοῦ	1 201d
Ἔρωτος, ὅν ποτ' ἤκουσα γυναικὸς Μαντινικῆς Διοτίμας, ἣ	2
ταῦτά τε σοφὴ ἦν καὶ ἄλλα πολλά—καὶ Ἀθηναίοις ποτὲ	3
θυσαμένοις πρὸ τοῦ λοιμοῦ δέκα ἔτη ἀναβολὴν ἐποίησε τῆς	4
νόσου—ἣ δὴ καὶ ἐμὲ τὰ ἐρωτικὰ ἐδίδαξεν· ὃν οὖν ἐκείνη	5
ἔλεγε λόγον, πειράσομαι ὑμῖν διελθεῖν ἐκ τῶν ὡμολογημένων	6
ἐμοὶ καὶ Ἀγάθωνι, αὐτὸς ἐπ' ἐμαυτοῦ, ὅπως ἂν δύνωμαι.	7
δεῖ δή, ὦ Ἀγάθων, ὥσπερ σὺ διηγήσω, διελθεῖν αὐτὸν πρῶτον,	8
τίς ἐστιν ὁ Ἔρως καὶ ποῖός τις, ἔπειτα τὰ ἔργα αὐτοῦ.	9 201e
δοκεῖ οὖν μοι ῥᾷστον εἶναι οὕτω διελθεῖν, ὥς	10
ποτέ με ἡ ξένη ἀνακρίνουσα διῄει. σχεδὸν γάρ τι καὶ ἐγὼ	11

---

1   σέ = Agathon. In the previous section Socrates was cross-examining Agathon about claims Agathon made in his speech.

τὸν δὲ λόγον: the verb that governs this accusative (διελθεῖν in line 6) is so long delayed by the introduction to Diotima that Socrates has in effect to start again. He inserts a relative clause ὅν . . . (lines 5–6), for which this may be seen as the antecedent, but has to repeat λόγον, incorporating it into the relative clause (see note on line 6), apparently because the digressions have created too great a distance between the antecedent and the relative pronoun.

2   Μαντινικός -ή -όν = from Mantinea, a region in Greece

Διοτίμα -ας ἡ = Diotima (see reading 9 introduction)

4   θυσαμένοις: mid. of θύω = arrange sacrifices for one's own behalf

*λοιμός -οῦ ὁ = plague, pestilence. This was presumably the plague that took place in 430 B.C.E., near the beginning of the Peloponnesian War, so the event described here happened in 440 B.C.E., when Socrates was around 29 years old.

δέκα ἔτη: identify the case. What use of this case is this (*Essentials* §80)?

ἀναβολή -ῆς ἡ = postponement, delay

6   λόγον: an example of an "incorporated" antecedent, whereby the antecedent instead of preceding the relative clause actually becomes part of it. This is a fairly straightforward example that should be easy to translate (Smyth 1956: §§2536–38).

7   ἐμοί and Ἀγάθωνι: the form of ὡμολογημένων in line 6 explains the use of the dative (*Essentials* §114)

ἐπ' ἐμαυτοῦ = by myself (very emphatic with αὐτός)

11   ἀνακρίνω = examine closely, question, interrogate

σχεδὸν . . . τι = σχεδόν (take with τοιαῦτα in line 12)

πρὸς αὐτὴν ἕτερα τοιαῦτα ἔλεγον οἷάπερ νῦν πρὸς ἐμὲ   12

Ἀγάθων, ὡς εἴη ὁ Ἔρως μέγας θεός, εἴη δὲ τῶν καλῶν·   13

ἤλεγχε δή με τούτοις τοῖς λόγοις οἷσπερ ἐγὼ τοῦτον, ὡς   14

οὔτε καλὸς εἴη κατὰ τὸν ἐμὸν λόγον οὔτε ἀγαθός.   15

    Καὶ ἐγώ, "Πῶς λέγεις," ἔφην, "ὦ Διοτίμα; αἰσχρὸς ἄρα ὁ   16

Ἔρως ἐστὶ καὶ κακός;"   17

    Καὶ ἥ, "Οὐκ εὐφημήσεις;" ἔφη· "ἢ οἴει, ὅτι ἂν μὴ καλὸν   18

ᾖ, ἀναγκαῖον αὐτὸ εἶναι αἰσχρόν;"   19

    "Μάλιστά γε."   20   202a

---

12   ἕτερα = other (rather than "different," which would contradict the overall point)

13   εἴη: explain the use of this mood here (*Essentials* §158)

    τῶν καλῶν: there is an interesting ambiguity in the language here. τῶν καλῶν is usually interpreted as an objective genitive with ἔρως, love "of beautiful things," a very common use of the genitive in the *Symposium*. But the genitive phrase might also be interpreted as a partitive genitive used as a predicate: "Ἔρως is one of the beauties." (See Smyth 1956: §1319 on the predicate use of a partitive gen.; and compare the sentence at reading 9C.40–41: ἔστιν γὰρ δὴ τῶν καλλίστων ἡ σοφία = for wisdom is indeed one of the most beautiful things.) The second interpretation makes more sense in the immediate context, as Socrates here is describing the mistaken views that he shared with Agathon until Diotima taught him otherwise. Diotima disputes not that love is "of beautiful things" (she agrees it is, nor is this a major point of Agathon's speech) but rather that "Ἔρως is himself one of the beauties," a point that she argues explicitly against (line 15) just as she will go on to argue that Eros is not a great god (reading B.1–26). Later, following her arguments against the beauty and divinity of Eros, Diotima reinterprets τῶν καλῶν as an objective genitive, to fit her conception (reading 9D.5).

    *ἐλέγχω = put to the test, cross-examine; dispute, refute (cf. English "elenchus," a word commonly used in philosophical writing to describe Socrates' questioning of his interlocutors)

16   πῶς λέγεις; = What do you mean? (λέγω frequently has this sense)

18   εὐφημέω: though etymologically this word means "speak auspiciously" (i.e., in a way suiting a ritual or religious context), it more often means "be silent" (so that you won't speak inauspiciously) (cf. English "euphemism"). The opposite of blaspheme, the word is typically used in a ritual or religious context, asking for silence. The breadth of meaning gives a certain ambiguity to Diotima's words: they might be taken as a polite form of "shut up" and/or a request that he speak in a way more respectful to the god he is speaking of.

    ὅτι = ὅ τι (as is customary in Plato)

20   Μάλιστά γε = absolutely!, a common strong affirmative

"῏Η καὶ ἂν μὴ σοφόν, ἀμαθές; ἢ οὐκ ᾔσθησαι ὅτι ἔστιν   21

τι μεταξὺ σοφίας καὶ ἀμαθίας;"   22

"Τί τοῦτο;"   23

"Τὸ ὀρθὰ δοξάζειν καὶ ἄνευ τοῦ ἔχειν λόγον δοῦναι οὐκ   24

οἶσθ᾽," ἔφη, "ὅτι οὔτε ἐπίστασθαί ἐστιν—ἄλογον γὰρ πρᾶγμα   25

πῶς ἂν εἴη ἐπιστήμη; —οὔτε ἀμαθία—τὸ γὰρ τοῦ ὄντος   26

τυγχάνον πῶς ἂν εἴη ἀμαθία; —ἔστι δὲ δήπου τοιοῦτον ἡ   27

ὀρθὴ δόξα, μεταξὺ φρονήσεως καὶ ἀμαθίας."   28

"Ἀληθῆ," ἦν δ᾽ ἐγώ, "λέγεις."   29

"Μὴ τοίνυν ἀνάγκαζε ὃ μὴ καλόν ἐστιν αἰσχρὸν εἶναι,   30   202b

μηδὲ ὃ μὴ ἀγαθόν, κακόν. οὕτω δὲ καὶ τὸν Ἔρωτα ἐπειδὴ   31

αὐτὸς ὁμολογεῖς μὴ εἶναι ἀγαθὸν μηδὲ καλόν, μηδέν τι   32

μᾶλλον οἴου δεῖν αὐτὸν αἰσχρὸν καὶ κακὸν εἶναι, ἀλλά τι   33

μεταξύ," ἔφη, "τούτοιν."   34

"Καὶ μήν," ἦν δ᾽ ἐγώ, "ὁμολογεῖταί γε παρὰ πάντων μέγας   35

θεὸς εἶναι."   36

"Τῶν μὴ εἰδότων," ἔφη, "πάντων λέγεις, ἢ καὶ τῶν εἰδότων;"   37

"Συμπάντων μὲν οὖν."   38

---

21   ῏Η: interrogative particle; do not translate

    ἄν = ἐάν (contracted). This is very common and recurs elsewhere in this reading.

24   *δοξάζω = think, have an opinion [δόξα], conjecture. The articular infinitive τὸ . . . δοξάζειν is
      the subject of the indirect statement introduced by οὐκ οἶσθα ὅτι.

    λόγον δίδωμι = offer a reasoned explanation (something essential to knowledge in Platonic
      philosophy)

25   ἐπίστασθαί: pred. (the equivalent of an artic. inf., but without the def. art. because a pred.)
      (*Essentials* §182)

    ἄλογος -ον = without λόγος, without an account, without verbal explanation

25–26   τὸ . . . τυγχάνον = the thing that obtains by chance

26   τοῦ ὄντος = that which is, the true, the real (obj. of τυγχάνον)

33   οἴου from οἴομαι: what must the form be (*Essentials* §52)?

34   τούτοιν: dual gen. (*Essentials* §68)

35   Καὶ μήν = and yet

    παρά = among, by

38   σύμπας -πασα -παν = all together, all at once, all in a body

    μὲν οὖν: the two particles work together to create a strong affirmation = certainly, in fact . . .
      (Smyth 1956: §2901a)

Reading 9B

Diotima disputes Socrates' claim at the end of reading 9A that everyone considers Eros a great god by arguing that neither she nor Socrates could possibly think so based on their other beliefs about Eros. She goes on to categorize Eros as one of the δαίμονες (daimones), in a passage of particular interest for the history of religion as well as for the dialogue. (On δαίμονες, see introduction: "Religion in the *Symposium*.")

Vocabulary

- Make an effort to learn the principal parts of ἐγείρω and μείγνυμι.

δαιμόνιος -α -ον: having to do with δαίμονες, divine, possessed, strange, wonderful; δαιμόνιε is a common form of address, usually ironical in tone. Socrates speaks of τὸ δαιμόνιον ("the divine sign" or "personal spirit") that prevents him from making mistakes.

ἐγρήγορα: be awake; *perf. forms with pres. meaning from* ἐγείρω ἐγερῶ ἤγειρα; *mid.* ἠγρόμην ἐγρήγορα ἐγήγερμαι ἠγέρθην: awaken, wake up, rouse; *aor. mid.* ἠγρόμην: I awoke; *recognize also* ἐξηγρόμην: I awoke, I woke up

θνητός -ή -όν: mortal (cf. θνήσκω, θάνατος, ἀθάνατος, etc.)

ἱερεύς -έως ὁ: priest (cf. ἱερός); declines like βασιλεύς -έως ὁ (*Essentials* §46.3g)

καθεύδω (less commonly without prefix: εὕδω), also *imperf.* καθηῦδον and *fut.* καθευδήσω: sleep

μείγνυμι/μίγνυμι μείξω ἔμειξα—μέμειγμαι ἐμείχθην/ἐμίγην: mix; *note especially* συμμ(ε)ίγνυμι: mix together; *intrans.*: engage in social or sexual intercourse; meet in battle

Reading 9B (*Symposium* 202b10–203a8)

Καὶ ἣ γελάσασα "Καὶ πῶς ἄν," ἔφη, "ὦ Σώκρατες,	1
ὁμολογοῖτο μέγας θεὸς εἶναι παρὰ τούτων, οἵ φασιν αὐτὸν	2 202c
οὐδὲ θεὸν εἶναι;"	3
"Τίνες οὗτοι;" ἦν δ' ἐγώ.	4
"Εἷς μέν," ἔφη, "σύ, μία δ' ἐγώ."	5
Κἀγὼ εἶπον, "Πῶς τοῦτο," ἔφην, "λέγεις;"	6
Καὶ ἥ, "Ῥᾳδίως," ἔφη. "λέγε γάρ μοι, οὐ πάντας θεοὺς	7
φὴς εὐδαίμονας εἶναι καὶ καλούς; ἢ τολμήσαις ἄν τινα μὴ	8
φάναι καλόν τε καὶ εὐδαίμονα θεῶν εἶναι;"	9
"Μὰ Δί' οὐκ ἔγωγ'," ἔφην.	10
"Εὐδαίμονας δὲ δὴ λέγεις οὐ τοὺς τἀγαθὰ καὶ τὰ καλὰ	11
κεκτημένους;"	12
"Πάνυ γε."	13
"Ἀλλὰ μὴν Ἔρωτά γε ὡμολόγηκας δι' ἔνδειαν τῶν	14 202d
ἀγαθῶν καὶ καλῶν ἐπιθυμεῖν αὐτῶν τούτων ὧν ἐνδεής ἐστιν."	15
"Ὡμολόγηκα γάρ."	16
"Πῶς ἂν οὖν θεὸς εἴη ὅ γε τῶν καλῶν καὶ ἀγαθῶν ἄμοιρος;"	17
"Οὐδαμῶς, ὥς γ' ἔοικεν."	18
"Ὁρᾷς οὖν," ἔφη, "ὅτι καὶ σὺ Ἔρωτα οὐ θεὸν νομίζεις;"	19
"Τί οὖν ἄν," ἔφην, "εἴη ὁ Ἔρως; θνητός;"	20
"Ἥκιστά γε."	21

---

6   πῶς . . . λέγεις; see note on reading 9A.16. Diotima's response suggests that it could also be interpreted to mean "how can you say this?" Rose 1985: 47 suggests this is a deliberate misunderstanding on her part.

8   τινα: with partitive gen. θεῶν in line 9

8–9   μὴ φάναι: negated φημί = deny, say that . . . not

11   οὐ negates λέγεις

16   γάρ: in answers, generally marks assent or assurance (Smyth 1956: §2806)

17   θεός: the predicate, as the absence of the definite article suggests; the subject is ὁ . . . ἄμοιρος
*ἄμοιρος -ον = without any part of *gen.*, without share in (cf. *μοῖρα -ας ἡ = share, portion, allotment)

21   *Ἥκιστά γε (strong negative) = least of all, absolutely not; opposite of μάλιστά γε (reading 9A.20)

“Ἀλλὰ τί μήν;”   22

“Ὥσπερ τὰ πρότερα,” ἔφη, “μεταξὺ θνητοῦ καὶ ἀθανάτου.”   23

“Τί οὖν, ὦ Διοτίμα;”   24

“Δαίμων μέγας, ὦ Σώκρατες· καὶ γὰρ πᾶν τὸ δαιμόνιον   25

μεταξύ ἐστι θεοῦ τε καὶ θνητοῦ.”   26   203e

“Τίνα,” ἦν δ’ ἐγώ, “δύναμιν ἔχον;”   27

“Ἑρμηνεῦον καὶ διαπορθμεῦον θεοῖς τὰ παρ’ ἀνθρώπων   28

καὶ ἀνθρώποις τὰ παρὰ θεῶν, τῶν μὲν τὰς δεήσεις καὶ   29

θυσίας, τῶν δὲ τὰς ἐπιτάξεις τε καὶ ἀμοιβὰς τῶν θυσιῶν,   30

ἐν μέσῳ δὲ ὂν ἀμφοτέρων συμπληροῖ, ὥστε τὸ πᾶν αὐτὸ   31

αὐτῷ συνδεδέσθαι. διὰ τούτου καὶ ἡ μαντικὴ πᾶσα χωρεῖ   32

καὶ ἡ τῶν ἱερέων τέχνη τῶν τε περὶ τὰς θυσίας καὶ τελετὰς   33

καὶ τὰς ἐπῳδὰς καὶ τὴν μαντείαν πᾶσαν καὶ γοητείαν. θεὸς   34   203a

---

25   πᾶν τὸ δαιμόνιον = πάντες οἱ δαίμονες: a neuter singular adjective can be used to describe a
       collection of people or things (Smyth 1956: §1024)

27   ἔχον: neut. part. (agreeing with τὸ δαιμόνιον)

28–31 ἑρμηνεῦον and διαπορθμεῦον . . . ὄν: the neuter participles agree with τὸ δαιμόνιον

28   ἑρμηνεύω = interpret (cf. English “hermeneutics”)
       διαπορθμεύω = carry over or across, communicate

29   δέησις -εως ἡ = entreating, asking (i.e., a prayer) (cf. δέομαι)

30   ἐπίταξις -εως ἡ = injunction, command, order
       ἀμοιβή -ῆς ἡ = return, exchange, payback

31   συμπληρόω = fill in the gap

32   συνδέω = bind or tie together (*δέω = bind)

33   τῶν τε: the genitive definite article presumably agrees with ἱερέων. τε perhaps implies the
       repetition of τῶν περί after the repeated καίς in the next line.
       τελετή -ῆς ἡ = initiation, mystic rite, religious festival

33–34 It is tempting to see the selective use of the definite article in these lines (omitted on τελετάς and
       γοητείαν, included elsewhere) as creating three separate categories of priest: (1) τῶν περὶ
       τὰς θυσίας καὶ τελετάς, (2) τῶν περὶ τὰς ἐπῳδάς, and (3) τῶν περὶ τὴν μαντείαν πᾶσαν
       καὶ γοητείαν. But perhaps it is only stylistic.

34   ἐπῳδή -ῆς ἡ (ἐπί + ᾠδή) = song sung to or over: enchantment, charm, spell
       μαντεία -ας ἡ = prophesying, prophetic power (cf. μαντεύομαι and μαντικός)
       γοητεία -ας ἡ = sorcery, magic

δὲ ἀνθρώπῳ οὐ μείγνυται, ἀλλὰ διὰ τούτου πᾶσά ἐστιν ἡ   35

ὁμιλία καὶ ἡ διάλεκτος θεοῖς πρὸς ἀνθρώπους, καὶ ἐγρηγορόσι   36

καὶ καθεύδουσι· καὶ ὁ μὲν περὶ τὰ τοιαῦτα σοφὸς   37

δαιμόνιος ἀνήρ, ὁ δὲ ἄλλο τι σοφὸς ὢν ἢ περὶ τέχνας   38

ἢ χειρουργίας τινὰς βάναυσος. οὗτοι δὴ οἱ δαίμονες   39

πολλοὶ καὶ παντοδαποί εἰσιν, εἷς δὲ τούτων ἐστὶ καὶ ὁ   40

Ἔρως.”   41

---

36   διάλεκτος -ου ἡ = dialogue

36-37   ἐγρηγορόσι and καθεύδουσι: the most plausible explanation of both dative participles here is
        that πρὸς θεοὺς ἀνθρώποις has fallen out of the text after ἀνθρώπους (lines 28-29). The
        dative participles cannot modify θεοῖς, since mortals cannot communicate with the gods
        when the gods are asleep. The meaning surely must be when men are asleep (since the Greeks
        believed that gods conveyed messages through dreams).

39   χειρουργία -ας ἡ = working by hand, handicraft

        βάναυσος -ον = mechanical, technical (with generally negative connotations). Here, opposed to
        δαιμόνιος, it suggests uninspired and pedestrian.

Reading 9C

Diotima tells Socrates an allegorical story of Eros's birth from Πόρος (Resource) and Πενία (Poverty). This birth from two near opposites suits the in-between quality of Eros described in the previous section. Diotima explains the association of Eros with Aphrodite, more commonly his mother, by putting his conception at her birthday festivities. Radical changes of genealogy are not uncommon in Greek mythmaking, as seen in the two different accounts of Aphrodite's parentage that Pausanias makes use of in his speech (reading 4A). Diotima's characterization of Eros shares many features with the characterization of Socrates in the dialogue. Each speaker gives a version of Eros that reflects his own characteristics.

Vocabulary

ἀκόλουθος -ου ὁ: follower, attendant (cf. *ἀκολουθέω: follow, attend)

ἀπορία -ας ἡ: lack of resources, extreme distress, resourcelessness, need, poverty

διό *conj.*: wherefore, on which account, because of which

ἐπιβουλεύω + *dat. pers*: plotted against, plan or contrive (against), plot (against), scheme (against)

θεράπων -ωνος ὁ: helper, assistant, servant (cf. English "therapy")

κυέω κυήσω ἐκύησα κεκύηκα κεκύημαι ἐκυήθην *trans.*: bear *obj.* in the womb, be pregnant with, carry; *ingressive aor.*: conceive, become pregnant with; *intrans.*: be pregnant

μακρός -ά -όν: long, far

παιδίον -ου τό: little child, baby (diminutive of παῖς ὁ/ἡ)

πενία -ας ἡ: poverty; in the myth told here πενία is personified and so capitalized Πενία; *recognize also* πένης -ητος ὁ/ἡ: poor man (or woman), pauper (cf. English "penury)

πόρος -ου ὁ: way, means, resource, abundance, plenty; *in the myth told here* πόρος *is personified and so capitalized* Πόρος (cf. ἀπορέω, ἀπορία, πορίζω); *recognize also the numerous related words used in this story*: πόριμος -ον: able to provide, resourceful, inventive, contriving; ἄπορος: without resources; εὔπορος: rich in resources; εὐπορέω: be rich in resources (opposite of ἀπορέω)

φρόνιμος -ον: in one's right mind, sensible (cf. φρονέω and φρόνησις); *recognize also* ἄφρων -ον: out of one's mind, senseless

Reading 9C (*Symposium* 203a9–204c6)

"Πατρὸς δέ," ἦν δ' ἐγώ, "τίνος ἐστὶ καὶ μητρός;"	1
"Μακρότερον μέν," ἔφη, "διηγήσασθαι· ὅμως δέ σοι ἐρῶ.	2 203b
ὅτε γὰρ ἐγένετο ἡ Ἀφροδίτη, ἡστιῶντο οἱ θεοὶ οἵ τε ἄλλοι	3
καὶ ὁ τῆς Μήτιδος υἱὸς Πόρος. ἐπειδὴ δὲ ἐδείπνησαν,	4
προσαιτήσουσα οἷον δὴ εὐωχίας οὔσης ἀφίκετο ἡ Πενία, καὶ	5
ἦν περὶ τὰς θύρας. ὁ οὖν Πόρος μεθυσθεὶς τοῦ νέκταρος—	6
οἶνος γὰρ οὔπω ἦν—εἰς τὸν τοῦ Διὸς κῆπον εἰσελθὼν	7
βεβαρημένος ηὗδεν. ἡ οὖν Πενία ἐπιβουλεύουσα διὰ τὴν	8
αὑτῆς ἀπορίαν παιδίον ποιήσασθαι ἐκ τοῦ Πόρου, κατακλίνεταί	9
τε παρ' αὐτῷ καὶ ἐκύησε τὸν Ἔρωτα. διὸ δὴ καὶ	10 203c
τῆς Ἀφροδίτης ἀκόλουθος καὶ θεράπων γέγονεν ὁ Ἔρως,	11
γεννηθεὶς ἐν τοῖς ἐκείνης γενεθλίοις, καὶ ἅμα φύσει ἐραστὴς	12
ὢν περὶ τὸ καλὸν καὶ τῆς Ἀφροδίτης καλῆς οὔσης.	13
ἅτε οὖν Πόρου καὶ Πενίας υἱὸς ὢν ὁ Ἔρως ἐν τοιαύτῃ τύχῃ	14
καθέστηκεν. πρῶτον μὲν πένης ἀεί ἐστι, καὶ πολλοῦ δεῖ	15

---

1   πατρός . . . τίνος καὶ μητρός: genitives of source (*Essentials* §99)

3   ἑστιάω = receive at one's hearth or in one's house: entertain, feast, regale (cf. *ἑστία -ας ἡ = hearth, Hestia)

4   Μῆτις -ιδος ἡ = Metis, goddess of craft, cunning intelligence, mother of Athene, until Zeus swallows her so that he can possess μῆτις himself, the quality of intelligence most associated with Athene and, frequently, with the Athenians
    υός = υἱός

5   προσαιτέω = beg (fut. part. can be used without ὡς to indicate purpose)
    οἷον δή + *part.* (here) = ἅτε + *part.* (*Essentials* §174)
    εὐωχία -ας ἡ = good cheer, feast, party

6   νέκταρος: from νέκταρ -αρος ὁ = nectar; genitive because here μεθυσθείς seems to embrace an idea of fullness and verbs signifying "fullness" take genitives (Smyth 1956: §1369); μεθύσκω is more frequently accompanied by a dative (e.g., οἴνῳ = drunk on wine)

7   κῆπος -ου ὁ = garden, orchard

8   βεβαρημένος = weighed down; i.e., drunk, intoxicated (cf. βαρύς)

12   γενέθλια -ων τά = birthday festivities

14   υός: see note on line 4
    τύχη = position, situation

15   πολλοῦ δεῖ = he lacks much; i.e., is far from

ἁπαλός τε καὶ καλός, οἷον οἱ πολλοὶ οἴονται, ἀλλὰ σκληρὸς   16

καὶ αὐχμηρὸς καὶ ἀνυπόδητος καὶ ἄοικος, χαμαιπετὴς ἀεὶ   17   203d

ὢν καὶ ἄστρωτος, ἐπὶ θύραις καὶ ἐν ὁδοῖς ὑπαίθριος κοιμώμενος,   18

τὴν τῆς μητρὸς φύσιν ἔχων, ἀεὶ ἐνδείᾳ σύνοικος.   19

κατὰ δὲ αὖ τὸν πατέρα ἐπίβουλός ἐστι τοῖς καλοῖς καὶ τοῖς   20

ἀγαθοῖς, ἀνδρεῖος ὢν καὶ ἴτης καὶ σύντονος, θηρευτὴς   21

δεινός, ἀεί τινας πλέκων μηχανάς, καὶ φρονήσεως ἐπιθυμητὴς   22

καὶ πόριμος, φιλοσοφῶν διὰ παντὸς τοῦ βίου,   23

δεινὸς γόης καὶ φαρμακεὺς καὶ σοφιστής· καὶ οὔτε ὡς   24

ἀθάνατος πέφυκεν οὔτε ὡς θνητός, ἀλλὰ τοτὲ μὲν τῆς αὐτῆς   25   203e

ἡμέρας θάλλει τε καὶ ζῇ, ὅταν εὐπορήσῃ, τοτὲ δὲ ἀποθνήσκει,   26

πάλιν δὲ ἀναβιώσκεται διὰ τὴν τοῦ πατρὸς φύσιν, τὸ   27

δὲ ποριζόμενον ἀεὶ ὑπεκρεῖ, ὥστε οὔτε ἀπορεῖ Ἔρως ποτὲ   28

οὔτε πλουτεῖ, σοφίας τε αὖ καὶ ἀμαθίας ἐν μέσῳ ἐστίν.   29

ἔχει γὰρ ὧδε. θεῶν οὐδεὶς φιλοσοφεῖ οὐδ᾽ ἐπιθυμεῖ σοφὸς   30   204a

---

17   αὐχμηρός -ά -όν = dry, dusty, rough, squalid
     *ἀνυπόδητος -ον = unshod, barefoot, shoeless
     ἄοικος -ον = homeless
     χαμαιπετής -ές = sleeping on the ground
18   ἄστρωτος -ον = without bed or bedding
     ὑπαίθριος -ον = under the sky, in the open air
     κοιμάομαι = sleep
19   σύνοικος -ον = dwelling in the same house with *dat.*
20   ἐπίβουλος -ου ὁ = one who schemes after, one who plans to ensnare *dat.* (cf. ἐπιβουλεύω)
21   ἴτης -ου ὁ = one who goes, goer, hasty one; impetuous, bold actor
     σύντονος -ον = intense
     θηρευτής -ου ὁ = hunter, huntsman (cf. θήριον τό and θήρ ὁ)
22   ἐπιθυμητής -ου ὁ = one who longs for or desires, man of desire
24   γόης -ητος ὁ = one who howls out enchantments, sorcerer, enchanter, magician
     φαρμακεύς -έως ὁ = one who deals in medicines, drugs, or poisons; sorcerer, healer
24–25 ὡς ἀθάνατος . . . ὡς θνητός = like an immortal . . . like a mortal
25–26 τότε μεν . . . τότε δέ = at one time . . . at another
26   θάλλω = bloom
27   ἀναβιώσκομαι = come to life again
28   ὑπεκρέω = ὑπό + ἐκ + ῥέω = flow out from under, slip away

γενέσθαι—ἔστι γάρ—οὐδ᾽ εἴ τις ἄλλος σοφός, οὐ φιλοσοφεῖ.   31

οὐδ᾽ αὖ οἱ ἀμαθεῖς φιλοσοφοῦσιν οὐδ᾽ ἐπιθυμοῦσι σοφοὶ   32

γενέσθαι· αὐτὸ γὰρ τοῦτό ἐστι χαλεπὸν ἀμαθία, τὸ μὴ   33

ὄντα καλὸν κἀγαθὸν μηδὲ φρόνιμον δοκεῖν αὑτῷ εἶναι   34

ἱκανόν. οὔκουν ἐπιθυμεῖ ὁ μὴ οἰόμενος ἐνδεὴς εἶναι οὗ ἂν   35

μὴ οἴηται ἐπιδεῖσθαι."   36

　　"Τίνες οὖν," ἔφην ἐγώ, "ὦ Διοτίμα, οἱ φιλοσοφοῦντες, εἰ   37

μήτε οἱ σοφοὶ μήτε οἱ ἀμαθεῖς;"   38

　　"Δῆλον δή," ἔφη, "τοῦτό γε ἤδη καὶ παιδί, ὅτι οἱ μεταξὺ   39　204b

τούτων ἀμφοτέρων, ὧν ἂν εἴη καὶ ὁ Ἔρως. ἔστιν γὰρ δὴ τῶν   40

καλλίστων ἡ σοφία, Ἔρως δ᾽ ἐστὶν ἔρως περὶ τὸ καλόν,   41

ὥστε ἀναγκαῖον Ἔρωτα φιλόσοφον εἶναι, φιλόσοφον δὲ   42

ὄντα μεταξὺ εἶναι σοφοῦ καὶ ἀμαθοῦς. αἰτία δὲ αὐτῷ καὶ   43

τούτων ἡ γένεσις· πατρὸς μὲν γὰρ σοφοῦ ἐστι καὶ εὐπόρου,   44

μητρὸς δὲ οὐ σοφῆς καὶ ἀπόρου. ἡ μὲν οὖν φύσις τοῦ   45

δαίμονος, ὦ φίλε Σώκρατες, αὕτη· ὃν δὲ σὺ ᾠήθης Ἔρωτα   46

εἶναι, θαυμαστὸν οὐδὲν ἔπαθες. ᾠήθης δέ, ὡς ἐμοὶ δοκεῖ   47　204c

---

31　οὐ: redundant and reinforcing after οὐδ᾽. Do not translate both.

33　αὐτὸ . . . τοῦτο: acc. of respect with χαλεπόν; anticipates articular infinitive τὸ . . . δοκεῖν. What
　　use of αὐτός is this (*Essentials* §202)?

　　χαλεπόν: pred. adj.; neut. (instead of fem. agreeing with the subje. ἀμαθία) suggests "a difficult
　　thing"

33–34　μὴ ὄντα . . . φρόνιμον: concessive participle clause with an articular infinitive, accusative
　　because agreeing with the subject of the infinitive. The fact that μὴ ὢν καλὸς κἀγαθὸς μηδὲ
　　φρόνιμος δοκεῖ αὑτῷ εἶναι ἱκανός.

36　ἐπιδέομαι = δέομαι

39　δῆλον . . . καὶ παιδί: Diotima's teasing attitude toward Socrates' intelligence is characteristic

40–41　ὧν and τῶν καλλίστων: partitive genitives (pred. use); translate: "among *gen.*" (Smyth 1956:
　　§1319)

44　τούτων: gen. with αἰτία; καί is adverbial

44–45　πατρός and μητρός: what is this use of these genitives (*Essentials* §99)?

46–47　ὃν . . . εἶναι: the entire clause is an accusative of respect = and as for what you thought Eros
　　was . . .

τεκμαιρομένη ἐξ ὧν σὺ λέγεις, τὸ ἐρώμενον Ἔρωτα εἶναι,   48

οὐ τὸ ἐρῶν· διὰ ταῦτά σοι οἶμαι πάγκαλος ἐφαίνετο ὁ   49

Ἔρως. καὶ γὰρ ἔστι τὸ ἐραστὸν τὸ τῷ ὄντι καλὸν καὶ   50

ἁβρὸν καὶ τέλεον καὶ μακαριστόν· τὸ δέ γε ἐρῶν ἄλλην   51

ἰδέαν τοιαύτην ἔχον, οἵαν ἐγὼ διῆλθον."   52

---

48   τεκμαίρομαι = infer, judge

    τὸ ἐρώμενον ... οὐ τὸ ἐρῶν: Diotima's criticism of Socrates for thinking Eros was τὸ ἐρώμενον is an important innovation. It is certainly more traditional in Greek thought to characterize Eros with qualities appropriate to an ἐρώμενος. Notably, Agathon, himself an ἐρώμενος, makes the same assumption.

49   οἶμαι: purely parenthetical here; treat independently of the rest of the sentence

50   ἐραστός -ή -όν = loveable, beloved (distinguish from the masc. noun ἐραστής -οῦ ὁ)

50–51   τὸ τῷ ὄντι καλὸν ... μακαριστόν: despite the definite article, this must be the predicate

51   ἁβρός -ά -όν = delicate

    τέλεος -ον = perfect

    μακαριστός -ή -όν: deemed or considered happy

52   ἰδέα -ας ἡ = form, shape, appearance

    ἔχον: neut. part. subst.; the definite article is presumably omitted because it is a predicate here (with ἐστι understood as the main verb)

Reading 9D

Diotima explains that Socrates has been confused because he thought Eros was "the beloved" rather than "the lover." Socrates then asks Diotima what good love is to human beings. In response to her questioning, he determines that a lover of beautiful or good things desires that those things become his own, and that this will bring him happiness. Diotima and Socrates then ponder why we say some people are in love and others not, when everyone is looking for beautiful and good things that will bring them happiness. The passage ends with a challenging discussion of the way humans use language, giving the name of the whole thing "love" to a part of it. Diotima uses an analogy to the word ποίησις, which is normally applied in Greek to the art of poetry, and poet (ποιητής), although both words are about making or creating, as their etymology shows (from the verb ποιέω). Properly speaking, Diotima argues, the words should apply to all creating and creation.

Vocabulary

ἀπόκρισις -εως ἡ: answer (cf. ἀποκρίνομαι)
ἐρώτησις -εως ἡ: question (cf. ἐρωτάω)
ὀνομάζω ὀνομάσω ὠνόμασα ὠνόμακα ὠνόμασμαι ὠνομάσθην: name or speak of by name, call or address by name
ποίησις -εως ἡ: poetry, the art of poetry, creation, creativity (cf. ποιέω and ποιητής -οῦ ὁ)

Reading 9D (*Symposium* 204c7–205c10)

Καὶ ἐγὼ εἶπον, "Εἶεν δή, ὦ ξένη, καλῶς γὰρ λέγεις·	1
τοιοῦτος ὢν ὁ Ἔρως τίνα χρείαν ἔχει τοῖς ἀνθρώποις;"	2
"Τοῦτο δὴ μετὰ ταῦτ'," ἔφη, "ὦ Σώκρατες, πειράσομαί σε	3 204d
διδάξαι. ἔστι μὲν γὰρ δὴ τοιοῦτος καὶ οὕτω γεγονὼς ὁ	4
Ἔρως, ἔστι δὲ τῶν καλῶν, ὡς σὺ φής. εἰ δέ τις ἡμᾶς	5
ἔροιτο· Τί τῶν καλῶν ἐστιν ὁ Ἔρως, ὦ Σώκρατές τε	6
καὶ Διοτίμα; ὧδε δὲ σαφέστερον· ἐρᾷ ὁ ἐρῶν τῶν καλῶν·	7
τί ἐρᾷ;"	8
Καὶ ἐγὼ εἶπον ὅτι "Γενέσθαι αὑτῷ."	9
"Ἀλλ' ἔτι ποθεῖ," ἔφη, "ἡ ἀπόκρισις ἐρώτησιν τοιάνδε· Τί	10
ἔσται ἐκείνῳ ᾧ ἂν γένηται τὰ καλά;"	11
Οὐ πάνυ ἔφην ἔτι ἔχειν ἐγὼ πρὸς ταύτην τὴν ἐρώτησιν	12
προχείρως ἀποκρίνασθαι.	13
"Ἀλλ'," ἔφη, "ὥσπερ ἂν εἴ τις μεταβαλὼν ἀντὶ τοῦ καλοῦ	14 204e
τῷ ἀγαθῷ χρώμενος πυνθάνοιτο· Φέρε, ὦ Σώκρατες, ἐρᾷ ὁ	15
ἐρῶν τῶν ἀγαθῶν· τί ἐρᾷ;' "	16
"Γενέσθαι," ἦν δ' ἐγώ, "αὑτῷ."	17
"Καὶ τί ἔσται ἐκείνῳ ᾧ ἂν γένηται τἀγαθά;"	18
"Τοῦτ' εὐπορώτερον," ἦν δ' ἐγώ, "ἔχω ἀποκρίνασθαι, ὅτι	19

---

2   χρεία -ας ἡ = use (cf. χράομαι)

5   τῶν καλῶν: obj. gen. with Ἔρως

6, 8   Τί *adverbial* = why? in what way, in what respect?

9   Γενέσθαι: the full meaning of Ἐρᾷ [= ἐπιθυμεῖ] τὰ καλὰ γενέσθαι αὑτῷ can be inferred
          from the question
       αὑτῷ: dat. of possessor (*Essentials* §107). What does the rough breathing mean (see note on
          reading 6A.31 or *Essentials* §205)?

13   προχείρως = readily, offhandedly; i.e., without further thought

14   Ἀλλ' . . . ὥσπερ ἂν εἰ: implies in this context Ἀλλ' ἀπόκριναι ὥσπερ ἂν ἀποκρίναιο εἰ . . .
       μεταβάλλω = shift [to another set of terms], change [one's terms]

16   τί: see note on lines 6, 8

19   εὐπορώτερον: compar. adv. of εὔπορος

εὐδαίμων ἔσται."   20

"Κτήσει γάρ," ἔφη, "ἀγαθῶν οἱ εὐδαίμονες εὐδαίμονες, καὶ   21   205a
οὐκέτι προσδεῖ ἐρέσθαι 'Ἵνα τί δὲ βούλεται εὐδαίμων εἶναι   22
ὁ βουλόμενος;' ἀλλὰ τέλος δοκεῖ ἔχειν ἡ ἀπόκρισις."   23

"Ἀληθῆ λέγεις," εἶπον ἐγώ.   24

"Ταύτην δὴ τὴν βούλησιν καὶ τὸν ἔρωτα τοῦτον πότερα   25
κοινὸν οἴει εἶναι πάντων ἀνθρώπων, καὶ πάντας τἀγαθὰ   26
βούλεσθαι αὑτοῖς εἶναι ἀεί, ἢ πῶς λέγεις;"   27

"Οὕτως," ἦν δ' ἐγώ· "κοινὸν εἶναι πάντων."   28

"Τί δὴ οὖν," ἔφη, "ὦ Σώκρατες, οὐ πάντας ἐρᾶν φαμεν,   29
εἴπερ γε πάντες τῶν αὐτῶν ἐρῶσι καὶ ἀεί, ἀλλά τινάς φαμεν   30   205b
ἐρᾶν, τοὺς δ' οὔ;"   31

"Θαυμάζω," ἦν δ' ἐγώ, "καὶ αὐτός."   32

"Ἀλλὰ μὴ θαύμαζ'," ἔφη· "ἀφελόντες γὰρ ἄρα τοῦ ἔρωτός   33
τι εἶδος ὀνομάζομεν, τὸ τοῦ ὅλου ἐπιτιθέντες ὄνομα, ἔρωτα,   34
τὰ δὲ ἄλλα ἄλλοις καταχρώμεθα ὀνόμασιν."   35

---

21   κτῆσις -εως ἡ = acquisition, possession (cf. κτάομαι)
22   προσδεῖ (impers. verb) = it is also necessary, it is necessary in addition
      Ἵνα τί . . . ; = so that what . . . ? i.e., for what purpose . . . ? τί takes the place of a purpose cause here.
23   τέλος: happiness being an end in itself, apparently
25   Ταύτην . . . τοῦτον: the subjects of the indirect statement introduced by οἴει in line 26
      βούλησις -εως ἡ = wish, desire (cf. βούλομαι)
      πότερα: introduces a question with two alternatives (= πότερον). Do not translate.
26   κοινὸν . . . πάντων ἀνθρώπων: with a genitive of person κοινός can mean "shared by gen.,
      common to gen."
29   ἐρᾶν = are in love (inf. in an indir. statement). Diotima here comments on the Greek word ἐράω
      being normally limited to those who experience erotic love, not to all forms of desirous love.
      (In some cases, ἐράω/ἔρως extends beyond the realm of the erotic, but that use seems
      designed to highlight the power of the emotion.)
30–31 τινάς . . . τοὺς δ' = some . . . others
33   ἀφελόντες (from ἀφαιρέω) = separating off, distinguishing
33–34 ἔρωτός τι εἶδος = one manifestation of love
34   ἐπιτίθημι = attribute to, give to
      ἔρωτα: both an objective complement to εἶδος after ὀνομάζομεν and in apposition to τὸ τοῦ
      ὅλου . . . ὄνομα
35   καταχράομαι = use dat. for acc.

"Ὥσπερ τί;" ἦν δ' ἐγώ.   36

"Ὥσπερ τόδε. οἶσθ' ὅτι ποίησίς ἐστί τι πολύ· ἡ γάρ   37

τοι ἐκ τοῦ μὴ ὄντος εἰς τὸ ὂν ἰόντι ὁτῳοῦν αἰτία πᾶσά ἐστι   38

ποίησις, ὥστε καὶ αἱ ὑπὸ πάσαις ταῖς τέχναις ἐργασίαι   39   205c

ποιήσεις εἰσὶ καὶ οἱ τούτων δημιουργοὶ πάντες ποιηταί."   40

    "Ἀληθῆ λέγεις."   41

    "Ἀλλ' ὅμως," ἦ δ' ἥ, "οἶσθ' ὅτι οὐ καλοῦνται ποιηταὶ ἀλλὰ   42

ἄλλα ἔχουσιν ὀνόματα, ἀπὸ δὲ πάσης τῆς ποιήσεως ἓν   43

μόριον ἀφορισθὲν τὸ περὶ τὴν μουσικὴν καὶ τὰ μέτρα τῷ   44

τοῦ ὅλου ὀνόματι προσαγορεύεται. ποίησις γὰρ τοῦτο   45

μόνον καλεῖται, καὶ οἱ ἔχοντες τοῦτο τὸ μόριον τῆς ποιήσεως   46

ποιηταί."   47

    "Ἀληθῆ λέγεις," ἔφην.   48

---

37   ποίησις -εως ἡ = creation, making (but the discussion necessitates understanding that this word
           is normally used in Greek specifically of poetic creation—hence English "poetic")
       τι πολύ = something multiple (i.e., with many different manifestations)

37–38 ἡ . . . αἰτία: all the words between the definite article and the noun αἰτία are in the attributive
           position. Hence they define the kind of cause (αἰτία) under discussion.

39   ἐργασία -ας ἡ = work, activity

40   ποιηταί = makers, creators (but the discussion necessitates understanding that this word is
           normally used in Greek specifically of poets—hence English "poet"). What is the function of
           this noun (*Essentials* §73)?

44   μόριον -ου τό = small piece, portion
       ἀφορίζω = mark off with boundaries, set apart, define
       τὰ μέτρα = poetic meters, rhythms

45   προσαγορεύω = name, call by name

Reading 9E

Beginning where reading 9D left off, the discussion suggests that only people who have a sexual form of eros are described as lovers or said to be in love, when in fact the word ought to apply to many more people who experience strong desire for good and beautiful things. The passage develops a definition of the object of love as "to possess the good for oneself forever" and also contains the first mention of "birth in the beautiful," a central metaphor of subsequent passages.

Vocabulary

ἀλλότριος -α -ον: another's, alien (to), foreign (to), unfriendly (to)
ἴσχω: (1) hold, possess; (2) hold, check, curb, keep back, restrain
οἰκεῖος -α -ον: in or of the house, domestic, one's own, related
πρᾶξις -εως ἡ: doing, deed, transaction, business
σπουδάζω σπουδάσομαι ἐσπούδασα ἐσπούδακα ἐσπούδασμαι ἐσπουδήσθην: be concerned, be eager, make haste, be serious
σπουδή -ῆς ἡ: eagerness, zeal, effort, earnestness, seriousness, haste, speed

Reading 9E (*Symposium* 205d1–206b10)

"Οὕτω τοίνυν καὶ περὶ τὸν ἔρωτα. τὸ μὲν κεφάλαιόν ἐστι	1	205d
πᾶσα ἡ τῶν ἀγαθῶν ἐπιθυμία καὶ τοῦ εὐδαιμονεῖν ὁ μέγιστός	2	
τε καὶ δολερὸς ἔρως παντί· ἀλλ᾽ οἱ μὲν ἄλλῃ	3	
τρεπόμενοι πολλαχῇ ἐπ᾽ αὐτόν, ἢ κατὰ χρηματισμὸν ἢ κατὰ	4	
φιλογυμναστίαν ἢ κατὰ φιλοσοφίαν, οὔτε ἐρᾶν καλοῦνται	5	
οὔτε ἐρασταί, οἱ δὲ κατὰ ἕν τι εἶδος ἰόντες τε καὶ ἐσπουδακότες	6	
τὸ τοῦ ὅλου ὄνομα ἴσχουσιν, ἔρωτά τε καὶ ἐρᾶν καὶ ἐρασταί."	7	
"Κινδυνεύεις ἀληθῆ," ἔφην ἐγώ, "λέγειν."	8	

---

1   Οὕτω ... ἔρωτα: Diotima refers back to the point she made at the end of the previous reading about the words ποίησις and ποιητής, words that she argued ought to have a wider application but are generally applied to one specific form of "creation" only, namely, poetry.

   τὸ ... κεφάλαιον: adverbial accusative, more or less equivalent to ἐν κεφαλαίῳ

2   εὐδαιμονέω = be well off, be fortunate, be happy

2–3   ὁ ... ἔρως: in apposition to ἡ ... ἐπιθυμία

3   δολερός -ά -όν = deceitful, treacherous. The unexpected word choice leads scholars to suspect that Plato is quoting here, but the source is unknown. Eros is frequently depicted as cunning and deceitful, willing to stoop to anything to get the beloved.

   παντί: dat. of the possessor (*Essentials* §107)

4   πολλαχῇ: take with ἄλλῃ = in other ways, [which/that are] numerous

   ἐπ᾽ αὐτόν: i.e., to Eros

   κατά: used repeatedly in lines 4–6 to specify the arena in which love is expressed; the translation will vary depending on the translation of the governing verb: "in" or "through" or "in accordance with" should work in most translations, but be flexible

   χρηματισμός -οῦ ὁ = moneymaking, business

5   φιλογυμναστία -ας ἡ = love of exercise

   οὔτε ἐρᾶν καλοῦνται = are not called "in love," i.e., are not said to be in love

6   οἱ δέ: as opposed to οἱ μέν in line 3

   κατά: see note on line 4

   ἕν τι εἶδος = one certain species

   ἐσπουδακότες from σπουδάζω: what form must this be, and what is the force of the tense in Greek?

7   ἔρωτά ... ἐρασταί: the accusative ἔρωτα is in apposition to ὄνομα; the nominative ἐρασταί arises because though a predicate it describes the subject of the sentence (pred. nom.). The idiom ὄνομα ἴσχουσιν is virtually synonymous with καλοῦνται.

"Καὶ λέγεται μέν γέ τις," ἔφη, "λόγος, ὡς οἳ ἂν τὸ ἥμισυ   9

ἑαυτῶν ζητῶσιν, οὗτοι ἐρῶσιν· ὁ δ' ἐμὸς λόγος οὔτε ἡμίσεός   10   205e

φησιν εἶναι τὸν ἔρωτα οὔτε ὅλου, ἐὰν μὴ τυγχάνῃ γέ που,   11

ὦ ἑταῖρε, ἀγαθὸν ὄν, ἐπεὶ αὑτῶν γε καὶ πόδας καὶ χεῖρας   12

ἐθέλουσιν ἀποτέμνεσθαι οἱ ἄνθρωποι, ἐὰν αὑτοῖς δοκῇ τὰ   13

ἑαυτῶν πονηρὰ εἶναι. οὐ γὰρ τὸ ἑαυτῶν οἶμαι ἕκαστοι   14

ἀσπάζονται, εἰ μὴ εἴ τις τὸ μὲν ἀγαθὸν οἰκεῖον καλεῖ καὶ   15

ἑαυτοῦ, τὸ δὲ κακὸν ἀλλότριον· ὡς οὐδέν γε ἄλλο ἐστὶν οὗ   16

ἐρῶσιν ἄνθρωποι ἢ τοῦ ἀγαθοῦ. ἢ σοι δοκοῦσιν;"   17   206a

"Μὰ Δί' οὐκ ἔμοιγε," ἦν δ' ἐγώ.   18

"Ἆρ' οὖν," ἦ δ' ἥ, "οὕτως ἁπλοῦν ἐστι λέγειν ὅτι οἱ   19

ἄνθρωποι τἀγαθοῦ ἐρῶσιν;"   20

"Ναί," ἔφην.   21

"Τί δέ; οὐ προσθετέον," ἔφη, "ὅτι καὶ εἶναι τὸ ἀγαθὸν   22

αὑτοῖς ἐρῶσιν;"   23

"Προσθετέον."   24

"Ἆρ' οὖν," ἔφη, "καὶ οὐ μόνον εἶναι, ἀλλὰ καὶ ἀεὶ εἶναι;"   25

"Καὶ τοῦτο προσθετέον."   26

"Ἔστιν ἄρα συλλήβδην," ἔφη, "ὁ ἔρως τοῦ τὸ ἀγαθὸν αὑτῷ   27

εἶναι ἀεί."   28

"Ἀληθέστατα," ἔφην ἐγώ, "λέγεις."   29

---

9   τις ... λόγος: clearly refers to Aristophanes' myth (reading 6); the pretense that this story was
        known to Diotima supports the fictional status of this entire account.

12   ὄν: supplementary part. with τυγχάνῃ in line 11 (*Essentials* §170); neut. with implied subje. τὸ
        ἥμισυ ἢ τὸ ὅλον

12–14   ἐπεὶ ... εἶναι: apparently amputation for medical purposes

14   πονηρά = causing πόνος; i.e., painful, or harmful in some other way
        οἶμαι: parenthetical (as often)

15   εἰ μὴ εἴ = unless if ...

15–16   οἰκεῖον ... ἀλλότριον: identify this use of the adjective (*Essentials* §123)

17   τοῦ ἀγαθοῦ: parallel to οὐδέν γε ἄλλο, but attracted to the case of the relative οὗ in line 17

22, 24, 26   προσθετέος -α -ον: verbal adj. of προστίθημι = add

27   συλλήβδην *adv.* = in sum, in short (σύν + ληψ- → λαμβάνω, i.e., taken together)
        τοῦ: explain what the definite article is doing here (*Essentials* §182)

"Ὅτε δὴ τοῦτο ὁ ἔρως ἐστὶν ἀεί," ἦ δ' ἥ, "τῶν τίνα τρόπον   30   206b

διωκόντων αὐτὸ καὶ ἐν τίνι πράξει ἡ σπουδὴ καὶ ἡ σύντασις   31

ἔρως ἂν καλοῖτο; τί τοῦτο τυγχάνει ὂν τὸ ἔργον; ἔχεις   32

εἰπεῖν;"   33

"Οὐ μεντἂν σέ," ἔφην ἐγώ, "ὦ Διοτίμα, ἐθαύμαζον ἐπὶ   34

σοφίᾳ καὶ ἐφοίτων παρὰ σὲ αὐτὰ ταῦτα μαθησόμενος."   35

"Ἀλλὰ ἐγώ σοι," ἔφη, "ἐρῶ. ἔστι γὰρ τοῦτο τόκος ἐν   36

καλῷ καὶ κατὰ τὸ σῶμα καὶ κατὰ τὴν ψυχήν."   37

"Μαντείας," ἦν δ' ἐγώ, "δεῖται ὅτι ποτε λέγεις, καὶ οὐ   38

μανθάνω."   39

30–31   Ὅτε δή = since

      τῶν ... διωκόντων: subje. gen. with ἡ σπουδὴ καὶ ἡ σύντασις (*Essentials* §91)

31   σύντασις -εως ἡ: vehement effort, exertion

34   μεντἂν = μεντοι + ἄν

34–35   present contrary-to-fact condition with implied protasis = if I could ... (*Essentials* §162), implying
      a "no" answer to Diotima's question

35   φοιτάω = come regularly, visit repeatedly

      μαθησόμενος: identify the tense of the participle and explain its use (*Essentials* §172)

36   τόκος -ου ὁ = birth

38   μαντεία -ας ἡ = divination, the study of a prophetic remark to elicit its meaning

      δεῖται = needs *gen.*

      ὅτι ... λέγεις: the relative clause is the subject of the verb δεῖται (ὅτι = ὅ τι)

39   μανθάνω = understand (as often), but also echoing the sound of μαντείας

Reading 9F

Having defined Eros through its object in the previous reading and thus having completed the first part of the agenda she laid out in reading 9A.9 (τίς ἐστιν ὁ Ἔρως καὶ ποῖός τις), Diotima turns to the second half of that agenda (τὰ ἔργα αὐτοῦ). Reading 9F argues that Ἔρως aims not at beauty per se, but at reproduction and birth in beauty, that is, at a kind of immortality. This passage makes the bold claim that ἔρως is really desire for the only kind of immortality that mortals can obtain, by suggesting that the desire for intercourse is an (unconscious) desire to reproduce. It also attempts to draw a rather difficult analogy between the act of sexual intercourse and that of childbirth (lines 8–13 in particular); this occurs at least in part because Diotima makes equivalent the male activity of begetting (γεννάω) and the female activity of giving birth (τίκτω). Moreover, she wishes to draw a close analogy between the production of children and other forms of human creativity. There is consequently a three-way analogy here:

sexual desire	intercourse
pregnancy	labor and birth of children
intellectual aspirations	creation of intellectual products

But the precise relationships within those analogies are often hard to follow. Allen 1991: 71 comments that sometimes it seems that things are born before they are begotten.[35] Likewise, the notion that all people are pregnant in body and soul, though it makes sense as a way of talking about human potential, does away with the notion that sexual intercourse needs to take place prior to pregnancy, a fact well known to the Greeks.

Vocabulary

- Be sure to learn the principal parts of τρέφω.

ἀθανασία -ας ἡ: immortality (cf. ἀθάνατος)
γέννησις -εως ἡ: procreation, generation, engendering, producing (cf. γεννάω) (distinguish from γένεσις, which is related to γίγνομαι)

---

35. Burnyeat 1977 also makes engaging reading on some of the problems with Plato's conception.

διατίθεμαι (pass. of διατίθημι) + *adv.*: be [in a certain state], be disposed or affected [in a certain manner]; e.g., δεινῶς διατίθεμαι: I am terribly affected; ἐρωτικῶς διατίθενται: they are affected by erotic passion, they are passionately in love

ἡλικία -ας ἡ: time of life, age; prime of life, maturity

μοῖρα -ας ἡ: allotment, portion, share, fate; *personified as* αἱ Μοῖραι: the Fates, goddesses who oversee life and death; *recognize also* ἄμοιρος -ον: without a share of *gen.*

τρέφω θρέψω ἔτρεψα τέτροφα τέθραμμαι ἐθρέφθην/ἐτράφην: bring up from childhood, rear, nourish, nurse; *recognize also* ἐκτρέφω, *with essentially the same meaning*

τροφή -ῆς ἡ: upbringing, rearing; nourishment, food, feeding

Reading 9F (*Symposium* 206c1–207c7)

"ἀλλ' ἐγώ," ἦ δ' ἥ, "σαφέστερον ἐρῶ. κυοῦσιν γάρ," ἔφη,	1	206c
"ὦ Σώκρατες, πάντες ἄνθρωποι καὶ κατὰ τὸ σῶμα καὶ κατὰ	2	
τὴν ψυχήν, καὶ ἐπειδὰν ἔν τινι ἡλικίᾳ γένωνται, τίκτειν	3	
ἐπιθυμεῖ ἡμῶν ἡ φύσις. τίκτειν δὲ ἐν μὲν αἰσχρῷ οὐ	4	
δύναται, ἐν δὲ τῷ καλῷ. ἡ γὰρ ἀνδρὸς καὶ γυναικὸς	5	
συνουσία τόκος ἐστίν. ἔστι δὲ τοῦτο θεῖον τὸ πρᾶγμα,	6	
καὶ τοῦτο ἐν θνητῷ ὄντι τῷ ζῴῳ ἀθάνατον ἔνεστιν, ἡ κύησις	7	
καὶ ἡ γέννησις. τὰ δὲ ἐν τῷ ἀναρμόστῳ ἀδύνατον γενέσθαι.	8	
ἀνάρμοστον δ' ἐστὶ τὸ αἰσχρὸν παντὶ τῷ θείῳ, τὸ	9	206d
δὲ καλὸν ἁρμόττον. Μοῖρα οὖν καὶ Εἰλείθυια ἡ Καλλονή	10	

---

1   κυοῦσιν *intrans.* = are pregnant (review various meanings of this verb, which recurs throughout this passage). This metaphorical notion that all are pregnant in both body and soul suggests the human potential for both physical and intellectual productivity.

4–5   ἐν αἰσχρῷ . . . ἐν τῷ καλῷ: the gender ambiguity (neut. or masc.) seems deliberate. Given that Diotima is talking about both physical and intellectual productivity and about pregnancy and birth, it probably should be extended to include the feminine as well. Translations such as "in something ugly" or "in what is beautiful" can preserve some of that self-conscious ambiguity.

4–5   ἡ . . . συνουσία = intercourse, union, being together (both the specific sexual act and the more general notion seem to be implied)

5   τόκος -ου ὁ = childbirth (cf. τέτοκα from τίκτω). The nature of the equivalency drawn here is uncertain. Is the first essential to or a part of the second? Or are they loosely or metaphorically equivalents?

7   θνητῷ ὄντι: circumstantial part. with a concessive force = although mortal
τῷ ζῴῳ: obj. of ἔνεστιν = what is living (includes people and animals)
κύησις -εως ἡ = conception, pregnancy

7–8   ἡ κύησις καὶ ἡ γέννησις: in apposition to τοῦτο . . . τὸ πρᾶγμα (line 6)

8   τὰ δέ: τά is a demonstrative referring back to ἡ κύησις καὶ ἡ γέννησις
ἀνάρμοστος -ον = inharmonious; + *dat.* = inharmonious with, incompatible with
ἀδύνατόν (ἐστι) + *acc.* + *inf.*

9   ἀνάρμοστον δ' ἐστὶ τὸ αἰσχρόν: the definite article helps make the sentence structure clear

10   ἁρμόττω = fit together, join, be harmonious with
Εἰλείθυια -ας ἡ = Eileithyia, goddess of childbirth, who together with one of the Fates (Μοῖραι) is seen as present as birth
Καλλονή -ῆς ἡ = Beauty, a personification apparently manufactured to make a point. The argument seems to be that Beauty both leads to life (and thus is one of the Μοῖραι) and also makes birth actually easier and more pleasant (and thus is in essence Εἰλείθυια).

ἐστι τῇ γενέσει. διὰ ταῦτα ὅταν μὲν καλῷ προσπελάζῃ   11

τὸ κυοῦν, ἵλεών τε γίγνεται καὶ εὐφραινόμενον διαχεῖται   12

καὶ τίκτει τε καὶ γεννᾷ· ὅταν δὲ αἰσχρῷ, σκυθρωπόν τε   13

καὶ λυπούμενον συσπειρᾶται καὶ ἀποτρέπεται καὶ ἀνείλλεται   14

καὶ οὐ γεννᾷ, ἀλλὰ ἴσχον τὸ κύημα χαλεπῶς φέρει. ὅθεν δὴ   15

τῷ κυοῦντί τε καὶ ἤδη σπαργῶντι πολλὴ ἡ πτοίησις γέγονε   16

περὶ τὸ καλὸν διὰ τὸ μεγάλης ὠδῖνος ἀπολύειν τὸν ἔχοντα.   17   206e

ἔστιν γάρ, ὦ Σώκρατες," ἔφη, "οὐ τοῦ καλοῦ ὁ ἔρως, ὡς σὺ οἴει."   18

  "Ἀλλὰ τί μήν;"   19

  "Τῆς γεννήσεως καὶ τοῦ τόκου ἐν τῷ καλῷ."   20

  "Εἶεν," ἦν δ' ἐγώ.   21

  "Πάνυ μὲν οὖν," ἔφη. "τί δὴ οὖν τῆς γεννήσεως; ὅτι   22

---

11   τῇ γενέσει = for birth (dat. of advantage)
       προσπελάζω = draw near to *dat.*

12   ἵλεως -ων = gracious, propitious, cheerful
       εὐφραίνω = cheer, delight, gladden
       διαχέω = pour different ways, disperse; *pass.* = be melted, relax

13   ὅταν δὲ αἰσχρῷ, σκυθρωπόν τε = ὅταν δὲ αἰσχρῷ προσπελάζῃ τὸ κυοῦν, σκυθρωπόν τε
          γίγνεται (the parallel with ὅταν μὲν καλῷ . . . ἵλεων τε in lines 11-12 allows the reader to fill
          in missing elements)
       σκυθρωπός -ή -όν = angry-faced, sad-faced, sullen

14   *λυπέω = give pain to, pain, distress, grieve, vex, annoy
       συσπειράομαι = coil [oneself] up
       ἀνείλλομαι = roll [oneself] up

15   κύημα -ατος τό = that which is conceived, embryo, fetus

16   σπαργάω = be full to bursting, swell, be ripe
       πτοίησις -εως ἡ = excitement, vehement passion

17   ὠδίς ὠδῖνος ἡ = labor pain, pain
       ἀπολύω = set *acc.* free from *gen.* (*λύω = release, set free)
       τὸν ἔχοντα [supply ὠδῖνα]: obj. of ἀπολύειν

20   τόκος -ου ὁ = childbirth, birth (cf. τέτοκα from τίκτω)

21   Εἶεν: Rose 1985: 52 points out that this is not exactly a ringing endorsement, and Diotima's next
          words (Πάνυ μὲν οὖν) forcefully assert the correctness of the definition.

22   τί; = why . . . ? in what way . . . ?

ἀειγενές ἐστι καὶ ἀθάνατον ὡς θνητῷ ἡ γέννησις. ἀθανασίας   23

δὲ ἀναγκαῖον ἐπιθυμεῖν μετὰ ἀγαθοῦ ἐκ τῶν ὡμολογημένων,   24   207a

εἴπερ τοῦ ἀγαθοῦ ἑαυτῷ εἶναι ἀεὶ ἔρως ἐστίν.   25

ἀναγκαῖον δὴ ἐκ τούτου τοῦ λόγου καὶ τῆς ἀθανασίας τὸν   26

ἔρωτα εἶναι."   27

   Ταῦτά τε οὖν πάντα ἐδίδασκέ με, ὁπότε περὶ τῶν ἐρωτικῶν   28

λόγους ποιοῖτο, καί ποτε ἤρετο "Τί οἴει, ὦ Σώκρατες,   29

αἴτιον εἶναι τούτου τοῦ ἔρωτος καὶ τῆς ἐπιθυμίας; ἢ οὐκ   30

αἰσθάνῃ ὡς δεινῶς διατίθεται πάντα τὰ θηρία ἐπειδὰν γεννᾶν   31

ἐπιθυμήσῃ, καὶ τὰ πεζὰ καὶ τὰ πτηνά, νοσοῦντά τε   32

πάντα καὶ ἐρωτικῶς διατιθέμενα, πρῶτον μὲν περὶ τὸ συμμιγῆναι   33   207b

ἀλλήλοις, ἔπειτα περὶ τὴν τροφὴν τοῦ γενομένου,   34

καὶ ἕτοιμά ἐστιν ὑπὲρ τούτων καὶ διαμάχεσθαι τὰ ἀσθενέστατα   35

τοῖς ἰσχυροτάτοις καὶ ὑπεραποθνήσκειν, καὶ αὐτὰ τῷ   36

λιμῷ παρατεινόμενα ὥστ' ἐκεῖνα ἐκτρέφειν, καὶ ἄλλο πᾶν   37

ποιοῦντα. τοὺς μὲν γὰρ ἀνθρώπους," ἔφη, "οἴοιτ' ἄν τις ἐκ   38

λογισμοῦ ταῦτα ποιεῖν· τὰ δὲ θηρία τίς αἰτία οὕτως ἐρωτικῶς   39

διατίθεσθαι; ἔχεις λέγειν;"   40   207c

---

23   ἀειγενής -ές = everlasting
       ὡς θνητῷ = to the extent possible for a mortal
24   μετὰ ἀγαθοῦ with ἀθανασίας in line 23 = immortality together with the good
29   ποιοῖτο: explain the use of this mood (*Essentials* §159a)
32   *πεζός -ή -όν = traveling on foot
       πτηνός -ή -όν = feathered, winged
33   συμμιγῆναι: aor. pass. inf. of συμμίγνυμι = συμμείγνυμι = σύν + μείγνυμι. The verb is
       frequently used to refer to sexual or social intercourse, but also to other forms of close contact.
36   ὑπεραποθνήσκειν = ὑπερ + αποθνήσκειν: was used earlier by Phaedrus (reading 3B.1) about
       Alcestis's self-sacrifice
37   παρατείνω = stretch, strain
39   *λογισμός -οῦ ὁ = calculation, reasoning
       αἰτία + *acc.* + *inf.* = the reason for *acc.* to ——

Καὶ ἐγὼ αὖ ἔλεγον ὅτι οὐκ εἰδείην· ἦ δ' εἶπεν, "Διανοῇ   41
οὖν δεινός ποτε γενήσεσθαι τὰ ἐρωτικά, ἐὰν ταῦτα μὴ   42
ἐννοῇς;"   43

"Ἀλλὰ διὰ ταῦτά τοι, ὦ Διοτίμα, ὅπερ νυνδὴ εἶπον, παρὰ   44
σὲ ἥκω, γνοὺς ὅτι διδασκάλων δέομαι. ἀλλά μοι λέγε   45
καὶ τούτων τὴν αἰτίαν καὶ τῶν ἄλλων τῶν περὶ τὰ ἐρωτικά."   46

Reading 9G

The desire for genesis (i.e., sexual desire) is ultimately a kind of longing for immortality. For mortals, our only hope at immortality is to leave something new behind to replace the old, as when we leave behind offspring. But Diotima points out that even within individuals the new replaces the old. For example, hair grows in to replace what falls out. New emotions, habits, opinions, and memories replace the old. Even knowledge is not immortal, as we recognize when we practice or study things we have previously learned. Diotima boldly claims that the desire for immortality drives all mortal action.

Suggested Review

- uses of αὐτός (*Essentials* §§200–205)

Vocabulary

αἷμα αἵματος τό: blood (cf. English "hematology" and "hematoma")

διάκειμαι + *adv.*: διατίθεμαι + *adv.*: be [in a certain state], be disposed or affected [in a certain manner]

ἐς = εἰς

θρίξ τριχός ἡ: hair

κλέος -ους τό: rumor, report, news, reputation, fame; *recognize also* εὐκλεής -ές: of good report, famous, glorious

λήθη -ης ἡ: oblivion, forgetting (cf. English "the river Lethe" and λανθάνω)

μνήμη -ης ἡ: remembrance, memory (cf. English "mnemonic")

ὀστέον -ου τό (in Attic, contracts to τὸ ὀστοῦν, τὰ ὀστᾶ; see Smyth 1956: §235 for full declension): bone (cf. English "osteopath")

οὐδέποτε = οὔποτε

πονέω πονήσω ἐπόνησα πεπόνηκα πεπόνημαι ἐπονήθην: work hard, toil, suffer (cf. *πόνος ὁ)

σάρξ σαρκός ἡ: flesh (cf. English "sarcophagus")

Reading 9G (*Symposium* 207c8–208e1)

"Εἰ τοίνυν," ἔφη, "πιστεύεις ἐκείνου εἶναι φύσει τὸν ἔρωτα,   1

οὗ πολλάκις ὡμολογήκαμεν, μὴ θαύμαζε. ἐνταῦθα γὰρ   2

τὸν αὐτὸν ἐκείνῳ λόγον ἡ θνητὴ φύσις ζητεῖ κατὰ τὸ δυνατὸν   3   207d

ἀεί τε εἶναι καὶ ἀθάνατος. δύναται δὲ ταύτῃ μόνον, τῇ   4

γενέσει, ὅτι ἀεὶ καταλείπει ἕτερον νέον ἀντὶ τοῦ παλαιοῦ,   5

ἐπεὶ καὶ ἐν ᾧ ἓν ἕκαστον τῶν ζῴων ζῆν καλεῖται καὶ εἶναι   6

τὸ αὐτό—οἷον ἐκ παιδαρίου ὁ αὐτὸς λέγεται ἕως ἂν πρεσβύτης   7

γένηται· οὗτος μέντοι οὐδέποτε τὰ αὐτὰ ἔχων ἐν   8

αὑτῷ ὅμως ὁ αὐτὸς καλεῖται, ἀλλὰ νέος ἀεὶ γιγνόμενος, τὰ   9

δὲ ἀπολλύς, καὶ κατὰ τὰς τρίχας καὶ σάρκα καὶ ὀστᾶ καὶ   10

αἷμα καὶ σύμπαν τὸ σῶμα. καὶ μὴ ὅτι κατὰ τὸ σῶμα,   11   207e

ἀλλὰ καὶ κατὰ τὴν ψυχὴν οἱ τρόποι, τὰ ἤθη, δόξαι, ἐπιθυμίαι,   12

---

1   ἐκείνου: Apparently refers to the proposition formulated at 9F, line 20, i.e., [ὁ ἔρως ἐστι] τῆς
       γεννήσεως καὶ τοῦ τόκου ἐν τῷ καλῷ.

2   μὴ θαύμαζε: i.e., that τὰ θηρία οὕτως ἐρωτικῶς διατίθενται (reading 9F.39–40)
       ἐνταῦθα: i.e., in this example, in this case

3   τὸν αὐτὸν ἐκείνῳ λόγον = by the same logic as in that case (adverbial acc.); ἐκείνῳ refers back
       to the previous case, that of humans
       κατὰ τὸ δυνατόν = as much as is possible

6–7   ἐπεί . . . τὸ αὐτό: the thought begun in this clause is never completed (anacoluthon) (Smyth
       1956: §§3004–8). To complete this sentence, we would need a clause containing a thought such
       as "genesis is going on" or "the process continues" or the like.
       καὶ ἐν ᾧ = even in that time when, even when
       καλεῖται = is said to

7   οἷον = such as, for example
       παιδάριον -ου τό = little child; ἐκ παιδαρίου = from childhood

9–10 τὰ δέ = others (as though the previous clause were τὰ μὲν νέος ἀεὶ γιγνόμενος = always
       becoming new in some ways . . .)
       ἀπολλύς: masc. nom. part. of ἀπόλλυμι. The sense here is "losing" rather than killing or
       destroying, but the overall connotations of death and destruction associated with this word
       are important to the content of the passage.

11   μὴ ὅτι = not just (idiomatic phrase probably due to an ellipsis of a verb of speaking) (Smyth 1956:
       §2763)

ἡδοναί, λῦπαι, φόβοι, τούτων ἕκαστα οὐδέποτε τὰ   13

αὐτὰ πάρεστιν ἑκάστῳ, ἀλλὰ τὰ μὲν γίγνεται, τὰ δὲ ἀπόλλυται.   14

πολὺ δὲ τούτων ἀτοπώτερον ἔτι, ὅτι καὶ αἱ ἐπιστῆμαι   15

μὴ ὅτι αἱ μὲν γίγνονται, αἱ δὲ ἀπόλλυνται ἡμῖν, καὶ οὐδέποτε   16   208a

οἱ αὐτοί ἐσμεν οὐδὲ κατὰ τὰς ἐπιστήμας, ἀλλὰ καὶ   17

μία ἑκάστη τῶν ἐπιστημῶν ταὐτὸν πάσχει. ὃ γὰρ καλεῖται   18

μελετᾶν, ὡς ἐξιούσης ἐστὶ τῆς ἐπιστήμης· λήθη γὰρ   19

ἐπιστήμης ἔξοδος, μελέτη δὲ πάλιν καινὴν ἐμποιοῦσα ἀντὶ   20

τῆς ἀπιούσης μνήμην σῴζει τὴν ἐπιστήμην, ὥστε τὴν   21

αὐτὴν δοκεῖν εἶναι. τούτῳ γὰρ τῷ τρόπῳ πᾶν τὸ θνητὸν   22

σῴζεται, οὐ τῷ παντάπασιν τὸ αὐτὸ ἀεὶ εἶναι ὥσπερ τὸ   23

θεῖον, ἀλλὰ τῷ τὸ ἀπιὸν καὶ παλαιούμενον ἕτερον νέον   24   208b

ἐγκαταλείπειν οἷον αὐτὸ ἦν. ταύτῃ τῇ μηχανῇ, ὦ Σώκρατες,”   25

ἔφη, “θνητὸν ἀθανασίας μετέχει, καὶ σῶμα καὶ τἆλλα   26

πάντα· ἀθάνατον δὲ ἄλλῃ. μὴ οὖν θαύμαζε εἰ τὸ αὑτοῦ   27

ἀποβλάστημα φύσει πᾶν τιμᾷ· ἀθανασίας γὰρ χάριν παντὶ   28

αὕτη ἡ σπουδὴ καὶ ὁ ἔρως ἕπεται.”   29

---

13   *λύπη -ης ἡ = pain

15   *ἄτοπος -ον = strange, odd
        αἱ ἐπιστῆμαι = pieces of knowledge (here)

16–17   μὴ ὅτι … ἀλλὰ καί = not just … but even (see note on line 11)

18   μία ἑκάστη τῶν ἐπιστήμων = each individual piece of knowledge

19   *μελετάω = study, practice, review
        ὃ καλεῖται μελετᾶν = what is called "practice" (the rel. clause is the subje. of the sentence)
        ὡς ἐξιούσης = because of [its] going out
        ἐστὶ τῆς ἐπιστήμης = is "of knowledge"; obj. gen. with μελετᾶν

20   *ἔξοδος -ου ὁ = going out, departure (ἐξ + ὁδός; cf. English "exodus")
        *μελέτη -ης ἡ = study, practice, review
        καινήν from *καινός -ή -όν = new, fresh; goes with μνήμην in line 21

23, 24 τῷ: neut. def. art. (dat. of means) introducing articular infinitive (*Essentials* §182)

24   τὸ ἀπιόν: neut. subst. part. of ἄπειμι and the subje. of the articular inf.
        παλαιόομαι = παλαιὸς γίγνομαι

27   αὑτοῦ: what does the rough breathing mark on this word indicate (see note on reading 6A.31)?

28   ἀποβλάστημα -ατος τό = shoot, scion, offspring
        πᾶν: subje. of τιμᾷ

Καὶ ἐγὼ ἀκούσας τὸν λόγον ἐθαύμασά τε καὶ εἶπον,   30

"Εἶεν," ἦν δ' ἐγώ, "ὦ σοφωτάτη Διοτίμα, ταῦτα ὡς ἀληθῶς   31

οὕτως ἔχει;"   32

Καὶ ἥ, ὥσπερ οἱ τέλεοι σοφισταί, "εὖ ἴσθι," ἔφη, "ὦ   33   208c

Σώκρατες· ἐπεί γε καὶ τῶν ἀνθρώπων εἰ ἐθέλεις εἰς τὴν   34

φιλοτιμίαν βλέψαι, θαυμάζοις ἂν τῆς ἀλογίας περὶ ἃ ἐγὼ   35

εἴρηκα εἰ μὴ ἐννοεῖς, ἐνθυμηθεὶς ὡς δεινῶς διάκεινται ἔρωτι   36

τοῦ ὀνομαστοὶ γενέσθαι καὶ κλέος ἐς τὸν ἀεὶ χρόνον   37

ἀθάνατον καταθέσθαι, καὶ ὑπὲρ τούτου κινδύνους τε   38

κινδυνεύειν ἕτοιμοί εἰσι πάντας ἔτι μᾶλλον ἢ ὑπὲρ τῶν   39

παίδων, καὶ χρήματα ἀναλίσκειν καὶ πόνους πονεῖν οὑστινασοῦν   40   208d

καὶ ὑπεραποθνῄσκειν. ἐπεὶ οἴει σύ," ἔφη, "Ἄλκηστιν   41

ὑπὲρ Ἀδμήτου ἀποθανεῖν ἄν, ἢ Ἀχιλλέα Πατρόκλῳ ἐπαποθανεῖν,   42

---

31   ὡς ἀληθῶς = truly

33   τέλεος -ον = having reached its end, perfect, complete

The qualities that make Diotima "sophistical" are apparently her strong confident assurance (εὖ ἴσθι) in the face of Socrates' doubt (compare a similar exchange at reading 9F.21–22). Dover 1980: 155 points out that εὖ ἴσθι is used by sophists elsewhere in Plato and hypothesizes that Plato sees it as characteristic. This characterization of Diotima, though brief, should at least raise questions about whether she should be taken simply as a mouthpiece for either Plato or Socrates.

34   ἐπεί γε καί = since in fact. This phrase gives the explanation of εὖ ἴσθι; there is no other main clause.

35   *φιλοτιμία -ας ἡ = love and pursuit of honor, competitive spirit
        τῆς ἀλογίας = at the lack of reason, at the illogicality (gen. of cause) (*Essentials* §98)

36   διάκεινται: the subj. is οἱ ἄνθρωποι, an idea imported from line 34

37   τοῦ . . . γένεσθαι . . . καταθέσθαι: both are articular infinitives; objective genitives with ἔρωτι
        ὀνομαστός -ή -όν = named, mentioned, famous, glorious

38   καταθέσθαι from *κατατίθημι = place, put down; *mid.* = lay down in store

40   *ἀναλίσκω = use up, spend, lavish, or squander

41–42   Ἄλκηστις, Ἄδμητος, Ἀχιλλεύς, Πάτροκλος: Phaedrus previously discussed the self-sacrificing deaths of these four (see reading 3B and introduction)

42   ἀποθανεῖν ἄν: this infinitive in an indirect statement represents an indicative of the same tense. What tense is the infinitive, and what does this tense of the indicative imply with ἄν (*Essentials* §162)?

ἢ προαποθανεῖν τὸν ὑμέτερον Κόδρον ὑπὲρ τῆς   43

βασιλείας τῶν παίδων, μὴ οἰομένους ἀθάνατον μνήμην   44

ἀρετῆς πέρι ἑαυτῶν ἔσεσθαι, ἣν νῦν ἡμεῖς ἔχομεν; πολλοῦ   45

γε δεῖ," ἔφη, "ἀλλ᾽ οἶμαι ὑπὲρ ἀρετῆς ἀθανάτου καὶ τοιαύτης   46

δόξης εὐκλεοῦς πάντες πάντα ποιοῦσιν, ὅσῳ ἂν ἀμείνους   47

ὦσι, τοσούτῳ μᾶλλον· τοῦ γὰρ ἀθανάτου ἐρῶσιν."   48   208e

---

43   Κόδρος -ου ὁ = Kodros (Latin Codrus), legendary king of Athens. He gave up his life to save
        Athens when the Dorian descendants of Heracles invaded. The invaders were given an oracle
        at Delphi that they would be victorious as long as they spared the life of Kodros. Consequently,
        he disguised himself as a woodcutter and started a quarrel with the warriors, who killed him,
        not recognizing him as Kodros. The Athenians were victorious and subsequently worshiped
        Kodros as a hero.

45   ἀρετῆς: obj. of πέρι. How is that shown (*Essentials* §206)?

45–46   πολλοῦ δεῖ = far from it

47–48   ὅσῳ . . . τοσούτῳ *correl.* = by as much . . . by so much . . . ; i.e., the better they are, the more they
        do . . . (datives of degree of difference) (*Essentials* §111)

Reading 9H

Diotima makes a distinction between those pregnant in body (who are inclined toward women and sexual generation) and those pregnant in soul (who are inclined toward men [i.e., are pederasts] and the production of intellectual products). This seems to hearken back to the distinction made earlier by Pausanias between the heavenly and the common Eros. Diotima points out that those who produce intellectual things, like the poets Homer and Hesiod, have "children" that are far more long-lived that mortal children. Lawgivers like Solon (an Athenian famous for the wisdom of the laws he made in a turbulent period in Athens) and Lycurgus (who was credited with writing the Spartan constitution), much admired by Plato and other Athenian writers on politics, are included among those who win immortality through their intellectual creations.

Vocabulary

ἐπιτηδεύω ἐπιτηδεύσω ἐπετήδευσα ἐπιτήδευκα ἐπιτετήδευμαι: pursue, practice, make
   acc. one's business; + inf.: take care to ——
ζηλόω ζηλώσω ἐζήλωσα ἐζήλωκα ἐζήλωμαι ἐζηλώθην: envy, emulate; rival, vie with
κοινόω κοινώσω ἐκοίνωσα κεκοίνωκα κεκοίνωμαι ἐκοινώθην: make common, make a
   sharer in, communicate; mid.: communicate, share in gen. (cf. κοινός)
παιδεύω παιδεύσω ἐπαίδευσα πεπαίδευκα πεπαίδευμαι ἐπαιδεύθην: bring up or rear a
   child, educate (cf. παῖς ὁ)
παντοῖος -α -ον: of all sorts or kinds, manifold
προσήκω: (1) have arrived at; be near, at hand; (2) used impers. + dat.: it concerns dat.; + dat. +
   inf.: it is appropriate for dat. to ——, it is fitting for dat. to ——; (3) common as part.: belonging
   to, befitting, related to; οἱ προσήκοντες: relations, relatives
πω adv.: up to this time, yet (cf. οὔπω and οὐδέπω)

Reading 9H (*Symposium* 208e1–209e4)

"Οἱ μὲν οὖν ἐγκύμονες,"	1	208e
ἔφη, "κατὰ τὰ σώματα ὄντες πρὸς τὰς γυναῖκας	2	
μᾶλλον τρέπονται καὶ ταύτῃ ἐρωτικοί εἰσιν, διὰ παιδογονίας	3	
ἀθανασίαν καὶ μνήμην καὶ εὐδαιμονίαν, ὡς οἴονται, αὑτοῖς	4	
εἰς τὸν ἔπειτα χρόνον πάντα ποριζόμενοι· οἱ δὲ κατὰ τὴν	5	
ψυχήν—εἰσὶ γὰρ οὖν," ἔφη, "οἳ ἐν ταῖς ψυχαῖς κυοῦσιν ἔτι	6	209a
μᾶλλον ἢ ἐν τοῖς σώμασιν, ἃ ψυχῇ προσήκει καὶ κυῆσαι	7	
καὶ τεκεῖν· τί οὖν προσήκει; φρόνησίν τε καὶ τὴν ἄλλην	8	
ἀρετήν—ὧν δή εἰσι καὶ οἱ ποιηταὶ πάντες γεννήτορες καὶ	9	
τῶν δημιουργῶν ὅσοι λέγονται εὑρετικοὶ εἶναι· πολὺ δὲ	10	
μεγίστη," ἔφη, "καὶ καλλίστη τῆς φρονήσεως ἡ περὶ τὰ τῶν	11	
πόλεών τε καὶ οἰκήσεων διακόσμησις, ᾗ δὴ ὄνομά ἐστι	12	
σωφροσύνη τε καὶ δικαιοσύνη—τούτων δ' αὖ ὅταν τις ἐκ	13	

1	ἐγκύμων -ον = pregnant
3	παιδογονία -ας ἡ = the begetting of children
5	πάντα: acc. masc. sing. with χρόνον
5–6	οἱ δὲ κατὰ τὴν ψυχήν: balances οἱ μὲν … ἐγκύμονες … κατὰ τὰ σώματα ὄντες of the first half of the sentence; the parallelism allows inference of the missing elements ἐγκύμονες and ὄντες. But a long parenthetical statement εἰσὶ … ἀρετήν interrupts the thought begun here, which is not resumed until line 9 with ὧν δή εἰσι.
6	εἰσί = there are (a common translation when εἰσι begins the sentence) γὰρ οὖν = for, in fact (Smyth 1956: §2958)
7	ἅ: supply as an antecedent an object of κυοῦσιν in line 6
8–9	τὴν ἄλλην ἀρετήν = the rest of virtue
9	ὧν = τούτων (referring to φρόνησιν καὶ ἄλλην ἀρετήν) γεννήτωρ -ορος ὁ = engenderer, father (cf. γεννάω)
10	εὑρετικός -οῦ ὁ = inventor, discoverer
12	διακόσμησις -εως ἡ = setting in order, arranging
13	τούτων = pregnant with *gen.*; must depend on ἐγκύμων in line 14 (Rose 1985: 55 compares to adjectives denoting "full," which are also accompanied by the gen.)

νέου ἐγκύμων ᾖ τὴν ψυχήν, ἤθεος ὢν καὶ ἡκούσης τῆς   14   209b

ἡλικίας, τίκτειν τε καὶ γεννᾶν ἤδη ἐπιθυμῇ, ζητεῖ δὴ   15

οἶμαι καὶ οὗτος περιὼν τὸ καλὸν ἐν ᾧ ἂν γεννήσειεν· ἐν   16

τῷ γὰρ αἰσχρῷ οὐδέποτε γεννήσει.   17

        Τά τε οὖν σώματα τὰ   18

καλὰ μᾶλλον ἢ τὰ αἰσχρὰ ἀσπάζεται ἅτε κυῶν, καὶ ἂν   19

ἐντύχῃ ψυχῇ καλῇ καὶ γενναίᾳ καὶ εὐφυεῖ, πάνυ δὴ ἀσπάζεται   20

τὸ συναμφότερον, καὶ πρὸς τοῦτον τὸν ἄνθρωπον   21

εὐθὺς εὐπορεῖ λόγων περὶ ἀρετῆς καὶ περὶ οἷον χρὴ εἶναι   22

τὸν ἄνδρα τὸν ἀγαθὸν καὶ ἃ ἐπιτηδεύειν, καὶ ἐπιχειρεῖ   23   209c

παιδεύειν. ἁπτόμενος γὰρ οἶμαι τοῦ καλοῦ καὶ ὁμιλῶν   24

αὐτῷ, ἃ πάλαι ἐκύει τίκτει καὶ γεννᾷ, καὶ παρὼν καὶ ἀπὼν   25

μεμνημένος, καὶ τὸ γεννηθὲν συνεκτρέφει κοινῇ μετ' ἐκείνου,   26

ὥστε πολὺ μείζω κοινωνίαν τῆς τῶν παίδων πρὸς ἀλλήλους   27

οἱ τοιοῦτοι ἴσχουσι καὶ φιλίαν βεβαιοτέραν, ἅτε καλλιόνων   28

καὶ ἀθανατωτέρων παίδων κεκοινωνηκότες.   29

        Καὶ πᾶς ἂν   30

δέξαιτο ἑαυτῷ τοιούτους παῖδας μᾶλλον γεγονέναι ἢ τοὺς   31

---

14   ἐγκύμων -ον = pregnant

       ἤθεος -ου ὁ = youth just come to manhood, unmarried young man

14–15 ἡκούσης τῆς ἡλικίας: what is the form of ἡκούσης (from the verb ἥκω)? What must this
       construction then be (*Essentials* §176)?

19   ἂν: how can you be sure that this is contracted from ἐάν (*Essentials* §160)?

20   εὐφυής -ές = well-grown, shapely

21   συναμφότερον = σύν + ἀμφότερα (i.e., beauty of body and beauty of soul)

22   εὐπορέω = have plenty of *gen.*, be full of *gen.*

24   τοῦ καλοῦ: masculine; we are back in the pedagogical context of pederasty, where men educate
       handsome boys (καλοί) in virtue

26   συνεκτρέφω = σύν + ἐκτρέφω

27   κοινωνία -ας ἡ = commonality, fellowship

       τῆς τῶν παίδων = τῆς τῶν παίδων κοινωνίας = the fellowship of having children (gen. of
       comparison)

31   δέχομαι . . . μᾶλλον = take . . . more; i.e., prefer, choose

ἀνθρωπίνους, καὶ εἰς Ὅμηρον ἀποβλέψας καὶ Ἡσίοδον καὶ   32   209d

τοὺς ἄλλους ποιητὰς τοὺς ἀγαθοὺς ζηλῶν, οἷα ἔκγονα ἑαυτῶν   33

καταλείπουσιν, ἃ ἐκείνοις ἀθάνατον κλέος καὶ μνήμην παρέχεται   34

αὐτὰ τοιαῦτα ὄντα· εἰ δὲ βούλει," ἔφη, "οἵους Λυκοῦργος   35

παῖδας κατελίπετο ἐν Λακεδαίμονι σωτῆρας τῆς Λακεδαίμονος   36

καὶ ὡς ἔπος εἰπεῖν τῆς Ἑλλάδος. τίμιος δὲ   37

παρ' ὑμῖν καὶ Σόλων διὰ τὴν τῶν νόμων γέννησιν, καὶ ἄλλοι   38

ἄλλοθι πολλαχοῦ ἄνδρες, καὶ ἐν Ἕλλησι καὶ ἐν βαρβάροις,   39   209e

πολλὰ καὶ καλὰ ἀποφηνάμενοι ἔργα, γεννήσαντες παντοίαν   40

ἀρετήν· ὧν καὶ ἱερὰ πολλὰ ἤδη γέγονε διὰ τοὺς τοιούτους   41

παῖδας, διὰ δὲ τοὺς ἀνθρωπίνους οὐδενός πω."   42

---

32   τοὺς ἀνθρωπίνους = τοὺς ἀνθρωπίνους παῖδας

33   ἔκγονος -ον = sprung of, born of

35   εἰ δὲ βούλει: parenthetical (i.e., if you want [another example])

      οἵους: supply a verb (e.g., σκόπει οἵους or similar)

      Λυκοῦργος -ου ὁ = Lykourgos (Latin Lycurgus), legendary Spartan lawgiver, credited with establishing the admired Spartan constitution

36–37   σωτήρ -ῆρος ὁ = savior. Presumably Lycurgus's laws are considered "saviors" of Sparta, because they kept order in the state and allowed them to preserve their way of life, and are considered saviors of practically all Greece (ὡς ἔπος εἰπεῖν τῆς Ἑλλάδος), because of the Spartans' role in repelling the Persians in the Persian Wars.

38   Σόλων -ωνος ὁ = Solon, famous Athenian lawgiver

41   ὧν ... ἱερά = cults for these

42   τοὺς ἀνθρωπίνους: see line 32

      οὐδενός: parallel to gen. ὧν of previous line, dependent on ἱερά

Reading 91

This is arguably the portion of the dialogue with the greatest philosophical importance, as it contains Plato's most detailed account of the "forms" or "ideas" (Greek εἴδη) and the process of coming to apprehend them.

In the opening section, Diotima suggests that she is about to take the discussion to a new level. Using the language of initiation into the so-called mystery religions, Diotima suggests that Socrates, even if he has been initiated in τὰ ἐρωτικά, may not be able to take this last step and experience the final revelation. She then describes the long training that needs to be given to the young man in order to prepare him for this final step. It is a gradual training, moving up step by step (the metaphor is of a ladder) from specific examples of the beautiful to the apprehension of the beautiful in itself.

Beginning from love of and apprehension of beauty in a single individual, love for beauty becomes increasingly abstract, universal, and incorporeal, ultimately ending in a notion of a love for the beautiful-in-itself. This idea of the beautiful is abstracted from, but incorporated in, all individual instances of beauty. This conception of the beautiful is pure, eternal, and unchanging, not subject to generation or decay. It is moreover entirely universal and not in anyway relative; all who perceive it perceive it in the same way. It is indeed a rather mystical notion, and the religious language that surrounds it is appropriate. This conception of the beautiful-in-itself has been identified by philosophers as the most explicit model for the conception of the ideas or the forms (εἴδη) that Plato uses elsewhere and the most detailed discussion of how they may be apprehended.[36]

Suggested Review

- use of the impersonal δεῖ (*Essentials* §85 or §183)

Vocabulary

αὐξάνω/αὔξω αὐξήσω ηὔξησα ηὔξηκα ηὔξημαι ηὐξήθην: make large, increase, augment; *mid.-pass.*: increase, grow, wax

---

36. Patterson 1991 offers a close analysis of this discussion.

ἔνθα *adv.*: there

ἐξαίφνης *adv.*: suddenly

ἐπιτήδευμα -ατος τό: pursuit, business, practice (cf. ἐπιτηδεύω)

ἡγέομαι ἡγήσομαι ἡγησάμην—ἥγημαι ἡγήθην: (1) go before, lead; (2) consider, believe, think. Both meanings of this word occur in this passage!

καθοράω (κατα + ὁράω) κατόψομαι κατεῖδον καθεώρακα κατῶμμαι κατώφθην: look down upon, perceive, view

καταφρονέω + *gen. or acc.*: look down on, disdain, despise, scorn

κήδω κηδήσω ἐκήδησα κέκηδα κεκήδημαι: trouble, distress, vex; *mid.-pass.* + *gen.*: care for, be concerned for

μέχρι *prep.* + *gen.*, or *conj.*: until, up to

προθυμία -ας ἡ: eagerness (cf. πρόθυμος -ον)

τῳ = τινί; του = τινός

Reading 9I (*Symposium* 209e5–211b5)

"Ταῦτα μὲν οὖν τὰ ἐρωτικὰ ἴσως, ὦ Σώκρατες, κἂν σὺ   1

μυηθείης· τὰ δὲ τέλεα καὶ ἐποπτικά, ὧν ἕνεκα καὶ ταῦτα   2   210a

ἔστιν, ἐάν τις ὀρθῶς μετίῃ, οὐκ οἶδ' εἰ οἷός τ' ἂν εἴης.   3

ἐρῶ μὲν οὖν," ἔφη, "ἐγὼ καὶ προθυμίας οὐδὲν ἀπολείψω·   4

πειρῶ δὲ ἕπεσθαι, ἂν οἷός τε ᾖς."   5

The love of beauty in the body

"Δεῖ γάρ," ἔφη, "τὸν ὀρθῶς   6

ἰόντα ἐπὶ τοῦτο τὸ πρᾶγμα ἄρχεσθαι μὲν νέον ὄντα ἰέναι   7

ἐπὶ τὰ καλὰ σώματα, καὶ πρῶτον μέν, ἐὰν ὀρθῶς ἡγῆται   8

ὁ ἡγούμενος, ἑνὸς αὐτὸν σώματος ἐρᾶν καὶ ἐνταῦθα γεννᾶν   9

λόγους καλούς, ἔπειτα δὲ αὐτὸν κατανοῆσαι ὅτι τὸ κάλλος   10

τὸ ἐπὶ ὁτῳοῦν σώματι τῷ ἐπὶ ἑτέρῳ σώματι ἀδελφόν ἐστι,   11   210b

---

1   κἂν σύ = καὶ ἂν σύ = even you. Diotima's disparagement of Socrates' abilities is typical of her, but is particularly pronounced here.

2   μυέω = initiate into the mysteries of *acc.*

   τὰ τέλεα καὶ ἐποπτικά: Rowe's "the final revelation" (1998: 97) is an excellent translation; the phrase (literally = the complete and observed things) is used of the advanced stages of the mystery religions, when sacred objects were apparently revealed to the initiates. Unfortunately, we do not know the content of these revelations.

   καί (before ταῦτα): not connective here, puts emphasis on ταῦτα

   ταῦτα = ταῦτα ... τὰ ἐρωτικά of line 1 (i.e., everything Diotima has taught him up until now)

3   μέτειμι = go after, pursue

   οἷός τ' ἂν εἴης: supply μυηθῆναι (of which τὰ ... ἐποπτικά of line 2 is the obj.)

4   ἀπολείπω + *gen.* = be lacking in, be sparing of

5   πειρῶ: impera. (for alpha-contract endings, see *Essentials* §57)

   ἄν = ἐάν

6–16   δεῖ governs the construction of the entire paragraph

7–8   ἰόντα ἐπί/ἰέναι ἐπί = go after, go for; i.e., pursue

8   ὁ ἡγούμενος = the one guiding, the one leading. Diotima imagines that the young initiate will have a guide. In the mystery religions, there was a mystagogus to guide the new initiates.

9   αὐτὸν ... ἐρᾶν ... γεννᾶν: see note on lines 6–16

10   κατανοέω = observe well, understand

11   τῷ ἐπὶ ἑτέρῳ σώματι = τῷ ἐπὶ ἑτέρῳ σώματι κάλλει: dat. with ἀδελφόν = brother to, related to

καὶ εἰ δεῖ διώκειν τὸ ἐπ' εἴδει καλόν, πολλὴ ἄνοια μὴ οὐχ   12

ἕν τε καὶ ταὐτὸν ἡγεῖσθαι τὸ ἐπὶ πᾶσιν τοῖς σώμασι κάλλος·   13

τοῦτο δ' ἐννοήσαντα καταστῆναι πάντων τῶν καλῶν σωμάτων   14

ἐραστήν, ἑνὸς δὲ τὸ σφόδρα τοῦτο χαλάσαι καταφρονήσαντα   15

καὶ σμικρὸν ἡγησάμενον·   16

The love of beauty in the soul: institutions, types of knowledge

Μετὰ δὲ ταῦτα τὸ ἐν ταῖς   17

ψυχαῖς κάλλος τιμιώτερον ἡγήσασθαι τοῦ ἐν τῷ σώματι,   18

ὥστε καὶ ἐὰν ἐπιεικὴς ὢν τὴν ψυχήν τις κἂν σμικρὸν ἄνθος   19

ἔχῃ, ἐξαρκεῖν αὐτῷ καὶ ἐρᾶν καὶ κήδεσθαι καὶ τίκτειν λόγους   20   210c

τοιούτους καὶ ζητεῖν, οἵτινες ποιήσουσι βελτίους τοὺς   21

νέους, ἵνα ἀναγκασθῇ αὖ θεάσασθαι τὸ ἐν τοῖς ἐπιτηδεύμασι   22

καὶ τοῖς νόμοις καλὸν καὶ τοῦτ' ἰδεῖν ὅτι πᾶν αὐτὸ αὑτῷ   23

συγγενές ἐστιν, ἵνα τὸ περὶ τὸ σῶμα καλὸν σμικρόν τι   24

ἡγήσηται εἶναι·   25

---

12   ἄνοια -ας ἡ = lack of sense, lack of understanding, but in the context with ἐστι understood, it is
        probably easier to translate as an adjective = it is utterly senseless

12–13   μὴ οὐχ ... ἡγεῖσθαι = not to consider. After verbs of hindering and many other negative expres-
        sions, like ἄνοια here, it is common to see a redundant μή before the infinitive; it is not
        normally translated (Smyth 1956: §§2739–49).

14   τοῦτο δ' ἐννοήσαντα καταστῆναι: with an understood αὐτόν. δεῖ is still governing the overall
        construction.

        καταστῆναι = to become (intrans. root aor. inf. of καθίστημι)

15   τὸ σφόδρα τοῦτο = τὸ σφόδρα ἐρᾶν τοῦτο or similar (can be inferred from gen. ἑνός and
        overall context)

        χαλάω = relax, diminish

17–25   δεῖ continues to govern the structure of both this paragraph and the next

19   τις: refers to some hypothetical young *eromenos*

        κἂν = καὶ ἐάν: ἐάν is redundant, and καί does not link the second part of the clause to the first
        but gives emphasis = even if he has (but) a slight bloom

20   αὐτῷ: refers not to the *eromenos* of line 19, but to the *erastes* under instruction in *erotika*

        λόγους: obj. of both τίκτειν and ζητεῖν, antecedent of οἵτινες

23   τοῦτ' = τὸ ... καλόν and is in fact the subject of the clause introduced by ὅτι (prolepsis)
        (*Essentials* §208). The primary point here is that all beauty is related, in fact, is ultimately one
        and the same thing.

24   *συγγενής -ές = born with, congenital, related to

Μετὰ δὲ τὰ ἐπιτηδεύματα ἐπὶ τὰς ἐπιστήμας   26

ἀγαγεῖν, ἵνα ἴδῃ αὖ ἐπιστημῶν κάλλος, καὶ βλέπων πρὸς   27

πολὺ ἤδη τὸ καλὸν μηκέτι τὸ παρ' ἑνί, ὥσπερ οἰκέτης,   28   210d

ἀγαπῶν παιδαρίου κάλλος ἢ ἀνθρώπου τινὸς ἢ ἐπιτηδεύματος   29

ἑνός, δουλεύων φαῦλος ᾖ καὶ σμικρολόγος, ἀλλ' ἐπὶ   30

τὸ πολὺ πέλαγος τετραμμένος τοῦ καλοῦ καὶ θεωρῶν πολλοὺς   31

καὶ καλοὺς λόγους καὶ μεγαλοπρεπεῖς τίκτῃ καὶ διανοήματα   32

ἐν φιλοσοφίᾳ ἀφθόνῳ, ἕως ἂν ἐνταῦθα ῥωσθεὶς καὶ   33

αὐξηθεὶς κατίδῃ τινὰ ἐπιστήμην μίαν τοιαύτην, ἥ ἐστι καλοῦ τοιοῦδε."   34

---

27   ἀγαγεῖν: the return to mention of leading is a little surprising after the previous paragraph. Diotima alternates between thinking primarily of the educating lover and the beloved who is being educated, even within this single sentence, as the latter is surely the subject of the next verb ἴδῃ.

28   πολὺ ἤδη τὸ καλόν: the adjective πολύ is in the predicate position, so "the beautiful, multiple now" (as opposed to how it was perceived previously)

28–30 μηκέτι . . . φαῦλος ᾖ καὶ σμικρολόγος: the pieces of this sentence are hard to put together and have generated some scholarly dispute (Rowe 1998: 196–97). Probably the easiest thing to do is to make μηκέτι negate the subjunctive ᾖ and to make τὸ παρ' ἑνί [καλόν] the object of the participle ἀγαπῶν. παιδαρίου κάλλος . . . ἑνός is then a series of examples in apposition to τὸ παρ' ἑνί [καλόν]. Or, as Rowe suggests, take κάλλος as completing τὸ παρ' ἑνί.

28   οἰκέτης = slave, apparently implying narrow and petty, possibly because a slave serves a single master

29   παιδάριον -ου τό = young boy

30   δουλεύων: circumstantial part., here virtually the equivalent of an adverb = slavishly, acting in a slavelike way

       σμικρολόγος -ον = petty

31   τετραμμένος: from τρέπω (review principal parts)

       *θεωρέω = look at, view, behold (cf. English "theory" and θεάομαι); the implied object is τὸ πέλαγος.

32   λόγους: obj. of τίκτῃ (as is διανοήματα)

       μεγαλοπρεπής -ές = befitting a great man, magnificent

       διανόημα -ατος τό = thought, notion

33   *ἄφθονος -ον = without envy (cf. *φθόνος -ου ὁ = envy and *φθονέω = envy)

       ῥωσθείς from ῥώννυμι = strengthen, make strong and mighty (cf. *ῥώμη -ης ἡ = strength)

34   τοιοῦδε: i.e., the one that will be given in the next section

Love of the beautiful or of beauty itself

"Πειρῶ δέ μοι," ἔφη, "τὸν νοῦν προσέχειν ὡς οἷόν   35   210e

τε μάλιστα. ὃς γὰρ ἂν μέχρι ἐνταῦθα πρὸς τὰ ἐρωτικὰ   36

παιδαγωγηθῇ, θεώμενος ἐφεξῆς τε καὶ ὀρθῶς τὰ καλά, πρὸς   37

τέλος ἤδη ἰὼν τῶν ἐρωτικῶν ἐξαίφνης κατόψεταί τι θαυμαστὸν   38

τὴν φύσιν καλόν, τοῦτο ἐκεῖνο, ὦ Σώκρατες, οὗ δὴ   39

ἕνεκεν καὶ οἱ ἔμπροσθεν πάντες πόνοι ἦσαν, πρῶτον μὲν   40

ἀεὶ ὂν καὶ οὔτε γιγνόμενον οὔτε ἀπολλύμενον, οὔτε αὐξανόμενον   41   211a

οὔτε φθῖνον, ἔπειτα οὐ τῇ μὲν καλόν, τῇ δ' αἰσχρόν,   42

οὐδὲ τοτὲ μέν, τοτὲ δὲ οὔ, οὐδὲ πρὸς μὲν τὸ καλόν, πρὸς   43

δὲ τὸ αἰσχρόν, οὐδ' ἔνθα μὲν καλόν, ἔνθα δὲ αἰσχρόν, ὡς   44

τισὶ μὲν ὂν καλόν, τισὶ δὲ αἰσχρόν· οὐδ' αὖ φαντασθήσεται   45

αὐτῷ τὸ καλὸν οἷον πρόσωπόν τι οὐδὲ χεῖρες οὐδὲ ἄλλο   46

οὐδὲν ὧν σῶμα μετέχει, οὐδέ τις λόγος οὐδέ τις ἐπιστήμη,   47

οὐδέ που ὂν ἐν ἑτέρῳ τινι, οἷον ἐν ζῴῳ ἢ ἐν γῇ ἢ ἐν οὐρανῷ   48

ἢ ἔν τῳ ἄλλῳ, ἀλλ' αὐτὸ καθ' αὑτὸ μεθ' αὑτοῦ μονοειδὲς ἀεὶ   49   211b

ὄν, τὰ δὲ ἄλλα πάντα καλὰ ἐκείνου μετέχοντα τρόπον τινὰ   50

τοιοῦτον, οἷον γιγνομένων τε τῶν ἄλλων καὶ ἀπολλυμένων   51

μηδὲν ἐκεῖνο μήτε τι πλέον μήτε ἔλαττον γίγνεσθαι μηδὲ   52

πάσχειν μηδέν.   53

---

35   μοι = for me, for my sake, please (ethical dat.) (*Essentials* §113)

35–36   ὡς οἷόν τε μάλιστα = ὡς μάλιστα

37   παιδαγωγέω = attend as a παιδαγωγός, train and teach, educate
     ἐφεξῆς *adv.* = in order, in a row, one after another

39   τὴν φύσιν: acc. of respect with θαυμαστόν (note the different genders)
     τοῦτο ἐκεῖνο = this [is] that

40   ἕνεκεν: Ionic form of ἕνεκα

42   φθίνω/φθίω φθίσομαι = decline, decay, wane, waste away
     τῇ μὲν . . . τῇ δέ: as is typical, the feminine dative singular implies adverbial "way" = in one
     way . . . in another

43–44   πρὸς μὲν τό . . . πρὸς δὲ τό = for one purpose . . . for another

45   φαντάζομαι = become visible, appear, show oneself

49   μονοειδής -ές = of one form or kind, uniform

50–51   τοιοῦτον . . . οἷον *correl.* = such . . . that; introducing a (natural) result clause, using infinitives
     (γίγνεσθαι, πάσχειν) as verbs

Reading 9J

Diotima ends by describing contemplation of the beautiful-in-itself as the best goal of life and claims that perception of this beautiful alone will lead to the begetting and nurturing of true virtue and the individual's personal immortality. It seems a profoundly religious and mystical notion with clear influence on later religious thinkers, including Christian ones. Socrates ends by saying that he himself is persuaded by Diotima and therefore tries to persuade others that Eros is the best helper in this endeavor.

Vocabulary

εἴδωλον -ου τό: image, phantom
ἐσθής -ῆτος ἡ: garment, dress, clothing, raiment
καθαρός -ά -όν: clear of dirt, clean, spotless, unsoiled, pure (cf. English "catharsis")
κτῆμα κτήματος τό: possession (cf. κτάομαι)
φλυαρία -ας ἡ: silly talk, nonsense, foolery; *recognize also* φλυαρέω: talk foolishly
χρυσίον -ου τό: gold, piece of gold

Reading 9J (*Symposium* 211b5–212c3)

Ὅταν δή τις ἀπὸ τῶνδε διὰ τὸ ὀρθῶς παιδεραστεῖν	1
ἐπανιὼν ἐκεῖνο τὸ καλὸν ἄρχηται καθορᾶν, σχεδὸν	2
ἄν τι ἅπτοιτο τοῦ τέλους. τοῦτο γὰρ δή ἐστι τὸ ὀρθῶς ἐπὶ	3
τὰ ἐρωτικὰ ἰέναι ἢ ὑπ’ ἄλλου ἄγεσθαι, ἀρχόμενον ἀπὸ	4 211c
τῶνδε τῶν καλῶν ἐκείνου ἕνεκα τοῦ καλοῦ ἀεὶ ἐπανιέναι,	5
ὥσπερ ἐπαναβασμοῖς χρώμενον, ἀπὸ ἑνὸς ἐπὶ δύο καὶ ἀπὸ	6
δυοῖν ἐπὶ πάντα τὰ καλὰ σώματα, καὶ ἀπὸ τῶν καλῶν	7
σωμάτων ἐπὶ τὰ καλὰ ἐπιτηδεύματα, καὶ ἀπὸ τῶν ἐπιτηδευμάτων	8
ἐπὶ τὰ καλὰ μαθήματα, καὶ ἀπὸ τῶν μαθημάτων ἐπ’	9
ἐκεῖνο τὸ μάθημα τελευτῆσαι, ὅ ἐστιν οὐκ ἄλλου ἢ αὐτοῦ	10
ἐκείνου τοῦ καλοῦ μάθημα, ἵνα³⁷ γνῷ αὐτὸ τελευτῶν ὃ ἔστι καλόν.”	11
“ἐνταῦθα τοῦ βίου, ὦ φίλε Σώκρατες,” ἔφη ἡ Μαντινικὴ	12 211d
ξένη, “εἴπερ που ἄλλοθι, βιωτὸν ἀνθρώπῳ, θεωμένῳ	13
αὐτὸ τὸ καλόν. ὃ ἐάν ποτε ἴδῃς, οὐ κατὰ χρυσίον τε καὶ	14

---

1   τῶνδε frequently points forward to what is coming up, but it can be used, as here, to refer back to a subject already introduced, particularly when the speaker wants to put particular emphasis on it.

παιδεραστέω = παιδῶν ἐραστής εἰμι: the implication has been throughout that an older man is leading a younger man, and that both are learning about *eros* properly.

2   ἐπάνειμι = rise up, climb up

3   τι: with σχεδόν in line 2 (= σχεδόν)

5   ἐπανιέναι from ἐπάνειμι = rise up, climb up, defining the τοῦτο that is τὸ ὀρθῶς . . . ἰέναι

6   χρώμενον: with an implied sing. acc. pron. = someone, one

ἐπαναβασμός -οῦ ὁ = step of a stair

9   μάθημα -ατος τό = thing learned, lesson, piece of knowledge

10   τελευτῆσαι: the infinitive is parallel to ἐπανιέναι (defining τοῦτο; see note on line 5)

11   γνῷ: root aor. subju. (*Essentials* §64)

τελευτῶν: the circumstantial participle is virtually an adverb here = finally

12   τοῦ βίου: partitive gen. with ἐνταῦθα = at this moment of life; *literally* = in this place within life

13   εἴπερ που ἄλλοθι: this phrase is used several times in Plato clearly in the sense of "above all places" (Bury 1973: 131), although the literal meaning would seem to be "if indeed anywhere else."

βιωτός -ή -όν = livable, worth living; *neut. used impers.* = It is worth living for a human being. It is worthwhile for a person to live. i.e., Life is worth living.

14   κατά = on the same level with

---

37. I use Dover's text here rather than Burnet 1901.

ἐσθῆτα καὶ τοὺς καλοὺς παῖδάς τε καὶ νεανίσκους δόξει σοι   15

εἶναι, οὓς νῦν ὁρῶν ἐκπέπληξαι καὶ ἕτοιμος εἶ καὶ σὺ καὶ   16

ἄλλοι πολλοί, ὁρῶντες τὰ παιδικὰ καὶ συνόντες ἀεὶ αὐτοῖς,   17

εἴ πως οἷόν τ' ἦν, μήτ' ἐσθίειν μήτε πίνειν, ἀλλὰ θεᾶσθαι   18

μόνον καὶ συνεῖναι." "Τί δῆτα," ἔφη, "οἰόμεθα, εἴ τῳ γένοιτο   19

αὐτὸ τὸ καλὸν ἰδεῖν εἰλικρινές, καθαρόν, ἄμεικτον, ἀλλὰ   20   211e

μὴ ἀνάπλεων σαρκῶν τε ἀνθρωπίνων καὶ χρωμάτων καὶ   21

ἄλλης πολλῆς φλυαρίας θνητῆς, ἀλλ' αὐτὸ τὸ θεῖον καλὸν   22

δύναιτο μονοειδὲς κατιδεῖν; ἆρ' οἴει," ἔφη, "φαῦλον βίον   23

γίγνεσθαι ἐκεῖσε βλέποντος ἀνθρώπου καὶ ἐκεῖνο ᾧ δεῖ   24   212a

θεωμένου καὶ συνόντος αὐτῷ; ἢ οὐκ ἐνθυμῇ," ἔφη, "ὅτι ἐνταῦθα   25

αὐτῷ μοναχοῦ γενήσεται, ὁρῶντι ᾧ ὁρατὸν τὸ καλόν, τίκτειν   26

16	ἕτοιμος: anticipates the infinitives ἐσθίειν … συνεῖναι in lines 18–19
19–20	τῳ = τινι (dat. with γένοιτο + *inf.*) = [if] it should befall anyone to ——
20	εἰλικρινής -ές = unmixed, pure
	ἄμεικτος -ον = unmixed (cf. μείγνυμι)
21	ἀνάπλεως -ων = quite full of *gen.* (see Smyth 1956: §289 for declension)
	χρῶμα -ατος τό = color
23	μονοειδής -ές = uniform
24	ἐκεῖνο = τὸ καλόν, obj. of θεωμένου, not the antecedent of ᾧ, which is here suppressed
	ᾧ δεῖ = with whatever it is fitting [for him to use], apparently referring to the faculty of perception. It is not exactly clear how one comes to perceive the good in itself; it does not seem to be with the eyes so much as with the mind or soul. The enigmatic phrasing seems to reflect that uncertainty.
26	ἐνταῦθα … μοναχοῦ = in this one place alone
	αὐτῷ … γενήσεται … τίκτειν = it will befall him to give birth
	ᾧ ὁρατόν = with that through which it is visible. As with ᾧ δεῖ in line 24, the instrument of this "seeing" remains vague.

οὐκ εἴδωλα ἀρετῆς, ἅτε οὐκ εἰδώλου ἐφαπτομένῳ, ἀλλὰ   27

ἀληθῆ, ἅτε τοῦ ἀληθοῦς ἐφαπτομένῳ· τεκόντι δὲ ἀρετὴν   28

ἀληθῆ καὶ θρεψαμένῳ ὑπάρχει θεοφιλεῖ γενέσθαι, καὶ εἴπέρ   29

τῳ ἄλλῳ ἀνθρώπων ἀθανάτῳ καὶ ἐκείνῳ;"   30

    Ταῦτα δή, ὦ Φαῖδρέ τε καὶ οἱ ἄλλοι, ἔφη μὲν Διοτίμα,   31   212b

πέπεισμαι δ' ἐγώ· πεπεισμένος δὲ πειρῶμαι καὶ τοὺς ἄλλους   32

πείθειν ὅτι τούτου τοῦ κτήματος τῇ ἀνθρωπείᾳ φύσει συνεργὸν   33

ἀμείνω Ἔρωτος οὐκ ἄν τις ῥᾳδίως λάβοι. διὸ δὴ   34

ἔγωγέ φημι χρῆναι πάντα ἄνδρα τὸν Ἔρωτα τιμᾶν, καὶ   35

αὐτὸς τιμῶ τὰ ἐρωτικὰ καὶ διαφερόντως ἀσκῶ, καὶ τοῖς   36

ἄλλοις παρακελεύομαι, καὶ νῦν τε καὶ ἀεὶ ἐγκωμιάζω τὴν   37

δύναμιν καὶ ἀνδρείαν τοῦ Ἔρωτος καθ' ὅσον οἷός τ' εἰμί.   38

τοῦτον οὖν τὸν λόγον, ὦ Φαῖδρε, εἰ μὲν βούλει, ὡς ἐγκώμιον εἰς   39   212c

ἔρωτα νόμισον εἰρῆσθαι, εἰ δέ, ὅτι καὶ ὅπῃ χαίρεις ὀνομάζων,   40

τοῦτο ὀνόμαζε.   41

27–28 ἐφάπτομαι = take hold of *gen.*, grasp, apprehend

28   ἀληθῆ: supply ἀρετήν: οὐκ εἴδωλα ἀρετῆς ... ἀλλὰ ἀληθῆ ἀρετήν

28–29 τέκοντι and θρεψαμένῳ: participles with ἐκείνῳ in line 30, can be interpreted either as circumstantial participles or as indefinite substantive participles without significant difference in sense

29   ὑπάρχει + *dat.* + *inf.*: it is possible for *dat.* to ——

29–30 θεοφιλεῖ ... ἀθανάτῳ: pred. adjectives with γενέσθαι

        εἴπέρ τῳ ἄλλῳ ἀνθρώπων: parenthetical = if indeed for any human being at all

30   καὶ ἐκείνῳ; by delaying the demonstrative that completes the impersonal expression and setting it apart with an adverbial καί, Plato makes the final words of Diotima's speech more emphatic and dramatic (= "he too," "that man especially"). The question carries over from ἐνθυμῇ (line 25).

33   συνεργός -οῦ ὁ = coworker with *dat.* for *gen.*, one who works together with *dat.* in acquiring *gen.*

36   *ἀσκέω = practice; work curiously, form by art, fashion

40   εἰ δέ = or if you prefer (βούλει can be inferred from εἰ μὲν βούλει of the previous line)

Reading 10. Socrates as Satyr: Alcibiades' Drunken Satyr-Play

Alcibiades, one of the most prominent political figures of the second half of the fifth century and a close associate of the group (see introduction: "Historical Context of the Dialogue" and appendix 1), enters the party. Crowned in ivy and violets, very drunk, leaning on a flute-girl, and accompanied by reveling men (*komasts*), he evokes the god Dionysus. Thus, a flute-girl and drunkenness, both earlier dismissed from the party (reading 2), return with Alcibiades, taking us back to the earlier part of the dialogue. When Alcibiades goes on to crown with a garland of victory first Agathon and then Socrates, we are reminded of the contest between Agathon and Socrates to be judged by Dionysus (reading 2). This part of the *Symposium* is at least in part comedy, which is etymologically related to and grows out of the revel (κῶμος). Comedy is a revel-song. Alcibiades is clearly celebrating a *komos* when he arrives.

Alcibiades' speech, which playfully compares Socrates to a satyr or a silen-figure, in a game characteristic of Greek symposia, is one of the best surviving verbal portraits of Socrates, apart from Plato's *Apology*. The satyr or silen was in classical times part-man/part-horse, a somewhat homely and comical figure, with a characteristic snub nose and a horse's tail. Satyrs may be showing playing the aulos (fig. 23), Dionysus's instrument, a double-reed instrument, often translated "flute," although more similar to an oboe. Satyrs are attendants of Dionysus and represent the comical side of drunkenness (as opposed to centaurs, also half-man/half-horse, who, when drunk, become violent and dangerous). There are many amusing images of satyrs in Greek vase paintings, where they are characterized by lewd and laughable behavior. The term *silen* appears virtually interchangeable with *satyr*, though at times it is used to distinguish older satyrs. Most ancient portraits of Socrates give his face a rather satyrlike appearance (fig. 21), possibly under the influence of this speech, though there seems also to have been an actual physical resemblance (reading 10C). Alcibiades suggests that Socrates is actually most like small statues of silens that when opened up contained "treasures" (ἀγάλματα), probably small images of the god Dionysus. The ugly and comical silenus-figure thus *contains* the beautiful god. This was probably meant to represent the partaking of wine, which is frequently presented as an actual imbibing of the god himself. Unfortunately, we do not have any of statuettes of precisely this kind.

Theatrical themes are also clearly represented in this final reading. Apart from the comedy of the *komos* (revel), Socrates refers to Alcibiades' speech as a satyr-play (reading 11), the third form of drama performed in Classical Athens beside comedy and tragedy. Only one survives in

Fig. 23. Silen playing the aulos for the god Dionysus. Red-figure drinking cup from Vulci, ca. 490–480 B.C.E. Painter Macron. Signed by the potter Hieron. Photo: Ingrid Geske-Heiden. Inv. F2290. Antikensammlung, Staatliche Museen zu Berlin, Berlin, Germany. Photo credit: Bildarchiv Preussischer Kulturbesitz/Art Resource, New York.

Fig. 24. Marble head representing the Athenian general and politician Alcibiades as a beautiful youth. Inscription reads "Alkibiades, son of Klinios, Athenian." Ancient copy from a fourth-century B.C.E. Greek original. Location: Musei Capitolini, Rome, Italy. Photo credit: Vanni/Art Resource, New York.

its entirety, Euripides' *Cyclops*, which retells the story of Odysseus's encounter with the Cyclops told in *Odyssey 9*, but with the addition of a chorus of satyrs and their leader Papa Silenus, who add considerable humor to the tale as well as Dionysiac themes appropriate to the drama.

Alcibiades' *eros* for Socrates, which emerges in this speech, is clearly very different from the pure and abstract *eros* that Diotima describes as the *eros* viewed by the initiate in reading 9. It resembles far more closely the kind of love described by Aristophanes, love for a particular individual. All scholars have agreed that this contrast is very important, though they disagree on precisely how to take this. Certainly, Alcibiades is an obviously flawed character whom we are not asked to take as a role model, and yet his form of love is far more familiar and sympathetic to most human beings. Socrates in contrast is strange and unfamiliar in his form of love; the dialogue mentions his strangeness (ἀτοπία) and even his hubris several times, which raises questions about how comprehensible most human beings will find him.

Further Reading on Alcibiades' Drunken Satyr-Play

- Nussbaum 1986 and Allen 1991: 102–8 offer two particularly eloquent, though very different readings of this episode.
- on Alcibiades—Plutarch's *Life of Alcibiades and Thucydides*, book 6
- on satyrs—Lissarague 1987, 1990a, 1990b

Suggested Reviews

- principal parts of βαίνω and γιγνώσκω

  βαίνω βήσομαι ἔβην βέβηκα -βέβαμαι ἐβάθην = go, come, walk
  γιγνώσκω γνώσομαι ἔγνων ἔγνωκα ἔγνωσμαι ἐγνώσθην = perceive, mark, learn, recognize, know

- forms of root aorist (ἔβην and ἔγνων) (*Essentials* §64)
- principal parts of δάκνω and οἴγνυμι

  δάκνω δήξομαι ἔδακον δέδηχα δέδηγμαι ἐδήχθην = bite, sting
  οἴγνυμι/οἴγω οἴξω ᾦξα/(ἀν)έῳξα (ἀν)έῳγα ᾦχθην/(ἀν)εῴχθην = open

Reading 10A

Alcibiades enters drunk and leaning on a flute-girl.

Vocabulary

ἀναδέω ἀναδήσω ἀνέδησα ἀναδέδεκα ἀναδέδεμαι ἀνεδέθην: bind above; i.e., put something round the head, crown, garland

ἀναπαύομαι -παύσομαι ἀνεπαυσάμην—πέπαυμαι ἀνεπαύσθην: rest, take a break

αὐλητρίς -τρίδος ἡ: female aulos-player (usually translated "flute-girl"), figs. 4 and 5.

βοάω βοήσομαι ἐβόησα: shout (cf. *βοή -ῆς ἡ: shout)

δέχομαι δέξομαι ἐδεξάμην—δέδεγμαι -ἐδέχθην: receive, accept, welcome, expect

δέω δήσω ἔδησα δέδεκα δέδεμαι ἐδέθην: bind; cf. ἀναδέω; *note also* ὑποδέω: bind below,
i.e., put on shoes

εἴωθα: be accustomed to (perf. forms with pres. meaning); *recognize also* εἰωθότως *adv.*: in a
customary way, as usual

ἐξαίφνης *adv.*: suddenly

κωμαστής -οῦ ὁ: reveler, *komast*, one who celebrates the *komos* (revel following a drinking party)

μανία -ας ἡ: mania, madness, insanity (cf. μαίνομαι)

μεθύω: be drunk; pres. and imperf. forms only (cf. μεθύσκομαι, *aor.* ἐμεθύσθην: get drunk
and English "meth-")

μέμφομαι μέμψομαι ἐμεμψάμην: blame

ὀφθαλμός -οῦ ὁ: eye (cf. English "ophthalmologist")

στέφανος -ου ὁ: garland, crown; *recognize also* στεφανόω: garland, put on a garland, crown
(cf. English "Stephanie" and "Stephen")

συμπότης -ου ὁ: fellow-drinker, symposiast

ταινία -ας ἡ: band, ribbon, fillet

φθονέω φθονήσομαι (pass. meaning) ἐφθόνησα—ἐφθόνημαι ἐφθονήθην: begrudge, envy;
recognize also φθόνος -ου ὁ: envy

χαῖρε/χαίρετε: greetings! farewell!; a salutation in imperative form, used both to greet and to
say good-bye

Reading 10A (*Symposium* 212c4–213e6)

Εἰπόντος δὲ ταῦτα τοῦ Σωκράτους τοὺς μὲν ἐπαινεῖν, τὸν	1
δὲ Ἀριστοφάνη λέγειν τι ἐπιχειρεῖν, ὅτι ἐμνήσθη αὐτοῦ	2
λέγων ὁ Σωκράτης περὶ τοῦ λόγου· καὶ ἐξαίφνης τὴν αὔλειον	3
θύραν κρουομένην πολὺν ψόφον παρασχεῖν ὡς κωμαστῶν, καὶ	4
αὐλητρίδος φωνὴν ἀκούειν. τὸν οὖν Ἀγάθωνα, "Παῖδες," φάναι,	5
"οὐ σκέψεσθε; καὶ ἐὰν μέν τις τῶν ἐπιτηδείων ᾖ, καλεῖτε·	6 212d
εἰ δὲ μή, λέγετε ὅτι οὐ πίνομεν ἀλλ' ἀναπαυόμεθα ἤδη."	7
Καὶ οὐ πολὺ ὕστερον Ἀλκιβιάδου τὴν φωνὴν ἀκούειν ἐν	8
τῇ αὐλῇ σφόδρα μεθύοντος καὶ μέγα βοῶντος, ἐρωτῶντος	9
ὅπου Ἀγάθων καὶ κελεύοντος ἄγειν παρ' Ἀγάθωνα.	10
ἄγειν οὖν αὐτὸν παρὰ σφᾶς τήν τε αὐλητρίδα ὑπολαβοῦσαν καὶ	11
ἄλλους τινὰς τῶν ἀκολούθων, καὶ ἐπιστῆναι ἐπὶ τὰς θύρας	12
ἐστεφανωμένον αὐτὸν κιττοῦ τέ τινι στεφάνῳ δασεῖ καὶ	13 212e

---

1   τοὺς μὲν ἐπαινεῖν: indir. statement (like all the narrative sections in the dialogue); τοὺς μέν = the others (besides Aristophanes)

2   ἐμνήσθη from μιμνήσομαι (deponent) = make mention of *gen.* This presumably refers to Socrates' mention of the myth of the halves in reading 9E.9.

3   περὶ τοῦ λόγου: i.e., Diotima's (or possibly Aristophanes' in which case this phrase is an elaboration on ἐμνήσθη αὐτοῦ in the previous line)

    αὔλειος -α -ον = courtyard, leading to the αὐλή or courtyard

4   κρούω = strike, smite, knock on hard

6   *ἐπιτηδεῖος -ου ὁ = intimate friend

9   *αὐλή -ῆς ἡ = courtyard

10   κελεύοντος ἄγειν: context suggests "slaves" or "companions" as the object of κελεύοντος; or, as Rose 1985: 60 suggests, this may be a representation of the impera. ἄγετε in an indirect statement.

11   τήν τε αὐλητρίδα καὶ ἄλλους τινὰς τῶν ἀκολούθων: acc. subje. of the inf. ἄγειν

    *ὑπολαμβάνω = hold up, support from below (Alcibiades is apparently so drunk that he needs help walking)

13   ἐστεφανωμένον from στεφανόω. (Remember that a non-indicative form that appears to be augmented must be a form of the perfect. The epsilon cannot be the temporal augment, which goes only on past tenses of the indicative; it is a form of reduplication that belongs to the perfect stem.)

    κιττός -οῦ ὁ = ivy, characteristically worn by Dionysus and his followers

    δασύς -εῖα -ύ = shaggy, rough

ἴων, καὶ ταινίας ἔχοντα ἐπὶ τῆς κεφαλῆς πάνυ πολλάς, καὶ εἰπεῖν·   14

    "Ἄνδρες, χαίρετε· μεθύοντα ἄνδρα πάνυ σφόδρα   15

δέξεσθε συμπότην, ἢ ἀπίωμεν ἀναδήσαντες μόνον Ἀγάθωνα,   16

ἐφ' ᾧπερ ἤλθομεν; ἐγὼ γάρ τοι," φάναι, "χθὲς μὲν οὐχ   17

οἷός τ' ἐγενόμην ἀφικέσθαι, νῦν δὲ ἥκω ἐπὶ τῇ κεφαλῇ   18

ἔχων τὰς ταινίας, ἵνα ἀπὸ τῆς ἐμῆς κεφαλῆς τὴν τοῦ σοφωτάτου   19

καὶ καλλίστου κεφαλήν, ἀνειπὼν οὑτωσί, ἀναδήσω.   20

ἆρα καταγελάσεσθέ μου ὡς μεθύοντος; ἐγὼ δέ, κἂν ὑμεῖς   21

γελᾶτε, ὅμως εὖ οἶδ' ὅτι ἀληθῆ λέγω. ἀλλά μοι λέγετε   22   213a

αὐτόθεν, ἐπὶ ῥητοῖς εἰσίω ἢ μή; συμπίεσθε ἢ οὔ;"   23

    Πάντας οὖν ἀναθορυβῆσαι καὶ κελεύειν εἰσιέναι καὶ   24

κατακλίνεσθαι, καὶ τὸν Ἀγάθωνα καλεῖν αὐτόν. καὶ τὸν   25

ἰέναι ἀγόμενον ὑπὸ τῶν ἀνθρώπων, καὶ περιαιρούμενον ἅμα   26

τὰς ταινίας ὡς ἀναδήσοντα, ἐπίπροσθε τῶν ὀφθαλμῶν ἔχοντα   27

οὐ κατιδεῖν τὸν Σωκράτη, ἀλλὰ καθίζεσθαι παρὰ τὸν Ἀγάθωνα   28

ἐν μέσῳ Σωκράτους τε καὶ ἐκείνου· παραχωρῆσαι   29   213b

γὰρ τὸν Σωκράτη ὡς ἐκεῖνον κατιδεῖν. παρακαθεζόμενον   30

δὲ αὐτὸν ἀσπάζεσθαί τε τὸν Ἀγάθωνα καὶ ἀναδεῖν.   31

---

14   ἴον -ου τό = violet. Violets are associated with Athens.

16   ἀπίωμεν: what form is this? Given that this is a question, what use must it be (*Essentials* §148)?

17   ἐφ' ᾧπερ = for which very thing

18   οἷός τ' ἐγενόμην: the aorist equivalent of οἷός τ' εἰμί (since εἰμί has no aorist), thus suggesting not a continuous state of incapacity but a moment of incapacity. Rose 1985: 60 suggests: "I proved unable, it turned out that I was unable. . . ."

20   ἀνειπεῖν = say aloud, proclaim

23   αὐτόθεν = at once
    ἐπὶ ῥητοῖς = on the stated terms (i.e., on the terms he set in the previous lines, as a συμπότης)
    εἰσίω: see note on ἀπίωμεν, line 16

25   τόν (last word in line) = τοῦτον: the definite article was originally a demonstrative pronoun. This is, in fact, still true in Homer. The phrase πρὸ τοῦ likewise preserves the original force of the definite article.

26   περιαιρέομαι = take (off) around, unwrap

27   ἐπίπροσθε = πρόσθε

29   παραχωρέω = go aside, make room

30   ὡς . . . κατιδεῖν = ὡς . . . κατεῖδεν: the infinitive is sometimes used instead of a finite verb in subordinate clauses in indirect statements, presumably by attraction to the infinitive in the main clause (Smyth 1956: §2631).
    ἐκεῖνον = Alcibiades

Εἰπεῖν οὖν τὸν Ἀγάθωνα, "Ὑπολύετε, παῖδες, Ἀλκιβιάδην,   32

ἵνα ἐκ τρίτων κατακέηται."   33

"Πάνυ γε," εἰπεῖν τὸν Ἀλκιβιάδην· "ἀλλὰ τίς ἡμῖν ὅδε   34

τρίτος συμπότης;" καὶ ἅμα μεταστρεφόμενον αὐτὸν ὁρᾶν   35

τὸν Σωκράτη, ἰδόντα δὲ ἀναπηδῆσαι καὶ εἰπεῖν, "Ὦ Ἡράκλεις,   36

τουτὶ τί ἦν; Σωκράτης οὗτος; ἐλλοχῶν αὖ με ἐνταῦθα κατέκεισο,   37

ὥσπερ εἰώθεις ἐξαίφνης ἀναφαίνεσθαι ὅπου ἐγὼ ᾤμην   38   213c

ἥκιστά σε ἔσεσθαι. καὶ νῦν τί ἥκεις; καὶ τί αὖ ἐνταῦθα   39

κατεκλίνης; ὡς οὐ παρὰ Ἀριστοφάνει οὐδὲ εἴ τις ἄλλος   40

γελοῖος ἔστι τε καὶ βούλεται, ἀλλὰ διεμηχανήσω ὅπως παρὰ   41

τῷ καλλίστῳ τῶν ἔνδον κατακείσῃ."   42

Καὶ τὸν Σωκράτη, "Ἀγάθων," φάναι, "ὅρα εἴ μοι ἐπαμυνεῖς·   43

ὡς ἐμοὶ ὁ τούτου ἔρως τοῦ ἀνθρώπου οὐ φαῦλον πρᾶγμα   44

---

32   ὑπολύω = remove the sandals from *acc.*; *literally* = unbind below, the opposite of ὑποδέω

33   ἐκ τρίτων = in the third place (idiomatic)

34   ἡμῖν = with us (because of συμπότης, line 35)

36   ἀναπηδάω = jump up

      Ἡράκλεις = Heracles, the great Greek hero, a common expletive, particularly in comedy

37   τουτί = τοῦτο + *deictic iota* = this here

      ἦν: the imperfect is occasionally used to register the sudden recognition of a present fact or truth. Translate as a present (with a tone of shock!) (imperf. of a truth just recognized) (Smyth 1956: §1902). This construction typically, as here, uses some form of the verb "to be" and normally, though not here, is accompanied by ἄρα.

      ἐλλοχάω = lie in ambush for

38   εἰώθεις: pluperf. with alternative 2nd pers. ending, but translate as simple past, as εἴωθα regularly uses perf. forms with present meaning

      ἀναφαίνομαι = appear, turn up

41   οὐδὲ εἴ τις ἄλλος: i.e., nor beside some other person, if there is one here, who . . . (but abbreviated)

      ἔστι τε καὶ βούλεται [εἶναι]: a pair of verbs found elsewhere, emphasizing an individual's responsibility for being what he is (Dover 1980: 161); in this context, slightly disparaging of Aristophanes and others like him, who prefer to be funny rather than beautiful or good like the attractive Agathon.

43   ὅρα εἴ = consider whether . . . , but implying something more like "please . . . won't you?" or "I hope that . . ."

      ἐπαμύνω + *dat.* = defend, defend against attack. What does the circumflex on the form here (ἐπαμυνῶ) imply about the tense?

γέγονεν. ἀπ᾽ ἐκείνου γὰρ τοῦ χρόνου, ἀφ᾽ οὗ τούτου   45

ἠράσθην, οὐκέτι ἔξεστίν μοι οὔτε προσβλέψαι οὔτε διαλεχθῆναι   46   213d

καλῷ οὐδ᾽ ἑνί, ἢ οὑτοσὶ ζηλοτυπῶν με καὶ φθονῶν   47

θαυμαστὰ ἐργάζεται καὶ λοιδορεῖταί τε καὶ τὼ χεῖρε μόγις   48

ἀπέχεται. ὅρα οὖν μή τι καὶ νῦν ἐργάσηται, ἀλλὰ διάλλαξον   49

ἡμᾶς, ἢ ἐὰν ἐπιχειρῇ βιάζεσθαι, ἐπάμυνε, ὡς ἐγὼ   50

τὴν τούτου μανίαν τε καὶ φιλεραστίαν πάνυ ὀρρωδῶ."   51

      "Ἀλλ᾽ οὐκ ἔστι," φάναι τὸν Ἀλκιβιάδην, "ἐμοὶ καὶ σοὶ διαλλαγή.   52

ἀλλὰ τούτων μὲν εἰς αὖθίς σε τιμωρήσομαι· νῦν   53

δέ μοι, Ἀγάθων," φάναι, "μετάδος τῶν ταινιῶν, ἵνα ἀναδήσω   54   213e

καὶ τὴν τούτου ταυτηνὶ τὴν θαυμαστὴν κεφαλήν, καὶ μή μοι   55

---

46   ἠράσθην: aor. (ingressive) of ἔραμαι, a deponent form of ἐράω (which is used only in the pres. and
       imperf.), with the same meaning. Translate actively. On the ingressive aorist, see *Essentials* §144.

47   ζηλοτυπέω = be jealous

48   λοιδορέομαι = abuse
       τὼ χεῖρε: what must this form be (*Essentials* §67)?

48–49 τὼ χεῖρε μόγις ἀπέχεται: i.e., he almost resorts to violence

49   ὅρα . . . μή = see that [he] does not . . . , take care lest . . .
       διαλλάττω = reconcile

50   βιάζομαι = use force
       ἐπαμύνω = defend, defend against attack

51   φιλεραστία -ας ἡ = passionate love for his lover (*erastes*)
       ὀρρωδέω = shudder at, shrink from

52   διαλλαγή -ῆς ἡ = reconciliation

53   τούτων: presumably referring to Socrates' suggestion in the previous speech that he fears
       Alcibiades' violence
       εἰς αὖθις: virtually = αὖθις. It is not unusual to see the preposition εἰς (used in its temporal sense:
       "up to, until, near to") followed by a temporal adverb (LSJ under εἰς II). Greek prepositions
       originated as adverbs, a use that is still evident in Homer, and later became more closely tied to
       verbs (as prefixes) and nouns (as prepositions), but they retain some of that original adverbial force
       and can sometimes be used rather loosely to link words in a sentence other than verbs and nouns.
       τιμωρέομαι = avenge oneself on *acc.* for *gen.*

54   μεταδίδωμι = give a share of *gen.*

μέμφηται ὅτι σὲ μὲν ἀνέδησα, αὐτὸν δὲ νικῶντα ἐν λόγοις   56

πάντας ἀνθρώπους, οὐ μόνον πρῴην ὥσπερ σύ, ἀλλ᾽ ἀεί,   57

ἔπειτα οὐκ ἀνέδησα." καὶ ἅμ᾽ αὐτὸν λαβόντα τῶν ταινιῶν   58

ἀναδεῖν τὸν Σωκράτη καὶ κατακλίνεσθαι.   59

---

58   τῶν ταινιῶν: partitive gen., common with verbs signifying to touch, take hold of (Smyth 1956: §§1345–46)

Reading 10B

Alcibiades joins the group and appoints himself symposiarch. The symposiasts agree to let Alcibiades praise Socrates rather than love.

Vocabulary

ἄτοπος -ον: strange, odd; *recognize also* ἀτοπία -ας ἡ: strangeness
νήφω: be sober (pres. forms only except in late texts)
τιμωρέομαι τιμωρήσομαι ἐτιμωρησάμην — τετιμώρημαι: exact vengeance, avenge oneself on
χέω χεῶ ἔχεα κέχυκα κέχυμαι ἐχύθην: pour, shed; *recognize also* ἐκχέω: pour out

Reading 10B (*Symposium* 213e7–215a3)

Ἐπειδὴ δὲ κατεκλίνη, εἰπεῖν· "Εἶεν δή, ἄνδρες· δοκεῖτε   1
γάρ μοι νήφειν. οὐκ ἐπιτρεπτέον οὖν ὑμῖν, ἀλλὰ ποτέον·   2
ὡμολόγηται γὰρ ταῦθ' ἡμῖν. ἄρχοντα οὖν αἱροῦμαι τῆς   3
πόσεως, ἕως ἂν ὑμεῖς ἱκανῶς πίητε, ἐμαυτόν. ἀλλὰ φερέτω,   4
Ἀγάθων, εἴ τι ἔστιν ἔκπωμα μέγα. μᾶλλον δὲ οὐδὲν δεῖ,   5
ἀλλὰ φέρε, παῖ," φάναι, "τὸν ψυκτῆρα ἐκεῖνον," ἰδόντα αὐτὸν   6
πλέον ἢ ὀκτὼ κοτύλας χωροῦντα. τοῦτον ἐμπλησάμενον   7   214a
πρῶτον μὲν αὐτὸν ἐκπιεῖν, ἔπειτα τῷ Σωκράτει κελεύειν ἐγχεῖν   8
καὶ ἅμα εἰπεῖν· "Πρὸς μὲν Σωκράτη, ὦ ἄνδρες, τὸ   9
σόφισμά μοι οὐδέν· ὁπόσον γὰρ ἂν κελεύῃ τις, τοσοῦτον   10
ἐκπιὼν οὐδὲν μᾶλλον μή ποτε μεθυσθῇ."   11
    Τὸν μὲν οὖν Σωκράτη ἐγχέαντος τοῦ παιδὸς πίνειν. τὸν   12
δ' Ἐρυξίμαχον "Πῶς οὖν," φάναι, "ὦ Ἀλκιβιάδη, ποιοῦμεν;   13

---

2   ἐπιτρεπτέος -α -ον = permissible (verbal adj. in -τέος) (*Essentials* §127)
     ποτέον: verbal adj. of πίνω (*Essentials* §127)

3–4 ἄρχοντα: pred. acc. with ἐμαυτόν in the next line, modified by τῆς πόσεως. It was a standard
     practice at the symposium to have a symposiarch or overseer of the drinking.

4   φερέτω: understand τις or παῖς τις as the subject; the object is implied in the protasis (if-clause)

5   μᾶλλον δέ: signals Alcibiades' change of mind: "but no . . ."
     ἔκπωμα -ατος τό = cup

6   ψυκτήρ -ῆρος ὁ = cooler, a large vessel in which wine would be cooled, considerably larger than
     a standard drinking cup (cf. ψυχρός)

7   κοτύλη -ης ἡ = unit of liquid measure, about a cup (so eight is close to a half-gallon)
     χωροῦντα = could hold, had a capacity. What use of the participle is this (*Essentials* §178)?
     *ἐμπίπλημι ἐμπλήσω ἐνέπλησα = fill full; *mid.* = have filled for one

8   κελεύειν: understand "slave" as the object (as elsewhere); κελεύω takes an accusative object so
     the dative Σωκράτει must go with ἐγχεῖν = pour out for Socrates (dat. of advantage).

9   Πρὸς . . . Σωκράτη = against Socrates, directed at Socrates (with σόφισμα in the next line)

10   σόφισμα -ατος τό = clever trick (referring to the extra-large drinking vessel)
     οὐδέν: i.e., worthless

11   οὐδὲν . . . μὴ μεθυσθῇ: οὐ μή + subju. (or fut. indic.) is used to indicate emphatic denial
     (*Essentials* §151). Socrates must be the subject here.

13   Πῶς . . . ποιοῦμεν; The tone here is of outraged disbelief. Πῶς is best translated here "what . . . !?"
     rather than the more standard "how."

οὕτως οὔτε τι λέγομεν ἐπὶ τῇ κύλικι οὔτε τι ᾄδομεν, ἀλλ᾽ 14 214b

ἀτεχνῶς ὥσπερ οἱ διψῶντες πιόμεθα;" 15

Τὸν οὖν Ἀλκιβιάδην εἰπεῖν. "Ὦ Ἐρυξίμαχε, βέλτιστε 16

βελτίστου πατρὸς καὶ σωφρονεστάτου, χαῖρε." 17

"Καὶ γὰρ σύ," φάναι τὸν Ἐρυξίμαχον· "ἀλλὰ τί ποιῶμεν;" 18

"Ὅτι ἂν σὺ κελεύῃς. δεῖ γάρ σοι πείθεσθαι· 19

'ἰητρὸς γὰρ ἀνὴρ πολλῶν ἀντάξιος ἄλλων·' 20

ἐπίτατte οὖν ὅτι βούλει." 21

"Ἄκουσον δή," εἰπεῖν τὸν Ἐρυξίμαχον. "ἡμῖν πρὶν σὲ 22

εἰσελθεῖν ἔδοξε χρῆναι ἐπὶ δεξιὰ ἕκαστον ἐν μέρει λόγον 23

περὶ Ἔρωτος εἰπεῖν ὡς δύναιτο κάλλιστον, καὶ ἐγκωμιάσαι. 24 214c

οἱ μὲν οὖν ἄλλοι πάντες ἡμεῖς εἰρήκαμεν· σὺ δ᾽ ἐπειδὴ οὐκ 25

εἴρηκας καὶ ἐκπέπωκας, δίκαιος εἶ εἰπεῖν, εἰπὼν δὲ ἐπιτάξαι 26

Σωκράτει ὅτι ἂν βούλῃ, καὶ τοῦτον τῷ ἐπὶ δεξιὰ καὶ οὕτω 27

τοὺς ἄλλους." 28

"Ἀλλά," φάναι, "ὦ Ἐρυξίμαχε," τὸν Ἀλκιβιάδην, "καλῶς 29

μὲν λέγεις, μεθύοντα δὲ ἄνδρα παρὰ νηφόντων λόγους 30

---

14   ἐπὶ τῇ κύλικι = at the cup, i.e., while drinking

15   διψάω = be thirsty, thirst

16–17 Alcibiades has apparently not noticed Eryximachus previously. The tone here is ironic; Eryximachus
       is a bit too upright and temperate for Alcibiades' taste.

20   A quotation from Homer, *Iliad* 11.514.
       ἰητρός: the Ionic form of ἰατρός
       ἀντάξιος -α -ον = equivalent to *gen.*, the equal of *gen.*

21   ἐπιτάττω = κελεύω (but takes dat. = give an order to)

26   ἐπιτάξαι: aor. inf. of ἐπιτάττω (parallel to εἰπεῖν)

27   καὶ τοῦτον = καὶ τοῦτον [δεῖ ἐπιτάξαι]: τοῦτον refers to Socrates. The language here is
       compressed but would be easily understood by a Greek audience familiar with the conventions
       of the symposium. After Alcibiades has given orders to Socrates, it will be Socrates' turn, since
       he is now on Alcibiades' right, to give an order to the person on his right and so on.

30   μεθύοντα ἄνδρα: obj. of the inf. παραβάλλειν (line 31) and shorthand for τὸν μεθύοντος
       ἀνδρὸς λόγον

παραβάλλειν μὴ οὐκ ἐξ ἴσου ἦ. καὶ ἅμα, ὦ μακάριε, πείθει τί   31

σε Σωκράτης ὧν ἄρτι εἶπεν; ἢ οἶσθα ὅτι τοὐναντίον ἐστὶ   32   214d

πᾶν ἢ ὃ ἔλεγεν; οὗτος γάρ, ἐάν τινα ἐγὼ ἐπαινέσω τούτου   33

παρόντος ἢ θεὸν ἢ ἄνθρωπον ἄλλον ἢ τοῦτον, οὐκ ἀφέξεταί   34

μου τὼ χεῖρε."   35

　"Οὐκ εὐφημήσεις;" φάναι τὸν Σωκράτη.   36

　"Μὰ τὸν Ποσειδῶ," εἰπεῖν τὸν Ἀλκιβιάδην, "μηδὲν λέγε   37

πρὸς ταῦτα, ὡς ἐγὼ οὐδ' ἂν ἕνα ἄλλον ἐπαινέσαιμι σοῦ παρόντος."   38

　"Ἀλλ' οὕτω ποίει," φάναι τὸν Ἐρυξίμαχον, "εἰ βούλει·   39

Σωκράτη ἐπαίνεσον."   40

　"Πῶς λέγεις;" εἰπεῖν τὸν Ἀλκιβιάδην· "δοκεῖ χρῆναι, ὦ   41   214e

---

31　παραβάλλειν: the infinitive is the subject of the impersonal expression ἐξ ἴσου [ἐστι] = it is not fair (*Essentials* §182)

　　παρά + *acc*. . . . παραβάλλω = compare *acc*. with *acc*.

　　μὴ οὐκ . . . ἦ: μὴ οὐ + *subju. to indicate a doubtful negation* = I suspect that —— is not the case, I doubt that . . . (*Essentials* §150). Distinguish from οὐ μή + subju. in line 11 (*Essentials* §151).

　　τί: the accent is cast by the enclitic σε in the next line; internal accusative with πείθω + *double acc*. = persuade *acc. pers.* of *acc*.

32　ὧν: partitive gen. with τι (*Essentials* §93), an example of attraction to a suppressed antecedent (*Essentials* §133)

　　ἄρτι εἶπεν: Alcibiades is clearly referring to reading 10A.45–47

　　τοὐναντίον = τὸ ἐναντίον (crasis); best taken as a predicate here, despite the definite article. Supply a subject: "the truth" or "it." πᾶν is adverbial.

33　ἢ: take with τοὐναντίον in the previous line = the opposite of . . .

34　ἢ . . . ἢ . . . ἄλλον ἢ: note the range of meanings of ἢ in this line. ἢ . . . ἢ = either . . . or. Following ἄλλον, ἢ = than.

34–35　οὐκ ἀφέξεταί μου τὼ χεῖρε: i.e., will become violent (reading 10A.48–49)

35　μου: gen. of separation with ἀφέξεταί = from me

36　εὐφημέω: *literally* = speak well. It is closely associated with ritual contexts that ask for silence and should therefore be translated "be quiet."

37　Ποσειδῶν -ῶνος ὁ = Poseidon, god of the sea and of horses, apparently a favorite of wealthy youths of this period involved in horseracing, like Alcibiades (e.g., Pheidippides swears by Poseidon in Aristophanes' *Clouds* 83). Bury 1973: 142 suggests a possible pun on Poseidon as "drink-giver" (πόσις-δίδωμι). The oath does not appear elsewhere in Plato. The accusative case is normally used for oaths (*Essentials* §88). For the form, see Smyth 1956: §260.

38　πρὸς ταῦτα: πρός must have a hostile sense = against

Ἐρυξίμαχε; ἐπιθῶμαι τῷ ἀνδρὶ καὶ τιμωρήσωμαι ὑμῶν ἐναντίον;"   42

"Οὗτος," φάναι τὸν Σωκράτη, "τί ἐν νῷ ἔχεις; ἐπὶ τὰ   43

γελοιότερά με ἐπαινέσαι; ἢ τί ποιήσεις;"   44

"Τἀληθῆ ἐρῶ. ἀλλ᾽ ὅρα εἰ παρίῃς."   45

"Ἀλλὰ μέντοι," φάναι, "τά γε ἀληθῆ παρίημι καὶ κελεύω   46

λέγειν."   47

"Οὐκ ἂν φθάνοιμι," εἰπεῖν τὸν Ἀλκιβιάδην. "καὶ μέντοι   48

οὑτωσὶ ποίησον. ἐάν τι μὴ ἀληθὲς λέγω, μεταξὺ ἐπιλαβοῦ,   49

ἂν βούλῃ, καὶ εἰπὲ ὅτι τοῦτο ψεύδομαι· ἑκὼν γὰρ εἶναι οὐδὲν   50

ψεύσομαι. ἐὰν μέντοι ἀναμιμνῃσκόμενος ἄλλο ἄλλοθεν   51   215a

λέγω, μηδὲν θαυμάσῃς· οὐ γάρ τι ῥᾴδιον τὴν σὴν ἀτοπίαν   52

ὧδ᾽ ἔχοντι εὐπόρως καὶ ἐφεξῆς καταριθμῆσαι."   53

---

42   ἐπιθῶμαι from *ἐπιτίθεμαι = attack *dat.*

     ὑμῶν ἐναντίον = in front of you all

43   ἐπί + *acc.* = for the purpose of

45–46   *παρίημι = permit, give permission

48   *φθάνω = delay, lag behind

49   ἐπιλαμβάνομαι = seize upon, stop, arrest; with μεταξύ = interrupt

50   ἑκὼν . . . εἶναι = intentionally at any rate. εἶναι is an example of an infinitive used absolutely (i.e.,
     in a parenthetical sense, not part of the overall grammatical construction, similar to ὡς ἔπος
     εἰπεῖν) (Smyth 1956: §2012).

51   ἄλλο ἄλλοθεν = one thing from one place/part, another from another; i.e., disjointedly, in a
     disconnected and confused fashion

52   τὴν σὴν ἀτοπίαν: Socrates' ἀτοπία is mentioned several times in the dialogue

53   ὧδ᾽ ἔχοντι: review meaning of ἔχω + adv. The participle ἔχοντι depends on ῥᾴδιον and agrees
     with an understood indefinite pronoun = easy for [a person] being in this condition [i.e., very
     drunk], easy for someone who is in this condition.

     ἐφεξῆς *adv.* = in order, in an orderly fashion

     καταριθμέω = make an account of

Reading 10C

Alcibiades begins his speech by comparing Socrates to a satyr or silen (see reading 10 introduction).

Vocabulary

ἄγαλμα -ατος τό: (1) glory, delight, ornament; (2) statue or image of a god

αὐλός -οῦ ὁ: aulos, a musical instrument similar to an oboe, but usually translated "flute," an instrument associated with Dionysus that appears in many vase paintings, played by satyrs, symposiasts, and flute-girls at the symposium. It also accompanied dramatic performances (cf. αὐλητρίς ἡ); *recognize also* αὐλητής -οῦ ὁ: (male) aulos-player; αὐλέω: play an aulos

δάκρυον -ου τό: tear (*δακρύω: cry, weep)

εἰκών εἰκόνος ἡ: figure, image, likeness (cf. εἰκάζω and English "icon" and "iconoclast")

καρδία -ας ἡ: heart (cf. English "cardiologist" and "cardiovascular")

καρτερέω: be steadfast, strong, patient, stubborn; hold out, bear up, endure manfully

μέλω μελήσω ἐμέλησα μεμέληκα -μεμέλημαι -ἐμελήθην (cf. ἀμελέω, ἐπιμελέομαι): be a concern to *dat.*; *often impers.* + *dat.* + *gen.*: There is a concern to *dat.* for *gen.*; e.g., μέλει μοι τοῦδε: There is a concern to me for this. I am concerned about this.

οἴγνυμι/οἴγω οἴξω ᾦξα/(ἀν)έῳξα (ἀν)έῳγα ᾤχθην/(ἀν)εῴχθην: mainly found in compounds (e.g., ἀνοίγνυμι: open up, open; διοίγνυμι: open by dividing or splitting, split open)

σάτυρος -ου ὁ: satyr, part-man/part-horse followers of Dionysus, known for their lewd and comical behavior; *recognize also* σατυρικός: satyrlike

σιληνός -οῦ ὁ: silen, a half-man/half-animal creature, similar to a satyr; *also capitalized* Silenus, father of the satyrs; *recognize also* σιληνικός/σιληνωδής: silen-like or Silenus-like

Reading 10C (*Symposium* 215a4—216a8)

Σωκράτη δ᾽ ἐγὼ ἐπαινεῖν, ὦ ἄνδρες, οὕτως ἐπιχειρήσω,	1
δι᾽ εἰκόνων. οὗτος μὲν οὖν ἴσως οἰήσεται ἐπὶ τὰ γελοιότερα,	2
ἔσται δ᾽ ἡ εἰκὼν τοῦ ἀληθοῦς ἔνεκα, οὐ τοῦ γελοίου. φημὶ	3
γὰρ δὴ ὁμοιότατον αὐτὸν εἶναι τοῖς σιληνοῖς τούτοις τοῖς	4
ἐν τοῖς ἑρμογλυφείοις καθημένοις, οὕστινας ἐργάζονται οἱ	5 215b
δημιουργοὶ σύριγγας ἢ αὐλοὺς ἔχοντας, οἳ διχάδε διοιχθέντες	6
φαίνονται ἔνδοθεν ἀγάλματα ἔχοντες θεῶν. καὶ φημὶ αὖ	7
ἐοικέναι αὐτὸν τῷ σατύρῳ τῷ Μαρσύᾳ. ὅτι μὲν οὖν τό γε	8
εἶδος ὅμοιος εἶ τούτοις, ὦ Σώκρατες, οὐδ᾽ αὐτὸς ἄν που	9
ἀμφισβητήσαις· ὡς δὲ καὶ τἆλλα ἔοικας, μετὰ τοῦτο ἄκουε.	10
ὑβριστὴς εἶ· ἢ οὔ; ἐὰν γὰρ μὴ ὁμολογῇς, μάρτυρας παρέξομαι.	11
ἀλλ᾽ οὐκ αὐλητής; πολύ γε θαυμασιώτερος ἐκείνου.	12
ὁ μέν γε δι᾽ ὀργάνων ἐκήλει τοὺς ἀνθρώπους τῇ ἀπὸ τοῦ	13 215c

---

4   σιληνός -ου ὁ = image of a silen, small statue of a silen

5   ἑρμογλυφεῖον -ου τό = statuary workshop, place for carving statues (herms)

6   σύριγξ -ιγγος ὁ = syrinx or Pan-pipe (a musical instrument)
      διχάδε *adv.* = δίχα

7   φαίνονται . . . ἔχοντες: review meaning of φαίνομαι with participle
      ἔνδοθεν = (from) within

8   Μαρσύας -ου ὁ = Marsyas, a satyr famous as the inventor of the aulos, challenged the god Apollo
      to a musical contest, an act of hubris, and lost. He was flayed alive by Apollo in accordance with
      an agreement that the winner could do as he liked with the loser.

9   τὸ εἶδος: identify the form and usage (*Essentials* §82)

10   *ἀμφισβητέω = stand apart, dispute, disagree

11   ὑβριστής -οῦ ὁ: Agathon made the same accusation earlier (reading 2B.18). On Socrates' hubris in
      the *Symposium*, see Gagarin 1977.

13   ὁ μέν γε = this one, for his part. . . . The σὺ δ᾽ that responds to this doesn't occur until line 19.
      This prepares the reader for the comparison between Socrates and Marsyas.
      κηλέω = charm, fascinate, bewitch, seduce

στόματος δυνάμει, καὶ ἔτι νυνὶ ὃς ἂν τὰ ἐκείνου αὐλῇ—ἃ γὰρ   14

Ὄλυμπος ηὔλει, Μαρσύου λέγω, τούτου διδάξαντος—τὰ οὖν   15

ἐκείνου ἐάντε ἀγαθὸς αὐλητὴς αὐλῇ ἐάντε φαύλη αὐλητρίς,   16

μόνα κατέχεσθαι ποιεῖ καὶ δηλοῖ τοὺς τῶν θεῶν τε καὶ   17

τελετῶν δεομένους διὰ τὸ θεῖα εἶναι.   18

        Σὺ δ' ἐκείνου τοσοῦτον   19

μόνον διαφέρεις, ὅτι ἄνευ ὀργάνων ψιλοῖς λόγοις ταὐτὸν   20

τοῦτο ποιεῖς. ἡμεῖς γοῦν ὅταν μέν του ἄλλου ἀκούωμεν   21   215d

λέγοντος, καὶ πάνυ ἀγαθοῦ ῥήτορος, ἄλλους λόγους, οὐδὲν   22

μέλει ὡς ἔπος εἰπεῖν οὐδενί· ἐπειδὰν δὲ σοῦ τις ἀκούῃ ἢ τῶν   23

σῶν λόγων ἄλλου λέγοντος, κἂν πάνυ φαῦλος ᾖ ὁ λέγων,   24

ἐάντε γυνὴ ἀκούῃ ἐάντε ἀνὴρ ἐάντε μειράκιον, ἐκπεπληγμένοι   25

ἐσμὲν καὶ κατεχόμεθα.   26

---

15   Ὄλυμπος -ου ὁ = Olympos, mythical figure, the beloved and student of Marsyas

15–16 τὰ . . . ἐκείνου = his songs (presumably). This (rather than the rel. clause ὃς ἂν τὰ ἐκείνου
      αὐλῇ) is the subject of ποιεῖ and δηλοῖ in the next line. This is an instance of anacoluthon
      "not following," a form of grammatical inconsistency found in many Greek texts (Smyth 1956:
      §§3004–8). Alcibiades starts to speak of the musicians, but in the middle of the sentence revises
      his thought so that the songs rather than the player of them create the enchantment. The
      anacoluthon may reflect his drunken state, but serves Plato's purposes here, for he seems to want
      to emphasize the effect of Socrates' words, not only when spoken by Socrates but when reported
      by others, presumably including himself.

17   κατέχομαι = be held fast [as under a spell], be possessed, bewitched, captivated
      ποιέω + acc. + inf. = cause acc. to——

17–18 τοὺς . . . δεομένους: the object of both ποιεῖ and δηλοῖ with κατέχεσθαι as an objective
      infinitive (*Essentials* §180). The satyrs' aulos-music creates a response in those who are in need
      of divine help. Similarly, Alcibiades will imply, Socrates' words generate a response in those in
      need of his instruction.

18   τελετή -ῆς ἡ = mystic rite, religious festival

20   *ψιλός -ή -όν = bare, naked, unadorned, prosaic
      ταὐτὸν = τὸ αὐτό (crasis), def. art. + αὐτός (*Essentials* §191). ταὐτόν is an alternative to ταὐτό,
      especially in poetry (for metrical reasons) and to avoid hiatus (before words beginning with a
      vowel), but the presence of the moveable nu in Plato before words beginning with a consonant
      is very common.

21–22 Alcibiades echoes Apollodorus in reading 1B.

22   καὶ πάνυ ἀγαθοῦ ῥήτορος = even of/from a very good orator

26   κατέχομαι = be held fast [as under a spell], be possessed, bewitched, captivated

Ἐγὼ γοῦν, ὦ ἄνδρες, εἰ μὴ   27

ἔμελλον κομιδῇ δόξειν μεθύειν, εἶπον ὀμόσας ἂν ὑμῖν οἷα δὴ   28

πέπονθα αὐτὸς ὑπὸ τῶν τούτου λόγων καὶ πάσχω ἔτι καὶ   29

νυνί. ὅταν γὰρ ἀκούω, πολύ μοι μᾶλλον ἢ τῶν κορυβαντιώντων   30   215e

ἥ τε καρδία πηδᾷ καὶ δάκρυα ἐκχεῖται ὑπὸ τῶν   31

λόγων τῶν τούτου, ὁρῶ δὲ καὶ ἄλλους παμπόλλους τὰ   32

αὐτὰ πάσχοντας· Περικλέους δὲ ἀκούων καὶ ἄλλων ἀγαθῶν   33

ῥητόρων εὖ μὲν ἡγούμην λέγειν, τοιοῦτον δ' οὐδὲν ἔπασχον,   34

οὐδ' ἐτεθορύβητό μου ἡ ψυχὴ οὐδ' ἠγανάκτει ὡς ἀνδραποδωδῶς   35

διακειμένου, ἀλλ' ὑπὸ τουτουΐ τοῦ Μαρσύου πολλάκις δὴ   36

οὕτω διετέθην ὥστε μοι δόξαι μὴ βιωτὸν εἶναι ἔχοντι ὡς   37   216a

ἔχω. καὶ ταῦτα, ὦ Σώκρατες, οὐκ ἐρεῖς ὡς οὐκ ἀληθῆ. καὶ   38

27–28 εἰ μὴ ἔμελλον . . . = if I were not going to ——; i.e., if I were not virtually certain to ——

28   κομιδῇ (dat. of manner) = wholly, entirely

30   μοι: with καρδία, parallel to τῶν κορυβαντιώντων, indicating possession. Alcibiades is comparing his own heart's leaping and other physical responses with those of the inspired Corybantes.

       κορυβαντιάω = celebrate the rites of the Corybantes, apparently somewhat ecstatic rituals, involving aulos-playing and frenzied dancing, associated with the worship of Dionysus and the goddess Cybele, the Great Mother. In the *Ion*, Socrates describes the Corybantes as not in their senses; in Aristophanes' *Wasps* the son initiates his father into the cult of the Corybantes, hoping to cure him of his obsession with the law courts, whereupon his father enters the courtroom with a tympanum (drumlike instrument), reinforcing the association of the Corybantes with music and dance that we see here.

31   πηδάω = jump, leap

33   Περικλῆς -έους ὁ = Pericles, a prominent Athenian statesman, known for his effective oratory, and Alcibiades' adoptive father

34   εὖ with λέγειν not with ἡγούμην, as the context makes clear. Context allows inference of a subject "they" with λέγειν.

35   ἐτεθορύβητο from θορυβέω: pluperf. implies "was put into an enduring state of disturbance"
       *ἀγανακτέω = feel irritation
       ἀνδραποδώδης -ες = slavish, servile (ὡς ἀνδραποδωδῶς διακειμένου = because of being enslaved [with μου])

37   δόξαι: not from the noun δόξα but from the verb δοκέω. What form must it be?
       βιωτός -ή -όν = liveable, possible to live (verbal adjective in -τος used impersonally with dative = so that it seemed to me not to be possible to live.)
       ὡς: makes clear that both ἔχω and ἔχοντι are to be translated as ἔχω + adv.

ἔτι γε νῦν σύνοιδ᾽ ἐμαυτῷ ὅτι εἰ ἐθέλοιμι παρέχειν τὰ ὦτα,   39

οὐκ ἂν καρτερήσαιμι ἀλλὰ ταὐτὰ ἂν πάσχοιμι. ἀναγκάζει   40

γάρ με ὁμολογεῖν ὅτι πολλοῦ ἐνδεὴς ὢν αὐτὸς ἔτι ἐμαυτοῦ   41

μὲν ἀμελῶ, τὰ δ᾽ Ἀθηναίων πράττω. βίᾳ οὖν ὥσπερ ἀπὸ   42

τῶν Σειρήνων ἐπισχόμενος τὰ ὦτα οἴχομαι φεύγων, ἵνα μὴ   43

αὐτοῦ καθήμενος παρὰ τούτῳ καταγηράσω.   44

---

39   σύνοιδα ἐμαυτῷ = I know with myself; i.e., I know in my heart, I am conscious that

42   τὰ δ᾽ Ἀθηναίων = the things of the Athenians; i.e., work on behalf of the state

43   Σειρῆνες -ων αἱ = the Sirens, mythical female creatures who lure men to their death with their
       enchanting, inescapable song (*Odyssey* 11.36–200)

       ἐπίσχομαι = plug up, stop up

44   καταγηράω = grow old (cf. γῆρας -ως τό)

Reading 10D

Alcibiades continues his speech and his comparison of Socrates to a satyr. He introduces the image of carved satyr statuettes.

Vocabulary

ἀγνοέω ἀγνοήσω ἠγνόησα ἠγνόηκα ἠγνόημαι ἠγνοήθην: be ignorant, not know (cf. γιγνώσκω and English "agnostic")

ἔμβραχυ *adv.*: in short, briefly (cf. *βραχύς -εῖα -ύ: short, brief)

ἐντός *adv.*: within, inside (cf. ἐν and ἔνδον); *recognize also* ἔνδοθεν: from within

ἔξω *adv.*: outside, without (cf. ἐκ/ἐξ); *recognize also* ἔξωθεν: from without

πλῆθος -ους τό: number, crowd, mass, the people (cf. English "plethora")

πόσος -η -ον: how great, how much; *pl.*: how many? (cf. ὁπόσος, τόσος, τοσοῦτος, τοσόσδε)

σπουδάζω σπουδάσομαι ἐσπούδασα ἐσπούδακα ἐσπούδασμαι ἐσπουδήσθην *intrans.*: make haste, be earnest, be serious; *trans.*: do or pursue hastily, earnestly, seriously or zealously (cf. σπουδή)

χρυσοῦς -ῆ -οῦν: golden, gold (endings contracted from -εος -εη -εον) (see Smyth 1956: §290 for full declension of contracted adjectives)

Reading 10D (*Symposium* 216a8–217a2)

Πέπονθα δὲ	1	
πρὸς τοῦτον μόνον ἀνθρώπων, ὃ οὐκ ἄν τις οἴοιτο ἐν ἐμοὶ	2	216b
ἐνεῖναι, τὸ αἰσχύνεσθαι ὁντινοῦν· ἐγὼ δὲ τοῦτον μόνον	3	
αἰσχύνομαι. σύνοιδα γὰρ ἐμαυτῷ ἀντιλέγειν μὲν οὐ δυναμένῳ	4	
ὡς οὐ δεῖ ποιεῖν ἃ οὗτος κελεύει, ἐπειδὰν δὲ ἀπέλθω,	5	
ἡττημένῳ τῆς τιμῆς τῆς ὑπὸ τῶν πολλῶν. δραπετεύω οὖν	6	
αὐτὸν καὶ φεύγω, καὶ ὅταν ἴδω, αἰσχύνομαι τὰ ὡμολογημένα.	7	
καὶ πολλάκις μὲν ἡδέως ἂν ἴδοιμι αὐτὸν μὴ ὄντα ἐν ἀνθρώποις·	8	216c
εἰ δ᾽ αὖ τοῦτο γένοιτο, εὖ οἶδα ὅτι πολὺ μεῖζον ἂν ἀχθοίμην,	9	
ὥστε οὐκ ἔχω ὅτι χρήσωμαι τούτῳ τῷ ἀνθρώπῳ.	10	
Καὶ ὑπὸ μὲν δὴ τῶν αὐλημάτων καὶ ἐγὼ καὶ ἄλλοι πολλοὶ	11	
τοιαῦτα πεπόνθασιν ὑπὸ τοῦδε τοῦ σατύρου· ἄλλα δὲ ἐμοῦ	12	
ἀκούσατε ὡς ὅμοιός τ᾽ ἐστὶν οἷς ἐγὼ ᾔκασα αὐτὸν καὶ τὴν	13	
δύναμιν ὡς θαυμασίαν ἔχει. εὖ γὰρ ἴστε ὅτι οὐδεὶς ὑμῶν	14	

1–3	πρός = in reference to. Alcibiades seems to have been notorious for outrageous behavior that suggested to the Athenians the lack of a sense of shame.
4	σύνοιδα ἐμαυτῷ = I know with myself; i.e., I know in my heart that . . . , I am conscious that . . .
4–5	ἀντιλέγειν . . . ὡς οὐ δεῖ: to argue against him that I ought not
4–6	δυναμένῳ and ἡττημένῳ: both dative participles modifying ἐμαυτῷ serve as the verbs of indirect statements
6	*ἡττάομαι + *gen.* = be less than, be inferior to; i.e., be overcome by, give way to, yield to
	δραπετεύω = run away from, flee (in the manner of a runaway slave)
10	*ἔχω (with indir. question) = know (cf. Reading 6B, line 12 and note)
	ὅτι = ὅ τι
	χρήσωμαι: aor. subju. of χράομαι (deliberative); ὅτι χρήσωμαι = what I am to do with . . .
11	αὔλημα -ατος τό = piece of music for the aulos (here used metaphorically of Socrates' words)
12	ἄλλα: from ἄλλος *not* ἀλλά = but (compare position of accent); acc. of respect with ὅμοιος (line 13)
13	ᾔκασα from εἰκάζω
	καί: links the two clauses introduced by ὡς
13–14	τὴν δύναμιν ὡς: prolepsis (*Essentials* §208)
14	ἴστε: impera. (context suggests)

τοῦτον γιγνώσκει· ἀλλὰ ἐγὼ δηλώσω, ἐπείπερ ἠρξάμην.   15   216d

ὁρᾶτε γὰρ ὅτι Σωκράτης ἐρωτικῶς διάκειται τῶν καλῶν καὶ   16

ἀεὶ περὶ τούτους ἐστὶ καὶ ἐκπέπληκται, καὶ αὖ ἀγνοεῖ πάντα   17

καὶ οὐδὲν οἶδεν, ὡς τὸ σχῆμα αὐτοῦ. τοῦτο οὐ σιληνῶδες;   18

σφόδρα γε. τοῦτο γὰρ οὗτος ἔξωθεν περιβέβληται, ὥσπερ   19

ὁ γεγλυμμένος σιληνός· ἔνδοθεν δὲ ἀνοιχθεὶς πόσης οἴεσθε   20

γέμει, ὦ ἄνδρες συμπόται, σωφροσύνης; ἴστε ὅτι οὔτε εἴ τις   21

καλός ἐστι μέλει αὐτῷ οὐδέν, ἀλλὰ καταφρονεῖ τοσοῦτον   22

ὅσον οὐδ᾽ ἂν εἷς οἰηθείη, οὔτ᾽ εἴ τις πλούσιος, οὔτ᾽ εἰ ἄλλην   23   216e

τινὰ τιμὴν ἔχων τῶν ὑπὸ πλήθους μακαριζομένων· ἡγεῖται   24

δὲ πάντα ταῦτα τὰ κτήματα οὐδενὸς ἄξια καὶ ἡμᾶς οὐδὲν   25

εἶναι—λέγω ὑμῖν—εἰρωνευόμενος δὲ καὶ παίζων πάντα τὸν   26

βίον πρὸς τοὺς ἀνθρώπους διατελεῖ. σπουδάσαντος δὲ αὐτοῦ   27

καὶ ἀνοιχθέντος οὐκ οἶδα εἴ τις ἑώρακεν τὰ ἐντὸς ἀγάλματα·   28

ἀλλ᾽ ἐγὼ ἤδη ποτ᾽ εἶδον, καί μοι ἔδοξεν οὕτω θεῖα καὶ   29

---

16   τῶν καλῶν: masc., not neut.; gen. obj. of ἐρωτικῶς διάκειται, virtually equivalent to ἐρᾷ
      τούτους = τοὺς καλούς

18   ὡς τὸ σχῆμα αὐτοῦ = as far as his external appearance goes (acc. of respect). I depart from
      Burnet 1901 here and follow the punctuation and interpretation of Rose 1985: 65 and Rowe
      1998: 110, 207–8.

      σιληνώδης -ες = silen-like. The points of comparison seem to be the appearance of a constant state of
      erotic interest in what is physically beautiful accompanied by ignorance and lack of wisdom. These
      appearances are of course contradicted by what is inside, at least in the case of Socrates.

19   τοῦτο: i.e., a silen-like exterior
      περιβάλλομαι = put acc. around oneself, dress in acc.; perf. = have dressed oneself in acc.; i.e.,
      wear acc.

20   γλύφω = carve
      πόσης with σωφροσύνης (line 21): obj. of γέμει
      οἴεσθε: parenthetical

21   *γέμω = be full of gen.

24   *μακαρίζω = count blessed, consider beneficial (cf. μακάριος -α -ον)

26   εἰρωνεύομαι = dissemble, be ironic (in the Socratic sense); i.e., feign ignorance
      παίζω . . . πρός + acc. = tease, make fun of acc.

27   διατελέω + supplemental part. = continue ——ing

χρυσᾶ εἶναι καὶ πάγκαλα καὶ θαυμαστά, ὥστε ποιητέον εἶναι   30   217a
ἔμβραχυ ὅτι κελεύοι Σωκράτης.   31

---

30   ποιητέον: verbal adj. of ποιέω (*Essentials* §127)
    εἶναι: verb in result clause (*Essentials* §185)

31   ὅτι κελεύοι: explain the mood of κελεύοι here (*Essentials* §159a). This phrase echoes the words
    and sentiments of Aristodemus in reading 2A.9.

Reading 10E

Alcibiades describes his attempted seduction of Socrates.

Vocabulary

ἄγριος -α -ον: wild, savage, fierce, uncultivated, untamed (cf. *ἀγρός -οῦ ὁ: field, country;
 and English "agriculture")
ἄγροικος -ον: rustic, living in the country, boorish, crude, unsophisticated (cf. *ἀγρός -οῦ ὁ
 and οἰκέω)
δάκνω δήξομαι ἔδακον δέδηχα δέδηγμαι ἐδήχθην: bite, sting
καρτερός -ά -όν (= κρατερός): strong, brave, enduring, patient, steadfast; *recognize also*
 καρτερία -ας ἡ (= κρατερία): strength, endurance, patience. (cf. κρατέω)
κλίνη -ης ἡ: couch (cf. κατακλίνομαι: recline)
οἰκέτης -ου ὁ: house slave
ὀψέ *adv.*: late
ποιέω + *inf.*: cause to ——
πύλη -ης ἡ: gate

Reading 10E (*Symposium* 217a2–218b7)

ἡγούμενος δὲ αὐτὸν ἐσπουδακέναι	1	
ἐπὶ τῇ ἐμῇ ὥρᾳ ἕρμαιον ἡγησάμην εἶναι καὶ εὐτύχημα	2	
ἐμὸν θαυμαστόν, ὡς ὑπάρχον μοι χαρισαμένῳ Σωκράτει πάντ'	3	
ἀκοῦσαι ὅσαπερ οὗτος ᾔδει· ἐφρόνουν γὰρ δὴ ἐπὶ τῇ ὥρᾳ	4	
θαυμάσιον ὅσον. ταῦτα οὖν διανοηθείς, πρὸ τοῦ οὐκ εἰωθὼς	5	
ἄνευ ἀκολούθου μόνος μετ' αὐτοῦ γίγνεσθαι, τότε ἀποπέμπων	6	
τὸν ἀκόλουθον μόνος συνεγιγνόμην—δεῖ γὰρ πρὸς ὑμᾶς πάντα	7	217b
τἀληθῆ εἰπεῖν· ἀλλὰ προσέχετε τὸν νοῦν, καὶ εἰ ψεύδομαι,	8	
Σώκρατες, ἐξέλεγχε—συνεγιγνόμην γάρ, ὦ ἄνδρες, μόνος	9	
μόνῳ, καὶ ᾤμην αὐτίκα διαλέξεσθαι αὐτόν μοι ἅπερ ἂν	10	
ἐραστὴς παιδικοῖς ἐν ἐρημίᾳ διαλεχθείη, καὶ ἔχαιρον. τούτων	11	
δ' οὐ μάλα ἐγίγνετο οὐδέν, ἀλλ' ὥσπερ εἰώθει διαλεχθεὶς ἄν	12	
μοι καὶ συνημερεύσας ᾤχετο ἀπιών.	13	
Μετὰ ταῦτα συγγυμνάζεσθαι	14	
προυκαλούμην αὐτὸν καὶ συνεγυμναζόμην, ὥς τι	15	217c
ἐνταῦθα περανῶν. συνεγυμνάζετο οὖν μοι καὶ προσεπάλαιεν	16	

1–2 σπουδάζω ἐπί = be eager for

2 ὥρα: here and below = youth, and the attractions of youth, youthful beauty
  ἕρμαιον -ου τό = lucky discovery; windfall; gift from Hermes, god of windfalls
  εὐτύχημα -ατος τό = piece of good luck

3 ὑπάρχον from ὑπάρχει + *dat.* + *inf.* = it is possible for *dat.* to ——. Identifying the form of
  ὑπάρχον should help the reader to identify the construction (*Essentials* §177).

4 φρονέω ἐπί + *dat.* = take pride in *dat.*

5 θαυμάσιον ὅσον = to an amazing degree, to an amazing extent (adverbial acc.)

9 *ἐξελέγχω = refute

11 ἐρημία -ας ἡ = deserted place, solitude (cf. *ἔρημος -ον = deserted, desolate, solitary)

12 ἄν: with the imperfect indicative ᾤχετο (line 13) not to make it counterfactual but to indicate
  repetition (iterative ἄν) = he would go off . . . (Smyth 1956: §§1790–91)

13 συνημερεύω = pass the day with

14 συγγυμνάζομαι = exercise together (*γυμνάζομαι = exercise)

15 προκαλέομαι = invite ahead of time, make a date with

16 περαίνω περανῶ = bring to an end, finish, accomplish
  προσπαλαίω = wrestle with

πολλάκις οὐδενὸς παρόντος· καὶ τί δεῖ λέγειν; οὐδὲν γὰρ   17

μοι πλέον ἦν. ἐπειδὴ δὲ οὐδαμῇ ταύτῃ ἤνυτον, ἔδοξέ μοι   18

ἐπιθετέον εἶναι τῷ ἀνδρὶ κατὰ τὸ καρτερὸν καὶ οὐκ ἀνετέον,   19

ἐπειδήπερ ἐνεκεχειρήκη, ἀλλὰ ἰστέον ἤδη τί ἐστι τὸ πρᾶγμα.   20

προκαλοῦμαι δὴ αὐτὸν πρὸς τὸ συνδειπνεῖν, ἀτεχνῶς ὥσπερ   21

ἐραστὴς παιδικοῖς ἐπιβουλεύων. καί μοι οὐδὲ τοῦτο ταχὺ   22

ὑπήκουσεν, ὅμως δ' οὖν χρόνῳ ἐπείσθη. ἐπειδὴ δὲ ἀφίκετο   23   217d

τὸ πρῶτον, δειπνήσας ἀπιέναι ἐβούλετο. καὶ τότε μὲν   24

αἰσχυνόμενος ἀφῆκα αὐτόν· αὖθις δ' ἐπιβουλεύσας, ἐπειδὴ   25

ἐδεδειπνήκεμεν διελεγόμην ἀεὶ πόρρω τῶν νυκτῶν, καὶ ἐπειδὴ   26

ἐβούλετο ἀπιέναι, σκηπτόμενος ὅτι ὀψὲ εἴη, προσηνάγκασα   27

αὐτὸν μένειν. ἀνεπαύετο οὖν ἐν τῇ ἐχομένῃ ἐμοῦ κλίνῃ, ἐν   28

ᾗπερ ἐδείπνει, καὶ οὐδεὶς ἐν τῷ οἰκήματι ἄλλος καθηῦδεν ἢ   29

ἡμεῖς. μέχρι μὲν οὖν δὴ δεῦρο τοῦ λόγου καλῶς ἂν ἔχοι   30   217e

---

17–18 οὐδὲν γὰρ μοι πλέον ἦν: *literally* = there was nothing more for me (i.e., I got no further; I accomplished nothing more). οὐδὲν πλέον + dative + linking verb seems to be a relatively common idiom in these vaguely sexual contexts. Variants occur in reading 11.12, 16–17.

18 οὐδαμῇ: dat. fem. sing. is frequently used as adv. = in no way
τ αύτῃ: dat. fem. sing. is frequently used as adv. = in this way, by this method
ἀνύτω = succeed

19 ἐπιθετέον: verbal adj. (*Essentials* §127) of *ἐπιτίθημι = make an attack on
κατὰ τὸ καρτερόν = with full strength
ἀνετέον: verbal adj. of ἀνίημι = let go, let alone (see note on ἐπιθετέον)

20 ἐνεκεχειρήκη: pluperf. from ἐγχειρέω = begin, take in hand
ἰστέον: verbal adj. of ὁράω (see note on ἐπιθετέον in line 19)

21 προκαλέομαι = invite ahead of time, make a date with
ἀτεχνῶς *adv.* = artlessly, unskillfully, without art or artifice

23 *ὑπακούω + *dat.* = obey, listen to, comply with. Verbs that mean obey, trust, or serve frequently take dative objects (cf. πείθομαι, πιστεύω, δουλεύω).

26 πόρρω = far into, deep into
τῶν νυκτῶν: the plural is explained by the night being divided into three watches, which are also called νύκτες (LSJ under νύξ I.3)

27 σκήπτομαι = make as an excuse

28 ἐχόμενος + *gen.* = touch, be next to. Verbs of taking hold frequently take genitive objects.

29 οἴκημα -ατος τό: in this context pretty much equivalent to οἰκία -ας ἡ

30 τοῦ λογοῦ: partitive with μέχρι . . . δεῦρο

καὶ πρὸς ὁντινοῦν λέγειν· τὸ δ' ἐντεῦθεν οὐκ ἄν μου ἠκούσατε   31

λέγοντος, εἰ μὴ πρῶτον μέν, τὸ λεγόμενον, οἶνος ἄνευ τε   32

παίδων καὶ μετὰ παίδων ἦν ἀληθής, ἔπειτα ἀφανίσαι Σωκράτους   33

ἔργον ὑπερήφανον εἰς ἔπαινον ἐλθόντα ἄδικόν μοι φαίνεται.   34

  Ἔτι δὲ τὸ τοῦ δηχθέντος ὑπὸ τοῦ ἔχεως πάθος   35

κἄμ' ἔχει. φασὶ γάρ πού τινα τοῦτο παθόντα οὐκ ἐθέλειν   36

λέγειν οἷον ἦν πλὴν τοῖς δεδηγμένοις, ὡς μόνοις γνωσομένοις   37

τε καὶ συγγνωσομένοις εἰ πᾶν ἐτόλμα δρᾶν τε καὶ λέγειν   38   218a

ὑπὸ τῆς ὀδύνης. ἐγὼ οὖν δεδηγμένος τε ὑπὸ ἀλγεινοτέρου   39

31–32 τὸ δ' ἐντεῦθεν ... λέγοντος: apodosis of the conditional sentence. Identify the type of condition (*Essentials* §162).

32 τὸ λεγόμενον = as the saying goes (LSJ under λέγω B III.10)

32–33 εἰ μὴ ... ἀληθής: protasis of the conditional sentence. Photius cites a proverb: οἶνος καὶ παῖδες ἀληθεῖς. Alcibiades here seems to play on the dual significance of παῖδες (both "children" and "slaves") (Dover 1980: 169).

33–34 ἔπειτα ... φαίνεται: adds an additional reason that Alcibiades is going to tell the story. Translate ἔπειτα as "and second" (responds to πρῶτον earlier in the sentence).

34 ὑπερήφανος -ον = conspicuous (above others)

*ἔπαινος -ου ὁ: noun from verb ἐπαινέω

ἐλθόντα: modifies an understood acc. subje. (ἐμέ) of the inf. ἀφανίσαι

35 δηχθέντος from δάκνω: identify the form and usage (*Essentials* §169)

ἔχις -εως ὁ = viper

38 *συγγιγνώσκω = understand, sympathize with, forgive *dat.*

39–46 The syntax here is particularly loose, probably deliberately reflecting Alcibiades' drunken state. He may also be supposed to be imitating the disorienting effects of snakebite. In any case, there is no main verb in this sentence. A main verb ἐρῶ (from λέγω not ἐράω) can be supplied; this seems to be implied. Alternatively, translate all nominative participles in this sentence (including πληγείς and δηχθείς in the parenthetical statement, which also lacks a main verb) as first person indicative verbs. This will help students to understand what he's saying as well as to capture some of the choppy flavor of the sentence. Students may also choose to preserve the drunken syntax; just don't expect to produce a grammatical English sentence.

39 ὀδύνη -ης ἡ = pain

δεδηγμένος τε: τε appears to connect δεδηγμένος to ὁρῶν following the long parenthesis (see note on lines 39–46)

ἀλγεινός -ή -όν = painful

καὶ τὸ ἀλγεινότατον ὧν ἄν τις δηχθείη—τὴν καρδίαν γὰρ   40

ἢ ψυχὴν ἢ ὅτι δεῖ αὐτὸ ὀνομάσαι πληγείς τε καὶ δηχθεὶς   41

ὑπὸ τῶν ἐν φιλοσοφίᾳ λόγων, οἳ ἔχονται ἐχίδνης ἀγριώτερον,   42

νέου ψυχῆς μὴ ἀφυοῦς ὅταν λάβωνται, καὶ ποιοῦσι δρᾶν   43

τε καὶ λέγειν ὁτιοῦν—καὶ ὁρῶν αὖ Φαίδρους, Ἀγάθωνας,   44

Ἐρυξιμάχους, Παυσανίας, Ἀριστοδήμους τε καὶ Ἀριστοφάνας·   45   218b

Σωκράτη δὲ αὐτὸν τί δεῖ λέγειν, καὶ ὅσοι ἄλλοι;   46

πάντες γὰρ κεκοινωνήκατε τῆς φιλοσόφου μανίας τε καὶ   47

βακχείας—διὸ πάντες ἀκούσεσθε· συγγνώσεσθε γὰρ τοῖς τε   48

τότε πραχθεῖσι καὶ τοῖς νῦν λεγομένοις. οἱ δὲ οἰκέται, καὶ   49

εἴ τις ἄλλος ἐστὶν βέβηλός τε καὶ ἄγροικος, πύλας πάνυ   50

μεγάλας τοῖς ὠσὶν ἐπίθεσθε.   51

---

40   τὸ ἀλγεινότατον: acc. of respect = in the most painful (part)

ὧν = τούτων ἅ: partitive gen./acc. of respect; attraction of the relative pronoun to the case of the suppressed antecedent (*Essentials* §§131–33)

41   πληγείς τε καὶ δηχθείς: see note on lines 39–46. There is no main verb in this parenthetical statement.

42   ἔχονται *mid.* = hold on tight, take hold

ἐχίδνη -ης ἡ = viper

*ἄγριος -α -ον = wild, savage, uncultivated, uncivilized

43   ψυχῆς: gen. obj. of λάβωνται (λαμβάνομαι + *gen.* = take hold of [physically])

ἀφυής -ές = without natural endowment; μὴ ἀφυοῦς = not without natural endowment; i.e., with some natural talent (litotes, or understatement, a characteristic rhetorical figure) (Smyth 1956: §3032)

48   βακχεία -ας ἡ = Bacchic revelry, Bacchic frenzy (The other members of the group are treated simultaneously as initiates to philosophy and as victims of snakebite.)

*συγγιγνώσκω = understand, sympathize with, forgive *dat.*

50   βέβηλος -ον = profane, uninitiated

*ἄγροικος -ον = of the fields, uncultivated, countrified, unsophisticated

50–51   πύλας . . . ἐπίθεσθε: i.e., block up your ears

Reading 10F

Alcibiades describes his night with Socrates.

Vocabulary

ἁλίσκομαι ἁλώσομαι ἑάλων/ἥλων ἑάλωκα/ἥλωκα: be taken, conquered

ἀλλάττω ἀλλάξω ἤλλαξα -ήλλαχα ἤλλαγμαι ἠλλάχθην/ἠλλάγην: change, alter; *mid.*:
    exchange *x* for *y*

ἀποστερέω ἀποστερήσω ἀπεστέρησα ἀπεστέρηκα ἀπεστέρημαι ἀπεστερήθην: rob,
    take away, deprive

ἀτιμάζω ἀτιμάσω ἠτίμασα ἠτίμακα ἠτίμασμαι ἠτιμάσθην: dishonor, slight

βέλος -ους τό: something thrown (cf. βάλλω), e.g., arrow, dart, javelin; missile

διάνοια -ας ἡ: thought, intention, purpose, intellect, mind

ἱμάτιον -ου τό: cloak, mantle; *pl.*: clothes

νώ νῶν *1st pers. dual pron.*: we two, us two; *nom./acc.* νώ; *dat./gen.* νῷν

ὀκνέω ὀκνήσω ὤκνησα: hesitate, be reluctant, shrink (from)

ὄμμα -ατος τό: eye

ὀργίζω ὀργιῶ ὤργισα—ὤργισμαι ὠργίσθην: make angry, irritate; *mid.-pass.*: become angry

οὐσία -ας ἡ: property

ὄψις -εως ἡ: sight, look, appearance

σίδηρος -ου ὁ: iron

τιτρώσκω τρώσω ἔτρωσα—τέτρωμαι ἐτρώθην: wound

ὑβρίζω ὑβριῶ ὕβρισα ὕβρικα ὕβρισμαι ὑβρίσθην: treat violently, insult, maltreat; *intrans.*:
    run riot, act criminally

χαλκεῖος -α -ον: bronze

χειμών -ῶνος ὁ: winter, winter storm

χρυσεῖος -α -ον: gold

Reading 10F (*Symposium* 218b8–219e5)

Ἐπειδὴ γὰρ οὖν, ὦ ἄνδρες, ὅ τε λύχνος ἀπεσβήκει καὶ   1

οἱ παῖδες ἔξω ἦσαν, ἔδοξέ μοι χρῆναι μηδὲν ποικίλλειν πρὸς   2   218c

αὐτόν, ἀλλ᾽ ἐλευθέρως εἰπεῖν ἅ μοι ἐδόκει· καὶ εἶπον κινήσας   3

αὐτόν, "Σώκρατες, καθεύδεις;"   4

   "Οὐ δῆτα," ἦ δ᾽ ὅς.   5

   "Οἶσθα οὖν ἅ μοι δέδοκται;"   6

   "Τί μάλιστα;" ἔφη.   7

   "Σὺ ἐμοὶ δοκεῖς," ἦν δ᾽ ἐγώ, "ἐμοῦ ἐραστὴς ἄξιος γεγονέναι   8

μόνος, καί μοι φαίνῃ ὀκνεῖν μνησθῆναι πρός με. ἐγὼ δὲ   9

οὑτωσὶ ἔχω· πάνυ ἀνόητον ἡγοῦμαι εἶναι σοὶ μὴ οὐ καὶ   10

τοῦτο χαρίζεσθαι καὶ εἴ τι ἄλλο ἢ τῆς οὐσίας τῆς ἐμῆς   11

δέοιο ἢ τῶν φίλων τῶν ἐμῶν. ἐμοὶ μὲν γὰρ οὐδέν ἐστι   12   218d

πρεσβύτερον τοῦ ὡς ὅτι βέλτιστον ἐμὲ γενέσθαι, τούτου δὲ   13

οἶμαί μοι συλλήπτορα οὐδένα κυριώτερον εἶναι σοῦ. ἐγὼ δὴ   14

τοιούτῳ ἀνδρὶ πολὺ μᾶλλον ἂν μὴ χαριζόμενος αἰσχυνοίμην   15

τοὺς φρονίμους, ἢ χαριζόμενος τούς τε πολλοὺς καὶ ἄφρονας."   16

   Καὶ οὗτος ἀκούσας μάλα εἰρωνικῶς καὶ σφόδρα ἑαυτοῦ τε   17

---

1   λύχνος -ου ὁ = lamp, light

    ἀπέσβηκει: intrans. pluperf. from ἀποσβέννυμι = be quenched, go out

2   ποικίλλω = embroider, embellish, speak elaborately

7   τί μάλιστα; = what exactly?

9   μνησθῆναι (from μιμνήσκω) = mention

10   ἀνόητος -ον = unreasonable

    μὴ οὐ: οὐ is redundant here; do not translate. Verbs and expressions of negative meaning often
        take the infinitive with a redundant οὐ to confirm the negative idea of the leading verb (Smyth
        1956: §§2745–46).

    σοί: obj. of χαρίζεσθαι in next line (context suggests)

11   τοῦτο χαρίζεσθαι = do this as a favor (implying a sexual favor, presumably)

13   ὡς ὅτι βέλτιστον = ὡς βέλτιστον (*Essentials* §198)

14   συλλήπτωρ -ορος ὁ = one that takes hold of with, partner, helper, assistant

17   εἰρωνικῶς = ironically

    ἑαυτοῦ = in his own way

καὶ εἰωθότως ἔλεξεν, "Ὦ φίλε Ἀλκιβιάδη, κινδυνεύεις τῷ   18

ὄντι οὐ φαῦλος εἶναι, εἴπερ ἀληθῆ τυγχάνει ὄντα ἃ λέγεις   19

περὶ ἐμοῦ, καί τις ἔστ' ἐν ἐμοὶ δύναμις δι' ἧς ἂν σὺ γένοιο ἀμείνων·   20   218e

ἀμήχανόν τοι κάλλος ὁρῴης ἂν ἐν ἐμοὶ καὶ τῆς   21

παρὰ σοὶ εὐμορφίας πάμπολυ διαφέρον. εἰ δὴ καθορῶν   22

αὐτὸ κοινώσασθαί τέ μοι ἐπιχειρεῖς καὶ ἀλλάξασθαι κάλλος   23

ἀντὶ κάλλους, οὐκ ὀλίγῳ μου πλεονεκτεῖν διανοῇ, ἀλλ'   24

ἀντὶ δόξης ἀλήθειαν καλῶν κτᾶσθαι ἐπιχειρεῖς καὶ τῷ   25

ὄντι "χρύσεα χαλκείων" διαμείβεσθαι νοεῖς. ἀλλ', ὦ   26   219a

μακάριε, ἄμεινον σκόπει, μή σε λανθάνω οὐδὲν ὤν. ἤ τοι   27

τῆς διανοίας ὄψις ἄρχεται ὀξὺ βλέπειν ὅταν ἡ τῶν ὀμμάτων   28

τῆς ἀκμῆς λήγειν ἐπιχειρῇ· σὺ δὲ τούτων ἔτι πόρρω."   29

Κἀγὼ ἀκούσας, "Τὰ μὲν παρ' ἐμοῦ," ἔφην, "ταῦτά ἐστιν, ὧν   30

οὐδὲν ἄλλως εἴρηται ἢ ὡς διανοοῦμαι· σὺ δὲ αὐτὸς οὕτω   31

βουλεύου ὅτι σοί τε ἄριστον καὶ ἐμοὶ ἡγῇ."   32

"Ἀλλ'," ἔφη, "τοῦτό γ' εὖ λέγεις· ἐν γὰρ τῷ ἐπιόντι χρόνῳ   33

βουλευόμενοι πράξομεν ὃ ἂν φαίνηται νῦν περί τε τούτων   34   219b

καὶ περὶ τῶν ἄλλων ἄριστον."   35

---

21   ἀμήχανος -ον = irresistible

22   εὐμορφία -ας ἡ = beauty of form, symmetry

24   *πλεονεκτέω = have or claim more than one's due from *gen.*

25   ἀλήθειαν καλῶν = true beauty, the reality of beauty

26   χρύσεα χαλκείων: the phrase *gold for bronze* quotes *Iliad* 6.236, where the Lydian warrior Glaucus exchanges his gold armor for the bronze armor of the Greek Diomedes, after the two discover that their ancestors were guest friends. Homer comments that Glaucus, in making such an uneven exchange lost his mind: Γλαύκῳ Κρονίδης φρένας ἐξέλετο Ζεύς = Zeus, the son of Kronos, took away Glaucus's sense (*Iliad* 6.234).

    διαμείβομαι = exchange *acc.* for *gen.*

28   [ἡ ...] τῆς διανοίας ὄψις = the perception of the mind, the mind's eyesight

    ἡ τῶν ὀμμάτων = ἡ τῶν ὀμμάτων ὄψις

29   *ἀκμή -ῆς ἡ = prime (cf. English "acme"); i.e., as a person ages and can no longer see well with his eyes, his mind becomes sharper

    ἐπιχειρέω *seemingly* = begin, a meaning that is more common for ἐγχειρέω, but the two words overlap considerably in meaning. The language here suggests that Socrates may be paraphrasing from poetry.

33   ἐπιών χρόνος = oncoming time; i.e., the future

Ἐγὼ μὲν δὴ ταῦτα ἀκούσας τε καὶ εἰπών, καὶ ἀφεὶς   36

ὥσπερ βέλη, τετρῶσθαι αὐτὸν ᾤμην· καὶ ἀναστάς γε, οὐδ'   37

ἐπιτρέψας τούτῳ εἰπεῖν οὐδὲν ἔτι, ἀμφιέσας τὸ ἱμάτιον   38

τὸ ἐμαυτοῦ τοῦτον—καὶ γὰρ ἦν χειμών—ὑπὸ τὸν τρίβωνα   39

κατακλινεὶς τὸν τουτουί, περιβαλὼν τὼ χεῖρε τούτῳ τῷ   40

δαιμονίῳ ὡς ἀληθῶς καὶ θαυμαστῷ, κατεκείμην τὴν νύκτα   41   219c

ὅλην. καὶ οὐδὲ ταῦτα αὖ, ὦ Σώκρατες, ἐρεῖς ὅτι ψεύδομαι.   42

ποιήσαντος δὲ δὴ ταῦτα ἐμοῦ οὗτος τοσοῦτον περιεγένετό   43

τε καὶ κατεφρόνησεν καὶ κατεγέλασεν τῆς ἐμῆς ὥρας καὶ   44

ὕβρισεν—καὶ περὶ ἐκεῖνό γε ᾤμην τι εἶναι, ὦ ἄνδρες δικασταί·   45

δικασταὶ γάρ ἐστε τῆς Σωκράτους ὑπερηφανίας—εὖ γὰρ   46

ἴστε, μὰ θεούς, μὰ θεάς, οὐδὲν περιττότερον καταδεδαρθηκὼς   47

ἀνέστην μετὰ Σωκράτους, ἢ εἰ μετὰ πατρὸς καθηῦδον ἢ   48   219d

ἀδελφοῦ πρεσβυτέρου.   49

　Τὸ δὴ μετὰ τοῦτο τίνα οἴεσθέ με διάνοιαν ἔχειν, ἡγούμενον   50

μὲν ἠτιμάσθαι, ἀγάμενον δὲ τὴν τούτου φύσιν τε καὶ   51

σωφροσύνην καὶ ἀνδρείαν, ἐντετυχηκότα ἀνθρώπῳ τοιούτῳ   52

---

37   τετρῶσθαι: from τιτρώσκω
38   ἐπιτρέπω = leave to *dat.*, permit, allow
      ἀμφιέσας: from ἀμφιέννυμι ἀμφιῶ ἠμφίεσα ἠμφίεσμαι ἠμφιέσθην = put *acc.* around, dress
      in *acc.*
39   τρίβων -ωνος ὁ = worn garment, threadbare cloak
40   τὼ χεῖρε: from χείρ χειρός ἡ. What must the form be (*Essentials* §67)? It's not unusual to see
      Greek χείρ where we use "arm."
41   δαιμόνιος -α -ον (of people) = possessed by a δαίμων, *hence* inhuman, strange, wonderful, but
      see also Diotima's characterization of Eros
43   τοσοῦτον: adverbial acc.
      *περιγίγνομαι = be superior to *gen.*
45   τι: enclitic τι; the rare accent on τι makes it emphatic = really something!
46   ὑπερηφανία -ας ἡ = arrogance
47   οὐδὲν περιττότερον: adverbial acc. = in no way more out of the ordinary . . . (*περιττός -ή -όν
      = beyond the regular number or size, out of the ordinary)
      καταδεδαρθηκώς from καταδαρθάνω = sleep soundly
50   τὸ δὴ μετὰ τοῦτο: adverbial acc. = in the time after this. It is not unusual to see a neuter definite
      article before an adverb or prepositional phrase expressing time, often with only very slight
      changes of meaning (Smyth 1956: §1611).

οἵῳ ἐγὼ οὐκ ἂν ᾤμην ποτ' ἐντυχεῖν εἰς φρόνησιν καὶ εἰς   53

καρτερίαν; ὥστε οὔθ' ὅπως οὖν ὀργιζοίμην εἶχον καὶ ἀποστερηθείην   54

τῆς τούτου συνουσίας, οὔτε ὅπῃ προσαγαγοίμην   55

αὐτὸν ηὐπόρουν. εὖ γὰρ ἤδη ὅτι χρήμασί γε πολὺ μᾶλλον   56   219e

ἄτρωτος ἦν πανταχῇ ἢ σιδήρῳ ὁ Αἴας, ᾧ τε ᾤμην αὐτὸν   57

μόνῳ ἁλώσεσθαι, διεπεφεύγει με. ἠπόρουν δή, καταδεδουλωμένος   58

τε ὑπὸ τοῦ ἀνθρώπου ὡς οὐδεὶς ὑπ' οὐδενὸς ἄλλου περιῇα.   59

53–54 οὐκ ἂν ᾤμην ποτ' ἐντυχεῖν: take ἄν with ἐντυχεῖν representing potential optative in indirect
statement. For the tendency of ἄν to be positioned near negatives and verbs of thinking, see
Smyth 1956: §1764.

εἰς (here) = in regards to

54–55 Optatives here signal deliberative questions in secondary sequence.

55 προσάγομαι = win over

56 ηὐπόρουν: from εὐπορέω (opposite of ἀπορέω)

57 ἄτρωτος -ον = impervious, incapable of being wounded (cf. τιτρώσκω)

Αἴας Αἴαντος ὁ = Aias (Latin Ajax), one of the great Greek heroes of the Trojan War, second to
Achilles, known as tough and (apparently) impervious to wounding; iron = weapon

57–8 ᾧ . . . μόνῳ: the antecedent is implied = the thing (i.e., Alcibiades' offering of his youthful beauty).
Socrates appears to be the understood subject of διεπεφεύγει so the relative clause is only
loosely attached to the main clause.

59 περιῇα: imperf. indic. 1st pers. sing. from περί + εἶμι

Reading 10G

Alcibiades describes Socrates at war.

Vocabulary

ἀμύνω ἀμυνῶ ἤμυνα: fend off, defend; *mid.*: defend oneself

ἀριστεῖα -ων τά *pl. used for sing.*: prize for valor, award for being ἄριστος, here frequently written τἀριστεῖα by crasis (*Essentials* §207)

ἀσφαλής -ές: unslipping, unerring, firm, secure, sure

ἑσπέρα -ας ἡ: evening

ἕως ἕω ἡ (= ἠώς): dawn, the goddess Eos, Dawn; *recognize also* ἕωθεν: from daybreak, from early dawn

θαρρέω (= θαρσέω): be of good courage, be of good cheer, be confident, bold (sometimes in a bad sense); particularly common in imperative: θαρρεῖ/θαρσεῖ: cheer up!

θέρος -ους τό: summer (cf. θερμός)

περίειμι (περί + εἰμί): be better than *gen.*, surpass *gen.*

στρατεία -ας ἡ: military campaign, expedition (cf. ὁ στρατηγός and ἡ στρατιά)

στρατιώτης -ου ὁ: soldier

στρατόπεδον -ου τό: camp, army camp

τλάω τλήσομαι ἔτλην τέτληκα: dare, endure, suffer hardship; *trans.*: undergo

φροντίζω φροντιῶ ἐφρόντισα πεφρόντικα: think, worry

Reading 10G (*Symposium* 219e5–221c1)

Ταῦτά τε γάρ μοι ἄπαντα προυγεγόνει, καὶ	1
μετὰ ταῦτα στρατεία ἡμῖν εἰς Ποτείδαιαν ἐγένετο κοινὴ	2
καὶ συνεσιτοῦμεν ἐκεῖ. πρῶτον μὲν οὖν τοῖς πόνοις οὐ	3
μόνον ἐμοῦ περιῆν, ἀλλὰ καὶ τῶν ἄλλων ἁπάντων—ὁπότ'	4
ἀναγκασθεῖμεν ἀποληφθέντες που, οἷα δὴ ἐπὶ στρατείας,	5
ἀσιτεῖν, οὐδὲν ἦσαν οἱ ἄλλοι πρὸς τὸ καρτερεῖν—ἔν τ' αὖ	6 220a
ταῖς εὐωχίαις μόνος ἀπολαύειν οἷός τ' ἦν τά τ' ἄλλα καὶ	7
πίνειν οὐκ ἐθέλων, ὁπότε ἀναγκασθείη, πάντας ἐκράτει, καὶ	8
ὃ πάντων θαυμαστότατον, Σωκράτη μεθύοντα οὐδεὶς πώποτε	9
ἑώρακεν ἀνθρώπων.	10
Τούτου μὲν οὖν μοι δοκεῖ καὶ αὐτίκα ὁ	11
ἔλεγχος ἔσεσθαι. πρὸς δὲ αὖ τὰς τοῦ χειμῶνος καρτερήσεις	12
—δεινοὶ γὰρ αὐτόθι χειμῶνες—θαυμάσια ἠργάζετο τά τε	13
ἄλλα, καί ποτε ὄντος πάγου οἵου δεινοτάτου, καὶ πάντων ἢ	14 220b

---

1	προγίγνομαι = happen before, happen first
2	Ποτείδαια -ας ἡ = Potidaea, a Greek city-state of military importance, since it occupies and guards the isthmus of Pallene. A colony of Corinth and a tribute-paying ally of Athens until its revolt in 432 B.C.E., when Corinth took the side of Sparta against the Athenians at the outbreak of the Peloponnesian War.
3	συσσιτέω (σύν + σιτέω) = eat with, take mess together (*σῖτος -ου ὁ = grain, bread, food)
5	ἀπολαμβάνω = cut off
	οἷα δὴ ἐπὶ στρατείας = οἷα δὴ ἐπὶ στρατείας γίγνεται: the syntax (rel. clause) requires a verb; the context suggests γίγνεται
6	ἀσιτέω = go without food (*σῖτος -ου ὁ = grain, bread, food)
	πρός (here) = in comparison to, next to, in the face of
7	εὐωχία -ας ἡ = party
	*ἀπολαύω = enjoy
12	*ἔλεγχος -ου ὁ = trial, test, proof
	πρός = with regard to *acc.*, as for *acc.*
	τοῦ χειμῶνος: obj. gen. (*Essentials* §92)
	καρτέρησις -εως ἡ = endurance, act of endurance
14	πάγος -ου ὁ = ice, frost
	οἷος+ *superl.* = of the most —— possible kind, of a very —— kind

οὐκ ἐξιόντων ἔνδοθεν, ἢ εἴ τις ἐξίοι, ἠμφιεσμένων τε   15

θαυμαστὰ δὴ ὅσα καὶ ὑποδεδεμένων καὶ ἐνειλιγμένων τοὺς   16

πόδας εἰς πίλους καὶ ἀρνακίδας, οὗτος δ᾽ ἐν τούτοις ἐξῄει   17

ἔχων ἱμάτιον μὲν τοιοῦτον οἷόνπερ καὶ πρότερον εἰώθει   18

φορεῖν, ἀνυπόδητος δὲ διὰ τοῦ κρυστάλλου ῥᾷον ἐπορεύετο   19

ἢ οἱ ἄλλοι ὑποδεδεμένοι, οἱ δὲ στρατιῶται ὑπέβλεπον   20

αὐτὸν ὡς καταφρονοῦντα σφῶν. καὶ ταῦτα μὲν δὴ ταῦτα·   21   220c

   Οἷον δ᾽ αὖ τόδ᾽ ἔρεξε καὶ ἔτλη καρτερὸς ἀνὴρ   22

ἐκεῖ ποτε ἐπὶ στρατιᾶς, ἄξιον ἀκοῦσαι. συννοήσας γὰρ   23

αὐτόθι ἕωθέν τι εἱστήκει σκοπῶν, καὶ ἐπειδὴ οὐ προυχώρει   24

αὐτῷ, οὐκ ἀνίει ἀλλὰ εἱστήκει ζητῶν. καὶ ἤδη ἦν μεσημβρία,   25

καὶ ἄνθρωποι ᾐσθάνοντο, καὶ θαυμάζοντες ἄλλος ἄλλῳ   26

ἔλεγεν ὅτι Σωκράτης ἐξ ἑωθινοῦ φροντίζων τι ἕστηκε.   27

---

15   ἠμφιεσμένων from ἀμφιέννυμι ἀμφιῶ ἠμφίεσα ἠμφίεσμαι ἠμφιέσθην = dress in; *mid.* =
       dress oneself in

16   θαυμαστὰ δὴ ὅσα = an amazing number of things (LSJ under ὅσος I.6)
       ὑποδέω = bind below; *hence in mid.* = put on or wear shoes
       ἐνειλιγμένων: from ἐνελίσσω = wrap up

17   πίλος -ου ὁ = felt
       ἀρνακίς -ιδος ἡ = sheepskin

19   φορέω = wear
       ἀνυπόδητος = barefoot (cf. ἀ + ὑπό + δέω)
       κρύσταλλος -ου ὁ = ice

20   ὑποδέω = bind below; *hence in mid.* = put on or (in perf.) wear shoes
       ὑποβλέπω = eye suspiciously, scornfully, or angrily

21   καὶ ταῦτα μὲν δὴ ταῦτα = well, that is that; so much for that (a fairly common formula of
       transition, suggesting movement to a new topic)

22   ἔρεξε from ῥέζω = do; ἔτλη from τλάω = dare. This line is based on two lines from the *Odyssey*
       (4.242, 271) describing Odysseus.

23   συννοήσας: ingressive aor. of συννοέω = think over, meditate on, reflect on (see note on reading
       6C.1)

24   προυχωρεῖ + dat. (impers. here) = it advances for *dat.*; i.e., *dat.* makes progress (προ + χωρέω)

25   μεσημβρία -ας ἡ = midday

27   ἐξ ἑωθινοῦ = ἕωθεν

τελευτῶντες δέ τινες τῶν Ἰώνων, ἐπειδὴ ἑσπέρα ἦν, δειπνήσαντες   28

—καὶ γὰρ θέρος τότε γ' ἦν—χαμεύνια ἐξενεγκάμενοι   29   220d

ἅμα μὲν ἐν τῷ ψύχει καθηῦδον, ἅμα δ' ἐφύλαττον αὐτὸν εἰ   30

καὶ τὴν νύκτα ἑστήξοι. ὁ δὲ εἱστήκει μέχρι ἕως ἐγένετο   31

καὶ ἥλιος ἀνέσχεν· ἔπειτα ᾤχετ' ἀπιὼν προσευξάμενος τῷ ἡλίῳ.   32

   Εἰ δὲ βούλεσθε ἐν ταῖς μάχαις—τοῦτο γὰρ δὴ   33

δίκαιόν γε αὐτῷ ἀποδοῦναι—ὅτε γὰρ ἡ μάχη ἦν ἐξ ἧς ἐμοὶ   34

καὶ τἀριστεῖα ἔδοσαν οἱ στρατηγοί, οὐδεὶς ἄλλος ἐμὲ ἔσωσεν   35

ἀνθρώπων ἢ οὗτος, τετρωμένον οὐκ ἐθέλων ἀπολιπεῖν, ἀλλὰ   36   220e

συνδιέσωσε καὶ τὰ ὅπλα καὶ αὐτὸν ἐμέ. καὶ ἐγὼ μέν, ὦ Σώκρατες,   37

καὶ τότε ἐκέλευον σοὶ διδόναι τἀριστεῖα τοὺς στρατηγούς,   38

καὶ τοῦτό γέ μοι οὔτε μέμψῃ οὔτε ἐρεῖς ὅτι ψεύδομαι·   39

ἀλλὰ γὰρ τῶν στρατηγῶν πρὸς τὸ ἐμὸν ἀξίωμα ἀποβλεπόντων   40

καὶ βουλομένων ἐμοὶ διδόναι τἀριστεῖα, αὐτὸς προθυμότερος   41

ἐγένου τῶν στρατηγῶν ἐμὲ λαβεῖν ἢ σαυτόν.   42

ἔτι τοίνυν, ὦ ἄνδρες, ἄξιον ἦν θεάσασθαι Σωκράτη, ὅτε ἀπὸ Δηλίου   43

φυγῇ ἀνεχώρει τὸ στρατόπεδον· ἔτυχον γὰρ παραγενόμενος   44

---

28   τελευτῶντες = adverbial τέλος

      Ἰώνες -ων οἱ = Ionians, allies of the Athenians on this campaign

29   καὶ γάρ: anticipates and explains what follows (ἐξενεγκάμενοι χαμεύνια)

      χαμεύνια -ων τά = bedrolls

30   ψύχος -ους τό = cool air (cf. ψυχρός)

      ἐφύλαττον ... εἰ = they watched ... [to see] whether

32   ἀνέχω = be up

33   εἰ δὲ βούλεσθε ἐν ταῖς μάχαις: context allows the reader to fill in the missing ideas (e.g.,
      ἀκοῦσαι τὰ ἔργα or similar)

34   ἀποδοῦναι = repay (for the favor he is about to describe)

37   συνδιασῴζω = help in saving

38   τἀριστεῖα: see vocabulary

40   ἀλλὰ γάρ = but in fact, but anyway (resuming the story)

      ἀξίωμα -ατος τό = reputation, status

43   Δηλίον -ου τό = Delium, a place in Boeotia. Part of a threefold assault made on Boeotia by the
      Athenians in 424 B.C.E. as part of the Peloponnesian War. The Athenians were defeated and
      forced to retreat. Thucydides 4.89–101 offers an account, with 4.96 describing the flight of the
      Athenians mentioned here.

ἵππον ἔχων, οὗτος δὲ ὅπλα. ἀνεχώρει οὖν ἐσκεδασμένων   45   221a

ἤδη τῶν ἀνθρώπων οὗτός τε ἅμα καὶ Λάχης· καὶ ἐγὼ περιτυγχάνω,   46

καὶ ἰδὼν εὐθὺς παρακελεύομαί τε αὐτοῖν θαρρεῖν,   47

καὶ ἔλεγον ὅτι οὐκ ἀπολείψω αὐτώ. ἐνταῦθα δὴ καὶ κάλλιον   48

ἐθεασάμην Σωκράτη ἢ ἐν Ποτειδαίᾳ (αὐτὸς γὰρ ἧττον   49

ἐν φόβῳ ἦ διὰ τὸ ἐφ' ἵππου εἶναι), πρῶτον μὲν ὅσον περιῆν   50

Λάχητος τῷ ἔμφρων εἶναι· ἔπειτα ἔμοιγ' ἐδόκει, ὦ Ἀριστόφανες,   51   221b

τὸ σὸν δὴ τοῦτο, καὶ ἐκεῖ διαπορεύεσθαι ὥσπερ   52

καὶ ἐνθάδε, "βρενθυόμενος καὶ τὠφθαλμὼ παραβάλλων,"   53

ἠρέμα παρασκοπῶν καὶ τοὺς φιλίους καὶ τοὺς πολεμίους,   54

δῆλος ὢν παντὶ καὶ πάνυ πόρρωθεν ὅτι εἴ τις ἅψεται τούτου   55

---

45   οὗτος δὲ ὅπλα [ἔχων]: i.e., he was a hoplite (foot soldier)

    ἀνεχώρει from ἀναχωρέω = retreat, go back. The singular verb suggests that the second name is added as an afterthought; Plato may be imitating spoken language.

    σκεδάννυμι σκεδάω ἐσκέδασα—ἐσκέδασμαι ἐσκεδάσθην = scatter, disperse

46   Λάχης -ητος ὁ = Laches, an Athenian general in 427–25 and 418 B.C.E. He appears as a strong fighter alongside the famous general Nicias in Plato's *Laches*, a dialogue on the subject of courage.

    περιτυγχάνω = ἐντυγχάνω

47   αὐτοῖν: dual dat. (*Essentials* §67)

48   αὐτώ: dual acc. (*Essentials* §67)

50   ὅσον περιῆν . . . : the relative clause depends on κάλλιον ἐθεασάμην

51   ἔμφρων -ον = in one's right mind, sensible, prudent, calm (contrast ἄφρων -ον = crazy, out of one's mind, without sense)

    ἔπειτα = second (the usual translation after πρῶτον)

51–52   τὸ σὸν δὴ τοῦτο = as this saying of yours goes. The construction is a form of accusative absolute, similar to that of τὸ λεγόμενον in reading 10E.32. τό + possessive adjective or genitive is a common way of introducing a quotation. Alcibiades quotes a description of Socrates in Aristophanes' *Clouds* 362.

52   ἐκεῖ: i.e., in Delium

53   ἐνθάδε: i.e., in the *Clouds* or in Athens

    βρενθύομαι = swagger

    τὠφθαλμὼ = τὼ ὀφθαλμώ: dual acc. of ὁ ὀφθαλμός (*Essentials* §67)

    τὠφθαλμὼ παραβάλλων = cast one's eyes sideways (the context suggests that this action implies self-confidence or even arrogance)

54   ἠρέμα *adv.* = calmly

55   ἅπτομαι: takes a gen. obj. (like many verbs implying physical touching)

τοῦ ἀνδρός, μάλα ἐρρωμένως ἀμυνεῖται. διὸ καὶ ἀσφαλῶς   56

ἀπήει καὶ οὗτος καὶ ὁ ἑταῖρος· σχεδὸν γάρ τι τῶν οὕτω   57

διακειμένων ἐν τῷ πολέμῳ οὐδὲ ἅπτονται, ἀλλὰ τοὺς   58

προτροπάδην φεύγοντας διώκουσιν.   59   221c

---

56   ἐρρωμένος -η -ον = healthy, stout, vigorous
57   σχεδὸν ... τι: the combination lends an approximate quality to the generalization made in this
       sentence = roughly speaking, in general ..., it is more or less the situation that. ... Dover
       1980: 175 translates "as a rule."
57-58   τῶν ... διακειμένων: see note on line 55
58   οὐδέ = not even (as often)
58-59   ἅπτονται ... διώκουσιν: both verbs have an anonymous "they" as the subject. Context allows
       inference of something like "enemy warriors."
59   προτροπάδην adv. = headforemost, with headlong speed

Reading 10H

Alcibiades winds up his speech.

Vocabulary

ἀπεικάζω = εἰκάζω
ἄπειρος -ον: inexperienced, untested (cf. πειράομαι)
θαῦμα θαύματος τό: wonder, marvel (cf. θαυμάζω, θαυμάσιος, θαυμαστός)
νήπιος -[α] -ον: childish, senseless, infantile, foolish
τείνω τενῶ ἔτεινα τέτακα τέταμαι ἐτάθην: stretch, strain, extend

Reading 10H (*Symposium* 221c2–222b7)

Πολλὰ μὲν οὖν ἄν τις καὶ ἄλλα ἔχοι Σωκράτη ἐπαινέσαι	1
καὶ θαυμάσια· ἀλλὰ τῶν μὲν ἄλλων ἐπιτηδευμάτων τάχ' ἄν	2
τις καὶ περὶ ἄλλου τοιαῦτα εἴποι, τὸ δὲ μηδενὶ ἀνθρώπων	3
ὅμοιον εἶναι, μήτε τῶν παλαιῶν μήτε τῶν νῦν ὄντων, τοῦτο	4
ἄξιον παντὸς θαύματος. οἷος γὰρ Ἀχιλλεὺς ἐγένετο, ἀπεικάσειεν	5
ἄν τις καὶ Βρασίδαν καὶ ἄλλους, καὶ οἷος αὖ	6
Περικλῆς, καὶ Νέστορα καὶ Ἀντήνορα—εἰσὶ δὲ καὶ ἕτεροι—	7
καὶ τοὺς ἄλλους κατὰ ταῦτ' ἄν τις ἀπεικάζοι· οἷος δὲ οὑτοσὶ	8 221d
γέγονε τὴν ἀτοπίαν ἄνθρωπος, καὶ αὐτὸς καὶ οἱ λόγοι αὐτοῦ,	9
οὐδ' ἐγγὺς ἂν εὕροι τις ζητῶν, οὔτε τῶν νῦν οὔτε τῶν	10
παλαιῶν, εἰ μὴ ἄρα εἰ οἷς ἐγὼ λέγω ἀπεικάζοι τις αὐτόν,	11
ἀνθρώπων μὲν μηδενί, τοῖς δὲ σιληνοῖς καὶ σατύροις, αὐτὸν	12
καὶ τοὺς λόγους.	13

---

1   ἐπαινέω: can take a double accusative = praise *acc. pers.* for *acc. thing*

2   τῶν μὲν ἄλλων ἐπιτηδευμάτων = concerning his other activities (probably gen. of connection [Smyth 1956: §1381], though the usage seems a bit loose). Alcibiades seems to mean that, although certain specific actions or practices of Socrates might resemble other people's, the totality of Socrates is completely individual.

τάχ' = perhaps (its regular meaning when it accompanies ἄν + opt.)

5–6   οἷος = τοιούτῳ οἷος = to the sort [of man] that. . . . The dative antecedent can be inferred from the verbs ἀπεικάσειεν and ἀπεικάζοι (which take the dat.).

6   Βρασίδας -ου ὁ = Brasidas, prominent and successful Spartan general during the Peloponnesian War

7   Νέστωρ -ορος ὁ = Nestor, old man hero (Greek) of the Trojan War, known for his past exploits and present good advice

Ἀντήνωρ -ορος ὁ = Antenor, Trojan old man, remarkable for advocating the return of Helen to the Greeks

8   κατὰ ταῦτα = in accordance with the same things, according to the same principles. Explain the form ταῦτα (*Essentials* §191, §207).

10   οὐδ' ἐγγύς (supply τινα) = no one even close

10–11 οὔτε τῶν νῦν οὔτε τῶν παλαιῶν: partitive with implied τινα

11   εἰ μὴ ἄρα εἰ: the sense of this combination is hard to render in decent English. Dover's suggestion (1980: 175) is good: "unless perhaps if. . . ."

Καὶ γὰρ οὖν καὶ τοῦτο ἐν τοῖς πρώτοις παρέλιπον, ὅτι   14

καὶ οἱ λόγοι αὐτοῦ ὁμοιότατοί εἰσι τοῖς σιληνοῖς τοῖς διοιγομένοις.   15

εἰ γὰρ ἐθέλοι τις τῶν Σωκράτους ἀκούειν λόγων, φανεῖεν   16   221e

ἂν πάνυ γελοῖοι τὸ πρῶτον· τοιαῦτα καὶ ὀνόματα καὶ   17

ῥήματα ἔξωθεν περιαμπέχονται, σατύρου δή τινα ὑβριστοῦ δοράν.   18

ὄνους γὰρ κανθηλίους λέγει καὶ χαλκέας τινὰς καὶ   19

σκυτοτόμους καὶ βυρσοδέψας, καὶ ἀεὶ διὰ τῶν αὐτῶν τὰ   20

αὐτὰ φαίνεται λέγειν, ὥστε ἄπειρος καὶ ἀνόητος ἄνθρωπος   21

πᾶς ἂν τῶν λόγων καταγελάσειεν. διοιγομένους δὲ ἰδὼν ἄν   22   222a

τις καὶ ἐντὸς αὐτῶν γιγνόμενος πρῶτον μὲν νοῦν ἔχοντας   23

ἔνδον μόνους εὑρήσει τῶν λόγων, ἔπειτα θειοτάτους καὶ   24

πλεῖστα ἀγάλματ᾽ ἀρετῆς ἐν αὑτοῖς ἔχοντας καὶ ἐπὶ πλεῖστον   25

τείνοντας, μᾶλλον δὲ ἐπὶ πᾶν ὅσον προσήκει σκοπεῖν   26

τῷ μέλλοντι καλῷ κἀγαθῷ ἔσεσθαι.   27

　　Ταῦτ᾽ ἐστίν, ὦ ἄνδρες, ἃ ἐγὼ Σωκράτη ἐπαινῶ· καὶ αὖ   28

---

14   παραλείπω = leave out, pass by, neglect

17–18   ὀνόματα καὶ ῥήματα = words and phrases

18   περιαμπέχομαι = be dressed in *acc.*; the subject must be οἱ λόγοι, so clearly a metaphor
　　　δορά -ᾶς ἡ = hide, skin

19   ὄνος -ου ὁ/ἡ = ass, donkey
　　　κανθήλιος -ου ὁ = pack ass (functions here to specify the kind of ὄνος)
　　　χαλκεύς -έως ὁ = bronze-worker

20   σκυτοτόμος -ου ὁ = leather-cutter, shoemaker
　　　βυρσοδέψης -ου ὁ = tanner

21   ἀνόητος -ον = not understanding, foolish

22   ἄν: the presence of ἄν is hard to explain, and scholars do not agree on the usage, though they do seem to agree that it lends a slightly hypothetical quality to this sentence. ἄν occurs with the future indicative in future conditions in Homer, but is rare in Attic prose. Perhaps the less than standard grammar expresses Alcibiades' drunkenness and emotionally overwrought state; the sentence was going to be hypothetical originally and became more concrete.

23   ἐντὸς αὐτῶν γιγνόμενος: the metaphorical notion of "being" within the opened statuettes (= Socrates' words) is somewhat peculiar (rather than just looking into them), but seems to express a penetration and intimacy appropriate to the context.

ἃ μέμφομαι συμμείξας ὑμῖν εἶπον ἅ με ὕβρισεν. καὶ μέντοι   29

οὐκ ἐμὲ μόνον ταῦτα πεποίηκεν, ἀλλὰ καὶ Χαρμίδην   30   222b

τὸν Γλαύκωνος καὶ Εὐθύδημον τὸν Διοκλέους καὶ ἄλλους   31

πάνυ πολλούς, οὓς οὗτος ἐξαπατῶν ὡς ἐραστὴς παιδικὰ   32

μᾶλλον αὐτὸς καθίσταται ἀντ᾽ ἐραστοῦ. ἃ δὴ καὶ σοὶ   33

---

29   ἃ μέμφομαι: the antecedent ταῦτα, the object of συμμείξας, is suppressed.

συμμείγνυμι = mix together with

ἅ με ὕβρισεν: this relative clause is in apposition to ἃ μέμφομαι, elaborating and clarifying it. The neuter plural ἅ stands in for the cognate accusative (*Essentials* §77) that so often accompanies ὑβρίζω: so ἅ ... ὕβρισεν = the wrongs which/that he did me, the criminal acts he perpetrated against me. Socrates is the subject, as the context makes clear. This is clearly paradoxical as the Athenians would not have thought refraining from sex with a free youth was a form of hubris (quite the reverse!).

30–31   Χαρμίδης ὁ Γλαύκωνος = Charmides, son of Glaucon. Charmides, Plato's maternal uncle, is the eponymous character of another Platonic dialogue on the subject of *sophrosyne* set almost immediately following the army's return from Potidaea in 432 (reading 10E.2). He is called "the great beauty of the day," "the most temperate of the young men of today," and "the inferior to none in quality" (*Charmides* 157d). Socrates describes himself as catching flame, possessed of the appetite of a wild beast, upon seeing inside Charmides' garments. But, by the end of the dialogue, Charmides professes himself charmed by Socrates (176b) and orders Socrates not to resist him (176d). Charmides was accused of profaning the mysteries alongside Alcibiades (see introduction: "Historical Context of the Dialogue"). His father, Glaucon, is the grandfather of Plato and his brother, Glaucon, but he is already dead in the *Charmides* and therefore cannot be the same Glaucon mentioned in the *Symposium's* opening frame.

31   Εὐθύδημος ὁ Διοκλέους = Euthydemos, son of Diocles, described in Xenophon's *Memorabilia* as the *eromenos* of Critias (Plato's uncle and later one of the Thirty) (1.2.29). The *Memorabilia* calls him τὸν καλόν and says he surpasses his contemporaries in his learning with the potential to be the best in speech and action (4.2.1). It also recounts his early interactions with Socrates in some detail (4.2–3). There is a Platonic dialogue named *Euthydemus*, but this character, a sophist from Chios, is not the one mentioned here.

32   ἐξαπατῶν ὡς ἐραστής: the deceptive nature of love and the predatory lover are standard topics of Greek writing and thinking about Eros

παιδικά pred. nom. with καθίσταται = he is made the boy-darling, he takes on the role of boy-toy

33   ἃ δή: i.e., which is why

λέγω, ὦ Ἀγάθων, μὴ ἐξαπατᾶσθαι ὑπὸ τούτου, ἀλλ᾽ ἀπὸ   34

τῶν ἡμετέρων παθημάτων γνόντα εὐλαβηθῆναι, καὶ μὴ κατὰ   35

τὴν παροιμίαν ὥσπερ νήπιον παθόντα γνῶναι.   36

---

34   μὴ ἐξαπατᾶσθαι, ἀλλ᾽ εὐλαβηθῆναι, and μὴ . . . γνῶναι: μή makes clear that all of these
        infinitives have imperatival force: "I tell you not to . . ." etc.

35   πάθημα -ατος τό = πάθος τό

36   παροιμία -ας ἡ = proverb, byword, adage. The proverb referred to here is πάθει μάθος (learning
        by suffering), which is commonly alluded to on the tragic stage.

        νήπιος -ου ὁ = fool, ignoramus, child

Reading 11. The End of the Symposium

A final coda brings the *Symposium's* themes to a fitting close: drama, drunkenness, disorder, Dionysus, Eros, issues of narration, the sobriety of Socrates—all are evoked in the short span. Alcibiades' speech meets with laughter, an element that has been important throughout the dialogue. But fittingly, given its themes, Socrates labels it not comedy (though it could well be taken as a *komos*-song, performed as it is by a *komast*) but a satyr-drama, a drama that normally follows the tragic performances.

When Socrates accuses Alcibiades not of being exceptionally honest and forthright, as the other symposiasts believe, but of composing the entire speech purely to cause trouble between Socrates and Agathon, a shuffle between Agathon, Alcibiades, and Socrates results, which puts Socrates in the middle and raises questions about who is *erastes* and who is *eromenos* in the group. Like Eros himself, Socrates emerges as the intermediary figure between the two other men, at once lover and beloved.

A crowd of revelers enters, and Dionysiac disorder ensues. It is clearly a komos of sorts, bringing the drinking party to its end. Apollodorus's source Aristodemus falls asleep at this point, waking only at cockcrow. In a state between sleeping and wakefulness, he observes that only Socrates and the two dramatists are still awake and still drinking, passing the drinking bowl to their right; the other guests have either left or are asleep. Socrates still appears to be sober and entirely unaffected by having been up all night drinking, illustrating the truth of Alcibiades' claims about his toughness and resistance. The content of the single detail that Aristodemus remembers of their discussion has seemed particularly important to scholars: Socrates is forcing the two dramatists to acknowledge that the same man is best qualified by his skill (*techne*) to write comedy and tragedy, so that the man who is the best comic poet must also be the best tragic poet. Although modern readers familiar with Shakespeare may find this proposition perfectly plausible, it would have seemed bizarre in Athens at this time, where the writing of tragedies and comedies was highly specialized, and no one did both. Although it seems to contradict things Socrates says elsewhere in Plato's dialogues about tragedy and comedy (*Republic*), the argument is at least compatible with points Socrates makes elsewhere about the need for the dramatic poet, since he is credited with teaching virtue, to know virtue, something Socrates consistently denies to both traditional and contemporary poets of Greece (*Ion* and *Republic*). The assumption underlying the argument seems to be that to know what is καλός is the most important requirement for writing either dramatic form. Socrates may also be referring to Plato's own art; for indeed in the *Symposium*, Plato

Fig. 25. Disorder reigns! *Komos* scene: men dancing. Exterior view of an Attic red-figure kylix (drinking cup) attributed to Douris, ca. 490–480 B.C.E. from Vulci. Inv. 1843,1103.45 British Museum, London, England. © Trustees of the British Museum.

has created a new art form that embodies all three dramatic forms: tragedy, comedy, and, in the speech of Alcibiades, satyr-drama, as Socrates explicitly comments. In this brief final scene, Plato offers perhaps a final reflection on his own achievement.

Further Reading on Plato as Composer of Tragedy and Comedy

- Clay 1975 and Patterson 1982

Suggested Review

- principal parts and usage of λανθάνω

  λανθάνω λήσω ἔλαθον λέληθα = escape notice of *acc.* in ——ing, be unknown, unseen, unnoticed by *acc.* in ——ing

Vocabulary

διατρίβω διατρίψω διέτριψα διατέτριφα διατέτριμμαι διέτρίβην/διετρίφθην: spend
   time, pass the time (cf. διατριβη -ης ἡ: pastime)
ἓ *acc. refl. pron.*: him(self), her(self), it(self) (cf. ἑαυτόν)
καταδαρθάνω—κατέδαρθον καταδεδάρθηκα: fall asleep, sleep

Reading 11 (*Symposium* 222c1–223d12)

Εἰπόντος δὴ ταῦτα τοῦ Ἀλκιβιάδου γέλωτα γενέσθαι	1	222c
ἐπὶ τῇ παρρησίᾳ αὐτοῦ, ὅτι ἐδόκει ἔτι ἐρωτικῶς ἔχειν τοῦ	2	
Σωκράτους. τὸν οὖν Σωκράτη, "Νήφειν μοι δοκεῖς," φάναι,	3	
"ὦ Ἀλκιβιάδη. οὐ γὰρ ἄν ποτε οὕτω κομψῶς κύκλῳ περιβαλλόμενος	4	
ἀφανίσαι ἐνεχείρεις οὗ ἕνεκα ταῦτα πάντα εἴρηκας,	5	
καὶ ὡς ἐν παρέργῳ δὴ λέγων ἐπὶ τελευτῆς αὐτὸ ἔθηκας,	6	
ὡς οὐ πάντα τούτου ἕνεκα εἰρηκώς, τοῦ ἐμὲ καὶ Ἀγάθωνα	7	
διαβάλλειν, οἰόμενος δεῖν ἐμὲ μὲν σοῦ ἐρᾶν καὶ μηδενὸς ἄλλου,	8	222d
Ἀγάθωνα δὲ ὑπὸ σοῦ ἐρᾶσθαι καὶ μηδ' ὑφ' ἑνὸς ἄλλου.	9	
ἀλλ' οὐκ ἔλαθες, ἀλλὰ τὸ σατυρικόν σου δρᾶμα τοῦτο	10	
καὶ σιληνικὸν κατάδηλον ἐγένετο. ἀλλ', ὦ φίλε Ἀγάθων,	11	
μηδὲν πλέον αὐτῷ γένηται, ἀλλὰ παρασκευάζου ὅπως	12	
ἐμὲ καὶ σὲ μηδεὶς διαβαλεῖ."	13	
Τὸν οὖν Ἀγάθωνα εἰπεῖν, "καὶ μήν, ὦ Σώκρατες,	14	
κινδυνεύεις ἀληθῆ λέγειν. τεκμαίρομαι δὲ καὶ ὡς κατεκλίνη ἐν	15	222e
μέσῳ ἐμοῦ τε καὶ σοῦ, ἵνα χωρὶς ἡμᾶς διαλάβῃ. οὐδὲν οὖν	16	

---

1   *γέλως -ωτος ὁ = laughter

2   *παρρησία -ας ἡ = frankness

4–5   ἄν . . . ἐνεχείρεις: carefully identify the form of ἐνεχείρεις and explain the use of ἄν (*Essentials* §162)

         κομψός -ή -όν = elegant

         κύκλῳ περιβάλλομαι = go around in a circle; the presence of the adverb κομψῶς suggests that he refers to the way Alcibiades returns to the satyr comparison at the end of his speech, creating a ring composition

6   πάρεργον -ου τό = subordinate or secondary business, afterthought

7–8   τοῦ . . . διαβάλλειν: artic. inf. in apposition to τούτου of the previous line (*Essentials* §182)

8   διαβάλλω (here) = make quarrel

10–11   τὸ σατυρικὸν δρᾶμα = satyr-play, a form of mythological drama, with a chorus of satyrs, performed following three tragedies during the Dionysiac festivals. The reference to the imagery of Alcibiades' speech is obvious; it also seems to play with the dramatic themes of the entire dialogue.

12   μηδὲν πλέον αὐτῷ γένηται: see note on reading 10E.17–18

13   διαβάλλω: see note on line 8

15   *τεκμαίρομαι = notice, observe, perceive from certain signs or tokens

16   διαλαμβάνω = separate, divide

πλέον αὐτῷ ἔσται, ἀλλ' ἐγὼ παρὰ σὲ ἐλθὼν κατακλινήσομαι."   17

"Πάνυ γε," φάναι τὸν Σωκράτη, "δεῦρο ὑποκάτω ἐμοῦ   18
κατακλίνου."   19

"Ὦ Ζεῦ," εἰπεῖν τὸν Ἀλκιβιάδην, "οἷα αὖ πάσχω ὑπὸ τοῦ   20
ἀνθρώπου. οἴεταί μου δεῖν πανταχῇ περιεῖναι. ἀλλ' εἰ   21
μή τι ἄλλο, ὦ θαυμάσιε, ἐν μέσῳ ἡμῶν ἔα Ἀγάθωνα κατακεῖσθαι."   22

"Ἀλλ' ἀδύνατον," φάναι τὸν Σωκράτη. "σὺ μὲν γὰρ ἐμὲ   23
ἐπῄνεσας, δεῖ δὲ ἐμὲ αὖ τὸν ἐπὶ δεξί' ἐπαινεῖν. ἐὰν οὖν   24
ὑπὸ σοὶ κατακλινῇ Ἀγάθων, οὐ δήπου ἐμὲ πάλιν ἐπαινέσεται,   25
πρὶν ὑπ' ἐμοῦ μᾶλλον ἐπαινεθῆναι; ἀλλ' ἔασον,   26
ὦ δαιμόνιε, καὶ μὴ φθονήσῃς τῷ μειρακίῳ ὑπ' ἐμοῦ   27   223a
ἐπαινεθῆναι· καὶ γὰρ πάνυ ἐπιθυμῶ αὐτὸν ἐγκωμιάσαι."   28

"Ἰοῦ ἰοῦ," φάναι τὸν Ἀγάθωνα, "Ἀλκιβιάδη, οὐκ ἔσθ' ὅπως   29
ἂν ἐνθάδε μείναιμι, ἀλλὰ παντὸς μᾶλλον μεταναστήσομαι   30
ἵνα ὑπὸ Σωκράτους ἐπαινεθῶ."   31

"Ταῦτα ἐκεῖνα," φάναι τὸν Ἀλκιβιάδην, "τὰ εἰωθότα·   32
Σωκράτους παρόντος τῶν καλῶν μεταλαβεῖν ἀδύνατον ἄλλῳ.   33
καὶ νῦν ὡς εὐπόρως καὶ πιθανὸν λόγον ηὗρεν, ὥστε παρ'   34
ἑαυτῷ τουτονὶ κατακεῖσθαι."   35

---

18   ὑποκάτω = next to [on the right hand side], beneath *gen*. Socrates encourages Agathon to move
away from Alcibiades, who currently lies between them, to the right side of Socrates, so that
Socrates will lie between the two handsome young men.

23-28   Socrates here plays with the conventions of the symposium, which have been consistently followed,
whereby the one to the right of the last speaker follows him in speaking. Agathon must lie to
his right rather than to his left.

25   ὑπό (here) = ὑποκάτω in line 18

29   οὐκ ἔσθ' ὅπως = there is no way that
ἰοῦ ἰοῦ = cry of joy: hooray (oddly, in other contexts, it seems to be a cry of sorrow!)

30   παντός: neut. gen. of comparison with μᾶλλον
μετανίστημι = remove; *mid*. = remove oneself, move aside

32   ἐκεῖνα: modifies τὰ εἰωθότα

33   μεταλαμβάνω = have or get a share of *gen*., partake of *gen*.

34   *πιθανός -ή -όν = calculated to persuade, persuasive

Τὸν μὲν οὖν Ἀγάθωνα ὡς κατακεισόμενον παρὰ τῷ   36   223b

Σωκράτει ἀνίστασθαι· ἐξαίφνης δὲ κωμαστὰς ἥκειν παμπόλλους   37

ἐπὶ τὰς θύρας, καὶ ἐπιτυχόντας ἀνεῳγμέναις ἐξιόντος   38

τινὸς εἰς τὸ ἄντικρυς πορεύεσθαι παρὰ σφᾶς καὶ κατακλίνεσθαι,   39

καὶ θορύβου μεστὰ πάντα εἶναι, καὶ οὐκέτι ἐν   40

κόσμῳ οὐδενὶ ἀναγκάζεσθαι πίνειν πάμπολυν οἶνον. τὸν   41

μὲν οὖν Ἐρυξίμαχον καὶ τὸν Φαῖδρον καὶ ἄλλους τινὰς ἔφη   42

ὁ Ἀριστόδημος οἴχεσθαι ἀπιόντας, ἓ δὲ ὕπνον λαβεῖν,   43

καὶ καταδαρθεῖν πάνυ πολύ, ἅτε μακρῶν τῶν νυκτῶν οὐσῶν,   44   223c

ἐξεγρέσθαι δὲ πρὸς ἡμέραν ἤδη ἀλεκτρυόνων ᾀδόντων, ἐξεγρόμενος   45

δὲ ἰδεῖν τοὺς μὲν ἄλλους καθεύδοντας καὶ οἰχομένους,   46

Ἀγάθωνα δὲ καὶ Ἀριστοφάνη καὶ Σωκράτη ἔτι   47

μόνους ἐγρηγορέναι καὶ πίνειν ἐκ φιάλης μεγάλης ἐπὶ δεξιά.   48

τὸν οὖν Σωκράτη αὐτοῖς διαλέγεσθαι· καὶ τὰ μὲν ἄλλα ὁ   49

Ἀριστόδημος οὐκ ἔφη μεμνῆσθαι τῶν λόγων—οὔτε γὰρ ἐξ   50   223d

ἀρχῆς παραγενέσθαι ὑπονυστάζειν τε—τὸ μέντοι κεφάλαιον,   51

ἔφη, προσαναγκάζειν τὸν Σωκράτη ὁμολογεῖν αὐτοὺς τοῦ   52

αὐτοῦ ἀνδρὸς εἶναι κωμῳδίαν καὶ τραγῳδίαν ἐπίστασθαι   53

ποιεῖν, καὶ τὸν τέχνῃ τραγῳδοποιὸν ὄντα καὶ κωμῳδοποιὸν   54

---

38   ἐπιτυγχάνω = ἐντυγχάνω

ἀνεῳγμέναις: θύραις can be inferred from gender and number

38–39 ἐξιόντος . . . τινός: what is the construction here (*Essentials* §176)? The phrase explains
ἀνεῳγμέναις.

39   εἰς τὸ ἄντικρυς = straight on in, right on in

40   *μεστός -ή -όν = full, filled, filled full

45   ἀλεκτρυών -όνος ὁ = cock, rooster

ἐξεγρόμενος: nom. agreeing with ὁ Ἀριστόδημος, as is normal when the subject of indir.
statement is the same as the subject of the main verb.

46   καί: i.e., or else. The two participles are linked because the activities are united in being distinct
from that pursued by Aristophanes, Agathon, and Socrates, not because anyone could have
actually been doing both of these things.

48   φιάλη -ης ἡ = broad, flat vessel, bowl

51   ὑπονυστάζω = nod off

52–53 τοῦ αὐτοῦ ἀνδρὸς εἶναι . . . ἐπίστασθαι: pred. gen. of characteristic (*Essentials* §104; Smyth
1956: §1304)

εἶναι. ταῦτα δὴ ἀναγκαζομένους αὐτοὺς καὶ οὐ σφόδρα   55
ἑπομένους νυστάζειν, καὶ πρότερον μὲν καταδαρθεῖν τὸν   56
Ἀριστοφάνη, ἤδη δὲ ἡμέρας γιγνομένης τὸν Ἀγάθωνα. τὸν   57
οὖν Σωκράτη, κατακοιμίσαντ' ἐκείνους, ἀναστάντα ἀπιέναι,   58
καὶ ἓ ὥσπερ εἰώθει ἕπεσθαι, καὶ ἐλθόντα εἰς Λύκειον,   59
ἀπονιψάμενον, ὥσπερ ἄλλοτε τὴν ἄλλην ἡμέραν διατρίβειν,   60
καὶ οὕτω διατρίψαντα εἰς ἑσπέραν οἴκοι ἀναπαύεσθαι.   61

---

56   νυστάζω = nod in sleep, nap, slumber
58   κατακοιμίζω = lull to sleep
59   καὶ ἓ ... ἕπεσθαι: this clause refers to Aristodemus and is apparently parenthetical as the subject
      of the action of the next participle, ἐλθόντα, is again Socrates
      Λύκειον -ου τό = the Lyceum (the wolf-place), the sanctuary of Apollo Lykeios, which lies to the
      east outside the city wall of Athens. Elsewhere in the dialogues (*Euthyphro* 2a1; *Lysis* 203a1, b2;
      Euthydemus 271a1), Plato speaks of the Lyceum as a place frequented by Socrates. It was later the
      site of Aristotle's school.
60   ἀπονίζω = wash off
      ἄλλοτε = at another time, at other times

Part 2
Review Exercises

The exercises are intended to be done following the designated reading in order to reinforce the vocabulary and grammar points used in that reading. For best results, the reading's vocabulary should be studied prior to attempting the exercises for that reading. It is probably also a good idea to read through the designated section(s) in *Essentials* before doing the exercises.

I have provided a set of exercises to accompany each of the first five reading selections (1A, 1B, 2A, 2B, 2C) but only four additional sets of exercises, one each for reading selections 3A–3B, 4A–4B, 5A–5B, and 6A–E, on the assumption that students need more systematic review early in the course and can then be weaned off the exercises to focus more exclusively on Plato's text and its interpretation with only spot review of grammar. Teachers can, however, delay doing some of the reviews until later in the course, if that seems desirable.

More exercises are provided than most classes will find necessary or desirable. Students with a very firm foundation in grammar may need very few or none of the regular exercises but may enjoy doing a few of the challenge passages for reinforcement of grammar. Less confident classes will profit from more regular reviews and perhaps an occasional challenge passage undertaken as a group exercise. Teachers need to consider their individual class's needs carefully in assigning exercises.

Asterisked (*) words are common Greek words that are worth learning if the student is otherwise feeling in control of the material. Many of them are part of the required vocabulary to be learned or reviewed in later chapters.

Unless otherwise stated, the Exercises are translation exercises designed to give students practice with the stated concept. Students should study the concept under review using their first year textbook or *Essentials* and then translate the sentences.

Review Exercise 1A

a. Indirect statement with infinitive (*Essentials* §184)

- οὔ φημι (I say that . . . not, I deny that . . .)

1. ἐκεῖνος δ᾽ ἔφη καὶ σὲ εἰδέναι τοῦτο.
2. οἱ δὲ μαθηταὶ **οἴονται** ταῦτ᾽ οὔπω μαθεῖν σαφῶς.
   *οἴομαι: think
3. οὔ φημι τῷ δείπνῳ παραγενέσθαι ἐκείνῃ τῇ νυκτί.
4. ἔφην δὲ **τῇ ὑστεραίᾳ** τῷ δείπνῳ παραγενήσεσθαι.
   *ὑστεραία -ας ἡ: next day, following day
5. πρὸ δὲ τοῦ ἡγούμην τὴν συνουσίαν γεγονέναι τοῦ αὐτοῦ ἔτους.
6. καὶ μὴν **οἶμαι ἀθλιώτατος** ἀνθρώπων τότε μὲν ἔγωγ᾽ εἶναι, νῦν δὲ σέ.
   *οἶμαι = οἴομαι: think
   *ἄθλιος -α -ον: wretched, miserable
7. πολλάκις Σωκράτης οὐκ ἔφη σοφὸς εἶναι.
8. ἡγοῦμαι Σωκράτη ἐρωτικώτατον φιλοσόφων τότ᾽ εἶναι.
9. πρὸ τῆς ἐκκλησίας ὁ στρατηγὸς ἤγγειλεν ἢ εἰς τὴν πόλιν ἄξειν **Λακεδαιμονίους** ἢ **αὐτοῦ** ἀποκτενεῖν.
   *Λακεδαιμόνιοι -ων οἱ: Spartans
   *αὐτοῦ *adv.*: on the spot, there
10. ὁ κῆρυξ ἔφη πάντα ἃ ἐρωτᾷς ἐν τῇ πρῴην ἐκκλησίᾳ ἤδη ἀγγελθῆναι.
11. οἱ ξένοι ἔφασαν πορρώθεν ἥκειν· τοὺς δ᾽ ἑταίρους τοὺς ὄπισθεν **πορευομένους** τῇ **ὑστεραίᾳ** ἀφίξεσθαι.
    *πορεύομαι: travel, make one's way
    *ὑστεραία -ας ἡ: next day, following day
12. ἆρα **νεωστὶ** ἡγῇ τὴν συνουσίαν γεγονέναι ταύτην ἣν ἐρωτᾷς ὥστε καὶ ἡμᾶς παραγενέσθαι;
    *νεωστί *adv.*: recently
13. Σωκράτης οὐδέν φησιν ἄλλο ἐπίστασθαι ἢ τὰ ἐρωτικά. ἆρ᾽ οἴει παίζειν αὐτόν;
14. πάντες ἡγούμεθα τοῦτον τὸν θεὸν οὔπω τετιμημένον ἱκανῶς εἶναι.
15. ὁ νεανίας ἡγεῖτο τοῦτον τὸν θεὸν οὔπω τετιμημένον ἱκανῶς εἶναι.

b. Participle forms (*Essentials* §§25–40)

1. Give the masculine nominative singular participle and the feminine and neuter nominative singular endings for the regular verb λύω in each category.

	active	middle	passive
present	λύων, *[handwriting]*	λυόμενος, -η, -ον	λυου *[handwriting]* -η, -ον
future	λύσων, λύσουσα	λυσόμενος *[handwriting]*	λυσόμενος, -η, -ον
aorist	λύσας	λυσασα -η, -ον	λυθεσων
perfect	λελυκώς	λελυκυῖα	λελυκός

2. Though the translation of participles can vary considerably depending on context, give a possible translation of a participle of λύω (release, loose; *mid.*: ransom) appropriate for each tense and voice. (*Essentials* §167)

	active	middle	passive
present	releasing	*[for]* releasing *[ransom]*	being released
future	about to release	about to release *[ransom]*	about to *[be]* release
aorist	having released	having ransomed	having been ransom *[released]*
perfect	which has *[been]* released	which has ransomed	which has been released

3. Choose one participle from the active column (e.g., aorist active) and one participle from the middle column (e.g., present middle) and decline each in full for the regular verb λύω.

Active example

	masculine	feminine	neuter
nom. sing.	λύσας	λύσασα	λύσαν
gen. sing.	λύσαντος	λυσάσης	λύσαντος
dat. sing.	λύσαντι	λυσάσῃ	λύσαντι
acc. sing.	λύσαντα	λύσασαν	λύσαν
nom. pl.	λύσαντες	λύσασαι	λύσαντα
gen. pl.	λυσάντων	λυσασῶν	λυσάντων
dat. pl.	λύσασι(ν)	λυσάσαις	λύσασι(ν)
acc. pl.	λύσαντας	λυσάσας	λύσαντα

[Handwritten notes at bottom of page:]

λύων λύουσα λῦον   λυόμενος, -η, -ον ←

λύσων λύσουσα λῦσον   λυόμενος, -η, -ον

λύσας λύσασα λῦσον   λυσάμενος, -η, -ον

λελυκώς, λελυκυῖα, λελυκός   λυθείς λυθεῖσα

λυθέν

Middle example

	masculine	feminine	neuter
nom. sing.	λελυμένος	λελυμένη	λελυμένον
gen. sing.	λελυμένον	λελυμένης	λελυμένον
dat. sing.	λελυμένῳ	λελυμένῃ	λελυμένῳ
acc. sing.	λελυμένον	λελυμένην	λελυμένον
nom. pl.	λελυμένοι	λελυμέναι	λελυμένα
gen. pl.	λελυμένων	λελυμένων	λελυμένων
dat. pl.	λελυμένοις	λελυμέναις	λελυμένοις
acc. pl.	λελυμένους	λελυμένας	λελυμένα

c. Circumstantial, supplementary, and substantival participles (*Essentials* §§166–75)

1. ἐγὼ γὰρ ἐτύγχανον πρῴην εἰς ἄστυ ἰών.
2. τῶν οὖν φίλων τις ἰδὼν Σωκράτη οἴκοθεν ἰόντα ἐκάλεσεν ἐπὶ δεῖπνον.
3. **ἅτε** γὰρ οὐ παραγενόμενος ὁ διηγούμενός σοι οὐκ εἶχε περὶ τοῦ δείπνου οὐδὲν σαφὲς λέγειν.
   *ἅτε + *part*.: on account of, because of
4. ἀκούσας τινός ὄπισθε καλοῦντος ἔμεινα.
5. ὁ οὖν Ἀριστόδημος διηγούμενος ἤρχετο.
6. οἱ δ' ὑμῖν διηγούμενοι ἔτυχον οὐδὲν σαφὲς εἰδότες.
7. καὶ μὴν Σωκράτης δῆλος ἦν παίζων.
8. "ποῖ καὶ πόθεν εἶ," **ἦν δ' ἐγώ**, "οὕτω καλὸς γεγενημένος;" "οἴκοθεν εἰς ἄστυ εἶμι," ἦ δ' ὅς, "ὡς ζητήσων Σωκράτη."
   *ἦν δ' ἐγώ: I said
9. οἱ δὲ νεανίαι οὐ λανθάνουσι τοὺς φύλακας Ἀθήνηθε φεύγοντες.
10. παντάπασιν ὁ λέγων φαίνεταί μοι οὐδὲν εἰδὼς περὶ τῆς συνουσίας ἣν ἐρωτᾷς.
11. **ἅτε** παῖδες ἔτι ὄντες, οὗτοι σαφῶς οὔπω λέγειν ἔχουσιν.
    *ἅτε + *part*.: on account of, because of
12. **εἰς** δ' Ἀγάθωνος ὁ Ἀριστόδημος ἄρτι ἦλθε **κληθεὶς** ὑπὸ Σωκράτους ἐπὶ δεῖπνον.
    *εἰς + *gen*. *name*: to *gen*.'s [house]
    *κληθείς from καλέω
13. ὁ **χρήσιμ'** εἰδώς, οὐχ ὁ πολλ' εἰδώς, σοφός. (Aeschylus, frag. 390 Radt)
    *χρήσιμος -η -ον: useful, good, worthwhile
14. οὐδεὶς τῶν **θνητῶν** οἶδε πάντα τὰ γιγνόμενα καὶ τὰ γενόμενα καὶ τὰ γενησόμενα.
    *θνητός -οῦ ὁ: mortal
15. μικραὶ **χάριτες** ἐν **καιρῷ** μέγισται τοῖς λαμβάνουσι. (Democritus, frag. 94 D-K)
    *χάρις -ιτος ἡ: favor
    *καιρός -οῦ ὁ: critical moment

16. οὐκ ἔξεστιν ἀνθρώποις λαθεῖν τοὺς θεοὺς ἀδικοῦσιν.

17. ὁ βασιλεὺς ἀπῆλθεν, **ἐξηπατηκέναι** μὲν **οἰόμενος**, **ἐξηπατημένος** δὲ μᾶλλον παντάπασιν.

     *ἐξαπατάω: deceive

     *οἴομαι: think

d. Verb drills: μένω, πυνθάνομαι, and ἀκούω

After reviewing the principal parts of these three verbs, translate or identify fully each of the following verb forms (space is provided for both). A parenthetical (2) indicates an ambiguous form, with two possible identifications/distinct translations.

1. μένεις   _____

2. μενεῖς   _____

3. ἔμενες   _____

4. ἔμεινας   _____

5. μείνας   _____

6. μεμένηκας   _____

7. μένε   _____

8. μενέτω   _____

9. μεῖναι   _____

10. μένομεν   _____

11. μενοῦμεν   _____

12. πυνθάνονται   _____

13. ἐπύθοντο   _____

14. ἐπυνθάνοντο   _____

15. πέπυσαι   _____

16. πεπυσμένοι εἰσιν _____   _____

17. πεύσονται _____   _____

18. ἐπεπύσμην _____   _____

19. πυνθάνεσθε (2) _____   _____

_____   _____

20. πυνθανέσθων _____   _____

21. ἀκούσεται _____   _____

22. ἤκουσαν _____   _____

23. ἀκήκοας _____   _____

24. ἠκούσθημεν _____   _____

25. ἤκουον (2) _____   _____

_____   _____

26. ἀκούσας _____   _____

27. ἤκουσας _____   _____

28. ἀκοῦσαι _____   _____

29. ἀκούων _____   _____

30. ἀκουσθήσεται _____   _____

Review Exercise 1B

a. Genitive absolute (*Essentials* §176)

1. πάλαι δ᾽ αὕτη ἡ συνουσία ἐγένετο παίδων ἔτι ὄντων ἡμῶν.
2. πάντων δ᾽ ὁμολογησάντων ὁ πορευόμενος ἤρχετο διηγούμενος τὸν λόγον.
3. γενομένων δὲ τούτων πρῶτον ἔτος τοῦ πολέμου τοῦδε **ἐτελεύτα**.
   *τελευτάω: end, come to an end
4. τοῦ δ᾽ ἀθλίου **ἱκέτου** δεομένου τοσοῦτον ὁ Ἀχιλλεὺς **ἤχθετο** ὥστ᾽ οὐκ ἐλέησεν.
   *ἱκέτης -ου ὁ: suppliant
   *ἄχθομαι: be vexed, angry
5. μεγάλων ἔργων πραχθέντων δεῖ ἡμᾶς τιμᾶν τοὺς πράξαντας.
6. τούτων πάλαι πολλὰ ἤδη ἔτη πρὸς ὑμᾶς οὐδὲν ἀληθὲς λεγόντων, τὴν δίκην σαφῶς κρῖναι οὐκ ἔχετε. (adapted from Socrates, *Apology*)
7. ἤδη **ἑσπέρας** γιγνομένης ὁ στρατηγὸς τοὺς ἄνδρας εἰς τὴν μάχην ἤγαγεν.
   *ἑσπέρα -ας ἡ: evening
8. τούτων ἐν τῇ ἀγορᾷ ἀποδειχθέντων οἱ πλουσιώτατοι τῶν πολιτῶν ἤρχονται **κατασκευάζοντες** ναῦς ὡς πόρρω πορευσομένας ἐπὶ τήνδε τὴν νῆσον.
   *κατασκευάζω: equip
9. τοσοῦτο πάθος οἱ Ἀθηναῖοι ἔπασχον ἀνθρώπων τ᾽ **ἔνδον** ἀποθνησκόντων καὶ γῆς **ἔξω δῃουμένης**.
   *ἔνδον *adv.*: within; i.e., inside the city
   *ἔξω *adv.*: outside; i.e., in the surrounding countryside
   δῃόω: lay waste to
10. οἱ ἄνδρες ἐν τῇ πόλει παντάπασιν **ἤχθοντο** μαινομένων ἐν τοῖς **ὄρεσι** τῶν γυναικῶν. ἔνιοι δ᾽ ἐπειρῶντο λαθεῖν τὰς γυναίκας ὄπισθεν **πέτρων** καὶ **δένδρων κρυπτόμενοι** ὀλίγῳ χωρίς, βουλόμενοι ὁρᾶν ἃ αὗται ἐποίουν.
    *ἄχθομαι: be upset, vexed, or angry
    *ὄρος -ους τό: mountain
    *πέτρα -ας ἡ: rock, crag
    *δένδρον -ου τό: tree
    *κρύπτω: hide
11. ἡδέως μέντοι ὡμολόγησαν καλέσαντος ἐμοῦ παραγενήσεσθαι τῇ ὑστεραίᾳ.
12. τούτου δ᾽ ἐν τῇ πόλει ἀγγελθέντος πάντες οἱ πολῖται πλὴν τοῦδε παντάπασιν ἐφοβήθησαν.

b. Relative clauses (*Essentials* §§129–35)

Circle the relative pronoun or adjective (in one case) in each sentence; identify by case, number, and gender; and translate the sentence.

1. πολλὰ ἔτη ἐβουλόμην πυθέσθαι τὸ δεῖπνον ἐν ᾧ Σωκράτης εἶπεν ἄλλως τε καὶ περὶ τῶν ἐρωτικῶν.
2. τῇ δὲ συνουσίᾳ οὐ παρεγενόμην ταύτῃ ἣν ἄρτι ἤρεσθε.
3. ἆρα τούτῳ τῷ δείπνῳ παρεγένετο ὅς σοι διηγεῖτο;
4. ἆρ' οὐ βούλει ἀκοῦσαι ἃ ὁ ἄθλιος ξένος πρὸ τοῦ θανάτου ἤγγειλεν;
5. ὃν γὰρ θεοὶ φιλοῦσιν, ἀποθνῄσκει νέος. (Menander, frag. 125.1 Kock)
6. οὐκ ἔστιν ὅστις τὴν τύχην οὐ **μέμφεται**. (Menander SECB 611)
    *μέμφομαι: blame
7. πειράσομαι ἆρα ὑμῖν κακοδαίμοσι πάντα δοῦναι ὧν δεῖσθε. ὑμᾶς γὰρ ἀθλίους ὄντας παντῶς ἐλεῶ.
8. ἐκεῖνος οὐδὲν εἶχε σαφὲς ἀγγέλλειν ἡμῖν, ὅπερ ἐξ ἀρχῆς πάντες ἐφοβούμεθα.
9. τρία ἔτη ἐζητοῦμεν ὅστις τῇ πάλαι συνουσίᾳ παραγενόμενος τοὺς ἐρωτικοὺς λόγους ἤκουσεν.
10. οὐκ ἔχω φιλεῖν ὅστις ἥδεται ἀεὶ λέγων.
11. καίπερ πειρώμενος οὐκ ἔχω, ὡς ἔοικε, **μεμνῆσθαι** ὧν πρῴην ἐπυθόμην.
    *μέμνημαι *perf. forms with pres. meaning*: remember
12. φιλοσόφων ὅσων ἀκήκοα ὁ Σωκράτης μάλιστα παίζων ἥδεται, ὡς ἔμοιγε δοκεῖ.
13. "ἀλλ' οἴει," ἦ δ' ὅς, "ὦ Σώκρατες, τοὺς θεοὺς ὠφελεῖσθαι ἀπὸ τούτων ἃ παρ' ἡμῶν λαμβάνουσιν;"
14. "πότε," ἦ δ' ὅς, "αὕτη ἡ συνουσία ἐγένετο;" κἀγὼ εἶπον, "τῇ ὑστεραίᾳ ἢ ᾗ τὰ **ἐπινίκια** ἔθυεν Ἀγάθων τῇ πρώτῃ τραγῳδίᾳ νικήσας."
    ἐπινίκια -ων τά: victory sacrifices, sacrifices to the gods in thanks for a victory
15. οὐδέπω τρία ἔτη ἐστίν ἀφ' οὗ ἐγὼ ἠρξάμην ζητῶν σαφῶς εἰδέναι ὅ τι ἂν ἐκεῖνος λέγῃ καὶ διανοῆται ἑκάστης ἡμέρας.
16. καὶ πρὸ τοῦ Σωκράτη γε ἔνια ἠρόμεθα ὧν ἐκείνου τοῦ ξένου ἠκούσαμεν.
17. ἐμοὶ γὰρ οὐκέτ' ἔστιν εἰς ὅ τι βλέπω πλὴν σοῦ. (Tecmessa to Ajax, Sophocles' *Ajax* 514–15)
18. ἐγὼ μέντοι ὑμῖν πειράσομαι τοῦτ' αὐτὸ ὃ διανοοῦμαι νῦν ἔτι μᾶλλον δηλῶσαι.
19. καὶ μὴν **ἥδομαι** ἀκούων Σωκράτους διηγουμένου περὶ τῶν ἐρωτικῶν ὧν γυναικός τινος ἐπύθετο νέος ὤν.
    *ἥδομαι: enjoy

c. Challenge passages

1. ὁ ἀδικῶν τοῦ ἀδικουμένου κακοδαιμονέστερος. (Democritus, frag. 45 D-K)

2. ἀνὴρ γὰρ ὅστις ἥδεται λέγων ἀεὶ
   λέληθεν αὑτὸν τοῖς **συνοῦσιν** ὢν **βαρύς**. (Sophocles[?],[38] frag. 103 Pearson)
   > *συνών ὁ: associate, companion (cf. συνουσία ἡ)
   > *βαρύς -εῖα -ύ: heavy, burdensome

3. πάντες ἄρα, ὡς ἔοικεν, Ἀθηναῖοι τοὺς νεανίας καλοὺς κἀγαθοὺς ποιοῦσι πλὴν
   ἐμοῦ, ἐγὼ δὲ μόνος διαφθείρω. (Socrates in Plato's *Apology* 25a9–10)

4. πάντων δ᾽ ὅσα ἐστ᾽ **ἔμψυχα** καὶ **γνώμην** ἔχει,
   γυναῖκές ἐσμεν ἀθλιώτατον **φυτόν**. (Medea in Euripides' *Medea* 230–31)
   > ἔμψυχος -ον: alive
   > *γνώμη -ης ἡ: sense, reason
   > *φυτόν -οῦ τό: thing born

5. ἐρωτηθεὶς διὰ τί οἱ μὲν φιλόσοφοι ἐπὶ τὰς τῶν πλουσίων θύρας ἔρχονται, οἱ δὲ
   πλούσιοι ἐπὶ τὰς τῶν φιλοσόφων οὐκέτι, Ἀρίστιππος ὁ φιλόσοφος τόδ᾽ εἶπεν
   "ὅτι οἱ μὲν ἴσασιν ὧν δέονται, οἱ δὲ οὐκ ἴσασιν." (Diogenes Laertius about Aristippus
   the Cynic)

6. παντάπασι κακοδαίμων ὁ ἄνθρωπος ᾧτινι μὴ **διαμένουσιν** οἱ **πειραθέντες** φίλοι,
   καθὰ Δημοκρίτης ὁ φιλόσοφος πάλαι εἶπεν.
   > διαμένω: wait through, remain steadfast (the prefix δια- frequently just intensifies
   > the meaning of the verb, as here)
   > πειραθέντες from πειράω: test, try, put to the test

7. τὴν **τοι Δίκην** λέγουσι παῖδ᾽ εἶναι χρόνου,
   δείκνυσι δ᾽ ἡμῶν ὅστις ἐστὶ μὴ κακός. (Euripides, *Antiope*, frag. 222 Nauck)
   > τοι: so
   > Δίκη -ης ἡ: Dike, the goddess Justice

8. Ὅμηρον ὃς ἐγένετο τῶν Ἑλλήνων σοφώτερος πάντων παῖδες **φθεῖρας** ἀποκτείνοντες
   ἐξηπάτησαν εἰπόντες· ὅσα εἴδομεν καὶ ἐλάβομεν, ταῦτα ἀπολείπομεν, ὅσα δὲ
   οὔτε εἴδομεν οὔτ᾽ ἐλάβομεν, ταῦτα φέρομεν.
   > φθείρ φθειρός ὁ: this word gives the answer to the riddle, which is supposed to
   > have killed Homer in his frustration, but don't kill yourself over it; see glossary
   > *ἐξαπατάω: deceive

9. ἐκεῖνον οὐ φιλῶ ὃς **οἰνοποτάζων** περὶ τοῦ τε θανάτου καὶ τοῦ πολέμου λέγει, ἀλλ᾽
   ὅστις τάς τε **Μούσας** καὶ ἔργα **χρυσέας Ἀφροδίτης ᾄδει.**
   > οἰνοποτάζω: drink wine
   > *Μοῦσαι -ῶν αἱ: Muses, goddesses of poetry
   > *χρύσεος -α -ον: golden
   > Ἀφροδίτη -ης ἡ: Aphrodite, goddess of love
   > *ᾄδω: sing of

38. This passage was attributed to Sophocles by Stobaeus, its ancient source, but some scholars are skeptical that the play
to which it belonged was written by Sophocles. Kannicht and Snell 1981 place it among fragments by unknown authors:
Adespota f.1.(c).

10. **Μοῦσαι** καὶ **Χάριτες**, **κοῦραι** Διός, αἵ ποτε **Κάδμου**
       ἐς γάμον ἐλθοῦσαι καλὸν **ἀείσατε ἔπος**
    "**ὅττι** καλὸν φίλον ἐστί, τὸ δ' οὐ καλὸν οὐ φίλον ἐστί·"
       τοῦτ' **ἔπος** ἀθανάτων ἦλθε διὰ **στομάτων** (an elegy by Theognis 15–18)
          *Μοῦσαι -ῶν αἱ: Muses
          Χάριτες -ων αἱ: Graces
          κούρη -ης ἡ = κορή -ῆς ἡ
          Κάδμος -ου ὁ: Cadmus
          *ἐς = εἰς
          *ἀείδω: sing
          *ἔπος -ους τό: word
          ὅττι = ὅ τι
          *στόμα -ατος τό: mouth

Review Exercise 2A

a. Common independent uses of the subjunctive: hortatory, prohibitive, deliberative (*Essentials* §§147–49)

1. ποῖ **τῆς γῆς** ἴωμεν; ποῖ τρεπώμεθα; οὐδαμοῦ γὰρ τὴν **σωτηρίαν** ἡμῖν ὁρῶ.
   τῆς γῆς: partitive gen. (*Essentials* §93)
   *σωτηρία -ας ἡ: safety, deliverance
2. αὐτίκα δὲ χωρῶμεν εἰς Ἀγάθωνος.
3. νῦν δ᾽ αὖ **ἀναλάβωμεν** τὰ πρῶτα λεχθέντα, δι᾽ ἃ δεῦρ᾽ ἥκομεν ἄρτι.
   ἀναλαμβάνω: take up; i.e., reconsider
4. τί διανοῶμαι πάντων περὶ ἐμὲ μαινομένων;
5. μὴ φοβηθῆτε τοῦτον τὸν κακοδαίμονα μηδαμῶς.
6. δειπνῶμεν καὶ διαλεγώμεθα σὺν τοῖς δικαίοις.
7. μήποτε λάβῃς γυναῖκας εἰς **συμβουλίαν**. (Menander SECB 486)
   συμβουλία -ας ἡ: counsel
8. οὕτω φῶμεν ἢ ἄλλως σοι δοκεῖ;
9. τί εἴπω; πῶς ἄρχωμαι λέγων καὶ πότε παύσωμαι; ἐν γὰρ τοιούτοις οὐδεὶς ἔχει
   λέγειν ἱκανῶς.
10. μήτε τὸν μαινόμενον μήτε τὸν γέλοιον μηδαμῶς ἐλεήσῃς. τὴν γὰρ **αἰσχύνην** ἰδεῖν
    οὐχ οἷοί τ᾽ εἰσιν.
    *αἰσχύνη -ης ἡ: disgrace, shame
11. μὴ κατακλιθῇς παρὰ τοὺς **φαύλους**.
    *φαῦλος -η -ον: worthless
12. οὔπω δῆλον, ἦν δ᾽ ἐγώ, ἀλλὰ σκεπτώμεθα εἰ ἀληθῆ ἄρτι ἔλεγες.
13. σκοπῶμεν δὴ καὶ κρινῶμεν τόν τε **ἡδονῆς** καὶ τὸν **φρονήσεως** βίον ἰδόντες χωρίς.
    *ἡδονή -ῆς ἡ: pleasure
    *φρόνησις -εως ἡ: mind, thought
14. μὴ **Πλοῦτον** εἴπῃς· **οὐχὶ** θαυμάζω θεὸν
    ὃν **χὠ** κάκιστος ῥᾳδίως **ἐκτήσατο**. (Euripides, frag. 20.1–2 Nauck)
    *Πλοῦτος -ου ὁ: Wealth
    *οὐχί = οὐ
    χὠ = καὶ ὁ
    ἐκτήσατο: acquires (gnomic aor. [*Essentials* §145], from *κτάομαι: acquire)

15. νῦν μὲν **πίνοντες τερπώμεθα**, καλὰ λέγοντες.
    ἄσσα δ' ἔπειτα ἔσται, ταῦτα **θεοῖσι μέλει**. (Theognis 1047–48)
    *πίνω: drink
    τέρπομαι: enjoy, take pleasure
    ἄσσα = ἄττα = ἄτινα
    θεοῖσι = θεοῖς
    *μέλει: are a concern to *dat.*

b. Common dependent uses of the subjunctive: ἄν in generalizing or indefinite clauses, in purpose clauses, in fear (for the future) clauses (*Essentials* §§152–54)

1. γελᾷ δ' ὁ **μῶρος, κἄν** τι μὴ γέλοιον ᾖ. (Menander SECB 165)
   μῶρος -α -ον: foolish
   κἄν = καὶ ἐάν
2. ἡμεῖς ἄρα ἴωμεν εἰς Ἀγάθωνος ὅπως δειπνήσωμεν αὐτοῦ σὺν τοῖς ἑταίροις
   διαλεγόμενοι καὶ κατακείμενοι.
3. πολλάκις ὁ Σωκράτης ἀποστὰς ὅποι ἂν τύχῃ αὐτόθι ἕστηκεν καὶ οὔ τι κινεῖται.
4. φοβούμεθα μὴ οἱ πολέμιοι ἡμᾶς οὐκ ἐλεήσωσιν.
5. αὐτόθι μενοῦμεν ἕως ἂν Σωκράτης ἀφίκηται σὺν τοῖς ἄλλοις.
6. ἐνθάδε μένωμεν ἕως ἂν οἱ ἄλλοι **ἔνδον** δείπνωσιν.
   *ἔνδον *adv.*: within
7. τὸν **εὐτυχεῖν** δοκοῦντα μὴ **ζήλου**, πρὶν ἂν **θανόντ'** ἴδῃς. (Euripides, *Herakleidae* 865–66)
   εὐτυγχάνω: fare well
   *ζηλόω: envy
   θανόντ' = ἀποθανόντα
8. ἐπειδὰν πυθώμεθα τὰ γεγενημένα, αὐτίκα ὑμῖν ἀγγελοῦμεν.
9. [ἐγὼ] εἶπον **μηδένα** τῶν ὄπισθεν κινεῖσθαι πρὶν ἂν ὁ πρόσθεν ἡγῆται. (military instruc-
   tions reported by the general who gave them, Xenophon, *Cyropaedia* 2.2.8)
   μηδένα: what does μηδένα rather than οὐδένα imply?
10. φοβοῦμαι μὴ δεῦρ' ἀφίκωνται οἱ πολέμιοι αὐτίκα.
11. μὴ κρίνετε, ἵνα μὴ κριθῆτε· ἐν ᾧ γὰρ **κρίματι** κρίνετε κριθήσεσθε, καὶ ἐν ᾧ μέτρῳ
    μετρεῖτε μετρηθήσεται ὑμῖν. (Matthew 7.1–2)
    κρίμα -ατος τό: judgment
    *μετρέω: measure
    μετρηθήσεται *impers.*: there will be a measuring
12. ὅπως ἂν σὺ κελεύῃς, οὕτως ποιήσω αὐτίκα.
13. ἡ μήτηρ φοβεῖται μὴ ὁ ἄθλιος υἱὸς ἀποθάνῃ πρὸ τῆς πόλεως ἐν τῇδε τῇ μάχῃ.
14. οὐδαμοῦ ὁ **χρηστὸς** χωρὶς σοφίας γενήσεται, ὅπου ἂν σκοπῇς.
    *χρηστός -ή -όν: good, worthy
15. μὴ τοὺς δίκῃ νικῶντας **ἐξωθῶμεν** ἵνα τοὺς ὄπισθεν εἰς τὸ πρόσθεν ἄγωμεν.
    ἐξωθέω: push aside

16. ὅταν μὲν ἄνευ νοῦ **θαρρῇ** ἄνθρωπος, βλάπτεται, ὅταν δὲ σὺν νῷ, ὠφελεῖται.
     *θαρρέω: be bold, be brave

17. καὶ τοίνυν, ἐὰν δύνωμαι, πάντα ὡς σαφέστατα διηγεῖσθαι πειράσομαι.

18. βασιλεὺς **αἱρεῖται** οὐχ ἵνα ἑαυτοῦ καλῶς ἐπιμελῆται, ἀλλ᾽ ἵνα οἱ ἑλόμενοι δι᾽ αὐτὸν
     εὖ πράττωσι. (Xenophon, *Memorabilia* 3.2.3)
          αἱρεῖται *pass.*: is chosen

19. χρὴ ὑμᾶς, ὦ ἄνδρες δικασταί, **εὐλαβεῖσθαι** μὴ ὑπὸ τούτου **ἐξαπατηθῆτε** ὡς δεινοῦ
     ὄντος λέγειν.
          *εὐλαβέομαι: take care, be cautious
          *ἐξαπατάω: deceive

c. Verb drills: λέγω and ἄγω

After reviewing the principal parts of these two verbs, translate or identify fully each of the
following verb forms (space is provided for both). A parenthetical (2) indicates an ambiguous
form, with two possible identifications/distinct translations.

1. εἶπε   _3rd sg. aor. act._   _aor. 2nd s. imp. act._

2. εἰπέ   _aor 2nd s. imp. act._   _____

3. ἐρεῖ   _____   _____

4. εἴρηκε   _____   _____

5. ἐρρήθη   _3 sg. aor. passive_   _____

6. ἔλεγεν   _____   _____

7. λεγέτω   _____   _____

8. ἐλέχθησαν   _____   _____

9. ἐρῶ   _____   _____

10. λέγομεν   _____   _____

11. εἴπομεν   _____   _____

12. εἴρηται (pass.) _____   _____

13. λέξασα   _____   _____

14. λέξων   _____   _____

15. ἄγε   _____   _____

16. ἄξετε   _____   _____

17. ἠγάγετε   *2nd pl. aor. act.*   _____

18. ἀχθείς   *aor. pass. part.*   _____

19. ἤχθησαν   _____   _____

20. ἄγεσθαι (2)   _____   _____

        _____   _____

21. ἄγειν   _____   _____

22. ἀγαγεῖν   *aor. act. if*   _____

23. ἤγετε   _____   _____

24. ἄγετε (2)   _____   _____

        _____   _____

d. Sight-reading: an edifying tale from Aesop

ἀνθρώπων ἕκαστος δύο **πήρας** φέρει, τὴν μὲν **ἔμπροσθεν**, τὴν δὲ ὄπισθεν, **γέμει** δὲ κακῶν **ἑκατέρα**· ἀλλ᾽ ἡ μὲν ἔμπροσθεν **ἀλλοτρίων** γέμει, ἡ δ᾽ ὄπισθεν τῶν αὐτοῦ τοῦ φέροντος. καὶ διὰ τοῦτο οἱ ἄνθρωποι τὰ μὲν ἐξ αὐτῶν κακὰ οὐχ ὁρῶσι, τὰ δὲ **ἀλλότρια** πάνυ **ἀκριβῶς θεῶνται**.

> πήρα -ας ἡ: sack
> *ἔμπροσθεν = πρόσθεν
> γέμω: be full of *gen.*, be loaded with *gen.*
> *ἑκάτερος -α -ον: each [of two]
> *ἀλλότριος -α -ον: another's
> *ἀκριβής -ές: accurate
> *θεάομαι: behold

e. Challenge passages

Neoptolemos to Philoctetes after persuading him to leave the island and cave that he has inhabited for the entire Trojan War (Sophocles, Philoctetes *645–46)*

ἀλλ᾿ εἰ δοκεῖ, χωρῶμεν, ἐνδόθεν λαβὼν
ὅτου σε **χρεία** καὶ **πόθος** μάλιστ᾿ ἔχει.
   *ὅτου = οὗτινος
   *χρεία -ας ἡ: need
   *πόθος -ου ὁ: desire, longing

Philoctetes to Neoptolemos (Sophocles, Philoctetes *635–36)*

ἀλλ᾿, ὦ **τέκνον**, χωρῶμεν, ὡς ἡμᾶς πολὺ
πέλαγος ὁρίζῃ τῆς Ὀδυσσέως νεώς.
   *τέκνον -ου τό: child
   *πέλαγος -ους τό: sea
   ὁρίζω: separate or divide *acc.* from *gen.*

Socrates to Anytus, who has just accused the sophists of corrupting the young (adapted from Plato, Meno *92a)*

πότερον δὴ οὖν φῶμεν κατὰ τὸν σὸν λόγον εἰδότας τούτους **ἐξαπατᾶν** καὶ διαφθείρειν τοὺς νέους, ἢ λεληθέναι καὶ ἑαυτούς; καὶ οὕτω μαίνεσθαι οἰόμεθα τούτους, οὓς ἔνιοί φασι σοφωτάτους ἀνθρώπων εἶναι;
   *ἐξαπατάω: deceive

Review Exercise 2B

a. Sight-reading: ancient quotations on wine, water, and drinking

Menander (SECB 26)

ἀνδρῶν δὲ φαύλων **ὄρκον** εἰς ὕδωρ γράφε.
  *ὄρκος -ου ὁ: oath

Pindar (Olympian *1*)

ἄριστον μὲν ὕδωρ

The philosophy of Epicurus, as presented by Christian critics (1 Corinthians 15.32)

φάγωμεν καὶ πίωμεν· **αὔριον** γὰρ ἀποθνῄσκομεν.
  *αὔριον: tomorrow

b. Optative replacing subjunctive in secondary sequence: purpose clauses, fear clauses, generalizations about the past (*Essentials* §159)

1. καὶ μὴν ἐβουλόμην παρὰ Ἀριστοφάνην κατακεῖσθαι ἵνα πολλὰ γέλοια ἀκούοιμι.
2. αἱ οὖν **θεώμεναι** παντάπασιν ἐφοβοῦντο μὴ οἱ πολέμιοι τὴν πόλιν κενὴν ἀνδρῶν λίποιεν.
  *θεάομαι: watch
3. ὅποι ὁ στρατηγὸς ἔλθοι, τὰς οἰκίας κενὰς καὶ λειφθέντας ηὗρεν.
4. χθὲς ἐζητοῦμεν σε ἵνα ἐπὶ δεῖπνον καλέσαιμεν, ἀλλ' οὐχ οἷοί τ' ἦμεν οὐδαμοῦ σε εὑρεῖν.
5. ὅσοι δὲ τὸ ὕδωρ ἐκ τοῦ τῆς **Λήθης** ποταμοῦ πίοιεν **ἐπελάθοντο** πάντων.
  Λήθη -ης ἡ: Forgetfulness, Lethe, the river of forgetfulness in the Underworld
  *ἐπιλανθάνομαι: forget
6. τοιαῦτα δ' ἐκ τοῦ **μάντεως** ἀκούσας ἐκεῖνος ἐφοβήθη μὴ ἡ μήτηρ ἀποθάνοι τῇ ὑστεραίᾳ.
  *μάντις -εως ὁ: prophet

7. ἔνιοι δὲ διηγοῦντο ὅσα τε καὶ οἷα πάθοιεν καὶ ἴδοιεν ἐν τῇ ὑπὸ τῆς γῆς **πορείᾳ**.

    πορεία -ας ἡ: journey (cf. πορεύομαι)

8. ἔλεγε τοὺς μὲν ἄλλους ἀνθρώπους **ζῆν** ἵν᾽ ἐσθίοιεν· αὐτὸς δὲ ἐσθίειν ἵνα ζῷη.

    (Diogenes Laertius about Socrates)

    ζῆν *irreg. inf. of* *ζάω: live

9. ὁπότε πρὸς τὸν πότον τρέποιντο, οὗτοι οἱ φαῦλοι ἀεὶ σφόδρα ἔπινον.

10. ὅποι τὸ ὕδωρ μὲν ῥέοι, πλήρης **παντοίων ἄνθων** ἦν ἡ γῆ. ὅποι δὲ μή, κενὴ **δένδρων**

    τε καὶ **φυτῶν**.

        *παντοῖος -α -ον: of all sorts

        *ἄνθος -ους τό: bloom

        *δένδρον -ου τό: tree

        *φυτόν -οῦ τό: plant

11. αὐτόθι δ᾽ ἡ στρατιὰ ἔμενεν ἕως ὁ στρατηγὸς ἀφίκοιτο σὺν **βοηθείᾳ**.

    *βοήθεια -ας ἡ: help, assistance, auxiliary troop

12. οἱ Ἀθηναῖοι ἔπειθον αὐτοὺς μὴ ποιεῖσθαι μάχην πρὶν οἱ σύμμαχοι παραγένοιντο.

13. ἐφοβούμην ἄρα μὴ **πλοῦτος** χωρὶς σοφίας τοὺς κακοδαίμονας οὐκ ὠφελοίη.

    *πλοῦτος -ου ὁ: wealth

c. Optative in indirect statements and questions in secondary sequence (*Essentials* §158)

1. ἠρόμην αὐτὸν ὅποι ἴοι οὕτω καλὸς γεγενημένος.

2. Σωκράτης πολλάκις ἔλεγεν ὅτι ἐρωτικώτατος ἀνθρώπων εἴη.

3. ὁ Ἀριστόδημος εἶπεν ὅτι οὐδαμοῦ ὁρῴη Σωκράτη ὄπισθεν ἑπόμενον.

4. ἐκείνῃ τῇ ἡμέρᾳ ἠγγέλθη ἐν τῇ ἐκκλησίᾳ ὅτι νενικημένοι εἶεν οἱ Λακεδαιμόνιοι καὶ

    ὁ βασιλεὺς τεθναίη.

5. οὐχ οἷοί τ᾽ ἦμεν κρῖναι ὁπότερος **τούτοιν τοῖν παρόντοιν** εἴη δυνατώτερος ᾄδειν.

    οὕτω γὰρ καλῶς ἀμφότεροι ᾖδον.

        τούτοιν τοῖν παρόντοιν: gen. masc. dual

6. ἐρωτηθεὶς ποῦ **τῆς Ἑλλάδος** ἴδοι ἀγαθοὺς ἄνδρας, "ἄνδρας μέν," εἶπεν, "οὐδαμοῦ,

    παῖδας δ᾽ ἐν **Λακεδαίμονι**." (Diogenes Laertius about Diogenes the Cynic)

        τῆς Ἑλλάδος: partitive gen. (*Essentials* §93) from Ἑλλάς -άδος ἡ: Greece, Hellas

        Λακεδαίμων -ονος ἡ: Lakedaimonia, Sparta

7. ὁ ἄνθρωπος εἶπεν ὅτι γέλοιόν τι πρῴην πάθοι.

8. εἰσελθὼν εἰς τοῦ Ἀγάθωνος ὁ Σωκράτης αὐτίκ᾽ ἤρετο ὅπου οἱ ἄλλοι δειπνοῦντες

    κατακλίνοιντο.

9. οἱ ἑταῖροι τὸν Σωκράτη ἤροντο ὅπου κατακεῖσθαι βούλοιτο.

10. πρὸς τὸν πυθόμενον τί πρότερον γεγόνοι, νὺξ ἢ ἡμέρα, "ἡ νύξ," ἔφη, "**μία** ἡμέρᾳ

    πρότερον." (Diogenes Laertius about Thales, the first so-called pre-Socratic philosopher)

        *μία: one

11. ἠρώτησέ τις αὐτὸν εἰ λήθοι θεοὺς ἄνθρωπος ἀδικῶν· "ἀλλ᾽ οὐδὲ διανοούμενος,"
    ἔφη. (Diogenes Laertius about Thales)
12. ἐρωτηθεὶς ποῖον **οἶνον** ἡδέως πίνοι, ἔφη "τὸν **ἀλλότριον**." (Diogenes Laertius about
    Diogenes the Cynic)
        *οἶνος -ου ὁ: wine
        *ἀλλότριος -α -ον: another's

d. Independent uses of the optative: wishes, potential optative (*Essentials* §§155–56)

1. τίς δικαίως ἂν τοιοῦτον ἐλεήσειε;
2. σφόδρα μεθύοντα ἄνδρα **δέξαισθε** ἂν συμπότην, ἢ ἀπίω;
       *δέχομαι: receive, welcome
3. εἰ γὰρ ἡ **κύλιξ** αὖθις τοῦ οἴνου πληρωθείη.
       κύλιξ -ικος ἡ: kylix, drinking cup
4. ὁ καλῶς ἄρα **πεπαιδευμένος** ᾄδειν τε καὶ **ὀρχεῖσθαι** δυνατὸς ἂν εἴη καλῶς. οὐχ
   ὁμολογοίης ἄν;
       *παιδεύω: educate
       *ὀρχέομαι: dance
5. ψευδεῖς μάρτυρες ἀπόλοιντο.
6. μήποτε γενοίμην γέλοιος τοῖς ἐχθροῖς.
7. οἱ δικασταί μ᾽ ἐλεήσειαν καὶ **ἀποψηφίσαιντο**.
       ἀποψηφίζομαι: vote to acquit

e. Verb drills: πίνω and ἐσθίω

After reviewing the principal parts of these two verbs, translate or identify fully each of the following verb forms (space is provided for both). A parenthetical (2) indicates an ambiguous form, with two possible identifications/distinct translations.

1. ἐπίομεν   _____

2. πιόμεθα   _____

3. ἐπίνομεν   _____

4. πίνωμεν   _____

5. τί πίω;   _____

6. τί ποθῇ;

7. πεπώκαμεν

8. πέποται (pass.)

9. ἐπέποτο (pass.)

10. ποθήτω

11. ποθήσεται

12. πινέτω

13. ἐδόμεθα

14. ἐφάγομεν

15. φάγωμεν

16. ἠσθίομεν

17. ἐσθίομεν

18. ἐσθίετε (2)

19. ἐδηδόκατε

20. φάγοιτε

21. ἐσθίουσα

22. φαγών

23. φάγε

24. ἐδήδεσται (2)

Review Exercise 2C

a. Indicative + ἄν (*Essentials* §162)

1. εἰ ἡ σοφία ἐκ τοῦ πληρεστέρου εἰς τὸ κενώτερον ἡμῶν ῥᾶον ῥεῖν ἐδύνατο, πάντες ἐβουλόμεθα ἂν κατακεῖσθαι παρὰ Σωκράτη.
2. εἰ μὴ σοφόν τι ηὗρες, οὔπω ἂν ἐπαύσω ζητῶν.
3. εἰ μὴ χθὲς ἔγωγε σφόδρα ἔπιον, τήμερον ἡδόμην ἂν μᾶλλον τοῦτον τὸν οἶνον πίνων.
4. εἰ δ᾽ ὁ ἔρως ἐποίει τοὺς ἀνθρώπους δυνατέρους λέγειν, οἷοί τ᾽ ἦμεν ῥᾶον ἂν ἐγκωμιάζειν.
5. πλέων οἶνος πρῴην ἂν ἐπόθη, εἰ δυνατώτεροι πίνειν ἦμεν.
6. εἰ δ᾽ ἐμεμνήμην, ἄν ὑμῖν ἔλεγον.
7. εἰ χεῖρας εἶχον οἱ ἵπποι, ὁμοίας ἵπποις ἂν θεῶν **ἰδέας** ἐποίουν. (Xenophanes of Colophon, adapted)
   ἰδέα -ας ἡ: image, form, shape
8. θεῶν μὴ σωσάντων ἀπεθάνομεν ἂν ἐν τῇδε τῇ μάχῃ.
9. ὀφθεὶς ὑπὸ τοῦ ἐμοῦ πατρὸς ἂν ᾐσχυνήθην.
10. ἐρωτηθεὶς τοιαῦτα, τί ἂν εἶπες;
11. οὐκ οἶδα περὶ ὧν πυνθάνεσθε· ἡδέως γὰρ ἔλεγον ἄν.
12. εἰ δ᾽ οἱ πολέμιοι τὴν πόλιν εἷλον, αἱ ἔνδον ἂν εἰς **δούλειαν** ἤχθησαν.
    δούλεια -ας ἡ: slavery

b. Subjunctive + ἄν (*Essentials* §160)

1. **ἢν ἐγγὺς** ἔλθῃ θάνατος, οὐδεὶς βούλεται **θνῄσκειν**. (Euripides, *Alcestis* 671–72)
   *ἢν = ἐάν
   *ἐγγύς: near
   *θνῄσκω = ἀποθνῄσκω
2. ἐὰν δ᾽ ἔχωμεν χρήμαθ᾽, ἕξομεν φίλους. (Menander SECB 238)
3. ὅποι ἂν ἔλθωμεν, ἀγγελῶμεν τοὺς λόγους ἐκείνου.
4. ὅποι ἂν ἔλθωμεν, ἀγγελοῦμεν τοὺς λόγους ἐκείνου.
5. ἀνὴρ μὲν ὅταν τοῖς ἔνδον ἄχθηται συνών, **ἔξω** ἰέναι δύναται· ἡμῖν δ᾽ **ἀνάγκη** πρὸς μίαν **ψυχὴν βλέπειν**. (Medea's lament, adapted)

*ἔξω: outside

*ἀνάγκη + *dat.* + *inf.*: it is necessary for *dat.* to ——

*ψυχή -ῆς ἡ: soul; *here essentially*: person

*βλέπω: look

6. τῷ ἀνδρὶ ὃν ἂν ἕλησθε πείσομαι. (Xenophon, *Anabasis* 1.3.15)

7. ἐκεῖνος ὁ φαῦλος αὐτόθι κατακείσεται ἕως ἂν ἡ **κύλιξ** οἴνου πληρῶται.

　　κύλιξ -ικος ἡ: kylix, drinking cup

8. πίνωμεν ἕως ἂν ὁ **κρατὴρ** κενὸς γένηται.

　　κρατήρ -ῆρος ὁ: krater, mixing bowl

9. ὅποι ἂν ἴῃς μέμνησο ἡμῶν.

10. ἀρετὴ δὲ **κἂν θάνῃ** τις οὐκ ἀπόλλυται.

　　ζῇ δ᾽ οὐκέτι ὄντος **σώματος**. (Euripides, frag. 734.1–2 Nauck)

　　κἂν = καὶ ἐάν

　　*θάνῃ = ἀποθάνῃ

　　ζῇ *pres. act. indic. 3rd pers. sing. of* *ζάω: live

　　*σῶμα -ατος τό: body

11. μὴ ἀπέλθητε πρὶν ἂν ἀκούσητε τὰ τοῖς ἔνδον βεβουλευμένα.

12. ὁπότερ᾽ ἂν ποιῶμεν, ἐκεῖνος ἔσται δυνατὸς ῥᾷστα ποιεῖν.

13. ἃ δ᾽ ἂν διδῶσ᾽ ἑκόντες, ὠφελούμεθα. (Euripides, *Ion* 380 -οἱ θεοί is the subj. of διδῶσ᾽)

14. καίπερ κληθεὶς εἰς τοῦ Ἀγάθωνος οὐκ εἶμι πρὶν ἂν καὶ σὺ ἐθέλῃς ὄπισθεν ἕπεσθαι.

15. **ἢν** πόλεμον αἱρῆσθε, μηκέτι ἥκετε δεῦρο ἄνευ **ὅπλων**.

　　*ἢν = ἐάν

　　*τὰ ὅπλα: weapons

16. ἃ δ᾽ ἂν ἑκὼν ἑκόντι ὁμολογήσῃ, φασὶν οἱ τῆς ἡμετέρας πόλεως νόμοι δίκαια εἶναι.

c. Optative + ἄν (*Essentials* §161)

1. τί γὰρ γένοιτ᾽ ἂν **ἕλκος** μεῖζον ἢ φίλος κακός; (Sophocles, *Antigone* 653)

　　ἕλκος -ους τό: wound

2. οὐ συμφαίης ἂν **λύπην** ἐνάντιον ἡδονῇ;

　　*λύπη -ης ἡ: pain, suffering

3. τῷ δ᾽ ὄντι ὠφελοίη ἂν ἐμέ τε καὶ τοὺς ἄλλους τούσδε, εἰ ὑμεῖς οἱ δυνατώτατοι πίνειν οὐ μέλλετε πίεσθαι.

4. τί δ᾽ ἂν φοβοίμην ᾧ **θανεῖν** οὐ **μόρσιμον**; (Prometheus in Aeschylus's *Prometheus Bound* 933)

　　*θανεῖν = ἀποθανεῖν

　　μόρσιμος -ον: fated

5. οὐδεὶς ἐναντία σοι φαίη ἄν, ἀλλ᾽ πάντες που συνφαῖμεν ἄν, εἰ συμβουλεύοις ἡμῖν μὴ πίνειν ἀμετρίως. ἢ ἀντιλέγεις;

6. οὐδεὶς ἑκὼν τὰ φαῦλα καὶ γιγνώσκων **προὔλοιτο** ἄν.

　　προὔλοιτο = προ + ἕλοιτο

7. θεῶν διδόντων οὐκ ἂν **ἐκφύγοις** κακά. (Eteocles in Aeschylus, *Seven against Thebes* 719)
    ἐκφεύγω = ἐκ + φεύγω

8. εἰ τοὺς ἀδικηθέντας, πάτερ, φευξόμεθα, τίσιν ἂν **βοηθήσαιμεν** ἄλλοις ῥαδίως;
    (Menander, frag. 283.1–2 Kock)
    *βοηθέω: help, to aid *dat.*

9. ἐγὼ ἄρα σοι ἡδέως διαλεγοίμην ἄν, ἡγούμενός σε βέλτιστ᾽ ἂν σκοπεῖσθαι ἄλλως τε
    καὶ περὶ ἀρετῆς.

10. οὐδεὶς ἂν τῶν **καλῶν κἀγαθῶν Περσῶν** ἑκὼν ὀφθείη **πεζὸς** ἰών.
    καλῶν κἀγαθῶν: noble, upper-class
    Περσαί -ῶν οἱ: Persians
    *πεζός -ή -όν: on foot, pedestrian

d. Challenge passages: mixed constructions

Prayer to Pan (Plato, Phaedrus 279b–c)

Ὦ φίλε Πάν τε καὶ ἄλλοι ὅσοι **τῇδε** θεοί, δοίητέ μοι καλῷ γενέσθαι **τἄνδοθεν**· ἔξωθεν
δὲ ὅσα ἔχω, τοῖς **ἐντὸς** εἶναί μοι φίλια. πλούσιον δὲ νομίζοιμι τὸν σοφόν· τὸ δὲ **χρυσοῦ
πλῆθος** εἴη μοι ὅσον μήτε φέρειν μήτε ἄγειν δύναιτο ἄλλος ἢ ὁ σώφρων.
    τῇδε: in this place, here
    τἄνδοθεν = τὰ ἔνδοθεν: the parts within; i.e., heart and mind, soul
    ἔξωθεν: outside, external
    *ἐντός: inside
    *χρυσός -οῦ ὁ: gold
    *πλῆθος -ους τό: quantity, amount

Socrates to Alcibiades (adapted from pseudo-Plato, Alcibiades 1.105e)

νεωτέρῳ μὲν οὖν ὄντι σοι, ὥς ἐμοὶ δοκεῖ, οὐκ εἴα ὁ θεός με διαλέγεσθαι, ἵνα μὴ **μάτην**
διαλεγοίμην. νῦν δ᾽ **ἐφῆκεν**. νῦν γὰρ ἂν μου ἀκούσαις.
    *μάτην *adv.*: in vain, without result
    ἐφίημι: encourage, urge

Sympotic fragment by Anacreon, a lyric poet of the sixth century B.C.E.

φέρ᾽ ὕδωρ, φέρ᾽ οἶνον, ὦ παῖ, φέρε δ᾽ **ἀνθεμόεντας** ἡμῖν
στεφάνους· **ἔνεικον**, ὥς δὴ πρὸς Ἔρωτα **πυκταλίζω**.
    ἀνθεμόεις -εν: blooming
    *στέφανος -ου ὁ: garland, crown
    ἔνεικον = ἐνεγκέ *aor. impera.*
    πυκταλίζω *subju.* + πρός: box against

Democritus, frag. 87 D-K

τὸν φαῦλον **παραφυλάττειν** δεῖ, μὴ **καιροῦ** λάβηται.
      παραφυλάττω: guard against
      *καιρός -οῦ ὁ: critical moment, opportunity

Athenian general Laches talking about Socrates' courage during the Athenians' retreat from Delium, after being routed by the Spartans (Alcibiades also speaks of this later in the Symposium)

ἐν γὰρ τῇ ἀπὸ Δηλίου φύγῃ μετ᾽ ἐμοῦ **συνανεχώρει**, κἀγώ σοι λέγω ὅτι εἰ οἱ ἄλλοι ἤθελον τοιοῦτοι εἶναι, ὀρθὴ ἂν ἡμῶν ἡ πόλις ἦν καῖ οὐκ ἂν ἔπεσε τότε τοιοῦτον **πτῶμα**.
      συναναχωρέω: retreat with
      πτῶμα -ατος τό: misfortune, fall, calamity (cognate acc.; *Essentials* §77)

Tecmessa, wife of Ajax, to their son, when Ajax has gone off to kill himself (Sophocles, Ajax 809–12)

οἴμοι, τί **δράσω**, **τέκνον**; οὐχ **ἰδρυτέον**.
ἀλλ᾽ εἶμι κἀγὼ **κεῖσ᾽** ὅποιπερ ἂν **σθένω**.
χωρῶμεν, **ἐγκονῶμεν**, οὐχ **ἕδρας ἀκμὴ**
σῴζειν **θέλοντας** ἄνδρα γ᾽ ὃς [ἂν] **σπεύδῃ θανεῖν**.
      *οἴμοι: oh me! woe is me!
      *δράω: do
      *τέκνον -ου τό: child
      οὐχ ἰδρυτέον: I must not rest (verbal adj.; *Essentials* §125, §127)
      *κεῖσ᾽ = ἐκεῖσε
      σθένω: be strong enough, be capable of managing
      ἐγκονέω: hurry
      οὐχ ἕδρας ἀκμὴ [ἐστι]: it is not the time for rest for *acc.*
      *θέλω = ἐθέλω
      ὃς [ἂν]: tragedy sometimes dispenses with the ἄν that normally accompanies this
        construction, and apparently did here, though texts vary
      *σπεύδω: hasten, hurry
      *θανεῖν = ἀποθανεῖν

Theognis 498–99

ἄφρονος ἀνδρὸς ὁμῶς καὶ σώφρονος οἶνος ὅταν δὴ
    πίνῃ ὑπὲρ **μέτρον**, **κοῦφον ἔθηκε** νόον.
        *ἄφρων -ον: senseless
        *μέτρον -ου τό: measure, portion
        *κοῦφος -η -ον: light, giddy
        ἔθηκε: gnomic aor.—translate as pres. (*Essentials* §145)

pseudo-Plato, **Alcibiades** *1.107a1–c3 (adapted)*

Σωκράτης: πότερον οὖν, ὅταν περὶ **γραμμάτων** Ἀθηναῖοι βουλεύωνται, πῶς ἂν ὀρθῶς
    γράφοιεν, τότε ἀναστήσῃ αὐτοῖς συμβουλεύσων;
Ἀλκιβιάδης: οὐδαμῶς.
Σωκράτης: ὅταν οὖν περὶ τίνος βουλεύωνται; οὐ γάρ που ὅταν γε περὶ **οἰκοδομίας**.
Ἀλκιβιάδης: οὐ μέντοι.
Σωκράτης: **οἰκοδόμος** γὰρ ταῦτά γε σοῦ βέλτιον συμβουλεύσει.
Ἀλκιβιάδης: ναί.
Σωκράτης: οὐδὲ μὴν ὅταν περὶ **μαντικῆς** βουλεύωνται;
Ἀλκιβιάδης: οὔ.
Σωκράτης: **μάντις** γὰρ αὖ ταῦτα ἄμεινον ἢ σύ.
Ἀλκιβιάδης: ναί.
Σωκράτης: ἐάν τέ γε σμικρὸς ἢ μέγας ᾖ, ἐάν τε καλὸς ἢ αἰσχρός, ἔτι τε **γενναῖος** ἢ
    ἀγεννής.
Ἀλκιβιάδης: πῶς γὰρ οὔ;
Σωκράτης: εἰδότος γὰρ οἶμαι περὶ ἑκάστου ἡ συμβουλή, καὶ οὐ πλουτοῦντος.
Ἀλκιβιάδης: πῶς γὰρ οὔ;
Σωκράτης: ἀλλ᾽ ἐάντε **πένης** ἐάντε πλούσιος ᾖ ὁ **παραινῶν**, οὐδὲν **διοίσει** Ἀθηναίοις
    ὅταν περὶ τῶν ἐν τῇ πόλει βουλεύωνται, πῶς ἂν **ὑγιαίνοιεν**, ἀλλὰ ζητήσουσιν
    ἰατρὸν εἶναι τὸν **σύμβουλον.**
Ἀλκιβιάδης: **εἰκότως** γε.

  *γράμμα -ατος τό: letter, writing
  οἰκοδομία -ας ἡ: house building
  οἰκοδόμος -ου ὁ: house builder
  *μαντική -ῆς ἡ: prophecy
  *μάντις -εως ὁ: seer, prophet
  *γενναῖος -α -ον: noble, wellborn
  ἀγεννής -ές: ignoble
  *πένης -ητος ὁ: poor man, pauper
  *παραινέω: offer advice
  *διαφερω: differ, make a difference, matter
  *ὑγιαίνω: be sound, be healthy
  *ἰατρός -οῦ ὁ: doctor
  σύμβουλος -ου ὁ: adviser, co-counselor
  *εἰκότως *adv.*: probably

e. Verb drills: ὁράω, αἱρέω, and ἔρχομαι

After reviewing the principal parts of these three verbs, translate or identify fully each of the
following verb forms (space is provided for both). A parenthetical (2) indicates an ambiguous
form, with two possible identifications/distinct translations.

1. εἶδες   2nd sg. aor. act.

2. ἰδοῦ   imp.

3. ἑώρακας   2nd sg. perf. act.

4. ὤφθης

5. ὀφθείς

6. ὄψει

7. ὤψαι (2)

8. ὅρα

9. ὁρᾷς

10. ὁρῴης

11. ὁρᾶν

12. ὀφθήσῃ

13. ἴδῃς   subj. pres. aor. 2nd sg. act. aor.

14. ἴδοις   opt. 2nd sg. aor.

15. αἱρεῖν   pres. inf.

16. αἵρει   pres. sg. imp.

17. αἱρεῖται (2) pres. mid/pass. 3rd sg. act.

18. αἱρείτω

19. ἑλεῖν

20. εἷλεν   _aor. 3rd sg. ind_   _____

21. αἱροίη   _____   _____

22. ἑλόμενος   _____   _____

23. αἱρήσων   _____   _____

24. ἑλών   _____   _____

25. ᾑρηκώς   _____   _____

26. ᾕρηκε   _____   _____

27. ᾕρηντο (2)   _____   _____

28. ᾑρέθη   _aor passive 3rd. sg_   _____

29. ἐλήλυθας   _____   _____

30. ἐλεύσεται   _____   _____

31. ἤλθετε   _aor aor. 2nd. pl. ind_   _____

32. εἰληλύθης   _____   _____

Review Exercise 3

Ancient scholion (drinking song)

σύν μοι πῖνε **συνήβα** συνέρα **συστεφανηφόρει**,
σύν μοι μαινομένῳ **μαίνεο**, σὺν σώφρονι **σωφρόνει**.
     συνηβάω: be young together
     συστεφανηφορέω: wear garlands together
     μαίνεο = Attic μαίνου
     σωφρονέω: be moderate, be controlled

a. Common uses of the accusative (*Essentials* §§76–88)

1. τίνα τρόπον ἀποθάνω; βούλομαι γὰρ εὖ τελευτᾶν τὸν βίον.
2. αὐτίκα Ζεὺς διεμηχανήσατο μηχανὴν ᾗ τοὺς ἀνθρώπους ἂν ποιήσειε πολὺ βελτίους.
3. οὐδέ τι σαφῶς ἴσμεν ὅπως ἔσται **τάδε ἔργα**. (Homer, *Iliad* 2.252)
     τάδε ἔργα = τάδε τὰ ἔργα
4. ἆρα τὴν συνουσίαν ἡγῇ ἄρτι γεγονέναι ταύτην, ὥστε καὶ ἐμὲ παραγενέσθαι;
5. σύμφασι γὰρ ὡς ἔπος εἰπεῖν πάντες οἵ τε ἰδιῶται καὶ οἱ ποιηταὶ τὸν Ἔρωτα ἐν τοῖς πρεσβύτατον εἶναι.
6. τοῦτον δ᾽ ἡ κορὴ οὕτως ἠγάπα ὥστε πατέρα τὸν γέροντα ἐκάλει.
7. γυνή τις Σωκράτη τὰ ἐρωτικὰ ἐδίδαξεν.
8. οὐκ ἔστιν οὐδένα τοῦτο μηχανᾶσθαι, ὅπως ἀποφεύξεται θάνατον.
9. ἄπειμι τοινυν· οὔτε γὰρ σὺ **τἄμ᾽** ἔπη
  τολμᾷς **ἐπαινεῖν** οὔτ᾽ ἐγὼ τοὺς σοὺς τρόπους. (Electra's sister to Electra in Sophocles' *Electra* 1050–51)
     τἄμ᾽ = τὰ ἐμά
     *ἐπαινέω: praise
10. ὦ παῖ, τὴν **μορφὴν** μὲν **ἔφυς** καλός, τοὺς τρόπους δὲ κακός.
     *μορφή -ῆς ἡ: shape
     *ἔφυν: be born, be by nature (root aor. of φύω)
11. πολλὰς δ᾽ ἡμέρας μεγάλας **θυσίας** ἐθύομεν τοῦ τὴν πόλιν σωθῆναι χάριν.
     *θυσία -ας ἡ: sacrifice

12. φημὶ ἄνδρα ἀγαθὸν αἰσχύνεσθαι ἄν, νὴ Δία, εἴ τι αἰσχρὸν ποιῶν δῆλος γίγνοιτο ἢ πάσχων ὑπό του δι' ἀνανδρίαν.

13. ἔδει ἕκαστον τὸν Ἔρωτα ὡς κάλλιστον ἐπὶ δεξιὰ ἐγκωμιάζειν.

14. μὴ δ' ἀποκτείνας τὸν Ἕκτορα ὁ Ἀχιλλεὺς οὐκ ἀπέθανεν ἂν ἐν ἀλλοτρίᾳ γῇ.

b. Common uses of the genitive (*Essentials* §§89–105)

1. πρεσβύτατος τῶν τότε ἦν ὁ Νέστωρ, ἔτη γεγονὼς **ἑκάτον**.
   *ἑκάτον *indecl. adj.*: one hundred

2. τὸν Διόνυσον ἑλώμεθα δικάστην τῆς ἡμετέρας σοφίας.

3. ἐπὶ τὸ **ἄκρον** ἀνέβη ὁ ἀνὴρ πρίν τινας αἰσθέσθαι τῶν πολεμίων.
   ἄκρον -ου τό: peak, mountain

4. νὴ Δία, τὴν ψυχὴν σφόδρα πάσχω, ἄτε ἐρῶν **πονηροῦ** παιδός.
   *πονηρός -ή -όν: knavish, wicked

5. οὐδεὶς **θνητῶν** πώποτ' **ἔφυ** πάντα μάκαρ.
   *θνητός -ή -όν: mortal
   *ἔφυν: was born, be by nature (root aor. of φύω)

6. οὐκ ἄγαμαι τὸν τοῦ πλούτου ἐρῶντα. ὁ γὰρ τοῦ πλούτου ἔρως ἐστιν κράτιστός τε καὶ ἥκιστος τῶν **ἐπιθυμιῶν**.
   *ἐπιθυμία -ας ἡ: desire (cf. ἐπιθυμέω)

7. διὰ τὴν τῆς γυναικὸς φιλίαν ὁ Ἄδμητος οὐκ αὐτίκα τελευτήσει.

8. **θέλων** καλῶς ζῆν μὴ τὰ τῶν φαύλων **φρόνει**. (Menander SECB 324)
   *θέλω = ἐθέλω
   *φρόνεω: think about, show consideration toward

9. σοφία πλούτου κτῆμα τιμιώτερον. ψυχῆς οὐδέν ἐστι τιμιώτερον. (Menander SECB 715, 843)

10. ἀλλ' ἡδύ τοι σωθέντα μεμνῆσθαι **πόνων**. (Euripides, *Andromeda*, frag. 133 Nauck)
    *πόνος -ου ὁ: toil, labor, suffering

11. **πενίαν** φέρειν οὐ παντός, ἀλλ' ἀνδρὸς σοφοῦ. (Menander SECB 633)
    *πενία -ας ἡ: poverty

12. τιμωρησάμενοι οὖν οἱ στρατιῶται πάλιν εἰς τὸ **στρατόπεδον** ἀναχώρησαν τῆς νυκτός.
    *στρατόπεδον τό: camp

13. εἴκοσι δραχμῶν **ἐπριάμην** τοῦτον τὸν ἵππον, ἀλλὰ οὐκ ἄξιός ἐστι τοσούτου.
    *ἐπριάμην: I bought

14. πολλοῦ ποιοῦμαι ἀκηκοέναι ἃ ἀκήκοα τοῦ Πρωταγόρου.

15. ἄτε πρεσβύτατος τῶν θεῶν ὤν, ὁ Ἔρως καὶ τιμιώτατός ἐστι.

16. Ἔρως δὲ τῶν θεῶν δικαίως **βασιλεύει**· οὗ γὰρ πάντες ὡς ἔπος εἰπεῖν ἐγένοντο.
    βασιλεύω: be king of, rule

17. ὁ μὲν μέγας ποταμὸς τοῦ **λύματος** πληροῦται, ἡ δὲ μικρὴ **κρηνὴ** ῥεῖ **καθαροῦ** ὕδατος.
    λῦμα -ατος τό: dirt removed by washing, pollution
    *κρηνή -ῆς ἡ: spring
    *καθαρός -ά -όν: pure

18. οὐδεὶς πώποτ᾽ εἰς τοσοῦτ᾽ **ἀναιδείας** ἀφίκετο ὥστε τοσοῦτό τι τολμῆσαι ποιεῖν.
      ἀναιδεία -ας ἡ: shamelessness
19. τῆς μὲν **ἀνδρείας** τὸν νεανίαν ἄγαμαι, τῆς δὲ **σωφροσύνης** τὸν γέροντα.
      *ἀνδρεία -ας ἡ: courage, bravery
      *σωφροσύνη -ης ἡ: moderation, temperance, self-control
20. **ἀνθῶν** στεφάνους φέρε, οὐ **χρυσοῦς**.
      *ἄνθος -ους τό: bloom, flower
      *χρυσοῦς -ῆ -οῦν (contracted from χρύσεος -α -ον): gold, made of gold
21. τὸν μὲν **χείμωνα** πληρεῖς οἱ ποταμοί, τοῦ δὲ **θέρους** πολλάκις **δέουσιν** ὕδατος.
      *χείμων -ωνος ὁ: winter
      *θέρος -ους τό: summer
      δέω: lack, need *gen.*
22. **ζηλῶ** σε τοῦ νοῦ, τῆς δ᾽ ἀνανδρίας μισῶ.
      *ζηλόω: envy
23. ἄρχων ἀγαθὸς οὐδὲν **διαφέρει** πατρὸς ἀγαθοῦ. (Xenophon, *Cyropaedia* 8.1.1)
      *διαφέρω: be different from *gen.*

c. Challenge passages

Theognis 873–76

οἶνε, τὰ μὲν σ᾽ **αἰνῶ**, τὰ δὲ **μέμφομαι**· οὐδέ σε **πάμπαν**
    οὔτε ποτ᾽ **ἐχθαίρειν** οὔτε φιλεῖν δύναμαι.
ἐσθλὸν καὶ κακὸν **ἐσσι**. τίς ἂν σέ γε **μωμήσαιτο**,
    τίς δ᾽ ἂν **ἐπαινήσαι** μέτρον ἔχων **σοφίης**;
                *αἰνέω: praise
                *μέμφομαι: blame
                *πάμπαν = πάνυ
                ἐχθαίρω = μισέω (cf. ἐχθρός)
                *ἐσθλός -ή -όν: noble, good
                ἐσσι = Attic εἶ (from εἰμί)
                μωμάομαι = μέμφομαι
                *ἐπαινέω: praise
                *σοφίη -ης ἡ = Attic σοφία -ας ἡ

Pentheus and Dionysus (Euripides, Bacchae 655–56)

Πε. σοφὸς σοφὸς σύ, πλὴν ἃ δεῖ σ᾽ εἶναι σοφόν.
Δι. ἃ δεῖ μάλιστα, ταῦτ᾽ ἔγωγ᾽ **ἔφυν** σοφός.
                *ἔφυν: was born, be by nature (root aor. of φύω)

Theognis 901–2

ἔστιν ὁ μὲν χείρων, ὁ δ᾽ ἀμείνων ἔργον ἕκαστον·
    οὐδεὶς δ᾽ ἀνθρώπων αὐτὸς ἅπαντα σοφός.

Plato, Laches 194d

ταῦτα ἀγαθὸς ἕκαστος ἡμῶν, ἅπερ σοφός, ἃ δὲ ἀμαθής, ταῦτα δὲ κακός.

Odysseus to Athene (Sophocles, Ajax 125–26)

ὁρῶ γὰρ ἡμᾶς οὐδὲν ὄντας ἄλλο πλὴν
εἴδωλ᾽, ὅσοιπερ ζῶμεν, ἢ **κούφην σκίαν**.
        *εἴδωλον -ου τό: phantom
        *κοῦφος -η -ον: light, insubstantial, fleeting
        σκία -ας ἡ: shadow

The presocratic philosopher Thales is referred to; the stone is apparently the lodestone, which has magnetic properties

τῶν πάλαι φιλοσόφων τις τὸν λίθον ἔφη ψυχὴν ἔχειν ὅτι τὸν **σίδηρον** κινεῖ.
        *σίδηρος -ου ὁ: iron

Er's accounts of the Underworld, upon experiencing a near-death experience (adapted from Plato's "Myth of Er" in Republic 10.621a–b)

αἱ ψυχαὶ ἀφίκοντο, ἤδη **ἑσπέρας** γιγνομένης, παρὰ τὸν τῆς **Λήθης** ποταμόν. μέτρον
μὲν οὖν τι τοῦ ὕδατος πᾶσιν **ἀναγκαῖον** ἦν πιεῖν, οἱ δὲ **φρονήσει** μὴ σῳζομενοι πλέον
ἔπινον τοῦ μέτρου· ὁ δὲ σφόδρα πιὼν πάντων ἐπελανθάνετο.
        *ἑσπέρα -ας ἡ: evening
        Λήθη -ης ἡ: Forgetfulness, Lethe, the river of forgetfulness in the Underworld
        *ἀναγκαῖος -α -ον: necessary
        *φρόνησις -εως ἡ: good sense, judgment

Theognis 1365–66

ὦ παίδων κάλλιστε καὶ **ἱμεροέστατε** πάντων,
        στῆθ᾽ αὐτοῦ καί μου **παῦρ᾽ ἐπάκουσον** ἔπη.
        ἱμεροείς -εσσα -εν: desirable
        παῦρος -α -ον = ὀλίγος -η -ον
        ἐπακούω = ἐπί + ἀκούω: hearken to, heed

Socrates (Apology 32e)

ἆρ᾽ οὖν ἄν με οἴεσθε **τοσάδε** ἔτη **διαγενέσθαι** εἰ ἔπραττον τὰ **δημοσία**, καὶ πράττων ἀξίως ἀνδρὸς ἀγαθοῦ ἐβοήθουν τοῖς δικαίοις καὶ ὥσπερ χρὴ τοῦτο περὶ πλείστου ἐποιούμην;

        τοσόσδε: so many, this many
        διαγίγνομαι: survive
        δημοσία τά: public matters, public business

Review Exercise 4

Theognis 1327–30

ὦ παῖ, ἕως ἂν ἔχῃς λείαν γένυν, οὔποτέ σ᾽ αἰνῶν
  παύσομαι, οὐδ᾽ εἴ μοι μόρσιμόν ἐστι θανεῖν.
σοί τε διδόντ᾽ ἔτι καλόν, ἐμοί τ᾽ οὐκ αἰσχρὸν ἐρῶντι αἰτεῖν.
    λεῖος -α -ον: smooth
    γένυς -υος ἡ: cheek, chin, jaw
    αἰνέω = ἐπαινέω
    μόρσιμος -ον: fated, doomed

Theognis 841–42

οἶνος ἐμοὶ τὰ μὲν ἄλλα χαρίζεται, ἓν δ᾽ ἀχάριστος,
  εὖτ᾽ ἂν θωρήξας μ᾽ ἄνδρα πρὸς ἐχθρὸν ἄγῃ.
    ἀχάριστος -ον: unpleasing
    εὖτε = ὅτε
    θωρήσσω: arm with a breastplate; *metaphorically*: make drunk and belligerent

a. Common uses of the dative (*Essentials* §§106–18)

1. ἐκεῖνος δὲ πολὺν οἶνον ἡμῖν ἔδωκεν ἐπιβουλεύων. ἡμᾶς γὰρ τῷ οἴνῳ βαρεῖς καὶ ἐν
   γῇ κειμένους ἔμελλε βαλεῖν λίθοις.
2. ἐμοί ἐστι τὰ παιδικὰ τῷ ὄντι πονηρὰ ὄντα.
3. βούλομαι δ᾽ ὑμᾶς μεμνῆσθαι τῶν ἐμοὶ πεπραγμένων.
4. ταύτην μὲν τὴν ἡμέραν αὐτοῦ ἔμειναν, τῇ δ᾽ ὑστεραίᾳ ταῖς ναυσὶν ἀπῆλθον.
5. ἐκεῖνος δ᾽ ᾤχετο ἀπιὼν τῆς νυκτός. πάλιν δ᾽ εἰς τὴν πόλιν σπουδῇ μεγάλῃ ἐπορεύετο.
6. οἴει τὸ θανεῖν τῷ ζῆν εἶναί τι ἐναντίον, ὥσπερ τῷ ἐγρηγορέναι τὸ καθεύδειν;
    *ἐγρήγορα: be awake; *perf. forms with pres. meaning*: has awakened, be awake
7. ἤδη μὲν καὶ πρόσθεν, νῦν δὲ πολλῷ ἄμεινον οἶδα ὅτι τοῖς φαύλοις οὐδεμί᾽ ἐστὶ χάρις.
8. μή μοι ἀνὴρ εἴη γλώσσῃ φίλος, ἀλλὰ καὶ ἔργῳ. (Theognis 979–80)
    *γλῶσσα -ης ἡ: tongue
9. οὗτοι οἱ φαῦλοι ὑμῖν ἀληθές γε ὡς ἔπος εἰπεῖν οὐδὲν εἰρήκασιν.

311

10. **μακρῷ** ἀρίστη τῶν ὑφ᾽ ἡλίῳ ἡ Ἄλκηστις, καθὰ Εὐριπίδης εἶπεν.

   *μακρός -ά -όν: far

11. οἱ Ἕλληνες τὸν **Ὀλυμπιάδα** νικήσαντα ἐτίμων **χρυσοῖς** στεφάνοις.

   Ὀλυμπιάδα: at Olympia, at the Olympic games

   *χρυσοῦς -ᾶ -οῦν: golden

12. τῇ μὲν γὰρ γυναικὶ κάλλιον ἔνδον μένειν ἢ **θυραυλεῖν**, τῷ δ᾽ ἀνδρὶ αἴσχιον ἔνδον μένειν ἢ τῶν **ἔξω** ἐπιμελεῖσθαι. (Xenophon, *Oeconomicus* 7.30)

   θυραυλέω: be outside

   *ἔξω *adv.*: outside

13. "τοσούτῳ ἥδιον ζῶ," ὅς δ᾽ ἦ, "ὅσῳ πλείω **κέκτημαι**."

   *κέκτημαι: possess; *perf. with pres. meaning from* κτάομαι: acquire, possess, has acquired

14. τῷ οὖν **τόξῳ** ὄνομα βίος, ἔργον θάνατος. (Heraclitus, frag. 48 D-K)

   τὸ τόξον: bow (important to understanding this passage is that another Greek word for bow is βιός)

15. δοκεῖ τούτῳ διαφέρειν ἀνὴρ τῶν ἄλλων **ζῴων**, τῷ τιμῆς **ὀρέγεσθαι**. (Xenophon, *Hiero* 7.3)

   *ζῷον τό: animal

   ὀρέγομαι + *gen.*: reach for, desire

16. καὶ μὴν τὰ μέν γε χρὴ τέχνῃ **πράσσειν**, τὰ δὲ ἡμῖν ἀνάγκῃ καὶ τύχῃ **προσγίγνεται**. (fragment of an unknown tragedy by Agathon)

   *πράσσω = Attic πράττω

   *προσγίγνομαι + *dat.*: come to, happen to

b. Result clauses (*Essentials* §185)

1. τὸν πάντα λόγον οὐ πάλαι ἤκουσα, ὥστε σαφέστατα εἰπεῖν ὑμῖν νῦν δύναμαι.
2. οὔποτε γὰρ δήπου οὕτως αἰσχρὸς ἂν εἴην ὥστε τολμῆσαι ψεύσασθαι πρὸς τοὺς δικαστάς.
3. τοιοῦτος ἦν ὁ Ἀλκιβιάδης ὥστε ὑπὸ πάντων θαυμάζεσθαι παντάπασιν.
4. θανοῦσα δὲ ὑπὲρ τοῦ ἀνδρὸς Ἄλκηστις ἔργον οὕτω καλὸν ἠργάσατο, ὥστε αὐτῇ ἔδοσαν μεγάλην τίμην οἱ θεοί.
5. τοιοῦτον οὐκ ἔστι ἡ σοφία ὥστε ἐκ ἄλλου εἰς ἄλλον ἡμῶν ῥᾳδίως ῥεῖν.
6. ἐκεῖνος ἄλλους τοσούτῳ **ὑπερεβάλλετο** ὥστε **ἐνάντιος** αὐτῷ οὐδεὶς ἐτόλμα ἐλθεῖν.

   ὑπερβάλλομαι: outdo, surpass

   *ἐνάντιος -α -ον: opposite, against, opposing

c. Common uses of the infinitive (*Essentials* §§179–85)

1. ἔγωγ᾽ οὐκ εἶχον πυθέσθαι οὐδὲν σαφὲς περὶ τῶν ἐρωτικῶν λόγων.
2. τοῖς πολίταις χρὴ ἡμᾶς ἀγγεῖλαι ἃ πεπύσμεθα.

3. τίς οὕτως ἐστὶ δεινὸς λέγειν ὥστε σε πεῖσαι λέγων ὡς ἡμεῖς σοι **ἐπιβουλεύομεν**;
   (Xenophon, *Anabasis* 2.5.15)

   *ἐπιβουλεύω + *dat*.: plot against

4. ἑταῖρος γὰρ Σωκράτους πολλὰ ἔτη ὤν, δικαιότατος εἶ τοὺς λόγους αὐτοῦ
   ἀπαγγέλλειν.

5. οὐδεὶς τῶν παρόντων οὕτω σοφὸς ἦν ὥστε τὴν ἀλήθειαν ἰδεῖν.

6. ὑμᾶς ἐπὶ δεῖπνον καλεῖν μέλλω πρὶν τὸ ἔτος τελευτᾶν.

7. τίς τῶν Ἑλλήνων οὕτως αἰσχρὸς εἴη ἂν ὥστε τὸν ξένον ἀποκτεῖναι ἢ τὴν γυναῖκα
   αὐτοῦ κλέψαι;

8. ὁ δὲ **Σόλων** ὁ ἄριστος τῶν πάλαι ἔφη τὸν μὲν λόγον **εἴδωλον** εἶναι τῶν ἔργων.

   ὁ Σόλων: Solon, an Athenian poet, statesman, and sage (seventh–sixth century
   B.C.E.)

   εἴδωλον τό: phantom, ghost, [mere] image

9. ἄξιον ἀνθρώπους ὄντας ἐπ' ἀνθρώπων **συμφοραῖς** μὴ γελᾶν, ἀλλ' **ὀλοφύρεσθαι**,
   καθάπερ φιλόσοφός τίς ποτε εἶπεν.

   *συμφορά -ᾶς ἡ: mishap, misfortune

   ὀλοφύρομαι: lament

10. πρὸ τοῦ θανεῖν πειράσομαι πάντα σαφῶς ὑμῖν διηγήσασθαι ἅπερ πρῴην ἤκουσα.

11. πότε οἷοί τ' ἐσόμεθα ταῦτα τὰ πράγματα σαφῶς κρῖναι;

12. μέγα κακὸν τὸ μὴ δύνασθαι φέρειν κακόν, καθάπερ ὁ Βίων ὁ σοφὸς πάλαι εἶπεν.

13. ὑμῖν πᾶσιν ἐρῶ ἀληθῶς περὶ τοῦ **μεθύσκεσθαι**.

    μεθύσκομαι: become drunk

14. οὐκοῦν τὸ θύειν **δωρεῖσθαί** ἐστι τοῖς θεοῖς, τὸ δ' εὔχεσθαι αἰτεῖν τοὺς θεούς;
    (Socrates in Plato, *Euthyphro* 14c)

    δωρέομαι: give gift(s)

15. ὁ πατὴρ ἠνάγκασέ με πάντα τὰ **Ὁμήρου ἔπη** μαθεῖν καὶ νῦν δυναίμην ἂν Ἰλιάδα
    ὅλην καὶ Ὀδύσσειαν **ἀπὸ στόματος** εἰπεῖν. (son of the general Nicias in Xenophon,
    Symposium 3.5)

    Ὅμηρος ὁ: Homer, poet of the *Iliad* and *Odyssey*

    *ἔπος τό: word

    ἀπὸ στόματος: i.e., without consulting a text, by heart

16. οὐδὲν γλυκύτερόν ἐστιν ἢ πάντ' εἰδέναι. (Menander, *Arbitrants*, frag. 849–50.2 Kock)

17. σοφοί τινες πάλαι ἔφασαν δεῖν ἕκαστον θνητὸν γνῶναι ἑαυτόν.

18. ἀγαθὸν οὐ τὸ μὴ ἀδικεῖν ἀλλὰ τὸ μηδὲ ἐθέλειν. (Democritus, frag. 62 D-K)

19. ὁ οὖν Ἀγάθων πολλάκις ἐκέλευεν ἡμᾶς μεταπέμψασθαι τὸν Σωκράτη ὄπισθεν
    ἰόντα.

20. φαῦλοι **βροτῶν** γὰρ τοῦ **πονεῖν ἡσσώμενοι**
    θανεῖν ἐρῶσιν. (fragment of an unknown tragedy by Agathon)

    *βροτός -ου ὁ: mortal

    *πονέω: toil, labor, suffer

    ἡσσάομαι = Attic *ἡττάομαι: be overcome by *gen*.

d. Challenge passages

An exchange from Sophocles' tragedy Philoctetes *108–9*

Neoptolemos is Achilles' son and therefore an honest young man; Odysseus is, of course, as cunning as ever. They are trying to get the bow of Heracles away from Philoctetes, so that they can use it to take Troy in accordance with a prophecy. But Philoctetes hates Odysseus and the Greek leadership because they abandoned him wounded on a desert island, so his foul-smelling wound and cries of distress would not bother them any more.

Νεοπτολεμος: οὐκ αἰσχρὸν ἡγεῖ **δῆτα** τὸ ψευδῆ λέγειν;
Ὀδυσσευς: οὐκ εἰ τὸ σωθῆναί γε τὸ ψεῦδος φέρει.

    δῆτα: then (inferential)

A famous epigram by Simonides on the tomb of the dead Spartans at Thermopylae

ξεῖν᾽, ἄγγειλον Λακεδαιμονίοις ὅτι **τῇδε**
   κείμεθα, τοῖς **κείνων ῥήμασι** πειθόμενοι.

    τῇδε: in this place
    κείνων = ἐκείνων
    ῥῆμα -ατος τό: thing said, word, comment

Theognis 1119–22

ἥβης μέτρον ἔχοιμι, φιλοῖ δέ με Ἀπόλλων
   Λητοίδης καὶ Ζεύς ἀθανάτων βασιλεύς,
ὄφρα δίκη ζώοιμι κακῶν **ἔκτοσθεν** ἁπάντων,
   ἥβῃ καὶ πλούτῳ **θυμὸν ἰαινόμενος**.

    *ἥβη -ης ἡ: youth
    Λητοίδης *nom.*: son of Leto
    *ὄφρα = ἵνα
    ἔκτοσθεν: apart from
    *θυμός -οῦ ὁ: heart, spirit
    ἰαινόμαι: delight, please

Euripides, frag. 1029 Nauck (adapted)

οὐκ ἔστιν ἀρετῆς κτῆμα τιμιώτερον·
οὐ γὰρ πέφυκε δοῦλος οὔτε χρημάτων
οὔτ᾽ **εὐγενείας** οὔτε **θωπείας ὄχλου**.
ἀρετὴ δ᾽ ὅσῳ περ μᾶλλον ἂν χρῆσθαι **θέλῃς**
τοσῷδε μείζων **αὔξεται τελουμένη**.

εὐγενεία -ας ἡ: good breeding
θωπεία -ας ἡ: flattery
ὄχλος -ου ὁ: crowd, mob
θέλω = ἐθέλω
τοσόσδε τοσήδε τοσόνδε: so much
αὔξομαι: grow
τελέομαι: come to maturity

Review Exercise 5

a. Common uses of ὡς (*Essentials* §§192–99)

1. ὁ Ὅμηρος ἄριστός τε καὶ θειότατος τῶν ποιητῶν, ὡς οἶμαι.
2. σκοπώμεθα τίνι τρόπῳ ἂν ὡς ῥᾷστα καὶ ἁπλώτατα τοιαύτην μηχανὴν μηχανῷτο.
3. ὡς μέγα τὸ μικρόν ἐστιν ἐν **καιρῷ** δοθέν. (Menander SECB 872)
   καιρός -οῦ ὁ: critical moment, right time
4. εὐθὺς δ᾽ οὖν ἐμὲ ὁ πατὴρ ὡς εἶδεν ὧδ᾽ εἶπεν σφόδρα ὀνειδίζων.
5. ἐξ ἀρχῆς ὑμῖν ὡς ἐκεῖνος διηγεῖτο καὶ ἐγὼ ἐπιχειρήσω διηγήσασθαι.
6. παρασκευασμένοι γάρ εἰσιν, ὡς οἶμαί, ἐρᾶν οἱ ἐντεῦθεν ἀρχόμενοι ὡς τὸν βίον ἅπαντα συνεσόμενοι, ἀλλ᾽ οὐκ ἐξαπατήσαντες, λαβόντες ὡς νέον, καταγελάσαντες οἰχήσεσθαι ἐπ᾽ ἄλλον ἀποτρέχοντες.
7. ὁρᾶτε τὸν τύραννον ὡς ἄπαις γέρων
   φεύγει· **φρονεῖν** δὲ θνητὸν ὄντ᾽ **οὐ χρὴ μέγα**. (Euripides, *Alkmeon in Corinth*, frag. 76 Nauck)
   *φρονέω μέγα: think big, be presumptuous
   οὐ χρὴ: it is necessary . . . not
8. ὡς κἂν φαῦλος ᾖ τἄλλ᾽, εἰς ἔρωτα πᾶς ἀνὴρ σοφώτατος. (Euripides, *Antigone*, frag. 162.2–3 Nauck)
9. ποιητής τις πάλαι εἶπεν ὡς ὁ ἔρως οὐ συνείη τοῖς **γήρως πόνοις**, ἀλλὰ τοῖς **ἥβης** ἄνθεσιν.
   *γῆρας -ως τό: old age
   *πόνος -ου ὁ: toil, suffering
   *ἥβη -ης ἡ: youth
10. καὶ ἅμα ταῦτ᾽ εἰπὼν ἀνέστη ὡς μὴ μέλλοιτο τὰ ἀναγκαῖα.
11. ἐκεῖνοι δ᾽ ἔπεμψαν τὸν κήρυκα ὡς ἀπαγγελοῦντα ὡς οἱ πολέμιοι τῇ πόλει ἐπεχείρουν.
12. οὐδὲν γὰρ ὧδε **ζῷον ἀναιδὲς** εἶναι φιλεῖ ὡς ὁ Ἀλκιβιάδης.
    *ζῷον -ου τό: living creature, animal
    *ἀναιδής -ές: shameless
13. ἀεὶ τὸν ὁμοῖον ἄγει θεὸς ὡς τὸν ὁμοῖον. (Homer, *Odyssey* 17.218)
14. μέμνησο νέος ὢν ὡς γέρων ἔσῃ ποτέ. (Menander SECB 485)
15. ὁρᾷς τὴν τῶν θεῶν δύναμιν, ὡς ῥᾳδίως φιλεῖ ἀπολεῖν θνητοὺς οὑστινασοῦν, μὴ κοσμίους ὄντας. πρὸ τοῦ γὰρ ὡς ἰσχυρὸς καὶ γενναῖος Αἴας ἦν. νῦν δὲ καρποῦται τὰ μεγίστη ὀνείδη καταγελώντων ὧδε τῶν ἐχθρῶν.

b. Verbal adjectives in -τέος (*Essentials* §§125–27)

1. "οὔπω δῆλον," ἦν δ᾽ ἐγώ, "ἀλλ᾽ ὅτι τοῦτο σκεπτέον εἰ ἀληθῆ λέγεις, δῆλον."
2. ἐπαινεῖν μὲν οὖν δεῖ ἀμφοτέρους θεούς, ἃ δ᾽ οὖν ἑκάτερος **εἴληχε** πειρατέον εἰπεῖν.
     εἴληχα *perf. of* *λαγχάνω: obtain by lot
3. ἡμῖν ποτέον, στεφάνους οἰστέον, ἀστέον.
4. μηχανητέον ὅπως ἐκεῖνος ἂν διαφύγῃ.
5. οὐ τὸ ζῆν περὶ πολλοῦ ποιητέον, ἀλλὰ τὸ εὖ ζῆν.
6. ὅστις πατὴρ πρὸς παῖδας ἐκβαίνει πικρός, τὸ **γῆρας** τούτῳ οἰστέον βαρύ.
     *γῆρας -ως τό: old age
7. ἐγὼ γὰρ εἶμι ἐκεῖσ᾽ ὅποι πορευτέον. (Sophocles, *Ajax* 690)
8. ΟΔΥΣΣΕΥΣ: ἡ ὁδὸς πορευτέα.
     ΦΙΛΟΚΤΗΤΗΣ: οὔ φημ᾽.
     ΟΔΥΣΣΕΥΣ: ἐγὼ δὲ φημί· πειστέον τάδε. (Odysseus trying to persuade a very unwilling
     Philoctetes to go to Troy, in Sophocles' *Philoctetes* 993–94)
9. ἀπολογητέον δή, ὦ ἄνδρες Ἀθηναῖοι, καὶ ἐπιχειρητέον ὑμῶν ἐξελέσθαι τὴν
     διαβολὴν ἣν ὑμεῖς ἐν πολλῷ χρόνῳ ἔσχετε ταύτην ἐν οὕτως ὀλίγῳ χρόνῳ. (Plato,
     Apology of Socrates 18e–19a)
     *διαβολή -ῆς ἡ: slander

c. Challenge passages

An epigram by Plato

ἀστέρας εἰσαθρεῖς Ἀστὴρ ἐμός· εἴθε γενοίμην
    οὐρανός, ὡς πολλοῖς **ὄμμασιν** εἰς σὲ βλέπω.
        *ἀστήρ ἀστέρος ὁ: star (also a proper noun in this epigram)
        εἰσαθρέω: look at, gaze upon
        *ὄμμα ὄμματος τό: eye

Anecdote about the presocratic philosopher Thales (adapted from Plato, Theaetetus 174a)

Θαλῆν ἀστρονομοῦντα καὶ ἄνω βλέποντα, πέσοντα εἰς **φρέαρ**, Θρᾷττά τις, δεινὴ
καὶ καλὴ **θεράπαινα** οὖσα, λέγεται καταγελάσαι ὀνειδίζουσα ὡς τὰ μὲν ἐν οὐρανῷ
προθυμοῖτο εἰδέναι, τὰ δ᾽ ὄπισθεν αὐτοῦ καὶ παρὰ πόδας λανθάνοι αὐτόν.
        Θαλῆς -εω ὁ: Thales, an early presocratic philosopher (ca. 585 B.C.E.), one of the
            seven sages of Greece
        ἀστρονομέω: study the stars
        φρέαρ -ατος τό: well
        *θεράπαινα -ης ἡ: female servant

Euripides, frag. 875 Nauck

ὦ **Κύπρις**, ὡς ἡδεῖα καὶ **μοχθηρός** [εἶ].

      Κύπρις -ιδος ἡ: Cypris, another name for Aphrodite

      μοχθηρός -όν: painful, toilsome, rascally

Humiliated and full of shame from the temporary insanity that drove him to slaughter cattle, thinking that they were his enemies, Ajax is mulling over his future (Sophocles, Ajax 470–73)

πεῖρα τις ζητητέα

τοιάδ᾽ ἀφ᾽ ἧς γέροντι δηλώσω πατρὶ

μή τοι φύσιν γ᾽ **ἄσπλαγχνος** ἐκ **κείνου** γεγώς.

αἰσχρὸν γὰρ ἄνδρα τοῦ **μακροῦ χρήιζειν** βίου.

      πεῖρα -ας ἡ: attempt

      τοιόσδε τοιάδε τοιόνδε: of such a kind as this

      ἄσπλαγχνος -ον: gutless, cowardly

      *κείνου = ἐκείνου

      *μακρός -ά -όν: long

      χρήιζω: desire *gen. obj.*

Ajax's famous announcement that he will make peace with his enemies, the sons of Atreus and Odysseus (Sophocles, Ajax 666–68)

τοιγὰρ **τὸ λοιπὸν** εἰσόμεθα μὲν θεοῖς

εἴκειν, μαθησόμεθα δ᾽ **Ἀτρείδας σέβειν**·

ἄρχοντές εἰσιν, ὥσθ᾽ **ὑπεικτέον**, τί μή;

      τὸ λοιπόν: what remains; i.e., the future

      εἴκω: yield to *dat.*

      Ἀτρείδαι -ων οἱ: sons of Atreus

      σέβω: respect, honor

      ὑπείκω: yield

Dialog between Dikaiopolis and Ktesiphon (Aristophanes, Acharnians 394–402)

   Dikaiopolis goes to the house of Euripides to get rags to help him appeal to the Athenians' pity more successfully. Euripides' slave Ktesiphon answers the door and shows himself a master of Euripidean paradox of a Gorgianic type (see reading 7 introduction).

ΔΙΚΑΙΟΠΟΛΙΣ: ὥρα ᾽στὶν ἤδη **καρτερὰν** ψυχὴν λαβεῖν,

   καί μοι **βαδιστέ**᾽ ἐστὶν ὡς Εὐριπίδην.

   παῖ παῖ.

ΚΗΦΙΣΟΦΩΝ: τίς οὗτος;

ΔΙΚΑΙΟΠΟΛΙΣ: ἔνδον ἔστ᾽ Εὐριπίδης;

ΚΗΦΙΣΟΦΩΝ: οὐκ ἔνδον ἔνδον ἐστίν, εἰ **γνώμην** ἔχεις.

ΔΙΚΑΙΟΠΟΛΙΣ: πῶς ἔνδον εἶτ᾽ οὐκ ἔνδον;

ΚΗΦΙΣΟΦΩΝ: ὀρθῶς ὦ γέρον.

ὁ νοῦς μὲν **ἔξω ξυλλέγων ἐπύλλια**
οὐκ ἔνδον, αὐτὸς δ᾽ ἔνδον **ἀναβάδην** ποιεῖ
τραγῳδίαν.

ΔΙΚΑΙΟΠΟΛΙΣ: ὦ **τρισμακάρι᾽** Εὐριπίδη,
ὅθ᾽ ὁ δοῦλος οὑτωσὶ σαφῶς **ἀπεκρίνατο**.

   *καρτερός -ά -όν: brave
   *βαδίζω: go, walk
   *γνώμη -ης ἡ: sense, reason
   *ἔξω adv.: outside
   ξυλλέγω: collect (ξυλ = συλ)
   ἐπύλλιον -ου τό: wordlet, little word (diminutive of ἔπος)
   ἀναβάδην adv.: aloft, on high
   τρισμακάριος -α -ον: thrice-blessed, three times blessed
   *ἀποκρίνομαι: answer

Prayer to Eros (Euripides, Andromeda, frag. 136 Nauck)

σὺ δ᾽ ὦ θεῶν τύραννε κἀνθρώπων Ἔρως,
ἢ μὴ δίδασκε τὰ καλὰ φαίνεσθαι καλά,
ἢ τοῖς ἐρῶσιν **εὐτυχῶς συνεκπόνει**
μοχθοῦσι μόχθους ὧν σὺ δημιουργὸς εἶ.
καὶ ταῦτα μὲν δρῶν τίμιος θνητοῖς ἔσῃ,
μὴ δρῶν δ᾽ **ὑπ᾽ αὐτοῦ τοῦ διδάσκεσθαι φιλεῖν**
ἀφαιρεθήσῃ χάριτας αἷς τιμῶσί σε.

   εὐτυχῶς: successfully
   συνεκπονέω: help dat. to work through
   μοχθέω: suffer
   μόχθος -ου ὁ: toil, hardship, distress
   ὑπ᾽ αὐτοῦ τοῦ διδάσκεσθαι φιλεῖν: by the very fact of their being taught to love

Opening lines of the Hippocratic treatise On Ancient Medicine (rewritten in Attic and slightly adapted)

Περὶ **ἀρχαίας** ἰατρικῆς

ὁπόσοι μὲν ἐπεχείρησαν περὶ ἰατρικῆς λέγειν ἢ γράφειν, **ὑπόθεσιν** αὐτοὶ αὐτοῖς **ὑποθέμενος** τῷ λόγῳ, θερμὸν ἢ ψυχρὸν ἢ ὑγρὸν ἢ ξηρὸν ἢ ἄλλο τι ὃ ἂν ἐθέλωσιν, εἰς βραχὺ ἄγοντες τὴν ἀρχὴν τῆς αἰτίας τοῖς ἀνθρώποις νόσων τε καὶ θανάτου, καὶ πᾶσι τὴν αὐτήν, ἐν ᾗ δύο **ὑποθέμενοι**, ἐν πολλοῖς μὲν καὶ οἷσι λέγουσι **καταφανεῖς** εἰσὶ ἁμαρτάνοντες, μάλιστα δὲ ἄξιον μέμψασθαι, ὅτι [ἁμαρτάνουσιν] **ἀμφὶ** τέχνης οὔσης, ᾗ χρῶνταί τε πάντες ἐπὶ τοῖς μεγίστοις καὶ τιμῶσι μάλιστα τοὺς ἀγαθοὺς **χειροτέχνας** καὶ δημιουργούς. εἰσὶν δὲ δημιουργοὶ οἱ μὲν φαῦλοι, οἱ δὲ πολλὸν διαφέροντες.

   *ἀρχαῖος -α -ον: ancient
   ὑπόθεσις -εως ἡ: fundamental principle
   ὑποτίθημι: lay down
   καταφανής -ές = κατάδηλος
   *ἀμφί *prep.* + *gen.*: concerning
   χειροτέχνης -ου ὁ: artisan, handicraftsman

Praise of Aphrodite (Euripides, frag. 898 Nauck)

τὴν Ἀφροδίτην οὐχ ὁρᾷς ὅση θεός;
ἣν οὐδ᾽ ἂν εἴποις οὐδὲ **μετρήσειας** ἂν
ὅση πέφυκε κἀφ᾽ ὅσον διέρχεται.
αὕτη τρέφει σὲ κἀμὲ καὶ πάντας **βρότους**.
τεκμήριον δέ, μὴ λόγῳ μόνον μάθῃς,
ἔργῳ δὲ δείξω τὸ **σθένος** τὸ τῆς θεοῦ.
ἐρᾷ μὲν **ὄμβρου** γαῖ᾽, ὅταν ξηρὸν **πέδον**
ἄκαρπον αὐχμῷ **νοτίδος ἐνδεῶς** ἔχῃ.
ἐρᾷ δ᾽ ὁ **σεμνὸς** οὐρανὸς πληρούμενος
ὄμβρου πεσεῖν εἰς γαῖαν Ἀφροδίτης ὕπο·
ὅταν δὲ **συμμιχθῆτον** ἐς ταὐτὸν δύο,
φύουσιν ἡμῖν πάντα καὶ τρέφουσ᾽ ἅμα,
δι᾽ ὧν **βρότειον** ζῇ τε καὶ **θάλλει** γένος.

   *μετρέω: measure
   *βρότος -ου ὁ: mortal
   *σθένος -ους τό: strength
   ὄμβρος -ου ὁ: rainstorm
   *πέδον -ου τό: ground
   ἄκαρπος -ον: fruitless
   αὐχμός -ου ὁ: drought
   νοτίς νοτίδος ἡ: moisture
   *ἐνδεής -ές: in need of *gen.*
   *σεμνός -ή -όν: august, grand, holy
   συμμιχθῆτον *aor. pass. subju. dual*: are mixed together
   βρότειος -α -ον *adj.*: mortal
   *θάλλω: bloom

d. Verb drills: πίπτω and φέρω

After reviewing the principal parts of these two verbs, translate or identify fully each of the following verb forms (space is provided for both). A parenthetical (2) indicates an ambiguous form, with two possible identifications/distinct translations.

1. ἔπιπτον (2)   _____   _____

    _____   _____

2. πεσοῦνται   _____   _____

3. πέσοιεν   _____   _____

4. πέσωσι   _____   _____

5. πίπτε   _____   _____

6. πεσεῖν   _____   _____

7. πεπτώκασι   _____   _____

8. πίπτων   _____   _____

9. οἴσομεν   _____   _____

10. ἠνέγκαμεν   _____   _____

11. φερέσθω (2)   _____   _____

    _____   _____

12. ἐνηνόχαμεν   _____   _____

13. ἐνεχθῶμεν   _____   _____

14. ἐνηνέγμεθα (2)   _____   _____

    _____   _____

15. ἐνέγκαι (2)   _____   _____

                        _____   _____

16. ἐφέρομεν   _____   _____

17. ἐφερόμεθα (2)   _____   _____

                        _____   _____

18. φερόμενοι (2)   _____   _____

                        _____   _____

19. φέρωμεν   _____   _____

20. οἴσεσθαι   _____   _____

21. οἰσομένην   _____   _____

22. ἐνέγκοι   _____   _____

23. ἐνεχθεῖεν   _____   _____

24. ἐνήνεχθαι (2)   _____   _____

                        _____   _____

Review Exercise 6

a. Accusative absolute (*Essentials* §177)

1. οὐκ ἐξὸν τοῖς θνητοῖς δὶς ζῆν οὔτ' **ἀνηβᾶν**, καρπώμεθα τὴν ἡμέραν ἡσθέντες τῷ τῆς **ἥβης** ἄνθει.
   ἀνηβάω: be young
   *ἥβη -ης ἡ: youth

2. **θάρσει**, δέον εὖ φέρειν **συμφορὰς** τὸν γενναῖον.
   *θαρσέω: be brave
   συμφορά -ας ἡ: downfall, disaster

3. οὐκ ἄγαμαι τοὺς πλουσίους, ἐξὸν καὶ τῷ κακίστῳ ῥᾷστα κτᾶσθαι τὸν πλοῦτον.

4. δόξαν τῷ δήμῳ ταῖς Μούσαις χάριν δοῦναι, τῇ ὑστεραίᾳ οἱ ἄρχοντες ταύτας τὰς θυσίας ἔθηκαν.

5. οὐ **προσῆκον** τοῖς θνητοῖς εἰδέναι τὰ θεῖα, ἀνδρὸς σώφρονός ἐστι ζητεῖν τὰς ἀνθρωπείας ἐπίστημας.
   προσήκει: it is fitting for *dat.* to ——

6. μετρίως πίνωμεν, οὐκ ὂν σῶφρον σφόδρα μεθύσκεσθαι.

7. θνῄσκω **παρόν** μοι μὴ θανεῖν ὑπὲρ **σέθεν**. (Alcestis to Admetus in Euripides' *Alcestis* 284)
   *πάρεστι: it is possible
   σέθεν = σοῦ

8. ὅστις δὲ **πράσσει** πολλὰ μὴ **πράσσειν** παρόν
   μῶρος, παρὸν ζῆν ἡδέως **ἀπράγμονα**. (Euripides, *Antiope*, frag. 193 Nauck)
   πράσσω = πράττω
   *μῶρος -α -ον: foolish
   ἀπράγμων -ον: without πράγματα, free of trouble, free of serious business

9. αὐτόθεν αὐτίχ' ὁρμᾶτε, οὐκ ἐν γυναιξὶ τοὺς νεανίας δέον ἀλλ' ἐν **σιδήρῳ** κἂν **ὅπλοις** τιμὰς ἔχειν.
   *σίδηρος -ου ὁ: iron
   ὅπλα -ων τά: weapons

10. πολλοὶ ἐν πολέμῳ βοηθήσαντες ἑταίρῳ ἢ **οἰκείῳ τραύματα** ἔλαβον καὶ ἀπέθανον, οἱ δ' οὐ βοηθήσαντες, δέον, ὑγιεῖς ἀπῆλθον. ἢ ἀντιλέγοις ἄν;
    *οἰκεῖος -ου ὁ: relative, family member
    *τραῦμα -ατος τό: wound

b. Fear clauses (*Essentials* §154, §159c)

1. οἱ Ἀθηναῖοι ἐφοβοῦντο μὴ Σωκράτης τοὺς νεανίας διάφθειροι.
2. οἱ Ἀθηναῖοι ἐφοβοῦντο μὴ Σωκράτης τοὺς νεανίας διέφθειρεν.
3. φοβοῦμαι μὴ οὗτος ὁ νεανίας πάντα τὸν οἶνον πίῃ.
4. φοβοῦμαι μὴ οὗτος ὁ νεανίας πάντα τὸν οἶνον ἔπιεν.
5. οἱ ἑταῖροι ἐφοβοῦντο μὴ ἱκανὸν σῖτον οὐχ εὕροιεν.
6. ὁ Ὀδυσσεὺς ἐφοβεῖτο οὐ μὴ ἐν μάχῃ θάνοι ἀλλὰ μὴ ἐν τῇ θαλάττῃ.
7. σκοπῶμεν **κοινῇ**, ὦ 'γαθέ, καὶ μὴ φοβηθῇς μὴ λίπω σε.
   *κοινῇ: in common, together, jointly

c. Numbers trivia (*Essentials* §§70–71)

1. **πόσαι** αἱ Μοῦσαι ἦσαν;
   *πόσοι -αι -α; how many?
2. πόσαι αἱ Χάριτες ἦσαν;
3. πόσαι αἱ Μοῖραι ἦσαν;
4. πόσοι ὀφθαλμοὶ τῷ Κύκλωπι ἦσαν;
5. πόσα σχέλη τῷ ἀρχαίῳ ἀνθρώπῳ ἦσαν, καθὰ ὁ Ἀριστοφάνης;
6. πόσα ὦτά σοι εἰσιν;
7. πόσα ἔτη οἱ Ἀχαιοὶ ἐμάχοντο πρὸ τῶν Τροίας τείχων;
8. πόσα ἔτη ἡ Πηνελοπεία ἔμενεν;
9. πόσοι οἱ θεοὶ ἔχοντες οἰκίας ἐν Ὀλύμπῳ;
10. πόσοι υἱοὶ τῷ Πριάμῳ ἦσαν; πόσαι θυγατέρες τῇ Νιόβῃ;
11. πόσα γένη, καθὰ ὁ Ἡσίοδος;
12. πόσοι αὐχένες τῷ κύνι Κερβέρῳ εἰσιν;
13. πόσοι στρατηγοὶ ἔβησαν ἐπὶ Θήβας;
14. ὀνόμαζε δύο τῶν ἑπτὰ σοφῶν.
15. τῶν μὲν βαρβάρων ἑξακισχίλιοι καὶ τετρακόσιοι ἄνδρες καὶ Ἀθηναίων δὲ ἑκατὸν καὶ
    ἐνενήκοντα καὶ δύο. (the number of men who died at Marathon, according to Herodotus)

d. Challenge passage

This fragment from the comic poet Eubulus is preserved in Athenaeus's *Deipnosophists* (The Sophists at Dinner). The god Dionysus is describing the effects of wine, per mixing bowl (krater). The effects of each krater are put in the genitive, and this structure is repeated throughout the poem. Knowledge of the ordinal numbers is assumed (*Essentials* §70). A translation is given in the introduction.

"μέτρον ἄριστον" ἢ "μηδὲν ἄγαν" (Measure is best or Nothing in excess.)
ὁ κωμῳδὸς Εὔβουλος ποιεῖ τὸν Διόνυσον λέγοντα.

ΔΙΟΝΥΣΟΣ

τρεῖς γὰρ μόνους κρατῆρας ἐγκεραννύω	1
τοῖς εὖ φρονοῦσι· τὸν μὲν ὑγιείας ἕνα	2
ὃν πρῶτον ἐκπίνουσι, τὸν δὲ δεύτερον	3
ἔρωτος ἡδονῆς τε, τὸν τρίτον δ' ὕπνου,	4
ὃν ἐκπιόντες οἱ σοφοὶ κεκλημένοι	5
οἴκαδε βαδίζουσ'. ὁ δὲ τέταρτος οὐκέτι	6
ἡμέτερός ἐστ' ἀλλ' ὕβρεος, ὁ δὲ πέμπτος βοῆς·	7
ἕκτος δὲ κώμων, ἕβδομος δ' ὑπωπίων,	8
‹ὁ δ'› ὄγδοος κλητῆρος, ὁ δ' ἔνατος χολῆς,	9
δέκατος δὲ μανίας ὥστε κἀκβάλλειν ποιεῖ·	10
πολὺς γὰρ εἰς ἓν μικρὸν ἀγγεῖον χυθεὶς	11
ὑποσκελίζει ῥᾷστα τοὺς πεπωκότας.	12

---

1   *κρατήρ -ῆρος ὁ = krater, mixing bowl
      ἐγκεραννύω = mix
2   *φρονέω = think
      τὸν μὲν ... ἕνα: understand κρατῆρα ἐγκεραννύω from the previous line
3   ἐκπίνω = ἐκ + πίνω
4   *ὕπνος -ου ὁ = sleep (cf. English "hypnotist")
7   ὕβρεος (from ὕβρις) = ὕβρεως
      *βοή -ῆς ἡ = shout, shouting
8   *κῶμος -ου ὁ = komos, revel
      ὑπώπιον -ου τό = black eye
9   κλητήρ -ῆρος ὁ = summoner or witness who gave evidence that summons had been served
      χολή -ῆς ἡ = anger (cf. English "choleric")
10   *μανία -ας ἡ: cf. English "mania"
      κἀκβάλλειν = καὶ ἐκβάλλειν seemingly = throw furniture [out the window?] or possibly throw
          up (see n12 in introduction: "The Symposium as a Social Institution")
11   ἀγγεῖον -ου τό = cup
      χυθείς from *χέω = pour
12   ὑποσκελίζω = trip up

Appendix 1. Major Characters in the Symposium

NOTE: For full references and more detail, see Nails 2002.

Agathon (born after 450?–died ca. 401/400? B.C.E.). Host of the party. Athenian tragedian, no plays surviving and only represented in a few brief fragments[39] but important enough to receive the attention of Plato, Aristophanes, and Aristotle. According to Athenaeus (5.217a), Agathon's first victory in the tragic contests, the occasion for the party described in the *Symposium*, took place at the Lenaea of 416 B.C.E. (see introduction: "Drama of the *Symposium*" and n8). The *Symposium* treats him as young and very attractive; he is the *eromenos* (beloved) of the elder Pausanias. He is also mentioned as Pausanias's *eromenos* in another Platonic dialogue, the *Protagoras*, with a dramatic date of approximately 435 B.C.E. (Alcibiades is said to be just getting his first beard). Their lasting relationship is treated as unusual in a culture where most homosexual relationships were apparently short-term. If Plato is being careful with chronology (something Athenaeus questions), Agathon is around thirty in the *Symposium*,[40] still young in a culture where men often did not marry until their thirties, though older than the typical *eromenos*.

Aristophanes' comedy, *Thesmophoriazusae*, produced in 411 B.C.E., mocks both Agathon himself and his poetic style as effeminate. Perhaps the beardlessness that Aristophanes implies in the *Thesmophoriazusae* (33–34, 189–92) encourages the perception of Agathon as an eternally youthful *eromenos*. This effeminacy also may suggest a connection between Agathon and the god Dionysus, often presented in this period as an effeminate youth (Euripides' *Bacchae*).[41] The *Thesmophoriazusae* also associates Agathon with the better-known tragic playwright Euripides, his contemporary. Like Euripides, Agathon left Athens for Macedon in the later years of the war, an event lamented by Aristophanes in the *Frogs* (84) and mentioned in the *Symposium* as having occurred many years before. The *Symposium* explicitly associates Agathon's style with that of the sophist and rhetorician Gorgias, who also influenced Euripides. Aristotle tells us in addition that Agathon was the first to use invented plots and characters in his tragedies rather than the mythical content standard in the fifth century and to introduce choral lyrics that were unconnected to the plot of the tragedy in which they appeared (*Poetics* 1451b19, 1456a).

39. Testimonia and fragments can be found in Snell 1986: 155–68. Two brief fragments from Agathon appear in review exercise 4.a.16 and 4.c.20.

40. It is hard to imagine that Pausanias would have brought an *eromenos* younger than twelve to meet Protagoras and the other sophists.

41. For an interesting discussion of the significance of Dionysus's effeminacy, see Jameson 1993.

Alcibiades (451–404 B.C.E.). Late arrival at the party. Major political figure of the second half of the fifth century B.C.E., elected general repeatedly. Handsome, wealthy, charming, influential in the assembly, effective as a general, but got himself in trouble with his extravagance and recklessness. Orphaned as a child and adopted by Pericles, the preeminent statesman of fifth-century Athens. Close associate of Socrates for a period. Notable for his role in the disastrous Sicilian Expedition, Athens' ambitious attempt to extend the Peloponnesian War into a new part of the Greek world (see introduction: "Historical Context of the Dialogue").

After the Sicilian Expedition and Alcibiades' defection to Sparta (see introduction: "Historical Context of the Dialogue"), the Athenians forgave Alcibiades sufficiently, or needed his military help desperately enough, that in 407 he was reappointed general at Athens, despite having in the meantime used his friendship with a prominent Persian to cause trouble for both Athens and Sparta and having supported an oligarchic revolution in Athens! Despite several military successes, the Athenians soon replaced him with other less capable generals, and he fled to Persia, where he was murdered. The Athenians' love-hate relationship with Alcibiades is nicely illustrated in Aristophanes' *Frogs*, where Dionysus says of the city and Alcibiades: "It desires him, it hates him, it wants to have him" (ποθεῖ μέν, ἐχθαίρει δέ, βούλεται δ' ἔχειν) (*Frogs* 1425). The erotic overtones are not accidental; Alcibiades was certainly sexually attractive, as well as sexually promiscuous, as his biographer Plutarch emphasizes, giving additional importance to his inclusion in this dialogue on eros.

Thucydides 6.15 offers a summary sketch of Alcibiades' historical significance in the context of his discussion of the Sicilian Expedition: "The most ardent supporter of the expedition was Alcibiades, the son of Clinias. He wanted to oppose Nicias, with whom he had never seen eye to eye in politics and who had just now made a personal attack on him in his speech. Stronger motives still were his desire to hold the command and his hope that it would be through him that Sicily and Carthage would be conquered—successes that would at the same time bring him personally both wealth and honor. For he was very much in the public eye, and his enthusiasm for horse breeding and other extravagances went beyond what his fortune could supply. This, in fact, later on had much to do with the downfall of the city of Athens. For most people became frightened at a quality in him that was beyond the normal and showed itself both in the lawlessness of his private life and habits and in the spirit in which he acted on all occasions. They thought that he was aiming at becoming a dictator, and so they turned against him. Although in a public capacity his conduct of the war was excellent, his way of life made him objectionable to everyone as a person; thus they entrusted their affairs to other hands, and before long ruined the city" (translated by Rex Warner).

Plutarch recounts his life in often amusing detail in his biography of Alcibiades in *Parallel Lives*. Nussbaum 1986 offers an interesting interpretation of the role of Alcibiades in the dialogue.

Apollodorus. Narrator of the dialogue. A devotee of Socrates, but only a boy in 416 B.C.E. (like Plato himself) and therefore not present at the symposium. He appears in other dialogues of Plato's: in the *Apology* as a member of an audience of Socrates' supporters (34a) and as part of a small group who want Socrates to propose that he pay a fine on their security as an alternate punishment to death (38b). At *Phaedo* 59a–b and 117b, he is presented as losing control of himself at Socrates' deathbed, in a way presented as typical of him, by breaking down in such a storm of weeping that everybody else in the room starts crying too, except for Socrates, who hints that he is acting like a woman and tells them all to control themselves (also Xenophon, *Apology* 27–28). Apollodorus's reputation for being soft (μαλθακός) is mentioned at *Symposium* 173d (reading 1B.26). Some read this as μανικός (crazy), possessed in the manner of many Socratic philosophers of a mad passion for philosophy, as described by Alcibiades (reading 10E).

Aristodemus. A follower of Socrates who was present at the symposium, primarily as an observer. Apollodorus's primary source for the story. He is described as small, shoeless, and among the foremost lovers of Socrates at the time. Like Alcibiades, an uninvited member of the group. Unlike Alcibiades, a rather modest and colorless figure whose essential reliability seems to be confirmed by Socrates in the opening of the *Symposium*. He is mentioned in Xenophon, *Memorabilia* 1.4.2. where he is also called τὸν μικρόν; Xenophon also reports that he does not sacrifice to the gods or use divination and mocks those who do.

Aristophanes (born ca. 450?–died ca. 385 B.C.E.). The most successful Athenian writer of Old Comedy, the comedic form of fifth-century Athens, distinctive for its large choruses, inventive plots, irreverent and bawdy humor, and costuming (which included padded rear ends and stomachs, grotesque masks, and enormous phalluses). Author of eleven surviving comedies, including his best known play, the sex farce *Lysistrata*, and *Clouds*, a play that openly mocks Socrates as a fuzzy-headed intellectual and sophist. In Plato's *Apology*, a re-creation of the defense speech that Socrates gave at his trial, Socrates implies that the *Clouds* contributed to his bad reputation in Athens and thus ultimately to his death. Given Aristophanes' mocking treatment of Agathon in his *Thesmophoriazusae* (see Agathon), his presence here as a friend and associate of these men is interesting. Aristophanes' *Frogs*, produced in 405 B.C.E., shares the *Symposium*'s interests in Dionysus, drama, and the role of Alcibiades in the city's decline. It also speaks of missing Agathon, who has left Athens for Macedon.

Diotima. A foreign woman (ξένη) of Mantinea, a polis in Arcadia on the Peloponnesus. Socrates credits her with educating him in love (τὰ ἐρωτικά). The only female "speaker" in the *Symposium*, her words are reported through several male intermediaries. She seems to be a kind of priestess or prophetess, an important female role. Although Socrates never labels her as such, she is associated repeatedly with the art of prophecy (μαντική), uses the language of initiation into the Mysteries, and is shown winning for the Athenians a postponement of the plague in 440 B.C.E. at the sacrifices. Her speech uses a considerable amount of religious imagery and language. Her name means "Zeus-honored" or "Zeus-honoring" and may play off the historical name of a famous *hetaera* associated with Alcibiades, Timandra. As far as we know, not a historical figure but an invention of Plato's. The *Symposium* is our only source of information on Diotima.

Eryximachus. A doctor. Son of another doctor, Acumenus. He appears in Plato's *Protagoras* alongside Phaedrus as a follower of the sophist Hippias of Elis. Plausibly the *erastes* of Phaedrus, certainly a very close friend. Socrates refers to him in talking to Phaedrus as "your friend" (ἑταῖρος) in the *Phaedrus* 268a, and Phaedrus cites the advice of Eryximachus's father in his first speech in that dialogue. In Andocides' speech, *On the Mysteries*, an Eryximachus is accused by an informant of being involved in the mutilation of the herms (Andocides 1.35). This has led some scholars to think that the *Symposium* depicts the occasion on which the events leading to these charges occurred (see introduction: "Historical Context of the Dialogue").

Pausanias of Cerameis. Appears in Plato's *Protagoras* alongside Agathon, to whom Socrates implies he is particularly attached, listening to the sophist Prodicus (315d–e). He is generally considered to be the lover of Agathon, with whom he apparently had a long-term relationship of a kind not typical of normal pederastic relationships. Socrates criticizes him in Xenophon's *Symposium* for exaggerating the positive aspects of pederasty (8.32–35), presumably an allusion to Plato's *Symposium*, though the dramatic date of Xenophon's *Symposium* is earlier, leading Athenaeus to criticize Xenophon for his chronology.

Phaedrus. Notable primarily for his youth and passionate interest in rhetoric. In the *Protagoras* he is shown, alongside Eryximachus, as part of a group around the sophist Hippias of Elis. As with Agathon, his presence on that occasion seems to suggest that he was in his late twenties or close to thirty in the *Symposium* (see Agathon). Phaedrus also appears in Plato's dialogue *Phaedrus* as an admirer and follower of the prominent orator Lysias, known as a master of the simple style of oration. The *Phaedrus*, if it has a dramatic date at all, must be quite close in time to the *Symposium* and deals with similar themes. Phaedrus was accused alongside Alcibiades and others of profaning the Mysteries (see introduction: "Historical Context of the Dialogue") and fled into exile; his association with the mutilation of the herms is dubious (Nails 2002: 233–34).

Socrates (born 470/469, died 399 B.C.E.). Major Athenian philosopher of the fifth century who left no writing of his own but profoundly influenced other thinkers and philosophers through personal contact, most directly Plato (427–347 B.C.E.) and his contemporary Xenophon (ca. 428–354 B.C.E.), both of whom wrote dialogues that provide a lasting record of Socrates and his methods. Known particularly for a teaching style that consisted of questioning and never asserting and for his insistence that he did not know anything. In 399, he was tried by an Athenian jury for impiety; Plato's *Apology* offers a fictionalized version of the speech he gave in his defense and is the most memorable and distinctive defense of his life and choices. Socrates was convicted and sentenced to die; a moving account of how he met this death is given in Plato's *Phaedo*.

Appendix 2. Time Line of Events
Relevant to the Symposium

All dates B.C.E.

470/469	birth of Socrates
440	date of Diotima's visit to Athens (fictional?)
435	dramatic date of Plato's *Protagoras*: present are Socrates, Alcibiades (just getting his beard), Pausanias and Agathon, Eryximachus and Phaedrus
432	revolt of Potidaea, a Greek polis and an Athenian ally subjected to tribute, and invasion of Potidaea by the Athenian army, including Alcibiades and Socrates (*Symposium* 219e5–220e = reading 10G.1–32).
431	Peloponnesian War breaks out between Athens and Sparta and their allies
430	plague at Athens
424	Athenians, including Alcibiades and Socrates, forced to retreat at Delium (*Symposium* 220e–221c = reading 10G.43–59)
423	first production of Aristophanes' *Clouds*, mocking Socrates, came in third (quoted in *Symposium* 221b3 = reading 10G.53)
416	Agathon's first victory in the tragic contests
	dramatic date of Plato's *Symposium*
415	mutilation of the herms on the eve of Sicilian Expedition
	Sicilian Expedition under the leadership of Nicias and Alcibiades
	recall of Alcibiades to Athens to stand trial on charges of profaning the Mysteries
	Alcibiades flees to Sparta and advises Gylippus (Spartan general)
413	Spartans under Gylippus defeat and massacre Athenians in Sicily
411	Aristophanes' *Thesmophoriazusae* (mocks Agathon)
407	Alcibiades chosen general
406	Alcibiades deposed
	Euripides dies
	Sophocles dies
405	Euripides' *Bacchae* produced posthumously (Dionysiac themes)
	Aristophanes' *Frogs* (Dionysiac themes)
404	surrender of Athens to Sparta
	end of the Peloponnesian War

Appendix 3. Seating Arrangement at Agathon's Symposium

The diagram assumes a standard seven-couch arrangement. Rectangles represent couches that normally hold two males. The number of couches could be either somewhat larger (eleven) or smaller (five), but seven couches are standard in Athenian houses, and this fits well enough with what is said in the dialogue. The unnamed guests also might be distributed differently around the room. The only gap in the reports of the speeches is that between Phaedrus and Pausanias, but Aristodemus fails to mention that he is not reporting his own speech (or Apollodorus neglects to pass that on), so we may not be informed of every gap. We also cannot be sure how many of the guests are alone on their couches, so it is possible that Aristophanes and Pausanias share a couch. Some scholars see the movement to the right that is mentioned several times in the dialogue as indicating a clockwise direction, but I follow Dover 1980: 11 and others in using the perspective of the drinkers reclining on their left elbows, rather than the perspective of the scholar looking at the page.

ἔσχατος Socrates + Agathon [Alcibiades later, between them]	Eryximachus + Aristodemus	Aristophanes [+ unnamed guest or Pausanias?]

entry to the room

Pausanias? + unnamed guest?

πρῶτος
Phaedrus
[+ unnamed guest?]

unnamed guests

unnamed guests?

Appendix 4. Structure of the Symposium

1. The opening frame: dialogue between Apollodorus and ἑταῖρος (reading 1)
2. The drinking party: the narration of Aristodemus (as reported by Apollodorus) (reading 2)
3. The first five speeches praising Eros (readings 3–7)[42]
4. Socrates questions Agathon (reading 8) and reports the speech of Diotima (reading 9)
5. Alcibiades enters and praises Socrates (reading 10)
6. The end of the evening and the morning after (reading 11)

speaker (reading)	pederastic relations	or rhetorician	associated sophist major sources	major points
Phaedrus (3)	ἐρώμενος (youth)	Lysias (*Phaedrus*) Hippias (*Protagoras*)	traditional myth, poetry	Eros is the oldest of the gods and instills virtue
Pausanias (4)	ἐραστής (older man)	Prodicus (*Protagoras*)	laws and customs (νόμοι)	two Erotes: the heavenly and the common
Eryximachus (5)	ἐραστής (older man)	Hippias (*Protagoras*)	medicine and other sciences (τέχναι)	Eros is in all parts of the cosmos and unites opposites
Aristophanes (ἄτοπος?) (6)	apparently no relationship	apparently no association mocks them in *Clouds*	comedy (a new myth)	Eros is a healer of our divided original nature
Agathon (7)	ἐρώμενος (youth)	Gorgias (*Symposium*) Prodicus (*Protagoras*)	tragedy (innovation)	Eros is the youngest of the gods and possesses all the cardinal virtues

42. The nearby chart suggests some possible organizational principles underlying the first five speeches, which appear to form a group. The speeches seem simultaneously to create a progression forward and to form a ring composition, with Agathon's speech at the end hearkening back to Phaedrus's at the beginning. In addition, Aristophanes seems to be ἄτοπος, both out of place physically and lacking qualities shared by the other speakers. But this chart is far from definitive, and readers may well wish to explore other possible structuring principles.

Glossary

The order of the principal parts follows the traditional listing: (1) present, (2) future, (3) aorist, (4) perfect active, (5) perfect middle-passive, and (6) aorist passive:

λαμβάνω λήψομαι ἔλαβον εἴληφα εἴλημμαι ἐλήφθην = take, grasp, seize

The principal parts of verbs with prefixes are normally listed under the verb without its prefix; for example: principal parts of ἀνέχω are listed under ἔχω. I do not regularly provide the principal parts for verbs with predictable parts unless they are used repeatedly in the text. A dash (—) indicates that the principal part does not exist or is not used in Attic Greek. The dash marking a missing principal part is *not*, however, used at the end of the list:

πάσχω πείσομαι ἔπαθον πέπονθα = suffer, experience

Πάσχω is always active in meaning; therefore, it does not have a perfect middle-passive (principal part #5) or aorist passive (#6). This is true of many verbs, including most verbs of motion:

ἀφικνέομαι ἀφίξομαι ἀφικόμην — ἀφῖγμαι = arrive (at)

As a verb of motion, ἀφικνέομαι is always active in meaning. Thus, like πάσχω, it has only four principal parts. Unlike πάσχω, however, ἀφικνέομαι always uses middle endings; consequently its principal parts look somewhat different. (A verb that always uses middle endings but is translated actively is called a deponent verb or, more precisely, a middle deponent verb.)

Like πάσχω and ἀφικνέομαι, βούλομαι is always active in meaning:

βούλομαι βουλήσομαι —— βεβούλημαι ἐβουλήθην = wish, want

Βούλομαι is similar to ἀφικνέομαι in that it consistently uses middle endings, *except*, as the principal parts show, it uses an aorist *passive* (#6) rather than an aorist *middle* (#4). Βούλομαι is thus also a deponent verb, but is distinguished from verbs that use middle endings consistently by being called a passive deponent verb.

Like βούλομαι, ἄγαμαι is a passive deponent verb, as the ending -θην on the aorist form should suggest. This verb is not found in the future or perfect in Attic Greek. Consequently, it has only two principal parts:

ἄγαμαι, *aor.* ἠγάσθην = admire, wonder at

In both the glossary and notes, I give the most basic, root meaning first, so that it is often necessary to look at all the meanings to find the closest approximation of the one appropriate to the specific context. Daniel Garrison provides some wise advice this regard: "Any lexicon definition is an approximate equivalent, not an exact meaning. A translation which mechanically substitutes English 'meanings' for Greek words is courting disaster. Avoid 'translationese' by interpreting units of meaning rather than isolated words."[43]

Αα

ἅ: neut. pl. rel. pron., nom. or acc. of ὅς ἥ ὅ

ἀβελτερία -ας ἡ: silliness, stupidity

ἁβρός -ά -όν: delicate

ἁβρότης -ητος ἡ: delicacy, luxury

ἀγαθός -ή -όν: good, noble, brave

Ἀγάθων -ωνος ὁ: Agathon, Greek tragedian, host of the symposium (see introduction and appendix 1)

ἄγαλμα -ατος τό: (1) glory, delight, ornament; (2) statue or image of a god

ἄγαμαι, *aor.* ἠγάσθην: admire, wonder at, be astonished at (pass. deponent)

ἄγαμος -ον: unmarried, single

ἀγανακτέω: feel irritation, be displeased with or angry at

ἀγανός -ή -όν: mild, gentle, kind

ἀγαπάω ἀγαπήσω ἠγάπησα ἠγάπηκα ἠγάπημαι ἠγαπήθην: love (typically, of a more disinterested, less passionate sort than ἐράω), be fond of

ἀγαστός -ή -όν (verbal adj. of ἄγαμαι): to be admired, deserving admiration, admirable

ἀγγέλλω ἀγγελῶ ἤγγειλα ἤγγελκα ἤγγελμαι ἠγγέλθην: announce, bear a message, report

ἄγγελος -ου ὁ: messenger

ἀγένειος -ον: beardless

ἀγεννής -ές: ignoble, not well-born

ἀγνοέω ἀγνοήσω ἠγνόησα ἠγνόηκα ἠγνόημαι ἠγνοήθην: not know, be ignorant

ἀγορά -ᾶς ἡ: agora, marketplace

ἀγριαίνω ἀγριανῶ ἠγρίανα: be angry, be wild, be crazy; get angry at *dat.*

ἄγριος -α -ον: living in the fields, wild, untamed, savage, fierce

ἀγριότης -ητος ἡ: wildness, fierce

ἄγροικος -ον: of the country, rustic, crude, unsophisticated, uncultivated

ἄγω ἄξω ἤγαγον ἦχα ἦγμαι ἤχθην: lead or carry, convey, bring; live (a particular way, e.g., in peace, in war); ἄγε *impera.*: come!

ἀγωνίζομαι: compete, participate in a contest

ἀδεής -ές: without fear, fearless

ἀδελφή -ῆς ἡ: sister

ἀδελφός -οῦ ὁ: brother

ἄδηλος -ον: not seen or known, unclear, unknown, obscure

43. Daniel H. Garrison, *The Student's Catullus* (3rd ed.; Norman: University of Oklahoma Press, 2004), 189.

ἀδικέω ἀδικήσω ἠδίκησα ἠδίκηκα ἠδίκημαι ἠδικήθην: do wrong, act unjustly; *trans.*: wrong, treat unjustly, injure

ἀδικία -ας ἡ: injustice, wrongdoing, offense

ἄδικος -ον: unjust

Ἄδμητος -ου ὁ: Admetos (Latin Admetus), husband of Alkestis (Alcestis) (see reading 3 introduction)

ἀδύνατος -ον: impossible, unable, incapable; + *inf.*: unable to ——, incapable of ——ing

ᾄδω/ἀείδω ᾄσομαι/ἀείσομαι ᾖσα/ἤεισα—ᾖσμαι ᾔσθην: sing

ἄδωρος -ον: without gifts, unbribed, ungenerous, stingy with *gen.*, miserly with *gen.*

ἀεί (or αἰεί) *adv.*: always, forever, continually

ἀειγενής -ές: everlasting

ἀθανασία -ας ἡ: immortality

ἀθάνατος -ον: undying, immortal

ἄθεος -ον: without the gods, ungodly

Ἀθήναζε *adv.*: to Athens

Ἀθηναῖος -α -ον: Athenian

Ἀθήνηθε(ν) *adv.*: from Athens

ἄθλιος -α -ον: subject to the toils of conflict, wretched, miserable, pathetic

ἀθυμία -ας ἡ: want of spirit, faintheartedness, despondency

Αἴας Αἴαντος ὁ: Aias (Latin Ajax), Greek hero of the Trojan War

Ἅιδης -ου ὁ: Hades, god of the Underworld

αἰδοῖα -ων τά: genitals

αἰεί = ἀεί

αἷμα αἵματος τό: blood

αἰνέω -αἰνέσω/-αἰνέσομαι ᾔνεσα ᾔνεκα ᾔνημαι ᾐνέθην: praise

αἰνίττομαι: speak in riddles, speak enigmatically

αἱρέω αἱρήσω εἷλον (ἑλ-) ᾕρηκα ᾕρημαι ᾑρέθην: take, capture, take with the hand, grasp; *in erotic context*: seduce; *mid.*: choose, elect; *aor. pass.*: was chosen (usually)

αἰσθάνομαι αἰσθήσομαι ᾐσθόμην—ᾔσθημαι: perceive, apprehend by the senses, see, hear, feel *acc. or gen.*

αἴσχιστος -η -ον (superl. of αἰσχρός): most shameful, ugliest, very shameful, etc.

αἰσχίων -ον (compar. of αἰσχρός): more shameful, uglier, rather shameful, etc.

αἶσχος -ους τό: ugliness, shame, disgrace

αἰσχρός -ά -όν: causing shame, disgracing, ugly, shameful

Αἰσχύλος -ου ὁ: Aischylos (Latin Aeschylus), Athenian tragedian

αἰσχύνη -ης ἡ: shame done one, disgrace, dishonor

αἰσχύνω αἰσχυνῶ ᾔσχυνα——ᾐσχύνθην: make ugly, disfigure, shame; *mid.-pass.*: feel ashamed, be ashamed at; + *acc. pers.*: feel shame before

αἰτέω αἰτήσω ᾔτησα ᾔτηκα ᾔτημαι ᾐτήθην: ask (for)

αἰτία -ας ἡ: cause, reason; + *acc. + inf.*: the reason for *acc.* to ——

αἴτιον -ου τό: cause, reason

αἴτιος -α -ον: blameworthy, culpable, responsible for *gen.*, guilty of *gen.*

ἀκαιρία -ας ἡ: unfitness of time, unseasonableness, bad timing

ἀκηκοώς -υῖα -ός: perf. act. part. of ἀκούω

ἄκλητος -ον: uncalled, uninvited, unbidden

ἀκμή -ῆς ἡ: point, edge, peak, prime

ἀκολασία -ας ἡ: licentiousness, intemperance

ἀκόλαστος -ον: licentious, intemperate, undisciplined

ἀκόλουθος -ον: following, attending on

ἀκόλουθος -ου ὁ: follower, attendant

Ἀκουμενός -οῦ ὁ: Akoumenos (Latin Acumenus), father of Eryximachos (Latin Eryximachus)

Ἀκουσίλεως -ω ὁ: Akousileos (Latin Acusilaus) of Argos, a shadowy figure of whom little is known, apparently a writer of genealogies

ἀκούω ἀκούσομαι ἤκουσα ἀκήκοα—ἠκούσθην: hear, listen to *acc. obj. or gen. source*

ἀκριβής -ές: exact, accurate, precise

ἀλγεινός -ή -όν: giving pain, painful, grievous

ἀλγέω: feel pain, suffer

ἀλεκτρυών -όνος ὁ: cock, rooster

ἀλήθεια -ας ἡ: truth, frankness, sincerity

ἀληθής -ές: true, truthful, honest

ἁλίσκομαι ἁλώσομαι ἑάλων/ἥλων ἑάλωκα/ἥλωκα: be taken, be conquered, be captured

Ἄλκηστις -ιδος ἡ: Alkestis (Latin Alcestis) (see reading 3B introduction)

Ἀλκιβιάδης -ου ὁ: Alkibiades (Latin Alcibiades), prominent fifth-century Athenian (see appendix 1 and introduction)

ἀλλά *conj.*: but, otherwise, except; ἀλλὰ γάρ: but in fact, but anyway, to resume my argument; ἀλλ᾽ οὖν: but then, however

ἀλλάττω ἀλλάξω ἤλλαξα -ήλλαχα ἤλλαγμαι ἠλλάχθην/ἠλλάγην: make other than it is, change, alter; *mid.*: exchange —— for ——

ἄλλῃ *fem. dat. sing. as adv.*: in another way, in another place, elsewhere

ἀλλήλων (gen. pl.); *dat.* -οις -αις; *acc.* -ους -ας -α: one another, each other

ἄλλο τι: something else, anything other; *introducing a question*: not . . . ? mustn't it be . . . ?

ἄλλοθεν *adv.*: from another place, from elsewhere

ἄλλοθι *adv.*: elsewhere, in another place

ἀλλοῖος -α -ον: of another sort or kind, different, other

ἄλλος -η -ο: other, another; ὁ ἄλλος the rest (of); ἄλλος . . . ἄλλος: one . . . (an)other

ἄλλοτε *adv.*: at another time, at other times; ἄλλοτε . . . ἄλλοτε: at one time . . . at another

ἀλλότριος -α -ον: another's, alien (to), foreign (to), hostile or unfriendly (to)

ἀλλοτριότης -ητος ὁ: alienation, estrangement

ἄλλως *adv.*: in another way or manner, otherwise; ἄλλως τε καί: especially, above all

ἀλογία -ας ἡ: lack of logic, illogicality, senselessness

ἄλογος -ον: without λόγος, without account, without logic or rationality

ἅλς ἁλός ὁ: salt; *sing.*: grain or lump of salt; *pl.*: table salt, salt prepared for use

ἁλῶναι: aor. inf. of ἁλίσκομαι

ἀλώσεσθαι: fut. inf. of ἁλίσκομαι

ἅμα *adv.*: at once; together, at the same time; *prep. + dat.*: at the same time as, together with; ἅμα ... ἅμα: at the same time, both ... and ... at once

ἀμαθής -ές: unlearned, ignorant, stupid, boorish

ἀμαθία -ας ἡ: ignorance, want of learning

ἁμαρτάνω ἁμαρτήσομαι ἥμαρτον ἡμάρτηκα ἡμάρτημαι ἡμαρτήθην: err, go astray, make a mistake, do wrong, miss

ἄμεικτος -ον: unmixed, pure

ἀμείνων -ον (compar. of ἀγαθός): better, abler, stronger, braver, quite good, etc.

ἀμελέτητος -ον: unpracticed, unprepared

ἀμελέω ἀμελήσων ἠμέλησα ἠμέληκα ἠμέλημαι ἠμελήθην: have no care for, be neglectful of, neglect

ἀμελής -ές: careless, uncaring, neglectful, heedless, negligent

ἀμετρίως *adv.*: immoderately

ἀμήτωρ (*gen.* ἀμήτορος): without a mother, motherless

ἀμήχανος -ον: without means or resource, irresistible

ἀμοιβή -ῆς ἡ: requital, recompense, compensation, return, payment

ἄμοιρος -ον: without any part of, without share in *gen.*

ἄμουσος -ον: without the Muses, Muse-less, uninspired, unpoetic, unmusical

ἀμύνω ἀμυνῶ ἤμυνα: keep off, ward off, defend; *mid.*: defend oneself

ἀμφιέννυμι ἀμφιῶ ἠμφίεσα — ἠμφίεσμαι ἠμφιέσθην: put around, clothe, dress in

ἀμφισβητέω: stand apart, disagree, differ

ἀμφισβητήσιμος -ον: doubtful, debatable, disputed

ἀμφότεροι -αι -α: both, each of two

ἄν (untranslatable particle affecting translation of verb mood; see *Essentials* §§160–62) + *indic.*: contrary-to-fact, unreal; + *opt.*: potential, hypothetical; + *subju.*: generalizing or indefinite

ἄν (sometimes) = ἐάν (contracted) when accompanied by subju.

ἀνά *prep. + acc.*: up, throughout, upon, up along, by; *as a prefix*: up, up to, upon, upward, back

ἀναβαίνω: go up, mount, ascend

ἀναβάλλω: throw or toss up

ἀνάβασις -εως ἡ: going up, mounting, ascent

ἀναβιώσκομαι: come back to life

ἀναβολή -ῆς ἡ: postponement

ἀναγκάζω ἀναγκάσω ἠνάγκασα ἠνάγκακα ἠνάγκασμαι ἠναγκάσθην: force, compel

ἀναγκαῖος -α -ον: necessary, with or by force, constraining; ἀναγκαῖόν ἐστι(ν); + *acc. + inf.*: it is necessary (for) *acc.* to ——

ἀνάγκη -ης ἡ: force, constraint, necessity; sometimes personified as a goddess; ἀνάγκη ἐστι(ν); + *acc. or dat. + inf.*: there is a necessity that *acc. or dat.* ——; it is necessary for *acc. or dat.* to ——

ἀναδέω: bind above; put a crown on, garland

ἀναθορυβέω: cry out loudly in support, shout in applause, send up a cheer ἀναισχυντία -ας ἡ: shamelessness

ἀναίσχυντος -ον: shameless, impudent

ἀνάκειμαι: be laid up, be dedicated

ἀνακογχυλιάζω: gargle

ἀνακρίνω: examine closely; *mid.*: question, interrogate

ἀναλαμβάνω: take up

ἀναλίσκω ἀναλώσω ἀνήλωσα ἀνήλωκα ἀνήλωμαι ἀνηλώθην: use up, spend, expend, lavish, squander

ἀναμιμνήσκω: remind *acc.* of *gen.*; *pass.*: remember

ἀνανδρία -ας ἡ: cowardice, lack of manliness

ἀνανθής -ές: without bloom

ἄναξ ἄνακτος ὁ: lord, chief, prince

ἀναπαύω: make to cease, stop or hinder from; *mid.*: cease, rest, take a break

ἀναπηδάω: jump up

ἀνάπλεως -ων: filled up, quite full of

ἀνάρμοστος -ον: unsuitable, incongruous, disproportionate, unharmonious

ἀναστάς -ᾶσα -άν: (root) aor. act. part. (intrans.) of ἀνίστημι

ἀναστήσῃ: fut. mid. indic. 2nd pers. sing. of ἀνίστημι

ἀνατίθημι: lay upon, attribute; set up, dedicate

ἀναφαίνομαι: appear, turn up

ἀναχωρέω: go up, go back, retreat

ἀναψυχή -ῆς ἡ: cooling off, period of refreshing; relief, recovery, rest, respite

ἀνδραποδώδης -ες: slavish, servile, abject

ἀνδρεία -ας ἡ: manliness, manhood, manly spirit, courage

ἀνδρεῖος -α -ον: manly, masculine, brave

ἀνδρόγυνος -ον: man-woman, having to do with both men and women, androgynous, hermaphroditic

ἀνδρόω: rear up into manhood, bring to manhood

ἀνέβην: aor. act. indic. 1st pers. sing. of ἀναβαίνω (root aor.)

ἀνείλλομαι: roll (oneself) up, curl up

ἀνεῖπον *aor.*: say aloud, proclaim

ἀνελευθερία -ας ἡ: want of freedom, slavishness, servility

ἀνεμέσητος -ον: without offense

ἄνεμος -ου ὁ: wind

ἄνευ *prep.* + *gen.*: without

ἀνευρίσκω: find out, discover

ἀνέχω: hold up, be up

ἀνεῳγμένος -η -ον: perf. mid.-pass. part. of ἀνοίγνυμι

ἀνήρ ἀνδρός ὁ: man

ἀνηῦρον: aor. act. indic. 1st pers. sing./3rd pers. pl. of ἀνευρίσκω

ἀνθίστημι: set against, compare; *mid.-pass. intrans.*: stand against, withstand, oppose

ἄνθος -ους τό: blossom, flower, bloom

ἀνθρώπειος -α -ον: of or belonging to man, human

ἀνθρώπινος -η -ον: of, from, or belonging to man, human

ἄνθρωπος -ου ὁ: human being, man

ἀνίημι: send up or forth, let go, let go forth

ἀνίστημι *trans.*: make stand up, raise up; *intrans.*: stand up, get up, arise

ἀνόητος -ον: mindless, foolish, unthinkable, unreasonable

ἄνοια -ας ἡ: want of understanding, folly

ἀνοίγνυμι/ἀνοίγω ἀνοίξω ἀνέῳξα ἀνέῳχα ἀνέῳγμαι ἀνεῴχθην: open, open up

ἀνοιχθείς -εῖσα -έν: aor. pass. part. of ἀνοίγνυμι

ἀνόμοιος -ον: unlike, dissimilar

ἀνομολογέομαι: agree upon

ἀντάξιος -α -ον: equivalent to *gen.*, equal of *gen.*

Ἀντήνωρ -ορος ὁ: Antenor, Trojan old man, remarkable for advocating the return of Helen to the Greeks

ἀντί *prep. + gen.*: instead of, for, over against, opposite

ἀντιβόλησις -εως ἡ: entreaty, prayer

ἄντικρυς *adv.*: straight on, right on

ἀντιλέγω: speak against *dat.*, gainsay, contradict

ἀνυπόδητος -ον: unshod, barefoot

ἀνύτω: effect, achieve, accomplish, complete

ἄνω *adv.*: up, upward, above

ἀξιομνημόνευτος -ον: worthy of mention

ἄξιος -α -ον: worthy, worthy of *gen.*, worth *gen.*, worth ——ing *inf.*

ἀξίωμα -ατος τό: that of which one is thought worthy, honor

ἄξω: fut. act. indic. 1st pers. sing. of ἄγω

ἄοικος -ον: homeless

ἀπαγγέλλω: report, announce, tell

ἄπαις (*gen.* ἄπαιδος): childless

ἁπαλός -ή -όν: soft to the touch, tender

ἁπαλότης -ητος ἡ: softness, tenderness

ἀπανθέω: cease to bloom, wither, fade

ἀπαντάω ἀπαντήσομαι ἀπήντησα ἀπήντηκα: meet, encounter, come or go to meet

ἅπαξ *adv.*: once

ἅπας ἅπασα ἅπαν (ἁπαντ-): all, the whole of, every (strengthened version of πᾶς πᾶσα πᾶν)

ἀπατάω ἀπατήσω ἠπάτησα ἠπάτηκα ἠπάτημαι ἠπατήθην: deceive, trick

ἀπέβην: aor. act. indic. 1st pers. sing. of ἀποβαίνω (root aor.)

ἀπεικάζω: liken to, compare

ἄπειμι (ἀπο- + εἰμί): be apart from, be away from

ἄπειμι (ἀπο- + εἶμι): go away, depart

ἀπεῖπον *aor.*: I renounced

ἄπειρος -ον: inexperienced

ἅπερ *rel. pron. (neut. pl.) + suffix* -περ: the very [ones] which/that . . .

ἀπερείδω: fix firmly, support; *mid.*: support oneself

ἀπέρχομαι: go away (from *gen.*), depart (from *gen.*), go back

ἀπεχθάνομαι: be hateful to, incur hatred, be roused to hatred

ἀπέχω: hold *acc.* off or away from *gen.*; keep *acc.* off or away from *gen.*

ἀπῆλθον: aor. act. indic. 1st pers. sing./3rd pers. pl. of ἀπέρχομαι

ἁπλοῦς -οῦν: single, simple

ἁπλῶς *adv.*: singly, in one way, simply

ἀπνευστί *adv.*: breathless

ἀπό/ἀφ᾽ *prep.* + *gen.*: from, away from, out of; *as a prefix*: away, from, forth, back

ἀποβαίνω: go away, go off, go forth

ἀποβάλλω: throw off, throw away

ἀποβλάστημα -ατος τό: shoot, scion, offspring

ἀποβλέπω: look fixedly at, look away from everything else at

ἀποδείκνυμι: show forth, reveal

ἀποδεῖξαι: aor. act. inf. of ἀποδείκνυμι

ἀποδέχομαι: receive from, get from, get back

ἀποδέω: bind fast

ἀποδιδράσκω: run away or off, escape

ἀποδίδωμι: give up or back, restore, return, pay back

ἀποδοῦναι: aor. act. inf. of ἀποδίδωμι

ἀποθανεῖν: aor. act. inf. of ἀποθνήσκω

ἀποθνήσκω ἀποθανοῦμαι ἀπέθανον τέθνηκα: die off, die

ἀποκρίνομαι ἀποκρινοῦμαι ἀπεκρινάμην—ἀποκέκριμαι: answer

ἀπόκρισις -εως ἡ: answer

ἀποκτείνω ἀποκτενῶ ἀπέκτεινα/ἀπέκτανον ἀπέκτονα: kill, slay

ἀπολαμβάνω: take or receive from, cut off

ἀπολαύω ἀπολαύσομαι ἀπέλαυσα ἀπολέλαυκα: have enjoyment of, enjoy, benefit from, profit from

ἀπολείπω: leave out, leave over or behind

Ἀπολλόδωρος -ου ὁ: Apollodoros, the opening speaker in the dialogue, the narrator

ἀπόλλυμαι ἀπολοῦμαι ἀπωλόμην: die; *perf.* ἀπόλωλα: be ruined

ἀπόλλυμι ἀπολέω ἀπώλεσα ἀπολώλεκα: destroy utterly, kill, slay

Ἀπόλλων -ωνος ὁ: Apollo, young male god of healing, prophecy, and music, among other things; son of Zeus and Leto

ἀπολογέομαι ἀπολογήσομαι ἀπελογησάμην—ἀπολελόγημαι: make a speech of defense, defend oneself in words

ἀπολύω: set loose from, set free of

ἀπονίζω: wash off

ἀποπέμπω: send off or away, dismiss

ἀποπέτομαι: fly off or away

ἀποπτάμενος -η -ον: aor. mid. part. of ἀποπέτομαι

ἀπορέω ἀπορήσω ἠπόρησα ἠπόρηκα ἠπόρημαι ἠπορήθην: be without means or resources, be at a loss, not know what to do

ἀπορία -ας ἡ: resourcelessness, lack of means, extreme distress, need, poverty

ἄπορος -ον: resourceless, without means, at a loss, poor, needy

ἀποσβέννυμι: put out, extinguish, quench

ἀποστάς -ᾶσα -άν: aor. act. part. of ἀφίστημι (intrans. root aor.)

ἀποστερέω: rob, take away, deprive, defraud

ἀποτελέω: bring quite to an end, complete

ἀποτέμνω: cut off, cut away

ἀποτρέπω: turn away

ἀποτρέχω: run off, run away

ἀποφαίνω: show forth, display, produce

ἀποφεύγω: flee from, escape, be acquitted

ἀπόφημι: speak out, deny, refuse

ἀποφηνάμενος -η -ον: aor. mid. part. of ἀποφαίνω

ἅπτω ἅψω ἧψα—ἧμμαι ἥφθην: (1) fasten, bind fast, fix upon; *mid.*: (more common) fix oneself upon, touch, grasp, reach, overtake, take hold of *gen. obj.*; (2) kindle, light on fire

ἀπών -οῦσα -όν: pres. part. of ἄπειμι (ἀπό + εἰμί)

ἄρα *inferential particle*: so, then, therefore, in fact

ἆρα *particle introducing a question; not translated*: ——?

ἀργία -ας ἡ: idleness, laziness, lack of work

ἀρετή -ῆς ἡ: goodness, excellence, courage, virtue

Ἄρης -εως (*poetic gen.* Ἄρεος) ὁ: Ares, god of war; *dat.* Ἄρει; *acc.* Ἄρη (poetic Ἄρεα)

ἀριθμός -οῦ ὁ: number

ἀριστεῖα -ων τά: prize for valor, award for being ἄριστος in battle

Ἀριστογείτων -ονος ὁ: Aristogeiton (Latin Aristogiton), one of the Athenian tyrannicides, *erastes* of Harmodios (reading 4B)

Ἀριστόδημος -ου ὁ: Aristodemos (Latin Aristodemus), a follower of Socrates, who narrates most of the *Symposium* to our narrator Apollodoros (see introduction)

ἄριστος -η -ον (superl. of ἀγαθός): best, bravest, very good, etc.

Ἀριστοφάνης -ους ὁ: Aristophanes, famous comic dramatist (see introduction and appendix 1)

Ἀρκάς -άδος ὁ: Arcadian, person from Arcadia

Ἁρμόδιος -ου ὁ: Harmodios (Latin Harmodius), one of the Athenian tyrannicides, *eromenos* of Aristogeiton (reading 4B)

ἁρμονία -ας ἡ: fastening, joining together, harmony

ἁρμόττω ἁρμόσω ἥρμοσα ἥρμοκα ἥρμοσμαι ἡρμόσθην: fit together, join, fit well

ἀρνακίς -ίδος ἡ: sheep's skin

ἀρρενωπία -ας ἡ: maleness, masculinity

ἄρρην -εν (or ἄρσην -εν): male

ἄρρητος -η -ον: unspoken, unsaid, not to be spoken, secret

ἄρσην -εν = ἄρρην -εν

ἄρτι *adv.*: just now, recently, exactly, straightaway

ἀρχαῖος -α -ον: from the beginning, original, ancient, archaic

ἀρχή -ῆς ἡ: beginning, origin, first cause, rule

ἄρχω ἄρξω ἦρξα ἦρχα ἦργμαι ἤρχθην: be first, begin, rule, govern; *mid.*: begin; + *supplemental part.*: begin —— ing; + *inf.*: begin to ——

ἄρχων -οντος ὁ: ruler, commander, chief, captain

ἄσας -ασα -αν: aor. act. part. of ᾄδω

ἀσελγαίνω: behave licentiously

ἀσθενής -ές: without strength, weak, feeble

ἀσιτέω: go without food, fast

ἀσκέω: work curiously, form by art, fashion

Ἀσκληπιός -οῦ ὁ: Asclepios (Latin Asclepius), the physician hero

ἀσκωλιάζω: hop, dance as at the Ἀσκώλια (part of a Dionysiac festival in Attica)

ἀσπάζομαι ἀσπάσομαι ἠσπασάμην: welcome, greet, embrace, cling to

ᾀστέος -α -ον (verbal adj. of ᾄδω): to be sung; *neut. used impers.*: one must sing, it is necessary to sing

ἄστρωτος -ον: without bed or bedding

ἄστυ -εως τό: city, town

ἀσφαλής -ές: not liable to slip or fall, immoveable, steadfast, firm, unerring, sure

ἀσχημοσύνη -ης ἡ: inelegance, lack of grace

ἀτάρ: but, yet

ἅτε + *part.*: because of —— ing, on account of —— ing

ἀτελής -ές: without end or goal, unaccomplished, unfulfilled

ἀτεχνής -ές = ἄτεχνος -ον: without art, ignorant of the rules of art, unskilled, simple; ἀτεχνῶς *adv.*: simply, utterly

ἀτιμάζω ἀτιμάσω ἠτίμασα ἠτίμακα ἠτίμασμαι ἠτιμάσθην: dishonor, esteem little, slight

ἀτοπία -ας ἡ: being out of the way, strangeness, oddness

ἄτοπος -ον: out of place, out of the way, strange, odd

ἄτρωτος -ον: unwounded

ἄττα: Attic for τινά

αὖ *adv.*: again, back, in turn, moreover

αὖθις *adv.*: back, back again, again, anew, moreover, in turn

αὔλειος -α -ον: of or belonging to the αὐλή (courtyard)

αὐλέω: play on the αὐλός (oboe-like instrument)

αὐλή -ῆς ἡ: courtyard

αὔλημα τό: piece of music for the αὐλός (oboe-like instrument)

αὐλητής -οῦ ὁ: αὐλός-player, flute-player

αὐλητρίς -ιδος ἡ: female αὐλός-player, flute-girl

αὐλός -οῦ ὁ: aulos, a double-reeded musical instrument similar to an oboe, but usually translated "flute"

αὐξάνω/αὔξω αὐξήσω ηὔξησα ηὔξηκα ηὔξημαι ηὐξήθην: make large, increase, augment; *mid.-pass.*: increase, grow, wax

αὔριον *adv.*: tomorrow

αὐτάρ *conj.*: but, then

αὐτή: fem. nom. sing. of αὐτός

αὐτή = ἡ αὐτή

αὕτη: fem. nom. sing. of οὗτος

αὐτίκα *adv.*: straightway, at once, immediately, directly

αὐτόθεν *adv.*: from the very spot; *of time*: at once

αὐτόθι *adv.*: on the spot, there

αὐτός -ή -ό: (1) *in nom. or intensifying the noun or pron.*: -self, the very (Latin *ipse*); (2) *by itself in cases other than nom., 3rd pers. pron.*: him, her, it, them; (3) *following def. art.*: the same (see *Essentials* §§200–205)

αὐτοῦ *adv.*: at this very place, here, there (also gen. of αὐτός)

αὐτοῦ -ῆς -οῦ (contracted from ἑαυτοῦ -ῆς -οῦ) *refl. pron.*: himself, herself, itself, oneself; *pl.*: themselves

αὐχήν -ένος ὁ: neck, throat

αὐχμηρός -ά -όν: dry, dusty, rough, squalid

ἀφ᾽ = ἀπό

ἀφαιρέω (ἀπό + αἱρέω): take away from, deprive

ἀφανίζω ἀφανιῶ ἠφάνισα ἠφάνικα ἠφάνισμαι ἠφανίσθην: make unseen, make disappear, hide from sight; *mid.-pass.*: become unseen, disappear

ἀφέξομαι: fut. mid. indic. 1st pers. sing. of ἀπέχω

ἀφῆκα: aor. act. indic. 1st pers. sing. of ἀφίημι

ἀφήσω: fut. act. indic. 1st pers. sing. of ἀφίημι

ἄφθονος -ον: without envy

ἀφίημι (ἀπό + ἵημι): send forth, discharge, send away, let go, let alone, neglect, permit

ἀφικνέομαι ἀφίξομαι ἀφικόμην—ἀφῖγμαι: come (to), arrive (at)

ἀφίστημι (ἀπό + ἵστημι): put away, remove; *intrans.*: stand off, away, or aloof from

ἀφορίζω: mark off with boundaries, set apart, define

ἀφροδίσιος -α -ον: belonging to Aphrodite, sexual

Ἀφροδίτη -ης ἡ: Aphrodite, goddess of love

ἀφροσύνη -ης ἡ: folly, thoughtlessness, senselessness

ἄφρων -ον: without sense, senseless, thoughtless

ἀφυής -ές: without natural talent, witless, dull

ἀφωνία -ας ἡ: speechlessness

Ἀχαιοί -ῶν οἱ: Achaioi (Latin Achaeans), Homeric name for the Greek warriors at Troy

ἀχαριστέω: not gratify, not indulge; be thankless, show ingratitude

ἄχθομαι ἀχθέσομαι ——— ἠχθέσθην: be vexed, be burdened, be grieved

Ἀχιλλεύς -ῆος ὁ: Achilleus (Latin Achilles), greatest Greek warrior of the Trojan War

Ββ

βαδίζω βαδιοῦμαι ἐβάδισα βεβάδικα: go slowly, walk

βαδιστέος -α -ον (verbal adj. of βαδίζω): to be walked; *neut. used impers.*: one must walk, it is necessary to walk

βαθύς -εῖα -ύ: deep

βαίνω -βήσομαι -ἔβην βέβηκα -βέβαμαι ἐβάθην: go, come, walk

βακχεία -ας ἡ: Bacchic frenzy

βαλλάντιον -ου τό: bag, pouch, purse

βάλλω βαλῶ ἔβαλον βέβληκα βέβλημαι ἐβλήθην: throw, hurl, shoot at, take a shot at, hit, strike

βάναυσος -ον: mechanical, technical, uninspired

βαπτίζω: dip in or under water, baptize

βάρβαρος -ου ὁ: one who cannot speak Greek, barbarian, non-Greek

βαρέω: weigh down

βαρύς -εῖα -ύ: heavy, weighty, deep

βασιλεία -ας ἡ: kingdom, dominion

βασιλεύς -έως ὁ: king

βασιλεύω: be king of *gen.*, rule *gen.*

βέβαιος -α -ον (also -ος -ον): firm, steady, steadfast, sure, certain

βέβηλος -ον: profane, uninitiated

βέλος -ους τό: missile, something thrown (cf. βάλλω), e.g., arrow, dart, javelin

βέλτιστος -η -ον: best

βελτίων -ιον: better

βία -ας ἡ: bodily strength, force, violence, power, might

βιάζομαι— ἐβιασάμην— βεβίασμαι: use force against, force, overpower

βίαιος -α -ον: forceful, violent

βίβλιον -ου τό: book

βίος -ου ὁ: life

βιωτός -ή -όν (verbal adj. of βιόω): to be lived, worth living

βλάπτω βλάψω ἔβλαψα βέβλαφα βέβλαμμαι ἐβλάβην/ἐβλάφθην: harm, injure

βλαύτη -ης ἡ: a kind of slipper or sandal

βλέπω βλέψομαι ἔβλεψα βέβλεφα βέβλεμμαι ἐβλέφθην: look (at), see

βοάω βοήσομαι ἐβόησα: cry aloud, shout

βοήθεια -ας ἡ: help, assistance, auxiliary troop

βοηθέω βοηθήσομαι ἐβοήθησα βεβοήθηκα βεβοήθημαι ἐβοηθήθην: come to aid, help, assist, aid *dat. obj.*

Βοιωτός -οῦ ὁ: Boeotian, person from Boeotia, a large district in central Greece, bordering on Attica

βουλεύω βουλεύσω ἐβούλευσα βεβούλευκα βεβούλευμαι ἐβουλεύθην: take counsel, deliberate, plan; *in past tenses*: determine, resolve

βούλησις -εως ἡ: will, wish

βούλομαι βουλήσομαι — — βεβούλημαι ἐβουλήθην: will, wish, be willing (pass. deponent)

βραδύς -εῖα -ύ: slow

Βρασίδας -ου ὁ: Brasidas, prominent and successful Spartan general during the Peloponnesian War

βραχύς -εῖα -ύ: short, little, brief; εἰς βραχύ: in brief, briefly

βρενθύομαι: swagger, walk in a bold or arrogant way

βυρσοδέψης -ου ὁ: tanner

βωμός -οῦ ὁ: any raised platform, stand, altar

Γγ

γαῖα -ας ἡ: earth; *capitalized*: Earth (personified), a goddess

γαλήνη -ης ἡ: stillness of the sea, calm

γαμέω γαμῶ ἔγημα γεγάμηκα γεγάμημαι: marry

γάμος -ου ὁ: marriage, wedding, wedding feast

γάρ *explanatory particle*: for (translate first in sentence or clause); γὰρ οὖν: for in fact

γαργαλισμός -οῦ ὁ: tickling

γαστήρ γαστ[ε]ρος ἡ: paunch, belly, stomach

γε *enclitic particle*: at least, at any rate (qualifies or emphasizes word it follows)

γεγονέναι: perf. act. inf. of γίγνομαι

γεγώς -υῖα -ός: perf. act. part. of γίγνομαι

γείτων -ονος ὁ/ἡ: neighbor

γελάω γελάσομαι ἐγέλασα — — ἐγελάσθην: laugh

γέλοιος -α -ον: causing laughter, laughable, ridiculous, funny

γέλως -ωτος ὁ: laughter

γελωτοποιέω: make laughter, stir up laughter

γέμω: be full

γενέθλιος -α -ον: of or belonging to one's birth; οἱ γενέθλιοι: birthday celebration

γενειάσκω: begin to get a beard

γένεσις -εως ἡ: origin, source, birth, race, descent

γενναῖος -α -ον: well-born, noble

γεννάω γεννήσω ἐγέννησα γεγέννηκα γεγέννημαι ἐγεννήθην: beget, engender, bring forth

γέννησις -εως ἡ: procreation, generation, engendering, producing

γεννήτωρ -ορος ὁ: engenderer, father

γένος -ους τό: race, kind, stock, family

γέρας -αος τό: prize or gift of honor

γέρων -οντος ὁ: old man

γεωργία -ας ἡ: agriculture, farming

γεωργός -οῦ ὁ: farmer

γῆ γῆς ἡ: earth; *capitalized*: Earth (personified), the goddess Gaia

γηραιός -ά -όν: aged, in old age, old

γῆρας -αος/-ως τό: old age

γίγας -αντος ὁ: giant

γίγνομαι γενήσομαι ἐγενόμην — — γεγένημαι/*2nd perf.* γέγονα (*part.* γεγώς): come into being, be born, happen, arise, become, be

γιγνώσκω γνώσομαι ἔγνων ἔγνωκα ἔγνωσμαι ἐγνώσθην: know, perceive, mark, learn, recognize

Γλαύκων -ωνος ὁ: Glaukon (Latin Glaucon), brother of Plato, mentioned in reading 1

γλυκύς -εῖα -ύ: sweet

γλύφω γλύψω ἔγλυψα—[γ]έγλυμμαι ἐγλύφθην/γλύφην: carve, cut out with a knife

γλῶσσα -ης ἡ: tongue

γνοίη: aor. act. opt. 3rd pers. sing. of γιγνώσκω (root aor.)

γνούς -οῦσα -όν: aor. act. part. of γιγνώσκω (root aor.)

γνῶ: aor. act. subju. 3rd pers. sing. of γιγνώσκω (root aor.)

γνώριμος -η -ον: well-known, familiar

γνώσομαι: fut. mid. indic. 1st pers. sing. of γιγνώσκω

γόης -ητος ὁ: one who howls out enchantments, sorcerer, enchanter, magician

γοητεία -ας ἡ: sorcery, magic

γονεύς -έως ὁ: father, ancestor, parent

Γοργίας -ου ὁ: Gorgias of Leontini, famous fifth-century sophist and rhetorician

γοῦν: at least then, at any rate, anyway

γράφω γράψω ἔγραψα γέγραφα γέγραμμαι ἐγράφην: write, inscribe, draw

γυμναστικός -ή -όν: having to do with athletic exercises, athletic

γυνή γυναικός ἡ: woman, wife

Δδ

δαιμόνιος -α -ον: having to do with δαίμονες; *of people*: possessed by a δαίμων, *hence* inhuman, strange, wonderful

δαίμων -ονος ὁ/ἡ: divine being, divine spirit, divinity, daimon

δάκνω δήξομαι ἔδακον δέδηχα δέδηγμαι ἐδήχθην: bite, sting

δάκρυον -ου τό: a tear, teardrop

δασύς -εῖα -ύ: thick with hair, hairy, shaggy, rough

δέ *postpositive conjunctive particle*: but, and (connects sentence or clause to previous sentence or clause)

δέδηγμαι: perf. mid.-pass. indic. 1st pers. sing. of δάκνω

δέδοται: perf. mid.-pass. indic. 3rd pers. sing. of δίδωμι

δέησις -εως ἡ: entreating, asking; prayer, entreaty, plea, statement of need or want (cf. verb δέομαι)

δεῖ + *acc.* + *inf.*: it is binding on *acc.* to ——, it is necessary for *acc.* to ——; δεῖ ὀλίγου: nearly, almost; δεῖ πολλοῦ: far from

δείδω δείσομαι ἔδεισα δέδοικα (2nd perf. δέδια with pres. meaning): fear

δείκνυμι/δεικνύω δείξω ἔδειξα δέδειχα δέδειγμαι ἐδείχθην: bring to light, display, show, exhibit

δεινός -ή -όν: awe-inspiring, awesome, awful, fearful, terrible, dread, dire, clever; + *inf.*: clever at ——ing

δειπνέω δειπνήσω ἐδείπνησα δεδείπνηκα δεδείπνημαι ἐδειπνήθην: dine

δεῖπνον -ου τό: dinner, dinner party, feast, principal meal

δεῖσθε: pres. mid. indic. 2nd pers. pl. of δέομαι

δέκα *indecl. adj.*: ten

δέκατος -η -ον: tenth

δεξιά -ᾶς ἡ: right hand; ἐπὶ δεξιά: to the right, in the right-hand direction (i.e., moving around the circle of guests from left to right, probably indicating counterclockwise, though some scholars interpret as clockwise; appendix 3)

δέομαι δεήσομαι —— δεδέημαι ἐδεήθην: want, ask (for), be in need (of), need *gen.* (pass. deponent) δέον + *acc.* + *inf.*: it being necessary for *acc.* to —— (neut. acc. part. of δεῖ creating an acc. abs.)

δέος δέους τό: fear, alarm, fright

δέρμα -ατος τό: skin, hide

δεσμός -οῦ ὁ: binding, bond, fetter

δεῦρο *adv.*: here, hither

δεύτερος -α -ον: second

δέχομαι δέξομαι ἐδεξάμην—δέδεγμαι -ἐδέχθην: take, accept, receive, receive graciously, welcome, expect

δέω δήσω ἔδησα δέδεκα δέδεμαι ἐδέθην: bind (see also impers. δεῖ and deponent δέομαι)

δή *particle emphasizing preceding word*: indeed, now, in truth; *sometimes ironical*: no doubt, of course

δῆλος -η -ον: clear, evident, visible, conspicuous; δῆλον ὅτι: it is clear that, obviously; δῆλός [ἐστί] + *part.*: be clearly ——ing, be obviously ——ing

δηλόω δηλώσω ἐδήλωσα δεδήλωκα δεδήλωμαι ἐδηλώθην: make visible or manifest, show, exhibit

δημιουργία -ας ἡ: workmanship, skilled craftsmanship

δημιουργός -οῦ ὁ: one who works for the people, skilled workman, handicraftsman

δῆμος -ου ὁ: people

δήπου (δή + που) *particle introducing a speculative note*: indeed perhaps, it indeed may be, I would indeed suppose

δῆτα: certainly, be sure, of course; οὐ δῆτα: certainly not; τί δῆτα; what then?

δηχθείς -εῖσα -έν: aor. pass. part. of δάκνω

διά *prep.* + *gen.*: through, by means of; + *acc.*: because of, during; διὰ τί; why . . . ?; *as a prefix*: through, thoroughly, apart, asunder

Δία: acc. of Ζεύς

διαβάλλω: throw over or across, carry over or across, slander, set at variance, make quarrel

διαβολή -ῆς ἡ: slander

διαγιγνώσκω: distinguish, discern

διαδικάζω: give judgment in a case; *mid.*: contest, compete

δίαιτα -ας ἡ: life, dwelling

διάκειμαι + *adv.*: be [in a certain state], be disposed or affected [in a certain manner]

διακόσμησις -εως ἡ: setting in order, arranging

διακωλύω: hinder, prevent

διαλαμβάνω: take or receive severally

διαλέγομαι διαλέξομαι/διαλεχθήσομαι —— διείλεγμαι διελέχθην: discuss, converse, talk through; + *dat.*: converse with *dat.*, talk to *dat.* (pass. deponent)

διάλεκτος -ου ἡ: discourse, discussion, debate, arguing

διαλλαγείς -εῖσα -έν: aor. pass. part. of διαλλάττω

διαλλαγή -ῆς ἡ: reconciliation

διαλλάττω: reconcile

διαμάχομαι: fight or strive with, struggle against

διαμείβω: exchange

διαμηχανάομαι: bring about, contrive

διαμνημονεύω: call to mind, remember

διανοέομαι διανοήσομαι — — διανενόημαι διενοήθην: think, have in mind, be minded, intend, purpose, expect (pass. deponent)

διανόημα -ατος τό: thought, notion

διάνοια -ας ἡ: thought, intention, purpose, belief, intellect, mind

διαπαύω: make to cease; *mid.*: cease

διαπορεύομαι: travel, journey

διαπορθμεύω: carry over or across

διαπράττομαι διαπράξομαι διεπραξάμην—διαπέπραγμαι: bring about, accomplish

διαπρίω: saw through

διαρθρόω: divide by joints, articulate, complete in detail

διασχίζω: cleave or rend asunder

διατελέω: bring quite to an end, accomplish, continue

διατέμνω: cut through, cut in two

διατίθημι: place separately, arrange; *pass. + adv.* be affected (in a certain way), be (in a certain state)

διατριβή -ης ἡ: way of spending time, way of life, pastime

διατρίβω: rub between, rub away, consume, waste, spend time

διαφερόντως *adv.*: in a different way, differently from, at odds with; superlatively, in a way surpassing others

διαφέρω: carry over or across, differ from *gen.*, be superior to *gen.*; *mid.*: differ, be at variance with, quarrel

διαφεύγω: flee, get away from, escape

διαφθείρω διαφθερῶ διέφθειρα διέφθαρκα διέφθαρμαι διεφθάρην: destroy utterly, corrupt

διαχέω: pour different ways, disperse

διδάσκαλος -ου ὁ: teacher, master

διδάσκω διδάξω ἐδίδαξα δεδίδαχα δεδίδαγμαι ἐδιδάχθην: teach

δίδωμι δώσω ἔδωκα/(δο-) δέδωκα δέδομαι ἐδόθην: give, grant; + *inf.*: grant, allow

δίειμι: go through, pass through, narrate, relate

διελθεῖν: aor. act. inf. of διέρχομαι

διέρχομαι: go through, pass through, narrate, relate, describe

διηγέομαι διηγήσομαι διηγησάμην—διήγημαι: narrate, relate, tell, describe, set out in detail

διῄει: imperf. act. indic. 3rd pers. sing. of δίειμι (= διέρχομαι)

δίκαιος -α -ον: right, just, fair, lawful, even

δικαιοσύνη -ης ἡ: righteousness, justice

δικαστής -οῦ ὁ: one who judges a case, juror, judge

δίκη -ης ἡ: custom, usage, justice, law case, punishment

διό *conj.*: wherefore, on which account, because of which

διοίγνυμι: open [particularly by dividing or splitting]; see ἀνοίγνυμι for principal parts

διοικίζω: cause to live apart

διοιχθέντες: aor. pass. part. masc. nom. pl. of διοίγνυμι

Διοκλέης -έους ὁ: Diokles, father of Euthydemos of Athens, mentioned by Alcibiades

Διόνυσος -ου ὁ: Dionysos (Latin Dionysus), god of wine and theater

Διός: gen. of Ζεύς

Διοτίμα -ας ἡ: Diotima, woman of Mantinea (see appendix 1 and reading 9 introduction)

διπλοῦς -οῦν: twofold, double

δίς adv.: twice, doubly

δίχα adv.: in two, asunder

διχάδε adv.: in two, asunder, apart

διψάω: be thirsty, thirst

διώκω διώξω ἐδίωξα δεδίωχα δεδίωγμαι ἐδιώχθην: pursue, prosecute

Διώνη -ης ἡ: Dione, goddess, mother of Aphrodite in the *Iliad*

δίωξις -εως ἡ: pursuit

δοκέω δόξω ἔδοξα—δέδογμαι -εδόχθην: (1) think, suppose, imagine, expect; (2) seem; *especially common used impers. + dat.*: δοκεῖ μοι: it seems to me, it seems good to me; *or + dat. + inf.*: ἐδόκει τῷ δήμῳ: it seemed good to the people to —— (i.e., the people decided to ——); ἡμῖν . . . ἔδοξε: we decided; but also personally: δοκῶ μοι: I seem to myself

δολερός -ά -όν: deceitful, treacherous

δόντες: aor. act. part. masc. nom. pl. of δίδωμι

δόξα -ης ἡ: that which is thought or seems, notion, opinion, reputation

δοξάζω: think, imagine, suppose, fancy, conjecture

δορά -ᾶς ἡ: skin, hide

δόσις -εως ἡ: gift

δουλεία -ας ἡ: slavery

δούλειος -α -ον: slavish, servile

δουλεύω δουλεύσω ἐδούλευσα δεδούλευκα δεδούλευμαι ἐδουλεύθην: be a slave, perform duties of a slave

δοῦλος -ου ὁ: slave

δοῦναι: aor. act. inf. of δίδωμι

δρᾶμα -ατος τό: deed, act, drama

δραπετεύω: run away

δραχμή -ῆς ἡ: drachma (unit of money: six obols, approximately three days' wages for a laborer)

δράω δράσω ἔδρασα δέδρακα δέδραμαι ἐδράσθην: do

δύναμαι δυνήσομαι — — δεδύνημαι ἐδυνήθην: be able

δύναμις -εως ἡ: power, might, strength, capacity

δυνατός -ή -όν: strong, mighty, able, possible; + *inf.*: able to ——, capable of ——ing

δύο (nom./acc.), δυοῖν (gen./dat.): two

δυσμένεια -ας ἡ: ill-will, enmity

δωρέω: give, present

δῶρον -ου τό: gift

δώσω: fut. act. indic. 1st pers. sing. of δίδωμι

Εε

ἕ *acc. refl. pron.*: him(self), her(self), it(self)

ἐάν: if (ever); in present general or future-more-vivid conditions

ἐάντε ... ἐάντε: whether ... or

ἑαυτοῦ -ῆς -οῦ *3rd pers. refl. pron.*: himself, herself, itself; *pl.*: themselves

ἐάω ἐάσω εἴασα εἴακα εἴαμαι εἰάθην: let, allow, permit; leave be, leave alone; ἐᾶν χαίρειν: let go, dismiss, send away

ἕβδομος -η -ον: seventh

ἐγγίγνομαι: be born or bred in, arise in

ἐγγύς *adv.*: near, nearby, nearly

ἐγγυτάτω/ἐγγύτατα *superl. adv.*: nearest

ἐγείρω ἐγερῶ ἤγειρα/*mid.* ἠγρόμην ἐγρήγορα ἐγήγερμαι ἠγέρθην: awaken, wake up, rouse; *aor. mid.* ἠγρόμην: I awoke; *perf.* ἐγρήγορα: I am awake

ἐγκαταλείπω: leave behind

ἐγκρατής -ές: with a firm hold, having mastery or control over oneself or others; *in positive sense*: self-disciplined; *in negative sense*: domineering, unyielding

ἐγκύμων -ον: pregnant

ἐγκωμιάζω ἐγκωμιάσω/-ομαι ἐνεκωμίασα ἐγκεκωμίακα ἐγκεκωμίασμαι ἐνεκωμιάσθην: praise, give an encomium, laud

ἐγκώμιον -ου τό: encomium, song or speech of praise

ἐγρήγορα: perf. act. indic. of ἐγείρω (perf. forms with pres. meaning)

ἐγχειρέω ἐγχειρήσω ἐνεχείρησα ἐγκεχείρηκα ἐγκεχείρημαι ἐνεχειρήθην: take in hand, undertake, try

ἐγχέω ἐγχεῶ ἐνέχεα ἐγκέχυκα ἐγκέχυμαι ἐνεχύθην: pour in

ἐγώ ἐμοῦ/μου ἐμοί/μοι ἐμέ/με: I, me

ἔγωγε (ἐγώ + γε): I at least, I for my part

ἕδος -ους τό: sitting-place, seat

ἔδοσαν: aor. act. indic. 3rd pers. pl. of δίδωμι

ἔδραμον: aor. act. indic. 1st pers. sing./3rd pers. pl. of τρέχω

ἐζήτουν: imperf. act. indic. 1st pers. sing./3rd pers. pl. of ζητέω

ἐθέλω ἐθελήσω ἠθέλησα ἠθέληκα: be willing, wish, want

ἔθηκας: aor. act. indic. 2nd pers. sing. of τίθημι

ἔθος -ους τό: custom, habit

εἰ: if, whether; εἰ γάρ *introducing wish*: if only, would that

εἶ: pres. indic. 2nd pers. sing. of εἰμί or fut. indic. 2nd pers. sing. of εἶμι

εἴασα: aor. act. indic. 1st pers. sing. of ἐάω

εἰδείην: pres. act. opt. 1st pers. sing. of οἶδα

εἰδέναι: pres. act. inf. of οἶδα

εἶδον: aor. act. indic. 1st pers. sing./3rd pers. pl. of ὁράω

εἶδος -ους τό: that which is seen, form, shape, figure

εἴδωλον -ου τό: image, phantom

εἰδώς -υῖα -ός (εἰδότος): act. part. of οἶδα (perf. forms with pres. meaning) εἶεν: well then! very well! or pres. opt. 3rd pers. sing. of εἰμί

εἴθε *introducing wish*: if only . . . , would that . . .

εἰκάζω εἰκάσω ἤκασα—ἤκασμαι ἠκάσθην: make like to, represent by a likeness, portray, conjecture, infer

εἰκός -ότος τό: that which is like truth, that which is likely, probable, or reasonable

εἴκοσι(ν) *indecl. adj.*: twenty

εἰκότως *adv.*: probably

εἰκών -όνος ἡ: figure, likeness, image, portrait

Εἰλείθυια -ας ἡ: Eileithyia, goddess of childbirth

εἰλικρινής -ές: unmixed, without alloy, pure

εἷλον: aor. act. indic. 1st pers. sing./3rd pers. pl. of αἱρέω

εἰμί ἔσομαι: be, exist, *imperf.* ἦ(ν), *part.* ὤν οὖσα ὄν, *inf.* εἶναι, *impers.* ἔστιν + *inf.*: it is possible to ——

εἶμι: I will go, *imperf.* ᾖα, *part.* ἰών ἰοῦσα ἰόν, *inf.* ἰέναι: go (with no futurity implied)

εἶναι: pres. inf. of εἰμί: to be

εἰπέ: aor. act. impera. 2nd pers. sing. of λέγω: tell! say!

εἴπερ (strengthened form of εἰ): if indeed, if truly

εἶπον: aor. act. indic. 1st pers. sing./3rd pers. pl. of λέγω

εἴρηκα: perf. act. indic. 1st pers. sing. of λέγω

εἴρημαι: perf. mid.-pass. indic. 1st pers. sing. of λέγω

εἰρήνη -ης ἡ: peace, time of peace

εἰρωνεύομαι: dissemble, pretend, be ironic

εἰρωνικός -ή -όν: dissembling, ironic

εἰς *prep.* + *acc.*: into, to, onto, for; + *gen. name*: to *name's*, to the [house/temple/abode] of *name*; *as a prefix*: into, in, to

εἷς μία ἕν: one

εἰσάγω: lead in or into, introduce

εἴσειμι: go or come into, enter

εἰσέρχομαι: go in or into, enter

εἰσηγέομαι: bring in, introduce

εἰσίω: pres. act. subj. 1st pers. sing. of εἴσειμι

εἶτα *adv.*: then, next

εἴτε . . . εἴτε: either . . . or, whether . . . or

εἶχον: imperf. act. indic. 1st pers. sing./3rd pers. pl. of ἔχω

εἴωθα *perf. forms with pres. meaning*: be accustomed to

εἰωθότως *adv.*: in customary wise, as usual

ἐκ/ἐξ *prep.* + *gen.*: from, out of, away from; since (time), because of; *as a prefix*: out, away, off; utterly

ἕκαστος -η -ον: every, every one, each, each one

ἑκατόν *indecl. adj.*: one hundred

ἑκάτερος -η -ον: each [of two], each [singly]; *normal in pred. position*: e.g., ἑκάτερον τὸν ἔρωτα: each [kind of] love, each of the two loves ἐκβαίνω: walk out from, leave, go forth, depart from, disembark

ἐκβάλλω: throw out, throw up

ἔκγονος -ον: born of, sprung from

ἐκδέχομαι: take or receive from

ἐκεῖ *adv.*: there, in that place

ἐκεῖνος -η -ο: that; *often used alone as virtual equivalent of 3rd pers. pron.*: he, she, it

ἐκεῖσε *adv.*: thither, to that place, there

ἐκκλησία -ας ἡ: assembly

ἐκλάμπω: shine or beam forth

ἐκλεαίνω: smooth out, smooth away

ἐκλέγω: pick or single out, select

ἐκπεπληγμένος -η -ον: perf. mid.-pass. part. of ἐκπλήττω

ἐκπέπωκα: perf. act. indic. 1st pers. sing. of ἐκπίνω

ἐκπίνω: drink out of, quaff, drain

ἐκπλαγείς -εῖα -έν: aor. pass. part. of ἐκπλήττω

ἐκπλήγνυμι = ἐκπλήττω

ἐκπλήττω ἐκπλήξω ἐξέπληξα ἐκπέπληγα ἐκπέπληγμαι ἐξεπλάγην/ἐξεπλήγην: strike out of, drive away from, amaze, astonish

ἔκπωμα -ατος τό: drinking cup

ἐκτελέω: bring quite to an end, accomplish, achieve

ἐκτομή -ῆς ἡ: castration

ἐκτός *adv.*: outside *or prep. + gen.*: out of, far from

ἕκτος -η -ον: sixth

ἐκτρέφω: bring up from childhood, rear up, nourish, nurse

ἐκτυπόω: model or work in relief

Ἕκτωρ -ορος ὁ: Hektor (Latin Hector), greatest Trojan warrior

ἐκφανής -ές: showing itself, manifest, evident

ἐκφέρω: carry out, bring out

ἐκφεύγω: flee out or away from, escape

ἐκχέω: pour out

ἑκών -οῦσα -όν: willing(ly), of free will, readily

ἐλάττων -ον: smaller, less

ἔλεγχος -ους τό: trial, test, proof, cross-examining, testing, elenchus

ἐλέγχω ἐλέγξω ἤλεγξα—ἐλήλεγμαι ἠλέγχθην: disgrace, put to shame, cross-examine, test

ἐλεέω (*aor.* ἠλέησα): pity, show mercy to, have pity on

ἐλεῖν: aor. act. inf. of αἱρέω

ἐλευθερία -ας ἡ: freedom

ἐλεύθερος -α -ον: free, not enslaved

ἐλθών -οῦσα -όν: aor. act. part. of ἔρχομαι

Ἑλλάς -άδος ἡ: Greece, Hellas

ἐλλείπω: leave in, leave behind; come short of, be inferior to

Ἕλλην -ηνος ὁ: Greek, Hellene

ἐλλόγιμος -ον: worthy of note, famous

ἐλλοχάω: lie in ambush for

ἔλοιτο: aor. mid. opt. 3rd pers. sing. of αἱρέω

ἐλπίζω ἐλπιῶ ἤλπισα — — ἠλπίσθην: hope, expect

ἐλπίς -ίδος ἡ: hope, expectation

ἔλωμαι: aor. mid. subju. 1st pers. sing. of αἱρέω

ἔμαθον: aor. act. indic. 1st pers. sing./3rd pers. pl. of μανθάνω

ἐμαυτοῦ -ῷ -όν *1st pers. refl. pron.*: me, myself

ἔμβραχυ *adv.*: in short, briefly

ἐμέ (acc. of ἐγώ): me

ἔμεινα: aor. act. indic. 1st pers. sing. of μένω

ἔμμετρος -ον: in meter, in verse

ἐμνήσθην: aor. pass. (with act. meaning) indic. 1st pers. sing. of μιμνῄσκω

ἐμοί (dat. of ἐγώ): to me, for me

ἔμοιγε = ἐμοί + *particle* γε

ἐμός -ή -όν: my, mine

ἐμοῦ (gen. of ἐγώ): of me, my

ἐμπίπλημι ἐμπλήσω ἐνέπλησα: fill full; *mid.*: have filled for oneself

ἐμποδίζω: put the feet in bonds, fetter, hinder, stop

ἐμποιέω: make in, create in

ἔμπροσθε(ν) *adv.*, or *prep. + gen.*: before, in front (of)

ἔμφρων -ον: in one's mind or senses; sensible, thoughtful

ἔμφυτος -ον: implanted, innate, inborn, natural

ἐν *prep. + dat.*: in, among, on, at; *+ gen.*: in the house of, at *gen.'s*

ἕν: neut. nom./acc. sing. of εἷς

ἕνα: acc. masc. sing. of εἷς

ἐναντίον *adv.*, or *prep. + gen.*: against, opposite, in the presence of, in front of

ἐναντιόομαι: contradict, deny

ἐναντίος -α -ον: opposite, opposed, hostile

ἔνατος -η -ον: ninth

ἐνδεής -ές: in need of, lacking

ἔνδεια -ας ἡ: want, need, lack

ἔνδοθεν *adv.*: from within, within

ἔνδον *adv.*, or *prep. + gen.*: in, within, in the house, at home

ἔνειμι: be in *dat.*; ἔνεστι(ν) *+ dat. + inf.*: it is possible for *dat.* to ——

ἕνεκα *prep. + gen.*: on account of, for the sake of, because of, for (gen. obj. usually precedes prep.)

ἕνεκεν: Ionic form of ἕνεκα

ἐνελίσσω: roll up in

ἐνενήκοντα *indecl. adj.*: ninety

ἐνενόησα: aor. act. indic. 1st pers. sing. of ἐννοέω

ἐνέτυχον: aor. act. indic. 1st pers. sing./3rd pers. pl. of ἐντυγχάνω

ἐνεχείρεις: imperf. act. indic. 2nd pers. sing. of ἐγχειρέω

ἔνθα *adv.*: here, there; ἔνθα μέν . . . ἔνθα δέ: here . . . there

ἐνθάδε *adv.*: here, there, thither

ἐνθένδε *adv.*: hence, from this quarter

ἔνθεος -ον: full of the god, inspired, possessed

ἐνθυμέομαι ἐνθυμήσομαι — — ἐντεθύμημαι ἐνεθυμήθην: lay to heart, consider well; take to heart, be concerned at (pass. deponent)

ἐνί = ἐν

ἑνί: masc./neut. dat. sing. of εἷς

ἐνιαυτός -οῦ ὁ: year, any long period of time, cycle, period

ἐνίζω: sit in, on, or among

ἔνιοι -αι -α: some

ἐνίοτε *adv.*: sometimes

ἐννέα *indecl. adj.*: nine

ἐννοέω: have in one's thoughts, think, consider, reflect; *ingressive aor.*: realize, conceive an idea

ἑνός: masc./neut. gen. sing. of εἷς

ἐνταῦθα *adv.*: here, there

ἐντεῦθεν *adv.*: hence or thence, from this point

ἐντεύξομαι: fut. mid. indic. 1st pers. sing. of ἐντυγχάνω

ἐντίθημι: put in or into

ἐντός *adv.*: within, inside

ἐντυγχάνω (+ *dat. obj.*): light upon, encounter, fall in with, meet with, obtain

ἐντύχῃ: aor. act. subju. 3rd pers. sing. of ἐντυγχάνω

ἐξ = ἐκ

ἐξαιρέω: take out of *gen.*, strip *gen.* of

ἐξαίφνης *adv.*: suddenly

ἐξακισχίλιοι -αι -α: six thousand

ἐξαπατάω: deceive or beguile thoroughly, trick

ἐξαρκέω: be quite enough for, suffice for; *used impers.* + *dat.*: it is enough for *dat.*; it satisfies *dat.*

ἐξαρνέομαι: deny utterly (pass. deponent)

ἐξεγείρω: awaken; *aor. mid.*: wake up

ἐξέγρεσθαι: aor. mid. inf. of ἐξεγείρω

ἔξειμι: go out, come out

ἐξελέγχω: convict, confute, refute

ἐξελέσθαι: aor. mid. inf. of ἐξαιρέω

ἐξενεγκάμενος -η -ον: aor. mid. part. of ἐκφέρω

ἐξεργάζομαι: work out, make completely, finish off, bring to perfection

ἔξεστι + *dat.* + *inf.*: it is possible for *dat.* to ——

ἐξευρίσκω: find out, discover

ἐξῆς *adv.*: in order, one after another

ἔξοδος -ου ὁ: going out, departure

ἐξόν *neut. part. of impers.* ἔξεστι *usually introducing acc. abs.*: it being possible, since it is possible, when it is possible, although it is possible ἐξορίζω: send beyond the frontier, banish

ἐξουσία -ας ἡ: power or authority, means, resources

ἔξω adv., or prep. + gen.: outside, outside of

ἕξω: fut. act. indic. 1st pers. sing. of ἔχω

ἔξωθεν adv.: from without

ἔοικα perf. forms with pres. meaning: seem, appear, be like

ἑορτή -ῆς ἡ: feast or festival, holiday

ἔπαθον: aor. act. indic. 1st pers. sing./3rd pers. pl. of πάσχω

ἐπαινέω: praise, applaud, commend; + double acc.: praise acc. pers. for neut. acc. thing

ἔπαινος -ου ὁ: praise, speech of praise, commendation, approval

ἐπαμύνω: defend, defend against attack

ἐπαναβασμός -οῦ ὁ: step of a stair

ἐπάνειμι: go back, return, rise, climb up

ἐπαποθνῄσκω: die with or after

ἐπέθεσαν: aor. act. indic. 3rd pers. pl. of ἐπιτίθημι

ἐπεί conj.: after, since, when

ἐπειδάν conj.: whenever

ἐπειδή conj.: when, since, because

ἐπειδήπερ = ἐπειδή + -περ

ἔπειμι: be upon

ἔπειμι: come on, approach, encroach, attack

ἐπείπερ (ἐπεί + suffix -περ) conj.: since in fact, since really, seeing that

ἐπείσθην: aor. pass. indic. 1st pers. sing. of πείθω

ἔπειτα adv.: then, thereupon, next, in the future; πρῶτον . . . ἔπειτα: first . . . second

ἐπέρχομαι: come upon, come near, come suddenly upon; attack, approach

ἔπεσον: aor. act. indic. 1st pers. sing./3rd pers. pl. of πίπτω

ἐπί prep. + acc.: against, at, toward, to, for, after, in quest of; + gen.: on, upon, in the time of; + dat.: at, near, for, for the purpose of; as a prefix: against, upon, toward, on top of, after

ἐπιβάτης -ου ὁ: one who mounts or embarks, the soldier on board a fighting ship, the warrior in a chariot

ἐπιβουλεύω: plan or contrive (against), plot (against), scheme (against) + dat. pers. plotted against

ἐπίβουλος -ον: treacherous, conniving, plotting against

ἐπιδείκνυμι: show, exhibit, make public, display

ἐπιδέομαι: want, lack

ἐπιδημέω: be at home, come home [from foreign travel]

ἐπίδοσις -εως ἡ: potential for growth

ἐπιεικής -ές: reasonable, fitting, meet, suitable

ἐπίθεσθε: aor. mid. impera. 2nd pers. pl. of ἐπιτίθημι

ἐπιθετέος -α -ον (verbal adj. of ἐπιτίθημι): to be put on, to be imposed on; neut. used impers.: one must put on or impose, it is necessary to put on

ἐπιθυμέω ἐπιθυμήσω ἐπεθύμησα ἐπιτεθύμηκα: set one's heart upon, desire, with gen. obj.

ἐπιθυμητής -οῦ ὁ: one who longs for or desires

ἐπιθυμία -ας ἡ: desire, yearning, longing

ἐπιθῶμαι: aor. mid. subju. 1st pers. sing. of ἐπιτίθημι

ἐπίκουρος -ου ὁ: ally, assistant

ἐπιλαμβάνομαι: seize upon, arrest

ἐπιλανθάνομαι ἐπιλήσομαι ἐπελαθόμην ἐπιλέληθα ἐπιλέλησμαι: forget, *with gen. or acc. obj.*

ἐπιλήσμων -ον: forgetful

ἐπιμέλεια -ας ἡ: care, attention diligence

ἐπιμελέομαι ἐπιμελήσομαι —— ἐπιμεμέλημαι ἐπιμελήθην: take care of *gen. obj.* (pass. deponent)

ἐπιμελής -ές: careful or anxious about; in charge of; ἐπιμελὲς ποιέομαι + *inf.*: make it a care/practice to ——

ἐπινίκιος -ον: of victory, triumphal; τὸ ἐπινίκιον: song or other celebration of victory

ἐπιπίπτω: fall upon or over, befall

ἐπίπνοος -ον: breathed upon, inspired

ἐπιπορεύομαι: journey over, travel on, go or march to

ἐπίπροσθεν *adv.*: before

ἐπίσταμαι ἐπιστήσομαι ——— ἠπιστήθην: know; + *inf.*: know how to —— (pass. deponent)

ἐπιστήμη -ης ἡ: knowledge, understanding, skill, experience, wisdom

ἐπίσχω: hold or direct toward; keep in, check

ἐπίταξις -εως ἡ: injunction, command, order

ἐπιτάσσω = ἐπιτάττω

ἐπιτάττω: command, order

ἐπιτήδειος -α -ον: made for an end or purpose, fit or adapted for it, suitable, convenient

ἐπιτήδευμα -ατος τό: pursuit, business, practice, habit, custom

ἐπιτηδεύω ἐπιτηδεύσω ἐπετήδευσα ἐπιτήδευκα ἐπιτετήδευμαι: pursue, practice, make *acc.* one's business; + *inf.*: take care to ——

ἐπιτίθημι: lay, put, or place upon, impose; attack

ἐπιτρεπτέος -α -ον (verbal adj. of ἐπιτρέπω): to be permissible, to be allowed; *neut. used impers.*: one must permit, one must allow, it is necessary to permit

ἐπιτρέπω: entrust to, permit, allow

ἐπιτυγχάνω: hit the mark, meet

ἐπιχειρέω ἐπιχειρήσω ἐπεχείρησα ἐπικεχείρηκα ἐπικεχείρημαι ἐπεχειρήθην + *dat.*: put one's hand on or to, make an attempt on, attack; + *inf.*: try to ——

ἐπιχειρητέος -α -ον (verbal adj. of ἐπιχειρέω): to be attempted; *neut. used impers.*: one must attempt, it is necessary to try

ἐπιχώριος -α -ον: in or of the country, in the province of

ἐποιούμην: imperf. mid.-pass. indic. 1st pers. sing. of ποιέω

ἕπομαι ἕψομαι ἑσπόμην: follow + *dat. obj.*

ἐπονομάζω: give a name to, name or call after, name *x* after *y*

ἐποπτικά -ῶν τά: highest mysteries, second-level rites of initiation in the Eleusinian Mysteries

ἔπος -ους τό: word; ὡς ἔπος εἰπεῖν: so to speak, virtually, almost ἐπριάμην: aor. equivalent of ὠνέομαι

ἑπτά *indecl. adj.*: seven

ἐπῳδή -ῆς ἡ: song sung to or over; enchantment, charm, spell

ἐπωνυμία -ας ἡ: name given after a person or thing, nickname, significant name

ἐραστής -οῦ ὁ: lover, passionate follower

ἐραστός -ή -όν: loveable, beloved

ἐράω, *imperf.* ἤρων: be in love, love *gen. obj.* [erotically], desire

ἐργάζομαι ἐργάσομαι ἠργασάμην—εἴργασμαι ἠργάσθην: work, labor, do, accomplish, build, make, produce

ἐργασία -ας ἡ: work, activity, labor

ἔργον -ου τό: work, deed, task

ἐρέσθαι: aor. mid. inf. of ἔρομαι

ἐρέω: fut. act. indic. 1st pers. sing. of λέγω

ἐρημία -ας ἡ: deserted place, solitude, desert, wilderness

ἐρίζω: argue, quarrel, contest

ἔριον -ου τό: wool

ἕρμαιον -ου τό: godsend, windfall, piece of luck (believed to come from the god Hermes)

ἑρμηνεύω: interpret

ἑρμογλυφεῖον -ου τό: statuary workshop, place for carving herms (special statues representing Hermes)

ἔρομαι ἐρήσομαι ἠρόμην: ask, enquire

ἐρρήθη: aor. pass. indic. 3rd pers. sing. of λέγω

ἐρρωμένος -η -ον: in good health, stout, vigorous

Ἐρυξίμαχος -ου ὁ: Eryximachos (Latin Eryximachus), doctor and guest at the symposium (see appendix 1)

ἔρχομαι εἶμι/ἐλεύσομαι ἦλθον ἐλήλυθα: come, go

ἐρῶ (fut. of λέγω): I will say or speak

ἐρώμενος -ου ὁ (subst. pass. part. of ἐράω): beloved (standard term for the younger male in male couples)

ἔρως -ωτος ὁ: love, desire

Ἔρως -ωτος ὁ: Eros, boy-god of love and desire

ἐρωτάω ἐρωτήσω ἠρώτησα ἠρώτηκα ἠρώτημαι ἠρωτήθην: ask, question; + *acc. pers.*: question *acc. pers.*; + *acc. thing*: ask about *acc. thing*; + *double acc.*: ask *acc. pers.* about *acc. thing*

ἐρωτηθείς -εῖσα -έν: aor. pass. part. of ἐρωτάω

ἐρώτημα -ατος τό: question

ἐρώτησις -εως ἡ: question, questioning

ἐρωτικός -ή -όν: amatory, having to do with love or desire, erotic

ἐς = εἰς

ἐσθής -ῆτος ἡ: garment, dress, clothing, raiment

ἐσθίω ἔδομαι ἔφαγον ἐδήδοκα ἐδήδομαι ἠδέσθην: eat

ἔσομαι: fut. mid. indic. 1st pers. sing. of εἰμί

ἑσπέρα -ας ἡ: evening

ἐσπουδακέναι: perf. act. inf. of σπουδάζω

ἔστε *conj.*: up to the time that, until

ἐστεφανωμένος -η -ον: perf. mid.-pass. part. of στεφανόω

ἔστηκα *perf. form of* ἵστημι *with pres. meaning*: stand

ἐστι(ν): pres. indic. 3rd pers. sing. of εἰμί

ἑστιάω: receive at one's hearth or in one's house; entertain, feast, regale

ἔστιν + *acc.* + *inf.*: it is possible for *acc.* to ——

ἔσχατος -η -ον: last, furthest, most extreme, outermost, end, final

ἑταιρίστρια -ας ἡ: lesbian(?); meaning of word uncertain, has been inferred from context

ἑταῖρος -ου ὁ: comrade, companion, mate

ἐτέθην: aor. pass. indic. 1st pers. sing. of τίθημι

ἕτερος -α -ον: one of two, other, different; ἕτερος . . . ἕτερος: one . . . the other

ἔτι *adv.*: still, yet, as yet; *negated*: longer; ἔτι καὶ νῦν: still now, even now

ἑτοῖμος -η -ον: at hand, ready, prepared, available

ἔτος -ους τό: year

εὖ *adv.*: well

εὐανθής -ές: with beautiful blooms, rich in flowers, with fresh flowers

εὐαρίθμητος -ον: easy to count, easily counted

εὐδαιμονέω: be well off, be fortunate, be happy

εὐδαιμονία -ας ἡ: prosperity, good fortune, wealth, happiness

εὐδαιμονίζω: call or account happy

εὐδαίμων -ον: blessed, happy, lucky, attended by a good daimon

εὕδω εὐδήσω: sleep, lie down to sleep

εὐετηρία -ας ἡ: goodness of season, good season

Εὐθύδημος -ου ὁ: Euthydemos (Latin Euthydemus), Athenian youth (see note on reading 10H.31)

εὐθύς -εῖα -ύ: straight, direct, straightforward; *commonly used adverbially*: straightaway, immediately

εὐκλεής -ές: of good report, famous, glorious

εὐλάβεια -ας ἡ: caution

εὐλαβέομαι εὐλαβήσομαι — — — ηὐλαβήθην: be cautious, circumspect, take care, beware (pass. deponent)

εὐμένεια -ας ἡ: goodwill, favor, kindness

εὔμοιρος -ον: blest with possessions, blest with a share

εὐμορφία -ας ἡ: beauty of form, symmetry

εὐπορέω: be rich in resources, be well-equipped with ideas, strategies, words, or other kinds of resources, prosper (for principal parts see ἀπορέω)

εὔπορος -ον: abundant in resources, fluent, resourceful, ingenious, inventive

εὐπρεπής -ές: attractive

εὑρεῖν: aor. act. inf. of εὑρίσκω

εὑρετικός -ή -όν: inventive, ingenious; ὁ εὑρετικός: inventor

εὑρίσκω εὑρήσω ηὗρον ηὕρηκα ηὕρημαι ηὑρέθην: find, discover

εὐρύστερνος -ον: broad-breasted

εὐσέβεια -ας ἡ: reverence toward the gods, piety

εὐσεβέω: live or act piously and reverently

εὐσχημοσύνη -ης ἡ: elegance, graceful manner

εὐτύχημα -ατος τό: piece of good luck, happy issue, success

εὐφημέω: use words of good omen or abstain from words of ill omen, keep silent

εὐφραίνω: cheer, delight, gladden

εὐφυής -ές: well-grown, shapely

εὔχομαι εὔξομαι ηὐξάμην—ηὖγμαι: pray, boast

εὐώδης -ες: sweet-smelling, fragrant

εὐωχία -ας ἡ: good cheer, feasting

ἐφ᾽ = ἐπί

ἐφάπτω: bind on or to; *mid.*: take hold of, touch, grasp, apprehend *gen.*

ἐφεξῆς *adv.*: in order, in a row, one after another

ἔφη: imperf. act. indic. 3rd pers. sing. of φημί

ἔφησθα: imperf. act. indic. 2nd pers. sing. of φημί

Ἐφιάλτης -ου ὁ: Ephialtes, one of a pair of giants who tried to assault the gods, mentioned at
   Iliad 5.385 and *Odyssey* 11.308

ἐφίστημι: set or place upon, put in charge of; *mid. intrans.*: stand next to

ἐφοίτων: imperf. act. indic. 1st pers. sing./3rd pers. pl. of φοιτάω

ἔφυ *intrans.*: aor. act. indic. 3rd pers. sing. of φύω

ἐφυμνέω: sing or chant after or over

ἔχθιστος -η -ον (superl. of ἐχθρός): most hated, most hateful, very hateful, etc.

ἐχθίων -ιον (compar. of ἐχθρός): most hateful, more hated, rather hateful, etc.

ἐχθρός -ά -όν: hated, hateful

ἐχθρός -οῦ ὁ: enemy, personal enemy (as opposed to οἱ πολέμιοι, the enemy with whom one
   is at war)

ἔχιδνα -ης ἡ: adder, viper

ἔχις -ιος or -εως ὁ: adder, viper

ἔχω (*imperf.* εἶχον) ἕξω/σχήσω ἔσχον ἔσχηκα -ἔσχημαι ἐσχέθην: (1) have, hold; (2) + *inf.*:
   be able to ——; (3) + *adv.*: be [such], be in [such] state, e.g., πῶς ἔχεις; How are you? εὖ
   ἔχω: I am well, χαλεπῶς ἔχω: I am in a bad state; (4) οὐκ ἔχω + ὅπως, πῶς, ποῦ, etc.: I
   don't know how . . . , where . . . , etc.

ἔωθεν *adv.*: from dawn, from early morning

ἑωθινός -ή -όν: in the morning, early

ἑώρακα: perf. act. indic. 1st pers. sing. of ὁράω

ἕως *conj.*: while; until, till

ἕως ἕω ἡ: dawn, morning

Ζ ζ

ζάω ζήσω: live, *pres.* ζῶ ζῇς . . . , *imperf.* ἔζων ἔζης . . . , *part.* ζῶν ζῶσα ζῶν, *inf.* ζῆν

Ζεύς Διός ὁ: Zeus, king of the gods; *acc.* Δία, *dat.* Διί

ζηλοτυπέω: be jealous

ζηλόω ζηλώσω ἐζήλωσα ἐζήλωκα ἐζήλωμαι ἐζηλώθην: envy, emulate; rival, vie with ζηλωτός -ή -όν: enviable, to be emulated, worthy of imitation

ζῆν: pres. act. inf. of ζάω

ζητέω ζητήσω ἐζήτησα ἐζήτηκα ἐζήτημαι ἐζητήθην: seek, seek for

ζῷον -ου τό: living being, animal

Ηη

ἤ conj.: or; *preceded by compar. adj. or adv.*: than; ἤ ... ἤ: either ... or; *in a question*: whether ... or

ἦ adv.: in truth, truly; in a question, often left untranslated (Latin *num*) *or* what? pray? can it be? see also εἰμί or ἠμί

ᾖ: pres. subju. 3rd pers. sing. of εἰμί

ᾗ adv.: which way, where, whither, in or at what place; also dat. sing. fem. of ὅς ἥ ὅ

ἤγαγον: aor. act. indic. 1st pers. sing./3rd pers. pl. of ἄγω

ἠγάπα: imperf. act. indic. 3rd pers. sing. of ἀγαπάω

ἤγγειλα: aor. act. indic. 1st pers. sing. of ἀγγέλλω

ἡγεμονεύω: lead, guide

ἡγεμών -όνος ὁ: one who leads, leader, guide

ἡγέομαι ἡγήσομαι ἡγησάμην—ἥγημαι ἡγήθην: (1) go before, lead the way; (2) consider, believe, think

ἠγώνισαι: aor. mid. indic. 2nd pers. sing. of ἀγωνίζομαι

ἠδέ conj.: and

ᾔδει: past indic. 3rd pers. sing. of οἶδα

ἡδέως adv.: sweetly, pleasantly, gladly

ἤδη adv.: by this time, before this, already, now

ᾔδη: past indic. 1st pers. sing. of οἶδα

ἥδιστος -η -ον (superl. adj. of ἡδύς): sweetest, most pleasant, very sweet, etc.

ἡδίων -ον (compar. adj. of ἡδύς): sweeter, more pleasant, rather sweet, etc.

ἥδομαι ἡσθήσομαι — — — ἥσθην: enjoy (pass. deponent)

ἡδονή -ῆς ἡ: delight, enjoyment, pleasure

ἡδύς ἡδεῖα ἡδύ: sweet, pleasurable

ἤθεος -ου ὁ: a youth just come to manhood, unmarried young man

ἦθος -ους τό: accustomed place, habit, custom; *pl.*: character, disposition

ἥκιστος -η -ον: least; *neut. pl. often used adverbially*: least of all, not at all (cf. μάλιστα)

ἤκουσα: aor. act. indic. 1st pers. sing. of ἀκούω

ἥκω ἥξω: have come, be present, be here

ἦλθον: aor. act. indic. 1st pers. sing./3rd pers. pl. of ἔρχομαι

ἡλικία -ας ἡ: time of life, age; prime of life, maturity

ἡλικιώτης -ου ὁ: equal in age, age-mate, peer

ἥλιος -ου ὁ: sun

Ἦλις -ιδος ἡ: Elis, a region in Greece on the northwest Peloponnesus

ἡμεῖς ἡμῶν ἡμῖν ἡμᾶς: we, us

ἠμέληται: perf. pass. indic. 3rd pers. sing. of ἀμελέω

ἡμέρα -ας ἡ: day

ἡμέτερος -α -ον: our

ἠμί: I say; *especially* ἦ δ' ὅς: he said; ἦν δ' ἐγώ: I said

ἥμισυς -εια -υ: half

ἤν = ἐάν

ἦν: (1) imperf. indic. 1st pers./3rd pers. sing. of εἰμί or (2) imperf. act. indic. 1st pers. sing. of ἠμί, usually in the phrase ἦν δ' ἐγώ: I said

ἡνίκα *rel. adv.*: at which time, when

ἥξω: fut. act. indic. 1st pers. sing. of ἥκω

ἠπόρουν: imperf. act. indic. 1st pers. sing./3rd pers. pl. of ἀπορέω

Ἡράκλεις: voc. of Herakles (Latin Heracles or Hercules), great Greek hero; used as an expletive

Ἡράκλειτος -ου ὁ: Herakleitos (Latin Heraclitus), presocratic philosopher

ἠράσθην: aor. (ingressive) of ἐράομαι, the mid. deponent of ἐράω: I fell in love, I conceived a passion

ἠργάσατο: aor. mid. indic. 3rd pers. sing. of ἐργάζομαι

ἠρέμα *adv.*: motionlessly, quietly, gently, softly

ἠρξάμην: aor. mid. indic. 1st pers. sing. of ἄρχομαι

ἠρόμην: I asked (aor.); defective verb, occurring in Attic only in aor. and fut. ἐρήσομαι; ἐρωτάω is used for other tenses

ἥρως ἥρωος/ἥρω ὁ: warrior, hero

ἠρώτων: imperf. act. indic. 1st pers. sing./3rd pers. pl. of ἐρωτάω

ἦσαν: imperf. indic. 3rd pers. pl. of εἰμί

ἡσθείς -εῖσα -έν: aor. part. of ἥδομαι (pass. with act. meaning)

ἤσθημαι: perf. mid. indic. 1st pers. sing. of αἰσθάνομαι

Ἡσίοδος -ου ὁ: Hesiod, a major Greek poet; author of *Theogony* and *Works and Days*; probably ca. seventh century B.C.E.

ἡσυχάζω: be quiet, be still, be at rest

ἡσυχία -ας ἡ: stillness, rest, quiet

ᾐσχυνήθην: aor. indic. 1st pers. sing. of αἰσχύνομαι

ἠτιμάσθαι: perf. pass. inf. of ἀτιμάζω

ἡττάομαι + *gen.*: be less than, be inferior to; give way to, yield to

ἥττων -ον: less, weaker

ηὗδον: imperf. act. indic. 1st pers. sing./3rd pers. pl. of εὕδω (= καθεύδω)

ηὔλει: imperf. act. indic. 3rd pers. sing. of αὐλέω

ηὐπόρουν: imperf. act. indic. 1st pers. sing./3rd pers. pl. of εὐπορέω

ηὗρον: aor. act. indic. 1st pers. sing./3rd pers. pl. of εὑρίσκω

Ἥφαιστος -ου ὁ: Hephaistos (Latin Hephaestus), the smith god

ἤχθησαν: aor. pass. indic. 3rd pers. pl. of ἄγω

Θθ

θάλαττα -ης ἡ: sea

θάλλω θαλῶ ἔθαλον τέθηλα: bloom

θάνατος -ου ὁ: death

θανεῖν: aor. act. inf. of θνήσκω

θαρρέω/θαρσέω: be of good courage, take courage; be confident, be bold

θάρρος/θάρσος -ους τό: courage, boldness

θάττων -ον/θάσσων -ον (compar. of ταχύς): quicker, swifter, rather swift, etc.

θαῦμα -ατος τό: wonder, marvel

θαυμάζω θαυμάσομαι ἐθαύμασα τεθαύμακα τεθαύμασμαι ἐθαυμάσθην: wonder, marvel at, be astonished, be surprised, admire wonderingly

θαυμάσιος -α -ον: wondrous, wonderful, marvelous

θαυμαστός -ή -όν: to be wondered at, wondrous, wonderful, surprising

θεά -ας ἡ: goddess

θεάομαι θεάσομαι ἐθεασάμην—τεθέαμαι: look on, gaze at, view, behold, watch, be a spectator of

θεατός -ή -όν (verbal adj. of θεάομαι): to be gazed at, to be watched, to be visible

θέατρον -ου τό: theater

θεῖος -α -ον: divine, holy, sacred

θέλγω: enchant, charm

θέλω = ἐθέλω

θέμενος -η -ον: aor. mid. part. of τίθημι

θέμις -ιτος ἡ: that which is laid down or established by custom, law, right, custom; acc. θέμιν

-θεν as suffix: from ——

θεός -οῦ ὁ/ἡ: god, goddess

θεοφιλής -ές: dear to the gods

θεραπεύω θεραπεύσω ἐθεράπευσα τεθεράπευκα τεθεράπευμαι ἐθεραπεύθην: help, attend, serve

θεράπων -ονος ὁ: helper, attendant, servant

θερμός -ή -όν: hot, warm

θέρος -ους τό: summer, summertime

θέσις -εως ἡ: setting, placing, arranging

Θέτις -ιδος ἡ: Thetis, goddess and mother of Achilles

θέω: run

θεωρέω θεωρήσω ἐθεώρησα τεθεώρηκα τεθεώρημαι ἐθεωρήθην: look at, view, behold, contemplate

Θῆβαι -ων αἱ: Thebes, plural name for singular city, as often; city of great importance in Greek myth; known as the city against which the "Seven" marched

θῆλυς -εια -υ: female

θηρευτής -οῦ ὁ: hunter, huntsman

θηρίον -ου τό: wild animal, beast

θνήσκω θανοῦμαι ἔθανον τέθνηκα: die, be dying; perf.: be dead

θνητός -ή -όν: liable to death, mortal

θορυβέω: make a noise or uproar, create disorder, trouble, disturb, cheer

θόρυβος -ου ὁ: noise, uproar, clamor

θρέψας -ασα -αν: aor. act. part. of τρέφω

θρίξ τριχός ἡ: hair

θυγάτηρ θυγάτ(ε)ρος ἡ: daughter
θύρα -ας ἡ: door
θυσία -ας ἡ: offering, sacrifice
θύω θύσω ἔθυσα τέθυκα τέθυμαι ἐτύθην: sacrifice, make [sacrifices]

Iι

ἰάομαι ἰάσομαι ἰασάμην — ἴαμαι ἰάθην: heal, cure
ἰατρική -ῆς ἡ (abbreviated from ἡ ἰατρικὴ τέχνη): the medical art, medicine
ἰατρικός -ή -όν: medical, having to do with medicine or doctors
ἰατρός -οῦ ὁ: doctor, healer
ἰδέα -ας ἡ: form, shape, appearance
ἴδῃς: aor. act. subju. 2nd pers. sing. of ὁράω
ἰδιώτης -ου ὁ: private person, layman, nonprofessional
ἱδρύω ἱδρύσω ἵδρυσα ἵδρυκα ἵδρυμαι ἱδρύθην: establish, settle
ἰδών ἰδοῦσα ἰδόν (ἰδόντος): aor. act. part. of ὁράω
ἰέναι: pres. inf. of εἶμι
ἱερεύς -έως ὁ: priest, sacrificer
ἱερόν -οῦ τό: sacred place, temple, sanctuary; pl.: sacred things, offerings, sacrifice, holy rites
ἱερός -ά -όν: sacred, holy, divine
ἵζω: sit
ἵημι ἥσω -ἧκα/(-ἕ) -εἷκα -εἷμαι -εἵθην: set going, put in motion
ἰητρός -οῦ ὁ (Ionic form of ἰατρός): doctor, healer
ἴθι: come! from εἶμι (impera. 2nd pers. sing.); often followed by another imperative (cf. ἄγε and
     φέρε)
ἱκανός -ή -όν: sufficient, able, enough, becoming, befitting, sufficing
ἱκετεία -ας ἡ: supplication
ἱκέτης -ου ὁ: suppliant
ἵλεως -ων: propitious, gracious, kindly
ἱμάτιον -ου τό: outer garment, cloak, mantle; pl.: clothes
ἵμερος -ου ὁ: longing or yearning after, desire
ἵνα conj. + subju. or opt. (purpose clause): in order that, so that
ἴοι: opt. 3rd pers. sing. of εἶμι
ἴον -ου τό: violet
ἰοῦ: cry of sorrow or (more rarely) joy: boo hoo or hooray
ἵππος -ου ὁ/ἡ: horse
ἴσθι: impera. 2nd pers. sing. of οἶδα or εἰμί
ἴσμεν: pres. indic. 1st pers. pl. of οἶδα
ἴσος -η -ον: equal (to), the same as dat.
ἵστημι: set, place; στήσω: shall set; ἔστησα: set, caused to stand; ἔστην root aor.: stood;
     ἔστηκα perf. forms with pres. meaning: stand; ἑστώς perf. part.; ἕσταμαι ἐστάθην: was set;
     trans.: make to stand, set, place, appoint, establish; intrans.: stand, take a stand, stop, be set,
     be placed
ἱστουργία -ας ἡ: art of weaving

ἰσχυρός -ά -όν: strong, mighty, powerful

ἰσχύς -ύος ἡ: strength

ἴσχω: (1) hold, possess; (2) hold, check, restrain, curb

ἴσως adv.: (1) equally, in like manner; (2) perhaps (often accompanied in Attic by ἄν or τάχ᾽ ἄν)

ἴτης -ου ὁ: one who goes, impetuous, hasty one, impudent fellow

ἴω: subju. 1st pers. sing. of εἶμι

ἰών ἰοῦσα ἰόν (ἰόντος): pres. act. part. of εἶμι

Ἴων Ἴωνος ὁ: Ionian, person from Ionia

Ἰωνία -ας ἡ: Ionia, region of Greece on coast of Asia Minor, now Turkey

Κκ

κἀγαθός = καὶ ἀγαθός (crasis); often in the expression καλὸς κἀγαθός: beautiful and good, but suggesting well-bred and well-brought up, upper crust

κἀγώ = καὶ ἐγώ (crasis)

καθά adv.: according as, just as

καθάπερ (intensified version of καθά) adv.: just exactly as

καθαρός -ά -όν: clear of dirt, clean, spotless, unsoiled, pure

καθέστηκεν: intrans. perf. forms with pres. meaning: 3rd pers. sing. of καθίστημι

καθεύδω καθευδήσω: lie down to sleep, sleep

καθεώρακα: perf. act. indic. 1st pers. sing. of καθοράω

καθηγέομαι: go before, act as guide, lead the way

κάθημαι perf. forms with pres. meaning: sit

καθίζομαι/καθέζομαι καθιζήσομαι ἐκαθισάμην: sit down, be seated

καθίστημι: set down, place; + adv.: bring into —— state; intrans. + adv.: be in —— state; + nom. noun: become noun

καθοράω (κατα + ὁράω) κατόψομαι κατεῖδον καθεώρακα κατῶμμαι κατώφθην: look down upon, perceive, view

καί: (1) (connecting two things syntactically the same) and; (2) also, even, actually, in fact; καὶ γάρ: in fact; yes, certainly; καὶ δή: and really; as a matter of fact; καὶ δὴ καί: moreover; καὶ μήν: and anyway; what's more; look now; καί . . . καί: both . . . and

καινός -ή -όν: new, fresh

καίπερ + part.: although, albeit

καιρός -οῦ ὁ: critical moment, opportunity, right time

κακηγορέω: speak badly of

κακία -ας ἡ: badness, baseness, cowardice, wickedness

κακοδαίμων -ον: possessed by a bad daimon, ill-fated, ill-starred, unfortunate, unhappy

κακός -ή -όν: bad, ugly, evil

καλάπους καλάποδος ὁ: shoemaker's last, tool for making shoes

καλέω καλῶ ἐκάλεσα κέκληκα κέκλημαι ἐκλήθην: call, summon, invite, name

κάλλιστος -η -ον (superl. of καλός): most beautiful, best, very beautiful, etc.

κάλλιων -ον (compar. of καλός): more beautiful, better, rather beautiful, etc.

καλλονή -ῆς ἡ: beauty

κάλλος -ους τό: beauty

καλλωπίζω: make the face beautiful, beautify, embellish

καλός -ή -όν: beautiful, good; καλὸς κἀγαθός: beautiful and good, but suggesting well-bred
    and well-brought up, upper crust

κἄμ' = καὶ ἐμέ (crasis + elision)

κἀμοί = καὶ ἐμοί (crasis)

κἄν = καὶ ἄν or καὶ ἐάν

κανθήλιος -ου ὁ: pack-ass

κἀνθρώπων = καὶ ἀνθρώπων (crasis)

καρδία -ας ἡ: heart

καρπόω: bear fruit; mid.: gather fruit, reap; enjoy the fruits of

καρτερέω: be steadfast, patient, staunch, hold out, bear up, endure manfully

καρτέρησις -εως ἡ: patient endurance

καρτερία -ας ἡ: strength, endurance, patience

καρτερός -ά -όν: strong, staunch, brave, enduring, patient, steadfast

κατά prep. + acc.: down toward, down along, according to, in respect to, in, on, by, throughout;
    + gen.: below, down from, downward, against; as a prefix: down, against, utterly or thoroughly

καταγέλαστος -ον: deserving mocking or derisive laughter, ridiculous, absurd

καταγελάω + gen.: laugh at derisively, jeer or mock at, ridicule

καταγηράσκω: grow old

καταγραφή -ῆς ἡ: drawing, delineation, engraving

καταδαρθάνω, aor. κατέδαρθον: sleep soundly, fall asleep

κατάδηλος -ον: quite manifest, plain, visible

καταδικάζω: give judgment against, convict, condemn

καταδουλόω: reduce to slavery, enslave

καταζάω: live out one's life

καταισχύνω: disgrace, dishonor, put to shame; mid.: feel shame before

κατάκειμαι: lie down, recline

κατακλίνω: lay down, make lie down; mid.-pass.: lie down, recline

κατάκλισις -εως ἡ: reclining

κατακομίζω: lull to sleep

καταλαμβάνω: seize upon, come upon, overtake

καταλείπω: leave behind

καταλύω: put an end to, dissolve, destroy

καταμανθάνω: learn or observe well

κατανοέω: observe well, understand

καταριθμέω: make an account of

κατάρχω: make a beginning of, begin

κατασκευάζω κατασκευάσω κατεσκεύασα κατεσκεύακα κατεσκεύασμαι κατεσκευάσθην:
    prepare, get ready, equip, build, establish, outfit

καταστήσας -ασα -αν: aor. act. part. (trans.) of καθίστημι

κατατίθημι: place, put down; mid.: lay down in store

καταφρονέω + *gen. or acc.*: think down upon, look down on, despise

καταχράομαι + *dat.*: use, use up, consume

κατεῖδον: aor. act. indic. 1st pers. sing./3rd pers. pl. of καθοράω

κατέχω: hold fast; *pass.*: be held fast, be possessed

κατιδών -οῦσα -όν: aor. act. part. of καθοράω

κάτω: down, downward, under; *in the context of couches in the symposium*: next to

κεῖμαι κείσομαι: lie, lie dead; *sometimes used instead of pass. of* τίθημι: be placed, be made, be established

κελεύω κελεύσω ἐκέλευσα κεκέλευκα κεκέλευμαι ἐκελεύσθην: urge, exhort, bid, command, order

κενός -ή -όν: empty, void; + *gen.*: void of, empty of

κενόω: empty out, drain

κένωσις -εως ἡ: emptying, emptiness

κεραυνόω: strike with thunderbolt(s)

Κέρβερος -ου ὁ: Cerberus, mythological three-headed dog who guards the Underworld

κέρδος -ους τό: gain, profit, advantage

κεφάλαιος -α -ον: of the head, chief, principal; *hence* κεφάλαιον -ου τό: gist, main point; ἐν κεφαλαίῳ: in sum

κεφαλή -ῆς ἡ: head, uppermost part

κῆδος -ους τό: care, concern

κήδω κηδήσω ἐκήδησα κέκηδα κεκήδημαι: trouble, distress, vex; *mid.-pass.*: care for, be concerned for *gen.*

κηλέω: charm, bewitch, enchant, beguile, fascinate

κῆπος -ου ὁ: garden, orchard

κῆρυξ -υκος ὁ: herald

κιθαρῳδός -οῦ ὁ: one who plays and sings to the cithara (stringed instrument), citharode

κινδυνεύω κινδυνεύσω ἐκινδύνευσα κεκινδύνευκα κεκινδύνευμαι ἐκινδυνεύθην: risk, venture; + *inf.*: be in danger of ——ing, risk or hazard ——ing; *often with idiomatic sense*: come close to ——ing, be likely to ——, chance to ——

κίνδυνος -ου ὁ: danger, risk, hazard, venture, enterprise

κινέω κινήσω ἐκίνησα κεκίνηκα κεκίνημαι ἐκινήθην: set in motion, move, urge on, shake or nudge; *mid.*: move (oneself), stir

-κις *suffix*: —— times

κιττός -οῦ ὁ: ivy

κλέος τό (no gen.): rumor, report, news, reputation, fame

κλέπτω κλέψω ἔκλεψα κέκλοφα κέκλεμμαι ἐκλάπην: steal

κληθείς -εῖσα -έν: aor. pass. part. of καλέω

κλίνη -ης ἡ: that on which one lies, couch or bed

Κόδρος -ου ὁ: Kodros (Latin Codrus), legendary king of Athens

κοιμάω: lull or hush to sleep, put to sleep

κοίμησις -εως ἡ: sleeping, lying down to sleep

κοινῇ *dat. fem. sing. as adv.*: in common, jointly

κοινός -ή -όν: common, shared; + *gen. pers*.: shared by *gen*., common to *gen*.; + *gen. thing*: sharing in *gen*.

κοινόω κοινώσω ἐκοίνωσα κεκοίνωκα κεκοίνωμαι ἐκοινώθην: make common, make a sharer in, communicate; *mid*.: communicate, share in *gen*.

κοινωνέω: have or do in common with, have a share of or take part in *gen*.

κοινωνία -ας ἡ: communion, association, partnership, fellowship

κοίτη -ης ἡ: marriage bed, bed

κολακεία -ας ἡ: flattery, fawning

κομιδῇ *dat. fem. sing. as adv*.: wholly, entirely

κομψός -ή -όν: well-dressed, elegant, fine

κόρη -ης ἡ: girl, maiden

κορυβαντιάω: be filled with Corybantic frenzy, celebrate the rites of a Corybant, act like a Corybant

κόσμιον -ου τό: decorum, moderation

κόσμιος -α -ον: well-ordered, regular, moderate

κόσμος -ου ὁ: (1) order; (2) ornament, decoration; (3) universe, cosmos

κοτύλη -ης ἡ: unit of liquid measure, about a cup

κράατα -ων τά: heads

κραιπαλάω: be hungover

κρανίον -ου τό: head, skull

κρᾶσις -εως ἡ: mixing, blending, compounding

κρατέω κρατήσω ἐκράτησα κεκράτηκα κεκράτημαι ἐκρατήθην: be strong, excel, surpass, overcome, rule *gen*.

κράτιστος -η -ον: strongest, mightiest, most powerful

κρείττων -ον: stronger, mightier, more powerful

κρίνω κρινῶ ἔκρινα κέκρικα κέκριμαι ἐκρίθην: judge

κρούω: strike, smite, knock on hard

κρύσταλλος -ου ὁ: ice

κτάομαι κτήσομαι ἐκτησάμην — κέκτημαι ἐκτήθην: acquire, procure for oneself, get, gain; *perf. forms with pres. meaning*: possess (i.e., have acquired)

κτῆμα -ατος τό: anything gotten, piece of property, possession, acquisition

κτῆσις -εως ἡ: possession, acquisition

κτητός -ή -όν (verbal adj. of κτάομαι): to be possessed, to be acquired

κυβερνάω: act as pilot or helmsman, steer, guide, govern

κυβερνήτης -ου ὁ: captain, steersman, helmsman, guide, governor

κυβιστάω: tumble head foremost, tumble, somersault, cartwheel

Κυδαθηναιεύς -έως ὁ: man from Kydathenaion, one of the city demes of Athens

κυέω κυήσω ἐκύησα κεκύηκα κεκύημαι ἐκυήθην *trans*.: bear *obj*. in the womb, be pregnant with, carry; *ingressive aor*.: conceive, become pregnant with; *intrans*.: be pregnant

κύημα -ατος τό: that which is conceived, embryo, fetus

κύησις -εως ἡ: conception, pregnancy

κύκλος -ου ὁ: ring, circle, any circular body or motion, wheel, orbit κυκλοτερής -ές: round, circular

Κύκλωψ -ωπος ὁ: Cyclops, one-eyed giant of Greek mythology

κύλιξ -ικος ἡ: cup, drinking cup, wine cup, kylix

κύριος -α -ον: authoritative, masterly; *of things*: critical, important

κύων κυνός ὁ/ἡ: dog

κωλύω κωλύσω ἐκώλυσα κεκώλυκα κεκώλυμαι ἐκωλύθην: prevent, hinder

κωμαστής -ου ὁ: reveler

κωμῳδέω: represent in a comedy, make into a comedy, satirize, lampoon

κωμῳδία -ας ἡ: comedy

κωμῳδοποιός -οῦ ὁ: maker of comedies, comic poet

κωμῳδός -οῦ ὁ: comic poet, writer of comedies

Λλ

λαβεῖν: aor. act. inf. of λαμβάνω

λαθεῖν: aor. act. inf. of λανθάνω

λάθρᾳ *fem. dat. sing. as adv.*: secretly, covertly, by stealth, treacherously

Λακεδαιμόνιος -α -ον: Spartan, Lacedaemonian

Λακεδαίμων -ονος ἡ: Sparta, Lacedaemonia

λαμβάνω λήψομαι ἔλαβον εἴληφα εἴλημμαι ἐλήφθην: take, get, capture, grasp, understand; + δίκην παρά + *gen.*: punish gen.

λαμπρός -ά -όν: bright, brilliant, radiant

λανθάνω λήσω ἔλαθον λέληθα: escape notice [of *acc.* in ——ing], be unknown, unseen, unnoticed [by *acc.* in ——ing]

Λάχης -ητος ὁ: Laches, Athenian general during the Peloponnesian War

λεαίνω: smooth, polish

λέγω ἐρῶ/λέξω εἶπον/ἔλεξα εἴρηκα εἴρημαι ἐρρήθην/ἐλέχθην: say, speak, talk, tell; speak of *acc.*, say *acc.* of *acc.*, mean, esp. in phrase πῶς λέγεις; what do you mean?

λείπω λείψω ἔλιπον λέλοιπα λέλειμμαι ἐλείφθην: leave, abandon, leave out, omit

λεκτέος -η -ον (verbal adj. of λέγω): to be said, to be spoken; *neut. used impers.*: one must say, one must speak, it is necessary to say

λέληθα: perf. act. indic. 1st pers. sing. of λανθάνω

λήγω λήξω ἔληξα: stop, stay, abate, cease from

λήθη -ης ἡ: oblivion, forgetting

λίθος -ου ὁ: stone

λιμήν λιμένος ὁ: harbor

λιμός -οῦ ὁ: hunger, famine, starvation

λιπών -οῦσα -όν: aor. act. part. of λείπω

λίσπη -ης ἡ: token cut in half by two friends, each of whom keeps one as a tally

λογισμός -οῦ ὁ: counting, reckoning, calculation

λόγος -ου ὁ: word, speech, account, reckoning, story, plot, argument, principle

λοιδορέομαι: abuse

λοιμός -οῦ ὁ: plague, pestilence

λοιπός -ή -όν: remaining, the rest, left, left behind

λούω: wash

λύγξ λυγγός ἡ: hiccup(s), bout of hiccups

Λυκοῦργος -ου ὁ: Lykourgos (Latin Lycurgus), legendary Spartan lawgiver, credited with establishing the admired Spartan constitution

λυπέω: give pain to, pain, distress, grieve, vex, annoy

λύπη -ης ἡ: pain

λύρα -ας ἡ: lyre, seven-stringed musical instrument

λύχνος -ου ὁ: lamp

λύω λύσω ἔλυσα λέλυκα λέλυμαι ἐλύθην: release, loose

Μμ

μά + acc.: by acc.! no, by acc.! (in negative oaths)

μαθεῖν: aor. act. inf. of μανθάνω

μάθημα -ατος τό: that which is learnt, lesson

μαθησόμενος -η -ον: fut. mid. part. of μανθάνω

μαθητής -οῦ ὁ: student

μαίνομαι μανήσομαι/μανοῦμαι ἐμηνάμην μέμηνα μεμάνημαι ἐμάνην: rage, be furious, be mad, be madly drunk, rave

μάκαρ (gen. μάκαρος): blessed, happy

μακαρίζω: bless, deem or pronounce happy

μακάριος -α -ον: blessed, happy; μακάριε (voc. used frequently in Plato with slightly mocking tone): my friend, my fine friend, or similar

μακαριστός -ή -όν: deemed happy, considered happy

μακρός -ά -όν: long, far

μάλα adv.: very, very much, exceedingly

μαλακός -ή -όν: soft, gentle, mild, effeminate

μαλθακίζομαι: be softened, become softened, be soft

μαλθακός -ή -όν: soft, gentle, mild

μάλιστα (superl. adv. of μάλα): very much, especially, most of all, absolutely, most certainly

μᾶλλον (compar. adv. of μάλα): rather, more; μᾶλλον ἤ: more than, rather than; μᾶλλον δέ: but no . . . , but rather

μανθάνω μαθήσομαι ἔμαθον μεμάθηκα: learn

μανία -ας ἡ: madness, frenzy

μαντεία -ας ἡ: divination, prophetic power, oracle, prophecy

μαντεύομαι μαντεύσομαι ἐμαντευσάμην — μεμάντευμαι: communicate in the manner of an oracle, speak oracularly, divine, prophecy, presage

μαντικός -ή -όν: of or for a soothsayer or his art, prophetic, oracular; ἡ μαντική (abbreviated from ἡ μαντική τέχνη): the prophetic art

Μαντινικός -ή -όν: from Mantinea

μάντις -εως ὁ: soothsayer, seer, prophet

Μαρσύας -ου ὁ: Marsyas, satyr famous as inventor of the αὐλός (see note on reading C1.8) μαρτυρία -ας ἡ: witness, testimony, evidence

μαρτύριον -ου τό: testimony, proof

μάρτυς μάρτυρος ὁ/ἡ: witness; *dat. pl.* μάρτυσι(ν)

μάχη -ης ἡ: battle, fight, combat

μάχομαι μαχέ[σ]ομαι ἐμαχεσάμην—μεμάχημαι: fight

με: acc. of ἐγώ

μεγαλοπρεπής -ές: befitting a great man, magnificent

μεγαλοφροσύνη -ης ἡ: greatness of mind, *either positive*: confidence *or negative*: arrogance

μέγας μεγάλη μέγα: big, great

μέγιστος -η -ον (superl. of μέγας): greatest, largest, very great, etc.

μέθη -ης ἡ: strong drink, drunkenness

μεθύσκω: make drunk, intoxicate, inebriate; *mid.*: get drunk, become intoxicated

μεθύω: be drunk

μείγνυμι/μίγνυμι μείξω ἔμειξα—μέμειγμαι ἐμείχθην/ἐμίγην: mix

μείζων -ον (compar. of μέγας): greater, larger, quite great, etc.

μειράκιον -ου τό: male of approximately 14–21, teenaged boy, young man

μέλας μέλαινα μέλαν: black

μελετάω: study, practice, review, exercise

μελέτη -ῆς ἡ: study, practice, review, exercise

μέλλω μελλήσω ἐμέλλησα: be about to do, think of doing, intend to do; delay; ὁ μέλλων χρόνος: the future time

μέλος -ους τό: limb

μέλω: be an object of care or thought; *often impers. with gen.* + *dat.*: μέλει μοι τοῦδε: there is a care to me for this; i.e., I care for this, this is a concern to me

μέμνημαι *perf. forms with pres. meaning*: remember

μέμφομαι μέμψομαι ἐμεμψάμην: blame, censure, find fault with

μὲν . . . δέ: on the one hand . . . on the other hand; *with def. art.*: ὁ μὲν . . . ὁ δέ: one . . . the other; οἱ μὲν . . . οἱ δέ: some . . . others; μὲν οὖν: *in affirmation*: certainly, in fact; *in correction*: no, but; when used independently of δέ can carry an implied contrast with an unexpressed idea

μένος -ους τό: might, force, strength, prowess, courage

μέντοι: (1) certainly, at any rate; (2) however, still, nevertheless

μένω μενῶ ἔμεινα μεμένηκα: wait, stay, remain; *trans.*: wait for

μέρος -ους τό: part, share, turn

μεσημβρία -ας ἡ: midday, noon

μέσον -ου τό: middle

μέσος -η -ον: middle, in the middle of, mid-

μεσόω: from the middle, be in or at the middle; + *supplemental part.*: be in the middle of ——ing

μεστός -ή -όν: full, filled, filled full

μετά *prep.* + *acc.*: after, amid; + *gen.*: with; + *dat.*: in the company of, in the midst of, among; *as a prefix*: among, between, sharing, representing change from one state or place to another μεταβάλλω: throw into a different position, change

μεταδίδωμι: give a share of

μεταλαμβάνω: have or get a share of, partake of

μετανίστημι: remove; *intrans.*: move

μεταξύ *adv. or prep. + gen.*: between

μεταπέμπω: send after

μεταστρέφω: turn about, turn round, turn

μετατίθημι: place among, place differently, move, alter

μέτειμι: go among or between

μετέχω *+ gen.*: partake of, enjoy a share of, share in, take part in

μέτριος -α -ον: within measure, moderate

μέτρον -ου τό: measure, portion

μέχρι *prep. + gen.*: until, up to, to a given point; *or conj.*: until

μή: not; *+ impera. or prohibitive subju.*: don't ——; *+ part.*: if not . . . unless; *after verb of fearing*: lest, that

μηδαμῇ *fem. dat. sing. as adv.*: in no way, not at all

μηδαμῶς *adv.*: in no way, not at all

μηδέ: but not, and not, not even; but don't, and don't, don't even, etc. (see μή)

μηδείς μηδεμία μηδέν: no one, nothing, none

μηκέτι: no more, no longer (see μή)

μήν: indeed, truly; καὶ μήν: and indeed, moreover, what is more, and in fact; τί μήν; what then?

μήποτε: never, don't ever, etc. (see μή)

μήτε . . . μήτε: neither . . . nor; don't . . . nor, etc. (see μή)

μήτηρ μητ(ε)ρός ἡ: mother

Μῆτις -ιδος ἡ: Metis (Craftiness, Cunning), mother of Athene swallowed and incorporated by Zeus

μηχανάομαι μηχανήσομαι ἐμηχανσάμην—μεμηχάνημαι: devise, contrive, bring about

μηχανή -ῆς ἡ: device, scheme, instrument, machine, contrivance

μία: fem. nom. sing. of εἷς

μικρός -ά -όν: small, little

μιμνήσκω μνήσομαι ἔμνησα—μέμνημαι ἐμνήσθην: remind, put in mind; *mid.-pass.*: remember

μισέω: hate

μνάομαι: court, woo

μνημεῖον -ου τό: monument, memorial, reminder

μνήμη -ης ἡ: remembrance, memory

μνημονεύω: remember, call to mind

μόγις *adv.*: with toil and pain, scarcely, barely

μοι: dat. of ἐγώ

μοῖρα -ας ἡ: allotment, portion, share, fate; personified as αἱ Μοῖραι: the Fates, goddesses who oversee life and death

μοιχεύτρια -ας ἡ: adulteress

μοιχός -οῦ ὁ: adulterer, debaucher

μοναχοῦ *adv.*: alone, only

μόνιμος -α -ον: staying in one place, stable, steadfast

μονοειδής -ές: of one form or kind, uniform

μόνος -η -ον: only, alone, solitary

μόριον -ου τό: small piece, portion

μου: gen. of ἐγώ

Μοῦσα -ης ἡ: Muse, goddess of poetry, music, and dance

μουσική -ῆς ἡ (abbreviated from ἡ μουσικὴ τέχνη): any art over which the Muses presided: poetry, music, and dance

μουσικός -ή -όν: having to do with the Muses, musical, poetic

μυέω: initiate into the mysteries

μῦθος -ου ὁ: story, tale

μῶρος -α -ον: foolish

Νν

ναί: yes

ναῦς νέως ἡ: ship; *irreg. declension: sing. gen.* νέως, *dat.* νηί, *acc.* ναῦν; *pl. nom.* νῆες, *gen.* νεῶν, *dat.* ναυσί, *acc.* ναῦς

ναύτης -ου ὁ: sailor

νεανίας -ου ὁ: youth, young man

νεανίσκος -ου ὁ: youth, young man

νέκταρ -αρος τό: nectar, drink of the gods

νέος -α -ον: young, youthful, new

Νέστωρ -ορος ὁ: Nestor, old man hero of the Trojan War

νεωστί *adv.*: recently, lately, just now

νεώτατος -η -ον (superl. of νέος): youngest, newest, very young, etc.

νεώτερος -α -ον (compar. of νέος): younger, newer, rather young, etc.

νή + *acc.*: by *acc.*!; νὴ Δία: by Zeus

νηνεμία -ας ἡ: windlessness, stillness in the air, calm

νήπιος -α -ον: infantile, babyish, newborn, foolish, childish

νῆσος -ου ἡ: island

νήφω: be sober, drink no wine

νικάω νικήσω ἐνίκησα νενίκηκα νενίκημαι ἐνικήθην: win, conquer, prevail, vanquish

νίκη -ης ἡ: victory

Νιόβη -ης ἡ: Niobe, famous for boasting that she had more children than the goddess Leto, whose divine children, Apollo and Artemis, then proceeded to kill all of hers, six boys and six girls in the *Iliad*, seven of each in Ovid's *Metamorphoses*, five or ten in other accounts

νοέω νοήσω ἐνόησα νενόηκα νενόημαι ἐνοήθην: think; perceive, notice; intend

νόημα -ατος τό: perception, thought

νομίζω νομιῶ ἐνόμισα νενόμικα νενόμισμαι ἐνομίσθην: consider, believe; hold as a custom or belief, use customarily, practice

νόμιμος -η -ον: conforming to custom or law

νομοθετέω: make law

νόμος -ου ὁ: law, custom, usage, ordinance

νόος -ου ὁ = νοῦς

νοσέω: be sick, ail

νόσημα -ατος τό: sickness, disease, plague

νόσος -ου ἡ: sickness, disease, malady

νοσώδης -ες: sickly, diseased, ailing

νουθετέω: put in mind, admonish, warn, advise

νοῦς νοῦ ὁ: mind, attention, thought, sense; *dat.* νῷ, *acc.* νοῦν; τὸν νοῦν παρέχω: pay attention to; ἐν νῷ ἔχω: have in mind; κατὰ νοῦν (also found uncontracted: νόος)

νῦν *adv.*: now, at this time

νυνδή *adv.* = νῦν strengthened by δή: just now, at this very time

νυνί *adv.*: now, at this moment

νύξ νυκτός ἡ: night

νυστάζω: nod in sleep, nap, slumber

νώ (nom./acc.) νῷν (gen./dat.) *1st pers. dual pron.*: we two, us two

νῷ: dat. sing. of νοῦς

νῶτον -ου τό: back

Ξ ξ

ξένη -ης ἡ: female guest, foreign woman

ξένος/ξεῖνος -ου ὁ: foreigner, stranger, guest-friend, guest

ξηρός -ά -όν: dry

Ο ο

ὁ ἡ τό: the (def. art.); ὁ μὲν . . . ὁ δέ: the one . . . the other; οἱ μὲν . . . οἱ δέ: some . . . others (*Essentials* §§186–91)

ὅ: nom./acc. neut. sing. of ὅς ἥ ὅ

ὅα: neut. pl. of ὅον

ὄγδοος -η -ον: eighth

ὅδε ἥδε τόδε: this, this here

ὁδός -οῦ ἡ: road, way, journey

ὀδύνη -ης ἡ: pain, hurt

ὅθεν *rel. adv.*: from whom, from which, from where; *often used as demonst. rather than rel.*: from this, hence

οἷ *adv.*: to where, to which, to whom

οἴγνυμι/οἴγω οἴξω ᾦξα/(ἀν)έῳξα (ἀν)έῳγα ᾤχθην/(ἀν)εῴχθην: open

οἶδα εἴσομαι: know; *past* ᾔδη (pluperf. forms with imperf. meaning); *part.* εἰδώς εἰδυῖα εἰδός (εἰδοτ-); *inf.* εἰδέναι (perf. forms with pres. meaning)

οἴει: pres. mid. indic. 2nd pers. sing. of οἴομαι

οἰηθείη: aor. opt. 3rd pers. sing. of οἴομαι (pass. forms with act. meaning)

οἴκαδε *adv.*: to one's home, home, homeward

οἰκεῖος -α -ον: in or of the house, domestic, one's own, related

οἰκειότης -ητος ἡ: kinship, intimacy, family relationship, close relationship

οἰκέτης -ου ὁ: inmate of one's house, house-slave; *pl.*: family members

οἰκέω οἰκήσω ᾤκησα ᾤκηκα ᾤκημαι ᾠκήθην *trans.*: inhabit, occupy, settle, manage, govern; *intrans.*: live, lie [in a place], be governed

οἴκημα -ατος τό: any inhabited place, dwelling place, dwelling, house

οἴκησις -εως ἡ: dwelling, habitation (in both abstract and concrete senses)

οἰκία -ας ἡ: house, dwelling, building

οἰκίζομαι: make one's home, inhabit, settle

οἴκοθεν *adv.*: from one's house, from home

οἴκοι *adv.*: at home, in the house

οἶμαι = οἴομαι

οἶνος -ου ὁ: wine

οἴομαι οἰήσομαι — — — ᾠήθην (often contracted to οἶμαι, *imperf.* ᾤμην): suppose, think, deem, imagine (pass. deponent)

οἶος -α -ον: alone, lone, lonely

οἷος -α -ον: what sort of, such, such as, of such a sort; correl. with τοιοῦτος: e.g., τοιοῦτο οἵῳ: the sort of thing with which; in exclamations: what kind of . . . ! e.g., οἷα αὖ πάσχω ὑπὸ τοῦ ἀνθρώπου: What outrageous things I suffer at the hands of the fellow!

οἷός τ᾽ εἰμι: be able

οἷοσπερ -απερ -ονπερ: of the very same sort (as)

οἶσθα: pres. indic. 2nd pers. sing. of οἶδα

οἰστέος -α -ον (verbal adj. of φέρω): to be borne, to be worn; *neut. used impers.*: it is necessary to bear, one must wear, etc.

οἴχομαι οἰχήσομαι: be off, be gone, have gone; frequently with a part. that reinforces its meaning, e.g., οἴχομαι φεύγων: I am off and fleeing; οἴχεται θανών: he is dead and gone; ᾤχετο ἀπιών: he was off and gone

ὀκνέω: hesitate, be reluctant, shrink (from)

ὀκρίβας -αντος ὁ: platform, dais

ὀκτώ *indecl. adj.*: eight

ὀλιγάκις *adv.*: seldom

ὀλίγος -η -ον: few, little, scanty, small

ὅλος -η -ον: whole, complete

ὀλοφύρομαι: lament

Ὄλυμπος -ου ὁ: (1) Olympos, beloved of the satyr Marsyas; (2) Mt. Olympus, home of the gods

ὄλωλα *perf. forms with pres. meaning*: I am destroyed (from ὄλλυμι)

Ὅμηρος -ου ὁ: Homer, poet of the *Iliad* and *Odyssey*

ὁμιλέω: be in company with, consort with *dat.*

ὁμιλία -ας ἡ: being together, communion, intercourse, converse, company

ὄμμα -ατος τό: eye

ὄμνυμι ὀμοῦμαι ὤμοσα ὀμώμοκα ὀμώμο(σ)μαι ὠμό(σ)θην: swear

ὅμοιος -α -ον: like, resembling, alike, similar to, equal to ὁμοίως *adv.*: in the same way, alike, like, equally to

ὁμολογέω ὁμολογήσω ὡμολόγησα ὡμολόγηκα ὡμολόγημαι ὡμολογήθην: agree (with), say the same (as), speak as one (with) (+ *dat. pers. agreed with and/or acc. thing agreed to*)

ὁμολογία -ας ἡ: agreement

ὁμολογουμένως *adv.*: by general agreement, conformably with

ὁμόνοια -ας ἡ: sameness of mind or thought, unity, concord

ὁμόσας -ασα -αν: aor. act. part. of ὄμνυμι

ὀμφαλός -οῦ ὁ: navel

ὅμως *adv.*: all the same, nevertheless, notwithstanding, still

ὄναρ τό: dream, vision in sleep (only nom. and acc.)

ὀνειδίζω ὀνειδιῶ ὠνείδισα ὠνείδικα—ὠνειδίσθην: throw reproach upon, reproach, rebuke, blame

ὄνειδος -ους τό: reproach, censure, blame

ὀνίνημι ὀνήσω ὤνησα: profit, benefit, help, assist

ὄνομα -ατος τό: name

ὀνομάζω ὀνομάσω ὠνόμασα ὠνόμακα ὠνόμασμαι ὠνομάσθην: name or speak of by name, call or address by name

ὀνομαστός -ή -όν: named, mentioned, famous, glorious

ὄνος -ου ὁ: ass, donkey

ὄντα -ων τά: existing things, the present

ὄντι: masc./neut. dat. pres. part. of εἰμί; τῷ ὄντι: really, in truth, in fact

ὀντινοῦν: masc. acc. sing. of ὁστισοῦν

ὀξύς -εῖα -ύ: sharp, keen, high-pitched

ὄον -ου τό: sorb-apple

ὅπῃ *fem. dat. sing. as adv.*: in whatever way

ὀπῃοῦν *fem. dat. sing. as adv.*: howsoever, in anyway whatsoever

ὄπισθε(ν) *adv.*: after, behind, in back; *or prep. + gen.*: behind

ὅπλον -ου τό: tool, implement, shield; *pl.*: weapons, arms

ὁπόθεν *rel. adv.*: from where, from what place

ὅποι *rel. adv.*: where (to); to which place, whither

ὁποῖος -α -ον: of what sort or quality, what sort of; ὁποῖος ... τις: what sort of a

ὁπόσος -η -ον: as much as, as many as, however much, however many

ὁπόταν *conj. + subju.*: whenever, when

ὁπότε *conj.*: when, whenever

ὁπότερος -α -ον: which [of two]

ὁποτέρωσε *rel. adv.*: to whichever [of two sides]

ὅπου *rel. adv.*: where

ὅπως: as, in such manner as, how; *in indir. question*: how; *+ subju. or opt.*: purpose clause: so that, in order that; *+ fut. indic.*: see to it that —— (issuing directive)

ὀπωστιοῦν *adv.*: in anyway whatsoever

ὁρατός -ή -όν: be seen, visible

ὁράω ὄψομαι εἶδον ἑώρακα ὦμμαι ὤφθην: see

ὄργανον -ου τό: instrument, tool

ὀργίζω ὀργιῶ ὤργισα—ὤργισμαι ὠργίσθην: make angry, provoke to anger, irritate; *mid.-pass.*: be or become angry

ὀρθός -ή -όν: straight, correct, upright, safe (because not knocked down)

ὁρίζω ὁριῶ ὥρισα ὥρικα ὥρισμαι ὡρίσθην: mark with a boundary, define, divide or separate from (as a boundary)

ὅρκος -ου ὁ: oath

ὁρμάω ὁρμήσω ὥρμησα ὥρμηκα ὥρμημαι ὡρμήθην: set in motion, urge, stir up, rouse; *intrans.*: start, begin

ὀρρωδέω: shudder at, shrink from

Ὀρφεύς -έως ὁ: Orpheus, legendary musician who traveled to the Underworld (see reading 3B introduction)

ὅς ἥ ὅ: (1) *rel. pron.*: who, which, that; (2) *demonst. pron.*: he, that one

ὅσαπερ (*neut. pl. of rel. adj.* ὅσος + *suffix* -περ): as many [things] as in fact, all those [things] which/that indeed

ὅσος ὅση ὅσον *rel. adj.*: as much as, as great as; *pl.*: as many as, all those who/which/that

ὅσπερ ἥπερ ὅπερ *intensified rel. pron.* (declines like ὅς ἥ ὅ): the very one who, the very thing which/that; the very one that

ὀστέον -ου τό: bone (in Attic, contracts to τὸ ὀστοῦν, τὰ ὀστᾶ; see Smyth 1956: §235 for declension)

ὅστις ἥτις ὅ τι *indef. rel. pron.*: who, what, anyone who, anything which/that, whoever, whatever

ὁστισοῦν ἡτισοῦν ὁτιοῦν: anybody/anything whatsoever, anybody/anything at all

ὅταν (ὅτε + ἄν) *conj.* + *subju.*: whenever

ὅτε *conj.*: when, since

ὅτι: that, because; + *superl.*: as —— as possible; in Plato, the equivalent of ὅ τι

ὅ τι: neut. nom./acc. sing. of ὅστις ἥτις ὅ τι

ὁτιοῦν: neut. nom./acc. sing. of ὁστισοῦν

ὅτου ὅτῳ ὅτων ὅτοις: alternative gen. and dat. forms of ὅστις

οὐ οὐκ οὐχ οὐχί: no, not

οὗ: where; also gen. masc./neut. sing. rel. pron. of ὅς ἥ ὅ

οὐδαμῇ *fem. dat. sing. as adv.*: nowhere, in no way

οὐδαμοῦ *adv.*: nowhere

οὐδαμῶς *adv.*: in no way

οὖδας -εος τό: ground, earth

οὐδέ *adv.*: but not, and not, not even

οὐδείς οὐδεμία οὐδέν: no one, nothing, none, no ——; οὐδέν ἐστι: be worthless, be insignificant

οὐδέποτε *adv.*: never

οὐδέπω *adv.*: and not yet, not as yet

οὐκ = οὐ (before a vowel)

οὐκέτι *adv.*: no more, no longer

οὔκουν *adv.*: not therefore, so not

οὐκοῦν *adv.*: therefore, then, accordingly

οὖν *adv.*: so, then, therefore, really, at all events, in fact

οὗπερ: masc./neut. gen. sing. of ὅσπερ

οὔποτε *adv.*: never

οὔπω *adv.*: not yet

Οὐρανία -ας ἡ: Ourania (Latin Urania), the heavenly one, one of the nine Muses

οὐράνιος -α -ον: having to do with Ouranos, heavenly

οὐρανός -οῦ ὁ: heaven; *capitalized*: personified Heaven, the god Ouranos (Latin Uranus)

οὖς ὠτός τό: ear

οὐσία -ας ἡ: that which is one's own, one's substance, property

οὔτε *adv.*: and not; οὔτε . . . οὔτε: neither . . . nor

οὗτος αὕτη τοῦτο: this; *pl.*: these (*Essentials* §11)

οὗτος *as informal address*: hey you!

οὑτοσί αὑτηί τουτοί: this one here [pointing]

οὕτω/οὕτως *adv.*: in this way, thus, so (especially with an adj. or another adv.)

οὑτωσί *adv.*: in this way here

οὐχ = οὐ (before a vowel with a rough breathing)

οὐχί = οὐ (in Attic)

ὀφείλω ὀφειλήσω ὠφείλησα ὠφείληκα—ὠφειλήθην: owe; 2nd aor. ὤφελον: ought

ὀφθαλμός -οῦ ὁ: eye

ὀφθείς -εῖσα -έν: aor. pass. part. of ὁράω

ὀφθῆναι: aor. pass. inf. of ὁράω

ὀφλισκάνω ὀφλήσω ὦφλον ὤφληκα: owe, bring on oneself

ὄχλος -ου ὁ: crowd, throng, mob

ὀψέ *adv.*: after a long time, late, at length

ὄψις -εως ἡ: sight, look, appearance, aspect (in the sense of external appearance)

ὀψοποιικός -ή -όν: food-making, culinary

Ππ

πάγκαλος -ον: all beautiful, all good and noble

πάγος -ου ὁ: ice, frost

πάθημα -ατος τό: anything that befalls one, suffering, calamity, misfortune, experience

πάθος -ους τό: suffering, experience, incident, accident

παθών -οῦσα -όν: aor. act. part. of πάσχω

παιδαγωγέω: attend as a παιδαγωγός, train and teach, educate

παιδαγωγός -οῦ ὁ: pedagogus, a person, usually a slave, in charge of accompanying children to and from school and elsewhere (cf. παίδ- and ἄγω)

παιδάριον -ου τό: little boy, young child

παιδεραστέω: love boys, be a boy-lover

παιδεραστής -οῦ ὁ: pederast, lover of παῖδες (see introduction: "Pederasty at Athens")

παιδεραστία -ας ἡ: pederasty, love of παῖδες (see introduction: "Pederasty at Athens")

παιδεύω παιδεύσω ἐπαίδευσα πεπαίδευκα πεπαίδευμαι ἐπαιδεύθην: bring up or rear a child, educate

παιδιά -ᾶς ἡ: childish play, sport, game

παιδικά -ῶν τά *pl. used for sing.*: darling, the beloved in a pederastic relationship, favorite, young beloved

παιδίον -ου τό: little or young child

παιδογονία -ας ἡ: begetting of children

παιδοποιία -ας ἡ: procreation of children

παίζω παίσομαι ἔπαισα πέπαικα πέπαισμαι: tease, joke, play; παίζω . . . πρός + *acc.*: make fun of *acc.*

παῖς παιδός ὁ/ἡ: child, slave, boy up to eighteen years old (or even beyond)

παιών -ῶνος ὁ: paean, song of praise

πάλαι *adv.*: long ago

παλαιόομαι: become old, become obsolete

παλαιός -ά -όν: old in years, aged, ancient

πάλιν *adv.*: back, backward, again

παμπολύς παμπολλή παμπολύ: very much, very great; *pl.*: very many

πάνδημος -ον: of or belonging to all the people, common, ordinary, vulgar, promiscuous

πάντα: acc. masc. sing. or nom./acc. neut. pl. of πᾶς πᾶσα πᾶν

παντάπασι(ν) *adv.*: all in all, altogether, wholly, absolutely

πανταχῇ *fem. dat. sing. as adv.*: everywhere, in every way

πανταχόθεν *adv.*: from all places, from all quarters, on every side

πανταχοῦ *adv.*: everywhere

πάντῃ *fem. dat. sing. as adv.*: in every direction, in every way

παντί: masc./neut. dat. sing. of πᾶς

παντοδαπός -ή -όν: of every kind, of all sorts, manifold, varied

παντοῖος -α -ον: of all sorts or kinds, manifold

πάντως *adv.*: altogether, entirely

πάνυ *adv.*: altogether, entirely, very (much); πάνυ γε: very much so; οὐ πάνυ: not at all

παρά *prep.* + *gen.*: from the side of, from, by; + *dat.*: beside, alongside of; + *acc.*: to the side of, beside, alongside of; *as a prefix*: beside, by, aside, amiss

παραβάλλω: throw beside or by, throw to; *of eyes*: cast askance

παραγγέλλω: urge on, recommend, exhort

παραγίγνομαι: be present, be by or near, attend upon, come to, arrive at *dat.*

παραινέω: advise, recommend

παρακαθίζομαι: sit down beside

παρακελεύομαι: order, exhort, urge

παρακέλευσις -εως ἡ: encouragement, exhortation, cheering on

παραλείπω: leave on one side, leave remaining, pass by, neglect

παραπαίω: *trans.*: strike on the side; *intrans.*: strike aside, fall aside, be out of one's wits

παρασκευάζω: get ready, prepare (for principal parts see κατασκευάζω)

παρασκοπέω: look aside at

παραστάτης -ου ὁ: one who stands by, defender

παρασχεῖν: aor. act. inf. of παρέχω

παρατείνω: stretch out along or beside, extend, strain

παραχωρέω: go aside, make room, give way, retire

παρείχει *impers.*: it is practicable

πάρειμι: be by or present; *part. frequently used substantively* οἱ παρόντες: those present; τὰ παρόντα, τὸ παρόν: present circumstances, the present, things now; ἐν τῷ παρόντι: in the present

πάρεργον -ου τό: subordinate or secondary business, appendage, appendix

παρέρχομαι: go by; ὁ παρελθὼν χρόνος: time past

παρέχω: hold beside, hold in readiness, furnish, provide, supply

παρῇ: pres. subju. 3rd pers. sing. of πάρειμι

παρίημι: let drop beside or at the side, let fall, pass over, permit

παροιμία -ας ἡ: byword, common saying, proverb, maxim, saw

παρρησία -ας ἡ: freespokenness, openness, frankness

παρών -οῦσα -όν: pres. part. of πάρειμι

πᾶς πᾶσα πᾶν: all, every; ὁ πᾶς —: the whole —, the entire —

πάσχω πείσομαι ἔπαθον πέπονθα: suffer, experience

πατήρ πατ(ε)ρος ὁ: father

Πάτροκλος -ου ὁ: Patroklos (Latin Patroclus), close friend of Achilles

Παυσανίας -ου ὁ: Pausanias, second speaker in the dialogue, lover of Agathon

παύω παύσω ἔπαυσα πέπαυκα πέπαυμαι ἐπαύ(σ)θην: make to cease, stop; *mid.*: stop, cease; + *gen.*: cease from; + *part.*: stop —ing

πέδιον -ου τό: plain

πεζός -ή -όν: traveling on foot

πείθω πείσομαι ἔπεισα/ἔπιθον πέπεικα/πέποιθα πέπεισμαι ἐπείσθην: persuade; *mid.*: trust, obey, believe *dat. obj.*

πειρατέος -η -ον (verbal adj. of πειράω): to be attempted; *neut. used impers.*: one must attempt, it is necessary to try, etc.

πειράω πειράσω ἐπείρασα πεπείρακα πεπείραμαι ἐπειράθην: attempt, endeavor, try, test (more common in the mid. with same meaning as act.)

πείσομαι: fut. mid. indic. 1st pers. sing. of πάσχω or πείθω

πειστέος -α -ον (verbal adj. of πείθω): to be persuaded or obeyed; *neut. used impers.*: one must obey, it is necessary to obey, etc.

πέλαγος -ους τό: sea

πελάζω: draw near, approach

πέμπτος -η -ον: fifth

πέμπω πέμψω ἔπεμψα πέπομφα πέπεμμαι ἐπέμφθην: send, dispatch

πένης -ητος ὁ: one who works for his daily bread, day-laborer, poor man

πενία -ας ἡ: poverty, need; personified as mother of Eros in Diotima's myth

πέντε *indecl. adj.*: five

πέπεισμαι: perf. mid.-pass. indic. 1st pers. sing. of πείθω

πέπονθα: perf. act. indic. 1st pers. sing. of πάσχω

πέπυσμαι: perf. mid. indic. 1st pers. sing. of πυνθάνομαι

περ/-περ *enclitic particle or suffix adding force to the word it follows*: indeed, the very, much, etc.

περαίνω: bring to an end, finish, accomplish, execute

περί *prep.* + *acc.*: about, concerning; + *gen.*: around, about, concerning; + *dat.*: in, on, about

περιαιρέω: take off something that surrounds, take off an outer coat, take away, strip off

περιαμπέχω: put round about, clothe

περιβάλλω: throw round; *mid.*: put *acc. clothing* around oneself, dress oneself

περιγίγνομαι: be superior to, overcome

περίειμι (περί + εἰμί): be around, surpass *gen.*

περίειμι (περί + εἶμι): go around

περιῇα: imperf. act. indic. 1st pers. sing. of περί + εἶμι

Περικλῆς -έους ὁ: Pericles, a prominent Athenian statesman and general; Alcibiades' adoptive father

περιμένω: wait for, await

περιπτύσσω: enfold, enwrap

περιττός -ή -όν: beyond the regular number or size, out of the ordinary

περιτυγχάνω: light upon, fall in with, meet with

περιφερής -ές: moving round, revolving, surrounding

περιφέρω: carry around

πέφυκα *perf. forms with pres. meaning*: be [by nature] (from φύω)

πῃ *fem. dat. sing. as adv.*: in some way, somehow

πηδάω πηδήσομαι ἐπήδησα πεπήδηκα: leap, spring, bound, jump; throb

Πηνελόπεια -ας ἡ: Penelope, wife of Odysseus, famous for waiting for her husband for twenty years

πιθανός -ή -όν: calculated to persuade, persuasive

πικρός -ά -όν: bitter, pointed, sharp, keen

πίλναμαι: draw near, approach

πῖλος -ου ὁ: felt, wool or hair made into felt

πίνω πίομαι ἔπιον πέπωκα πέπομαι ἐπόθην: drink

πίπτω πεσοῦμαι ἔπεσον πέπτωκα: fall

πιστεύω πιστεύσω ἐπίστευσα πεπίστευκα πεπίστευμαι ἐπιστεύθην: trust, believe *dat.*

πλεῖστος -η -ον (superl. of πολύς): most, largest, greatest

πλείων -ον (compar. of πολύς): more, larger, greater

πλέκω πλέξω ἔπλεξα πέπλεχα πέπλεγμαι ἐπλέχθην/ἐπλάκην: braid, weave, twine, twist

πλεονεκτέω: have or claim more than one's due, get or have too much; be greedy, grasping, arrogant

πλεονεξία -ας ἡ: greediness, lust for more [power, money, etc.]

πλευρά -ᾶς ἡ: rib

πλέω πλεύσομαι ἔπλευσα πέπλευκα πέπλευσμαι ἐπλεύσθην: sail

πλέων -ον = πλείων -ον

πληγείς -εῖσα -έν: aor. pass. part. of πλήττω

πλῆθος -ους τό: great number, throng, crowd, multitude

πλήν *prep.* + *gen.*: except; *or adv.*: except, besides

πλήρης -ες: full

πληρόω πληρώσω ἐπλήρωσα πεπλήρωκα πεπλήρωμαι ἐπληρώθην: make full, fill (with) *gen.*

πλησιάζω: bring near, be near *dat.*

πλησμονή -ῆς ἡ: filling or being filled, fullness, satiety

πλήττω πλήξω ἔπληξα πέπληγα πέπληγμαι ἐπλάγην/ἐπλήγην: strike, smite

πλούσιος -α -ον: rich, wealthy

πλουτέω: be rich, be wealthy

πλοῦτος -ου ὁ: wealth

πόδα: acc. sing. of πούς

πόδες: nom. pl. of πούς

ποθεν *enclitic indef. adv.*: from some place or other

πόθεν *interrogative adv.*: from where . . . ?

ποθέω: long for, yearn after

πόθος -ου ὁ: longing, yearning, fond desire or regret

ποι *enclitic indef. adv.*: to wherever, to somewhere

ποῖ *interrogative adv.*: (to) where . . . ?

ποιέω ποιήσω ἐποίησα πεποίηκα πεποίημαι ἐποιήθην: do, make, create; + *inf.*: cause to ——;
    περὶ πολλοῦ ποιοῦμαι: value highly; τοὺς λόγους . . . ποιοῦμαι: make words, i.e., discuss

ποίησις -εως ἡ: poetry, the art of poetry, creation, creativity

ποιητής -οῦ ὁ: one who makes, creator, poet

ποικίλλω: work in various colors, embroider, make elaborate

ποικίλος -η -ον: many-colored, variegated, complexly wrought, intricate, riddling, ambiguous

ποιός -ά -όν *enclitic indef. adj.*: of a certain nature, kind, of quality; of some sort

ποῖος -α -ον: of what nature? of what sort?

πολεμέω: wage war with, fight, be at war

πολέμιος -α -ον: of or belonging to war; *as subst.* οἱ πολέμιοι: the enemy, those with whom one
    is at war (as opposed to personal enemies)

πόλεμος -ου ὁ: war, battle

πόλις -εως ἡ: city, city-state

πολίτης -ου ὁ: citizen

πολιτικός -ή -όν: political, having to do with the city

πολλάκις *adv.*: many times, often

πολλαχῇ *adv.*: in many ways

πολλαχοῦ *adv.*: in many places

Πολύμνια -ας ἡ: Polymnia or Polyhymnia, one of the nine Muses

πολύς πολλά πολύ: much, many

πονέω πονήσω ἐπόνησα πεπόνηκα πεπόνημαι ἐπονήθην: work hard, do work, toil, suffer

πονηρός -ή -όν: bad, wretched, wicked, toilsome, painful, grievous

πόνος -ου ὁ: toil, work, task, labor; *pl.*: pains, griefs

πορεία -ας ἡ: walking, mode of walking or running, gait, mode of travel, journey

πορευτέος -α -ον (verbal adj. of πορεύω): to be traversed or traveled over; *neut. used impers.*:
    one must go or travel, it is necessary to go, etc.

πορεύω πορεύσω ἐπόρευσα πεπόρευκα πεπόρευμαι ἐπορεύθην: make go, carry, convey,
    bring, supply; *mid.*: go, travel, march, walk

πορίζω ποριῶ ἐπόρισα πεπόρικα πεπόρισμαι ἐπορίσθην: bring, convey; bring about, contrive; furnish, provide; *mid.*: acquire, procure, get

πόριμος -ον: able to provide, resourceful, inventive, contriving

πόρος -ου ὁ: way, means, resource; personified as father of Eros in Diotima's myth

πόρρω *adv.*: far, far off

πόρρωθεν *adv.*: from afar, from a distance

Ποσειδῶν -ῶνος ὁ: Poseidon, god of the sea; brother of Zeus and one of the twelve Olympian gods

ποσί(ν): dat. pl. of πούς

πόσις -εως ἡ: drink

πόσος -η -ον: how great? how much? *pl.*: how many?

ποταμός -οῦ ὁ: river

ποτέ *enclitic indef. adv.*: at some time or other, at some time, once, ever, some day

πότε *in direct and indir. questions*: when

Ποτειδαία -ας ἡ: Poteidaia (Latin Potidaea), a Greek city-state in northern Greece

ποτέος -α -ον (verbal adj. of πίνω): to be drunk; *neut. used impers.*: one must drink, it is necessary to drink

πότερος -α -ον: introducing a direct alternative question (often not translated); introducing indirect questions: which of the two? whether?

πότνια -ας ἡ: mistress, queen, lady

πότος -ου ὁ: drinking, drinking bout

που *enclitic indef. adv.*: anywhere, somewhere, *but often simply introduces a speculative note into a passage*: I suppose, I guess

ποῦ: where?

πούς ποδός ὁ: foot

πρᾶγμα -ατος τό: deed, act, thing, matter, affair, situation; *pl.*: troubles, circumstances, business

πρᾶξις -εως ἡ: deed, transaction, business

πραότης -ητος ἡ: mildness, gentleness

πράττω πράξω ἔπραξα πέπραγα/πέπραχα, πέπραγμαι ἐπράχθην: do, act, accomplish

πρέπει *impers.* + *acc.* + *inf.*: it is fitting for *acc.* to ——

πρεπόντως *adv.*: in fit manner, befittingly, beseemingly, gracefully

πρεσβεύω: be the elder or eldest; *trans.*: place as elder, show honor to, esteem

πρεσβύτατος -η -ον: eldest, most esteemed; + *dat.*: most important to/esteemed by

πρεσβύτερος -α -ον: elder, more esteemed; + *dat.*: more important to/esteemed by

πρεσβύτης -ου ὁ: old man, elder

Πρίαμος -ου ὁ: Priam, old king of Troy, who had fifty sons

πρίν *adv.*: before, previously; *conj.* + *inf.*: before; + *subju.* + ἄν *or opt.*: until, before

πρό *prep.* + *gen.*: before, in front of, for, on behalf of; πρὸ τοῦ: before this, previously

προαιρέομαι: choose first, prefer

προαποθνήσκω: die before or first

προαφίσταμαι: fall off or revolt before; *intrans.*: stop first, come away first

προβάλλω: throw before, throw forward, put forward

προβεβλῆσθαι: perf. mid.-pass. inf. of προβάλλω

προγίγνομαι: happen before, happen first

πρόγονος -ου ὁ: forefather, predecessor, ancestor

πρόειμι: go forward, go on, go in advance

προθυμέομαι: be ready, willing, eager for *acc.* or to *inf.*

προθυμία -ας ἡ: readiness, willingness, eagerness, zeal

πρόθυμος -ον: ready, willing, eager, zealous

πρόθυρον -ου τό: front door, porch, vestibule

προκαλέω: invite ahead of time, make a date

προλέγω: say beforehand, say in advance

πρός *prep.* + *acc.*: to, toward, for the purpose of, with a view to, in reference to; + *gen.*: from, in the name of; + *dat.*: in addition to, near, at; *as a prefix*: to, toward, in addition

προσάγομαι: win over

προσαγορεύομαι: name, call by name

προσαιτέω: ask besides, beg

προσαναγκάζω: force or constrain to

προσβλέπω: look at

προσδεῖ *impers.*: it is still necessary

προσδοκία -ας ἡ: expectation, anticipation

πρόσειμι: be in addition, also be

προσέρχομαι: come or go to (*usually dat.*)

προσεύχομαι: offer prayers or vows

προσέχω: hold to, offer; + τὸν νοῦν: pay attention to

προσήκω: (1) have arrived at; be near, at hand; (2) *used impers.* + *dat.*: it concerns *dat.*; + *dat.* + *inf.*: it is appropriate for *dat.* to —, it is fitting for *dat.* to —; (3) *common as subst. part.*: belonging to, befitting, related to

πρόσθεν *prep.* + *gen.*: before, in front of; *or adv.*: before, forward, to the front; formerly, previously

προσθετέος -α -ον (verbal adj. of προστίθημι): to be added; *neut. used impers.*: one must add, it is necessary to add, etc.

προσίστημι *intrans.*: go to

προσοιστέος -α -ον (verbal adj. of προσφέρω): to be applied, to be dealt with, to be performed; *neut. used impers.*: one must apply, it is necessary to perform, etc.

προσπαλαίω: wrestle with

προσπελάζω: make approach, bring near to; *mid.*: draw near to

προστάττω: order, command

προστίθημι: apply

προσφέρω: bring to or upon, apply to, approach, have dealings with

πρόσωπον -ου τό: face, visage, countenance

προτεραία -ας ἡ (abbreviated from ἡ προτεραία ἡμέρα): day before

πρότερος -α -ον: before, previous, first [of two]; πρότερον *adv.*: previously, first

προτροπάδην *adv.*: headforemost, with headlong speed

προὔλοιτο: aor. mid. opt. 3rd pers. sing. of προαιρέομαι

προυρρήθην: aor. pass. indic. 1st pers. sing. of προλέγω

προχείρως *adv.*: readily

προχωρέω: go or come forward, advance

πρῴην *adv.*: lately, just now, day before yesterday

πρῶτος -η -ον: first (*often adverbially in neut. sing. acc.*); τὸ πρῶτον: at first

πταίρω πταρῶ ἔπταρα/ἔπταρον: sneeze

πταρμός -οῦ ὁ: a sneeze

πτηνός -ή -όν: feathered, winged

πτοίησις -εως ἡ: excitement, vehement passion

πύλη -ης ἡ: one wing of a pair of double gates, gate

πυνθάνομαι πεύσομαι ἐπυθόμην—πέπυσμαι: learn by hearsay or by inquiry; ask, inquire; hear (of or about)

πῦρ πυρός τό: fire

πω *enclitic particle*: up to this time, yet

πώποτε *adv.*: ever yet

πως *enclitic adv.*: somehow, in some way, in any way, at all, by any means

πῶς *interrogative adv.*: how? in what way or manner?

Ρρ

ῥᾴδιος -α -ον: easy

ῥᾷστος -η -ον (superl. of ῥᾴδιος): easiest, very easy

ῥᾴων -ον (compar. of ῥᾴδιος): easier, rather easy

ῥέζω: do, act, deal

ῥέω ῥυήσομαι/ῥεύσομαι ἔρρευσα ἐρρύηκα—ἐρρύην: flow, run, stream, gush (Attic uses aor. pass. forms for aor. act.)

ῥηθείς -εῖσα -έν: aor. pass. part. of λέγω

ῥηθήσεσθαι: fut. pass. inf. of λέγω

ῥῆμα -ατος τό: that which is said or spoken, word, saying

ῥητός -ή -όν: stated, specified; ἐπὶ ῥητοῖς: on set terms

ῥήτωρ ῥήτορος ὁ: public speaker, pleader, rhetor, orator, politician

ῥίς ῥινός ἡ: nose

ῥυθμός -οῦ ὁ: measured motion, time, rhythm

ῥυτίς -ίδος ἡ: a fold or pucker, wrinkle

ῥώμη -ης ἡ: bodily strength, strength, might

ῥώννυμι: strengthen, make strong and mighty

Σσ

σάρξ σαρκός ἡ: flesh

σατυρικός -ή -όν: satyr, satyrlike

σάτυρος -ου ὁ: satyr, half-man/half-horse follower of Dionysus, known for lewd and comical behavior

σαυτοῦ -ῷ -όν *refl. pron.*: yourself, you (contracted from σεαυτοῦ)

σαφής -ές: clear, plain, distinct, manifest, sure, unerring

σαφῶς *adv.*: clearly

σέ/σε: acc. of σύ

σεαυτοῦ -ῷ -όν *refl. pron.*: yourself

Σειρήν -ῆνος ἡ: Siren, legendary singer who lures men to their death by her enchanting song

σελήνη -ης ἡ: moon (Selene)

σεμνός -ή -όν: august, dignified, majestic, pompous

σή: nom. fem. sing. of σός -ή -όν

σημαίνω σημανῶ ἐσήμηνα σεσήμαγκα σεσήμασμαι ἐσημάνθην: signify

σιγάω σιγήσομαι ἐσίγησα σεσίγηκα σεσίγημαι ἐσιγήθην: be silent

σίδηρος -ου ὁ: iron

σιληνικός -ή -όν: silen-like, Silenus-like

σιληνός -ου ὁ: silen, a mythological half-man/half-animal creature, similar to a satyr; *capitalized*: Silenus, father of the satyrs

σιληνώδης -ες: silen-like, Silenus-like

σῖτος -ου ὁ; *pl.* σῖτα -ων τά: wheat, grain; food

σιωπάω: be silent, be quiet

σκεδάννυμι σκεδάω ἐσκέδασα—ἐσκέδασμαι ἐσκεδάσθην: scatter, disperse

σκέλος -ους τό: leg

σκέπτομαι σκέψομαι ἐσκεψάμην—ἔσκεμμαι: look about, look carefully, consider

σκήπτω: prop, stay; *mid.*: make as an excuse

σκληρός -ά -όν: hard, harsh, rough, harsh

σκοπέω: look at or after, look carefully, consider (in pres. and imperf. only, other tenses use forms of σκέπτομαι)

σκοτεινός -ή -όν: dark, obscure, riddling

σκυθρωπός -ή -όν: angry-faced, sad-faced, sullen

σκῦτος -ους τό: skin, hide, leather, piece of leather

σκυτοτόμος -ου ὁ: leather-cutter, worker in leather, shoemaker

σμικρόλογος -ον: petty

σμικρός -ά -όν (= μικρός): small, little

σοι/σοί: dat. of σύ

Σόλων -ωνος ὁ: Solon, Athenian lawgiver and poet

σός σή σόν: your, yours

σου/σοῦ: gen. of σύ

σοφία -ας ἡ: cleverness, skill, wisdom

σόφισμα -ματος τό: piece of cleverness, cunning trick

σοφιστής -οῦ ὁ: sophist, professional wiseman, master of one's craft or art, an adept

σοφός -ή -όν: wise, skilled in any handicraft or art, cunning, clever; + *inf.*: good at ——ing

σπαργάω: be full to bursting, swell, be ripe

σπεύδω σπεύσω ἔσπευσα: hurry, make haste

σπονδή -ῆς ἡ: drink offering, libation

σπουδάζω σπουδάσομαι ἐσπούδασα ἐσπούδακα ἐσπούδασμαι ἐσπουδήσθην: be serious, be concerned, be eager, make haste

σπουδή -ῆς ἡ: eagerness, zeal, effort, earnestness, seriousness, haste, speed στάδιον -ου τό: (1) stade, unit of measurement equivalent to 606.75 English feet; (2) stadium (because the race course at Olympia was one stade long)

στένω: groan, moan; *trans.*: bemoan, lament

στέφανος -ου ὁ: crown, garland

στεφανόω: put round, crown, garland

στῆθος -ους τό: breast, chest

στήλη -ης ἡ: upright stone, post, slab, monument, stele

στόμα -ατος τό: mouth

στρατεία -ας ἡ: military expedition, campaign

στρατηγός -οῦ ὁ: leader or commander of an army, general

στρατιά -ᾶς ἡ: army

στρατιώτης -ου ὁ: soldier

στρατόπεδον -ου τό: military camp, soldiers' camping ground

στρογγύλος -η -ον: round, spherical

σύ σοῦ σοί σέ: you

συγγενής -ές: born with, congenital, natural, inborn

συγγίγνομαι: be with

συγγιγνώσκω: think with, agree with, understand, sympathize with, forgive *dat.*

συγγυμνάζω: exercise together

συγκατάκειμαι: lie with or together

συλλήβδην *adv.*: taken all together, collectively, in sum, in short

συλλήπτωρ -ορος ὁ: partner, accomplice, assistant

συμβαίνω: befall; + *dat.* + *inf. used impers.*: fall randomly to *dat.* to ——

συμβιόω: live with, live together

σύμβολον -ου τό: sign, token

συμβουλεύω + *dat.*: advise, counsel, recommend to

συμβουλή -ῆς ἡ: advice, counsel

σύμμαχος -ου ὁ: ally

συμμείγνυμι = συμμίγνυμι

σύμμετρος -ον: accommodating

συμμίγνυμι: mix together, commingle (for principal parts see μείγνυμι)

σύμπας -πασα -παν: all together, all at once, all in a body

συμπίνω -πίομαι -έπιον -πέπωκα -πέπομαι -ἐπόθην: drink together, join in a drinking bout with

συμπλέκω: twine, weave, braid together

συμπληρόω: fill in the gap

συμπλοκή -ῆς ἡ: intertwining, embrace

συμπότης -ου ὁ: fellow drinker, companion at the symposium

συμφέρω: bring together, gather, collect; *mid.*: come together, meet, agree with

σύμφημι: assent, approve; agree with

συμφορά -ᾶς ἡ: attendant circumstance (usually of a negative kind), misfortune, calamity

συμφυσάω: blow together, conflate, fuse

συμφύω: make to grow together; *intrans.*: grow together

σύν *prep.* + *dat.*: along with, in company with, together with, with the help of; *as a prefix*: together with, fellow——

συναγωγεύς -έως ὁ: one who brings together, unifier

συναμφότερος -α -ον: both together

συναναχωρέω: retreat with

συνδειπνέω: dine with, dine together

συνδέω: bind or tie together

συνδιασῴζω: help in saving

συνδιατρίβω: spend time with *dat.*

συνεγιγνόμην: imperf. mid. indic. 1st pers. sing. of συγγίγνομαι

σύνειμι (σύν + εἰμί): be together

σύνειμι (σύν + εἶμι): come together

συνεκτρέφω: bring up along with, rear together

συνέλκω: draw together, draw up, contract

συνεράω: love together

συνεργός -οῦ ὁ: associate, partner in work

συνέρχομαι: go together or in company

συνῄδη: past 1st pers. sing. of σύνοιδα

συνημερεύω: pass the day together or with

συνίστημι: set together, combine, associate, unite, band together

συννοέω: meditate, reflect upon

σύνοδος -ου ἡ: meeting, events that bring us together

σύνοιδα: share in knowledge with *dat.*; + *part. of indir. statement*: share in the knowledge that

σύνοικος -ον: dwelling in the same house with

συνουσία -ας ἡ: being together with, gathering, society, conversation, companionship, company

συντακείς -εῖσα -έν: aor. pass. part. of συντήκω

σύντασις -εως ἡ: vehement effort, exertion

συντήκω συντήξω συνέτηξα συντέτηκα—συνετάκην: fuse into one mass, weld together

σύντονος -ον: strained tight, intense

σῦριγξ σύριγγος ἡ: syrinx, pipe, Pan's pipe

σύσπαστος -η -ον: drawn together, closed by drawing together

συσπειράομαι: coil up

συσσιτέω: eat with

σφεῖς σφῶν σφίσι σφᾶς (*neut. nom./acc.* σφέα) *3rd pers. pron.*: they

σφόδρα *adv.*: very, very much, exceedingly

σχεδόν *adv.*: close, near, nearly, almost

σχῆμα -ατος τό: form, figure, appearance

σῴζω σώσω ἔσωσα σέσωκα σέσω(σ)μαι ἐσώθην: save, preserve

Σωκράτης -ους ὁ: Socrates, the famous fifth-century philosopher (see introduction and appendix 1)

σῶμα -ατος τό: body

σωτήρ -ῆρος ὁ: savior, deliverer, preserver

σωτηρία -ας ἡ: safety, deliverance

σωφρονέω: be of sound mind, be chaste, moderate, or temperate

σωφροσύνη -ης ἡ: soundness of mind, moderation, temperance, self-discipline

σώφρων -ον: of sound mind, temperate, moderate, self-disciplined, chaste, sober

Ττ

τἀγαθά = τὰ ἀγαθά (crasis)

ταινία -ας ἡ: band, ribbon, fillet

τάλας τάλαινα τάλα: wretched, miserable

τἀληθῆ = τὰ ἀληθῆ (crasis)

τἆλλα = τὰ ἄλλα (crasis)

τάξις -εως ἡ: arrangement, order, battle order, line of battle

τἀριστεῖα = τὰ ἀριστεῖα (crasis)

ταριχεύω: preserve

ταῦτα: nom./acc. neut. pl. of οὗτος

ταύτῃ *fem. dat. sing. as adv.*: in this way

ταὐτόν = τὸ αὐτό(ν) (crasis); the use of nu, even when the word is followed by a consonant, is common in Plato

τάχα *adv.*: (1) quickly, presently, forthwith; (2) perhaps (in Attic especially when it accompanies ἄν)

ταχύς -εῖα -ύ: quick, fast, swift, fleet

τε: and; τε . . . τε: both . . . and; τε . . . καί: both . . . and; X τε Y τε Z τε = X and Y and Z etc. *note especially* the position of τε: it follows the word or words being joined: e.g., τά τ’ ὦτα τόν τε νοῦν τά τ’ ὄμματα = τὰ ὦτα *and* τὸν νοῦν *and* τὰ ὄμματα

τεθνάναι: perf. act. inf. of θνῆσκω

τείνω τενῶ -έτεινα -τέτακα -τέταμαι -ετάθην: stretch, extend, strain

τεῖχος -ους τό: wall, especially a city wall

τεκμαίρομαι: infer, judge; ordain, decree

τεκμήριον -ου τό: sure sign or token, evidence, proof

τεκών -οῦσα -όν: aor. act. part. of τίκτω

τέλεος -ον: having reached its end, finished, complete, perfect

τελετή -ῆς ἡ: initiation, mystic rite, religious festival

τελευτάω τελευτήσω ἐτελεύτησα τετελεύτηκα τετελεύτημαι ἐτελευτήθην: complete, finish, end; accomplish; die

τελευτή -ῆς ἡ: finish, end, completion, accomplishment

τελέω: make perfect, complete

τέλος -ους τό: end, goal, result; *often used without def. art. as adv.*: finally, at last

τεμάχιον -ου τό: slice

τέμνω τεμῶ ἔτεμον τέτμηκα τέτμημαι ἐτμήθην: cut

τέταρτος -η -ον: fourth

τετρακόσιοι -αι -α: four hundred

τετραμμένος -η -ον: perf. mid.-pass. part. of τρέπω

τετρωμένος -η -ον: perf. mid.-pass. part. of τιτρώσκω

τέτταρες τέτταρα: four

τέττιξ τέττιγος ὁ: cicada

τέχνη -ης ἡ: art, skill, craft

τεχνικός -ή -όν: artistic, skilful, skilled, workmanlike

τέως: as long as, while, until

τῇδε *fem. dat. sing. as adv.*: in this way, in this place, here

τηλικοῦτος -αύτη -οῦτο: so great, so much

τήμερον *adv.*: today

τίθημι θήσω ἔθηκα/(θε-) τέθηκα τέθειμαι ἐτέθην: set, put, place, arrange

τίκτω τέξομαι ἔτεκον τέτοκα: give birth, bring into the world, bear

τιμάω τιμήσω ἐτίμησα τετίμηκα τετίμημαι ἐτιμήθην: pay honor to, hold in honor, honor, revere, reverence

τιμή -ῆς ἡ: honor, that which is paid in token of worth or value

τίμιος -α -ον: prized, valued, valuable, honored, honorable

τιμωρέω τιμωρήσω ἐτιμώρησα τετιμώρηκα τετιμώρημαι ἐτιμωρήθην: avenge, help; *mid.*: exact vengeance on, avenge oneself upon, punish

τινα/τινά: masc. acc. sing. or neut. nom./acc. pl. of τις/τι

τίνω τ(ε)ίσω ἔτ(ε)ισα τέτ(ε)ικα -τέτεισμαι -ετ(ε)ίσθην: pay

τις τι *as adj.*: a/an, a certain, some, any; *as subst.*: *masc./fem.*: anyone, someone, a certain person; *neut.*: something, anything; οὔ τι: in no way, not at all

τίς τί: *as adj.*: what ——? which——?; *as subst.*: *masc./fem.*: who?; *neut.*: what? why?

τιτρώσκω τρώσω ἔτρωσα — τέτρωμαι ἐτρώθην: wound

τλάω τλήσομαι ἔτλην τέτληκα: take upon oneself, bear, suffer, undergo

τμῆμα -ατος τό: part cut off, section, piece

τμῆσις -εως ἡ: cutting

τοι *enclitic particle*: let me tell you, surely, verily

τοιγάρ: so then, wherefore, therefore, accordingly

τοιγάρτοι: stronger version of τοιγάρ, typically used at the beginning of a speech or narrative

τοίνυν: therefore, accordingly

τοιόσδε τοιάδε τοιόνδε: such as this [following], such as this [here]; of the kind described next; *pl.*: such as these

τοιοῦτος τοιαύτη τοιοῦτο(ν): such as this; of this kind, of this sort; with correl. οἷος: of such a kind . . . as; of such a kind . . . that; with correl. ὥστε: of such a kind . . . that, such . . . that

τοῖσδε: dat. masc./neut. pl. of ὅδε

τόκος -ου ὁ: childbirth

τολμάω τολμήσω ἐτόλμησα τετόλμηκα τετόλμημαι ἐτολμήθην: dare, undertake, venture

τομή -ῆς ἡ: end left after cutting, stump

τοξική -ῆς ἡ (abbreviated from ἡ τοξικὴ τέχνη): art of archery

τόξον -ου τό: bow (in archery)

τόπος -ου ὁ: place

τόσος -η -ον: so great, so vast, so big, so much; *pl.*: so many

τοσόσδε τοσήδε τοσόνδε: as great as this, as much as this; *pl.*: as many as these

τοσοῦτος τοσαύτη τοσοῦτον: so great, so much, this much; *pl.*: so many, this many; *neut. sing. acc. often used adverbially*: so much, to such an extent, to this extent; with correl. ὅσος: as much . . . as . . . ; *pl.*: as many . . . as . . . (suggesting a large amount); with correl. ὥστε: so much . . . that . . . , to such an extent that . . . ; *pl.*: so many . . . that

τότε *adv.*: at that time, then

τοτέ *indef. adv.*: at times, now and then; τοτὲ μὲν . . . τοτὲ δέ: at one time . . . at another, now . . . then

του (from τις τι) = τινός

τοῦδε: gen. masc./neut. sing. of ὅδε

τοὐναντίον = τὸ ἐναντίον (crasis)

τουτί (τοῦτο + deictic iota): this here

τοῦτο: nom./acc. neut. sing. of οὗτος

τραγῳδία -ας ἡ: tragedy

τραγῳδοποιός -οῦ ὁ: maker of tragedies, tragic poet, tragedian

τρεῖς τρία: three

τρέπω τρέψω ἔτρεψα/ἐτραπόμην τέτροφα τέτραμμαι ἐτρέφθην/ἐτράπην: turn or direct, make turn [in flight]; *mid.-pass.*: turn or direct oneself, go, turn in flight

τρέφω θρέψω ἔθρεψα τέτροφα τέθραμμαι ἐθρέφθην/ἐτράφην: nourish, feed, nurse, bring up, rear

τρέχω δραμοῦμαι ἔδραμον δεδράμηκα δεδράμημαι: run

τρία: nom./acc. neut. pl. of τρεῖς

τρίβων -ωνος ὁ: worn garment, threadbare cloak

τρίς *adv.*: thrice, three times

τρισμύριοι -αι -α: thrice ten thousand (30,000)

τρίτος -η -ον: third

Τροία -ας ἡ: Troy, city on the northern coast of Asia Minor, famous for withstanding the Greek attack for ten years

τρόπος -ου ὁ: way, turn, manner, style, direction, course; *pl.*: ways, manners, habits, character

τροφή -ῆς ἡ: upbringing, rearing; nourishment, food, feeding

τρυφή -ῆς ἡ: luxury, softness, delicacy, daintiness

τυγχάνω τεύξομαι ἔτυχον τετύχηκα/τέτευχα + *gen. obj.*: happen upon, meet with by chance, gain, obtain; + *supplemental part.*: happen to be ——ing, happen to ——; + *dat. pers.*: happen to, befall

τύπτω τυπτήσω: strike

τυραννίς -ίδος ἡ: tyranny, absolute rule by one man, often with the attendant notion that he is unrestrained by constitution or laws

τύραννος -ου ὁ: tyrant, absolute sovereign, man who has come to power through unconstitutional means

τυφλός -ή -όν: blind

τύχη -ης ἡ: fortune, luck, chance, happenstance

τύχω: aor. act. subju. 1st pers. sing. of τυγχάνω

τῳ (from τις τι) = τινί

τῷ ὄντι: really, truly

Υυ

ὑβρίζω ὑβριῶ ὕβρισα ὕβρικα ὕβρισμαι ὑβρίσθην: treat violently, treat hubristically, wax wanton, run riot, commit a crime

ὕβρις -εως ἡ: wantonness, wanton violence or insolence, aggression, criminal act

ὑβριστής -οῦ ὁ: violent, overbearing person; wanton, insolent man; criminal

ὑγιαίνω ὑγιανῶ ὑγίανα: be healthy

ὑγίεια -ας ἡ: health, soundness

ὑγιεινός -ή -όν: good for the health, wholesome, sound, healthy

ὑγιής -ές: healthy, sound

ὑγρός -ά -όν: wet, moist, running, fluid

ὕδωρ ὕδατος τό: water

ὑεῖ: alternative dat. sing. of υἱός

ὑέος: alternative gen. sing. of υἱός

υἱός -οῦ ὁ: son

ὑμεῖς ὑμῶν ὑμῖν ὑμᾶς: you (pl.)

ὑμέτερος -α -ον: your, yours

ὑμνέω ὑμνήσω ὕμνησα ὕμνηκα ὕμνημαι ὑμνήθην: sing, laud, sing of, hymn, celebrate in song

ὕμνος -ου ὁ: song, hymn

ὑπαίθριος -ον: under the sky, in the open air

ὑπακούω: listen, hearken to, heed, obey dat.

ὑπάρχω: begin, make a beginning; impers. ὑπάρχει + dat. + inf.: it is possible for dat. to ——

ὑπεκρέω: flow out from under, slip away

ὑπέρ prep. + gen.: on behalf of, for, over, above; + acc.: over, beyond; as a prefix: beyond, excessively, over, above

ὑπεράγαμαι: admire excessively, be exceedingly pleased

ὑπεραποθνῄσκω: die for

ὑπερβάλλω: throw over or beyond a mark, overshoot, surpass

ὑπερηφανία -ας ἡ: arrogance, disdain

ὑπερήφανος -ον: conspicuous, surpassing, overweening

ὑπηρετέω: do service on board ship, do rower's service, do hard service, serve

ὑπισχνέομαι ὑποσχήσομαι ὑπεσχόμην—ὑπέσχημαι: promise

ὕπνος -ου ὁ: sleep

ὑπό prep. + gen.: by, from under, under the influence of, at the hands of, because of; + dat.: under, beneath, under the rule or influence of; + acc.: under, toward, beneath, along under, up under; as a prefix: under, about

ὑποβλέπω: look up from under, eye suspiciously, scornfully, or angrily

ὑποδέω: bind or fasten under; pass.: be shod, wear shoes

ὑποκάτω adv.: below, under

ὑποκριτής -οῦ ὁ: actor

ὑπολαμβάνω: take up by getting under, undercut, prop up, take over

ὑπολείπω: leave behind, leave remaining

ὑπολύω: unbind below; remove the sandals from *acc.*

ὑπονυστάζω: nod off, fall asleep gradually

ὑπόσχεσις -εως ἡ: undertaking, engagement, promise

ὑστεραία -ας ἡ (abbreviated from ἡ ὑστεραία ἡμέρα): the day after, the next day

ὕστερος -α -ον: following, next, latter, later

Φφ

φάγω: aor. act. subju. 1st pers. sing. of ἐσθίω

Φαῖδρος -ου ὁ: Phaidros (Latin Phaedrus), the first speaker at the symposium (see appendix 1)

φαίνω φανῶ ἔφηνα πέφηνα πέφασμαι ἔφαν(θ)ην: reveal, show, make appear; *mid. + part.*: be seen to ——, be shown to ——, be obviously ——ing; + *inf.*: appear to ——, seem to —— (but not actually to be)

Φαληρεύς -έως ὁ: man from Phalerum, demotic name of Apollodorus

Φαληρόθεν *adv.*: from Phalerum, one of the 170 demes of Attica

φάναι: pres. act. inf. of φημί

φανερός -ά -όν: open to sight, visible, manifest, evident

φανός -ή -όν: visible, bright, glorious

φαντάζομαι: become visible, appear, show oneself

φαρμακεύς -έως ὁ: one who deals in medicines, drugs, or poisons; sorcerer, healer

φαρμάττω: drug, enchant, deceive

φάσκω: say, affirm, assert

φάσμα -ατος τό: apparition, phantom

φαῦλος -η -ον: slight, paltry, insignificant; *of people*: worthless, common, vulgar

φέρω οἴσω ἤνεγκον/ἤνεγκα ἐνήνοχα ἐνήνεγμαι ἠνέχθην: bear, bring, lead, carry, wear; φέρε: come!

φεύγω φεύξομαι ἔφυγον πέφευγα: flee, take flight, run away

φημί φήσω ἔφησα, *imperf.* ἔφην, *part.* φάς φᾶσα φάν (φάντ-), *inf.* φάναι: say, declare; οὔ φημί: deny, say that . . . not

φθάνω φθήσομαι ἔφθασα/ἔφθην: come or do first or before, anticipate

φθείρ φθειρός ὁ: louse; *pl.*: lice

φθίνω/φθίω φθίσομαι: decline, decay, wane, waste away

φθονέω: bear ill will or malice, bear a grudge, be envious or jealous, begrudge

φιάλη -ης ἡ: broad, flat vessel; bowl

φίλανδρος -ον: man-loving, husband-loving

φιλάνθρωπος -ον: loving humankind, humane, benevolent, kindly

φιλεραστής -οῦ ὁ: lover-lover, friend to a lover, someone fond of a lover

φιλεραστία -ας ἡ: love for a lover, affection for one's ἐραστής

φιλέω φιλήσω ἐφίλησα πεφίληκα πεφίλημαι ἐφιλήθην: love, regard or treat with affection, kiss; + *inf.*: be inclined to ——, tend to, be accustomed to ——

φιλία -ας ἡ: friendly or familial love, affection, friendship

φίλιος -α -ον: of or from a friend, friendly, dear, beloved

φιλογυμναστία -ας ἡ: fondness for gymnastic exercises, love of exercise

φιλογυναίκης -ες: women-loving, fond of women

φιλόδωρος -ον: fond of giving, bountiful

φίλος -η -ον: loved, beloved, dear

φίλος -ου ὁ: friend

φιλοσοφέω: love knowledge and pursue it, philosophize, be a philosopher, live the life of a philosopher

φιλοσοφία -ας ἡ: love of knowledge and wisdom, philosophy

φιλόσοφος -ου ὁ: philosopher

φιλοτιμέομαι: love or seek after honor, be ambitious

φιλοτιμία -ας ἡ: love of honor, ambition

φιλούμενε: pres. mid.-pass. part. voc. sing. of φιλέω

φίλτατος -η -ον (superl. of φίλος): dearest, most beloved

φλυαρέω: talk nonsense, play the fool

φλυαρία -ας ἡ: silly talk, nonsense, foolery

φοβέομαι φοβήσομαι — — πεφόβημαι ἐφοβήθην: fear, be afraid of (pass. deponent)

φοβερός -ά -όν: frightening, fearful

φόβος -ου ὁ: fear, flight

Φοῖνιξ -ικος ὁ: Phoinix, one of the sources for the story of the *Symposium*

φοιτάω: come regularly, visit repeatedly

φορέω: bear or carry constantly, wear

φράζω φράσω ἔφρασα πέφρακα πέφρασμαι ἐφράσθην: tell, utter, mention, point out, show

φρήν φρενός ἡ: mind, understanding

φρονέω φρονήσω ἐφρόνησα πεφρόνηκα πεφρόνημαι ἐφρονήθην: think, have understanding, be wise or prudent; intend; + *neut. adj.*: think [a certain way], be disposed [a certain way]; e.g., φίλα φρονέω: be friendly (to); μέγα φρονέω: think big, be proud or arrogant

φρόνημα -ατος τό: one's mind, spirit, high spirit, boldness, arrogance; *pl.*: thoughts, purposes

φρόνησις -εως ἡ: intention, thought, sense; good sense, thoughtfulness, wisdom, understanding; *also sometimes with negative sense:* pride, presumption, arrogance

φρόνιμος -ον: in one's right mind, sensible

φροντίζω φροντιῶ ἐφρόντισα πεφρόντικα: think, consider, take thought, have a care, worry; + *gen.*: think of, worry about

φυγή -ῆς ἡ: flight

φυλακτέος -α -ον (verbal adj. of φυλάττω): to be watched or guarded; *neut. used impers.*: one must take care, one must watch carefully

φύλαξ φύλακος ὁ: watcher, guard, sentinel, guardian

φυλάττω φυλάξω ἐφύλαξα πεφύλαχα πεφύλαγμαι ἐφυλάχθην: guard, keep watch, watch closely

φύσις -εως ἡ: nature; *especially common* as *dat.* φύσει: by nature

φυτόν -οῦ τό: that which has grown, plant, tree

φύω φύσω ἔφυσα/ἔφυν πέφυκα: bring forth, produce, put forth; *mid.-pass. root aor.* ἔφυν: grow, be born, be [by nature]; *perf.* πέφυκα: be [by nature], be inclined [by nature]

φωνέω: speak

φωνή -ῆς ἡ: sound, tone, voice, language

Χχ

χαίρω χαιρήσω—κεχάρηκα κεχάρ[η]μαι ἐχάρην (deponent in aor.): rejoice, be glad, be delighted; *impera.*: greetings! farewell!

χαλάω: slacken, loosen, relax

χαλεπός -ή -όν: difficult, hard to bear, painful, sore, grievous; χαλεπῶς ἔχω: I am in a painful state

χαλκεία -ας ἡ (abbreviated from ἡ χαλκεία τέχνη): art of bronze-working

χάλκειος -α -ον: bronze, brazen

χαλκεύς -έως ὁ: worker in bronze or copper, smith

χαμαιπετής -ές: falling to the ground, sleeping on the ground

χαμεύνιον -ου τό: bedroll

Χάος -ους/-εος τό: Chaos, one of the earliest gods according to Hesiod's *Theogony*

χαρίζομαι χαριοῦμαι ἐχαρισάμην—κεχάρισμαι + *dat.*: gratify, give pleasure to, do a favor for

χάρις -ιτος ἡ: favor, grace, charm, gratitude; χάριν + (*preceding*) *gen.*: for the sake of *gen.*, e.g., ἀθανασίας χάριν: for the sake of immortality; *capitalized*: the Graces, traditionally three in number

χειμών -ῶνος ὁ: winter, winter storm

χείρ χειρός ἡ: hand, arm; *dat. pl.* χερσί(ν)

χειρουργία -ας ἡ: working by hand, handicraft

χείρων χεῖρον: worse

χερσί: dat pl. of χείρ

χέω χεῶ ἔχεα κέχυκα κέχυμαι ἐχύθην: pour, shed

χθές *adv.*: yesterday

χλιδή -ῆς ἡ: delicacy, daintiness, luxury, effeminacy

χορευτής -οῦ ὁ: member of a chorus, choral dancer

χορός -οῦ ὁ: round dance, choral dance or song, chorus

χράομαι χρήσομαι ἐχρησάμην—κέχρημαι ἐχρήσθην + *dat.*: use, enjoy, deal with, experience, be subject to; consult an oracle

χρεία -ας ἡ: use

χρή, *imperf.* (ἐ)χρῆν, *fut.* χρῆσται, *inf.* χρῆναι, *indecl. part.* χρεών, *subju.* χρῇ, *opt.* χρείη: it is fated, necessary for *acc.* to *inf.*

χρῆμα -ατος τό: thing that one uses; *pl.*: money

χρηματισμός -οῦ ὁ: moneymaking, business

χρηματιστικός -ή -όν: fitted for moneymaking

χρῆναι: inf. of χρή

χρῆσθαι: inf. of χράομαι

χρήσιμος -η -ον: useful, serviceable, good for use, good, apt or fit

χρηστός -ή -όν: good, valuable, useful, serviceable, upright, helpful

χρόας: poetic acc. of χρώς ὁ

χρόνος -ου ὁ: time

χρυσεῖος -α -ον: gold, golden

χρύσεος -α -ον/-οῦς -ῆ -οῦν: gold, golden (see Smyth 1956: §290 for declension of contracted version)

χρυσίον -ου τό: gold, piece of gold

χρῶμα -ατος τό: surface, skin, color

χρώς χρωτός ὁ: skin, complexion

χωρέω χωρήσομαι/χωρήσω ἐχώρησα κεχώρηκα κεχώρημαι ἐχωρήθην: go, make way, proceed

χωρίζω: separate, part, sever, divide

χωρίς *adv.*: separately, asunder, apart, by oneself or by themselves; *or prep.* + *gen.*: without, apart from, beside

Ψψ

ψευδής -ές: lying, false, untrue

ψεύδομαι ψεύσομαι ἐψευσάμην—ἔψευσμαι: speak falsely, lie

ψεῦδος -ους τό: lie, falsehood, untruth

ψῆττα -ης ἡ: a kind of flatfish, sole, turbot

ψηφίζομαι ψηφιοῦμαι ἐψηφισάμην—ἐψήφισμαι: vote

ψιλός -ή -όν: bare, naked, unadorned, prosaic

ψόγος -ου ὁ: blame, censure

ψόφος -ου ὁ: sound, noise

ψυκτήρ -ῆρος ὁ: wine cooler

ψυχή -ῆς ἡ: breath, life, soul

ψύχος -ους τό: cool air, cold

ψυχρός -ά -όν: cold, chill, frigid

Ωω

ὦ + *voc. as form of address*: O!

ὠγαθέ = ὦ ἀγαθέ (crasis)

ὧδε *adv.*: in this way, so, thus, as follows

ᾠδή -ῆς ἡ: song, ode

ὠδίς ὠδῖνος ἡ: labor-pain, pain

ᾠήθη: aor. indic. 3rd pers. sing. of οἶμαι (pass. deponent)

ὠκύς -εῖα -ύ: swift

ὦμεν: pres. subju. 1st pers. pl. of εἰμί

ὡμολογημένος -η -ον: perf. pass. part. of ὁμολογέω

ὤμοσα: aor. act. indic. 1st pers. sing. of ὄμνυμι

ὤν οὖσα ὄν (ὄντος): pres. part. of εἰμί

ὧν: gen. masc./fem./neut. pl. of ὅς

ὠνέομαι ὠνήσομαι ἐπριάμην—ἐώνημαι ἐωνήθην: buy

ᾠόν -οῦ τό: egg

ὥρα -ας ἡ: season, time, hour, youth

ὡρμημένος -η -ον: perf. mid.-pass. part. of ὁρμάω

ὡς + *indic.*: as, when; + *superl.*: as —— as possible; *introducing indir. statement*: that; how; + *fut. part.*: in order to, so that, since; ὡς ἀληθῶς; truly; ὡς ἔπος εἰπεῖν: so to speak, virtually, practically, almost (*Essentials* §§192–99)

ὡσαύτως *adv.*: in like manner, just as, in the same way (as)

ὦσι(ν): pres. subju. 3rd pers. pl. of εἰμί

ὠσί(ν): dat. pl. of οὖς

ὥσπερ *adv.*: just like, just as if, even as, like

ὥστε *conj.* + *inf. or indic. to express a result*: so that, with the result that, such that, that, as, as being

ὦτα τά: nom./acc. pl. of οὖς

Ὦτος -ου ὁ: Otos, one of a pair of giants who made an assault on the gods (see Ἐφιάλτης)

ὠφελέω ὠφελήσω ὠφέλησα ὠφέληκα ὠφέλημαι ὠφελήθην: help, benefit; *pass.* + ἀπό + *gen.*: derive benefit from *gen.*, be helped by *gen.*

ὠφελία -ας ἡ: profit

ᾠχόμην: imperf. mid. indic. 1st pers. sing. of οἴχομαι

Index of English Terms

Index of Greek Terms

NOTE: *For Greek names and other words that are transliterated into English, as well as for cross-references to English words, see the Index of English Terms.*

Ἀγάθων, declension of, 37. *See also* Agathon
ἀγαπή, 23
ἀλλ᾽ οὐ, 160n27
ἄλλο τι, 169
ἄν: = ἐαν, 113n17, 132n12, 182n18, 214n19; practice with usage accompanied by different moods (review exercise 2C), 299–301
ἀτοπία, 107, 229, 240n52
αὐλητρίς. *See* Flute-girl
αὐλός. *See* Aulos

βούλεται λέγειν, 104n3

γάρ, as assent in brief answers, 176n19

δαίμων. *See* Daimon
δῆλον ὅτι, 147n14

εἴπερ που ἄλλοθι, 223n13
εἰς αὖθις, 234
ἑκὼν εἶναι, 240n50
ἐραστής. *See* Erastes
ἐρώμενος. *See* Eromenos
ἔρως. *See* Eros
ἑταίρα. *See* Hetaera
ἑταῖρος (unnamed companion of Apollodorus), 9, 27, 27n17, 37; speeches of, 41–42
εὐφημέω, 182n18, 239n36

ἡμετέροις αὐτῶν, 134n30

καὶ μήν, in drama, 33n5
καλὸς κάγαθός, 62
κατά as prefix, 58n3
κεῖμαι, forms of, 46
κῶμος. *See* Komos

μάλιστα: + γε, 182n20; with numerals, 52n3
μὲν οὖν, 177n41, 183n38

μή: + ὅτι, 208n11; + οὐχί, redundant with verb of negative meaning, 154n27–28; redundant before infinitive, 219n12–13, 256n10

ὀλίγου, 161n39
ὅπως ἄν + subju. in Plato, 165n16–17
ὅπως μή + fut. indic. to express fear, 133n21
ὅρα: + εἰ, 233n43; + μή, 234n49
ὅς ἥ ὅ as demonstrative pronoun, 33n5
ὅτι: introducing direct quotation, 35n14; = ὅ τι in Plato, 67n12, 120n11, 182n18, 200n38, 247n10; + superlative, 132n5
οὐ: + δήπου . . . , 138n19; + future indicative in a question, 33n4; + τι, 113n14
-ουν (suffix), 139n34
οὗτος, as a form of address, 33n4

παιδικά, 18, 21, 65
παῖς/παῖδα/παῖδας implied from context, 52n2, 237n4, 237n8
πέφυκα, 147n15
ποίησις, 193, 196n37
ποτέ, 41n25
πῶς, 48n19, 237n13

Σωκράτης, declension of, 37. *See also* Socrates

τι, enclitic accented with grave for emphasis, 41n20, 258n45
τί δέ, 171n16–17

ὕβρις. *See* Hubris

φιλία, 5, 23, 73n5, 89n13

ὡς, practice with common uses of (review exercise 5), 316

CPSIA information can be obtained
at www.ICGtesting.com
Printed in the USA
LVOW03s2344240817
546282LV00002B/2/P